Microsoft

Working with Microsoft Dynamics™ CRM 4.0, Second Edition

Jim Steger
Mike Snyder

PUBLISHED BY
Microsoft Press
A Division of Microsoft Corporation
One Microsoft Way
Redmond, Washington 98052-6399

Library of Congress Control Number: 2008920564

Printed and bound in the United States of America.

1 2 3 4 5 6 7 8 9   QWT   3 2 1 0 9 8

Distributed in Canada by H.B. Fenn and Company Ltd.

A CIP catalogue record for this book is available from the British Library.

Microsoft Press books are available through booksellers and distributors worldwide. For further information about international editions, contact your local Microsoft Corporation office or contact Microsoft Press International directly at fax (425) 936-7329. Visit our Web site at www.microsoft.com/mspress. Send comments to mspinput@microsoft.com.

Microsoft, Microsoft Press, Active Directory, ActiveX, BizTalk, Excel, FrontPage, Hotmail, IntelliSense, Internet Explorer, Jscript, Microsoft Dynamics, MSDN, MSN, Outlook, PivotChart, PivotTable, SharePoint, SQL Server, Visio, Visual Basic, Visual C#, Visual SourceSafe, Visual Studio, Windows, Windows Live, Windows NT, Windows Server, and Windows Vista are either registered trademarks or trademarks of Microsoft Corporation in the United States and/or other countries. Other product and company names mentioned herein may be the trademarks of their respective owners.

The example companies, organizations, products, domain names, e-mail addresses, logos, people, places, and events depicted herein are fictitious. No association with any real company, organization, product, domain name, e-mail address, logo, person, place, or event is intended or should be inferred.

This book expresses the author's views and opinions. The information contained in this book is provided without any express, statutory, or implied warranties. Neither the authors, Microsoft Corporation, nor its resellers, or distributors will be held liable for any damages caused or alleged to be caused either directly or indirectly by this book.

Acquisitions Editor: Ben Ryan
Project Editor: Valerie Woolley
Editorial Production: ICC Macmillan Inc.
Technical Reviewer: Corey O'Brian; Technical Review services provided by Content Master, a member of CM Group, Ltd.
Cover: Tom Draper Design

Body Part No. X14-51561

Table of Contents

What do you think of this book? We want to hear from you!

Microsoft is interested in hearing your feedback so we can continually improve our books and learning resources for you. To participate in a brief online survey, please visit:

www.microsoft.com/learning/booksurvey

Part II Customization

Part III **Extending Microsoft Dynamics CRM**

What do you think of this book? We want to hear from you!

Microsoft is interested in hearing your feedback so we can continually improve our books and learning resources for you. To participate in a brief online survey, please visit:

www.microsoft.com/learning/booksurvey

Foreword

Over the last two years, Microsoft Dynamics CRM has led a revolution in the world of customer relationship management software and solutions. Designed from the ground up to offer rapid business adoption through a flexible and agile technology solution, Microsoft Dynamics CRM extends everyday productivity applications such as Microsoft Office Outlook to help businesses reach new heights in finding, keeping, and growing customer relationships.

The revolution continues with Microsoft Dynamics CRM 4.0.

With its revamped, multitenant architecture, innovative new business process automation studio, and features for global organizations including multilanguage and multicurrency transactions, Microsoft Dynamics CRM 4.0 provides compelling features and capabilities for today's global business.

From small businesses to the largest enterprises, Microsoft Dynamics CRM 4.0 offers unmatched flexibility, security, and scalability for those looking to establish a common customer information system in your organization.

Mike Snyder and Jim Steger again have provided a comprehensive, yet easy-to-follow guide for learning the new Microsoft Dynamics CRM 4.0 application. I continue to be amazed by their ability to take complex topics such as business systems design, business process automation, and Web services programming and distill them into a set of practical examples commonly found in customer deployments of Microsoft Dynamics CRM. In addition, they provide outstanding application and customization guides that can be embraced across various user groups and communities.

For users of Microsoft Dynamics CRM, this guide provides you with the information and tools necessary to become a system master.

For system implementers and customizers, you will find a comprehensive resource guide for extending the everyday Microsoft Dynamics CRM 4.0 application to meet your unique business needs.

Last, for information technology administrators, this text provides a great reference guide for planning, implementing, and maintaining your Microsoft Dynamics CRM system.

Working with Microsoft Dynamics CRM 4.0 , Second Edition is sure to lead your organization through all phases of the system development life cycle—from envisioning, planning, developing, and stabilizing to deploying and maintaining your customer relationship management system. This book does a great job explaining the basics, but truly shines in making it possible for you to take the next step in terms of solution design and development. Each customer deployment of Microsoft Dynamics CRM 4.0 will benefit from a resource guide such as this text.

I hope you find this guide both as informative and fun to read as I have during the process of developing this text.

I wish you all the best in your successful deployment of Microsoft Dynamics CRM 4.0.

Sincerely,
Bill Patterson
Director, Product Management
Microsoft Dynamics CRM
Microsoft Corporation

Acknowledgments

We want to thank all of the people that assisted us in writing this book. If we accidentally miss anyone, we apologize in advance. We would like to extend a special thanks to the following people:

- **Bill Patterson**   Bill sponsored the book project and helped make sure that all the pieces fell into place correctly. He also agreed to help us by writing the book's foreword.

- **Phil Richardson**   Getting this book completed on schedule would not have been possible without Phil's amazing assistance. From his help with early builds of the product, to coordinating Microsoft Dynamics CRM team resources and providing technical feedback throughout the process, Phil's contribution to this process was truly amazing.

- **Neil Erickson**   We asked Neil, our Sonoma Partners network administrator, to build more Microsoft Dynamics CRM environments than we care to admit. Toward the end, it seemed like he was constantly building out test systems for us! We want to thank Neil for his endless patience and support in providing us access to the test systems we needed to evaluate the software.

In addition, we want to thank these members of the Microsoft Dynamics CRM product team who helped us at one point or another during the book project:

Kam Baker	Jeff Kelleran	Irene Pasternack
Andrew Becraft	Donald La	Dominic Pouzin
Rohit Bhatia	Amy Langlois	Dave Porter
Andrew Bybee	Chris Laver	Manisha Powar
Jim Daly	Patrick Le Quere	Michael Scott
Rich Dickinson	Elliot Lewis	John Song
Ajith Gande	Michael Lu	Derik Stenerson
Barry Givens	Andy Magee	Praveen Upadhyay
Humberto Lezama Guadarrama	Ed Martinez	Mahesh Vijayaraghavan
Nishant Gupta	Dinesh Murthy	Sumit Virmani
Peter Hecke	Kevin Nazemi	Brad Wilson
Akezyt Janedittakarn	Michael Ott	Charlie Wood

Thank you to the following Sonoma Partners colleagues who assisted with reviewing the content and providing feedback:

Brad Bosak	Brendan Landers	Kara O'Brien
Brian Baseggio	Peter Majer	Kristie Reid
Rob Jasinski	Andrew Myers	Tammy Wolak

Of course, we also want to thank the folks at Microsoft Press who helped support us throughout the book-writing and publishing process:

- **Ben Ryan**   Ben championed the book project and was gracious enough to allow us to include our Sonoma Partners branding on the book cover.

- **Valerie Woolley**   Once again, working with Valerie has been a delight. She did a great job of helping us get the work done in time. She also went above and beyond to cram the schedule so that we could get the book in print for the Microsoft Convergence conference.

- **Christina Yeager**   Christina copy edited the book for us to ensure consistency with the Microsoft Press guidelines.

We also would like to thank Michael Ryder for managing the editing and production process and ensuring a successful delivery of the book.

Last but not least, we want to thank Corey O'Brien. As the technical editor for the book, Corey worked around the clock to confirm the technical accuracy of the text. This included reviewing and testing all of our code samples and double-checking our facts.

Mike Snyder's Acknowledgments

I want to thank my wife, Gretchen, who tolerated the long nights and weekends that this book consumed over the past few months. Despite the fact that I kept disappearing into my office to sneak out some work, she supported me 100 percent from start to finish. Even though my kids won't be able to read this note for years, I want to thank my children who provided me with the motivation to undertake this project. I also want to recognize my parents and my wife's parents who assisted my family with various baby-sitting stints. I would like to thank all of my co-workers at Sonoma Partners who helped pick up the slack created by my time commitment to this book.

Jim Steger's Acknowledgments

First and foremost, I wish to thank my wife, Heidi, for her patience and for allowing me to endure this long and hectic process again. I could not have completed this endeavor with-out her unwavering support, understanding, and encouragement. I want to thank both of my children, who were on their best behavior for their mom during these past few months, which allowed me the extra time required to write! I would also like to personally thank Phil Richardson of Microsoft who took the time to review code, provide builds, and answer my numerous questions. I also received input from numerous members of the Microsoft Dynamics CRM development team, and I want to extend my thanks to them as well. Finally, I wish to express my gratitude to my associates at Sonoma Partners who really stepped up their effort and understanding while I was forced to prioritize my writing over some of my day-to-day duties.

Introduction

We love Microsoft Dynamics CRM 4.0, and hopefully by the time you finish reading this book, you will love Microsoft Dynamics CRM, too. We understand if you're skeptical about the possibility of falling for a piece of software, but we want you to know right up front that our goal is to show you all of the wonderful and amazing benefits the Microsoft Dynamics CRM application can provide for your business.

Who Is This Book For?

We wrote this book for the people responsible for implementing Microsoft Dynamics CRM at their organization. If you're the person responsible for setting up or configuring Microsoft Dynamics CRM software on behalf of other users at your company, this book is for you. You might be an information technology professional or simply a Power User from the sales or marketing department. You should be comfortable with technical concepts and understand the role of various Microsoft technologies such as Microsoft Exchange Server, Microsoft Active Directory, and Microsoft SQL Server. You don't need to be a coding expert to benefit from this book, but we hope that you can edit an XML file and that you understand how relational databases work.

In addition to project managers, software developers looking to extend and customize Microsoft Dynamics CRM will enjoy our review of the Microsoft Dynamics CRM software development kit. We include multiple code samples that software developers can immediately build and deploy to their own Microsoft Dynamics CRM installations. And, of course, you can also extend our code examples to include your own unique modifications specific for your business.

This book can also help prospective customers with their software selection process as they evaluate the customization options that Microsoft Dynamics CRM offers. If you want to learn more about the software's capabilities before you make a purchase decision, we hope that this book provides some of the technical details you're looking for.

Who is this book not for? It's *not* for end users interested in learning how they will use Microsoft Dynamics CRM on a day-to-day basis because their company just went live with the software. If you don't have System Administrator rights, you won't be able to perform most of the steps in this book, so it probably won't provide much benefit for you. If you're not sure whether you have System Administrator rights, well, then, this book probably isn't for you either. We are in the process of writing a book for Microsoft Dynamics CRM users, so please check online at the Microsoft Web site for the availability of that book if you're interested in that topic.

This book also *does not* tell you how to install the Microsoft Dynamics CRM software and troubleshoot any installation-related issues. We don't cover upgrading an existing Microsoft Dynamics CRM 3.0 installation to Microsoft Dynamics CRM 4.0. The Microsoft Dynamics CRM Implementation Guide gives excellent and detailed advice on the installation and upgrade processes, so there's no need for us to repeat that information here.

Organization of This Book

We divided *Working with Microsoft Dynamics CRM 4.0* into 3 parts and 10 chapters. The three parts break down as follows:

- **Part 1, Overview and Setup**   Provides a quick overview of the various components of Microsoft Dynamics CRM and explains how to configure some of the more frequently used areas of the software.

- **Part 2, Customization**   Goes deep into how you can modify Microsoft Dynamics CRM to match the way your business works. Topics include adding new data fields, revising the user interface, creating reports, and automating business processes by using workflow.

- **Part 3, Extending Microsoft Dynamics CRM**   Explains how you can create your own custom code that will integrate with Microsoft Dynamics CRM through its predefined software interface. This part includes lots of code samples and examples that you can implement immediately at your organization.

Obviously, software developers and development managers can receive the most benefit from Part 3, but we explain the coding and extensions concepts so that everyone can understand the examples even if you don't understand the coding syntax.

In resources such as the Implementation Guide, the software development kit (SDK), the User Interface Style Guide, and the online Help, Microsoft Dynamics CRM 4.0 includes more than 1,500 pages of product documentation on how to use the software. This book is *only* 640 pages, so obviously it can't possibly cover every nook and cranny of how Microsoft Dynamics CRM works. Rather, our goal is to focus on the key areas most companies will need to set up, customize, and extend the software while providing plenty of examples and real-world advice. This book assumes that you can install the software and that you have a decent understanding of how to navigate the user interface. Consequently, if you want to learn more about using the software (as opposed to customizing the software), we recommend that you take advantage of the many Microsoft training options available for Microsoft Dynamics CRM such as eCourses, classroom training, and the Foundation Library. Because of this book's space constraints, we decided not to repeat any information or samples already covered in the product documentation. Therefore, we frequently refer you to the SDK and the Implementation Guide.

One last thought regarding the organization of this book: We tried to eliminate any "marketing fluff" so that we can cram as much information as possible in this book. To that end, you will not read the reasons why customer relationship management (CRM) projects fail or read a discussion about the future of CRM software. We're straightforward and direct people, so we appreciate it when books present information in the same manner. Hopefully, you like this style, too.

Prerelease Software

We wrote most of this book using preproduction versions of Microsoft Dynamics CRM 4.0. Microsoft released the final version of Microsoft Dynamics CRM 4.0 (build number 4.0.7333.3) just a week or two before we submitted the final copy to our editor, but we did review and test our examples using the final release. However, you might still find minor differences between the production release and the examples and screenshots included in this book. In addition, at the time this book went to print, Microsoft did not yet release additional utilities and tools related to Microsoft Dynamics CRM, such as the mobile solution and the integration with Microsoft Dynamics ERP products. Consequently, we were not able to include those topics in the book.

Microsoft Dynamics CRM Live

As you learn in this book, Microsoft Dynamics CRM offers several different deployment options, including a Microsoft-hosted version of the software named Microsoft Dynamics CRM Live. This book deals primarily with the on-premise version of Microsoft Dynamics CRM because Microsoft Dynamics CRM Live was still in a preproduction mode at the time this book went to press. Both versions of the software work identically in almost all areas, but we do highlight key known differences between the on-premise and hosted versions. Unfortunately, we could not provide exact details in many areas because Microsoft Dynamics CRM Live is a moving target in regard to how the final production version will manifest. If you're interested in Microsoft Dynamics CRM Live, we suggest that you check *http://www.crmlive.com* for the latest information about that product.

System Requirements

We recommend that you refer to the Microsoft Dynamics CRM Implementation Guide for detailed system requirements. From a high level, you'll need the following hardware and software to run the code samples in this book:

Client

- Microsoft Windows XP with Service Pack 2 (SP2) or the Windows Vista operating system

- Microsoft Internet Explorer 6 SP1 or Internet Explorer 7

- Microsoft Visual Studio 2005 or Microsoft Visual Studio 2008 (for the code samples)

- Microsoft Office 2003 with SP3 or the 2007 Microsoft Office System with SP1 (if you want to use Microsoft Dynamics CRM for Microsoft Office Outlook)

Server

- Microsoft Windows Server 2003 or Microsoft Windows Small Business Server 2003

- Microsoft SQL Server 2005

- Computer/processor: Dual 1.8-gigahertz (GHz) or higher Pentium (Xeon P4) or compatible CPU

- Memory: 1 gigabyte (GB) of RAM minimum, 2 gigabytes (GB) or more of RAM recommended

- Hard disk: 400 megabytes (MB) free space

- Network card: 10/100 megabits per second (Mbps) minimum, dual 10/100/1000 Mbps recommended

Code Samples

This book features a companion Web site that makes available to you all the code used in the book. The code samples are organized by chapter, and you can download code files from the companion site at this address:

http://www.microsoft.com/mspress/companion/9780735623781/

Find Additional Content Online

As new or updated material becomes available that complements your book, it will be posted online at the Microsoft Press Online Developer Tools Web site. The type of material you might find includes updates to book content, articles, links to companion content, errata, sample chapters, and more. The Web site will be available soon at *http://www.microsoft.com/ learning/books/online/developer* and will be updated periodically.

Support for This Book

Microsoft Press provides support for books and companion content at the following Web site:

http://www.microsoft.com/learning/support/books/

Questions and Comments

If you have comments, questions, or ideas regarding the book or the companion content, or if you have questions that are not answered by visiting the sites previously listed, please send them to Microsoft Press via e-mail to

mspinput@microsoft.com

Or via postal mail to

Microsoft Press
Attn: *Working with Microsoft Dynamics CRM 4.0* Editor
One Microsoft Way
Redmond, WA 98052-6399

Please note that product support is not offered through these mail addresses. For further information regarding Microsoft software support options, please go to *http://support.microsoft.com/directory/* or call Microsoft Support Network Sales at (800) 936-3500.

Part I
Overview and Setup

No two businesses in the world are exactly the same, each uses a unique set of tools and processes to manage their customers. Therefore companies need to make sure that their customer management software can easily adjust and conform to their needs. Microsoft Dynamics CRM 4.0 offers powerful configuration tools so that customers can modify and customize the software, yet administrators can use these tools through a simple and easy-to-learn Web interface.

The first three chapters of this book will cover Part 1 "Overview and Setup". We will give you some background on Microsoft Dynamics CRM 4.0 and then we'll introduce some of the key Microsoft CRM terminology and concepts you'll use throughout the entire book. After the background, we'll jump right into the details of how to set up and configure common areas of the application. Before you read Chapters 2 and 3 you should install Microsoft Dynamics CRM, develop a comfort level navigating through the user interface, and have a rough idea of how your company wants to implement your CRM strategy. For the most part, you'll find the configuration and settings administration tools we cover in Part 1 located under the Settings section of Microsoft Dynamics CRM. Of course, you'll need the appropriate security privileges to access the Settings area. In the last chapter of Part 1, we'll go into the details of configuring information security and data access in Microsoft Dynamics CRM.

Part 2 of this book will explain how you can customize Microsoft Dynamics CRM. The last part of this book, Part 3, will review how you can create custom code for more complex Microsoft CRM customization and integration needs.

Chapter 1
Microsoft Dynamics CRM 4.0 Overview

We know that you're eager to get into the details of how Microsoft Dynamics CRM 4.0 works and learn more about its great customization capabilities. Before we can jump into those details, we need to cover a little background information about Microsoft Dynamics CRM and introduce some of the core concepts and terminology used throughout this book.

Life Without Customer Relationship Management

Think back to a particularly bad customer service experience you have had. Maybe you called a customer service phone number and were transferred to five different people, and every single person asked you the same questions so that you had to keep repeating the same answers over and over again. Or perhaps a salesperson pulled together a proposal for you but forgot to include your preferred customer pricing in the quote. Or maybe a credit card company mailed you an application for a new account, even though you've had an account with that company for 10 years. You probably thought to yourself, "Why doesn't this company know who I am?" Do any of these situations sound familiar?

As its name implies, the goal of *customer relationship management* (CRM) is to enable businesses to manage each and every customer experience better. More important, CRM strategy recognizes that customer experiences span over time and that a typical customer might interact with your business 50 to 100 times in the course of your relationship. Ideally, your company could provide each customer a personalized experience based on the customer's unique history of interactions with you. For example, you wouldn't ask longstanding customers if they would like to open an account; when customers call your customer service department, you wouldn't have to ask them to answer the same questions over and over again; and your most valuable customers would always receive preferred pricing.

> **Important** The purpose of CRM is to enable businesses to track and manage all of their customer interactions over the lifetime of the customer relationship. CRM is a business strategy, and companies typically use a CRM software system as a technology platform to help implement their CRM strategy, processes, and procedures.

In today's competitive business environment, mistreated customers can easily find other vendors or suppliers that are eager to replace you. However, if you give your customers a personalized experience, they're more likely to value their relationship with you and continue to patronize your business. The CRM philosophy makes so much sense, so why do so many companies force good customers to suffer through bad experiences every day?

As you probably know, it's very difficult for companies to embrace a CRM strategy and create consistently great customer experiences. Some of the factors that make a CRM strategy difficult to implement include the following:

- **Multiple customer management systems** Almost every company uses more than one system (such as sales tracking, warehouse management, or financial accounting) to run its business. Most of these systems can't easily communicate with each other to seamlessly share data. Therefore, you can imagine how salespeople using a sales tracking system might not know that a customer just opened an urgent customer service issue in your customer service system.

- **Remote workers** Even if your company is lucky enough to use a single system to track all of your customer interactions, remote and offsite workers may not have the ability to access data in the customer management system.

- **Rapidly changing business processes** You may recognize the saying, "The only thing constant in life is change," by French author François de la Rochefoucauld. This expression really hits home in regard to the business processes of our Internet-enabled world. No sooner does a company finalize a customer management process than it must reconsider how that methodology will change in the next month, quarter, or year. Rapidly changing business processes challenge employees to adjust quickly, but most CRM systems can't react and do not adjust as quickly as the business needs them to.

- **Multichannel customer interactions** Customers expect to be able to work with your company using any communication channel that they prefer. With the proliferation of different technologies, these customer communication channels can include Web sites, phone, fax, e-mail, mail, and instant messaging. If a company wants to track all of a customer's interactions, its customer management system must work with each of these technologies.

- **Difficult and rigid systems** Adopting a CRM strategy usually requires a company to select a technology system as its customer management platform. Earlier CRM systems earned the reputation of being difficult to use and complex to install. Even worse, companies could only customize their CRM systems to their business needs if they invested large sums of money and time in consultants who would customize the software for them.

CRM isn't a particularly new concept and it has earned somewhat of a bad reputation among businesses. These are just some of the reasons responsible for its less-than-stellar track record over the years.

So, what would happen if a company *could* successfully implement a CRM strategy and software? What types of benefits might the company receive?

- CRM could track customer interests and purchase history over time, and then proactively generate new marketing initiatives for customers based on their unique histories.

- CRM could log a history of a customer's service requests so that a service technician could easily view all of those requests when the customer calls with a new issue. Reviewing a customer's service history might help the technician resolve a customer's new issue much more quickly.

- A manager could view all of the interactions with a customer across various functional areas such as sales, marketing, and customer service. People typically refer to this cross-functional history as a *360-degree view* of the customer.

- Marketing managers could analyze and report on the effectiveness of their marketing lists and campaigns to determine how they should reallocate future marketing investments.

- An analyst could use business intelligence tools to segment customers and prospects to identify trends and create predictive models for sales and customer service planning.

This list doesn't include all of the benefits of CRM, but it's clear that a successful CRM implementation can provide many short-term and long-term benefits for any business.

Introducing Microsoft Dynamics CRM

Microsoft saw the need for a better CRM software platform and created a solution called Microsoft Dynamics CRM. Microsoft designed this software for companies of all sizes to use as their technology platform for implementing CRM strategies. Microsoft first released Microsoft Dynamics CRM (version 1.0) in late 2002 and has continued to update the software over the past years with new releases and feature packs. This book covers the latest release of the software, Microsoft Dynamics CRM 4.0, in addition to the CRM offering named Microsoft Dynamics CRM Live (available at *http://www.crmlive.com*) hosted by Microsoft. This chapter gives you a brief overview of the Microsoft Dynamics CRM software to explain how it helps companies implement CRM strategies. We discuss the following topics:

- Software design goals
- Deployment options and editions
- Licensing
- Front office vs. back office
- System requirements

After we cover Microsoft Dynamics CRM from a high-level perspective, the subsequent chapters explain how you can configure, customize, and extend the software to meet your company's unique business needs.

> **More Info** This book explains how to configure and customize the Microsoft Dynamics CRM software, but we do not instruct you on CRM strategies because they can vary widely by industry and company size. If you're interested in learning more about the philosophies and methodologies behind CRM, we suggest that you read one of the many books that discuss these topics in a non-software-specific manner. We wrote this book for people who are responsible for managing and deploying Microsoft Dynamics CRM.

Software Design Goals

Microsoft designed Microsoft Dynamics CRM to resolve the common issues that historically caused problems during CRM deployments. Some of the issues we've already mentioned include offsite workers who need remote access to data, multichannel customer communications, and rigid software design. To solve these problems, Microsoft Dynamics CRM targeted three software design themes:

- Works the way you do
- Works the way your business does
- Works the way Information Technology (IT) expects it to

Works the Way You Do

Earlier CRM systems forced users to track information in multiple systems because the CRM software didn't include all of the functionality that users need to complete their job such as e-mail, calendaring, task management, and spreadsheet programs. People performed their work using productivity tools such as Microsoft Office Outlook, Microsoft Office Excel, and Microsoft Office Word, but then they had to copy customer data into their CRM system! This extra step caused negative user feedback because it slowed down users, created additional work, and forced them to learn an entirely new tool.

To address this problem, Microsoft Dynamics CRM works directly in Office and Outlook so that users can perform their usual job functions *and* track data in Microsoft Dynamics CRM at the same time. Microsoft Dynamics CRM is a server-based product that you install and run on a Web server, and users can install the Microsoft Dynamics CRM for Outlook software to work directly in Outlook, as shown in Figure 1-1. You can see that Microsoft Dynamics CRM adds a toolbar to Outlook and also adds Microsoft Dynamics CRM folders to the Outlook folder list.

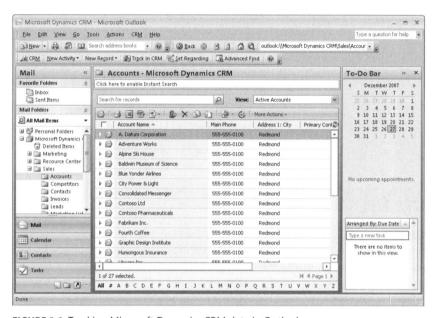

FIGURE 1-1 Tracking Microsoft Dynamics CRM data in Outlook

If your users know how to use Outlook, they already know how to use the key customer management tools in Microsoft Dynamics CRM, such as contacts, tasks, appointments, and e-mail. Figure 1-2 shows the Microsoft Dynamics CRM toolbar that users use to compose an e-mail message in Outlook, and then they can simply click the Track in CRM button to save a copy of the message to the Microsoft Dynamics CRM database.

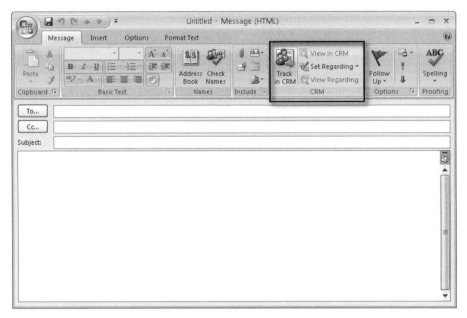

FIGURE 1-2 The Track in CRM button for saving data to Microsoft Dynamics CRM

This tracking concept applies not only to e-mail messages, but also to calendar items, contacts, and tasks. By offering this native Outlook experience to users, Microsoft Dynamics CRM lets users work with their usual tools *and* easily track and manage CRM data.

Real World Believe it or not, many companies still require their employees to copy information from their Outlook e-mail messages and paste it into their CRM systems. It sounds crazy, but this process is implemented at many companies, both big and small. The Microsoft Dynamics CRM native Outlook integration eliminates the need for this extra work.

Even if your company doesn't use Outlook, or if you use Microsoft Office Outlook Web Access, Microsoft Dynamics CRM provides you with additional user interface options:

- Microsoft Internet Explorer Web browser
- Mobile access through handheld devices such as cellular phones and personal digital assistants (PDAs)

More Info At the time this book went to press, Microsoft had not finalized the exact details regarding the mobile interface of Microsoft Dynamics CRM. Therefore, we will exclude that topic from this book, but check the Microsoft Web sites for updates regarding this module.

Microsoft Dynamics CRM also integrates directly with additional business productivity tools, such as the following:

- Excel
- Word
- Microsoft Exchange Server
- Microsoft SharePoint products
- Microsoft Office Communication Server

As one example of this integration between products, Figure 1-3 shows how Microsoft Dynamics CRM can display the Microsoft Office Communication Server presence indicator directly in the Microsoft Dynamics CRM user interface. From the presence icon, users can quickly determine the status of their co-workers, including schedule availability, out-of-office notifications, and so on. Users can also start an instant message conversation, an audio call, or an online meeting as well.

FIGURE 1-3 Microsoft Dynamics CRM integrates with Microsoft Office Communication Server to display user presence and access to additional actions

We explain the details of Microsoft Dynamics CRM integration with Excel, Word, and Exchange Server in later chapters.

By providing a tight integration with tools that your users already know, Microsoft Dynamics CRM provides an extremely rapid learning curve to ensure maximum user adoption. More important, it's designed to work the way that your users work.

> **More Info** At the time this book went to press, Microsoft had not finalized the integration between Microsoft Dynamics CRM 4.0 and Microsoft SharePoint products. In Microsoft Dynamics CRM 3.0, Microsoft released a SharePoint list Web part that customers could use to display Microsoft Dynamics CRM grids directly on a SharePoint Web page.

Works the Way Your Business Does

So, you've seen how Microsoft Dynamics CRM works hard to make life easier for the people who use the system on a day-to-day basis. Microsoft Dynamics CRM also offers several benefits designed to accommodate the way that businesses work. In particular, these benefits include the following:

- **Web-based configuration tools**   Because your business processes change rapidly, you can quickly and easily customize Microsoft Dynamics CRM by using Web-based configuration tools. In addition to configuring forms and adding fields, you can create entirely new types of data to track and manage in Microsoft Dynamics CRM without writing a single line of code.

- **Robust security model**   Microsoft Dynamics CRM uses a role-based security model to provide you with incredibly detailed and flexible security configuration options. You can structure the system so that users access and edit only the information they need for their jobs. Yet, the security model remains agile enough to allow users to create ad-hoc teams for collaborative work on projects and customer accounts.

- **Open programming interfaces**   Because businesses use more than one system for their operations, Microsoft Dynamics CRM offers an open programming interface so that you can connect Microsoft Dynamics CRM with almost any type of external application, such as your company Web site, a financial system, or a company intranet. The Microsoft Dynamics CRM programming interface uses Web services, so you can use almost any integration technology or platform that meets your needs.

- **Business process automation**   Microsoft Dynamics CRM includes a Workflow module to automate business processes and repetitive tasks, such as automatically creating follow-up tasks for new leads or escalating overdue customer service issues to a manager. You set up these business workflows by using a Web-based user interface, so you can easily customize and revise them without programming code when your business needs to shift quickly.

- **Supports global deployments**   If your business includes users throughout the world, Microsoft Dynamics CRM supports multiple languages and multiple currencies in a single database so that all your users use a single Microsoft Dynamics CRM deployment. Each user sees the localized language, date format, and currency settings appropriate for his or her region of the world.

> **More Info**   Part II, "Customizing," and Part III, "Extending Microsoft Dynamics CRM," explain how you can customize Microsoft Dynamics CRM to match your business processes and procedures.

Works the Way Information Technology Expects It To

If you're in the Information Technology (IT) department, we're sure you've worked with some difficult systems. Maybe the software used some proprietary database format that only three people in the world understand, or maybe the software was so fragile that you didn't want to upgrade it for fear of breaking it! Microsoft Dynamics CRM is designed to work with the existing tools, applications, and infrastructure that IT professionals use every day. Some of the Microsoft Dynamics CRM benefits specific to IT include these:

- **Industry-standard technologies**   Microsoft Dynamics CRM uses industry-standard network management technologies for its foundation. Microsoft Dynamics CRM can be configured to use Microsoft Active Directory directory services and Integrated Windows authentication for user and password management. This integration makes it easier for administrators because users won't need a separate login and password to access Microsoft Dynamics CRM.

- **Wizard-driven deployment**   When you install Microsoft Dynamics CRM, the software checks for all of the system prerequisites and tells you which adjustments you may need to make. Depending on your network environment, you can install the Microsoft Dynamics CRM software with just a handful of clicks!

- **Failover and disaster recovery**   Microsoft Dynamics CRM supports clustering for Web, database, and e-mail server environments, so you can feel confident about the safety of your mission-critical data.

- **Zero-footprint clients**   Users can access Microsoft Dynamics CRM through Microsoft Internet Explorer and still access all of the software's rich functionality. Remote users can log on to their Microsoft Dynamics CRM system and access their customer data anywhere they can access the Internet.

- **Automation support**   You can install Microsoft Dynamics CRM from a command line or by using Terminal Services. Microsoft Dynamics CRM also supports thin-client environments such as Citrix and roaming profiles.

- **Multiple deployment options**   Microsoft Dynamics CRM offers multiple options for how you can deploy the software. You can purchase the software and install it on premise in your local network, or you can rent the software on a monthly basis through

Microsoft or a third party and the hosting company will manage all of the hardware, software, network, and security issues on your behalf. You can also switch from one deployment model to another if your business needs change over time. Regardless of the deployment option you select, you can always configure the security settings so that your remote and offsite workers can log on and access the system with no problems.

- **Server role deployment**   With Microsoft Dynamics CRM, you can split the various server roles (such as the DeploymentService, DiscoverService, HelpServer, Application Server, and so on) onto different servers to distribute the application load. Splitting the Microsoft Dynamics CRM server roles to different machines can be appropriate for customers with large or complex deployments.

- **Support for various types of e-mail**   In addition to working with Microsoft Exchange Server, Microsoft Dynamics CRM also supports any Post Office Protocol 3 (POP3) e-mail system for incoming mail and any Simple Mail Transfer Protocol (SMTP) e-mail system for outgoing mail.

- **Multitenant architecture**   In some editions of Microsoft Dynamics CRM, customers can deploy multiple copies of Microsoft Dynamics CRM on the same set of hardware. By using this multitenant architecture, Information Technology departments can more easily support multiple organizations in their company.

In light of these benefits (and many more that we didn't list), you'll find that Microsoft Dynamics CRM works the way IT expects.

> **More Info** This book focuses on configuring and customizing Microsoft Dynamics CRM, but we do not cover the software installation and related troubleshooting because the Microsoft Dynamics CRM Implementation Guide provides more than 300 pages of information on these topics. You can learn more by downloading the latest version of the Implementation Guide at *http://go.microsoft.com/fwlink/?LinkID=104413*.

Deployment Options and Editions

One of the great benefits that Microsoft Dynamics CRM offers customers is the power of choice in regard to purchasing and deploying the software. From a high level, customers can obtain and deploy Microsoft Dynamics CRM using one of three methods:

- Purchase perpetual software licenses and deploy the software on premise
- Pay for the software on a hosted basis through Microsoft Dynamics CRM Live
- Pay for the software on a hosted basis through a Microsoft hosting partner

Although all three options offer the same core functionality of Microsoft Dynamics CRM, there are some notable differences between the deployment options that you should consider when deciding which deployment model best fits your company. See Table 1-1.

TABLE 1-1 Differences Between the Deployment Options

	On premise	Microsoft Dynamics CRM Live	Partner hosted
Supports Integrated Windows authentication	Yes	No	Yes
Supports form-based authentication	Yes	No	Yes
Uses Windows Live ID authentication	No	Yes	No
Supports creation of custom attributes and entities	Yes	Yes	Yes
Supports configuration of security roles and business units	Yes	Yes	Yes
Supports modification of the Site Map and ISV.config	Yes	Yes	Yes
Supports data import and export	Yes	Yes	Yes
Allows access to the Microsoft Dynamics CRM Web services programmatically	Yes	Yes	Yes
Supports the use of IFRAMEs	Yes	Yes	Yes
Supports the hosting of custom pages on Microsoft Dynamics CRM server	Yes	No	Partner-specific
Supports the use of programming plug-ins	Yes	No	Partner-specific
Supports workflow	Yes	Yes	Yes
Supports custom workflow assemblies	Yes	No	Partner-specific

Some of these terms may be new to you, and we explain them in more detail throughout the book.

Generally speaking, Microsoft Dynamics CRM Live fits best with companies that have basic customization and configuration needs. Customers with complex programming or integration requirements probably fit better with the on-premise or partner-hosted options.

> **More Info** The hosted deployment model Microsoft Dynamics CRM Live does not allow some functionality such as plug-ins and workflow assemblies because of current security restrictions. Because plug-ins and workflow assemblies run custom programming code that you create, the hosting company must ensure that the custom code will not cause any problems in its data center. Without these types of code verification (or code isolation) tools in place at the time the book went to press, Microsoft Dynamics CRM Live will not permit you to use these areas of functionality. However, these types of constraints may evolve over time, so be sure to check with the hosting company for the latest information.

If you decide to deploy Microsoft Dynamics CRM on premise, you can purchase Microsoft Dynamics CRM in one of three editions:

- Microsoft Dynamics CRM 4.0 Workgroup Edition
- Microsoft Dynamics CRM 4.0 Professional Edition
- Microsoft Dynamics CRM 4.0 Enterprise Edition

Some of the key differences between the three editions include the following:

- The Workgroup Edition supports a maximum of five users, and you can deploy only a single organization running on a single server.
- Both the Professional Edition and the Enterprise Edition support an unlimited number of users.
- The Professional Edition supports a single organization, whereas the Enterprise Edition supports multiple organizations.
- The Enterprise Edition supports role-based service installation so that you can increase system performance by splitting the various Microsoft Dynamics CRM server roles (and their corresponding application load) over multiple servers.

If you choose to deploy Microsoft Dynamics CRM through Microsoft Dynamics CRM Live, there are currently two different editions available:

- **Microsoft Dynamics CRM Live Professional Edition**   Includes 5 gigabytes of data storage and access to all of Microsoft Dynamics CRM except for usage with Microsoft Dynamics CRM for Outlook with Offline Access
- **Microsoft Dynamics CRM Live Professional Plus Edition**   Includes 20 gigabytes of data storage and access to all of Microsoft Dynamics CRM including usage with Microsoft Dynamics CRM for Outlook with Offline Access

We expect that Microsoft Dynamics CRM Live will offer additional editions over time, so please be sure to check *http://www.crmlive.com* for the latest options and pricing.

Deploying Microsoft Dynamics CRM on Microsoft Windows Small Business Server 2003

Microsoft Windows Small Business Server is a specialized operating system version that bundles Windows Server 2003, Exchange Server 2003, and Microsoft Windows SharePoint Services so that they can be deployed on a single piece of hardware. Small Business Server 2003 Premium Edition also includes Microsoft SQL Server 2005 Workgroup Edition and ISA Server 2004. Because Microsoft Dynamics CRM requires a SQL Server database, you must deploy Microsoft Dynamics CRM with the Premium Edition.

Microsoft Windows Small Business Server offers great value for small businesses because the cost of the bundled product is thousands of dollars less than purchasing all of the components individually. Although deploying Small Business Server includes several great benefits, it does include some notable restrictions:

- Each domain can contain only one installation of Small Business Server 2003.

- Small Business Server 2003 does not support trusts between domains, and you must install the server at the root of the Active Directory forest.

- A Small Business Server 2003 domain cannot have any child domains.

- You cannot run Terminal Services in Application Server mode on Small Business Server 2003.

- You can connect a maximum of 75 users or devices to a Windows Small Business Server–based network. After you factor in performance consider-ations, a recommended maximum number of users for a Small Business Server can range from 40 to 50 users, depending on their usage and the system hardware.

Regardless of these constraints, Microsoft Dynamics CRM works perfectly well on Small Business Server 2003.

Licensing

Just as Microsoft Dynamics CRM offers multiple deployment options, Microsoft Dynamics CRM also offers flexibility in how you can purchase the software licenses. Microsoft Dynamics CRM requires two types of software licenses for each deployment: server licenses and Client Access Licenses (CALs). Every deployment must include at least one server license, and you must have one CAL for every active user in the system. Client Access Licenses are typically referred to as user licenses.

Customers can purchase CALs under one of two models:

- **Named User CALS**   The number of user licenses that you need depends on the number of *named users* in your system. The CAL is tied to a specific user, and that user can access Microsoft Dynamics CRM from any computer.

- **Device CALs**   Under this model, the CAL is tied to a specific device and different Microsoft Dynamics CRM users can access the system, as long as they access it from the same device. Device CALs fit best with multishift operations such as call centers and hospitals.

> **Important** Named user licensing is different from many other software programs that base
> their licensing on the number of concurrent users. Every active user in Microsoft Dynamics CRM
> consumes a license, regardless of how often he or she accesses the system or how many users
> log on at the same time. But don't worry, when necessary a system administrator can easily
> transfer user licenses from one user to another, such as when a user leaves the company or if an
> employee takes an extended leave of absence.

Regardless of whether you select the named user or device CAL model, three different types
of CAL licenses exist:

- **Full**   Users with a full CAL have access to all of Microsoft Dynamics CRM as defined by
  their business unit and security roles. (Chapter 3, "Managing Security and Information
  Access," explains the details of configuring user access.)

- **Read-only**   Users with a read-only CAL can read data in Microsoft Dynamics CRM, but
  they cannot modify or delete any records. Some documentation refers to this type of
  CAL as a *limited* user.

- **Administrative**   Users with an administrative CAL can modify the system settings and
  customize records, but they cannot modify any of the other records in the system.
  Administrative CALs are free of charge.

If your company deploys a Web farm with multiple Microsoft Dynamics CRM Web servers,
you must have a server license for every Web server running Microsoft Dynamics CRM.

External Connector License

If you want to share Microsoft Dynamics CRM data with external users such as your customers
or partners, you can purchase an *External Connector License* that allows you to share
Microsoft Dynamics CRM data with an unlimited number of third-party users and systems.
By using the External Connector License, you do not need to purchase a user license for each
external user. For example, you can create an extranet Web site where customers can log on
and retrieve Microsoft Dynamics CRM data in real time. You could also create a special Web
site for your partners to enter and update Microsoft Dynamics CRM data. It is important to
note that the External Connector License does not apply to your company's employees, it
applies only to external users such as customers, partners, and vendors. Internal employees
need a Microsoft Dynamics CRM CAL to access data in Microsoft Dynamics CRM.

> **Important** The External Connector License is only a software license, it does not include any
> software components; therefore, you must create your own custom portal and authentication
> mechanism to allow external users to access your Microsoft Dynamics CRM data.

The two primary versions of the External Connector License are as follows:

- **External Connector**   Allows external users full read-write access to Microsoft Dynamics CRM data

- **Limited External Connector**   Allows external users read-only access to Microsoft Dynamics CRM data

You will need an External Connector License for each server that hosts an external application. If you have multiple servers hosting external applications, you can mix and match the types of connector licenses as necessary.

The following types of users would not qualify for Microsoft Dynamics CRM usage under the External Connector License:

- All internal users

- External users acting in an internal capacity by using the Microsoft Dynamics CRM Web client or Outlook client interface

These types of users need to purchase a CAL to access Microsoft Dynamics CRM.

Volume Licensing

Of course, you can purchase the Microsoft Dynamics CRM software licenses through various Microsoft licensing programs such as Open Business, Open Value, Select, Enterprise Agreement, and Full-Package Product. We don't go into the details of these programs because licensing is a complex topic, but the key point is that you can purchase the software using whichever licensing program makes the most sense for your business.

> **Important**   When you purchase Microsoft Dynamics CRM licenses, you will receive software updates and new version rights at no charge for a period of time after your initial purchase. The length of time that you receive software updates depends on the licensing program that you use to purchase the licenses, but it ranges from one to three years. You can continue to receive software updates by purchasing Software Assurance for additional years. If you choose not to renew updates, you will still own the Microsoft Dynamics CRM software licenses in perpetuity.

When you purchase Microsoft Dynamics CRM software licenses through volume licensing programs such as Open Business, Open Value, Select, and Enterprise Agreements, you will receive a product ID key that you enter upon software installation. When you enter this product ID key, the software will allow you to have up to 100,000 users regardless of the number of licenses you have actually purchased. This may surprise you, but many Microsoft products rely on self-enforcement of licensing to make sure that you've purchased the correct number of licenses. As you probably already know, stiff penalties exist for noncompliance with software laws; therefore, you should periodically check the number of user licenses you have purchased against the number of user licenses you are actually using. Because the software user interface allows you to add users up to 100,000, you can accidentally add 50, 75, or even 100 more users than you have purchased licenses for!

Front Office vs. Back Office

Because CRM strategies revolve around tracking and managing customer interactions, CRM applications typically focus on customer touchpoints in departments such as sales, customer service, and marketing. Some people refer to these customer interfacing departments as the *front office* of a company. Consequently, you can refer to the departments that help support a business's operations but that don't interact directly with customers as the *back office*. Typical back-office departments include Information Technology, human resources, manufacturing, distribution, and accounting. Most people refer to software applications that help companies manage back-office operations as enterprise resource planning (ERP) applications. Just like CRM systems, implementing ERP applications requires a very careful and well-planned process to maximize the project's success.

The Microsoft Dynamics CRM functionality focuses mostly on front-office features, so it doesn't really include any back-office functionality as part of its default installation. Of course, you could customize the Microsoft Dynamics CRM software to include your own back-office functionality, but developing ERP functionality can prove extremely complex and expensive. Fortunately, Microsoft offers several ERP applications from the same division that created Microsoft Dynamics CRM.

> **Important** In addition to Microsoft Dynamics CRM, the Microsoft Dynamics division offers several ERP software products in its lineup.

Some of the current Microsoft Dynamics ERP products include these:

- Microsoft Dynamics GP
- Microsoft Dynamics SL
- Microsoft Dynamics NAV
- Microsoft Dynamics AX

Each of these products provides rich functionality, and choosing the right ERP product for your business requires careful consideration well beyond what we can explain in this book.

We mention these ERP products so that you know that Microsoft offers software for these back-office departments in case you're interested in automating that part of your business. In addition, Microsoft offers software integration between Microsoft Dynamics CRM and Microsoft Dynamics GP so that you can synchronize customer records, orders, and invoices between your front-office and back-office systems, as Figure 1-4 illustrates.

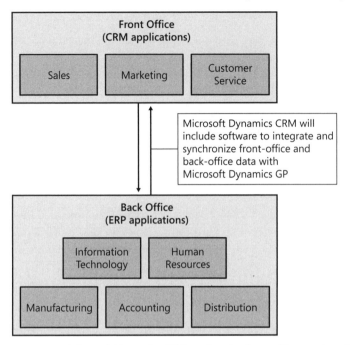

FIGURE 1-4 Microsoft Dynamics CRM synchronization and integration with Microsoft Dynamics GP

> **More Info** Microsoft Dynamics CRM 3.0 includes integration software named Microsoft
> Dynamics CRM Connector for Microsoft Dynamics GP to synchronize front-office and back-office
> data. The Microsoft Dynamics CRM Connector for Microsoft Dynamics GP uses Microsoft BizTalk
> Server 2004 Partner Edition and supports the synchronization of customer, address, product,
> price, order, and invoice data between the two systems. In addition, this integration software
> includes its own software development kit (SDK) so that you can customize the synchronization.
> The official name, pricing, and functionality of this integration software for Microsoft Dynamics
> CRM 4.0 had not been released at the time this book was written. However, Microsoft Dynamics
> CRM 3.0 offers the Microsoft Dynamics CRM Connector for Microsoft Dynamics GP software as
> a free download for customers. We're hopeful that Microsoft will offer the Microsoft Dynamics
> CRM 4.0 verison of this Microsoft Dynamics GP integration software at no charge as well.

System Requirements

As mentioned earlier, Microsoft Dynamics CRM uses industry-standard technologies such as
Windows Server, Active Directory, and SQL Server for its platform. You have great flexibility
in designing and configuring your Microsoft Dynamics CRM environment, and your final
system design will depend on several variables such as the following:

- Number of servers available and server hardware specifications
- Number of Microsoft Dynamics CRM users and their expected system usage

- Hardware specifications of your servers and your local area network performance

- Your network structure and security configurations, including firewalls and virtual private network (VPN) connections

- Amount of disaster recovery and failover systems needed in your deployment

Important Even though Microsoft designed Microsoft Dynamics CRM as an easy-to-use software application, this application requires a server environment to set up and install. This book includes a trial version of the software, but please do not attempt to install it onto a desktop computer.

The Microsoft Dynamics CRM 4.0 Implementation Guide lists some recommended deployment configurations based on the variables outlined previously. However, as a general rule of thumb, the Microsoft Dynamics CRM server environment requires the following components:

- Windows Server (2003 or 2000) or Small Business Server 2003 Premium Edition

- SQL Server 2005 with SQL Server Reporting Services

Of course, users accessing Microsoft Dynamics CRM must also meet certain minimum hardware and software requirements on their computers. Users need at least Internet Explorer 6 with Service Pack 1 (SP1) running on Windows XP with Service Pack 2 to access Microsoft Dynamics CRM using the Web client. Both Internet Explorer 7 and the Windows Vista operating system are supported as well. Microsoft Dynamics CRM for Outlook requires either Microsoft Office 2003 with SP3 or Microsoft Office 2007 with SP1. We don't include the exact hardware and software specifications in this book because they vary over time as Microsoft releases new versions of its software. Please consult the Microsoft Dynamics CRM Web site at *http://www.microsoft.com/crm* or the Implementation Guide for the latest hardware and software requirements.

More Info Some customers ask us about using Web browsers other than Internet Explorer, such as Mozilla Firefox or Apple Safari, with Microsoft Dynamics CRM. If you browse to a Microsoft Dynamics CRM Web site using a browser other than Internet Explorer, you get an error message stating that the browser isn't supported or you get a completely useless jumbled page. However, we did find a Firefox extension named IEtab (*http://ietab.mozdev.org*) that you can use to render pages in Firefox using the Internet Explorer engine. This trick relies on having Internet Explorer on the computer because IEtab simply displays an Internet Explorer window in a Firefox shell; therefore, some people say this doesn't qualify as running Microsoft Dynamics CRM in Firefox. However, the IEtab extension does provide a little bit of fun. Of course, this configuration is not supported by Microsoft, so we do not recommend deploying it in a production environment. Unfortunately, we have not yet found a trick or workaround to get Apple's Safari browser to display Microsoft Dynamics CRM correctly.

Core Concepts and Terminology

Now that you know some of the background of Microsoft Dynamics CRM, we can explain the details of the actual software. We cover the Microsoft Dynamics CRM core concepts and terminology in the following areas:

- User interfaces
- Entities
- Microsoft Dynamics CRM customizations

We briefly explain these areas as a quick tour so that we can dedicate as much space as possible in this book to cover customizing and extending Microsoft Dynamics CRM.

User Interfaces

Microsoft Dynamics CRM is a Web-based application built using the Microsoft .NET Framework technology platform. Because of its native Web architecture, users can access Microsoft Dynamics CRM through the Internet Explorer Web browser. Figure 1-5 shows what the interface looks like.

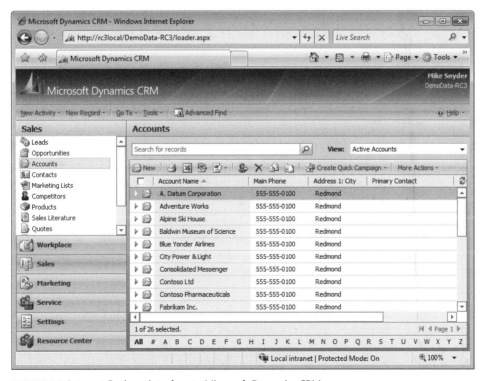

FIGURE 1-5 Internet Explorer interface to Microsoft Dynamics CRM

In addition to the Web interface (also known as the *Web client*), users can access Microsoft Dynamics CRM by installing the Microsoft Dynamics CRM client for Microsoft Office Outlook on a computer running Outlook. Because Microsoft Dynamics CRM for Outlook is optional, you can pick and choose which users should receive this software on their computer. You can deploy Microsoft Dynamics CRM for Outlook to all, none, or just some of your users. Figure 1-1, earlier in this chapter, shows a sample screenshot of Microsoft Dynamics CRM for Outlook. Microsoft Dynamics CRM for Outlook offers two versions:

- **Microsoft Dynamics CRM for Outlook** Designed for use with desktop computers that will remain connected to the Microsoft Dynamics CRM server at all times. Use this client for online-only scenarios and when multiple users log on to the same computer using different profiles.

- **Microsoft Dynamics CRM for Outlook with Offline Access** Designed for users of laptop computers who must disconnect from the Microsoft Dynamics CRM server but who still need to work with CRM data when they are offline. The software copies data from the Microsoft Dynamics CRM server to a Microsoft SQL Server 2005 Express Edition database installed on the user's computer so that the user can work while disconnected. When the user reconnects to the server, the Microsoft Dynamics CRM client bidirectionally synchronizes data between the Microsoft Dynamics CRM server and the user's SQL Server 2005 Express Edition database. The offline client can be used by only one user on a single computer. Microsoft Dynamics CRM refers to the processes of connecting and disconnecting from the server as *going offline* and *going online*.

> **Note** When we reference the Microsoft Dynamics CRM for Outlook in this book, we are refer-
> ring to *both* the standard and offline versions. The two clients offer nearly identical functionality
> except that the version with offline access allows users to work disconnected from the Microsoft
> Dynamics CRM server.

Users can access almost all of the Microsoft Dynamics CRM system functionality from either the Web client or from Microsoft Dynamics CRM for Outlook. Therefore, you can decide whether you want to deploy the Web client or Microsoft Dynamics CRM for Outlook, or if you want to offer both options to your users. Microsoft Dynamics CRM for Outlook can synchronize a user's Microsoft Dynamics CRM contacts and activities between the Microsoft Dynamics CRM server and a user's Outlook data. You can configure how often this synchronization occurs, and you can also filter the contact data that you want the software to synchronize on each user's behalf.

> **More Info** In addition to the end user interfaces, Microsoft Dynamics CRM includes additional
> tools for administrators to set up and manage the deployment. We cover some of the tools such
> as the Microsoft Dynamics CRM Data Migration Manager and the E-mail Router in Chapter 2,
> "Setup and Common Tasks."

Entities

Microsoft Dynamics CRM uses the term *entities* to describe the record types that it uses throughout the system. The concept of entities is easily one of the most important concepts to understand before you can customize Microsoft Dynamics CRM. Some people use the term *objects* to describe the concept of entities.

The default installation of Microsoft Dynamics CRM includes more than 150 different entities for tracking and managing different types of data. We don't have the space to list all of the default entities, but some of the more frequently used entities include the following:

- **Lead**   A potential customer that users can qualify or disqualify as a sales opportunity. When you qualify (convert) a Lead, Microsoft Dynamics CRM can automatically create an Account, Contact, and Opportunity record for you.

- **Contact**   A person who interacts with your organization. Contact records can be customers, but you can also track any type of contact, such as partners, suppliers, vendors, and so on.

- **Account**   A business or organization that interacts with your company. You can link an account's employees as contacts related to the account. In addition, you can create parent and child relationships between accounts to reflect divisions or departments within a single large account.

- **Case**   A customer service incident reported by a customer that your organization wants to track and manage until it's successfully resolved.

- **Activity**   An action or follow-up item that your users must complete, such as tasks, phone calls, letters, and e-mail messages. You can link activities to an entity to specify what the follow-up item regards.

- **Note**   Short text annotations that you can link to various entities throughout Microsoft Dynamics CRM.

- **Opportunity**   A potential sale for your organization. After a customer decides whether he or she will purchase from your company, you can mark the opportunity as won or lost.

Microsoft Dynamics CRM uses a *form* to display the attributes of a single entity record, as shown in Figure 1-6. Users can view and update entity records by editing the data that appears on the entity's form.

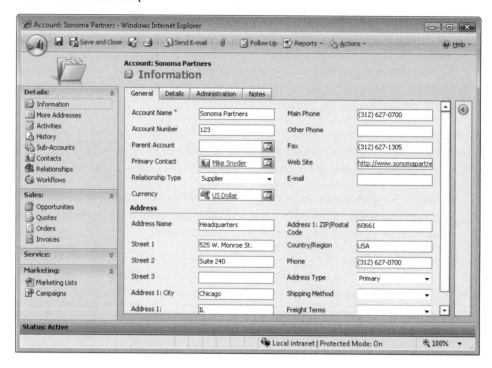

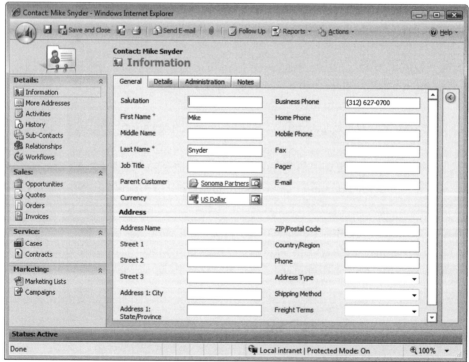

FIGURE 1-6 Account and Contact forms

In addition to an entity form that displays one record at a time, users can retrieve data for multiple entity records at the same time by using a *view*. Figure 1-7 shows the Open Opportunities view (in the Web client).

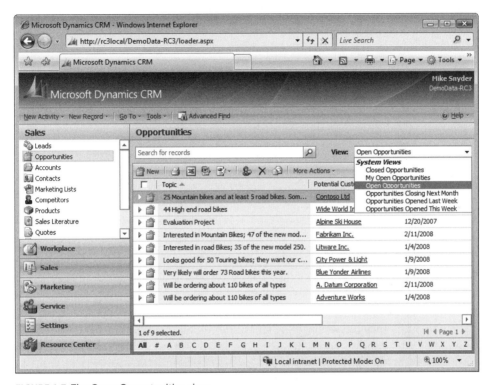

FIGURE 1-7 The Open Opportunities view

> **Important** Entities can have only one form, but you can create as many views as you want for each entity. Forms and views are two of the most important user interface components in the system, and you'll probably invest a lot of time customizing the forms and views for the entities in your Microsoft Dynamics CRM system.

Microsoft Dynamics CRM categorizes entities into four user interface areas: Workplace, Sales, Marketing, and Service. Table 1-2 summarizes the entities that appear in the various areas by default.

TABLE 1-2 Entities by Area

Workplace area	Sales area	Marketing area	Service area
Accounts	Accounts	Accounts	Accounts
Contacts	Contacts	Contacts	Contacts
Activities	Leads	Leads	Service Calendar
Calendar	Opportunities	Marketing Lists	Cases

TABLE 1-2 Entities by Area

Workplace area	Sales area	Marketing area	Service area
Queues	Marketing Lists	Campaigns	Knowledge Base
Articles	Competitors	Products	Contracts
Reports	Products	Sales Literature	Products
Announcements	Sales Literature	Quick Campaigns	Services
	Quotes		
	Orders		
	Invoices		
	Quick Campaigns		

> **Note** You can create new areas in the user interface and change where entities appear by editing the site map. For example, you could edit the site map so that the Announcements entity appears in the Sales and Marketing area in addition to the Workplace area. Refer to Chapter 6, "Entity Customization: Relationships, Custom Entities, and Site Map," for more information about editing the site map.

Your users will work with entity records mostly by using the various forms and views throughout the system. However, system administrators can review all of the configuration data related to an entity, such as its data attributes, its form, its views, and any relationships an entity may possess with other entities in Microsoft Dynamics CRM. You will use an entity editor to modify the record instead of making the changes directly in the Microsoft SQL Server database. By using the entity editor, Microsoft Dynamics CRM will automatically perform all of the behind-the-scenes modifications necessary to ensure that the software continues to function properly. Figure 1-8 shows the entity editor for the Account entity.

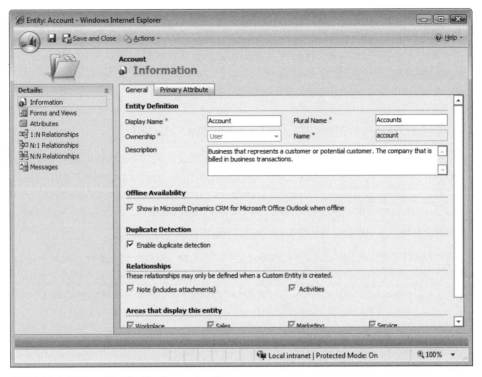

FIGURE 1-8 Entity editor for the Account entity

> **Important** Do not edit the Microsoft Dynamics CRM database directly in Microsoft SQL Server because that will probably cause unexpected results such as loss of data or unrepairable damage.

You can customize nearly half of the default entities that Microsoft Dynamics CRM creates, but there are some entities that you cannot customize because Microsoft Dynamics CRM uses them to manage the inner workings of the software. Chapter 4, "Entity Customization: Concepts and Attributes," Chapter 5, "Entity Customization: Forms and Views," and Chapter 6, "Entity Customization: Relationships, Custom Entities and Site Map," go into great detail about how to customize existing entities and create new entities to meet your business's needs.

> **Important** With Microsoft Dynamics CRM, you can customize entities, and you can also create entirely new entities that you can use to store additional types of data. System administrators use a Web-based interface to create new entities and customize existing entities without having to write a single line of programming code.

Microsoft Dynamics CRM Customizations

Microsoft Dynamics CRM offers great out-of-the-box functionality, but we believe one of its biggest benefits is the ease with which you can customize and revise the software to make it fit your business perfectly. Microsoft Dynamics CRM includes some of the most powerful, yet flexible, customization options available for any CRM program on the market. Some of the customization highlights include the following:

- **Entity customization and creation** Customize entities by adding, modifying, or deleting their various properties, such as attributes, forms, views, relationships, mappings, and system messages. You can also create entirely new custom entities. Chapters 4, 5, and 6 explore entity customization in detail.

- **Site map and ISV.config** You can revise the user interface and application navigation by adding new areas, links, and buttons to areas throughout the application. Chapter 6 explains how to work with the site map and Chapter 9, "Microsoft Dynamics CRM 4.0 SDK," details the ISV.config file.

- **Custom reports** Use SQL Server Reporting Services or Microsoft Dynamics CRM to modify the default reports, or you can create entirely new reports using the Microsoft Dynamics CRM Report Wizard. Reporting Services includes powerful reporting functionality, such as data caching, report snapshots, and automated report delivery. You can also create additional reporting and analysis tools by using the Filtered database views that Microsoft Dynamics CRM creates for entities such as Leads, Accounts, and Contacts. Chapter 7, "Reporting and Analysis," reviews the details regarding reporting in Microsoft Dynamics CRM.

- **Workflow rules** Use the workflow functionality to create rules that help automate business processes. Workflow rules can reference and incorporate data from your own custom .NET workflow assemblies. A sample workflow can accomplish something like this: "Make sure a salesperson calls and introduces himself or herself to every new account by automatically creating a phone call Activity due one day after an account is created." Chapter 8, "Workflow," explains creating and managing workflow rules in Microsoft Dynamics CRM.

- **Business logic integration** Programmatically access and update Microsoft Dynamics CRM data through Web services by creating your own custom code. By adhering to the Microsoft Dynamics CRM published application programming interfaces (APIs), your custom code can upgrade smoothly to future versions of Microsoft Dynamics CRM. You can create two-way integration between Microsoft Dynamics CRM and other systems, such as your company Web site or extranet, by using the SDK integration tools.

- **Pre-event and post-event plug-ins**   Create custom business logic with .NET assemblies that you can link directly to the Microsoft Dynamics CRM application logic. Chapter 9 details how to work with plug-ins.

- **Client extensions and scripting**   Tap into client-side events such as *OnLoad*, *OnSave*, and *OnChange*. You can attach your custom scripts to these client events, and Microsoft Dynamics CRM will trigger them for you. Client extensions can help improve your users' experience because you can add advanced data validation and automatic formatting when users enter data on forms. Automatically formatting a phone number is an example of a client extension. Chapter 10, "Form Scripting and Extensions" outlines how to work with client extensions and scripting.

Supported vs. Unsupported Customizations

Although Microsoft Dynamics CRM provides almost limitless customization options, you may encounter scenarios in which you want to customize the software in a manner not described in this book or in the product documentation. You may hear that these types of undocumented customizations are "unsupported," but what does that really mean? Unsupported customizations could fall into one of three categories:

- Microsoft has not tested the change and can't confirm whether it will cause problems.

- Microsoft has tested the change and knows that it will cause problems.

- The change might not cause problems now, but it might cause problems if you update your software with hot fixes, patches, or new releases of Microsoft Dynamics CRM.

Unfortunately, you can't really know into which category a particular customization will fall. Therefore, you may make an unsupported change and never experience a problem. However, it's more likely that unsupported customizations will cause problems sooner or later, potentially even months after the change is made. If you do experience a problem with an unsupported customization and you call Microsoft technical support, guess what they'll say? "That's unsupported, so we can't assist you." Of course, they are quite friendly people and they may give you a tip or two related to your request, but you should not expect any assistance from Microsoft technical support if you implement unsupported customizations. Some of the most obvious unsupported customizations include the following:

- Manually or programmatically interacting directly with the SQL Server database (other than through filtered views)

- Modifying any of the .aspx or .js files

- Installing or adding files to the Microsoft Dynamics CRM folders other than those folders explicitly permitted as defined in the software development kit

- Referencing or decompiling any of the Microsoft Dynamics CRM .dll files

Even though many "unsupported" customizations are technically possible to implement, you should carefully consider the risk/reward tradeoff of doing so. You should anticipate that your unsupported customizations could *possibly* break with Microsoft Dynamics CRM 4.0 hot fixes and that they *probably will* break with future versions of Microsoft Dynamics CRM.

Summary

CRM is a strategy that businesses implement to improve the quality of all their customer interactions. For companies using industry-standard technologies such as Active Directory, SQL Server, and Exchange Server, Microsoft Dynamics CRM is an excellent choice as the technology platform for implementation of CRM strategies. Microsoft designed Microsoft Dynamics CRM to address the common user and IT complaints related to earlier CRM applications. In particular, Microsoft Dynamics CRM uses all of the common tools that employees already use every day, such as Outlook, Internet Explorer, Word, and Excel. It also uses industry-standard network technologies such as Active Directory, SQL Server, and Exchange Server to help minimize the time required by IT professionals to deploy and administer the software.

Microsoft Dynamics CRM offers customers many different choices on how they can purchase and deploy the software. Customers can purchase perpetual licenses and deploy the software on premise, or they can use Microsoft Dynamics CRM through a Web-hosted service such as Microsoft Dynamics CRM Live.

Microsoft Dynamics CRM uses entities as the data storage mechanism for the record types in the software. You can customize the default system entities, including modifying their forms and views. You can also create entirely new custom entities to capture data about new record types unique to your business. In addition to entity customization, Microsoft Dynamics CRM offers a variety of customization and integration options.

Chapter 2
Setup and Common Tasks

Now that you understand some of the background, benefits, and architecture of Microsoft Dynamics CRM, we can delve into the details of setup and common tasks in the system. Because companies of varying sizes and industries use Microsoft Dynamics CRM, we concentrate on the information that typically applies to most businesses. At this point, we assume that you have already installed the software and that you can access it from the Web client and through the Microsoft Dynamics CRM client for Microsoft Office Outlook. In addition, we also assume that you are at least a little familiar with using the Microsoft Dynamics CRM user interface and you understand how to work with records to add activities, notes, and so on.

Tip Installing the Microsoft Dynamics CRM software is a topic beyond the scope of this book. The Microsoft Dynamics CRM 4.0 Implementation Guide provides excellent information on this topic. You can download the guide at *http://go.microsoft.com/fwlink/?LinkID=104413*.

We want to provide you with more information about the most commonly used day-to-day end user activities so that you can help guide users to make the most of your organization's investment in Microsoft Dynamics CRM. In addition, we explain the options available when you load your customer data into Microsoft Dynamics CRM.

Microsoft Dynamics CRM for Outlook

Without a doubt, the integration that Microsoft Dynamics CRM offers with Microsoft Office Outlook generates the most excitement and interest among our customers and prospects. People love that they can work directly with their customer relationship management (CRM) data in Outlook without needing to open a second software application. Unfortunately, the integration between Microsoft Dynamics CRM and Outlook also generates quite a few questions about how the two systems work together. We expect that you'll get a lot of questions about how the systems work together, too; therefore, we want to give you a detailed look at the integration. We cover the following topics in this section:

- Standard versus offline client

- Integration points

- Data synchronization

- Remote workers

In the next section, we also cover how to work with e-mail in Microsoft Dynamics CRM, which includes some overlap with Microsoft Dynamics CRM for Outlook.

Standard vs. Offline Client

As you learned in Chapter 1, "Microsoft Dynamics CRM 4.0 Overview," Microsoft Dynamics CRM offers two versions of the Outlook client:

- Microsoft Dynamics CRM for Outlook

- Microsoft Dynamics CRM for Outlook with Offline Access

The add-ins offer almost identical functionality, but one version allows users to work offline disconnected from the Microsoft Dynamics CRM server. Microsoft Dynamics CRM for Outlook with Offline Access uses significantly more system resources than the standard version of Microsoft Dynamics CRM for Outlook does. Therefore, we encourage you to install Microsoft Dynamics CRM for Outlook with Offline Access only if you know that the computer and user will definitely need to work offline.

With Microsoft Dynamics CRM for Outlook with Offline Access installed, users can click a button to *go offline*. When going offline, Microsoft Dynamics CRM for Outlook with Offline Access copies data from the server to a local Microsoft SQL Server 2005 Express Edition database located on the computer. The offline client will automatically install this database as part of its installation routine. Users see a progress window indicating the status of the synchronization process (Figure 2-1).

Once offline, users can continue working with Outlook and Microsoft Dynamics CRM data as usual, but when they view Microsoft Dynamics CRM pages, only data from the local database is displayed.

More Info When offline, Microsoft Dynamics CRM uses a local Web server named Cassini to display the Web pages. Cassini is a lightweight Web server built on the Microsoft .NET Framework.

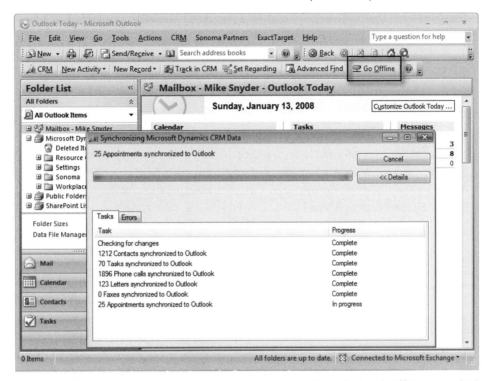

FIGURE 2-1 Users click Go Offline and Microsoft Dynamics CRM for Outlook with Offline Access displays a synchronization progress window

Microsoft Dynamics CRM for Outlook with Offline Access performs the offline synchronization process when users click the Go Offline button. If users forget to click the Go Offline button, they can still work with Microsoft Dynamics CRM data offline, but the data may be out-of-date depending on the last time it was synchronized with the offline database. To avoid this scenario, users can select a setting in the Local Data tab of the Personal Options of Microsoft Dynamics CRM for Outlook so that the system automatically updates local data in the background at regular intervals (such as every 15 minutes).

When users wish to connect to the Microsoft Dynamics CRM server, they click the Go Online button. Microsoft Dynamics CRM for Outlook with Offline Access will then perform another synchronization process. This process uploads data to the server that the user created or modified while offline. If Microsoft Dynamics CRM encounters a conflict scenario in which a user modified a record on the server while an offline user modified that same record, Microsoft Dynamics CRM uses the record with the latest modified date stamp to determine which record to keep. It automatically keeps one record or the other without prompting the user; it does not merge field-level changes of the two records. Microsoft Dynamics CRM will also fire any asynchronous plug-ins and workflow rules that apply to records created or modified while offline.

Two additional topics we want to highlight regarding Microsoft Dynamics CRM for Outlook with Offline Access include the following:

- Local data groups
- Offline constraints

Local Data Groups

If you work for a company with a very large Microsoft Dynamics CRM database (millions of records), you may wonder what happens when you go offline with Microsoft Dynamics CRM for Outlook with Offline Access. Does the software copy those millions of records to your laptop? How long does it take? Do you need a bigger hard drive?

Fortunately, users can configure exactly which data they want to download to their computer using the Local Data Groups setting. Microsoft Dynamics CRM for Outlook with Offline Access includes predefined local data filters for the various default system entities (Figure 2-2).

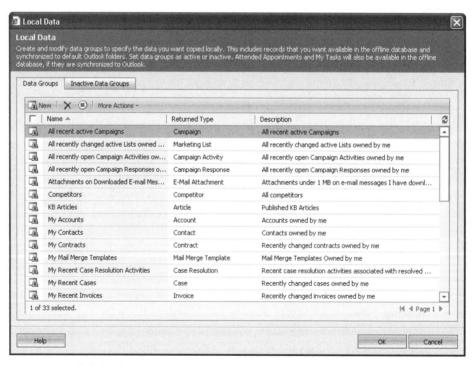

FIGURE 2-2 Default local data groups installed with Microsoft Dynamics CRM for Outlook with Offline Access

As you can see in Figure 2-2, Microsoft designed the default local data groups to restrict the amount of data the system takes offline. For example, on the Account and Contact records, the default settings download only active records that you own. Obviously, if you own millions of Accounts and Contacts, you should be careful about the amount of data you download when you go offline. As you would expect, very large offline data sets negatively affect system performance. To avoid downloading very large offline data sets, modify the local data group filters to only include the records you need while offline.

> **Tip**   The default local data group settings will only download reports that you own for offline use, so you may want to modify that setting to include any key reports that you need offline.

In addition, the default local data settings do not include *any* custom entity records that you create. Therefore, if your users want to work with custom entities offline, you must instruct them on how to include the specified records in their local data groups. Click Modify Local Data Groups to access the local data groups under the CRM item on the Outlook menu. To add new groups, simply click the New button on the grid toolbar. The Data Group dialog box opens, and then you can design a filter using the familiar Advanced Find user interface.

> **Important**   You must manually include custom entities in your local data groups if you want to work with those records while offline. Unfortunately, Microsoft Dynamics CRM does not include a tool or mechanism for administrators to modify local data groups for multiple users at one time. Therefore, you need to adjust the local data group on each computer that has Microsoft Dynamics CRM for Outlook with Offline Access installed.

For users with the standard (non-offline enabled) version of Microsoft Dynamics CRM for Outlook, local data groups apply only to the Contact record. Contacts in the local data group of the non-offline version can be synchronized into the user's Outlook contacts. Local data groups for other types of records don't apply because Microsoft Dynamics CRM for Outlook only synchronizes the contact records into users' Outlook file.

Offline Constraints

For the most part, both the standard and offline versions of Microsoft Dynamics CRM for Outlook provide nearly identical user experiences. However, Microsoft Dynamics CRM for Outlook with Offline Access does include a few constraints when running in the offline mode. These constraints include the following:

- Workflow rules do not run offline.
- Asynchronous plug-ins do not run offline.
- Duplicate detection does not work offline.
- You cannot import data when offline.
- You cannot access the system settings or customize entities while offline.
- You cannot access the Resource Center when offline.

- You cannot access the Service Calendar when offline.

- You cannot modify the Knowledge Base while offline, but you can access Knowledge Base articles.

When users go back online and connect to the Microsoft Dynamics CRM server, the system applies the appropriate workflow rules for the new or modified records. Therefore, be mindful of creating workflow rules that implement business-critical processes if some of your users work with data offline. Similarly, asynchronous plug-ins do not run offline. Microsoft Dynamics CRM runs asynchronous plug-ins against the appropriate records when users synchronize with the server after working offline. However, you can create synchronous plug-ins that will run offline in Microsoft Dynamics CRM for Outlook with Offline Access if you need that functionality.

Integration Points

Now we will review the details about how Microsoft Dynamics CRM for Outlook integrates with Outlook. After you install and configure the software, Microsoft Dynamics CRM for Outlook makes the following modifications to the Outlook interface:

- Adds the CRM toolbar

- Adds Microsoft Dynamics CRM folders

- Adds a CRM menu item

Figure 2-3 shows these modifications in the user interface.

FIGURE 2-3 Microsoft Dynamics CRM for Outlook modifications to Outlook user interface

As you can see in Figure 2-3, by clicking one of the Microsoft Dynamics CRM folders, you can display a CRM grid directly in Outlook. From here you can access CRM data just as you can through the Web client.

On the CRM menu, you can perform various tasks such as changing options, modifying local data groups, and importing data. With the CRM toolbar, you can quickly access functionality to create new records or activities, track records, or start Advanced Find.

In addition, Microsoft Dynamics CRM for Outlook adds a Track in CRM section to the following types of records: Tasks, Contacts, Appointments, and E-mail messages. When users click the Track in CRM button, they can relate the activity to the correct record in Microsoft Dynamics CRM by clicking Set Regarding and specifying a record. The regarding record can be any type of entity in Microsoft Dynamics CRM that supports a relationship to activities such as Leads, Cases, Accounts, Opportunities, and so forth (Figure 2-4). In addition, you can set the regarding value to custom entities that you create (assuming you configure the custom entity with a relationship to activities).

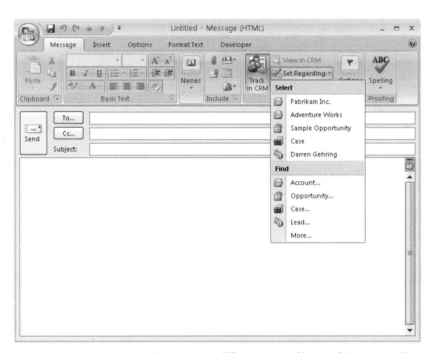

FIGURE 2-4 Setting the regarding record to different types of Microsoft Dynamics CRM records

By linking e-mail messages, appointments, and tasks to records in Microsoft Dynamics CRM, users can view those Outlook records in the list of activities related to that CRM record. Users can create records in Outlook and track them in Microsoft Dynamics CRM, or the activities can be created on the Microsoft Dynamics CRM server and then synchronized with a user's Outlook file. A typical example of this scenario is creating and assigning a task to a user using workflow (on the server), and then Microsoft Dynamics CRM for Outlook synchronizes that new task into a user's Outlook task list automatically.

Last, Microsoft Dynamics CRM for Outlook creates a new address book that users can access when writing e-mail messages (Figure 2-5). With this Microsoft Dynamics CRM address book, users can quickly access the e-mail addresses of the contacts in the database without requiring users to open another application to look up that information. To access the address book, simply click the To or Cc button when creating an e-mail message in Outlook and select the Microsoft Dynamics CRM Address Book in the drop-down list. You can modify which records Microsoft Dynamics CRM for Outlook will synchronize into your address book by changing the settings in the Address Book tab on the Options menu.

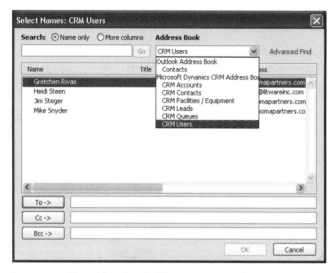

FIGURE 2-5 The address book of Microsoft Dynamics CRM records and e-mail addresses

> **More Info** The figures in this book show images of Microsoft Office Outlook 2007, but Microsoft Dynamics CRM for Outlook works with Outlook 2003 in a similar manner. However, the user interface for Outlook 2003 with Microsoft Dynamics CRM for Outlook will appear different.

CRM vs. Outlook Forms

As you can see, working with the customer records in Microsoft Dynamics CRM for Outlook is really no different from working with standard Outlook records. As we indicated, these are just Outlook forms with the additional Track in CRM button added. Therefore, users can learn the system quickly and become comfortable tracking data in Microsoft Dynamics CRM right away.

However, some Microsoft Dynamics CRM customers ask about customizing the Outlook forms to include additional types of data that they want to capture. For example, there might be some custom attributes on the Microsoft Dynamics CRM Contact record that they want to display in Outlook. If the record is already linked to a Microsoft Dynamics CRM record, the user can click the View in CRM button in the Outlook form and Microsoft Dynamics CRM for Outlook will open a new window displaying the full Microsoft Dynamics CRM form (complete with custom attributes and so forth).

> **Important** Users should click the View in CRM button to view the Microsoft Dynamics CRM form with all of the customized fields. Microsoft Dynamics CRM does not include any tools to customize the Outlook forms using custom attributes, and attempting this type of Outlook customization would require specific Outlook programming expertise.

If you desire, you can configure Microsoft Dynamics CRM for Outlook to display the Microsoft Dynamics CRM form when you create a new appointment, task, contact, or e-mail record from the CRM toolbar. You can enable this setting by clicking Options on the CRM menu, and then selecting which record types you want to use the Microsoft Dynamics CRM form instead of the Outlook form when you create a new record.

Activity Reminders

Outlook includes a reminder feature for tasks and appointments that automatically opens a message window on the date and at the time specified by the user. This reminder window is intended to ensure that the user notices the event and doesn't accidentally overlook it or forget to complete it. Microsoft Dynamics CRM for Outlook takes advantage of this Outlook feature by automatically creating reminder times for tasks and appointments created in Microsoft Dynamics CRM that synchronize with Outlook. The integration works in one of two ways depending on how the user creates the task or appointment:

- **Activity created in Microsoft Dynamics CRM**   Microsoft Dynamics CRM for Outlook automatically specifies the Outlook reminder time. For activities such as tasks and phone calls, the Outlook reminder time matches the activity due date and time. For appointments, Microsoft Dynamics CRM for Outlook will create the reminder time based on the default reminder settings configured for that user in Outlook (none, 15 minutes, 30 minutes, and so forth).

- **Activity created in Outlook and tracked in CRM**   For appointments and tasks, users can configure the reminder to suit preference. For tasks, they can configure the reminder time so that the reminder time does not need to match the task due date. For example, you might want a reminder 1 day before the task is due.

Microsoft Dynamics CRM does not store the Outlook reminder date and time as attributes of the activities. Therefore, users cannot access the Outlook reminder time on the Microsoft Dynamics CRM activity form. Additionally, users cannot turn off the automatic reminder creation for tasks, phone calls, letters, and faxes. Creating any of these activities with a due date creates a reminder in Outlook. The user can modify the Outlook reminder date and time after the activity synchronizes in Outlook, but updating the activity due date and time in the Microsoft Dynamics CRM Web client resets the reminder time to match the activity due date and time.

> **Caution** Reminder windows only appear when you're using Outlook; they will not appear in the Web client.

Outlook Web Access

Microsoft Dynamics CRM for Outlook works only with Outlook 2003 and Outlook 2007; it does not support integration with Outlook Web Access. Therefore, if your users use only Outlook Web Access, they cannot access the Microsoft Dynamics CRM integration functionality we have described.

However, if Microsoft Dynamics CRM for Outlook is installed, users can log on to Outlook Web Access and view the Microsoft Dynamics CRM data synchronized with their Outlook file such as CRM contacts, appointments, and tasks. However, the user will not see the Microsoft Dynamics CRM for Outlook user interface modifications such as the CRM toolbar, the Track in CRM buttons, and the Microsoft Dynamics CRM folders.

> **Caution** Microsoft Dynamics CRM for Outlook does not support integration with Outlook Web Access. To track Outlook data in Microsoft Dynamics CRM and synchronize data between Microsoft Dynamics CRM and Outlook, each user must install Microsoft Dynamics CRM for Outlook on a computer running Outlook 2003 or Outlook 2007.

Data Synchronization

The Microsoft Dynamics CRM for Outlook software synchronizes Microsoft Dynamics CRM data and Outlook data. Quite impressively, Microsoft Dynamics CRM for Outlook updates data bidirectionally so that users can modify records in either the Microsoft Dynamics CRM Web client or Microsoft Dynamics CRM for Outlook. Changes made in either system update the other the next time Microsoft Dynamics CRM for Outlook performs a synchronization.

Data synchronization generates a lot of questions, so we want to explain the following topics:

- Configuring data synchronization
- Deleting records

Configuring Data Synchronization

Figure 2-6 shows the Synchronization tab of Microsoft Dynamics CRM for Outlook.

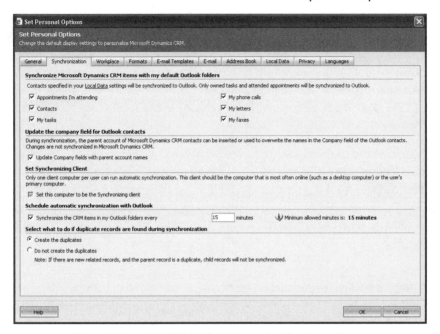

FIGURE 2-6 Microsoft Dynamics CRM for Outlook synchronization settings

Configuring synchronization is simple when you break down the options:

- **Appointments**   Only applies to appointments you're attending
- **Contacts**   Microsoft Dynamics CRM for Outlook synchronizes only contacts included in your local data group filters
- **Tasks**   Only applies to tasks you own
- **My Phone calls**   Only applies to phone calls you own
- **My Letters**   Only applies to letters you own
- **My Faxes**   Only applies to faxes you own

Because Outlook does not contain records for phone calls, letters, or faxes, Microsoft Dynamics CRM for Outlook synchronizes those records into Outlook tasks. Any record that you create in Outlook and for which you click the Track in CRM button is also included in the synchronization process because you will own that record in Microsoft Dynamics CRM.

Important Configuring local data groups in Microsoft Dynamics CRM for Outlook with Offline Access determines which records the system brings offline. In addition, Microsoft Dynamics CRM for Outlook and Microsoft Dynamics CRM for Outlook with Offline Access can synchronize the contact records in your local data groups with your Outlook contacts.

If you select the Update Company fields with parent account names, Microsoft Dynamics CRM for Outlook populates the contact's company name in Outlook. Unfortunately, the contact company name behaves differently from the other fields because Microsoft Dynamics CRM for Outlook does not perform a bidirectional synchronization of changes to the contact's company name. If you change a contact's company name in Outlook, Microsoft Dynamics CRM for Outlook will overwrite that change in the future with the contact's parent account name.

Figure 2-6 also shows that you can configure Microsoft Dynamics CRM for Outlook to synchronize automatically (the default interval is 15 minutes). This scheduled synchronization only applies changes from the server to your Outlook. Conversely, if you change a record in Microsoft Dynamics CRM for Outlook while online, that change will update the Microsoft Dynamics CRM server *immediately*. It does not wait for the next scheduled interval to make the update.

> **Important** Scheduling synchronization applies only to downloading changes from the server to your Outlook file. Changes made to records in Microsoft Dynamics CRM for Outlook when online update the data on the server immediately.

One other important factor you should consider regarding data synchronization is that the Microsoft Dynamics CRM for Outlook software updates your Outlook records only if a record was modified since the last synchronization. For example, assume that a fictional account named Fabrikam has 10 Contact records associated with it. As a result of a merger, Fabrikam changes its name to Contoso, Inc. If you update the account name in Microsoft Dynamics CRM, Microsoft Dynamics CRM records a modification to the Account record, but it won't alter the Contact records related to that account. Therefore, your contacts in Outlook will still use the old Fabrikam name in the company name field. However, each time someone updates one of the Contoso Contact records, Microsoft Dynamics CRM for Outlook will update the company name in Outlook to Contoso on the next data synchronization.

Deleting Records

After Microsoft Dynamics CRM for Outlook synchronizes data in the Outlook file, special rules apply to how the synchronization processes deleted records. For example, deleting a contact record in Outlook will *not* delete that contact record in Microsoft Dynamics CRM. Conversely, deleting a contact in Microsoft Dynamics CRM removes the synchronized contact from Outlook for all users except for the Outlook user who owns the record in Microsoft Dynamics CRM.

> **Important** Microsoft Dynamics CRM for Outlook uses various rules and conditions on deleted records to determine how the synchronization process should update Outlook and Microsoft Dynamics CRM.

Microsoft Dynamics CRM for Outlook processes deleted records as outlined in Table 2-1.

TABLE 2-1 Microsoft Dynamics CRM for Outlook Deletion Processing

Record	Action	Record state	Result
Contact	Delete in Microsoft Dynamics CRM	Any	Deleted from Outlook for all users except contact owner. Remains in Outlook of contact owner.
Contact	Delete in Outlook	Any	No change in Microsoft Dynamics CRM.
Task	Delete in Microsoft Dynamics CRM	Pending (not completed in Outlook)	Deleted from Outlook.
Task	Delete in Microsoft Dynamics CRM	Past (completed in Outlook)	Remains in Outlook.
Task	Delete in Outlook	Pending (open in Microsoft Dynamics CRM)	Deleted from Microsoft Dynamics CRM.
Task	Delete in Outlook	Past (completed or canceled in Microsoft Dynamics CRM)	No change to Microsoft Dynamics CRM.
Appointment	Delete in Microsoft Dynamics CRM	Pending (open in Microsoft Dynamics CRM)	Deleted from Outlook if Appointment start time is in the future.
Appointment	Delete in Microsoft Dynamics CRM	Past (completed or canceled in Microsoft Dynamics CRM)	Remains in Outlook.
Appointment	Delete in Outlook	Pending (open in Microsoft Dynamics CRM)	Deleted from Microsoft Dynamics CRM if deleted by appointment owner or organizer. Not deleted from Microsoft Dynamics CRM if deleted in Outlook by nonowners or nonorganizers.
Appointment	Delete in Outlook	Past (completed or canceled in Microsoft Dynamics CRM)	No change to Microsoft Dynamics CRM.

When a user deletes a contact in Outlook (which will not be deleted from Microsoft Dynamics CRM), and then someone subsequently modifies that contact record in Microsoft Dynamics CRM, Microsoft Dynamics CRM for Outlook will regenerate that contact in the user's Outlook file even though the user previously deleted it.

On a related note, deactivating Contact records in Microsoft Dynamics CRM does not remove the contacts from Outlook. Users must manually delete the deactivated contacts if they don't want them to appear in Outlook any longer.

E-Mail in Microsoft Dynamics CRM

As you would expect, Microsoft Dynamics CRM includes numerous features to help you track and manage e-mail communications with customers. From a high level, Microsoft Dynamics CRM can send and receive e-mail using one of two methods:

- The Web client
- Microsoft Dynamics CRM for Outlook

The options available to you depend on your e-mail infrastructure and how the network administrator installed the software. Microsoft Dynamics CRM supports a wide number of e-mail platforms, including Microsoft Exchange Server and any Post Office Protocol 3 (POP3)/Simple Mail Transfer Protocol (SMTP)–compliant e-mail server.

Microsoft Dynamics CRM includes a software application named Microsoft Dynamics CRM E-mail Router that acts as an interface between your e-mail system and Microsoft Dynamics CRM. The Microsoft Dynamics CRM E-mail Router also includes the E-mail Router Configuration Wizard to help you set up and configure e-mail for users. The Microsoft Dynamics CRM E-mail Router is *not* required for you to install Microsoft Dynamics CRM, but it does offer advanced e-mail routing and tracking features. If for some reason your organization cannot use the Microsoft Dynamics CRM E-mail Router, Microsoft Dynamics CRM for Outlook will perform similar routing and tracking functionality on each client computer. However, because it is a client application, users must keep Microsoft Dynamics CRM for Outlook open for the software to process the e-mail.

> **More Info** Because configuring e-mail and installing the Microsoft Dynamics CRM E-mail Router offers so many different deployment options, explaining these topics is beyond the scope of this book. Please refer to the Microsoft Dynamics CRM Implementation Guide for detailed instructions on how to install and configure the E-mail Router software.

After you configure Microsoft Dynamics CRM to work with your e-mail systems, you should understand these important areas:

- E-mail tracking
- E-mail templates
- Creating and sending mass e-mail messages

E-Mail Tracking

After you've successfully configured the various e-mail options in Microsoft Dynamics CRM, you can configure automatic e-mail tracking for both the organization and the individual users.

> **Important** All of the e-mail tracking settings we describe apply to the *automatic* tracking of e-mail. Regardless of the settings you choose, users with Microsoft Dynamics CRM for Outlook installed can manually track e-mail using the Track in CRM feature. Some customers prefer to rely on manual e-mail tracking so that the database contains only the key e-mail messages as determined by your users. With automatic tracking, Microsoft Dynamics CRM captures all of the messages, even if they are just short e-mail replies, personal notes, out-of-office replies, and so forth.

Organization Settings

You can access the organization e-mail settings in the E-mail tab of System Settings in the Administration area (Figure 2-7).

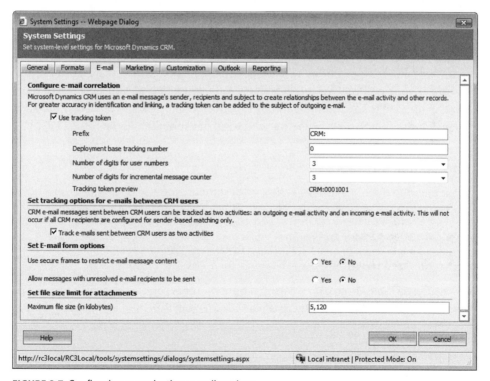

FIGURE 2-7 Configuring organization e-mail settings

From here, you can configure the various e-mail organization settings, and most of them are self-explanatory. For the e-mail correlation portion of these settings, you have one of two options:

- Smart matching only
- Smart matching with tracking tokens

If you leave the Use tracking token check box clear, Microsoft Dynamics CRM uses the smart matching feature to correlate e-mail messages automatically with the appropriate records. Smart matching uses an algorithm based on the e-mail sender, recipients, and message subject line to try to determine which record to use as the e-mail regarding record (Lead, Opportunity, Quote, and so forth). When matching on the e-mail message subject, the smart matching feature ignores prefixes (such as RE: and FW:) in addition to letter capitalization.

In you find that the accuracy of the smart matching feature does not meet your needs, you can choose to use the tracking token feature, which increases the accuracy of automatic e-mail matching. With the tracking token feature enabled, Microsoft Dynamics CRM adds a code in the subject line of e-mail messages sent from Microsoft Dynamics CRM.

In Figure 2-8, you can see that Microsoft Dynamics CRM automatically appended the tracking code "CRM:0002001" to the end of the e-mail subject line. This tracking code uniquely identifies the e-mail activity in the database. If a customer were to reply to this message, Microsoft Dynamics CRM would use the tracking token in the message subject as part of its matching algorithm to set the regarding field of the e-mail activity to the correct record. If you don't care for the default tracking token format, you can specify your own unique tracking token configuration by modifying the prefix and adjusting the number of digits for the components of the tracking token (as shown earlier in Figure 2-7).

Individual Settings

In addition to the organization-wide e-mail settings, you can configure e-mail tracking settings on a user-by-user basis. You edit individual e-mail settings in one of two places:

- Personal Options E-mail tab
- Microsoft Dynamics CRM User form

In the E-mail tab of each user's personal options, users can specify which e-mail messages they want to track in Microsoft Dynamics CRM (Figure 2-9).

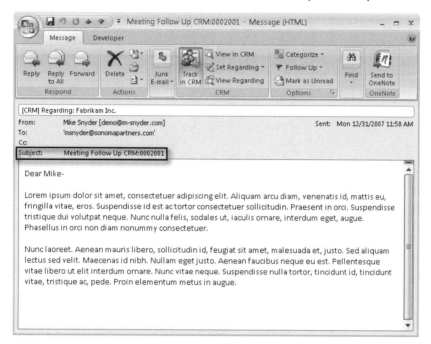

FIGURE 2-8 Tracking token in the subject line of an e-mail message

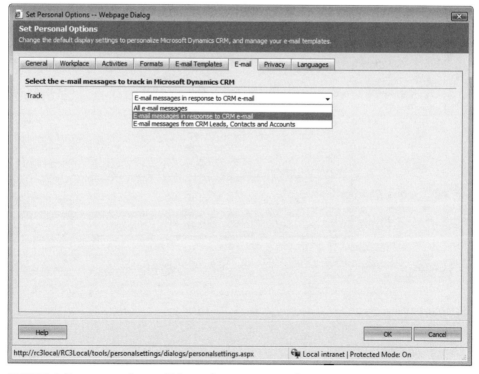

FIGURE 2-9 Users can configure which e-mail messages to track

The three options include the following:

- All e-mail messages
- E-mail messages in response to CRM e-mail
- E-mail messages from CRM Leads, Contacts, and Accounts

To turn off automatic e-mail tracking for a particular user, an administrator with the appropriate security credentials can modify the user's profile to set the incoming and outgoing e-mail access type to None (Figure 2-10). The default Microsoft Dynamics CRM security roles do not allow users to modify their own records, so typically a system administrator is required to configure these e-mail settings.

Tip Administrators can also use the Microsoft Dynamics CRM E-Mail Router Configuration Manager to update the user profile settings regarding incoming and outgoing e-mail access types. With this tool, administrators can update the settings for multiple users at one time.

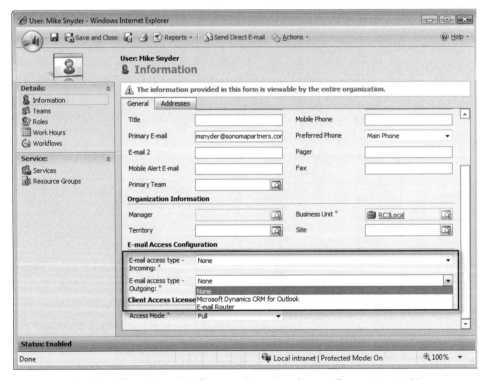

FIGURE 2-10 Turning off e-mail tracking for a user by setting the e-mail access type to None

E-Mail Templates

As their name implies, with e-mail templates you can create preformatted e-mail messages that you can reference in several areas throughout Microsoft Dynamics CRM. You can use e-mail templates in the following ways:

- **Insert templates into e-mail messages**   When users create e-mail messages in the Microsoft Dynamics CRM Web client, they can insert an e-mail template into the body of the message. Users can also insert multiple e-mail templates into a single e-mail message if necessary. Users cannot access e-mail templates when creating an e-mail message in Microsoft Dynamics CRM for Outlook.

- **Send direct e-mail by using templates**   Users can use e-mail templates to send the same e-mail message to multiple records. For example, you could use the Direct E-mail feature (which uses e-mail templates) to send the same message to 500 Contacts.

- **Reference e-mail templates in workflow rules**   Users can reference e-mail templates in Microsoft Dynamics CRM workflow to accomplish many types of business process automation techniques.

- **System Job notifications**   When Microsoft Dynamics CRM completes certain system jobs such as importing data or duplicate detection, it sends an e-mail confirmation message to administrators. You can use an e-mail template to modify the e-mail confirmation message.

In addition to being accessible from different areas of the Microsoft Dynamics CRM application, e-mail templates have the following unique features:

- **Data fields**   You can insert data fields into e-mail templates that Microsoft Dynamics CRM will dynamically populate on usage. For example, if you want to send an e-mail message to 20 people and address each recipient by his or her first name, you can insert a first name data field into the e-mail template. When Microsoft Dynamics CRM sends the message, it will automatically populate the data field with the first name value for each of the 20 recipients.

- **Personal and organization ownership**   E-mail templates can have individual or organization ownership, so security on each template can be set to just specific users or all users.

- **Template types**   For each e-mail template that you create, you must specify the single entity (such as leads or opportunities) to which the template applies. You can also create a global template for use with multiple entities.

You can create and use e-mail templates for many different entity types such as Leads, Opportunities, Accounts, Quotes, Orders, and service activities. You can also create e-mail templates for any custom entities that you create. Next, we explain the details of working with e-mail templates.

Creating or Modifying E-Mail Templates

Now that you understand some of the ways in which you can use e-mail templates in Microsoft Dynamics CRM, we will discuss how you create and set up new e-mail templates. Microsoft Dynamics CRM includes more than 20 e-mail templates in the default installation, including Lead Reply – Web Site Visit and Closed Case Acknowledgment.

You can modify these default templates or create entirely new e-mail templates that meet your needs. To view the e-mail templates that are currently in your system, browse to the Settings area of Microsoft Dynamics CRM and click Templates. A grid displays all of the e-mail templates and their types. Simply double-click any record to view a template, such as the Lead Reply – Trade Show Visit template shown in Figure 2-11.

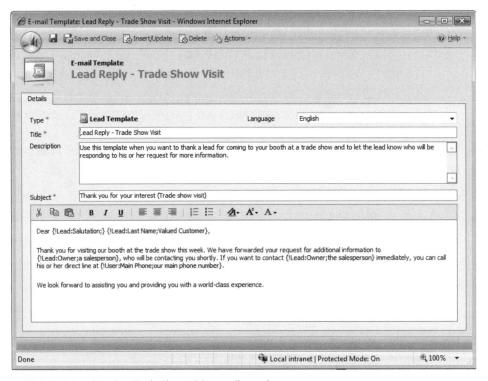

FIGURE 2-11 Lead Reply – Trade Show Visit e-mail template

You can see that a template contains several attributes, such as follows:

- **Type**   Whether the template is global or applies to only one entity.

- **Title**   Short title of the e-mail template that appears when users select a template.

- **Description**   Additional descriptive text that explains the function of the e-mail template. Users can access the description when they select a template.

- **Subject**   The Subject line of the e-mail message.

- **Body**   The body of the e-mail message. It isn't labeled on the form, but this is the large text box below the Subject line.

You can also see in Figure 2-11 that the e-mail template includes a highlighted data field like the following:

```
{!Lead: Last Name; Valued Customer}
```

Microsoft Dynamics CRM automatically converts this data field to the last name of the Lead for this record. The text before the colon refers to the entity, and the text after the colon specifies the attribute name. If a Lead record does not have a last name value, you can include a default value for the data field by entering text after the semicolon. In this example, Microsoft Dynamics CRM would insert the text *Valued Customer* in the e-mail message if there were no data in the last name field.

To add a new data field to an e-mail template, click the Insert/Update button on the form toolbar. The Data Field Values dialog box shown in Figure 2-12 appears.

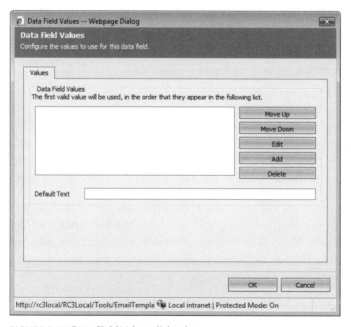

FIGURE 2-12 Data Field Values dialog box

When you click the Add button, another dialog box prompts you to select the Record Type and Field for the data field. Depending on the entity you selected for the e-mail template type, you can add fields from different related entities. For example, on Lead e-mail templates, you can add only fields from the Lead and User entities. However, for Opportunity e-mail templates, you can add fields from the Account, Contact, Opportunity, and User entities. After you select the field that you want to add and click OK, the field appears in the Data Field Values list. Then, you can specify the default value text (optional) by entering it in the Default Text box. When you click OK, Microsoft Dynamics CRM automatically creates the data field and adds it to the e-mail template.

> **Tip** You can add data fields to both the subject and body of an e-mail template.

If you want to add multiple data fields to an e-mail template, you must add them one at a time, as in this example:

```
{!Contact : Salutation;} {!Contact : Last Name;}
```

These data fields will insert the following text into an e-mail message for a sample Contact, Mr. Brian Valentine:

```
Mr. Valentine
```

However, if you add both data fields at the same time by using the Data Field Values dialog box, Microsoft Dynamics CRM will create one data field in the template, like this:

```
{!Contact : Salutation;Contact : Last Name;}
```

This data field inserts the following text for the same Contact:

```
Mr.
```

As you can see, Microsoft Dynamics CRM allows you to enter a dynamic data field for the default value of a different data field. In this example, *Contact: Last Name* is the default value for the *Contact: Salutation* data field. However, because the Contact record includes a value for the salutation, it does not need to output the default value of *Contact: Last Name*.

Creating a new e-mail template is straightforward. Click the New button on the grid toolbar, select the entity type for the e-mail template, and then enter the appropriate information in the template fields. After you set up your new template with attributes and data fields, click Save on the e-mail template toolbar. Microsoft Dynamics CRM immediately applies your changes to the e-mail template and users can access it.

> **Tip** When you enter and edit text in the e-mail template body, pressing Enter on your keyboard adds an extra line. If you want a single carriage return (instead of a new paragraph), press Shift+Enter instead.

Inserting Templates into E-Mail Messages

When you're writing an e-mail message in the Web client, you can click the Insert Template button to open the Insert Template dialog box, as shown in Figure 2-13. You must select at least one e-mail recipient before you can insert a template because Microsoft Dynamics CRM must know which template types apply to the message (based on the entity type of the recipients).

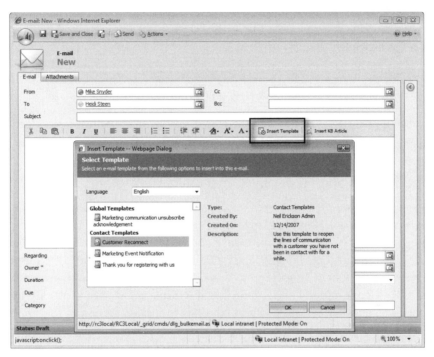

FIGURE 2-13 Inserting an e-mail template into an e-mail message

After you select an e-mail template, Microsoft Dynamics CRM automatically populates the template content in the body of the message and dynamically fills out any data fields that the e-mail template contains. This is a convenient feature if you want to edit or add additional content to an e-mail message before you send it (something you can't do with the Direct E-mail feature). If your e-mail message includes multiple recipients, Microsoft Dynamics CRM will prompt you with a dialog box to select one recipient as the e-mail template target when you insert a template into the message.

Caution Each time you insert an e-mail template into the body of an e-mail message, Microsoft Dynamics CRM updates the Subject line of the e-mail message to match the subject of the e-mail template. So, if you insert multiple templates, the subject is determined by the last template inserted. This is very convenient for writing new e-mail messages, but you should be aware of this behavior if you insert e-mail templates when you reply to messages.

Unfortunately, you cannot insert an e-mail template into an Outlook e-mail message even if you have the Microsoft Dynamics CRM for Outlook software installed.

Creating and Sharing Personal E-Mail Templates

The process we just explained creates an e-mail template that the entire organization can view and use. Users can also create personal templates for their own use.

Creating a personal e-mail template

1. On the application menu toolbar, click Tools, and then click Options.

2. In the E-mail Templates tab, click New on the grid toolbar.

If a user decides that he or she wants to share an e-mail template with the entire organization, the user can convert a personal template into an organization template at any time.

Inserting Images and Hyperlinks into E-Mail Templates

After you create a few e-mail templates, you'll probably notice that the editing tools for the e-mail message body are somewhat limited. For example, none of the buttons allow you to add a hyperlink or an image to the message. If you want to develop a more sophisticated e-mail template with multiple images, links, and so on, you can create HTML code with a development tool such as Microsoft Visual Studio 2008. However, if you try to copy and paste your HTML code into the e-mail template, it is displayed as plain text; your recipient will receive a bunch of HTML code instead of the formatted version of your message! Fortunately, by using a little trick you can easily copy and paste your custom HTML code into the e-mail template and still maintain the correct formatting.

For example, assume that you want to send a simple company newsletter to contacts in your database by using an e-mail template with the following requirements:

- Display the company logo in the message
- Display a hyperlink that readers can click to get more information

The following sample shows a company newsletter created in HTML using Visual Studio 2008. Next, you can copy (Ctrl+C) the sample newsletter and paste (Ctrl+V) it into the e-mail message body. The trick is to copy and paste the rendered HTML output, not the HTML code. You can accomplish this in a few ways:

- Copy and paste the formatted message from Visual Studio 2008 Design view
- Copy and paste the HTML Web page from a Microsoft Internet Explorer window

After you copy and paste the contents of the message into the e-mail template body, you will see the properly formatted e-mail message, complete with an image and a hyperlink. After you paste the code into the message, you can also add a data field to dynamically display the contact's first name in the newsletter. Figure 2-14 shows the finished e-mail message. Please note that if you use images, you need to make sure that the image references a URL that the e-mail recipient can access. This technique does not copy the image file into the file, it simply references the image URL from the HTML file.

Caution You cannot copy and paste HTML code from a text editor program such as Notepad into the e-mail template.

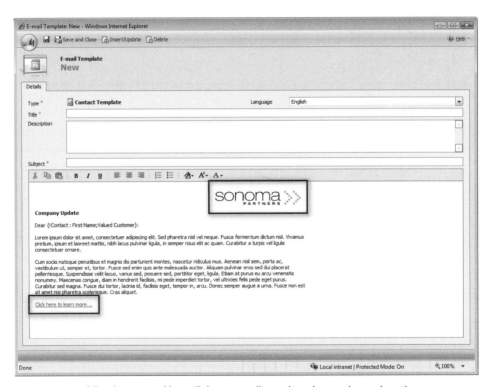

FIGURE 2-14 Adding images and hyperlinks to e-mail templates by copying and pasting

If you try this copy and paste technique but it does not work, confirm that you have the following element at the top of your HTML code.

```
<!DOCTYPE HTML PUBLIC "-//W3C//DTD HTML 4.0 Transitional//EN">
```

You can also try using the copy and paste technique with other HTML editor applications. We found that the success of this technique varies depending on the format that applications use to copy data to the Clipboard.

Creating and Sending Mass E-Mail Messages

Many Microsoft Dynamics CRM users would like to send an e-mail message to a large group of their prospects or customers, and of course Microsoft Dynamics CRM includes several tools for mass e-mailings. One key criterion for mass e-mail messages is that each message must be individually addressed to a recipient. For example, if you want to send an e-mail message to 500 contacts, you want the system to create 500 copies of the message each addressed to an individual recipient instead of generating one e-mail with 500 people in the To, CC, or BCC field. The three main methods for sending mass e-mail messages in Microsoft Dynamics CRM are the following:

- Direct E-mail

- Quick campaign

- Workflow rule

Each mass e-mailing method is explored in more detail in the following subsections.

Regardless of which option you select, Microsoft Dynamics CRM sends the e-mail messages through the outgoing e-mail server configured during the software installation. Therefore, use some discretion when sending a very large number of messages at one time because it can negatively affect the performance of your servers. Some factors that come into play include the hardware specifications on your servers, network performance, Internet bandwidth, and the amount of load on the server. Although no published specifications exist and the numbers can range wildly depending on your infrastructure, if you need to send more than 10,000 or 20,000 e-mail messages in one hour, we recommend that you explore the option of using third-party e-mail engines instead of Microsoft Dynamics CRM. You should also be mindful of the latest laws and legislation regarding bulk e-mail marketing including the federal CAN-SPAM law. You can learn more about these laws at *http://www.ftc.gov/spam/*. Sending large numbers of unsolicited e-mail messages from your e-mail servers can get your system blocked or blacklisted.

Direct E-Mail

By using the Direct E-mail feature, you can select recipients in a grid, and then choose an e-mail template that you want to send. As discussed, e-mail templates can include data fields that Microsoft Dynamics CRM dynamically populates with information specific to each recipient. You access the Direct E-mail feature from the grid toolbar for entities that support e-mail templates. Figure 2-15 shows the Direct E-mail button for the Contact entity.

FIGURE 2-15 The Direct E-mail button on the grid toolbar

When you click the Direct E-mail button, Microsoft Dynamics CRM opens the Send Direct E-mail dialog box, shown with sample data in Figure 2-16.

In this dialog box, you choose the e-mail template you want to send. Because e-mail templates are defined with an entity type, you can select only templates specific to the entity that you're working with or one of the global templates. So, in this example, you cannot send an Account or Lead template from this page because the Direct E-mail button was clicked on the Contact grid toolbar. To select a different e-mail template, simply click its name in the selection box.

After you select the e-mail template that you want to send, you can specify to which records to send the message. You can send the message to just the selected records, to all of the records on the current page, or to all of the records in the selected view.

Regardless of the value that you select, Microsoft Dynamics CRM will not send Direct E-mail messages to any Lead, Account, or Contact record if the Do Not Allow Bulk E-mails or Do Not E-mail attribute for the record is set to Do Not Allow. You can access these two settings in the Administration tab if you want to modify their values.

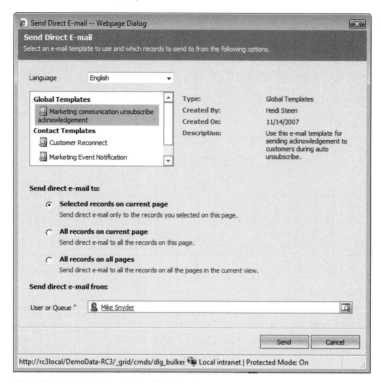

FIGURE 2-16 Send Direct E-mail dialog box

By default, Microsoft Dynamics CRM sets the sender of the e-mail message as the currently logged on user. You can change this value by clicking the lookup button and selecting a different user or queue.

Warning Be very careful when using the Direct E-mail feature! When you click the Send button, Microsoft Dynamics CRM sends the message immediately. There is no preview or cancel option, so make sure that your message is ready to send when you click Send.

In summary, Direct E-mail offers the following benefits and constraints:

- You can send Direct E-mail messages to many different entities such as Leads, Accounts, Contacts, Opportunities, Quotes, and Orders.

- Direct E-mail uses previously created e-mail templates.

- You cannot include an e-mail attachment with Direct E-mail messages.

- You can send Direct E-mail messages to selected records in a view or all the records in a view regardless of the number of pages in that view.

- You cannot preview your message before you send.

Quick Campaign

By using the Microsoft Dynamics CRM Quick Campaign feature, you can send a large number of e-mail messages to a group of recipients. To send a Quick Campaign e-mail message, simply select a group of records in a grid and click the Create Quick Campaign button on the grid toolbar. Then, select which records in the grid to include in the quick campaign. The selection options include the following:

- For selected records
- For all records on the current page
- For all records on all pages

After you select the records to include, Microsoft Dynamics CRM starts the Create Quick Campaign Wizard that walks you through creating a mass e-mailing. On the Select the Activity Type and Owners page, you can select the Send e-mail messages automatically and close corresponding e-mail activities option to send the e-mail messages automatically upon completion of the wizard (as shown in Figure 2-17). If you clear this option, Microsoft Dynamics CRM will create the e-mail messages as open activities but won't send them to recipients until someone sends each message individually.

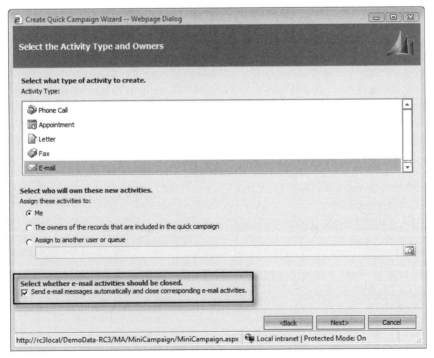

FIGURE 2-17 Specifying whether to send the quick campaign e-mail messages upon wizard completion

Quick campaigns also give you the option to record customer interest as *campaign responses*. A campaign response lets you record how a particular customer responded to one of your campaign efforts. You can create the campaign response record manually for each recipient, or you can use a data import process to load a larger number of records. In quick campaigns, Microsoft Dynamics CRM does not automatically create campaign responses for you.

In summary, quick campaigns offer the following benefits and constraints:

- They only apply to Leads, Accounts, Contacts, and Marketing List records.

- A wizard walks you through the creation of quick campaign e-mail messages.

- You cannot use e-mail templates when you send a quick campaign.

- You cannot include an attachment to an e-mail message created in a quick campaign.

- Quick campaigns save the group of records to which you sent the message in case you need to go back and reference that information later.

- You can create quick campaigns for non-e-mail activities such as tasks and phone calls.

- You can capture response data using the Campaign Response entity.

- You can send quick campaign e-mail messages to selected records in a view or all of the records in a view regardless of the number of pages in that view.

Workflow Rules

If neither the Direct E-mail nor the Quick Campaign feature meets your needs, you can use the Microsoft Dynamics CRM workflow engine for sending mass e-mail. Chapter 8, "Workflow," explains the details of setting up, configuring, and running a workflow rule to send e-mail, so we won't cover that here. However, we do want to highlight workflow as a viable option for mass e-mail because it offers a few benefits over Direct E-mail and quick campaigns:

- Workflow e-mail messages can use e-mail templates, or you can manually create the e-mail message.

- You can include file attachments (one or more) to a workflow e-mail message that you manually create.

- You can automatically send your workflow e-mail messages based on different trigger events that you configure in the workflow rule such as updating a field or changing a record status.

Unfortunately, using workflow for mass e-mail does include one significant constraint: You can only manually apply a workflow rule to a single page of records in a grid. Therefore, if you want to send a thousand e-mail messages, you must select all the records on a page, and then apply the workflow rule. Then, you must move to the next page of records and

repeat the process. If you configured Microsoft Dynamics CRM to
page, you need to repeat this process 10 times to send all thousar
manually applied workflow. However, you could configure the wo
automatically based on some other criterion in the record to avo

Tip You can display up to 250 records per page by changing the d
50 records per page. To access this setting, click Tools, and then clic
toolbar.

Third-party add-on ExactTarget for Microsoft Dynamics CRM

Although the out-of-the-box options for mass e-mailing in Microsoft Dynamics CRM
can meet most organizations' needs, a company named ExactTarget (*http://www.
exacttarget.com*) offers an add-on product for Microsoft Dynamics CRM that includes
many additional e-mail marketing features and benefits. ExactTarget offers its e-mail
marketing services on a hosted basis, and it created an integration with Microsoft
Dynamics CRM so that users can send e-mail through the ExactTarget service directly
from the Microsoft Dynamics CRM interface (see Figure 2-18).

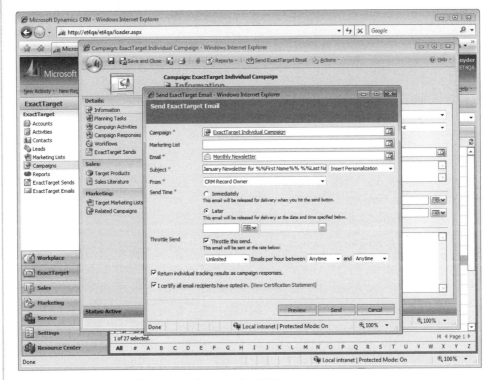

FIGURE 2-18 ExactTarget for Microsoft Dynamics CRM

By using the ExactTarget service for sending mass e-mail, Microsoft Dynamics CRM users can enjoy the following additional benefits:

- ExactTarget sends the e-mail messages through its servers, not through the outgoing e-mail server configured for Microsoft Dynamics CRM. This allows users to send a large volume of e-mail without affecting their internal network. Outsourcing the message delivery to ExactTarget also helps improve message deliverability because ExactTarget works with the various e-mail companies to ensure consistent delivery.

- ExactTarget automatically captures response data such as e-mail opens, clicks in messages, bounces, and unsubscribes. Almost all of the response data downloads into the Microsoft Dynamics CRM user interface so that you can report on it, access it using Advanced Find, and so on. The default ExactTarget for Microsoft Dynamics CRM installation includes data such as unique opens, total opens, unique clicks, deliverability rate, and bounce rate.

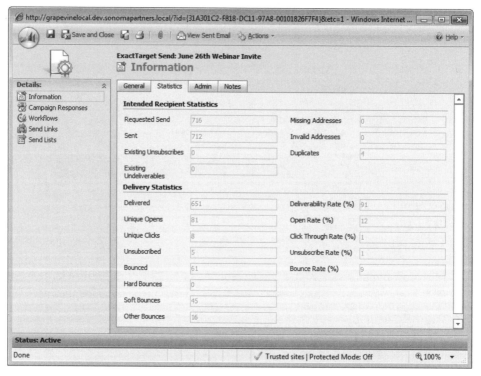

- Users have more control over the delivery of their mass e-mail messages because they can schedule a specific date and time to start the message send. In addition, users can throttle the e-mail to send only a certain number of messages per hour.

> ■ ExactTarget offers a proprietary user interface in which users can create and
>   design their e-mail messages to include images and hyperlinks.
>
> Companies looking for more advanced e-mail marketing in Microsoft Dynamics CRM
> should definitely consider the ExactTarget for Microsoft Dynamics CRM option.

Mass E-Mail Summary

Table 2-2 outlines some key differences of the mass e-mail options for Microsoft Dynamics CRM.

TABLE 2-2 Mass E-Mail Options Summary

	Direct E-mail	Quick campaigns	Workflow
Uses e-mail templates	Yes	No	Yes
Can include images and hyperlinks in the e-mail message	Yes	Yes	Yes
Available entities	Leads, Contacts, Opportunities, Accounts, Quotes, Orders, and so forth	Only Leads, Accounts, Contacts, and marketing lists	Any entity, including custom entities
E-mail recipient selection	All or some of the records in a view	All or some of the records in a view	Can only apply manual workflow to all records on a page (250 records max.)
Can include a file attachment	No	No	Yes
Works with campaign responses	No	Yes	No
Tracks e-mail opens	No	No	No
Tracks hyperlinks clicked in the e-mail message	No	No	No

Mail Merge

Microsoft Dynamics CRM offers a few options so that you can create a large number of
letters, envelopes, or labels quickly and easily. These options include the following:

■ Use the Microsoft Dynamics CRM Mail Merge feature.

■ Use the Mail Merge feature in Microsoft Office Word, using Microsoft Dynamics CRM
   filtered views as the data source.

■ Use the Mail Merge feature in Word, using Microsoft Dynamics CRM data exported to
   Microsoft Office Excel as the data source.

■ Write a Microsoft SQL Server Reporting Services report.

■ Create a custom letter generation application using the Microsoft Dynamics CRM
   software development kit.

Although you will probably use the Microsoft Dynamics CRM Mail Merge feature most of the time, the other options for document generation can meet specific needs that the Mail Merge feature does not. In this book, we focus on how to use the Microsoft Dynamics CRM Mail Merge feature.

In the Web client or Microsoft Dynamics CRM for Outlook, users can access the Mail Merge feature to generate Word documents for records in their databases. Users access the Mail Merge feature by clicking the Word button on the grid toolbar. By default, Microsoft Dynamics CRM includes templates for the Lead, Account, Contact, Quote, and Opportunity entities, but you can also create mail merge templates for custom entities. Users can also start the mail merge feature from a single record by clicking Mail Merge on the Actions menu of the entity record. When you start a mail merge, Microsoft Dynamics CRM automatically opens the Microsoft Dynamics CRM Mail Merge for Microsoft Office Word dialog box (Figure 2-19).

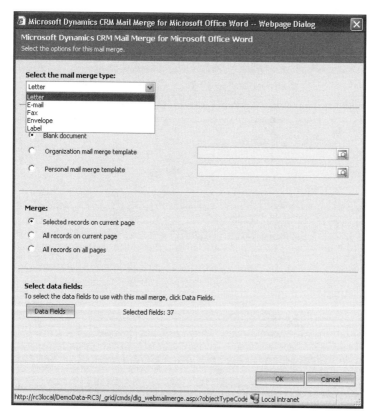

FIGURE 2-19 Microsoft Dynamics CRM Mail Merge for Microsoft Office Word dialog box

In this dialog box, you can choose to create a document from scratch or you can select an existing mail merge template. Microsoft Dynamics CRM includes approximately 10 mail merge templates.

You also select which records you want to include in the mail merge process. Similar to Direct E-mail, you can choose selected records only, all records on the current page, or all records on all pages.

Last, you select which data fields you want to include in the mail merge. If you select a mail merge template that already includes data fields, you don't need to respecify the data fields. However, if you create a new template from a blank document, you need to pick which fields you want to include. Please note the following when you select data fields:

- You can select fields from the entity, you're running the Mail Merge against including any custom attributes that you added.

- You can select fields from related entities, including custom entities and entities linked through custom relationships.

- You cannot select fields on a custom entity if that entity has an N:1 relationship with the Mail Merge entity.

- You can include a maximum of 62 data fields.

After you click OK, what you see next varies depending on whether you're running the mail merge on a computer that has the Microsoft Dynamics CRM for Outlook software running. If you're on a computer with Microsoft Dynamics CRM for Outlook open and running, Word starts and you'll see a list of the mail merge recipients to select from (Figure 2-20).

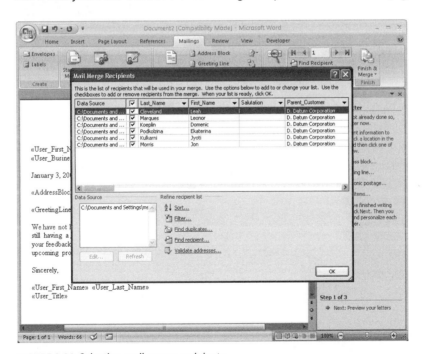

FIGURE 2-20 Selecting mail merge recipients

If you start a mail merge from a computer that does not have Microsoft Dynamics CRM for Outlook running, mail merge starts Word and displays a document that appears like the one shown in Figure 2-21.

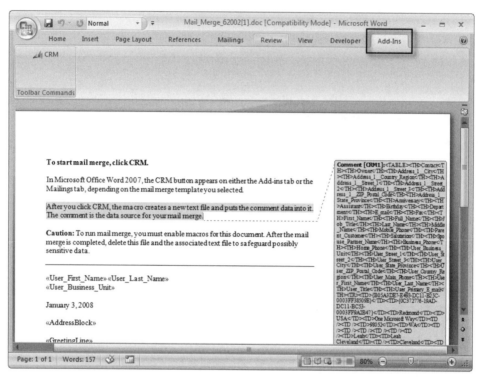

FIGURE 2-21 The interim document created when a mail merge is started on a computer that does not have Microsoft Dynamics CRM for Outlook running

When you click the CRM button located in the Add-ins tab, Word will run a macro that loads the mail merge data into the document, and then you will see the recipient list like the one shown earlier in Figure 2-20. Click OK to approve the recipients, or edit the list as necessary. From here, the mail merge behaves the same as the standard Word Mail Merge feature in which you can insert mail merge fields, modify the document, add rules, preview your letter, and so on.

Note Explaining the details of setting up and using the Word Mail Merge feature is beyond the scope of this book. We assume you're already familiar with the concepts and techniques related to using Word Mail Merge.

When the mail merge is complete, users with Microsoft Dynamics CRM for Outlook running have a few additional options. First, users can choose to upload the final version of the template to Microsoft Dynamics CRM. This upload can either create an entirely new template or it can modify the template you selected when you started the mail merge (Figure 2-22).

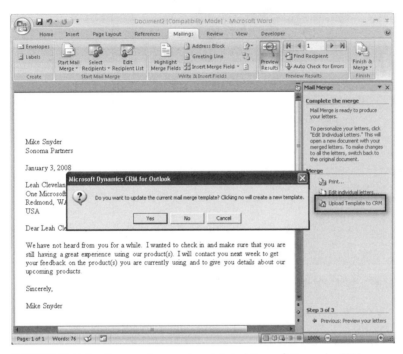

FIGURE 2-22 Uploading a mail merge template to Microsoft Dynamics CRM

Second, mail merge users with Microsoft Dynamics CRM for Outlook running can create Letter activities in Microsoft Dynamics CRM to record the completed mail merge. When users click the Print or Edit individual letters link, the Create Activities dialog box opens (Figure 2-23).

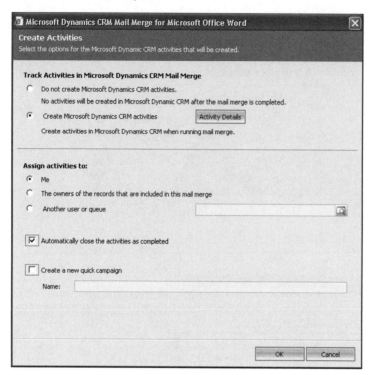

FIGURE 2-23 Create Activities dialog box in mail merge

You can click the Activity Details button to modify the subject of the completed Letter activity to better describe the purpose of the mail merge. In addition, Microsoft Dynamics CRM will automatically include the final version of the Word document (with merged data) as an attachment to the Letter activity.

Important Using mail merge on a computer with Microsoft Dynamics CRM for Outlook running allows users to upload the template to Microsoft Dynamics CRM and create Letter activities that automatically record the mail merge on the record's history. As long as Microsoft Dynamics CRM for Outlook is open and running, users can access these additional features from Outlook or through the Web client. However, if Outlook is closed, users cannot access these features in the Web client even though Microsoft Dynamics CRM for Outlook is installed on the computer.

In addition to creating a new mail merge template at the end of the mail merge process, you can also create and upload new templates by navigating to Settings, Templates, and then clicking Mail Merge Templates. From here, you can specify the name, associated entity, ownership, template language, data fields, and so on. When you upload the mail merge template, Microsoft Dynamics CRM reminds you that you must save the Word file as a Word XML file (.xml) before you can upload it.

Microsoft Dynamics CRM automatically creates a completed Letter activity for each of the records in your mail merge. When working with mail merge in Microsoft Dynamics CRM, you should consider the following:

- You can create mail merges only for Leads, Accounts, Contacts, Opportunities, Quotes, and custom entities.

- You can create your own custom mail merge templates.

- Mail merge templates can be owned by the organization or by an individual.

- If you're using Microsoft Dynamics CRM for Outlook, you can automatically create a completed Letter activity with the attached mail merge file for each recipient.

- If you're using Microsoft Dynamics CRM for Outlook, you can upload the modified template to Microsoft Dynamics CRM or you can upload the modified file as a new template.

Enabling mail merge for upgraded custom entities

If you upgraded from Microsoft Dynamics CRM 3.0 to Microsoft Dynamics CRM 4.0, you may notice that you cannot select your custom entity as the target for a mail merge template. However, if you create a new custom entity in Microsoft Dynamics CRM 4.0, you *can* select that custom entity as the mail merge template target. Microsoft decided not to enable mail merge by default for upgraded custom entities, and unfortunately you cannot reenable mail merge in the user interface. However, you can reenable mail merge by exporting the customizations.xml file for a custom entity and adding a new element named *IsMailMergeEnabled* to the .xml file (as shown here in XML Notepad 2007).

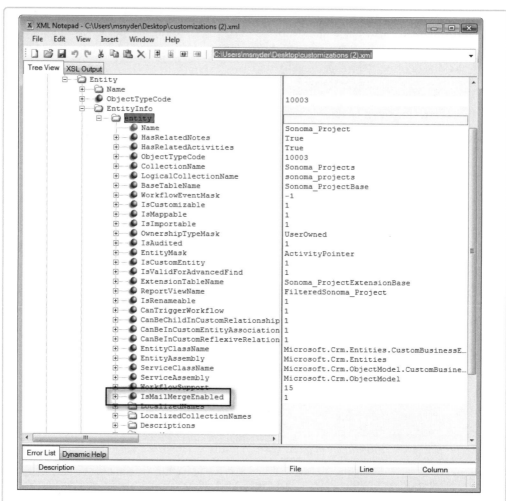

Simply set this new element value to 1, and then reimport the entity customizations and publish the entity. Then, you can select that custom entity as the target of a mail merge template.

Data Management

Very rarely does a company deploy Microsoft Dynamics CRM without any existing customer data. Even if you don't already have a software system with customer names, addresses, and so forth, you probably have a bunch of customer data in various Excel and Outlook files. Consequently, there's always a data import process to go along with each Microsoft Dynamics CRM deployment. Once you get all your data into Microsoft Dynamics CRM, guess what you find out? You discover that you have lots of duplicate records in your database that you want to remove! Don't worry. Microsoft Dynamics CRM includes several tools for data management including the following:

- Import Data Wizard
- Data Migration Manager
- Duplicate detection

The first two tools are for importing data into Microsoft Dynamics CRM. Deciding which tool you should use depends on what you're trying to accomplish. Table 2-3 outlines some of the key differences between the Import Data Wizard and the Data Migration Manager.

TABLE 2-3 Differences Between the Import Data Wizard and the Data Migration Manager

Category	Import Data Wizard	Data Migration Manager
Which users can access the tool	Configurable with security roles	Only Microsoft Dynamics CRM system administrators
Import data into custom entities and custom attributes?	Yes	Yes
Number of source data files	One per import	Multiple files per import
Imported record assignment	Must assign all records to one user	Can assign records to multiple users
Detect duplicates during import?	Yes	No
Set value of *CreatedOn* attribute from the source data?	No, the *CreatedOn* date will match the time of the record import	Yes
Select all data from a single import for deletion?	No	Yes
Automatically map source data to Microsoft Dynamics CRM fields?	Yes, will map based on column headings in source data	No
Picklist mapping	Includes a user interface tool to match source data to picklists	Must create a data map of picklist values
Customize Microsoft Dynamics CRM with new entities and attributes on the fly based on imported data?	No	Yes
Transform data during import?	No	Yes, includes string and date functions such as split, substring, replace, and concatenate
E-mail message notification upon import completion?	Yes	No

Next, we look at these various data management tools in more detail.

Import Data Wizard

As you probably noticed in Table 2-3, Microsoft designed the Import Data Wizard primarily for the end user to import data; it lacks some of the more powerful features included in the Data Migration Manager. However, the Import Data Wizard can meet most basic data import needs with its nice, simple user interface. Importing data with the Import Data Wizard always follows the same basic process:

1. Prepare the import file.

2. Create a data map.

3. Import the records.

4. View the results and correct failures.

Prepare the Import File

Obviously, before you can import anything, you need to gather the data into an electronic file. The import file should meet the following criteria:

- The data file must be in a delimited format, using either a comma, colon, semicolon, or tab as the delimiter. If any of your records use the delimiter in its record set, you need to add quotation marks or a single quotation mark as the data delimiter.

- You need one import file for each type of entity that you want to import. For example, if you want to import Leads, Accounts, and Contacts, you need three files.

- Because all records imported through the Import Data Wizard are assigned to a single owner, you should split up your import files accordingly. Alternatively, you can import all of the records to a single owner, and then reassign them after the import is complete.

- The first row of the data file should include column headings. If you set the column headings to match the attribute display names, the Import Data Wizard will automatically map the columns to the appropriate fields in Microsoft Dynamics CRM.

- The first column heading cannot be an entity name. For example, if you import Contacts, the first column header cannot be *Account* because that is an existing entity name.

- Be sure to include a column for each business-required field on the entity.

- Each import file must be 4 megabytes (MB) or smaller in file size.

- If you want to import data that relates to two or more entities together, the column that links the two records must match the primary attribute of the related record. For example, when you import Contacts, if you want to match them to Accounts, you must include the account name because the *name* attribute is the primary attribute of the Account entity.

> **Tip** In addition to including the primary attribute of the related entity (typically the name), you can also link imported records with existing related Microsoft Dynamics CRM records by including the globally unique identifier (GUID) in the appropriate column. You can find the GUID for a record by using a filtered view or database query, in addition to looking it up manually in the user interface for a single record. The GUID is a 32-digit hexadecimal number in the query string.

Create a Data Map

With your source data files ready, next you need to create a data map to correlate the data you're importing to the correct Microsoft Dynamics CRM data fields. You can create data maps in one of two ways:

- **Automatic**   During the Import Data Wizard process, Microsoft Dynamics CRM can automatically generate a data map for you if all of the columns in your source file match the attribute display names in Microsoft Dynamics CRM.

- **Manual**   You can navigate to the Settings and Data Management section of Microsoft Dynamics CRM to create a data map manually. In addition, you can create a manual data map on the fly in the middle of the Import Data Wizard.

Using the automatic map creation option can save you time, but it does have some limitations. For example, if you use the automatic data map, you must import *every* column from the source file into Microsoft Dynamics CRM—you cannot pick and choose which columns to import. In addition, you cannot selectively modify the automatic data map. You must accept all or none of the mappings that it provides for you.

To create a manual data map, navigate to the Settings and Data Management section of Microsoft Dynamics CRM, select Data Maps, and then click New on the grid toolbar. After you assign the name and select the entity record type, click Save and you can start mapping the attributes after you load your sample data. To access the data attribute mappings, simply click the Attributes link in the navigation pane.

> **More Info** The sample data file cannot be larger than 50 kilobytes in size.

Figure 2-24 shows a sample data map for an Account data source. As the figure illustrates, you can see all of the column headings from the sample data and the attributes of the

Account entity that we mapped them to. The right side of the window shows all of the attributes from the target entity. To create the map between the source data and the target entity, click the row in the Source area of where you want the data to map, click the corresponding attribute in the Target area, and then click the Map button. Alternatively, you can double-click the target attribute instead of clicking the Map button.

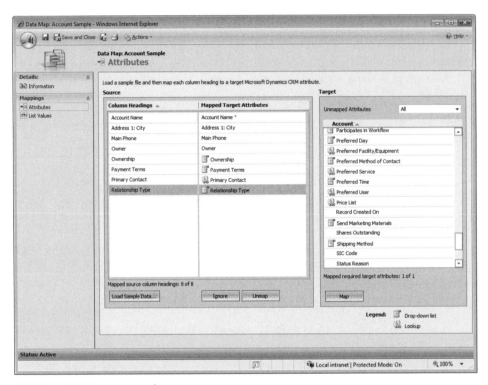

FIGURE 2-24 Data map example

You can also see that the Legend in the lower-right corner indicates whether a target attribute is a picklist (drop-down list) or a lookup field. In this example, we included three picklist fields, Ownership, Payment Terms, and Relationship Type, and one lookup field, Primary Contact. As we discussed earlier, be sure that the data in your source lookup fields matches the primary attribute (or the GUID) of the related entity, and then the records will map automatically. If your data map includes picklist attributes, you must click the List Values link to complete one additional step for each of the picklist fields to ensure that your data map works correctly. Figure 2-25 shows the List Values mapping screen.

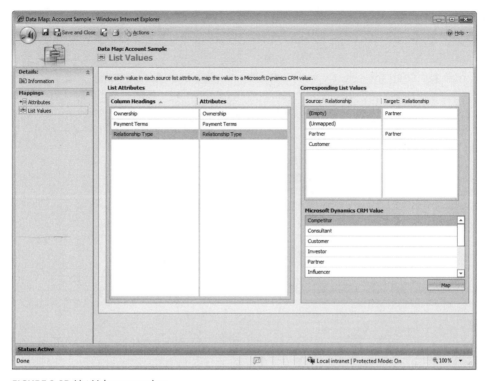

FIGURE 2-25 List Values mapping

For each row that you select in the List Attributes area, the values on the right side of the screen will update. The Corresponding List Values area shows which values appear in the sample file and includes (Empty) and (Unmapped) options. The Microsoft Dynamics CRM Value area lists all of the picklist values for the selected attribute. To get the data to map correctly, you need to match a Microsoft Dynamics CRM value for each Corresponding List Value.

Important If you're mapping data that contains picklists, be sure to include one record with every possible picklist value so that you can correctly map it in the user interface. If your sample file does not include a picklist value for you to map, it will receive the value you assign to the (Unmapped) option.

We recommend that you include mappings for all of the required fields on your target entity. After you've configured the data map, save the record and you're ready to import the data.

Tip You can activate or deactivate a data map on the More Actions menu on the data map grid toolbar, but this menu option is not available in a Data Map record. In addition, you can export and import data maps so that you can move them from one system to another (such as moving a data map from a test environment to a production environment).

Import the Records

With your source data file and data map complete, you're ready to import the data into Microsoft Dynamics CRM. To access the Import Data Wizard, click Tools on the application menu toolbar, and select Import Data. The Import Data Wizard opens and you can select your source file and specify the data and field delimiters used in your file. On the next page of the wizard, you select the entity into which you want to import. After you select the entity, the Import Data Wizard will try to perform an automatic data map for you (Figure 2-26).

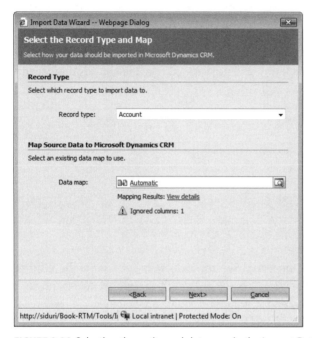

FIGURE 2-26 Selecting the entity and data map in the Import Data Wizard

If desired, you can also select the custom data map that you created. At this time, the Import Data Wizard displays possible warnings or errors related to your mapping. On the next page, you can select which user will own the imported records and whether you want to enable duplicate detection during import.

> **Caution** If you choose not to import duplicates, the Import Data Wizard will not prompt you to resolve duplicates during the import. Instead, it will not import the duplicate record and will create a log of unimported records for you to resolve later. The option to exclude or import duplicates only appears for entities with duplicate detection enabled.

On the last page of the Import Data Wizard, you can create a name for the import and decide whether you want Microsoft Dynamics CRM to send you an e-mail notification upon completion of the import process. After you set the values per your preference, click the Import button and let the Import Data Wizard do its magic.

View the Results and Correct Failures

To view the progress of a data import, users with proper security privileges can navigate to the Imports section of the Workplace, or go to the Systems Jobs area of Settings. As you would expect, you can view a list of all the import processes in these views. By double-clicking an import record, you can open a new window that provides more details about the import such as the data map used, the number of successful imports, number of failures, and so on.

Click the Failures link in the navigation pane to view a list of the records that failed to import correctly (Figure 2-27).

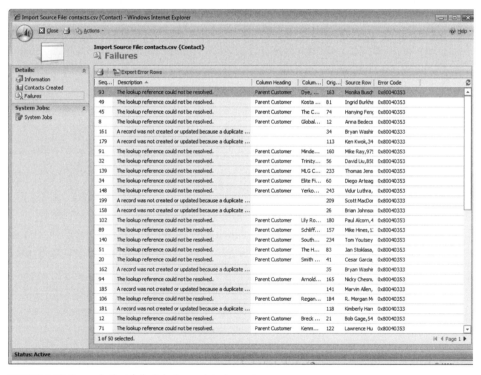

FIGURE 2-27 Records that failed during a data import

From here, you can learn more about the reason why the record failed during the import process. In addition, you can click the Export Error Rows button on the grid toolbar to download a comma-separated value file of these failed records (including all of their original source data) so that you can correct the errors and import the records.

Data Migration Manager

If you find that the Import Data Wizard won't meet your needs, Data Migration Manager offers more robust data import functionality. Data Migration Manager offers three main areas of functionality:

- Migrate data
- Delete migrated data
- Manage data maps

As explained previously, one of the main benefits Data Migration Manager offers is that you can import multiple source files at one time instead of importing one entity at a time. In addition, Data Migration Manager can customize Microsoft Dynamics CRM on the fly during the import process to add new entities, attributes, and so on.

> **Important** Data Migration Manager includes built-in data maps for Salesforce.com, Microsoft Office Outlook 2007 with Business Contact Manager, Microsoft Office Outlook 2003 with Business Contact Manager Update, and ACT! 6. Using these existing data maps will save you lots of time and headaches if you import data from one of these systems into Microsoft Dynamics CRM.

Data Migration Manager includes a simple wizard interface that walks you through the data import process (Figure 2-28). Although you must be a Microsoft Dynamics CRM system administrator to use this tool, you do not need any programming experience to perform complex data imports.

Explaining the Data Migration Manager in detail is beyond the scope of this book, but we recommend that you review the Help file included with the Data Migration Manager for additional information about some of the advanced functionality that this tool offers.

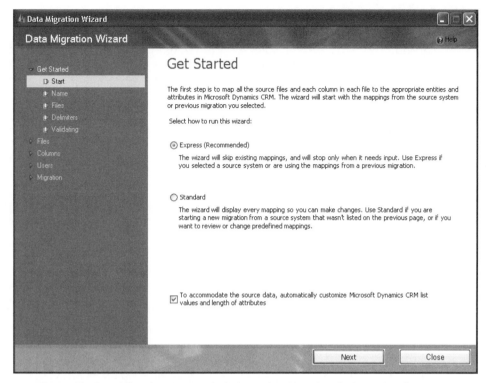

FIGURE 2-28 The Data Migration Manager includes a wizard interface for importing data

The Data Migration Manager encountered an error while setting up the temporary migration database

When we first started working with Data Migration Manager, we occasionally received an error stating, "The Data Migration Manager encountered an error while setting up the temporary migration database. Restart the Data Migration Manager, and then try migrating the data again."

This error was listed as a known Data Migration Manager issue, and we were able to correct it by deleting the *UserReplicationID* registry key and restarting Data Migration Manager. You can find this registry key in HKLM\SOFTWARE\Microsoft\Data Migration Wizard on 32-bit systems.

As a reminder, please exercise extreme caution when you edit your system registry because you can cause permanent damage to your system.

Duplicate Detection

After loading data into your system, of course you want to make sure that the database remains clean without lots of duplicate records. Fortunately, Microsoft Dynamics CRM includes duplicate detection functionality to help you maintain the integrity of your data. Duplicate detection consists of three main areas:

- Duplication detection settings
- Duplicate detection rules
- Duplicate detection jobs

You access almost all of the duplicate detection configuration in the Data Management section located in Microsoft Dynamics CRM Settings.

Duplication Detection Settings

You can enable duplicate detection for your organization and determine when Microsoft Dynamics CRM should perform the duplicate checks. The three options to configure these settings are the following:

- When a record is created or updated
- When Microsoft Dynamics CRM for Outlook goes from offline to online
- During a data import

You can choose to enable duplicate detection for some or all of these settings, but you cannot selectively apply these settings to specific entities. For example, if you enable duplicate detection for record creation and update, Microsoft Dynamics CRM will apply that setting to *all* entities. Assuming you enable duplicate detection for the organization, you can configure duplicate detection for individual entities as explained in Chapter 6, "Entity Customization: Relationships, Custom Entities, and Site Map."

Duplicate Detection Rules

Because every organization defines duplicates differently, Microsoft Dynamics CRM lets you configure your own duplicate detection rules per your specific business needs. After you define and publish a duplicate detection rule, Microsoft Dynamics CRM creates a *matchcode* for every record created or updated in the previous 5 minutes. This matchcode process runs continually in the background every 5 minutes, even for deactivated records. Microsoft Dynamics CRM uses matchcodes behind the scenes to look for duplicate records per your duplicate detection settings. Figure 2-29 shows a sample duplicate detection rule that we set up.

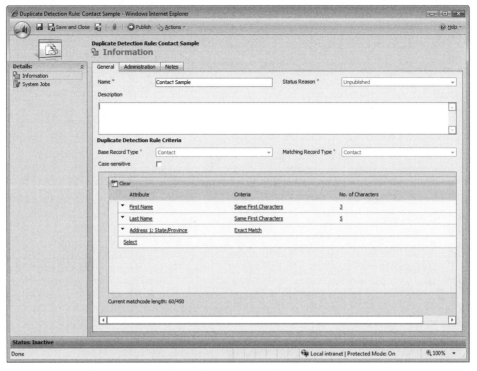

FIGURE 2-29 Duplicate detection rule configured on the Contact entity

In this example, Microsoft Dynamics CRM will identify a duplicate if all of the following conditions are met:

- The first three characters of the first name match
- The first five characters of the last name match
- All of the characters in the state/province field match

Unlike the Advanced Find tool, you cannot configure OR conditions in a duplicate detection rule, but can you set up multiple rules for a single entity. In addition, you can configure your rule to search cross-entity (such as Contact to Lead) and can specify whether the checks should be case-sensitive. Last, you need to consider that each attribute you add to your duplicate detection rule will add to the matchcode length, and Microsoft Dynamics CRM enforces a maximum matchcode length of 450. Each change to the rule will update the current matchcode length so that you can monitor where you stand in relation to the maximum. When you're finished configuring the rule, publish it by clicking the Publish button on the toolbar.

Then, if a user tries to enter a record that Microsoft Dynamics CRM determines is a duplicate, the user will see a dialog box like the one shown in Figure 2-30.

FIGURE 2-30 Duplicate detection warning dialog box

From here, the user can choose to save the record or cancel the create/update operation. Unfortunately, there is no way to merge the new or updated record into one of the duplicates identified by Microsoft Dynamics CRM.

Important Because the matchcode process runs every 5 minutes, if you rapidly create or update records that qualify as duplicates before the matchcodes can update, Microsoft Dynamics CRM will not immediately recognize those records as duplicates. To find these duplicates, you should use the duplicate job process that we explain next.

You may wonder if you can permanently dismiss this duplicate warning if you know for a fact that the record you updated is not a duplicate even though it meets the duplicate detection rules. Again, unfortunately, you cannot permanently dismiss a duplicate check for a record, so you will see this dialog box each time you update the record. In this scenario, we recommend that you tweak your duplicate detection rule to avoid the situation.

Duplicate Jobs

In addition to the duplicate detection settings, you can also configure Microsoft Dynamics CRM to perform a duplicate detection job on a scheduled interval to look for potential duplicates. To create a new duplicate detection job, navigate to the Data Management section of

Settings, and click Duplicate Detection Jobs. Next, click New, and Microsoft Dynamics CRM will open the Duplicate Detection Wizard. For each duplicate job, you can use the Advanced Find interface to create a subset of records on which to perform the duplicate check. You can also schedule the duplicate check job to repeat and run again on a scheduled interval such as every 7, 30, 90, 180, or 365 days. After Microsoft Dynamics CRM completes the duplicate job, you can open that job record and click View Duplicates in the navigation pane to resolve any duplicates found during the job.

Queues

Imagine that a sample organization, Adventure Works Cycle, has created the e-mail address *bikesupport@adventure-works.com* to handle all incoming customer support requests. The goal of this support alias is to allow the Adventure Works customer service representatives to monitor incoming support requests in a single location to make sure that everything is resolved in a timely manner. Microsoft Dynamics CRM uses the Queue feature to track and hold pending work items until they are assigned to a user. Adventure Works Cycle could create a queue called Bicycle Cases; then, every e-mail message sent to bikesupport@adventure-works.com would create a queue item in the Bicycle Cases queue. In addition to activities such as E-mails and Tasks, you can also assign Cases to a queue. Users can access the queues for your organization by browsing to the Queues subarea of the Workplace area.

Microsoft Dynamics CRM removes items from a queue when they're assigned to a user, or when a user accepts an item currently in the queue. If you assign a queue item to a user, the item will move to the Assigned folder until the user accepts it. When a user accepts an item, it moves to the user's In Progress folder until he or she completes the item. Microsoft Dynamics CRM automatically removes Cases and Activities from the In Progress folder when you complete them, except for completed E-mail activities. To remove a completed E-mail item from the In Progress folder, you must delete it. This does not delete the item, it just removes it from the In Progress folder. Figure 2-31 shows the queue flow chart.

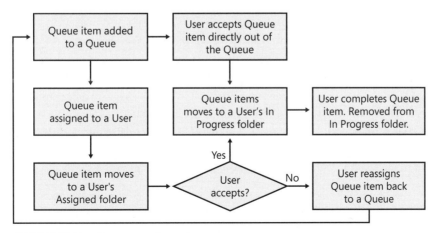

FIGURE 2-31 How items move through a queue

You can set up and manage queues by browsing to the Settings area, clicking Business Management, and then clicking Queues. You don't have to use an e-mail address for each queue, but you can configure this functionality by following the detailed instructions included in the Microsoft Dynamics CRM Implementation Guide.

The following are additional important points to consider regarding queues:

- You can use queues for any type of business activity that uses activities, including incoming sales requests and marketing tasks. You should not consider queues as strictly a customer service tool.

- Queues do not own records, so assigning an item to a queue will not change its ownership (or trigger the workflow assign event), but it will add the item to the queue.

- Although assigning an item to a queue does not change ownership, assigning a queue item to a user changes the ownership of the item.

- Items listed in the queue respect the Microsoft Dynamics CRM security settings regarding which records each user can read, write, delete, and so on. However, all users can view all the queues and all the items in queues (even though Microsoft Dynamics CRM won't allow them to open records to which they don't have access).

- If you set up an e-mail alias to automatically create queue items, Microsoft Dynamics CRM will not automatically create Cases for each e-mail message sent to the alias. You must do this manually or with custom programming code.

- A queue is not a customizable entity, so you cannot modify the columns that appear for the queue folders.

Although queues do involve a few minor constraints, they are a great tool to help your organization streamline and automate many business operations.

Summary

Microsoft Dynamics CRM offers excellent integration with Microsoft Office Outlook through the Microsoft Dynamics CRM for Outlook software. With Microsoft Dynamics CRM for Outlook installed, users can synchronize contacts, tasks, appointments, phone calls, letters, and faxes in Microsoft Dynamics CRM and Outlook. Conversely, users can update records in Outlook, and then Microsoft Dynamics CRM for Outlook will synchronize the changes to the server. By using Microsoft Dynamics CRM for Outlook with Offline Access, users can work while disconnected from the server. Microsoft Dynamics CRM also includes productivity tools that help users work more efficiently with e-mail and mail merges. Microsoft Dynamics CRM data management features include data import capabilities and duplicate detection processes.

Chapter 3
Managing Security and Information Access

If you've deployed multiple systems in the past, you already know that you must design your customer relationship management (CRM) solution to restrict information appropriately based on individual user permissions. Controlling how your users access customer data is a mission-critical component of any business application. Microsoft designed the Microsoft Dynamics CRM security model to support the following goals:

- Provide users with only the information they need to perform their jobs; do not show them data unrelated to their positions.

- Simplify security administration by creating security roles that define security user rights, and then assign users to one or more security roles.

- Support team-based and collaborative projects by enabling users to share records as necessary.

Microsoft Dynamics CRM provides an extremely granular level of security throughout the application. By customizing the security settings, you can construct a security and information access solution that will most likely meet the needs of your organization. The process to customize the Microsoft Dynamics CRM security settings requires that you configure your organization structure, decide which security roles your system users (employees) will have, and then define the security privileges associated with each security role.

Although you might not expect to, you will find yourself constantly tweaking and revising the security settings as your business evolves. Fortunately, the Microsoft Dynamics CRM security model makes it easy for you to update and change your security settings on the fly.

Mapping Your Needs

For the first step in planning security settings for your deployment, we recommend that you create a rough model of your company's current operational structure (by using a tool such as Microsoft Office Visio). For each section of your organizational layout, you should identify the approximate number of users and the types of business functions those users perform. You will need this rough organizational map to start planning how you want to set up and configure security in your Microsoft Dynamics CRM deployment.

> **Important** Your Microsoft Dynamics CRM business unit structure should not necessarily match your operational structure. You should configure the Microsoft Dynamics CRM business unit hierarchy to match your security needs, not to create an exact model of your organizational structure. Whereas the operational and Microsoft Dynamics CRM security business unit structures typically remain consistent for smaller organizations, midsize and enterprise organizations usually need to design a Microsoft Dynamics CRM business unit structure that does not match their organizational chart.

To put this type of organizational mapping into a real-world context, consider an example organization. Figure 3-1 shows the business structure for a fictional company named Adventure Works Cycle.

Each box in the figure represents a business unit in Microsoft Dynamics CRM, and you can structure parent and child relationships between business units. *Business units* represent a logical grouping of business activities, and you have great latitude in determining how to create and structure them for your implementation.

> **Tip** Sometimes people refer to business units by using the acronym BU.

One constraint of configuring business units is that you can specify only one parent for each business unit. However, each business unit can have multiple child business units. Also, you must assign every Microsoft Dynamics CRM user to one (and only one) business unit.

For each user in your organizational structure, you should try to define answers for questions such as the following:

- Which areas of Microsoft Dynamics CRM will the users need access to (such as Sales, Marketing, and Customer Service)?

- Do users need the ability to create and update records, or will read-only access suffice?

- Will you need to structure project teams or functional groups of users that work together on related records?

- Can you group users together by job function or some other classification (such as finance, operations, and executive managers)?

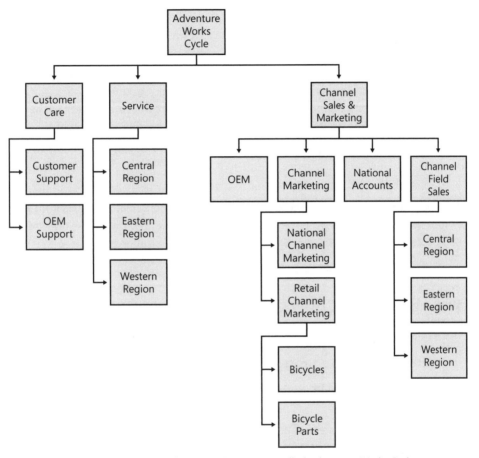

FIGURE 3-1 Organization structure for a sample company called Adventure Works Cycle

After you develop a feel for how your organization and users will use Microsoft Dynamics CRM, you can start to configure the Microsoft Dynamics CRM application to meet those needs.

Real World For smaller organizations, mapping out your Microsoft Dynamics CRM organization model might take only 15 minutes. However, you may want to budget a day or two to map out the security model for enterprise organizations with hundreds of users spread geographically throughout the country. You should also not expect to get the security model *done* because it will constantly change over time.

Don't spend too much time trying to perfect your organizational model right now. The goal of the exercise is to research and develop more details about how your organization intends to use Microsoft Dynamics CRM so that you can configure the security settings correctly. This organizational model won't be your final version, but it can help you think through and consider the ramifications of the security settings you choose.

Security Concepts

After you've developed a rough organizational model with information about the different types of users in your system, you must translate that information into Microsoft Dynamics CRM security settings. Before we explain how to configure the security settings in the software, we explain two of the key topics related to Microsoft Dynamics CRM security:

- Security model concepts
- User authentication

After you understand these concepts, we can get into the details of configuring the software to meet your specific needs. Because of the many security customization options offered in Microsoft Dynamics CRM, very rarely do we see an organizational structure that Microsoft Dynamics CRM security settings cannot accommodate.

Security Model Concepts

The Microsoft Dynamics CRM security model uses two main concepts:

- Role-based and object-based security
- Organizational structure

Role-Based and Object-Based Security

Microsoft Dynamics CRM uses security roles and role-based security as its core security management techniques. A *security role* describes a set of access levels and privileges for each of the entities (such as Leads, Accounts, or Cases) in Microsoft Dynamics CRM. All Microsoft Dynamics CRM users must have one or more security roles assigned to them. Therefore, when a user logs on to the system, Microsoft Dynamics CRM looks at the user's assigned security roles and uses that information to determine what the software will allow that user to do and see throughout the system. This is known as *role-based security*.

With this security model, you also can define different security parameters for the various records (such as Lead, Account, Contact, and so on) because each record has an owner. By comparing the business unit of the record owner with the security role and business unit of a user, Microsoft Dynamics CRM determines that user's security privileges for a single record. You can think of configuring access rights on the individual record level (not the entity level) as *object-based security*. Figure 3-2 illustrates this concept.

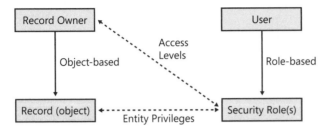

FIGURE 3-2 Role-based security and object-based security combine to determine user rights

In summary, Microsoft Dynamics CRM uses a combination of role-based and object-based security to manage access rights and permissions throughout the system.

Organizational Structure

In addition to security roles, Microsoft Dynamics CRM uses an organization's structure as a key concept in its security model. Microsoft Dynamics CRM uses the following definitions to describe an organization's structure:

- **Organization** The company that owns the deployment. The organization is the top level of the Microsoft Dynamics CRM business management hierarchy. Microsoft Dynamics CRM automatically creates the organization based on the name that you enter during the software installation. You cannot change or delete this information. You can also refer to the organization as the *root business unit*.

- **Business unit** A logical grouping of your business operations. Each business unit can act as parent for one or more child business units. In the sample organization in Figure 3-1, you would describe the Customer Care business unit as the parent business unit of the Customer Support and OEM Support business units. Likewise, you would refer to the Customer Support and OEM Support business units as child business units.

- **User** Someone who typically works for the organization and has access to Microsoft Dynamics CRM. Each user belongs to one (and only one) business unit, and each user is assigned one or more security roles.

Later in this chapter, we explain how these terms relate to setting up and configuring security roles.

User Authentication

Microsoft Dynamics CRM supports three different types of security methods to authenticate users when they try to log on to the system:

- Integrated Windows authentication
- Forms-based authentication
- Microsoft Windows Live ID

Customers that purchase Microsoft Dynamics CRM and deploy the software on premise will use Integrated Windows authentication, and they have the option to deploy a forms-based authentication for Internet-facing deployments of Microsoft Dynamics CRM as well. For on-premise deployments of Microsoft Dynamics CRM, each user who logs on to the system needs to use a Microsoft Active Directory account.

Only customers who use Microsoft Dynamics CRM Live will use Microsoft Windows Live ID to authenticate and log on to the system.

Integrated Windows Authentication

Microsoft Dynamics CRM uses Integrated Windows authentication (formerly called NTLM, and also referred to as Microsoft Windows NT Challenge/Response authentication) for user security authentication in the Web browser and in the Microsoft Dynamics CRM for Outlook interfaces. By using Integrated Windows authentication, users can simply browse to the Microsoft Dynamics CRM Web site and Microsoft Internet Explorer automatically passes their encrypted user credentials to Microsoft Dynamics CRM and logs them on. This means that users log on to Microsoft Dynamics CRM (authenticate) by using their existing Microsoft Active Directory directory domain accounts, without having to sign in to the Microsoft Dynamics CRM application explicitly. This integrated security provides great convenience for users because there's no need for them to remember an additional password just for the CRM system. Using Integrated Windows authentication also helps system administrators because they can continue to manage user accounts from Active Directory services. For example, disabling a user in the Active Directory directory service prevents him or her from logging on to Microsoft Dynamics CRM because the user's logon and password will not work anymore.

More Info Disabling or deleting users in Active Directory prevents them from logging on to Microsoft Dynamics CRM, but it does not automatically disable their user records in Microsoft Dynamics CRM. Because all active users count against your licenses, make sure that you remember to disable their user records in Microsoft Dynamics CRM to free their licenses. Also, if you change a user's name in Active Directory, you must manually update it in Microsoft Dynamics CRM. We strongly recommend that you deactivate the user in Microsoft Dynamics CRM before deactivating his or her Active Directory account.

Most companies install Microsoft Dynamics CRM on their local intranet in the same Active Directory domain that users log on to. By default, the User Authentication security settings in Microsoft Internet Explorer 7.0 automatically log users on to any intranet site that they browse to, including Microsoft Dynamics CRM. This default setting will work fine for almost all of your users.

However, you may find that you want to alter the default security settings to change how the Internet Explorer browser handles user authentication. Typical reasons to modify the Internet Explorer security settings include the following:

- You want to log on to Microsoft Dynamics CRM impersonating one of your users during setup and development.

- Your Microsoft Dynamics CRM deployment resides in a different Active Directory domain (or on the Internet) and you want to change the logon settings.

- You want to trust the Microsoft Dynamics CRM Web site explicitly to allow for pop-up windows.

To view your Internet Explorer 7.0 security settings, click Internet Options on the Tools menu in Internet Explorer. The Security tab in the Internet Options dialog box displays Web content zones, including Internet, Local intranet, Trusted sites, and Restricted sites, as shown in Figure 3-3.

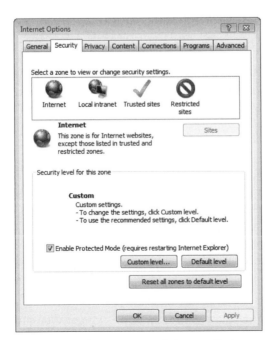

FIGURE 3-3 Web content zones in Internet Explorer

By altering the security settings, you can change how Internet Explorer passes your logon information to various Web sites, such as your Microsoft Dynamics CRM Web site.

Turning off automatic logon in the Local intranet zone

1. In the Security tab, click Local intranet, and then click Custom level.

2. In the Security Settings dialog box, scroll down until you see the User Authentication section, and then select Prompt for user name and password.

When you disable automatic logon, Internet Explorer does not automatically pass your user credentials to Microsoft Dynamics CRM (or any other Web site on your local intranet). Instead, it prompts you to enter your user name and password when you browse to the Microsoft Dynamics CRM server. This prompt gives you the opportunity to enter any user credentials that you want, including user credentials from a different domain. As an administrator, you may want to log on as a different user during your setup and configuration phase to confirm that your security settings are correct.

In addition to disabling automatic logon, you may want to add Microsoft Dynamics CRM as a trusted site in Internet Explorer or list it as part of your intranet zone. The steps and benefits of either are almost identical; so let's review adding Microsoft Dynamics CRM as a trusted site.

Adding a trusted site to Internet Explorer

1. In the Security tab, click Trusted sites, and then click Sites.

2. In the Trusted sites dialog box, enter the address of your Microsoft Dynamics CRM server (include the *http://* portion of the address), and then click Add. You may need to clear the Require server verification check box if your Microsoft Dynamics CRM deployment does not use *https://*.

3. Click OK.

Adding a trusted site to Internet Explorer accomplishes two things in regard to Microsoft Dynamics CRM:

- Internet Explorer will automatically pass your user credentials to the Web site and attempt to log you on. You may want to set this up for your Microsoft Dynamics CRM users who are not located on your local intranet (such as offsite or remote users) so that they do not have to enter a user name and password each time they browse to Microsoft Dynamics CRM.

- The Internet Explorer Pop-up Blocker allows pop-up windows for any Web site listed in your Trusted sites zone.

> **Caution** Intranet sites and trusted sites in Internet Explorer become quite powerful, so you must use caution when deciding which sites you will trust. For example, the default security settings for trusted sites in Internet Explorer automatically install signed Microsoft ActiveX controls on your computer.

Microsoft Dynamics CRM and Pop-up Blockers

Many users utilize a pop-up blocker add-in for Internet Explorer in an attempt to limit the number of pop-up advertisements they see when browsing the Internet. Unfortunately, some of these pop-up blockers may also block some of the Web browser windows that Microsoft Dynamics CRM uses. Consequently, you'll probably need to let your users know how to configure their pop-up blockers to allow pop-up windows from the Microsoft Dynamics CRM application.

One common pop-up blocker issue appears when running Microsoft Dynamics CRM in *application mode*. While in application mode, Internet Explorer will hide the browser's address, toolbars, and menu bars. Theoretically, this simplifies the user experience and makes it easier for users to work with Microsoft Dynamics CRM. However, some users don't like application mode because it behaves differently from a typical Web browser experience. Application mode is turned off by default in Microsoft Dynamics CRM 4.0, but you can activate it by selecting the Application Mode check box located in the Customization tab of the System Settings (accessed by browsing to Settings, clicking Administration, and then clicking System Settings). In application mode, the most common problem caused by pop-up blockers manifests when users initially log on to Microsoft Dynamics CRM. If your users say something like, "The window just disappeared" and you have Microsoft Dynamics CRM application mode enabled, you can safely assume that pop-up blocker software caused the problem. When users log on to Microsoft Dynamics CRM, a new browser window appears, and the original browser window closes. However, if the user's pop-up blocker stops the new window from appearing, it looks to the user like the original window simply disappeared because Microsoft Dynamics CRM closed the user's original browser window.

In addition to times when they start the Microsoft Dynamics CRM system in application mode, your users might also experience issues with pop-up blockers when Microsoft Dynamics CRM opens dialog boxes in various places throughout the system. Therefore, you should know how to resolve these pop-up blocker issues even if you're not running in application mode.

Internet Explorer 7.0 includes a pop-up blocker, but the default setting allows sites in the Local intranet and Trusted sites zones to open pop-up windows. If Internet Explorer does not recognize Microsoft Dynamics CRM as an intranet site, or if you don't want to add it as a trusted site, you can configure the pop-up blocker to allow pop-up windows from the Microsoft Dynamics CRM Web site (on the Tools menu, point to Pop-Up Blocker, and then click Pop-up Blocker Settings to enter the Microsoft Dynamics CRM address).

Some pop-up blockers do not allow you to enter a trusted address manually like the Internet Explorer pop-up blocker does. Therefore, you have to browse to the Web site you want to allow, and then click some sort of "Allow Pop-ups" button. However, because the Microsoft Dynamics CRM window disappears on initial logon, you may wonder how you could ever open the Web site to allow pop-ups. A simple trick is to browse to *http://<crmserver>/loader.aspx*, where *crmserver* is the address of your Microsoft Dynamics CRM Web server, and then Microsoft Dynamics CRM will start in the same Internet Explorer window instead of opening a new one. From this page, you can click the Allow Pop-ups button to always allow pop-ups for your Microsoft Dynamics CRM Web site.

Here's another trick related to pop-up windows: You can reference the same Microsoft Dynamics CRM Web site by using several different techniques. For example, you could access Microsoft Dynamics CRM by using any of the following:

- Computer (NetBIOS) name (Example: *http://crm*)
- Internet Protocol (IP) address (Example: *http://127.0.0.1*)
- Fully qualified domain name (Example: *http://crm.domain.local*)
- A new entry in your Hosts file (add by editing C:\WINDOWS\system32\drivers\etc\hosts)

Although all of these URLs take you to the same Microsoft Dynamics CRM server, Internet Explorer 7.0 treats each of these as different Web sites. Therefore, you could configure different security settings in Internet Explorer for each of these URLs. For example, you can browse to the NetBIOS name by using Integrated Windows authentication to log on as yourself, but you could configure Internet Explorer to prompt for a logon when you browse to the IP address to impersonate a user.

Forms-Based Authentication

Although many users will access Microsoft Dynamics CRM over a local intranet connection using Integrated Windows authentication, Microsoft Dynamics CRM also offers customers the option of deploying Microsoft Dynamics CRM as an Internet-facing deployment (often abbreviated as *IFD*). In an IFD scenario, customers could browse over the Internet to a custom URL address such as *http://crm.yourdomainname.com* to access your Microsoft Dynamics CRM system. Using this access method, users do not need to create a virtual private network (VPN) connection to your network. They could use any type of standard Internet connection to access their data remotely. When they browse to the external IFD URL that you configure, users see a logon screen like the one shown in Figure 3-4.

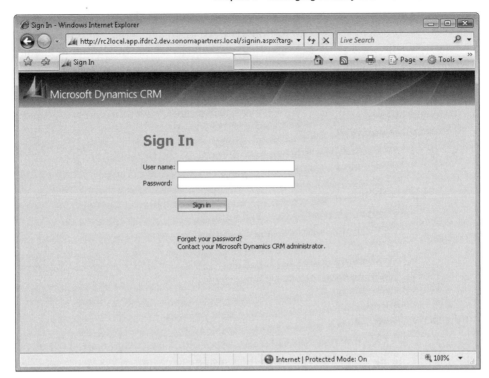

FIGURE 3-4 Internet-facing deployment logon screen

At the logon screen, the user can enter his or her Active Directory user name and password into the specified form fields. Microsoft refers to this method of user authentication as *forms-based authentication.*

More Info For detailed information about forms-based authentication, you can refer to the MSDN article titled "Explained: Forms Authentication in ASP.NET 2.0" located at *http://go.microsoft.com/fwlink/?LinkID=102281.*

After users log on to Microsoft Dynamics CRM by using the Web form, the system will behave in a nearly identical way as when users connect to the system over the local intranet using Integrated Windows authentication. However, some parts of the system such as the dynamic worksheets in Microsoft Office Excel will not work correctly unless the user also has Microsoft Dynamics CRM for Outlook installed on the computer.

Important When accessing Microsoft Dynamics CRM through forms-based authentication, some portions of the software such as dynamic worksheets will require that the user install Microsoft Dynamics CRM for Outlook.

The Microsoft Dynamics CRM Implementation Guide explains how to set up and configure an IFD server, so we won't repeat that material here. However, we want to highlight a few key points about an IFD deployment:

- Unfortunately, you can set up and configure an IFD only when you install Microsoft Dynamics CRM. You can't go back and add it later; therefore, you must decide very early if you will want to use this feature.

- If you do configure the IFD, it will work for all of the organizations on the Microsoft Dynamics CRM server. You cannot selectively pick and choose which organizations can log on remotely.

- All users who can log on to the local intranet can log on by using the IFD. You cannot specify that a user can log on only by using the local intranet.

In summary, forms-based authentication applies only to Microsoft Dynamics CRM users who access their system using an Internet-facing deployment.

Windows Live ID

As we previously stated, only Microsoft Dynamics CRM Live customers will use Windows Live ID to authenticate when they log on to their system. Microsoft offers Windows Live ID as a single sign-on service that businesses and consumers can use throughout various Internet Web sites. By allowing people to use a single logon and password, Windows Live ID simplifies the end-user experience regarding authentication.

More Info Microsoft previously referred to Windows Live ID as the Microsoft Passport Network. Windows Live ID works with MSN Messenger, MSN Hotmail, MSN Music, and many other Web sites.

When users browse to *http://www.crmlive.com* and choose to log on, they are prompted to enter their Windows Live ID credentials, as shown in Figure 3-5.

Please note that when you invite a user to your Microsoft Dynamics CRM Live organization, you must use the e-mail address of that user's Windows Live ID account.

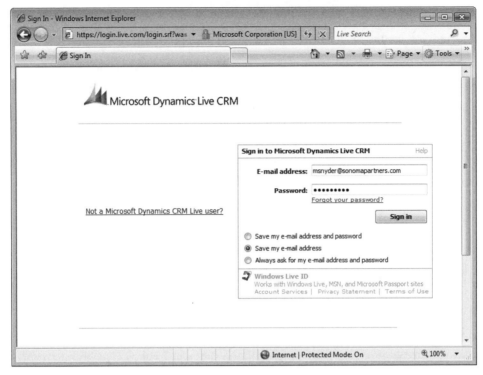

FIGURE 3-5 Entering Windows Live ID credentials on Microsoft Dynamics CRM Live

Managing Users

A user is someone with access to Microsoft Dynamics CRM who typically works for your organization. To manage users in Microsoft Dynamics CRM, browse to Administration in the Settings area, and click Users. For each user, you must complete the following security-related tasks:

- Assign one or more security roles to the user.
- Assign the user to one business unit.
- Assign the user to one or more teams (optionally).
- Assign a Client Access License type.

The combination of these four settings determines a user's access to information in Microsoft Dynamics CRM.

Note Although most of your users will be employees of your organization, you can create user accounts for trusted third-party vendors or suppliers if you want to grant them access to your system. Obviously, you should carefully structure the business units and security roles to make sure that third-party users don't see information that you don't want them to view.

As an administrator, in addition to adding new users you will also need to do the following:

- Disable old users and reassign their records to different users.

- Monitor the number of Microsoft Dynamics CRM licenses you're using to make sure you are compliant.

Tip If you change a user's business unit, Microsoft Dynamics CRM removes all of that user's security roles because roles can vary by business unit. In such a situation, remember to assign the user security roles again; otherwise, he or she won't be able to log on to Microsoft Dynamics CRM.

Reassigning User Records

As part of the usual course of business, employees will leave your organization and you'll need to adjust their user record in the system accordingly. When a user stops working with your Microsoft Dynamics CRM deployment, you should disable the user's record by clicking More Actions, and then clicking Disable on the user record menu bar. By disabling the user, he or she can no longer log on to your Microsoft Dynamics CRM system. However, disabling a user will not change his or her record ownership because disabled users can still own records.

Note To maintain data integrity, Microsoft Dynamics CRM does not allow you to delete users.

After disabling the user, you will also probably want to reassign his or her records to a different user in the system. By doing so, you can make sure that a different user will address any open activities or follow-ups that the previous user didn't complete yet. We recommend that you reassign the records using one of two methods:

- Bulk reassign
- Manually reassigning active records

Bulk Reassign

If you open a user record in Microsoft Dynamics CRM, you will see the Reassign Records option on the Actions menu. When you click this menu item, the dialog box shown in Figure 3-6 appears.

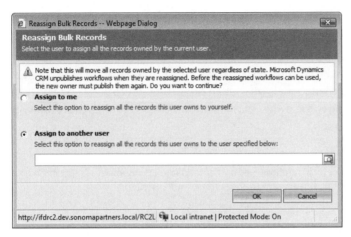

FIGURE 3-6 Reassign Bulk Records dialog box

When you select a different user and click OK, Microsoft Dynamics CRM reassigns all of the records from the old user to the new user you specified. Although this provides a quick and easy method to reassign records, it moves all of the old user's records regardless of their state. This typically does not accomplish what most customers want because it changes the owner of inactive records such as completed activities, qualified leads, won opportunities, and so on. This caused some confusion for one of our customers because it changed the data that appeared in the commission and sales activity reports! In addition, the bulk reassign can confuse users looking at the activity history for a particular account because the owner of the old inactive activities changes from the previous user to the new user.

Note Reassigning records only changes the owner of a record, it does not change the user who created or modified the record; that information stays intact.

In light of these constraints, we consider the Reassign Bulk Records option something of a brute force tool that you should use only in limited circumstances.

Manually Reassign Active Records

Although no one likes to see the word *manual* appear in any task description, we strongly encourage you to reassign the records manually from the old user to a new user instead of using the Reassign Bulk Records tool. By doing so, you maintain the history of the data linked to the previous user. At first this may appear easy to accomplish because you can simply select the active records for the various entities and assign them to a new owner. For example, you could select just the open leads, cases, and opportunities and assign them to a new owner. However, Microsoft Dynamics CRM maintains entity relationships between records so that actions taken against a parent record cascade down to its children records. For example, when you change the owner of an opportunity record, Microsoft Dynamics CRM automatically changes the owner of the activities related to that opportunity based on the relationship configuration.

More Info We explain entity relationships and cascading actions in detail later in Chapter 6, "Entity Customization: Relationships, Custom Entities, and Site Map."

By default, Microsoft Dynamics CRM cascades the reassign action to all of the children records in almost all of the entity relationships. In this scenario, if you change the owner of an Account, all of its related records such as Cases, Opportunities, Quotes, Orders, and so on will also receive the new owner even if those related records are inactive. Likewise, when Microsoft Dynamics CRM changes the owner of the related records, it will cascade that reassignment action to all of the children records of the Cases, Opportunities, Quotes, Orders, and so on. Again, that reassignment would also apply to both active and inactive records, which most customers would not want to happen.

To avoid this scenario, we recommend that you change the default entity relationship behaviors before you start reassigning records. You should configure the cascading behavior from Cascade All to Cascade Active so that it takes action only against active children records, as shown in Figure 3-7 for the Account to Task entity relationship.

Unfortunately, you can't change this entity relationship behavior for the entire system in one place. You need to configure the relationships manually for each of the various entity relationships.

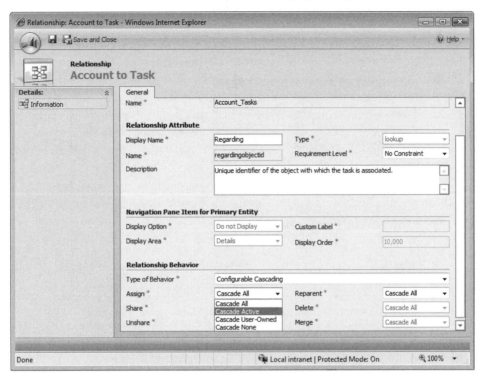

FIGURE 3-7 Changing the default relationship behavior between entities before reassigning records

Monitoring License Usage for Compliance

With the on-premise version of Microsoft Dynamics CRM, you need to keep track of the number of active Microsoft Dynamics CRM licenses your company uses to ensure that you do not use more licenses than you should. As we mentioned earlier, Microsoft Dynamics CRM licensing trusts customers to monitor their own usage because the volume license key grants you 100,000 users regardless of how many user licenses your company actually purchased.

> **Note** Microsoft Dynamics CRM Live licensing differs from on-premise licensing because it uses a hard enforcement on the number of user licenses. If you try to add more users than you have licenses for, the system will send you an error message and reject the action.

If you want to view a summary of your current active licenses, start the Microsoft Dynamics CRM Deployment Manager on the Microsoft Dynamics CRM Web server, and then click License. Right-click a license and select Properties (shown in Figure 3-8).

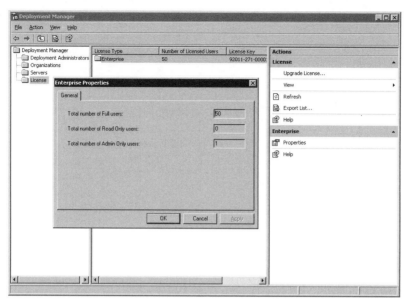

FIGURE 3-8 License summary in Microsoft Dynamics CRM Deployment Manager

As you can see in Figure 3-8, Microsoft Dynamics CRM reports the number of different users for each of the different license types: Full, Read Only, and Administrative. You must purchase the corresponding number of licenses to match the number of Full and Read-Only users in your system, but you do not need to purchase user licenses for administrative users.

Microsoft Dynamics CRM Enterprise Edition customers can set up multiple organizations in a single Microsoft Dynamics CRM deployment, and this license summary will display the total number of users across all of the organizations. Unfortunately, you cannot run this license summary tool for a single organization, so if you need this information detailed by organization, you must log on manually to each organization and perform a query to determine the number of active users in each category.

Security Roles and Business Units

As we explained earlier, Microsoft Dynamics CRM uses a combination of role-based security and object-based security to determine what users can see and do in the deployment. Instead of configuring security for each user one record at a time, you assign security settings and permissions to a security role, and then you assign one or more security roles to a user. Microsoft Dynamics CRM includes the following 13 predefined security roles:

- **CEO-Business Manager**   A user who manages the organization at the corporate business level

- **CSR Manager**   A user who manages customer service activities at the local or team level

- **Customer Service Representative**   A customer service representative (CSR) at any level

- **Marketing Manager**   A user who manages marketing activities at the local or team level

- **Marketing Professional**   A user engaged in marketing activities at any level

- **Sales Manager**   A user who manages sales activities at the local or team level

- **Salesperson**   A salesperson at any level

- **Schedule Manager**   A user who manages services, required resources, and working hours

- **Scheduler**   A user who schedules appointments for services

- **System Administrator**   A user who defines and implements the process at any level

- **System Customizer**   A user who customizes Microsoft Dynamics CRM records, attributes, relationships, and forms

- **Vice President of Marketing**   A user who manages marketing activities at the business unit level

- **Vice President of Sales**   A user who manages the sales organization at the business unit level

These default security roles include predefined rights and permissions typically associated with these roles so that you can save time by using them as the starting point for your deployment. You can edit any of the default security roles, except for System Administrator, to fit the needs of your business.

> **Tip**   You can also copy the default security roles by clicking Copy Role on the More Actions menu on the grid toolbar. Copying roles and then modifying the copies greatly reduces the setup time required to create new roles.

When you assign multiple security roles to a user, Microsoft Dynamics CRM combines the user rights so that the user can perform the highest-level activity associated with any of his or her roles. In other words, if you assign two security roles that have conflicting security rights, Microsoft Dynamics CRM grants the user the least-restrictive permission of the two. For example, consider a fictional Vice President of Sales named Connie Watson. Figure 3-9 shows that Connie has two security roles assigned to her: Salesperson and Vice President of Marketing.

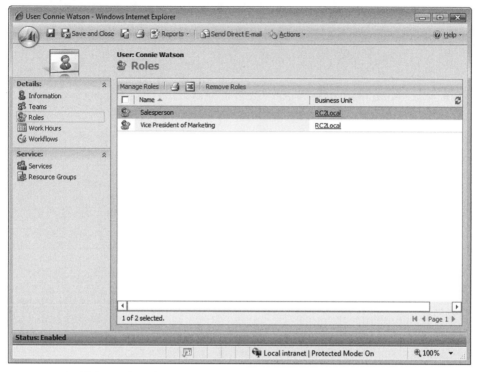

FIGURE 3-9 Multiple security roles assigned to a user

In the Microsoft Dynamics CRM default security roles, a user with only the Salesperson security role cannot create new announcements, but the Vice President of Marketing security role can. Because Microsoft Dynamics CRM grants the least-restrictive permission across all of a user's roles, Connie is able to create announcements in this example because she is also assigned the Vice President of Marketing security role.

Important Security roles combine together to grant users all of the permissions for all of their assigned security roles. If one of a user's security roles grants a permission, that user *always* possesses that permission, even if you assign him or her another security role that conflicts with the original permission.

Security Role Definitions

Before we explain how to modify security roles, we quickly cover the terminology related to security roles. To view and manage the settings for a security role, browse to Administration in the Settings area, and click Security Roles. Then, double-click one of the roles listed in the grid. Figure 3-10 shows the Salesperson default security role settings.

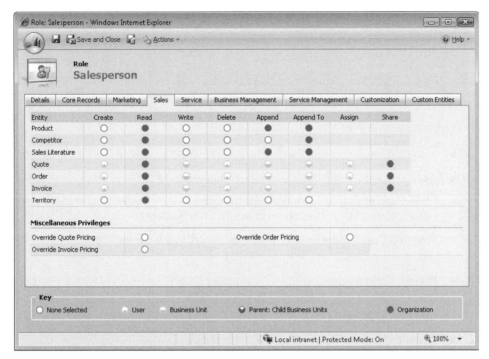

FIGURE 3-10 Salesperson security role settings

The columns in the top table represent entity privileges in Microsoft Dynamics CRM. *Privileges* give a user permission to perform an action in Microsoft Dynamics CRM such as Create, Read, or Write. The bottom section lists additional miscellaneous privileges including Override Quote Pricing and Override Invoice Pricing. Microsoft Dynamics CRM divides the privileges of a security role into subsets by creating tabs for the functional areas, such as Marketing, Sales, Service, and so on. Each tab in the security role editor lists different entity privileges and miscellaneous privileges for entities in Microsoft Dynamics CRM.

The colored circles in the security role settings define the access level for that privilege. *Access levels* determine how deep or high in the organizational business unit hierarchy the user can perform the specified privilege. For example, you could configure access levels for a security role so that a user could delete any record owned by someone in his or her business unit but only read records owned by users in different business units.

Important The actions that privileges grant to users (such as Create and Delete) do not vary by access level. For example, the Read privilege for the User access level offers the same action (functionality) as the Read privilege for the Organization access level. However, the different access levels determine on which records in Microsoft Dynamics CRM the user can execute the privilege.

In the following subsections, we explore configuring access levels for a security role in more detail.

Access Levels

As you can see in the key (located at the bottom of Figure 3-10), Microsoft Dynamics CRM offers five access levels:

- **None Selected**   Always denies the privilege to the users assigned to the role.

- **User**   Grants the privilege for records that the user owns, in addition to records explicitly shared with the user and records shared with a team to which the user belongs. We explain sharing records later in this chapter.

- **Business Unit**   Grants the privilege for records with ownership in the user's business unit.

- **Parent: Child Business Units**   Grants the privilege for records with ownership in the user's business unit, in addition to records with ownership in a child business unit of the user's business unit.

- **Organization**   Grants the privilege for all records in the organization, regardless of the business unit hierarchical level to which the object or user belongs.

> **Note** The User, Business Unit, and Parent: Child Business Units access levels do not apply to some privileges, such as Bulk Edit and Print (found in the Business Management tab under Miscellaneous Privileges), because the concept of user ownership or business units doesn't apply to those privileges. No user or business unit owns Bulk Edit or Print because they're just actions. Therefore, these types of privileges offer only two access levels: None Selected and Organization. In these scenarios, you can think of None Selected as "No" and Organization as "Yes" in regard to whether the user possesses that privilege.

Consider an example scenario to understand access levels in a real-world context. Figure 3-11 shows five business units, six users, and six Contact records.

We examine the impact of configuring different access levels for a single privilege (Contact Read) in the context of a fictional user named Gail Erickson. Gail belongs to the Service business unit, which is a child of the Adventure Works Cycle business unit and is also a parent of the Central Region business unit. Each of the Contacts shown is owned by the user record to which it is linked. Table 3-1 shows which Contact records Gail could read for each of the five possible access level configurations.

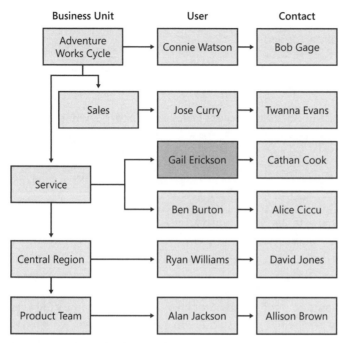

FIGURE 3-11 Access levels example

TABLE 3-1 Read Privileges for Gail Erickson by Access Level

Read privilege access level for the Contact entity	Bob Gage	Twanna Evans	Cathan Cook	Alice Ciccu	David Jones	Allison Brown
None	No	No	No	No	No	No
User	No	No	Yes	No	No	No
Business Unit	No	No	Yes	Yes	No	No
Parent: Child Business Units	No	No	Yes	Yes	Yes	Yes
Organization	Yes	Yes	Yes	Yes	Yes	Yes

For the Business Unit access level, Microsoft Dynamics CRM grants Gail the Read privilege for the Alice Ciccu contact because Ben Burton owns that record and he belongs to the same business unit as Gail. For the Parent: Child Business Units access level, Microsoft Dynamics CRM grants Gail the Read privilege for the David Jones and Allison Brown records because the Central Region and Product Team business units are children of the Service business unit that Gail belongs to, and both the David Jones and Allison Brown records are owned by users that belong to these child business units.

As this example illustrates, configuring access levels for a security role requires that you understand and consider the following parameters:

- The organization and business unit hierarchy

- Record ownership and the business unit that the record owner belongs to

- The business unit of the logged-in user

Table 3-2 summarizes how Microsoft Dynamics CRM grants and denies privileges based on these parameters.

TABLE 3-2 Privileges Granted Based on Access Level and Record Ownerships

Privilege access level	Record owned by user	Record owned by different user in same business unit	Record owned by user in any child business unit	Record owned by user in any nonchild business unit
None	Deny	Deny	Deny	Deny
User	Grant	Deny	Deny	Deny
Business Unit	Grant	Grant	Deny	Deny
Parent: Child Business Units	Grant	Grant	Grant	Deny
Organization	Grant	Grant	Grant	Grant

By now you should have a good understanding of how Microsoft Dynamics CRM determines whether to grant security privileges to users based on access levels. Now we discuss what each of the privileges means and the actions that they allow users to perform in the system.

Privileges

Privileges define what users can view and do in Microsoft Dynamics CRM, and you bundle privileges together in a security role definition. Some of the privileges describe actions that users can take against entity records such as delete or create, and other privileges define features in Microsoft Dynamics CRM such as Mail Merge and Export to Excel. In this section, we explore the following topics:

- Entity privileges

- Miscellaneous privileges

- Privilege impact on application navigation

Entity Privileges

As Figure 3-10 showed earlier, some privileges such as Create, Read, and Write apply to the entities in Microsoft Dynamics CRM. For each entity type and privilege, you can configure a different access level. The following list describes the actions that each privilege allows:

- **Create**   Permits the user to add a new record

- **Read**   Permits the user to view a record

- **Write**   Permits the user to edit an existing record

- **Delete**   Permits the user to delete a record

- **Append**   Permits the user to attach another entity to, or associate another entity with, a parent record

- **Append To**   Permits the user to attach other entities to, or associate other entities with, the record

- **Assign**   Permits the user to change a record's owner to a different user

- **Share**   Permits the user to share a record with another user or team

- **Enable/Disable**   Permits the user to enable or disable user and business unit records

> **More Info**   Not all of the entity privileges apply to all of the entities in Microsoft Dynamics CRM. For example, the Share privilege does not apply to any of the entities in the Service Management tab. The Enable/Disable privilege applies only to the Business Unit and User entities.

The Append and Append To actions behave a little differently from the other privileges because you must configure them on two different entities for them to work correctly. To understand the Append and Append To actions better, consider the analogy of attaching a sticky note to a wall. To configure the sticky note concept using Microsoft Dynamics CRM security privileges, you need to assign Append privileges to the sticky note and then configre Append To privileges to the wall. Translating that concept to Microsoft Dynamics CRM entities, if you want to attach (or append) a Contact to an Account, the user would need Append privileges for the Contact and Append To privileges for the Account record.

In Microsoft Dynamics CRM, you can also configure entity privileges for any custom entities that you create in your deployment. You can configure all five access levels for each custom entity for all of the entity privileges.

> ### Troubleshooting Entity Privilege Errors
>
> Sometimes when you're adjusting Microsoft Dynamics CRM security roles, you may later get an error message telling you that the user does not have permission to complete an action. You may think to yourself, "What in the world is this talking about?" After you review the security roles, you wonder which privilege could *possibly* be missing that would result in this error.
>
> Many times you will need to grant a user a security privilege that would not be obvious to you by simply looking at the security role configuration screens. For example, would you guess that you need the Append To Order privilege before you can create an Appointment record?

If you find yourself getting stuck trying to track down the appropriate privileges that a user needs to perform an action, we recommend that you refer to the Microsoft Dynamics CRM software development kit (SDK) because it contains documentation regarding the various privileges users need to complete certain actions. You can find this information in the Privileges by Message section of the SDK. For example, you'll see something like this for the privileges needed to create an appointment:

- prvAppendActivity
- prvAppendToAccount
- prvAppendToActivity
- prvAppendToContact
- prvAppendToContract
- prvAppendToIncident
- prvAppendToInvoice
- prvAppendToLead
- prvAppendToOpportunity
- prvAppendToOrder
- prvAppendToQuote
- prvAppendToService
- prvCreateActivity
- prvReadActivity
- prvShareActivity

Although at first this list appears a little cryptic, you can use this information as a starting point to determine which privileges the user will need in a security role to perform the desired action. Unfortunately, in Microsoft Dynamics CRM 3.0 we did find a few instances for which the SDK documentation did not list *all* of the necessary privileges. In those instances, we recommend you enable system tracing for the server. The trace should capture the exact privilege identifier, which you can use to look up the missing privilege. Chapter 9, "Microsoft Dynamics CRM 4.0 SDK," details how to accomplish this. Because this approach requires server and database administration rights, you can also rely on a more tedious trial-and-error method to toggle off and on the other privileges in the security role to figure out what the user needs.

Miscellaneous Privileges

In addition to entity privileges, Microsoft Dynamics CRM includes additional miscellaneous privileges in each tab of the security role editor. The privilege name often provides enough information about what the privilege covers, but sometimes the description can leave you guessing. This is especially true for miscellaneous privileges that relate to areas of the application that you may not use often. In the following list, we provide a little more description about each of the miscellaneous privileges and, in some cases, where to find the related feature.

- **Publish E-mail Templates**   Permits the user to make a personal e-mail template available to the organization. Users can access this feature by browsing to Templates in the Settings section, and opening a personal E-mail Template by double-clicking it. Then, they can click Make Template Available to Organization on the Actions menu.

- **Publish Reports**   Allows a user to make a report available (or viewable) to the entire organization. For Reporting Services reports, this privilege will also allow the user to publish the report to the Reporting Services Web server for external use.

- **Publish Duplicate Detection Rules**   Permits the user to publish duplicate detection rules configured in the data management section.

- **Add Reporting Services Reports**   Permits the user to upload an existing Reporting Services report file to Microsoft Dynamics CRM. Reporting Services files are in the RDL format. This privilege differs from the Create privilege of the Report entity, which refers to creating a new report by using the Report Wizard or by adding another file type (such as an Excel file or PDF report). Please note that Microsoft Dynamics CRM Live customers cannot upload custom reports to the server; they can only create reports using the Report Wizard.

- **Publish Mail Merge Templates to Organization**   Permits the user to make mail merge templates available to the entire organization. Individually owned mail merge templates follow the standard Microsoft Dynamics CRM security model.

- **Create Quick Campaign**   Permits the user to create a single activity and distribute it to multiple records by using a marketing quick campaign. The user also needs to have the correct security configuration to create the quick campaign activities.

- **Override Quote Pricing**   Permits the user to override the calculated price of a quote (based on products added to the quote) and manually enter new quote pricing. Users can access the Override Price button when they're editing a Quote Product attached to a Quote.

- **Override Invoice Pricing**   Permits the user to override the system-generated price of an invoice and manually enter new invoice pricing. Users can access the Override Price button when they're editing an Invoice Product attached to an Invoice.

- **Override Order Pricing**   Permits the user to override the system-generated price of an order and manually enter new order pricing. Users can access the Override Price button when they're editing an Order Product attached to an Order.

- **Publish Articles**   Permits the user to publish unapproved Knowledge Base articles. Users access the Approve (publish) button on the grid toolbar of the Unapproved Article Queue located in the Knowledge Base area.

- **Assign Role**   Permits the user to add or remove security roles to and from user records in the Settings section.

- **Bulk Edit**   Permits the user to edit multiple records at the same time. Users with this privilege can access the feature from an entity's grid toolbar. This feature does not apply to all entities.

- **Print**   Permits the user to create a printer-friendly display of a grid. Users with this privilege can access this feature by clicking the Print button on the grid toolbar. You cannot vary this privilege by entity type.

- **Merge**   Permits the user to merge two records into a single record. Users with this privilege can access the Merge feature from the grid toolbar.

- **Go Offline**   Permits a user with Microsoft Dynamics CRM for Outlook with Offline Access installed to work in an offline mode. Working offline creates a local copy of the database on the laptop. Because the user can remove the laptop (with the offline data) from work premises, the offline option raises a potential security question that you must consider.

- **CRM Address Book**   Permits a user of the Microsoft Dynamics CRM clients for Outlook to select CRM records from his or her address book in Outlook.

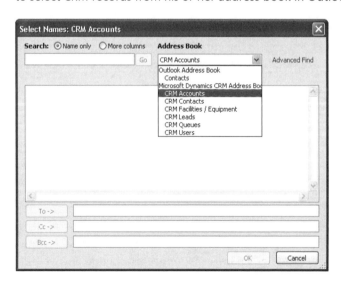

- **Update Business Closures**   Permits the user to modify business working hours and closure information. Users access the Business Closures information in the Settings area.

- **Language Settings**   Always a user to change their own language settings.

- **Assign Territory to User**   Permits the user to add or remove users from a sales territory. Users access the Sales Territories information in the Business Administration section of the Settings area.

- **Go Mobile**   Permits the user to synchronize Microsoft Dynamics CRM data with mobile devices.

- **Export to Excel**   Permits the user to export the grid data to Microsoft Office Excel. Users with this privilege access the Export to Excel feature from the grid toolbar.

- **Mail Merge**   Permits the user to create mail merge items such as letters, e-mail messages, envelopes, and labels. This privilege refers to creating mail merge items using Microsoft Dynamics CRM for Outlook .

- **Web Mail Merge**   Same as the Mail Merge privilege, but it permits the user to access the mail merge functionality in the Web interface without using Microsoft Dynamics CRM for Outlook.

- **Sync to Outlook**   Permits a user of Microsoft Dynamics CRM for Outlook to synchronize Microsoft Dynamics CRM data such as Contacts, Tasks, and Appointments to his or her Outlook file.

- **Send E-mail as Another User**   Permits the user to select a different user or queue for the From address of an e-mail message sent with the Microsoft Dynamics CRM Send Direct E-mail feature. The Send Direct E-mail button appears on grids only if the user has the following security privileges:

  - Read and Append privileges on the Activity entity

  - Append To privileges for the entity to which the user is sending direct e-mail (such as Contact or Account)

  - Read privileges on the E-mail Template entity

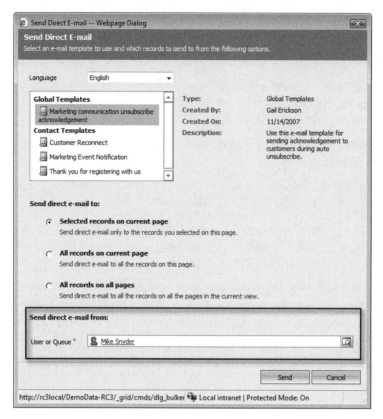

- **Send Invitation**   Permits a user to send an e-mail invitation to an employee to join the organization. This privilege applies only to Microsoft Dynamics CRM Live deployments.

- **Search Availability**   Permits the user to search for available times when scheduling a Service activity.

- **Browse Availability**   Permits the user to view the Service Calendar located in the Service area.

- **ISV Extensions**   Determines whether Microsoft Dynamics CRM displays customizations, such as custom menu items and toolbar buttons, from the ISV.config file to the user. Note that this setting applies to all or none of the ISV extensions—you cannot turn on specific ISV extensions by using this setting.

- **Execute Workflow Job**   In addition to proper permissions to the System Job entity, users need this privilege to execute manual workflow rules or automatic workflow rules.

- **Export Customizations**   Permits the user to export system customizations from Microsoft Dynamics CRM to a configuration file.

- **Import Customizations**   Permits the user to import a configuration file into Microsoft Dynamics CRM.

- **Publish Customizations**   Permits the user to publish customizations applied to an entity.

> **More Info**   At the time this book went to press, Microsoft had not yet released the mobile version of Microsoft Dynamics CRM 4.0. Therefore, we cannot definitively describe how the Go Mobile privilege will behave.

If you're still not sure what a specific privilege does or whether it will do what you want, you can easily test a privilege by simply selecting the access level for a security role, saving the role, and then logging on to Microsoft Dynamics CRM as a user with only that security role. Remember that if your personal account has a System Administrator role, you have Organization access level rights for all privileges, so don't log on as a System Administrator to test security privileges. Testing security privileges is a good example of when you may want to impersonate a different user when you log on to Microsoft Dynamics CRM. We explained earlier in the chapter how you can modify your Internet Explorer security settings so that Microsoft Dynamics CRM prompts you to enter a user name and password instead of using Integrated Windows authentication.

> **Note**   Miscellaneous privileges don't apply to custom entities that you create.

Field-Level Security

You configure privileges and access levels based on entire entity records in Microsoft Dynamics CRM, not on the individual attributes for each entity. For example, you cannot use security role configurations to specify that users can view a contact's name and phone number but not the social security number or home address. If users possess the Read privilege for a Contact record, they can view *all* of the Contact's attributes displayed on the form.

However, you can take advantage of the Microsoft Dynamics CRM robust programming model to dynamically hide attributes on a form or disable certain attributes based on the user's security role. You would use the form *onLoad* event to execute this type of custom script. Chapter 10, "Client-Side SDK," explains how to use the form *onLoad* event, and it includes example code. However, you should know about some caveats when using the form *onLoad* event to hide attributes on a form.

A user could still view the "hidden" data by performing an Advanced Find and adding the hidden column to his or her output result set. Users cannot edit data using this technique, but they can view all attributes of any entity that they have privileges to read. Users could also potentially view this hidden information by exporting to Excel or running reports that contain this information. The data in the field you are trying to hide is also still viewable to users if they connected to the Microsoft Dynamics CRM database using the filtered views feature (as explained in Chapter 7, "Reporting and Analysis"). Therefore, users could also still access the field you're trying to hide by clicking the print view of the record.

Therefore, using the form *onLoad* event doesn't really provide field-level security at all if you need to hide data from users, but you can use this technique to restrict users from editing specific attributes on the entity form. If you really need to restrict access to specific fields, we recommend that you create a custom entity related to the parent record and configure security for the custom entity to restrict access as appropriate. For example, you can create a custom entity related to the Contact record that you use to store sensitive information such as a person's social security number or credit card information.

Privilege Impact on Application Navigation

Microsoft Dynamics CRM includes more than 100 entities and thousands of features in the Sales, Marketing, and Customer Service areas. However, very few organizations will use *all* of the entities that Microsoft Dynamics CRM offers to track and manage their customer data. Consequently, users commonly request to see only the areas of the application that their organization actually uses. For example, if your organization doesn't use the Sales Literature or Invoices entities, your users won't want to see these entities as they navigate through the user interface.

Although it would be technically possible to use the site map to remove some areas of the navigation (Sales Literature and Invoices, in this example), the better solution is to modify user security roles and privileges, which also changes the user interface.

 Important You should modify security roles—instead of modifying the site map—to hide areas of Microsoft Dynamics CRM that your organization does not use. By modifying security roles, you also can change the display of the entity navigation pane, which is an area of the user interface that you cannot edit by using the site map. Chapter 6 explains the site map in more detail and discusses when you should modify it.

If you modify a security role and set the access level of the Read privilege for an entity to None Selected, Microsoft Dynamics CRM automatically removes that entity from the user interface for users with that security role, including the menu bar, the application navigation pane, and the entity record. Most of the 13 default security roles include an Organization access level for the Read privilege on all of the entities, so users will see all of the entities in the application navigation. Therefore, we recommend that you change the Read privilege access level to None Selected for any entity that you're not using in your deployment. By doing so, you create a streamlined user interface that can help new users learn the system more quickly and that lets existing users navigate more efficiently.

Tip To see the updated application navigation after you modify a security role, you may have to refresh your Web browser window or restart Outlook.

Figure 3-12 shows the Account record for a user with the default Customer Service Representative security role assigned. Because that role includes the Read privilege for most of the entities, the user can see all of the links in the entity navigation pane, such as Quotes, Orders, Invoices, Marketing Lists, and Campaigns.

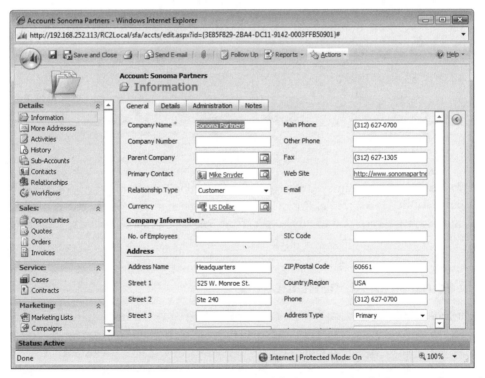

FIGURE 3-12 Account record as seen by a user with the default Customer Service Representative security role

In reality, most customer service representatives don't need to see all of this information on an Account record. Instead, assume that you want your customer service representatives to see only the information shown in the Details and Service groups. By modifying their security roles and setting the Read privilege to None Selected for the entities that you want to hide, the revised Account form can appear like the one shown in Figure 3-13.

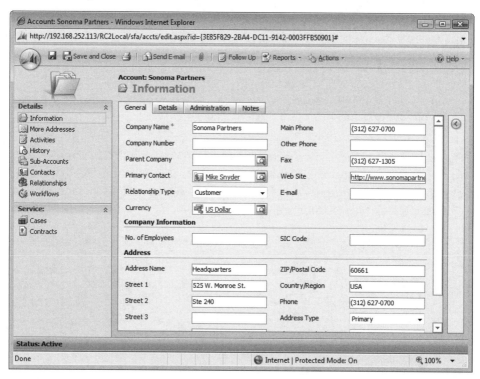

FIGURE 3-13 Account record as seen by a user with a revised Customer Service Representative security role

You can see that we removed the Sales and Marketing links from the navigation pane by modifying the security role. This provides a much cleaner user interface that your users will appreciate. Likewise, you could also revise the Salesperson security role so that salespeople see only entities that they need to perform their jobs.

Security Role Inheritance

If your deployment includes multiple business units, you must understand how Microsoft Dynamics CRM inherits security roles in the business unit hierarchy. When you create a new security role in a business unit, Microsoft Dynamics CRM creates an instance (copy) of that security role for every business unit that is a child of the business unit for which you created the new security role. If you try to edit the security role in one of the child business units, you will see a warning message stating, "Inherited roles cannot be modified or updated." You can edit only the parent security role, and then Microsoft Dynamics CRM automatically copies your changes to all of the security roles in the child business units. Consider the organization hierarchy of the sample organization Adventure Works Cycle, as shown in Figure 3-14.

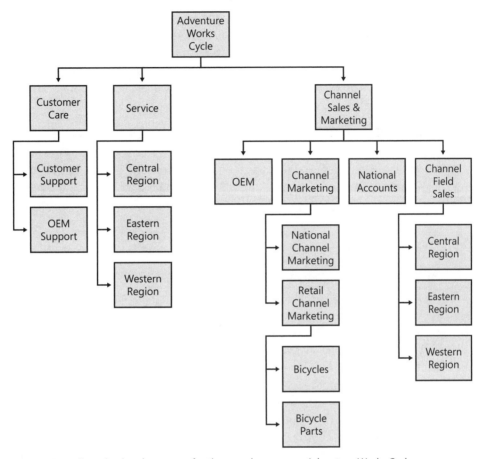

FIGURE 3-14 Organizational structure for the sample company Adventure Works Cycle

If you create a new security role called Director assigned to the Customer Care business unit, Microsoft Dynamics CRM automatically creates noneditable copies of the Director security role in the Customer Support and OEM Support business units because they are children of the Customer Care business unit. Any changes you make to the Director security role are automatically propagated to all of the Director security roles in the child business units. When you view the security roles for one of the other business units, such as Service or OEM, you do not see the Director security role listed because the Service and OEM business units are not children of the Customer Care business unit.

Tip When you create a new security role, Microsoft Dynamics CRM assigns the security role to the root business unit by default, so make sure that you remember to change the role's business unit by using the business unit lookup if you want to create a role in a nonroot business unit.

Every user belongs to only one business unit, and you can assign users security roles only from the business unit to which they belong. Therefore, in this example, you could not assign the Director security role to users who belong to any business unit other than Customer Care, Customer Support, and OEM Support. You can view all of the security roles for a single business unit by using the business unit view filter drop-down list to select a specific business unit.

Because Microsoft Dynamics CRM inherits security roles to children business units, you cannot make the privileges of a security role be different for each business unit. However, you can create a varying number of security roles for each business unit in your deployment. The ability to create unique security roles for each business unit gives you great flexibility to create and configure security roles to meet your organization's needs.

Sharing Records

Despite the numerous security options and configuration choices already discussed, you will probably encounter scenarios in which users need to share and collaborate on records that the business unit hierarchy does not support. Consider a fictional company called Coho Vineyard & Winery (the root business unit) that has two children business units named Vineyard and Winery. Coho Vineyard & Winery CEO Laura Owen (user assigned to root business unit) owns the Woodgrove Bank account. However, the security roles for Gretchen Rivas (assigned to Vineyard business unit) and Heidi Steen (assigned to Winery business unit) do not have the Write privilege for the Account entity. The CEO decides that she wants Gretchen and Heidi to work on a special project related to Woodgrove Bank for which they will need to edit the record. However, Laura doesn't want them to edit any other Account records that she owns other than Woodgrove Bank. This type of security configuration is not possible using the security configurations covered so far. If Laura gives Gretchen and Heidi privileges to edit Account records for the Organization, they would be able to edit *any* Account, not just the Woodgrove Bank record. Fortunately, Microsoft Dynamics CRM allows users to share records to accommodate exactly this type of collaboration scenario. *Sharing* records allows a user to grant privileges for a specific record so that other users can work with the shared record, even though they would not usually have the necessary privileges to do so.

To share records, users must have a security role assigned the appropriate Share privilege. To set up a share such as the one described in the Woodgrove Bank example, open the entity record and click Sharing on the More Actions menu of the entity menu bar. In the Share dialog box, select the users who you want to share this record with by clicking Add User/ Team. Use the Lookup tool to find the records that you want, and then click OK. Microsoft Dynamics CRM adds the users to the page, as shown in Figure 3-15.

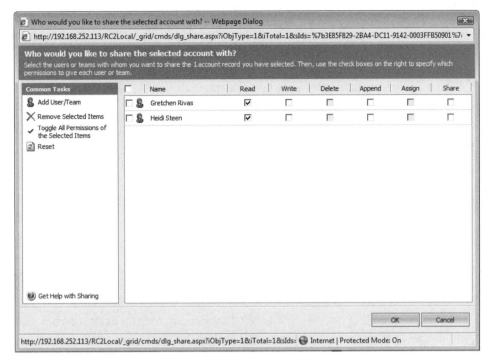

FIGURE 3-15 Sharing records with users

Next, specify which privileges you want to share with these users. In the Woodgrove Bank example, Laura Owen can select the Read and Write privileges so that Gretchen and Heidi can edit this record. Note that the Delete and Assign privilege check boxes are unavailable because Laura doesn't have those privileges for this record, and therefore cannot share them with any other user.

> **More Info** Users can't share a privilege if they do not possess the privilege themselves. For example, a user cannot share Delete privileges for a record if he or she does not have the Delete privilege for that record.

With this share in place, Gretchen and Heidi can now read and write just the Woodgrove Bank Account record. Of course, you can revoke a share at any time by simply opening the record and clearing the check boxes of the privileges that you want to revoke.

Teams

In the Coho Vineyard & Winery example, it is easy to set up the share because you need to select only two users. But what if Laura wants to share the Woodgrove Bank record with 100 users? What if she wants to share five different records with those same 100 users? It would be a pretty miserable and time-consuming process to share records manually one user at a time in these examples. Fortunately, with Microsoft Dynamics CRM you can set up and configure *teams* of users to expedite the sharing process. By sharing a record with a team instead of with individual users, you do not have to select user records manually for each share that you create. Rather, you simply select the team that you want to share with, and all of the users in that team participate in the share.

You can create and modify teams by browsing to Administration in the Settings area, and then clicking Teams. When you create a team, you specify the business unit that the team belongs to, and then you simply add members to the team.

> **Important** Although you assign a team to a business unit, you can add any user in the organization to a team, regardless of his or her business unit. You cannot change a team's business unit once it is created.

If you use a large number of teams, you can configure the security settings so that users see only a subset of all of the teams. To do this, configure the Team entity privilege in a user's security role with an access level appropriate for each team's business unit. For example, if you create a team that belongs to the root business unit but you grant a security role only with a User access level for the team privilege, users with that security role won't see that root business unit team in the user interface unless they personally created that team. By using this type of configuration, you can restrict the teams that each user is allowed to view (and share records with) in case you want to hide specific teams (such as executive or financial teams).

> **Caution** Once you create a team, you cannot delete or disable it. If you no longer want to use a team, all you can do is remove all of its members. Therefore, you should use some discretion when creating teams, or you can end up with a bunch of abandoned teams that contain no members.

You may wonder if it's possible to have a team own a record instead of just sharing a record with a team. Unfortunately, you cannot set a team as the owner of a record such as a Lead, Account, or Contact.

Sharing and Inheritance

When you share a record with a team or user, child entities of the shared record can inherit the same sharing settings as the parent record. In the Woodgrove Bank example, Gretchen and Heidi can edit the Account record and its related entities, such as Tasks, Phone Calls, and Notes, because they inherit the same share as their parent record.

More Info For shared records (directly shared or inherited), users receive only the shared privileges for the entity if they have at least a User access level for that entity. For example, if Heidi has an access level of None Selected for the Activity entity, she is not able to view activities related to Woodgrove Bank even if someone shares Read privileges with her for that Account record. Likewise, she needs to have at least a User access level for the Account entity to view the Woodgrove Bank account record after Laura shares it with her.

You can configure how Microsoft Dynamics CRM shares related records by editing the relationship behavior between two entities. For example, you may want Microsoft Dynamics CRM to inherit sharing with related entities such as Tasks but not with a different related entity such as Activities. Chapter 6 explains in detail how to configure relationship behaviors between entities.

Caution Be careful about relying on sharing inheritance that goes more than two levels deep because the security settings may not work as you expect. Microsoft Dynamics CRM Knowledge Base article 908504 refers to Microsoft Dynamics CRM 3.0, but it explains how sharing inheritance two levels or deeper can have unexpected results.

Summary

Microsoft Dynamics CRM includes a powerful and highly configurable security model that you can use to configure and restrict information access according to your business needs. The on-premise version of Microsoft Dynamics CRM uses Active Directory to manage user accounts and passwords. On-premise users accessing Microsoft Dynamics CRM by the local intranet authenticate with Integrated Windows authentication, whereas users accessing Microsoft Dynamics CRM by an Internet-facing deployment use forms-based authentication. All users of Microsoft Dynamics CRM Live use Windows Live ID as their user authentication method.

By combining role-based and object-based security settings with your organization's business unit structure, in Microsoft Dynamics CRM you can accommodate very complex security and information access needs. Microsoft Dynamics CRM also supports project-based and collaborative work by enabling users to share records with teams and individual users.

Part II
Customization

Part I of this book gave you a brief overview of Microsoft Dynamics CRM and showed you how to setup and configure some commonly used areas of the software. However, we would consider everything we've reviewed so far more as software "configuration" instead of "customizing". Part II of this book will get deep into the details of how you can customize Microsoft Dynamics CRM and provide you real world context of why you might need to perform these customizations. Just like Part I, you'll need to have System Administrator rights in your Microsoft Dynamics CRM system to perform almost all of the customizations we review in Part II. Any IT project manager or "power user" will have the technical skills necessary to perform all of the customizations we review in this part, even if you're not a programmer or developer.

If possible, we would highly recommend that you actually log in to Microsoft Dynamics CRM and try to follow along in the user interface as you read the material in these chapters.

Chapter 4

Entity Customization: Concepts and Attributes

Before we explain how to customize entities in Microsoft Dynamics CRM, we want to remind you why you need to customize your system. Assume your company is considering implementing Microsoft Dynamics CRM and you've installed the trial version of the software. As soon as you show the company owners or executives the user interface and they see one of the default forms (such as the Account form shown in Figure 4-1), the first words out of their mouth will be something like, "That's not the information we track about our customers. We would never use the Shipping Method and Freight Term fields, and where do we enter the SIC Code and the Number of Employees each customer has? Also, we don't call customers an Account; we refer to them as a Company."

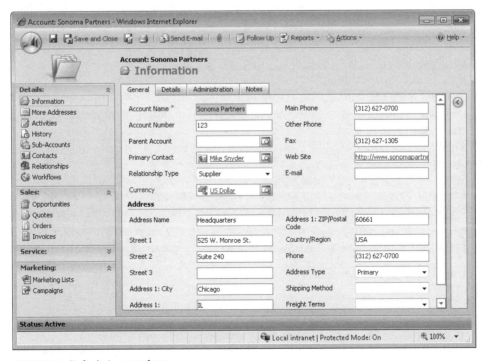

FIGURE 4-1 Default Account form

Ah-ha! It took only one meeting for your users to start demanding customizations to the Microsoft Dynamics CRM system to better match your business needs. However, in just a few minutes (literally) and without a single line of programming code, you could customize Microsoft Dynamics CRM so that your new form looks like the one shown in Figure 4-2.

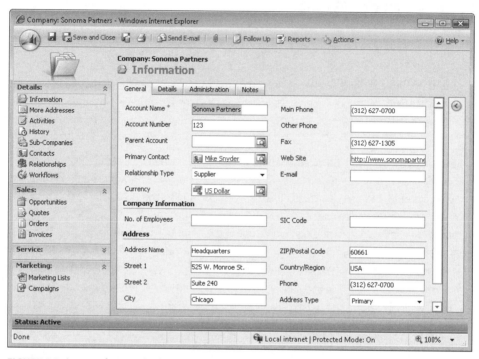

FIGURE 4-2 Account form revised with new fields and renamed Company

Implementing this type of customization in other customer relationship management (CRM) vendors' applications might take weeks of coding and testing. It might not even be possible to change some of the key system terminology such as renaming Account to Company. The Microsoft Dynamics CRM customization model can make these and other types of customizations seem almost trivial.

Microsoft Dynamics CRM offers an incredible number of system customization opportunities, and you can complete most of them through a Web-based interface without any programming expertise. In fact, Microsoft Dynamics CRM offers so many customization features we had to break the entity customization explanation into three separate chapters on the following topics:

- Concepts and attributes
- Forms and views
- Relationships and custom entities

In this chapter, we give you an overview of the concepts related to entity customization, and then start the entity customization explanation with entity attributes.

Customization Concepts

Microsoft Dynamics CRM is a horizontal platform that can be used by any company, regardless of industry or size. Because no two businesses use the same processes or track the same customer data, Microsoft designed the Microsoft Dynamics CRM software for easy customization by using a metadata-driven product architecture.

Metadata is defined as data about data. When users look up a customer or prospect, Microsoft Dynamics CRM runs behind the scenes to retrieve the record data from the metadata, which in turn retrieves information from the actual underlying system data. Microsoft Dynamics CRM stores its underlying system data in a relational database format using Microsoft SQL Server. Figure 4-3 illustrates a highly simplified representation of this metadata-driven concept.

FIGURE 4-3 Metadata product architecture

Of course, your users will never know that Microsoft Dynamics CRM uses a metadata architecture, but it's important that you know about it for several reasons:

- The metadata makes heavy use of Web services and XML data formats, so you see terminology related to those technologies in the Microsoft Dynamics CRM documentation and in this book (such as *entity* and *attribute*).

- With the metadata-driven architecture in Microsoft Dynamics CRM, you can quickly and easily make customizations that would be extremely difficult (or perhaps impossible) to implement in other CRM systems.

- Microsoft Dynamics CRM automatically manages the extremely complex details of the metadata on your behalf. If you attempt to make changes directly to the underlying system data in SQL Server, you run the risk of damaging the metadata and creating irreversible errors in your system.

To ensure that the metadata and its underlying SQL data always remain well structured, Microsoft Dynamics CRM offers two ways to customize your system. The first method is a Web-based interface specifically designed for you to manage metadata changes. The second method allows you to use the Microsoft Dynamics CRM software development kit (SDK) to programmatically alter the metadata. Both of these tools work in the predefined framework of Microsoft Dynamics CRM to update the metadata and its underlying SQL data correctly.

Note You learn more about the Microsoft Dynamics CRM SDK and altering the metadata programmatically in Chapter 9, "Microsoft Dynamics CRM 4.0 SDK."

In addition to helping you protect your software investment, using the Microsoft Dynamics CRM administration tools for your customizations includes additional benefits such as the following:

- The Web-based administration tools provide a simple and easy-to-understand interface.

- Microsoft technical support can assist you with any changes that you make using the customization tools.

- Your customizations should upgrade smoothly to future releases and updates of Microsoft Dynamics CRM.

- You can install third-party software add-ons for Microsoft Dynamics CRM.

You can see the benefits of the Microsoft Dynamics CRM metadata architecture and using the customization tools that Microsoft Dynamics CRM provides. Next, we talk about some of the key concepts and terminology related to customizations:

- Entities and attributes

- Security and permissions

- Publishing customizations

- Importing and exporting customizations

- Renaming a customizable entity

Entities and Attributes

If you have worked with relational databases such as Microsoft Office Access or SQL Server, you understand the meaning of the terms *table* and *column*. In the Microsoft Dynamics CRM metadata-driven XML-based terminology, you can mentally translate those concepts to *entity* and *attribute*, as shown in Table 4-1.

TABLE 4-1 Terminology Comparison

Relational database terminology	XML-based terminology
Table	Entity
Column	Attribute

Microsoft Dynamics CRM stores data in entities such as Accounts, Contacts, Leads, and Opportunities. The data related to an entity, such as a phone number for a contact, is an attribute of the entity.

Entities

When you install Microsoft Dynamics CRM, it creates more than 100 *system entities* (also known as *default entities* or *default system entities*) in the software, and of course you will want to customize many of them. Which types of customizations Microsoft Dynamics CRM allows you to make on system entities is predetermined at installation. For some system entities, you can perform only limited customizations, and for other system entities you cannot perform any customizations at all. In addition to the system entities and customizable entities, you can create entirely new entities, known as *custom entities*, in Microsoft Dynamics CRM. In summary, there are three types of entities:

- **System**   Microsoft Dynamics CRM uses more than 100 noncustomizable system entities (examples include Privilege, License, and Calendar) to manage the internal operations of the software. You cannot edit the settings of any of these entities, add new attributes, or delete these entities from the system.

- **Customizable entity**   Microsoft Dynamics CRM includes more than 50 customizable system entities. Account, Activity, and User are a few examples. These entities give you extensive customization capabilities, from adding attributes to changing the form layout. You can rename customizable entities. However, you cannot delete any of the customizable entities.

- **Custom entity**   You can modify custom entities just like you can modify the customizable entities, and you can also delete them. We explain custom entities in detail in Chapter 6, "Entity Customization: Relationships, Custom Entities, and Site Map."

To view all of the entities in your system, go to the Customization section of Microsoft Dynamics CRM and click Customize Entities. A grid appears that lists every entity in your deployment.

> **Tip** The terminology used in the grid's view selector can be confusing. The view choice of Customizable Entities will display both entities of type customizable entity and custom entity. In addition, sometimes Microsoft Dynamics CRM refers to customizable entities as system entities because they were created upon software installation. For example, if you try to delete a customizable entity such as Account, the error message states, "System entities cannot be deleted."

You can customize the following data for custom and customizable entities:

- Attributes
- Forms
- Views
- Relationships
- Messages

Attributes

Every entity possesses one or more attributes that store data about the entity. Microsoft Dynamics CRM uses two types of attributes: system and custom.

- **System**   As with system entities, Microsoft Dynamics CRM uses system attributes to manage the internal workings of the software. To ensure that the software always works correctly, Microsoft Dynamics CRM prevents you from deleting system attributes. However, you can modify some values of system attributes. For example, you can specify the requirement level (Business Required, Business Recommended, or No Constraint) for system attributes.

- **Custom**   As with custom entities, Microsoft Dynamics CRM includes the ability to add entirely new custom attributes. You can add or delete custom attributes on both customizable entities and custom entities, but you cannot add custom attributes to system entities.

Table 4-2 summarizes the customizations that you can perform on each type of entity.

TABLE 4-2 Customizations Allowed by Entity Type

Entity type	System (noncustomizable)	Customizable (system created)	Custom
Forms			
Add custom form	n/a	Only one form per entity	Only one form per entity
Modify form	n/a	Yes	Yes
Delete form	n/a	No	No
Views			
Add custom views	n/a	Yes	Yes
Modify views	n/a	Yes	Yes
Delete views	n/a	Yes	Yes
System Attributes			
Add system attributes	No	No	No
Modify system attributes	No	Yes: partial	Yes: partial
Delete system attributes	No	No	No
Custom Attributes			
Add custom attributes	No	Yes	Yes

TABLE 4-2 Customizations Allowed by Entity Type

Entity type	System (noncustomizable)	Customizable (system created)	Custom
Modify custom attributes	No	Yes	Yes
Delete custom attributes	No	Yes	Yes
Messages			
Add messages	No	No	No
Modify messages	No	Yes	n/a
Delete messages	No	No	n/a

Note that the SQL Server database that Microsoft Dynamics CRM uses limits the number of custom attributes that you can add to an entity. Most users won't run into a problem with this database limit, but you should recognize that it exists.

Calculating the Maximum Number of Attributes

Adding a new custom attribute in Microsoft Dynamics CRM adds a column in the SQL Server database. When you add many custom attributes to an entity, you might want to consider the number of bytes any single row uses. SQL Server 2000 enforces a limit of 8,060 bytes for any one record, but SQL Server 2005 automatically mitigates this constraint behind the scenes by using an overflow page concept. Because Microsoft Dynamics CRM 4.0 currently supports only SQL Server 2005, you don't have to worry about bumping into the row byte limit. However, it is important for you to know that it exists because Microsoft recommends you stay below the 8,060-byte threshold for database performance reasons. We explain here how to calculate the number of bytes in case you're curious.

Microsoft Dynamics CRM stores custom attributes in a SQL Server table separate from the system fields so that you can use almost all of the 8,060 bytes available for adding custom attributes. (Microsoft Dynamics CRM automatically adds one cross-reference column to link the custom attributes to the correct entity.) Microsoft Dynamics CRM also supports deletion of custom attributes so that you can delete fields if necessary.

The maximum number of bytes per row (which provides a guide for calculating the suggested maximum number of custom attributes for an entity in Microsoft Dynamics CRM) depends on the data types of the attributes in your table. Table 4-3 lists the data types and the number of bytes each data type consumes.

TABLE 4-3 **Bytes Required per Data Type**

Data type	Bytes required
Boolean	1
Datetime	8
Picklist	4
Integer	4
Float	8
Decimal	Varies between 5 and 17 depending on the precision chosen
Currency	8
Ntext	16
Nvarchar (n)	$n \times 2$ (where *n* is the length of the *nvarchar* field)

Obviously, the *nvarchar* fields take up the most space, so exercise caution when adding these to your CRM data. For example, if you were to add 25 custom *nvarchar* fields with a length of 100 characters each, you would be using 5,000 bytes ($25 \times 100 \times 2$) of the 8,060 bytes available (62 percent). If you add 25 custom *Boolean* fields, you use only 25 bytes (25×1) of the 8,060 available (0.3 percent).

Microsoft Dynamics CRM also does not enforce the row byte limit at the column level. Therefore, you can add two custom *nvarchar* attributes each with a length of 4,000 characters. This would calculate out to 16,000 bytes total (($4,000 \times 2$) + ($4,000 \times 2$)), which obviously violates the 8,060-byte SQL Server recommended maximum. Microsoft Dynamics CRM allows this because SQL Server enforces the byte limit for each individual row (record), not for the entire table. Therefore, if you added a record and populated the two *nvarchar* fields with 4,000 characters each, SQL Server 2005 would automatically manage the 8,060-byte overflow for you and you wouldn't receive an error message. However, we recommend that you try to prevent this scenario from occurring frequently because it might negatively affect database performance.

Security and Permissions

Users assigned the System Administrator role can perform all of the functions in the system, including making the customizations described in this chapter. However, you might want to let certain users customize the system, but you don't want to grant them System Administrator rights. Fortunately, in Microsoft Dynamics CRM you can configure security roles to specify who can perform various customizations. Microsoft Dynamics CRM includes two default security roles with system customization privileges: System Administrator and System Customizer. Figure 4-4 shows the default security settings for the System Customizer role.

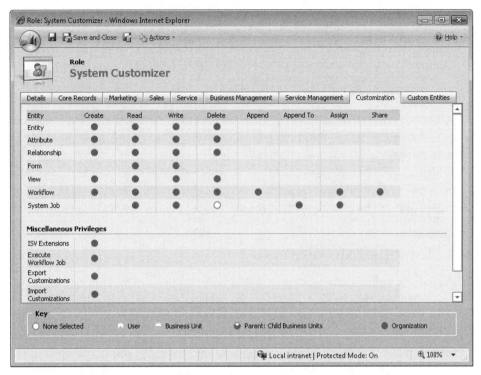

FIGURE 4-4 Default security settings for the System Customizer role

You can see from this screen shot that in Microsoft Dynamics CRM you can refine the customization rights on a more detailed level than just specifying "yes" or "no." For example, you might allow some of your users to create new attributes but not allow the same users to create new entities. You can also remove Delete permissions related to entity customization. If the person performing your customizations is new to Microsoft Dynamics CRM, we strongly recommend that you modify the default System Customizer role to remove all of the Delete permissions and do not assign the user to the System Administrator role. Microsoft Dynamics CRM is very forgiving in regard to mistakes made when you're modifying customizations, but you can't recover a deleted customization. If you spend 40 hours customizing a custom entity and someone accidentally deletes it, your work is gone forever. To change the security settings of the System Customizer role, simply click the appropriate option and save the security role (as you learned in Chapter 3, "Managing Security and Information Access").

> **Tip** Although you cannot undo a deletion, you can avoid an accidental loss of your customizations by proactively backing up your customizations. If someone does mistakenly delete your customizations, you could reimport your customizations from your backup file. Restoring your customizations from a backup will not recover any data deleted from the records, but you would save yourself the time of having to reconstruct the customizations. We suggest that you back up your customizations after each time you successfully publish your customizations. To create a backup of your customizations, simply export the customizations for all entities and save the file that Microsoft Dynamics CRM creates. We explain publishing, importing, and exporting customizations in more detail later in this chapter.

Later in this chapter, we review importing, exporting, and publishing your customizations. All users assigned System Administrator and the default System Customizer roles can perform these actions. In addition, you can toggle these privileges on and off individually for each security role. For example, you might allow one security role to import customizations but not to export or publish customizations. Mostly, you should plan on granting these privileges to users who will need to customize and configure your Microsoft Dynamics CRM system.

Publishing Customizations

When you perform customizations on Microsoft Dynamics CRM entities, your users will not immediately see the changes that you make. Rather, you decide when you want to *publish* the customizations so that users can see them. The ability to decide when you want to publish customizations makes your life easier because you can work on a set of interrelated customizations, and then make them available to all of your users at the same time. Even more convenient, in Microsoft Dynamics CRM you can select how you want to publish your customizations. You can publish customizations in one of three ways:

- A single entity at a time
- Two or more entities at the same time
- All publishable entities at one time

Microsoft Dynamics CRM makes publishing customizations a very simple process.

Publishing Process

When you publish an entity, Microsoft Dynamics CRM publishes all of the changes related to the entity, including all of the attributes, the attribute properties, the form, the views, the relationships, and so on. Here we walk you through the steps necessary to publish your customizations to users.

Publishing customizations for select entities

1. Go to the Customization section of Microsoft Dynamics CRM and click Customize Entities.

2. Select the entities that you want to publish. To select more than one entity, select the first entity, and then hold down the Ctrl key while selecting additional entities.

3. Click Publish on the grid toolbar. A message indicates that your customizations are being published.

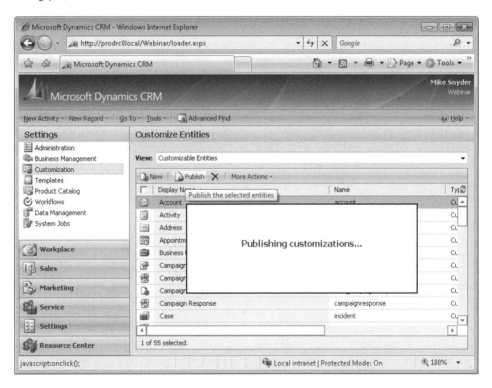

When the publish message disappears, all of the customizations that you just selected to publish will appear to your users. You can also publish customizations for a single entity by clicking Publish on the Actions menu in the entity editor, as illustrated in Figure 4-5.

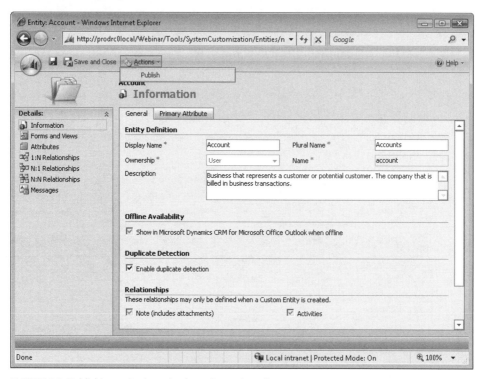

FIGURE 4-5 Publishing a single entity from the entity editor

Real World Microsoft Dynamics CRM is a Web application running on Microsoft Internet Information Services (IIS). Publishing customizations requires an update to the Microsoft Dynamics CRM metadata. Therefore, some users might experience glitches if they try to access Microsoft Dynamics CRM in the middle of the publishing process. If possible, try to publish your customizations when you know that users are not using Microsoft Dynamics CRM.

In addition to publishing select entities, you can also publish all entities at one time.

Publishing customizations for all entities

1. Go to the Customization section of Microsoft Dynamics CRM and click Customize Entities.

2. On the grid toolbar, click More Actions, and then click Publish All Customizations.

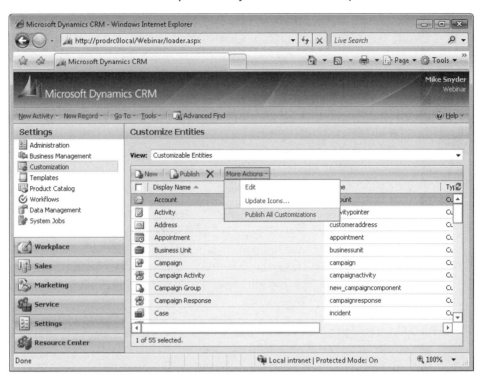

3. A message will appear indicating that your customizations are being published.

Publishing all of the entities takes more time than publishing just a few entities, so try to avoid publishing all customizations when many users are accessing Microsoft Dynamics CRM.

Another very important factor to consider before you publish all customizations is whether other system customizers (other than yourself) have made customizations that they don't want to publish yet. When you publish all customizations, you might unknowingly publish someone else's customizations before that person has finished and tested the changes. This type of situation can create system errors or user confusion. To be safe, we encourage you to publish only the entities that you change. You can't "unpublish" customizations, so make sure that you're ready before you click Publish!

Real World   Although you can publish changes whenever you want and as often as you want in Microsoft Dynamics CRM, frequent random changes to the system might cause confusion for your users. We recommend that you create a business process in which you queue and publish customizations on a scheduled interval that makes sense for your business (such as weekly, biweekly, or monthly). You can also help users understand the changes that you published to the system by creating an announcement in Microsoft Dynamics CRM. Announcements appear to users in the Workplace; you can use them to provide highlights of changes in the system.

Publishing Customizations to the Microsoft Dynamics CRM Laptop Client for Microsoft Office Outlook

Microsoft Dynamics CRM offers an offline version of the Microsoft Dynamics CRM client for Microsoft Office Outlook that allows users to work while totally disconnected from the network and the Microsoft Dynamics CRM server. But what happens when you publish changes and one or more of your offline users are not connected to the Microsoft Dynamics CRM server? Does this cause a problem the next time they connect their laptops to the server? Remarkably, Microsoft Dynamics CRM queues all of the published customization changes on the Web server and automatically deploys them to the Outlook client the next time the client synchronizes its software.

Microsoft Dynamics CRM can also handle the synchronization if you publish changes multiple times while the Outlook offline client is disconnected from your network for an extended period of time. Even if your company uses hundreds of Outlook offline clients, and users connect and disconnect from the network at random times unrelated to one another, the Microsoft Dynamics CRM synchronization engine smoothly manages the process for all of your users.

In effect, you don't need to worry about coordinating the publishing of your customizations when your Outlook offline users are connected to the network. Simply publish the customizations at your whim, and Microsoft Dynamics CRM does all the complicated synchronization work for you.

Importing and Exporting Customizations

With all of the customization options available in Microsoft Dynamics CRM, you could invest anywhere from 30 minutes to several thousand hours customizing the software. Fortunately, with Microsoft Dynamics CRM you can export some or all of your customizations, and then import them into a different Microsoft Dynamics CRM system. The import and export features save you valuable time because you won't have to repeat your customization work. You can also export your customizations proactively to make sure you always have a backup copy.

To access the customization import and export features, click Customization in the Settings section. We examine exporting customizations first, so click Export Customizations. By default, you'll see a list of the many different items that you can export (see Figure 4-6).

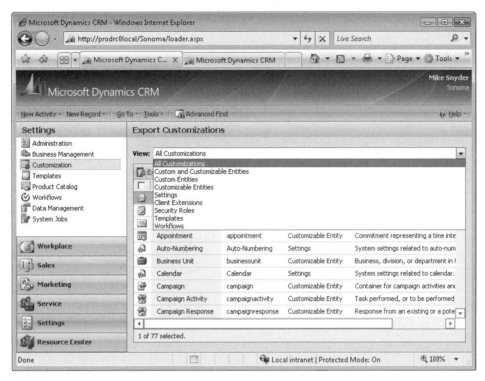

FIGURE 4-6 List of exportable customizations

In addition to all of the custom and customizable entities, you will also notice that you can export the following:

- **ISV.config**   Configuration file for customizing the navigation pane, toolbars, and menus

- **Site map**   The application navigation structure

- **Security roles**   The configuration for a specific security role

- **E-mail tracking**   System settings related to e-mail tracking such as max file attachment size, e-mail form options, e-mail tracking settings, and so on

- **Marketing**   System setting related to marketing such as unsubscribe notification, campaign responses, and so on

- **General**   System settings such as name format, decimal precision, and blocked file extensions

- **Calendar**   System settings related to calendar formatting and display

- **Customization**   System settings for schema prefix, application mode, and so on

- **Relationship roles**   All relationship roles

- **Auto-numbering**   System settings for automatic numbering of contracts, cases, quotes, invoices, and so on

- **Outlook synchronization**   System settings related to the Microsoft Dynamics CRM client for Microsoft Office Outlook such as the synchronization interval, e-mail promotion, and background synchronization options

- **Templates**   Article, contract, mail merge, and e-mail templates

- **Workflows**   Any workflow rules configured in the system.

Exporting one or more entity customizations

1. Go to the Customization section of Microsoft Dynamics CRM and click Export Customizations.

2. Select the item (or items) that you want to export.

3. On the grid toolbar, click Export Selected Customizations.

4. Microsoft Dynamics CRM displays the following message.

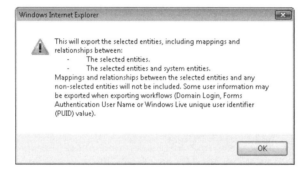

5. Click OK.

6. The following dialog box appears.

7. Select the destination location to save the customizations.zip file, and then click Save.

To export all of the customizations (for all of the items in the list), you can click the Export All Customizations button located under the More Actions button on the grid toolbar, and then proceed to step 7.

The customizations.zip file that Microsoft Dynamics CRM creates contains a single customizations.xml file. The system creates a .zip file to minimize the size of the file that it needs to export. If you open the customizations.xml file with a text editor or Microsoft Internet Explorer, you will see that this file includes all of the customizations (defined in XML format) related to the customizations that you selected to export. When you export an entity's customizations, those customizations include (but are not limited to) its attributes, forms, views, mappings, and relationships. However, Microsoft Dynamics CRM does not export nonmodifiable attributes in entities, relationships, attributes, or templates. This does not cause a problem because Microsoft Dynamics CRM doesn't need this information when it imports the customizations, so don't be surprised if you don't see those items in the customizations.xml file. After you export your customizations to the customizations.zip file, you can import these customizations into a different Microsoft Dynamics CRM system.

> **Tip** You can import either the .zip or the .xml file, whichever you prefer.

Importing customizations

1. Go to the Customization section of Microsoft Dynamics CRM and click Import Customizations.

2. Click Browse, and then select the customizations.zip file that you just exported. Click Open.

3. The full path to the customizations.zip file appears in the Import File text box. Click Upload.

4. Microsoft Dynamics CRM reads the customizations.zip file and confirms that it contains a valid structure to import. You will receive an error message if you try to import an invalid file. If the file passes the validation, Microsoft Dynamics CRM displays a list of entity customizations contained in the customizations.zip file.

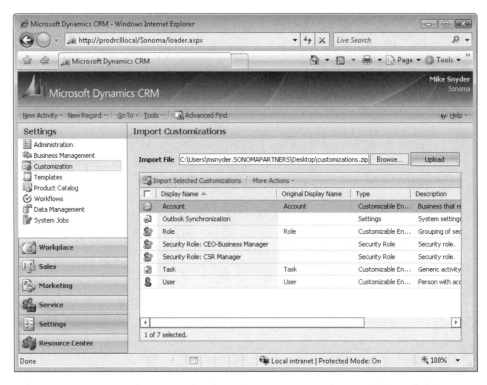

5. Select one or more entity customizations that you want to import. Then, click Import Selected Customizations on the More Actions menu.

6. You will receive a warning message that says, "The Import Customizations process can take several minutes to complete depending on the number of items being imported. Once the process begins it cannot be stopped or reverted. Do you want to continue importing customizations?" Click OK.

7. A message box indicates that customizations are importing.

8. When the import process completes, a message appears that says, "Customizations have been imported successfully." If a problem occurs, Microsoft Dynamics CRM also displays additional messages related to your customizations import.

9. Click OK.

Important Don't forget to publish your customizations after an import! The changes you imported to entities won't appear to users until you publish those entities. Changes to the other areas of the system such as security roles, templates, and so on are available immediately.

Import Customization Conflicts

Microsoft Dynamics CRM imports customizations by using an additive process. It adds any new customizations to the target system, but it won't remove the customizations that previously existed in the target system. Consider the following example to understand how the additive import process works.

Assume that you have a Microsoft Dynamics CRM system called System A that contains the following customizations:

- Custom entity B added
- Custom entity C added
- Account entity with custom attributes Y and Z added

You want to import the customizations that you set up on another system (called System B) into System A. You configured System B with the following customizations:

- Custom entity B added
- Custom entity E added
- Account entity with custom attributes D and Z added

If you exported all of the customizations from System B and then imported those customizations into System A, the final customizations on System A would be as follows:

- Custom entity B added
- Custom entity C added
- Custom entity E added
- Account entity with custom attributes D, Y, and Z added

As Figure 4-7 illustrates, Microsoft Dynamics CRM examines the customizations import file and determines that custom entity E and the Account custom attribute Z need to be added to the system.

However, note that Microsoft Dynamics CRM did *not* remove the original customizations in System A. In this example, a conflict would occur regarding custom entity B and custom attribute Y because you're trying to import customizations that already exist in the target system. This type of conflict is called a *collision*.

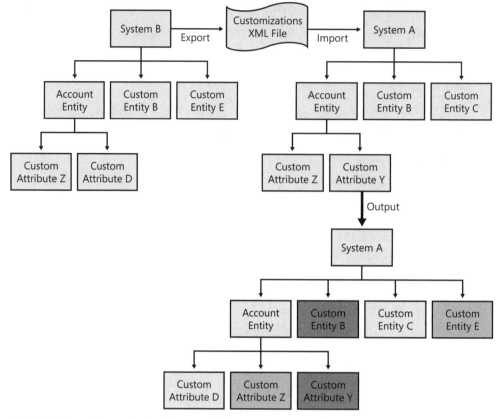

FIGURE 4-7 Importing customizations, an additive process

> **Important** Collisions occur when you try to import a customization (such as an entity, attribute, or view) and the schema name of that imported customization already exists in the target system.

Microsoft Dynamics CRM resolves collisions using one of three actions:

- **Overwrite** The data in the import file overwrites the data in the target system.
- **Error** Microsoft Dynamics CRM generates an error and aborts the import.
- **New object** Microsoft Dynamics CRM creates a new object in the target system.

Table 4-4 outlines the import collision conditions and the actions that Microsoft Dynamics CRM takes in each scenario.

TABLE 4-4 Import Conflicts and Microsoft Dynamics CRM Actions

Object	Collision condition	Collision action taken
Modifiable entity property	Same entity name, different property	Overwrite
Nonmodifiable entity property	Same entity name	Error
Attribute modifiable property	Same entity name, same attribute name	Overwrite
Attribute nonmodifiable property	Same entity name, same attribute name	Error
Form	Same name	Overwrite
Form	Different property	Overwrite
View	Same name	Overwrite
Advanced Find view	Same name	Overwrite
Quick Find view	Same name	Overwrite
Associated view	Same name	Overwrite
Attribute mapping	Different attribute mappings for a source/target pair	Overwrite
Template	Same name	Overwrite
ISV.config	Same name	Overwrite
Custom relationships modifiable property	Same primary/related entity, different property	Overwrite
Customer relationships modifiable property	Same name, different property	New object
Customer relationships nonmodifiable property	Same name, different property	Error

Table 4-4 shows that in most cases in which collisions occur, Microsoft Dynamics CRM overwrites the target system with the values from the import file. When a collision takes place on a nonmodifiable property, Microsoft Dynamics CRM generates an error during the import process.

Manually Editing Export Files

If you examine the customizations.xml export file for a single entity, you'll see the customizations for that entity. If you created 30 custom attributes, all 30 would be exported into the customizations.xml file. In the Microsoft Dynamics CRM user interface, you can choose which entities you want to export, but you can't choose which individual customizations you want to export on each entity. You will get all the customizations for each entity; if you want to export just the entity views, but not the attributes of the entity, you are out of luck.

Fortunately, Microsoft Dynamics CRM makes it pretty easy to work around this issue if you're familiar with editing .xml files. Because the customizations export is just a standard .xml file, you could manually edit the file to remove any of the customizations that you do not want before importing the file into a new system. In this example, you could manually remove 10 of the 30 custom attributes from the customizations.xml file, and then import the edited customizations.xml file into your target system. The target system would receive only those 20 custom attributes remaining in the customization file, instead of the original 30 custom attributes exported from your parent system. This manual editing concept also carries over to other customizations related to an entity, including forms, views, and so on.

> **Warning** Do not attempt to edit the customizations.xml file manually unless you're extremely comfortable working with XML files. If you do manually edit the file, the Microsoft Dynamics CRM software development kit (SDK) provides an XML schema so that you can validate whether your edited customizations.xml file remains well structured.

Manually editing the customizations.xml file gives you complete control over the customizations that you import into a new system. Remember that you can also programmatically import customizations with the Microsoft Dynamics CRM SDK if you find a need for that feature.

Renaming Entities

When you implement Microsoft Dynamics CRM, you might find that the system entity terminology does not exactly match your business terminology. For example, instead of referring to people as Contacts, your business might use the term *Clients* or *People*. Or you might refer to *Companies* or *Businesses* instead of Accounts. The metadata-driven structure of Microsoft Dynamics CRM offers you an easy method for renaming customizable entities.

To rename an entity, go the Customization section of Microsoft Dynamics CRM and click Customize Entities. Find the entity that you want to rename, and then double-click that entity to open the entity editor. You will see a Name field and a Plural Name field in the Entity Definition section of the form, as shown in Figure 4-8.

On this form, simply enter the new name and plural name of the entity, and then click Save. Microsoft Dynamics CRM uses the plural version of the name when referring to multiple records in the system, so make sure that you complete this field.

> **Important** You can rename an entity to almost any value that you want. The only naming requirement that Microsoft Dynamics CRM enforces is that you cannot use the name of another entity in the system. This might seem obvious enough, but it does cause some confusion. Microsoft Dynamics CRM contains many system entities such as Site, Organization, and Unit, but you might forget that these entity names already exist in Microsoft Dynamics CRM because they're not customizable entities. If you try to use an entity name that already exists, Microsoft Dynamics CRM will present an error message to you.

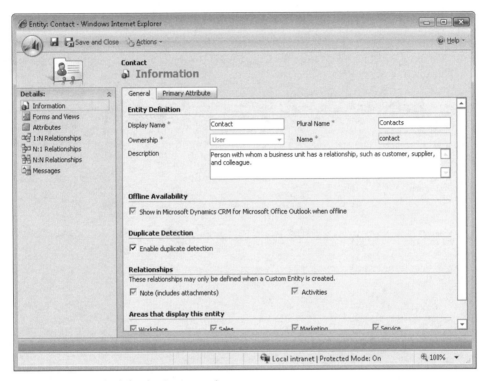

FIGURE 4-8 General tab for the Contact entity

After you rename the entity, you should also manually update the additional sections of Microsoft Dynamics CRM that reference the entity name so that the user interface remains consistent with the new name that you just assigned to the entity. You should update the following areas:

- Rename the entity view names (for example, change Active Contacts to Active Clients).

- Update form labels (for example, on the Account form, change Primary Contact to Primary Client).

- Change system messages (explained in the next section).

- Modify any reports that reference the entity name. (Modifying reports is explained in Chapter 7, "Reporting and Analysis.")

- Update the online Help content to display the new entity name.

After you finish making these changes, remember to publish all of the entities that you customized. Figure 4-9 shows how renaming the Contact entity Client correctly updates the application navigation pane. We also renamed the Active Contacts default view as Active Clients to remain consistent with the new entity name.

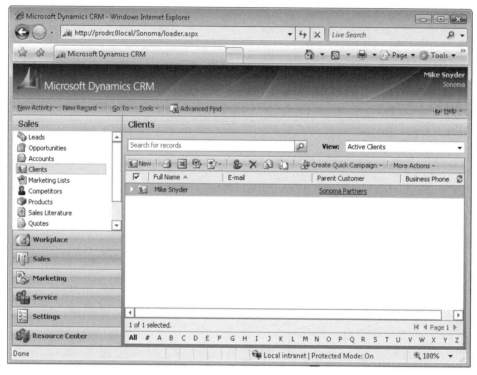

FIGURE 4-9 Contact entity renamed as Client

You can use this technique to rename any of the customizable entities, including activity type entities such as Task, Phone Call, Letter, and Appointment.

Changing System Messages

For each entity, Microsoft Dynamics CRM includes several predefined *system messages* that appear throughout the system. When you rename an entity, we recommend that you update these system messages to make them consistent with the new name. If you do not update the system messages, a user might see an error message regarding a Contact even though you renamed that entity Client. You can view all system messages of an entity in the Messages section of the entity editor, as shown in Figure 4-10.

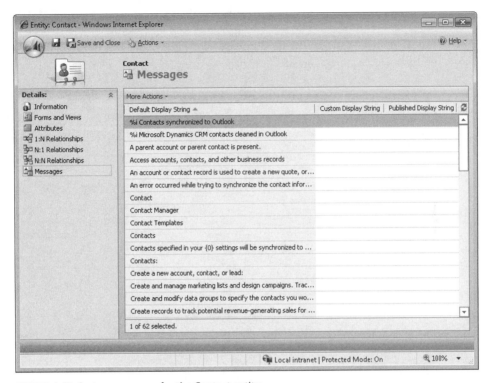

FIGURE 4-10 System messages for the Contact entity

To edit any one system message, simply double-click a record and enter the updated system message in the Custom Display String field. You can also add more descriptive information about the system message to help users.

You should note four important things about editing system messages:

- You cannot include hyperlinks in the Custom Display String field.

- Some system messages contain data placeholders, such as numbers in braces ({0}) or symbols and letters (%i). You should not remove or edit these data placeholders because Microsoft Dynamics CRM populates them with dynamic data when it displays the system message to users.

- Several entities use a large number of system messages. For example, Account entities use 57 messages and Contact entities use 62 messages. In addition, the same message might be used in several different locations throughout the system. Therefore, rely on your best judgment when you decide what text to enter for updating the Custom Display String.

■ Some areas of Microsoft Dynamics CRM use messages to display text where you might not usually consider the text a "message." For example, if you decide to rename the Account entity Company, you might also want to rename the Sub-Accounts link in the entity navigation pane as Sub-Companies.

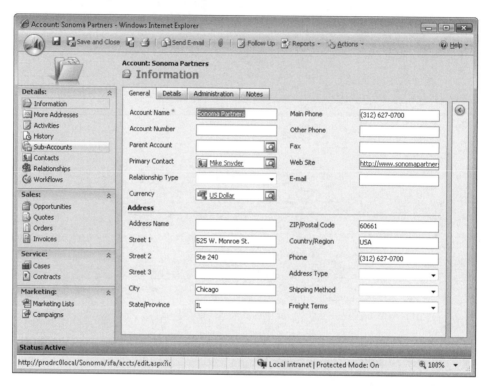

To make this change, navigate to the system messages of the Account entity, and then simply change the Custom Display String of Sub-Accounts to Sub-Companies. Likewise, if you decide to rename the Lead entity as Prospect, you would use a message to edit the text that appears on the Convert Lead button of the Lead form.

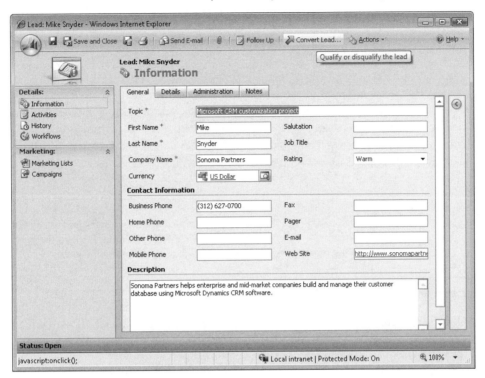

If you rename entities, carefully review and edit *all* of the system messages because messages might appear to users in places where you do not expect them.

Customizing Online Help

Microsoft Dynamics CRM includes Web-based online Help files that users can access from the Help menu. Of course, the online Help files reference the default entity names such as Account, Contact, Lead, and Opportunity. If you rename entities, the new entity names will not be reflected in the online Help documentation, which might cause confusion for your users. Fortunately, in Microsoft Dynamics CRM you can customize the online Help documentation to change the terminology to match your system. If you decide that you want to customize online Help, the Microsoft Dynamics CRM SDK includes detailed instructions on the process.

Advantages of Customizing Online Help

Users can access online Help directly from the Web client or either of the Outlook clients. By customizing the online Help, you can make the entity name in this documentation consistent with the user interface when you rename entities.

In addition to updating entity names in online Help documentation, you can add entirely new sections of online Help. If your system makes heavy use of custom entities and customization code, your users will benefit from online Help documentation that describes the full functionality of their customized system.

> **Tip** Users access context-sensitive help through the Help On This Page link that appears throughout Microsoft Dynamics CRM. You can add context-sensitive topics for custom entities that you create. The Microsoft Dynamics CRM software development kit explains the process of modifying the Help files in great detail, so we won't repeat that content here.

Issues Related to Customizing Online Help

Of course, customizing the online Help files seems like a good idea, but there are a few potential issues we want to bring to your attention. Online Help includes two versions:

- One for the Web client and Microsoft Dynamics CRM client for Microsoft Office Outlook

- One for the Microsoft Dynamics CRM client for Microsoft Office Outlook with Offline Access

Microsoft Dynamics CRM stores the online Help files for the Web client and Microsoft Dynamics CRM client for Microsoft Office Outlook in the Help folder of the Microsoft Dynamics CRM Web server.

The Microsoft Dynamics CRM client for Microsoft Office Outlook with Offline Access stores the Help files on the client computer so that users can access the information when they're disconnected from the server. The English version of these files can be found in the res\web\help\1033\OP folder under the default installation path for the client, which is c:\Program Files\Microsoft Dynamics CRM\Client. You can find the non-English Help files in the folder with the corresponding language ID code (1033 for English, 3082 for Spanish, etc.).

If you plan to modify the online Help files, we recommend that you copy the Microsoft Dynamics CRM installation files to a network location, and then modify the Help files in those folders. Then, when you install the Microsoft Dynamics CRM client for Microsoft Office Outlook with Offline Access, install the software from the network and the user will receive your customized Help instead of the default files.

Every time you install Microsoft Dynamics CRM or upgrade to a new release, the installation copies the new version of online Help over the existing online Help files. Therefore, remember to make backup copies of your customized Help files before you reinstall or upgrade your system.

> **Important** Microsoft Dynamics CRM Live customers cannot modify the online Help that appears for the Web client and Microsoft Dynamics CRM client for Microsoft Office Outlook, but they can modify the online Help for the Microsoft Dynamics CRM client for Microsoft Office Outlook with Offline Access.

Attributes

Attributes provide additional data about entities, and every entity in Microsoft Dynamics CRM contains multiple attributes. For example, the Contact entity uses attributes such as first name, last name, and phone number. Each attribute has a data type (such as *integer*, *money*, and *bit*) that determines the type of data that you can store in a field.

When you install Microsoft Dynamics CRM, the system creates more than 150 entities, and some entities possess up to 125 attributes. So, you're talking about potentially 18,750 data attributes right out of the box! But of course you know that even 18,750 attributes won't be enough for your business. Everyone wants a system as highly customized to their business as possible, and Microsoft Dynamics CRM makes it easy for you to add new attributes and customize the default attributes.

However, before you start customizing attributes, we review the terminology and concepts related to attributes.

Attribute Properties

Every attribute has multiple *attribute properties* that further define how the attribute behaves in Microsoft Dynamics CRM. Figure 4-11 shows the attribute editor and the properties of the attribute.

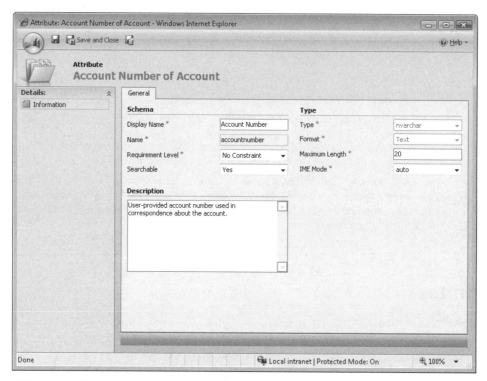

FIGURE 4-11 Attribute properties for a single attribute

The following attribute properties apply to every attribute:

- **Display name**   Sets the text that users see throughout Microsoft Dynamics CRM, such as on the forms, views, and in Advanced Find.

- **Name**   Displays the metadata schema name. The schema name also correlates to the column name in the underlying SQL Server database.

- **Requirement level**   Dictates the type of data validation that Microsoft Dynamics CRM enforces when users enter or update data on a form (Business Required, Business Recommended, or No Constraint).

- **Searchable**   Specifies whether this attribute will appear in the list of attributes for which users can search using an Advanced Find.

- **Type**   Specifies the data type of the attribute. Data types include *integer*, *picklist*, and *bit*, among others.

- **IME Mode**   IME stands for Input Method Editor (IME), and it relates to user text entry fields with various Asian languages. If you don't have a specific need to change the IME value, simply leave the default value of *auto*.

- **Description**   Text that describes the attribute. Your end users do not see this text, but system customizers do.

> **Tip** When you create a new custom attribute, you might be tempted to skip the Description field because it's optional. However, we strongly encourage you to invest an extra 20 to 30 seconds to enter a description of the purpose of this new attribute because it can save you time down the road when you (or someone who takes over the project from you) look at the attribute and wonder, "Why did we add this field?" As a bare minimum we suggest that you enter your name and the date that you created the attribute.

Depending on the data type of the attribute, some attributes include additional properties. Table 4-5 outlines the additional attribute properties and the data types to which they apply.

TABLE 4-5 Data Type–Specific Attribute Properties

Attribute property	Applies to these data types
Format	nvarchar, int, ntext, datetime
Maximum Length	nvarchar, ntext
List Value	bit, picklist
Default Value	bit, picklist
Minimum Value	int, float, money, decimal
Maximum Value	int, float, money, decimal
Precision	float, money, decimal

Next, we review each of these data types in detail to understand how they work in Microsoft Dynamics CRM.

Data Types

If you've worked with relational databases, you probably already understand *data types* in great detail, so we just review how they relate specifically to Microsoft Dynamics CRM. If you are not familiar with data types, it's critical for you to develop an understanding of how they work because data types drastically affect how Microsoft Dynamics CRM stores, manages, and displays data in the system. For example, Microsoft Dynamics CRM does not allow users to enter a text value such as "abc" into an attribute with a *money* data type. The attribute data types also determine how Microsoft Dynamics CRM sorts records and the types of operations that you can perform by using the Advanced Find feature.

Microsoft Dynamics CRM uses the following 14 data types to store attribute data:

- **nvarchar** Stores text and numeric data in one field.

- **picklist** Allows you to specify a predefined list of values for the attribute. Users see a drop-down list on the form.

- **bit** Stores data as one of two values, 0 or 1. In Microsoft Dynamics CRM, you can relabel the 0 and 1 values so that users see Yes and No, True and False, and so on. Many people use the word *Boolean* when referring to bit data types.

- *int*   Allows you to store only whole numbers, such as –2, –1, 0, 1, 2, and so on. Int is an abbreviation for integer.

- *float*   Stores approximate numeric values with a configurable number of decimals, such as 1.3333 or 3.145.

- *decimal*   Stores exact numeric values with decimals such as 1.5.

- *money*   Stores currency amounts.

- *ntext*   Stores text and numeric data in one field.

- *datetime*   Stores date and time data.

- *status*   System data type that stores status information about an entity.

- *state*   System data type that stores state information about an entity.

- *primarykey*   System data type that stores cross-reference information.

- *owner*   System data type that stores the entity's owner.

- *lookup*   System data type that stores information about related records.

Note Microsoft Dynamics CRM 4.0 now stores *ntext* values in SQL Server 2005 as an *nvarchar(max)* data type.

Microsoft Dynamics CRM automatically creates and manages the system data types, so you really don't have to worry about too much. However, you should know that they exist because you will see attributes with system data types listed on every entity.

Tip While both floats and decimals store real numbers, SQL Server stores float data as approximations whereas decimals are stored exactly as specified. Your users might not notice any difference between the *float* and *decimal* data types because they can both display values in the Microsoft Dynamics CRM user interface with configurable precision such as 1.25 or 5.786. Therefore, you may wonder which data type to use. Naturally, the answer will depend on what you want to do with the data. One possible guideline you can use is the following. Use a *decimal* data type when you require queries with sums across a large set of numbers or when performing comparisons in which you use the equal (=) or not equal (<>) operators. When you need to store fractions or numeric values you will be comparing with the greater than (>) or less than (<) operators, consider using a *float*. If you're really not sure how the data will be used, we recommend that you use a *float* data type.

We explain the different data types in more detail later in this chapter when we explain how to add custom attributes to an entity.

Requirement Levels

For every attribute, Microsoft Dynamics CRM defines a *requirement level*. The requirement level dictates the type of data validation that Microsoft Dynamics CRM should enforce when users enter or update data on a form. In addition to enforcing data validation, Microsoft Dynamics CRM automatically adds a label indicator to provide users with a visual cue regarding the requirement level of the attribute. Table 4-6 explains the three requirement levels and color coding.

TABLE 4-6 Requirement Levels

Requirement level	Description	Attribute label indicator on form
Business Required	Users must enter a value for this attribute. If they leave it blank, the system prompts them when they try to save.	Red asterisk
Business Recommended	Provides a visual cue to users that your business recommends completion of this field. Users can save the record with no data if necessary. Saving a record with no data in a Business Recommended field does not prompt or warn the user.	Blue plus sign
No Constraint	Indicates to users that no constraint exists on the data field.	Black with no indicator

If you specify an attribute as Business Required, you cannot remove it from the entity form. Likewise, you shouldn't set an attribute as Business Required if it isn't displayed on the form.

Reviewing the Current Schema

Before you start adding or modifying attributes, we recommend that you become familiar with the entity attributes that Microsoft Dynamics CRM creates upon installation. In other words, you should check the default database schema to determine whether a field already exists in the database before you create a new custom attribute.

> **Warning** Just because you do not see a field on the default forms, do not assume that the field doesn't exist in the database. The default forms contain only some of the attributes for each entity. For example, there are more than 50 Account attributes that do not appear on the default Account form.

Because Microsoft Dynamics CRM creates up to 18,750 attributes upon installation, we're sure that you're wondering what's the quickest way to determine which attributes already exist in the system. Microsoft Dynamics CRM provides two excellent tools to browse the attributes of an entity: the entity editor and the metadata browser.

Entity Editor

To browse the attributes of an entity by using the entity editor, go to the Customization section of Microsoft Dynamics CRM and click Customize Entities. You'll see a list of all the entities in Microsoft Dynamics CRM. When you double-click any record, the entity editor appears. Click Attributes to see a list of all the attributes for that entity, as shown in Figure 4-12.

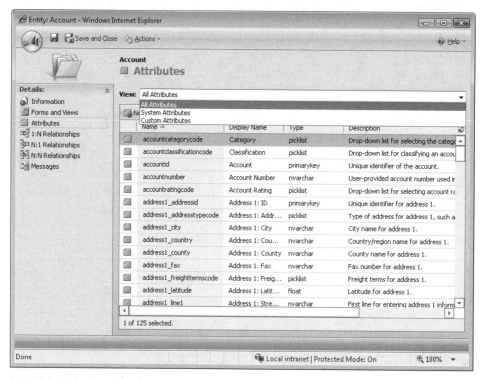

FIGURE 4-12 Attributes for the Account entity

Before you add a new attribute to an entity, you should review the list of attributes for that entity to make sure that a similar field doesn't already exist. If you want more detail about any one attribute, simply double-click the attribute to open the attribute editor. The attribute editor shows you all of the attribute properties for that attribute, including type, description, schema name, and so on.

Metadata Browser

In addition to the entity editor, you can use the Metadata Browser to quickly view all of the attributes for a given entity. To view the Metadata Browser (as shown in Figure 4-13), use a Web browser to navigate to *http://<*crmserver*>/sdk/list.aspx*, where *<crmserver>* is the name of your server.

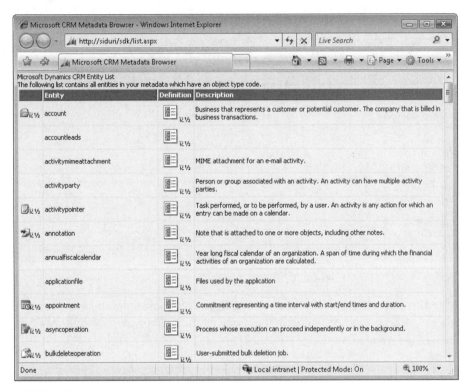

FIGURE 4-13 Metadata Browser

This Web-based Metadata Browser lists only the entities available through the SDK, so there is not necessarily a one-to-one correlation with the list of entities that you see in the Customization section. However, you will find all of the customizable entities and custom entities in the SDK list. If you can't find the entity you're looking for, note that the Metadata Browser displays the entity schema name instead of the name. For example, the Metadata Browser displays the Address entity under its schema name of "customeraddress." To view all of the attributes for an entity, click the icon in the Definition column. The Entity Navigator page for an entity displays all of the attribute and relationship information on one page, as shown in Figure 4-14.

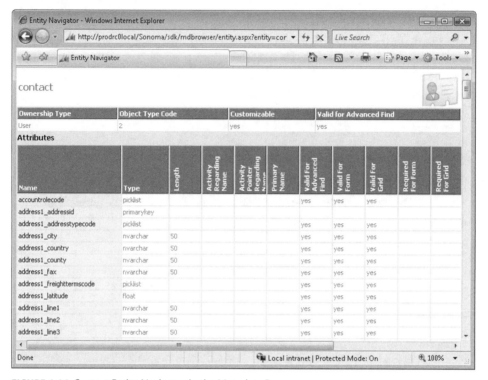

FIGURE 4-14 Contact Entity Navigator in the Metadata Browser

Depending on the type of attribute information you're looking for, this format might be more convenient for you than using the entity editor is. We prefer using the Metadata Browser for several reasons:

- You can view all of the attributes for an entity on one page.

- You can use Internet Explorer to search on the page (by using Ctrl+F) for specific terms that interest you.

- You can easily (and cleanly) copy and paste all of the entity attributes from the definition detail page into a Microsoft Office Excel worksheet if you want to work with them some more.

Although the Metadata Browser does list all of an entity's attributes, it unfortunately does not display all of the attribute properties. Some of the important attribute properties not shown in the Metadata Browser include Display Name, Type Format, and Requirement Level.

> **Caution** Because Microsoft Dynamics CRM stores all of its underlying system data in SQL Server, it is technically possible for you also to view the entity schemas in SQL Enterprise Manager. However, we don't recommend doing this because it creates additional work. The entity editor and the Metadata Browser display the metadata, which automatically consolidates the complex Microsoft Dynamics CRM data relationships into an easy-to-use format. By viewing the SQL Server tables directly, you bypass the metadata, which means that you have to reconstruct manually where Microsoft Dynamics CRM stores all of the data, which can be a time-consuming process.

Both the entity editor and the Metadata Browser give you all of the attributes for an entity, so you simply need to choose the format that you prefer.

Modifying, Adding, and Deleting Attributes

After you've reviewed the entities and you understand their attributes, you're ready to start making some changes. Attribute customizations fall into one of three categories:

- Modifying attributes
- Adding custom attributes
- Deleting attributes

Modifying Attributes

The simplest type of attribute customization you can perform is to modify an existing attribute. When you modify attributes, you actually modify the properties of the attribute. You make changes to the attribute properties in the attribute editor, as shown in Figure 4-15.

To change any one of the attribute properties, simply follow these steps.

Modifying an attribute property

1. Navigate to the entity that you want to customize, and then click Attributes.
2. Double-click the attribute that you want to modify. The attribute editor appears.
3. Update a value, and then click Save.
4. An "Updating Attribute" message appears. When the message disappears, your change is complete.

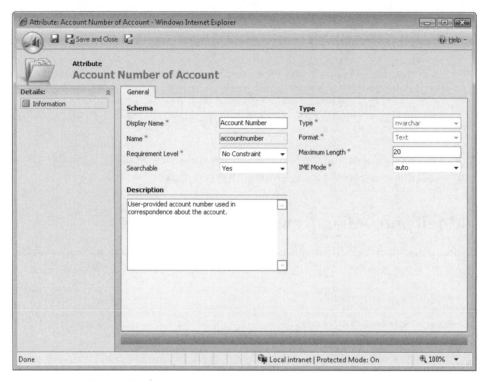

FIGURE 4-15 Attribute editor for Account Number attribute

As we explained earlier, your users will not see the changes you make until you publish your customizations.

Although Figure 4-15 might not clearly show it, Microsoft Dynamics CRM disables or makes unavailable some of the attribute property fields. As you probably expect, the unavailable property fields indicate that you cannot edit the attribute properties. You can never edit the schema name or data type for an existing attribute. In addition, Microsoft Dynamics CRM prevents you from editing attribute properties on the system entities. Of course, these few restrictions help ensure that the software always works correctly and that your system will upgrade smoothly to future releases of Microsoft Dynamics CRM.

When you're modifying attributes, take extra care when deleting the *picklist* values of existing attributes because you might permanently lose access to the data in the user interface. Consider a set of 75 records that use a custom picklist. The picklist contains three options: A, B, and C (with 25 records each). If you delete *picklist* value A, Microsoft Dynamics CRM deletes that value from the form so that no new records can select *picklist* value A. Unfortunately, the existing 25 records that displayed the value of A display a blank *picklist* value when you open them. Fortunately, Microsoft Dynamics CRM reminds you of this data deletion when you attempt to delete a *picklist* value. You cannot deactivate a *picklist* value if it's no longer in use, you can only delete it.

> **Tip** You can increase the length of a custom attribute field if necessary.

Adding Custom Attributes

As you can see, changing the properties of existing attributes really couldn't be any simpler. However, the real customization fun begins when you start adding your own custom attributes. Again, before you add a custom attribute, double-check all of the existing attributes of an entity to make sure a similar field doesn't already exist. When you're ready to add a custom attribute, follow these steps.

Adding a custom attribute

1. Go to the Customization section of Microsoft Dynamics CRM and click Customize Entities.

2. Double-click the entity that you want to modify.

3. In the navigation pane, click Attributes, and then click New on the grid toolbar.

4. The following form appears for you to complete.

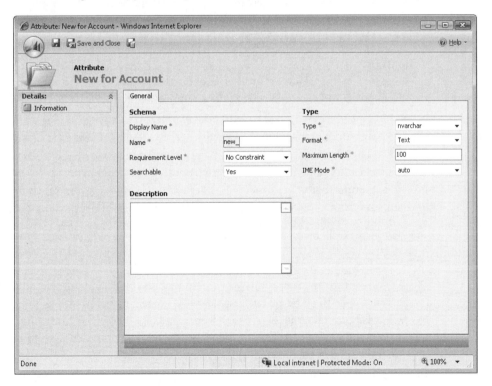

5. Click Save.

To create a custom attribute, you must enter the following attribute properties:

- Display name
- Schema name
- Requirement level
- Searchable (optional)
- Type
- Description (optional)
- IME Mode

We defined each of these properties earlier in this chapter, but now we cover the schema name and type in more detail.

Schema Name

The schema name represents the name of the attribute in the metadata. Every custom attribute includes a prefix value in the schema name (such as "New_customfield"). Microsoft Dynamics CRM creates the "New_" default schema prefix. When you create a custom attribute, notice that the schema prefix field is read-only and you can't edit it when you're creating an attribute.

> **Important** You can change the default schema prefix by navigating to Administration in the Settings section. Then, click System Settings and select the Customization tab. The prefix must contain between two and eight alphanumeric characters, and it cannot start with "mscrm."

When you enter text in the display name field and you lose focus on the field (by pressing the Tab key or clicking elsewhere on the page), Microsoft Dynamics CRM automatically fills in the rest of the schema name after the prefix. Because the schema name can consist of alphanumeric and underscore characters only, Microsoft Dynamics CRM removes any inappropriate characters. When you are creating a schema name, keep the following in mind:

- Your users will never see the schema name.
- You cannot change the schema name after you create the attribute.
- Any advanced customizations you create such as the SDK code, scripting, and reports will reference the schema name instead of the display name, so try to be consistent with casing (such as all lowercase, all Pascal case, or all camel case). Also, save your developers some keystrokes by keeping the name just long enough to describe its function but not so long that it takes forever to type.

Type

When creating new attributes, you can choose from one of eight data types, some of which you can use to specify further how Microsoft Dynamics CRM should format the data. Table 4-7 summarizes the data types and data formatting options available for custom attributes.

TABLE 4-7 Data Types and Formats for Custom Attributes

Attribute data type	Format	Description
nvarchar	E-mail	Displays text as a clickable mailto: hyperlink.
	Text	Displays text on one line.
	Text area	Displays a multiline text box with scrollbars.
	Ticker symbol	Displays text as a live hyperlink that starts a stock quote request on *http://moneycentral. msn.com.*
	URL	Displays text as a hyperlink. Microsoft Dynamics CRM automatically adds *https://* to whatever the user enters.
picklist	Picklist	Drop-down list control. You can use the additional buttons to add, modify, and delete *picklist* values. You can also specify a sort order and assign a default *picklist* value.
bit	Bit	Displays two possible options on the form. You can change No and Yes to new values such as True and False, and you can specify the order in which the values appear. You can also specify the default value. On the form editor, you can determine whether you want the text to appear with option buttons, a check box, or a drop-down list.
int	None	Whole numbers only (1, 2, 3, and so on). You can also set a minimum and maximum range for this value.
	Duration	Displays a picklist with 23 predefined *duration* values ranging from one minute to three days.
	Time zone	Displays a picklist from which users can select one of 75 different time zones from around the world.
	Language	
float	Float	Used to store numeric values with a configurable precision (such as 1.23 or 3.145) up to five digits. You can also specify a minimum and maximum range.

TABLE 4-7 Data Types and Formats for Custom Attributes

Attribute data type	Format	Description
decimal	Decimal	Used to store numeric values with a configurable precision (such as 1.23 or 3.145) up to 10 digits. You can also specify a minimum and maximum range.
money	Money	Used to store currency amounts. You can specify the precision and a minimum and maximum range.
ntext	None	Displays a multiline text box with scrollbars.
datetime	Date only	Date formatted as month, date, and year. A calendar control automatically appears on the form.
	Date and time	Date formatted as month, date, year along with hours and minutes. A calendar control and time selection drop-down list automatically appear on the form.

Figure 4-16 shows a mockup of how each of these data types appears to users on the entity form. As you can see, each data type saves and displays information differently, so it's important that you select the appropriate data type for your custom attribute.

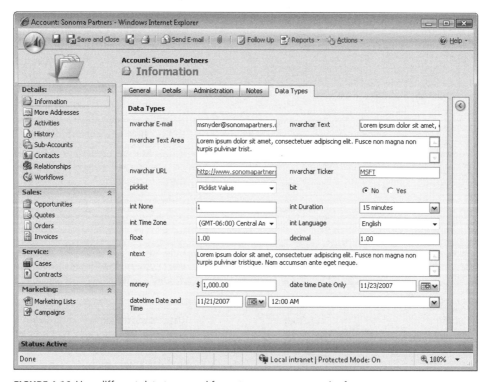

FIGURE 4-16 How different data types and formats appear on an entity form

More Info   Both the *ntext* and *nvarchar* data types store text and numeric data, and both data types format the data on the form by using a text area, so how should you decide which data type to use? For attributes with a length greater than eight characters, the *nvarchar* data type consumes more bytes in SQL Server. However, data stored using the *nvarchar* data type provides better performance than does data stored using *ntext*. Therefore, a good rule of thumb is to use the *nvarchar* data type attributes with up to 100 characters, and use *ntext* for attributes with more than 100 characters.

Attribute Icons

When you view a list of attributes for an entity, you can quickly distinguish the attributes that you created (custom) from the system attributes by looking at the icon in the far left column. Microsoft Dynamics CRM displays an icon for custom attributes that is different from the one used for system attributes.

Deleting Attributes

Because it's easy to add custom attributes, you might find yourself getting a little overzealous and adding more attributes than you need or want. Of course, you could simply remove any unused attributes from an entity's form, but they will still appear in Advanced Find, SDK, database, filtered views, and so on. If these extra attributes bother you and you decide to delete old or unused custom attributes, you'll find the process very simple.

Warning   Deleting a custom attribute also deletes all of the data stored in that field, and you cannot retrieve that data later. Be sure to take the appropriate steps to back up all of your data before deleting an attribute.

Before you delete any attributes, make sure that you remove from Microsoft Dynamics CRM any existing references to that attribute. To remove references to an attribute, do the following:

- Remove the attribute from the entity's form, and then publish the form.
- Remove the attribute from any reports that contain the attribute.
- Remove the attribute from any filter criteria used in views.
- Remove the attribute from any script or code references.

Fortunately, Microsoft Dynamics CRM does most of the hard work for you by automatically checking all the forms and views in the system. If you miss a reference to an attribute you want to delete, you'll see an error message like the one shown in Figure 4-17.

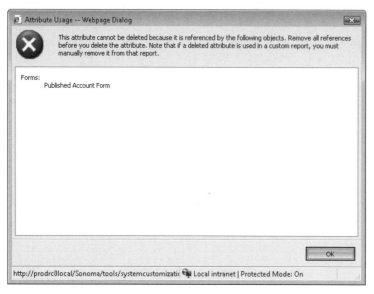

FIGURE 4-17 Error message shown when attempting to delete a referenced attribute

Even though Microsoft Dynamics CRM checks the forms and views for references to deleted attributes, you must scrub the reports and code yourself to remove any references to the deleted attribute.

After you're certain that you have removed all references to the attribute, you can delete the attribute by following these steps.

Deleting a custom attribute

1. Go to the Customization section of Microsoft Dynamics CRM and click Customize Entities.

2. Double-click the entity of the attribute that you want to delete.

3. Click Attributes, and then select the custom attribute that you want to remove.

4. Click the Delete button on the grid toolbar.

5. A warning message appears that says, "Deleting this attribute will result in loss of all data stored in it. Continue with the deletion of the attribute?" Click OK.

Attributes and Closing Dialog Boxes

Closing dialog boxes present a special case you need to consider when you're customizing entity attributes. A *closing dialog box* is a dialog box that appears when a user takes one of the following actions:

- Closes an activity such as Phone Call

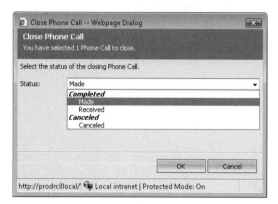

- Converts a Lead

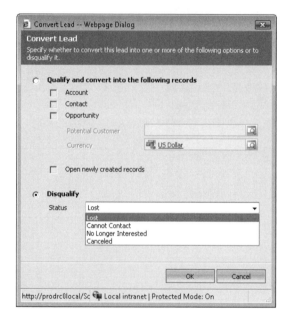

- Closes an Opportunity

- Resolves a Case

When a user initiates one of these actions, a closing dialog box prompts the user to specify how he or she wants to close the entity. It might not be obvious where you should customize the closing dialog box *picklist* values because these closing dialog boxes aren't entity forms, but they do display attributes of the entity. To edit the closing dialog box *picklist* values, you must modify the *statuscode* attribute (Status Reason display name) of the entity you're closing. We quickly show you how to edit the closing dialog box values for the Phone Call entity, and then you will know how to apply the same concept and process to the other closing dialog boxes referenced in the preceding list.

Important   For entities that users can close in Microsoft Dynamics CRM (such as Phone Calls and Letters), the *statuscode* attribute behaves a little differently from a standard *picklist* attribute. In these examples, you can specify different *picklist* values for each *statecode* value (Status Reason display name) where most picklists contain only one range of values. You can specify different *statuscode* picklist values for each of the three *statecode* values: Open, Completed, and Canceled.

Editing the Phone Call closing dialog box values

When you close activities such as Tasks and Phone Calls, a closing dialog box appears in which the user determines whether to mark the activity Completed or Canceled. The following procedure explains how to customize those *picklist* values.

1. Go to the Customization section of Microsoft Dynamics CRM and click Customize Entities.

2. Double-click the Phone Call entity.

3. In the navigation pane, click Attributes, and then double-click the statuscode schema name. The attribute editor appears.

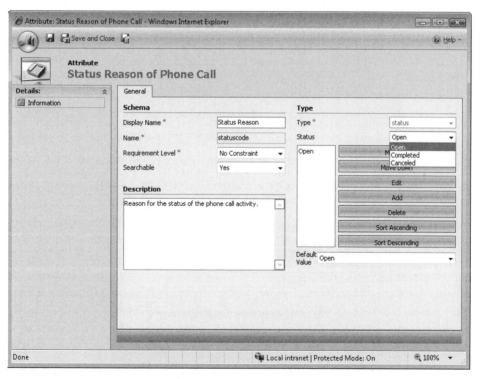

4. In the Status drop-down list, select Completed. The picklist values change from the Open value ("Open") to the Completed values ("Made", "Received").

5. Click Add, and then type **Left Message** in the Label field. Click OK.

6. In the State drop-down list, click Canceled. Then, click Add, and type **Wrong Number** in the Label field. Click OK. You will see that the "Wrong Number" picklist value is added under the "Canceled" value.

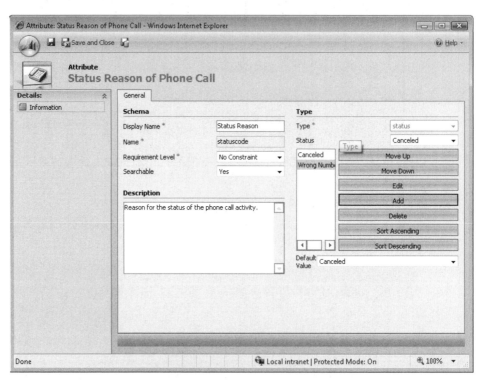

7. Click Save, and then click Close on the attribute editor toolbar.

8. Click Actions on the Phone Call entity editor menu bar, and then click Publish.

9. Now when your users close a Phone Call activity, they will see the following closing dialog box that incorporates your new customizations.

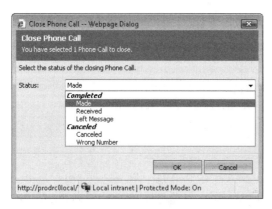

> **Important** If users click the Save As Completed button on the toolbar, they will not see the closing dialog box. In this case, Microsoft Dynamics CRM uses the *picklist* value that you specify as the default value of the Completed state. Because most users will probably click the Save As Completed button, make sure you choose the default value that you want.

Noneditable Status Reasons

Microsoft Dynamics CRM includes some entities with closing dialog boxes that behave differently from the ones just discussed, limiting your ability to customize them. For example, the campaign response displays a dialog box to convert records that appear similar to the examples we just covered, but you cannot modify the Close Response *picklist* values by modifying the Status Reasons. You can use the attribute editor to add new values to the Closed and Canceled statuses, but unfortunately those values won't appear in the user interface. To assign these values to campaign response records, you need to write some custom code using the SDK to assign these status reasons to records.

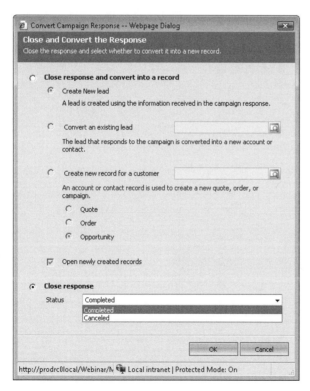

In addition, even though you can modify the status reasons for phone calls and letters, you cannot modify the status reasons for the Task, E-mail, and Appointment entities.

Summary

In this chapter, we explained the concepts, terminology, and processes related to customizing entities. Microsoft Dynamics CRM stores data as entities, and each entity possesses multiple attributes that define its characteristics. The software uses three different types of entities: system customizable, system noncustomizable, and custom. Every entity consists of multiple attributes, and Microsoft Dynamics CRM supports two different types of attributes: system and custom. Only users with the correct security rights, such as users with the System Administrator or System Customizer security roles, can perform customizations. After you complete your updates, you deploy your customizations to users using a publishing process. If you need to copy your customizations from one system to another, you can export your customizations to an .xml file that can be imported into a different system. In Microsoft Dynamics CRM, you also can easily rename the default system entities using terminology that better fits your business.

This chapter also explored the details related to entity attributes. Each entity attribute consists of common properties (such as display name and schema name), in addition to properties unique to the data type of the attribute. You can modify existing attributes in addition to creating or deleting new custom attributes.

Chapter 5

Entity Customization: Forms and Views

In Chapter 4, "Entity Customization: Concepts and Attributes," you learned the concepts and processes related to customizing entities in Microsoft Dynamics CRM. In this chapter, we go deeper into entity customization and give a detailed explanation of forms, activities, and views.

Customizing Forms

You already know that when a user opens a record, Microsoft Dynamics CRM displays the form for that record's entity. In addition, Microsoft Dynamics CRM displays a record's form whenever a user clicks the Information link in the navigation pane, as shown in Figure 5-1.

Most of the system entities use a form, but some of the noncustomizable system entities such as Case Resolution and Organization don't use a form because users don't view or update these records directly. In addition, some customizable system entities don't use a form either such as the following:

- Contract Template
- Customer Relationship
- Discount
- Discount List
- E-mail Template

- Opportunity Relationship

- Price List

- Price List Item

- Resource Group

- Team

- Territory

- Unit

- Unit Group

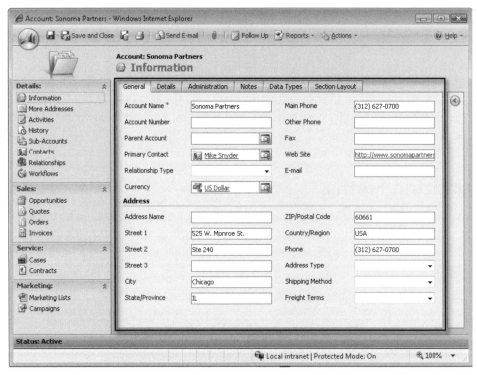

FIGURE 5-1 The Information link displays an entity's form

Microsoft Dynamics CRM uses one unique form per entity, so when you customize an entity's form keep in mind that all users will see the same form. For example, you cannot create one form that displays certain fields for sales users, and then create a second form that displays a different set of fields for customer service users.

> **Tip** One workaround for varying the form by user is to use the form *onLoad* event to dynamically hide or disable fields, sections, or tabs on the form based on the role of the user viewing the form. See Chapter 10, "Client–Side SDK," for more information about using the form *onLoad* event.

When you view the default Microsoft Dynamics CRM entity forms, you will notice that most data fields displayed on the form are just attributes of the entity. Of course, you probably will want to customize the default form layouts to add more than just attributes to meet the requests of your users. In Microsoft Dynamics CRM, you can customize the following areas of each form:

- Fields
- Field event scripts
- Tabs
- Sections
- IFrames
- Form event scripts
- Form design and layout

In this chapter, we explain all of the details related to configuring each of these areas of the form. Form customization follows the same process that you learned in Chapter 4 for attribute customization. After you set up the form exactly how you want it in the Customize Entities section, you must publish the entities you customized before users can see your changes. In addition, you must have the appropriate security permissions to edit forms and publish entities.

To access the entity form editor, follow these steps:

Accessing the form editor

1. In the Customization section of Microsoft Dynamics CRM, click Customize Entities.
2. Double-click the entity that you want to edit to open the entity editor.
3. Click Forms and Views.
4. Double-click Form to open the form editor.

You perform all form customizations in the form editor. Figure 5-2 shows the form editor user interface, using the Account form as an example.

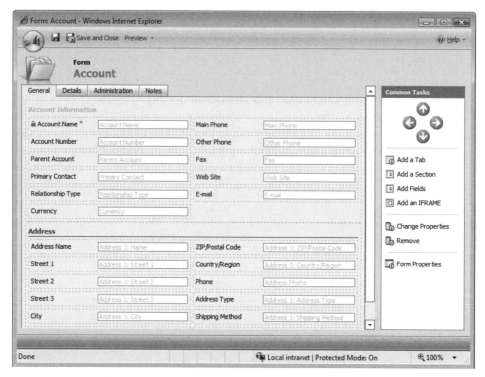

FIGURE 5-2 Form editor user interface

Forms consist of four components:

- **Tabs** By using *tabs*, you can organize the data fields for an entity into logical groupings. The default tabs for an entity typically include General, Details, Administration, and Notes.

- **Sections** In each tab, you can group information in *sections*. For each section, you can specify a section name and decide whether you want to display the section name and a divider on the form. In Figure 5-2, Account Information and Address are sections on the form. Note that Account Information is unavailable, indicating that the section name will not be displayed on the form.

- **Fields** *Fields* display the actual data related to an entity. Most, but not all, of the fields on a form are attributes of the entity.

- **IFrames** In Microsoft Dynamics CRM, you can display an *IFrame* (also known as an *inline frame*) on the form of an entity. You can think of an IFrame as a "window" in the form that you can use to display a different Web page inside the window frame. We explain IFrames in more detail and give examples later in this chapter.

In the form editor, notice that dotted lines encapsulate the different areas of the form. These dotted lines indicate the sections, fields, and IFrames. Obviously, the default form for each entity appears a little different because each entity contains unique attributes. However, all of the entity form editors use these two tools:

- Common Tasks
- Preview

As Figure 5-2 shows, you see the Common Tasks tools in the right-hand column of the form editor. You can access the Preview tool from the form editor menu bar. In the following sections, we explain how to use both of these tools when you're editing a form. After you understand what the form editor tools do, we go into greater detail about how you use these tools to set up and configure the following data related to a form:

- Form properties
- Sections
- Fields
- IFrames

Common Tasks

You can use the Common Tasks tools to edit everything on the form, including data fields, event scripts, and form layout. The Common Tasks tools consist of the following:

- **Directional arrows**   You can use the four green arrows to move the form components around on the form. The arrows can move fields, sections, tabs, and IFrames. To move a field, section, or IFrame, select it on the form; the dotted line around the area is then highlighted in green. Then, click an arrow to move the highlighted item to a new position. To move a tab, select it on the form, and then click an arrow to move it. The up and down arrows apply only to sections, fields, and IFrames; the left and right arrows apply only to tabs and fields.

- **Add a Tab**   With the Add a Tab tool, you can add a new tab to the form. Microsoft Dynamics CRM adds the new tab to the right of existing tabs. Note that you can add a maximum of eight tabs.

- **Add a Section**   With this tool, you can add a new section to a form. Microsoft Dynamics CRM always adds the new section below the last section in the currently selected tab.

- **Add Fields**   Use the Add Fields tool to select new fields to add to the form. When you click Add Fields, the dialog box displays only fields not already on the form; so if you don't see the field that you're looking for, it's probably already on the form somewhere. If you want to add a field to a specific section, select the section, and then click Add Fields.

- **Add an IFrame** With this tool, you can add an IFrame to the form.

- **Change Properties** You can use the Change Properties tool to change the properties of a form component, including tabs, sections, fields, and IFrames. You can also open the Change Properties dialog box by double-clicking a component in the form editor.

- **Remove** With this tool, you can remove a component (including tabs, sections, fields, and IFrames) from the form.

- **Form Properties** With this tool, you can specify scripts to run when Microsoft Dynamics CRM triggers form events and also configure the Form Assistant.

You can use the Common Tasks tools to lay out and design almost all of the information that appears on an entity's form. At first it might seem like a lot to learn, but the tools are very intuitive and straightforward, so we're sure you'll learn to use these Common Tasks tools quickly.

Form Preview

When you're done manipulating your form and you have everything where you want it, you can use the convenient form preview tool to evaluate how the form will appear to users before you publish it. Microsoft Dynamics CRM offers the following three types of form previews:

- **Create Form** Simulates how the form will appear and behave when users create a new record for the entity

- **Update Form** Simulates how the form will appear and behave when users edit an existing record

- **Read-Only Form** Shows how the form will appear to users who do not have permissions to edit a record

The form preview feature does more than just show you the form layout—you can also test any custom scripts that you added to the form. Microsoft Dynamics CRM offers you three different events for which you can create custom scripts:

- *onLoad* form event

- *onSave* form event

- *onChange* field event

Obviously, being able to test and debug your event scripts using the preview tool can save you time. When you start the form preview, Microsoft Dynamics CRM fires the *onLoad* event, which you can use to trigger your custom script. However, because the preview doesn't actually save a record, you can use the Simulate Form Save button on the form preview menu bar, which triggers the *onSave* form event. You can also fire the *onChange* field event by changing the field value and then changing the field focus (by pressing the Tab key to leave a field or by clicking a different field). If you don't change the field value, the *onChange* event will not fire.

 Note Sometimes the Microsoft Dynamics CRM user interface uses different casing for these events such as *OnLoad* and *onLoad*. The correct syntax for your code (which is case-sensitive) is *onLoad*, *onSave*, and *onChange*.

We explain adding custom scripts to events later in this chapter, and we provide numerous code examples that use these form and field events in Chapter 10.

Form Properties

With the Form Properties tool in Common Tasks, you can modify the form display settings and add custom scripts to the form's *onLoad* and *onSave* events. The Form Properties page contains three tabs (shown in Figure 5-3):

- Events
- Display
- Non-Event Dependencies

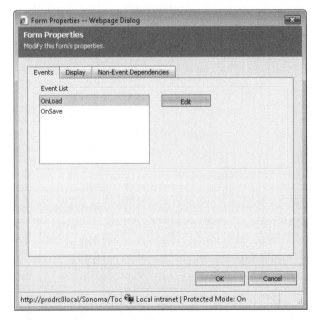

FIGURE 5-3 The Form Properties page

Events

You can add custom scripts that run when Microsoft Dynamics CRM triggers the *onLoad* or *onSave* event. When you add custom scripts to the form, you can manually specify which fields those scripts reference (in the Dependencies tab of the event). By indicating the script-dependent fields, Microsoft Dynamics CRM prevents other System Customizers from removing a field that a script uses. If you don't specify dependent fields and a user unknowingly removes a script-dependent field from a form, the script will fail.

Display

In this tab, you can specify whether you want to display the Form Assistant for an entity, and if the Form Assistant should be expanded by default. Microsoft Dynamics CRM includes a Form Assistant (Figure 5-4) so that users can quickly search for values in lookup fields without having to open another window.

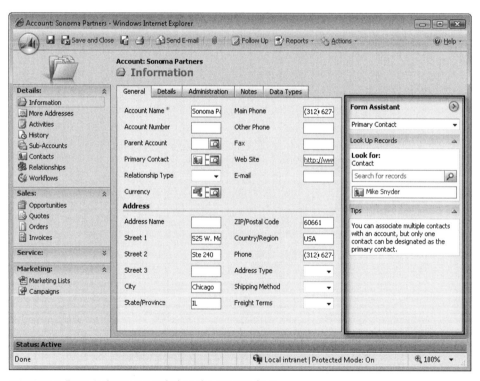

FIGURE 5-4 Form Assistant expanded on the Account form

However, you can also see in Figure 5-4 that the Form Assistant may cause some formatting issues with your form if your users run a low display screen resolution such as 800 × 600. In this example, users could not read the name of the account's primary contact in Figure 5-4 without collapsing the Form Assistant.

Consequently, Microsoft Dynamics CRM gives you the option to specify whether you want to enable the Form Assistant and if it should be expanded by default for a particular form's entity (see Figure 5-5).

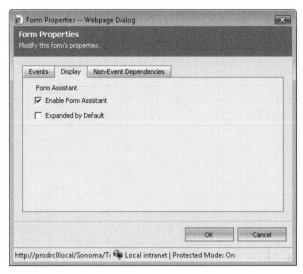

FIGURE 5-5 Form Assistant settings in the Display tab of the Form Properties dialog box

Non-Event Dependencies

If you are also using additional external (non-event) scripts, you can manually specify these fields as dependent.

As mentioned earlier, if a user tries to remove a field from a form that you specified as dependent (either on an event or a non-event), Microsoft Dynamics CRM denies the request and displays an error message similar to the one shown in Figure 5-6.

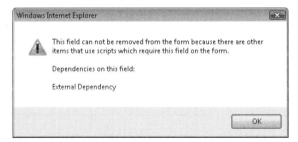

FIGURE 5-6 Error message displayed when a user tries to remove a dependent field from a form

> **Tip** Microsoft Dynamics CRM doesn't force you to specify dependent fields, but taking a little extra time to complete this step can save you a headache later. Therefore, we recommend that you always specify script-dependent fields.

Form Customization Example

Now that you understand how to add scripts by using the Form Properties page, we can walk through a few simple examples to illustrate how and why you may want to use the *onLoad* and *onSave* events.

When users create a new task in Microsoft Dynamics CRM, the default form appears like the one shown in Figure 5-7.

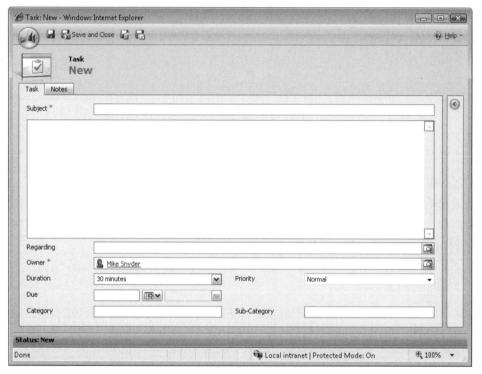

FIGURE 5-7 Default form for a new task

Based on the hundreds of Microsoft Dynamics CRM deployments we've completed, we know that customers frequently want to make the following changes to the form:

- Change the default duration from 30 minutes to blank.

- Automatically populate today's date in the Due Date field.

These two changes may seem simple at first, but digging deeper into the details of these fields reveals some issues. Because the Duration field looks like a picklist field, you may expect to be able simply to change the default value by editing the *Duration* attribute of the Task entity. However, even though the Duration field appears to be a picklist, it is actually a special integer field used on a variety of activities in Microsoft Dynamics CRM. For these

special fields, you cannot set a default value (or add picklist values) like you can fo
picklist fields.

> **Note** The Duration picklists used on activity forms such as Task and Phone Call behave differently from a typical picklist because users can dynamically enter their own values on the form instead of having to select from predefined values like they do for a regular picklist field.

You learned in Chapter 4 that *datetime* attribute data types do not have a default value. Because the Due Date field uses the *datetime* data type, you can't use the attribute editor to specify today's date as the default value in the Due Date field. Hence, you now have two issues to solve regarding the customer requests.

Despite the two problems, you can easily meet the customer's needs by using the *onLoad* event of the task entity's form. To do this, you add a simple script to the form's *onLoad* event, and Microsoft Dynamics CRM will run your script every time a user opens the Task form. When the script runs, it will programmatically change the value of the Duration and Due Date fields to the values that you specify. The last issue that you need to address with the script is making sure that you change the Duration and Due Date values only when users create a *new* Task. Obviously, you wouldn't want to change the Due Date and Duration values when a user opens a previously created Task. When you're done, every time a user creates a new Task, the script will set the Duration field to blank and the current date as the due date.

Now we describe how you would set up, test, and deploy this code.

Using the form's *onLoad* event to prefill Task Duration and Due Date

1. In the Customization section of Microsoft Dynamics CRM, click Customize Entities. Double-click the Task entity to open the entity editor.

2. Click Forms and Views, and then double-click Form to open the form editor for the Task entity.

3. Click Form Properties. On this page, you can choose to add a script to the form's *onLoad* or *onSave* event. As we mentioned previously, you want to use the *onLoad* event so that the script runs when users open a form.

4. Select *onLoad,* and then click Edit to open the Event Detail Properties page. On this page, enter the following code.

```
var CRM_FORM_TYPE_CREATE = 1;

switch (crmForm.FormType)
{
  case CRM_FORM_TYPE_CREATE:
    crmForm.all.actualdurationminutes.DataValue = null;
```

```
rmForm.all.scheduledend.DataValue = new Date();
reak;
ault:
/ do nothing
reak;
```

5. Now quickly review how this JavaScript code will programmatically set the values on the form. This code sets the *actualdurationminutes* field (the schema name for Duration) to null, which means blank. It also sets the *scheduledend* field (the schema name for Due Date) to the current date by using the JavaScript *Date( )* object. The *onLoad* event will run this script every time a user opens a form, but remember that you want to set the default values only when users create a *new* Task. Therefore, this code includes a *switch* statement so that your script runs only for the form type of 1. Microsoft Dynamics CRM assigns a form type value to each form (1: Create, 2: Update, 3: Read Only, and so on) so that you can tie this information to your scripts, as you do in this example. In this script, a form type of 2 indicates an Update form, so the script won't alter the Due Date or Duration field values.

6. After you enter the code, select the Event is enabled check box. This check box indicates whether Microsoft Dynamics CRM should run your script when it fires the *onLoad* event.

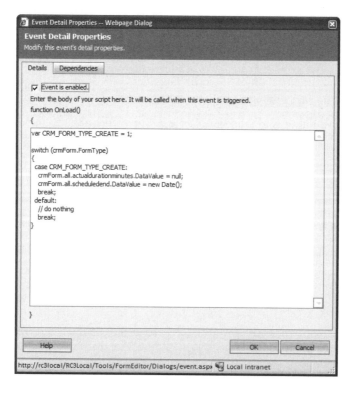

7. To set up the dependencies related to the code to ensure that no one accidentally removes the Duration or Due Date fields from the Task form (because the script would generate an error if those fields were missing), click the Dependencies tab.

8. The Available fields list displays all of the fields that appear on the Task form. To make Due Date and Duration dependent fields, select those values in the left column, and then click the >> button to move them into the Dependent Fields list.

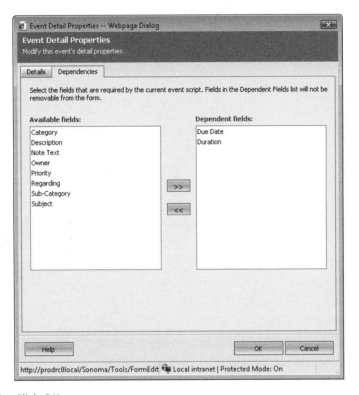

9. Click OK.

10. Click OK again to return to the task form editor.

11. Before you try to preview this script, save the changes you made by clicking Save.

12. To test the script on the create form, click Preview, and then click Create Form. The form should appear as shown here.

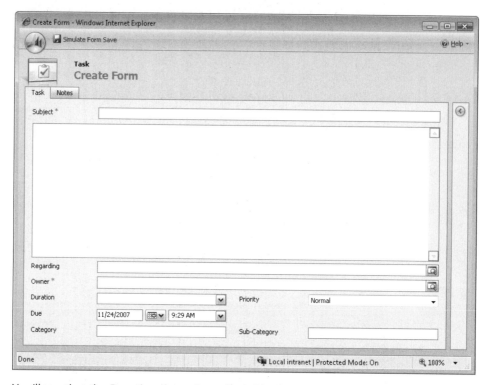

You'll see that the Duration drop-down list is blank, and the Due Date field displays today's date and time! You may need to resize the preview window to make it large enough to display all of the fields correctly.

13. If you test the script on the update form (click Preview, and then click Update Form), you'll see that the Due Date field does not default to today's date as you may expect. However, notice that the Duration field appears blank. When you use the Update Form preview, Microsoft Dynamics CRM shows you an update of a blank record, so it will always show picklists as blank. The script ran correctly, but the fact that Microsoft Dynamics CRM shows an update of a blank record may cause some little nuances such as blank picklists.

14. To publish the Task entity, return to the entity editor. Click Actions, and then click Publish on the top toolbar. That's it, you're done!

This example shows you how to tap into the form's *onLoad* event to manipulate field values before users see the form. Even if you didn't understand the syntax of this code example, you should understand the concepts of customizing your forms by adding custom scripts that tie into Microsoft Dynamics CRM form events. Figure 5-8 is a flow chart that shows how Microsoft Dynamics CRM processes the code in the example.

Of course, this example shows a very simple tweak to the Task form, but you can get creative with your own custom code. Chapter 10 goes into more detail on writing code that ties into events and shows you more examples of how you can customize your forms.

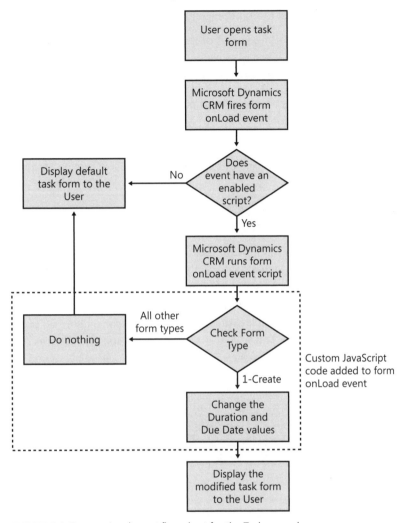

FIGURE 5-8 Form *onLoad* event flow chart for the Task example

Sections

By using form sections, you can group together and organize multiple data fields in a manner that makes the most sense for your users. Every field you add to a form must belong to a section, and you can have as many sections as you need on a form. Each section contains multiple properties:

- **Name**   The name of the section. It must be unique for each entity.

- **Label**   Specifies whether you want the section name to appear to users on the form. You can also specify whether you want to display a divider line under the section name on the form.

- **Location**   Specifies in which tab on the form the section should appear.

- **Layout**   Specifies the formatting layout of the fields in the section. After you create a section, you cannot change its layout. You can access the section's layout on the Formatting tab when you view a section's properties.

Working with sections is a pretty straightforward process, and only the layout properties require a more detailed explanation.

When you add a new section, you have the option of specifying its layout. In Microsoft Dynamics CRM, you can choose from one of two mutually exclusive section layouts:

- **Variable Field Width**   This layout displays all of the fields in the section in two columns. However, you can specify that specific fields (on a field-by-field basis) in the section span the width of both columns on the form.

- **Fixed Field Width**   A Fixed Field Width section layout gives you the option to specify one of five column formats. When you select one of these Fixed Field Width formats, the number of columns in that section remains fixed. So, unlike a Variable Field Width section, you cannot configure a field to span the width of multiple columns. Another way to think of Fixed Field Width layout is as a *variable height* section. All of the fields in a Fixed Field Width section will have the width that you specify when you create the section (1:2, 2:1, 1:1, 3, or 4). However, with the Fixed Field Width layout you can include text areas in a column and change the height of the column to meet your needs.

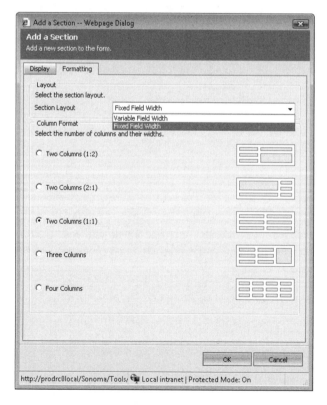

Tip With the Variable Field Width layout, you also can use the autoexpand feature on text area fields (explained in the section titled "Fields" later in this chapter). Microsoft Dynamics CRM defaults to Variable Field Width for new sections.

All of the default Microsoft Dynamics CRM forms use the Variable Field Width layout exclusively. We created a sample section layout that uses the Fixed Field Width to illustrate one potential design (Figure 5-9).

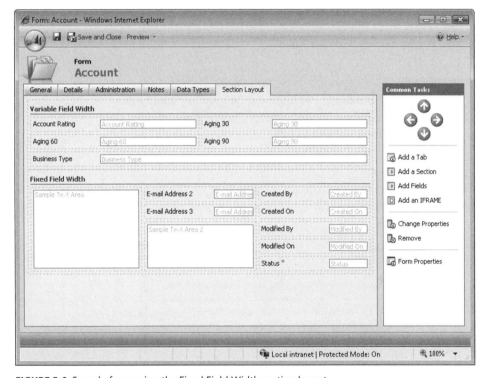

FIGURE 5-9 Sample form using the Fixed Field Width section layout

Another caveat regarding the Variable Field Width section layout is that you can vary only the height of text area fields. You cannot change the height of the other data type fields such as *integer*, *money*, *bit*, or *datetime*.

Tip After you create a section, you cannot change the layout later. If you need to change the section's layout, simply remove the fields from the section and delete it. You can then create a new section with the desired layout and add all of the fields to the new section.

Fields

Most of the fields displayed on a form are attributes of the entity. You add, modify, remove, and change the properties of a field by using the Common Tasks tools. For each field on a form, you can set the following properties related to that field (shown in the tabs in Figure 5-10):

- Display
- Formatting
- Name
- Events

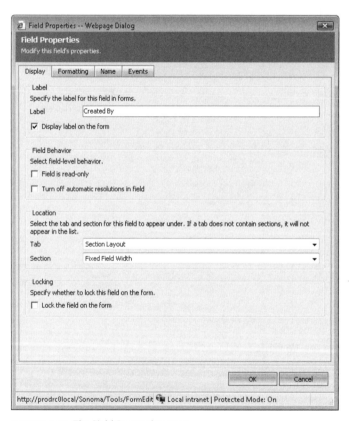

FIGURE 5-10 The Field Properties page

Display

You can adjust the following display settings for each field:

- **Label**   Use this section to set the text that appears on the form to the left of the field. You can hide the field label by clearing the Display label on the form check box.

- **Field Behavior**   Selecting the Field is read-only check box makes the field disabled on the form. This means that users can read the value of the field, but they cannot change it. If you select Turn off automatic resolutions in field box, Microsoft Dynamics CRM will not automatically try to match values in lookup fields. You may want to do this for performance reasons if a particular lookup field contains a very large number of records to match against.

- **Location**   Use this section to specify the tab and section where the field should appear on the form.

- **Locking**   Selecting the check box in this section prevents users (including yourself) from removing the field from the form. A lock icon appears next to the field label of a locked field. Of course, a user with permissions to customize a form could simply unlock a locked field and then remove it. Therefore, locking a field isn't foolproof, but it should indicate to others that the field shouldn't be removed from the form.

> **Tip** We use the lock field features to indicate that the field contains client-side script. This can save you a few clicks when you're working with a form because you'll see the lock icon displayed on the form, and you'll know that it contains a script without having to dig into the field's event properties.

Formatting

In the Formatting tab, you can set up additional formatting properties. For a field in a section that uses the Variable Field Width layout, you can use the Layout section to toggle between the one-column and two-column displays. If this section is disabled, the field is in a section that uses the Fixed Field Width layout.

bit **Data Types**   For fields of the *bit* data type, you can specify the formatting of the data field on the form. By default, Microsoft Dynamics CRM displays bit options such as yes/no and true/false with two radio (option) buttons. However, you can change this formatting to a check box or drop-down list if you like (see Figure 5-11).

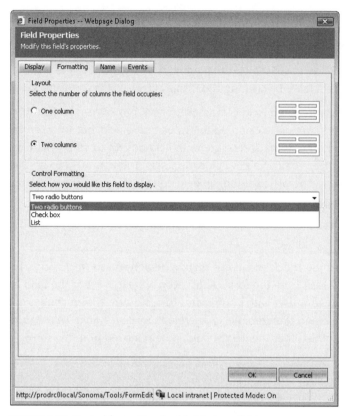

FIGURE 5-11   Control formatting for *bit* data type fields

***ntext* and *nvarchar* (Text) Data Types**   For fields of the *ntext* and *nvarchar* data types, you can also configure the row layout to change the number of rows of the text area to display on the form (see Figure 5-12).

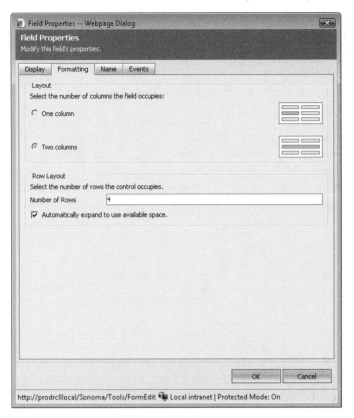

FIGURE 5-12 Row layout formatting for *ntext* and *nvarchar* (text) data types

For fields in a Variable Field Width section only, you can also specify whether an *ntext* field should automatically expand to use available space. If you select this check box, the form will override the number of rows you specified and expand to include more rows if they will fit in the window. You can use this autoexpand feature on only one *ntext* field per tab. Figure 5-13 shows two different forms and the benefit of using the autoexpand feature.

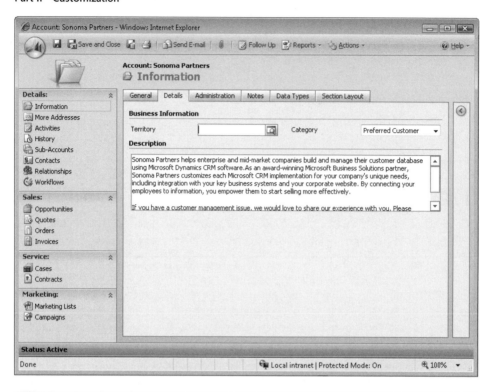

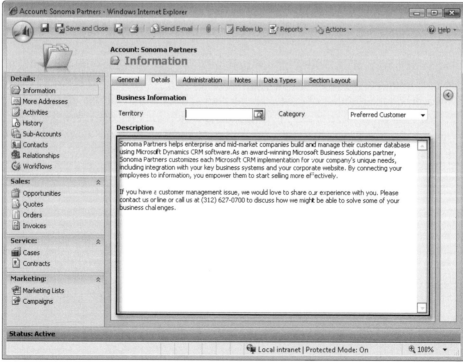

FIGURE 5-13 Comparing an autoexpand text area with a fixed height text area

As you can see in the figure, the form that uses the autoexpand feature provides the user with more space to enter and view information in the Description field. We recommend using the autoexpand option wherever possible.

Name

The Name tab displays the schema information for the attribute, including the display name, schema name, and description. To edit the display name and description information, you must update these values using the attribute editor for the entity, as explained in Chapter 4.

Events

As discussed earlier in this chapter, you can include custom scripts that Microsoft Dynamics CRM triggers on the field's *onChange* event. Here is a simple example of an *onChange* event to illustrate how you might use this feature. Many businesses assign a unique account number to each of their customers, and the example customer would like every account number to contain eight digits. Creating a custom *onChange* script that runs on the Account Number field is a good way to remind users that every account number should be eight digits in length.

Using the field's *onChange* event to enforce account number length

1. In the Customization section of Microsoft Dynamics CRM, click Customize Entities. Double-click the Account entity to open the entity editor.

2. Click Forms and Views, and then double-click Form to open the form editor for the Account entity.

3. Double-click the Account Number field on the form to open the Field Properties page. Click the Events tab.

4. Select onChange, and then click Edit to open the Event Detail Properties dialog box. Enter the following code.

```
var oField = event.srcElement;
if (typeof(oField) != "undefined" && oField != null)
{
   if (oField.DataValue.length != 8)
     alert("Account Number should be 8 characters.");
}
```

5. Select the Event is enabled check box to tell Microsoft Dynamics CRM to run this script when the field's *onChange* event fires.

6. To add Account Number as a dependent field so that the script always runs properly, click the Dependencies tab, select Account Number, and then click the >> button. Account Number moves to the Dependent fields list. Click OK.

7. On the Field Properties page, click OK.

8. Save the Account form.

9. To test this custom script, click Preview, and then click Create Form. The preview window appears.

10. Enter **1234567** into the Account Number field, and then press the Tab key. The following prompt appears, reminding you that account numbers should contain eight digits.

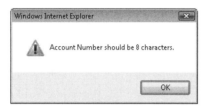

11. To publish the Account entity, simply return to the entity editor, click Actions on the menu bar, and then click Publish.

Again, don't worry too much about the syntax of the code. The point we're trying to communicate is how easy it is to add custom scripts to a field's *onChange* event.

> **More Info** In this example, the custom script reminds the user that the account number *should* be eight digits. However, a user could still enter any value for an account number and save the record. A customer may want this behavior. For example, perhaps not every Account is assigned an Account Number immediately, or perhaps some of the old Accounts have Account Numbers from a previous system that contained 10 digits. However, if the customer always wants to enforce the eight-digit account number requirement, you would have to create a slightly modified custom script and add it to the form's *onSave* event (instead of the field's *onChange* event). By adding a custom script to the form's *onSave* event, you can prevent users from creating or updating records that do not meet your business criteria.

Tweaking the Tab Order of Fields on a Form

When your users enter data on a form, they can use the Tab key to advance from one field to the next field on the form. To move back to the previous field on a form, they can press Shift+Tab. These keyboard functions allow users to enter form data much more quickly than they can by clicking from field to field with their mouse. As users press the Tab key, Microsoft Dynamics CRM moves the cursor from field to field down the column of a section, and then it moves to the top of the next column (left to right). When users reach the last field in a section, pressing the Tab key advances them to the upper-left field of the next section (see Figure 5-14).

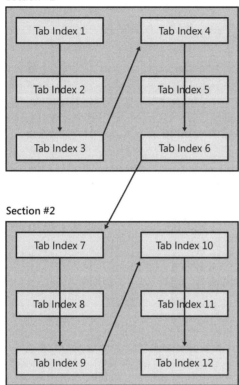

FIGURE 5-14 Microsoft Dynamics CRM field tab order on a Contact form

In standard HTML code, you can specify a tab index for each field on a form to control the order in which users move from field to field. Unfortunately, you cannot specify tab indexes on form fields in Microsoft Dynamics CRM. However, you can easily manipulate the tab sequence that users experience by understanding the Microsoft Dynamics CRM tab behavior and then getting clever with your use of form sections. Conceptually, you can create *invisible* sections on a form and place the form fields in the appropriate sections, depending on how you want users to proceed. You can make a section invisible by not displaying its name or the divider line on the form. Figure 5-15 shows how to change the tab order from the initial order shown in Figure 5-14.

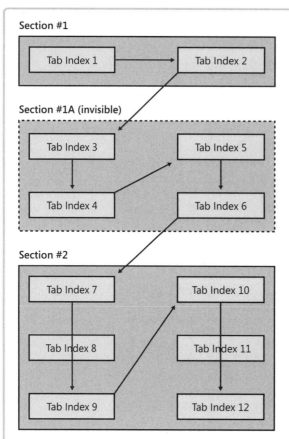

FIGURE 5-15 Modified tab order after adding an invisible section to the form

Adding the Section 1A, and then not displaying the section label and divider make this section appear invisible to your users. They will think they tabbed from the left field to the right field (in Section 1), but in reality, they tabbed from the bottom of the left column to the top of the right column of Section 1!

IFrames

In Microsoft Dynamics CRM, you can add IFrames (also known as *inline frames*) to an entity's form. IFrames open the door to almost unlimited customization capabilities in Microsoft Dynamics CRM forms. Conceptually, an IFrame creates a frame within a Web page that displays a second Web page. The Web page in the IFrame can be any Web page that you want, whether it is hosted on your server or not. In the context of Microsoft Dynamics CRM, you can add one or more IFrames to any entity's form. Figure 5-16 shows an example of an IFrame on an Account form that references a company logo displayed as an image.

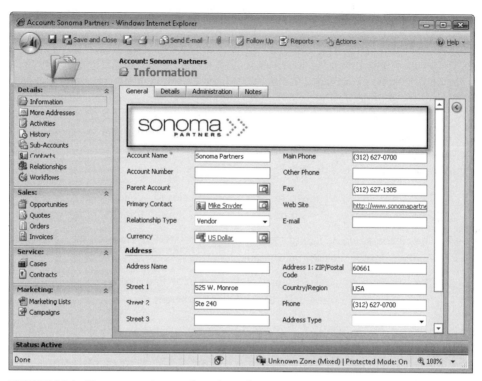

FIGURE 5-16 An IFrame on an Account form that references an image file

Although this is a very simple example, the key concept is that you can display non–Microsoft Dynamics CRM content *within the context of a record's form* by using an IFrame. Potential uses for an IFrame on a form include the following:

- Displaying external Web sites
- Displaying your own custom Web pages
- Displaying photos or images related to the record
- Displaying other Web sites on your intranet

The most important feature of the IFrame capability is that Microsoft Dynamics CRM can automatically append the IFrame Web address (Uniform Resource Locator, or URL) with additional information from Microsoft Dynamics CRM such as the record type, unique record ID, organization name, language preference, and so forth. By taking advantage of the additional dynamic information in the URL string, you can display Web content in the IFrame that is unique to the record you are looking at instead of displaying a generic URL.

> **Tip** IFrames reference a URL address. People usually use URLs to reference Web pages, but you can use the IFrame to reference anything that is URL addressable. For example, you can also use URLs to display images, Microsoft Office Word files, Microsoft Office Excel files, and so on. You can also specify protocols other than Hypertext Transfer Protocol (HTTP), such as HTTP Secure (HTTPS) or File Transfer Protocol (FTP).

Although the image displayed in Figure 5-16 gives a simple IFrame example, we can illustrate the benefits of using IFrames with a more complex real-world example. Many of our customers and prospects ask to modify the display of an Account record to show a highly customized view of the record. As you learned in Chapter 4, you can easily add and remove account attributes to the Account form, but this doesn't necessarily meet 100 percent of the customer scenarios. Consider the following requests:

1. The customer would like to see the open and closed activity records when users open an Account record without having to click the links in the navigation pane.

2. The customer would like to see the contacts related to the Account without clicking the Contacts link in the navigation pane.

3. The customer would like to display data from the financial and accounting system to see the Account's open balances and recent payments.

For requests 1 and 2, Microsoft Dynamics CRM stores this data, but you can't display it on the Account form because it isn't an account attribute. For request 3, the data may be stored in a different system entirely from Microsoft Dynamics CRM, so those values obviously can't be displayed using the standard entity form editor tools.

Fortunately, with the use of IFrames and a custom Web page, you can easily meet these types of customer requests. Figure 5-17 shows one possible implementation using a tool that we created called the *account overview*.

As you can see, the account overview displays all of the information requested by the customer in a single view!

Now that you understand the concept and some of the benefits of using IFrames in Microsoft Dynamics CRM forms, we'll review the details related to using an IFrame. Afterward, we will explain how we set up and configured the account overview example shown in Figure 5-17.

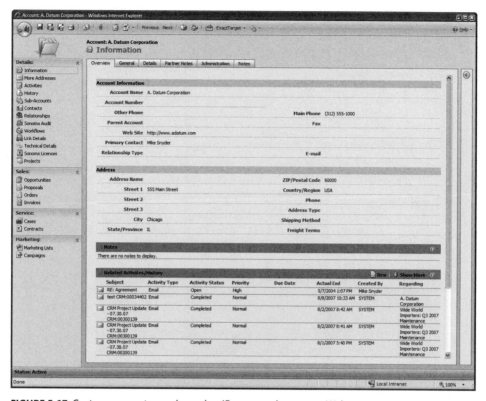

FIGURE 5-17 Custom account overview using IFrames and a custom Web page

When you click Add an IFRAME in the Common Tasks tool in the entity form editor, Microsoft Dynamics CRM prompts you to configure the following IFrame properties on the properties page, as shown in Figure 5-18:

- Name
- Label
- Security
- Location
- Layout
- Row Layout
- Scrolling
- Border
- Dependencies

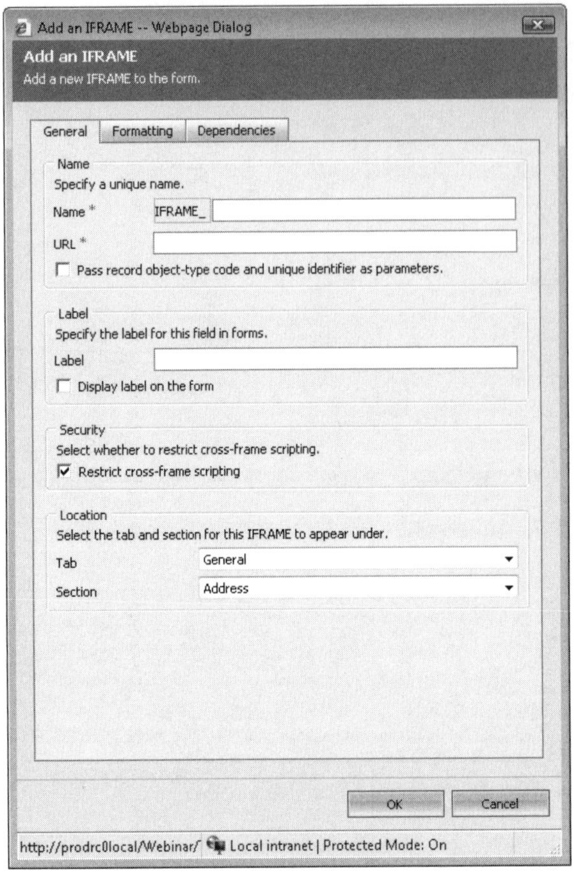

FIGURE 5-18 IFrame properties page

We'll review each of these properties in detail.

Name

In the Name section in the General tab, you specify the name of the IFrame and its URL.

- **Name** Notice that Microsoft Dynamics CRM automatically prefixes the value *IFRAME_* to your IFrame name. Unlike the attribute schema prefix that you can configure, you cannot alter this value. After you create an IFrame, you cannot change its name.

- **URL** In the URL field, you enter the address of the Web page or resource that you want to reference in the IFrame. You can specify a full URL (including the *http://*) or a relative URL.

- **Parameters** If you select the Pass record object-type code and unique identifier as parameters check box, Microsoft Dynamics CRM will append additional query string parameters to the IFrame URL. Table 5-1 shows how an IFrame URL would appear for a sample record with and without the parameters check box selected.

> **Tip** You can view the full URL of an IFrame that you create by right-clicking in the IFrame and clicking Properties. Refer to Chapter 9, "Microsoft Dynamics CRM 4.0 SDK," for an explanation of how to enable the right-click feature in Microsoft Dynamics CRM.

TABLE 5-1 Passing Parameters to IFrames

Parameters passed?	URL displayed in the IFrame
No	*http://www.adatum.com/sample.aspx*
Yes	*http://www.adatum.com/sample.aspx?type=1&typename=account&id={09CDE437-8D93-DC11-A8E4-0003FF9456FD}&orgname=book&userlcid=1033&orglcid=1033*

You can see that passing parameters appends the following data to the URL query string:

- **type** Every Microsoft Dynamics CRM entity has a corresponding object type code such as 1, 2, and so on that references entities (for example, 1 = Account, 2 = Contact, and so on). You can use the software development kit (SDK) metadata browser as one method to find the object type code number for each entity.

- **typename** Displays the user-friendly entity name.

- **id** Displays the globally unique identifier of the current record. Also referred to as the GUID (pronounced *goo-id*).

- **orgname** Displays the organization name.

- **userlcid** Displays the language code ID for the user (for use in multilingual deployments). User language code 1033 stands for English.

- **orglcid** Displays the language code ID for the organization.

With all of this additional information in the URL query string, you can tell exactly which record the user is looking at, which organization the user belongs to, the user's preferred language, and the organization's default language. From here, you can design your own custom Web pages that take advantage of this query string information to render information relevant to the record the user is viewing. We also want to highlight the fact that even though Table 5-1 shows a custom .aspx page, you don't need to create your custom Web pages using Microsoft technology. The Microsoft Dynamics CRM IFrame can append the parameters to any type of URL you give it, so you can create custom pages in the IFrame using the Web development platform of your choice.

> **Important** By passing parameters to IFrames, you can create custom Web pages that dynamically update to display data related to the open record. Your custom Web page must retrieve data from the additional query string parameters and update the Web page display accordingly.

Label

Similar to form sections, you can add a label to the IFrame on the form and specify whether to display this label to users.

Security

Because IFrames display content from another Web site, scripts from that alternate Web site could run and perform malicious or unintended behavior in Microsoft Dynamics CRM. By default, Microsoft Dynamics CRM blocks cross-frame scripts from the IFrame Web site. Chapter 10 explains cross-frame scripting and related security considerations in detail. For the most part, you should leave the Restrict cross-frame scripting check box selected unless you know that you need to allow cross-frame scripting.

Location

Use these properties to specify in which tab and section to display the IFrame.

Layout

Figure 5-19 shows the Formatting tab of the IFrame properties page.

Microsoft Dynamics CRM disables the layout option for IFrames. Consequently, IFrames in a Variable Field Width section will always span both columns, and IFrames in a Fixed Field Width section will always remain fixed to the width of the column they occupy.

Row Layout

Use this section to enter the number of rows that the IFrame should occupy. As with fields, you can also set the IFrame to automatically expand to the size of the window.

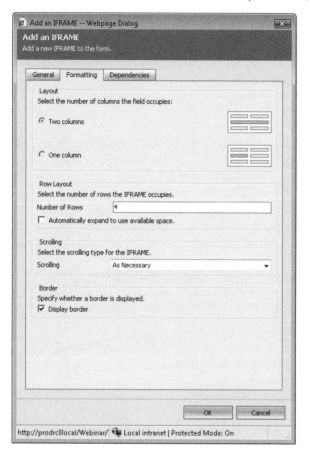

FIGURE 5-19 Formatting tab of the IFrame properties page

Scrolling

You can configure the scrolling type for each IFrame. Scrolling refers to adding a scroll bar to the IFrame so that users can move the page up and down in the IFrame. The three scrolling options are as follows:

- **As Necessary**   Microsoft Dynamics CRM automatically determines whether it needs to add scroll bars. If the content in the IFrame takes more vertical (or horizontal) space than the IFrame offers, Microsoft Dynamics CRM adds scroll bars.

- **Always**   Microsoft Dynamics CRM always includes horizontal and vertical scroll bars.

- **Never**   Microsoft Dynamics CRM never includes horizontal and vertical scroll bars.

We recommend that you leave the default option, As Necessary, selected.

Border

The IFrame Border property determines whether Microsoft Dynamics CRM displays a small, one-pixel blue border around the IFrame. This border exactly matches the style of the border that surrounds each of the data fields on the form.

Dependencies

If you use scripts in your IFrame that reference fields on the form, you can specify those fields as Dependent in the Dependencies tab. This prevents users from accidentally removing dependent fields from the form.

So, now that you understand a little more about setting up an IFrame, we can circle back to the account overview example shown in Figure 5-17 to show you how we built that. The Account form for the Overview tab includes a single IFrame named Overview (Figure 5-20).

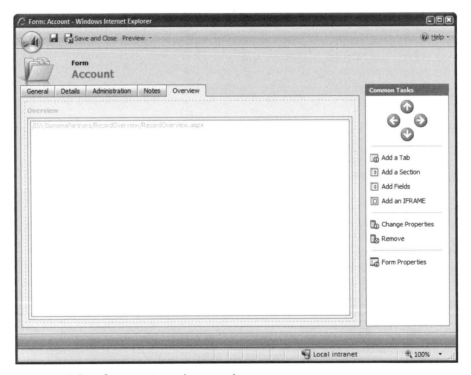

FIGURE 5-20 Form for account overview example

If you double-click this IFrame to view its properties, you'll see the configuration shown in Figure 5-21.

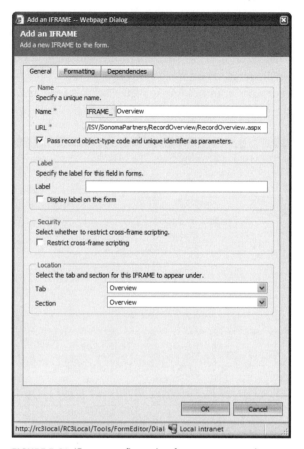

FIGURE 5-21 IFrame configuration for account overview example

We created a custom Web page named RecordOverview.aspx that reads the query string information to look up the exact record the user is viewing. From there, the custom page queries the associated records such as activities and contacts to display them on the page per our request. It's really pretty straightforward!

> **Important** By carefully matching the styles and colors of Microsoft Dynamics CRM on your custom Web pages embedded in IFrames, you can make custom Web pages "invisible" to your users so that they can't tell when they're working with the standard versus the custom Web pages. This leads to a better user experience, so we highly recommend that you try your best to match the fonts, colors, and so on.

IFrames are one of the most exciting form customization tools available in Microsoft Dynamics CRM because they open so many customization and integration options.

Displaying Related Records in an IFrame

In addition to the account overview example that uses a custom Web page to display related records, you can also use IFrames to reference existing Microsoft Dynamics CRM Web pages for the same purpose. In this example, you will display the activity history on the Lead form using IFrames along with the form *onLoad* event (Figure 5-22).

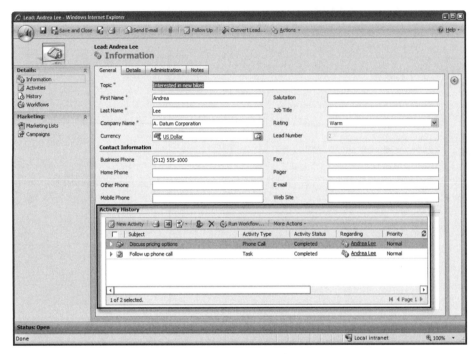

FIGURE 5-22 Displaying the activity history on the Lead form using IFrames

1. Open the lead form editor and add a section called **Activity History** and display the label. Then, add an IFrame named **ActivityHistory**. Type **about:blank** for the URL and make sure you select the Pass record object-type code and unique identifier as parameters check box. Finally, clear the Restrict cross-frame scripting option to allow the features of the activity history to function properly.

2. Click Form Properties, and then click *onLoad*. Add the following script:

```
//script to display activity history
var CRM_FORM_TYPE_CREATE = 1;
if (crmForm.FormType == CRM_FORM_TYPE_CREATE )
{
  document.all.IFRAME_ActivityHistory.src="about:blank";
}
else
```

```
{
  var navActivityHistory;
  navActivityHistory = document.all.navActivityHistory;
  if (navActivityHistory != null)
  {
    document.all.IFRAME_ActivityHistory.src="/sfa/leads/areas.aspx?oId="  +
    crmForm.ObjectId + "&oType=4&security=852023&tabSet=areaActivityHistory";
  }
  else
  {
    alert("navHistory Not Found");
  }
}
```

3. Click Event is Enabled, and then click OK twice.

4. Save the form, and then publish the Lead entity.

Even if you're not familiar with JavaScript, try to follow along with the code. Every time the Lead form opens, it fires the *onLoad* script, which then dynamically changes the IFrame URL from about:blank to the URL sfa/leads/areas.aspx appended with the unique parameters for the Lead record. The script also checks the form type to make sure that it doesn't perform this update when creating a new Lead for obvious reasons (there's no history or unique ID at that time).

So, this is a clever way to display the associated activity history on a form by using one of the Microsoft Dynamics CRM Web pages areas.aspx! Of course, this type of customization in which you reference existing .aspx pages is not officially supported by Microsoft, but it's a pretty low-risk customization that you may enjoy. You can also modify this script to work with other entities (including custom entities) by modifying the URL and oType as necessary. You can find the URL and oType information for other areas of the system by navigating to the entity activity history page, right-clicking the grid, and examining the URL in the properties value.

Customizing Views

Microsoft Dynamics CRM uses views to display multiple records at one time. You can customize almost all of the views used in Microsoft Dynamics CRM to display just the data that you want your users to see. In addition, you can also create entirely new views to display differ-ent data sets. First, we define the various components of a view, as shown in Figure 5-23:

- **Quick Find**   Users can enter search terms and click Find to search within the view.

- **View Filter**   This list shows all of the predefined views available to the user.

- **Grid** The grid displays the records for the view in rows and columns.

- **Grid toolbar** With the grid toolbar, users can perform additional actions on the records in the grid. Users can select more than one record at a time to perform these grid toolbar actions (such as assigning records or exporting data to Microsoft Office Excel).

- **Columns** Each view consists of one or more data columns. Users can click the column header to sort the view's records in ascending order (A to Z). Clicking the column header a second time sorts the records in the opposite order (descending, from Z to A).

- **Index** Users can click an Index letter to quickly filter the records shown in the view.

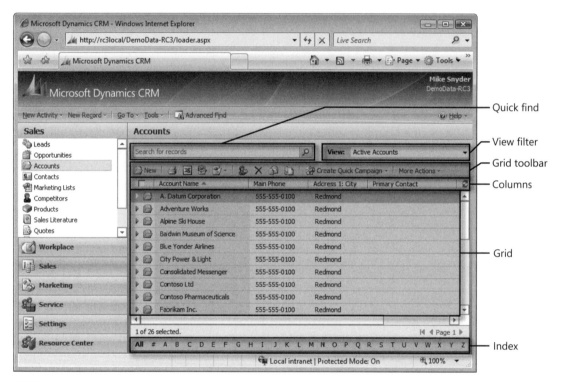

FIGURE 5-23 View components

To customize views, in the Customization section of Microsoft Dynamics CRM, click Customize Entities. Then, double-click the entity that you want to modify, and click Forms and Views in the navigation pane.

Tip People frequently use the term *grid* interchangeably with the term *view* in regard to Microsoft Dynamics CRM.

View Types

Microsoft Dynamics CRM uses three types of views:

- Public Views
- System-Defined Views
- Saved Views

Saved Views are different from the other two views because you do not manage them in the Customization section of Microsoft Dynamics CRM. Rather, you use the Advanced Find tools to create, modify, and delete Saved Views.

Public Views

Not surprisingly, any Microsoft Dynamics CRM user can access Public Views for an entity. All of the Public Views appear in the View Filter for each entity. You can also specify a Default Public View for each entity. The Default Public View loads the first time a user browses to an entity area. Therefore, if you want to create a new view for Accounts that every user will see the first time he or she browses to the Account workspace, create a new view and set it as the Default Public View for the Account entity. You can change the Default Public View in the entity editor by selecting the view that you want to make the default (single click it), and then clicking Set Default on the More Actions menu, as shown in Figure 5-24.

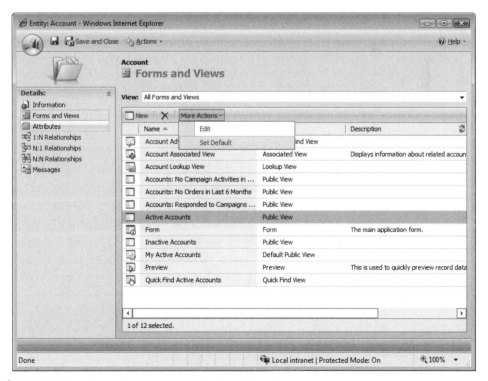

FIGURE 5-24 Setting a different view as the Default Public View

System-Defined Views

Microsoft Dynamics CRM includes five System-Defined Views:

- Associated View

- Advanced Find View

- Lookup View

- Quick Find View

- Preview

Similar to system entities, Microsoft Dynamics CRM automatically creates these System-Defined Views upon installation of the software. Each serves a unique purpose in the user interface, so the software constrains your ability to modify any System-Defined View. In particular, Microsoft Dynamics CRM implements a few notable customization restrictions with all of these views:

- Only one of each System-Defined View can exist for an entity.

- You cannot delete any of the System-Defined Views.

- You cannot use the user interface to configure filtering in the System-Defined Views because the system relationships define the records that Microsoft Dynamics CRM displays in each view.

> **Tip** Some system views contain filter information in the customization XML. For instance, the Associated View displays only active records. Should you want to display all records, regardless of state, you could export the entity's customization XML file, manually update the filter, and then import the revised customization file back into Microsoft Dynamics CRM. Chapter 9 provides an example of how to accomplish this type of customization.

Next, we discuss how Microsoft Dynamics CRM uses each of these views and how you can customize them.

Associated View   When you look at the records related to an entity, Microsoft Dynamics CRM displays the related active records using the Associated View. For example, when you view the Contacts related to an Account, Microsoft Dynamics CRM uses the Associated View of the Contact to display the records (Figure 5-25). When you look up the Sub-Accounts of an Account, Microsoft Dynamics CRM displays the Associated View of the Account entity.

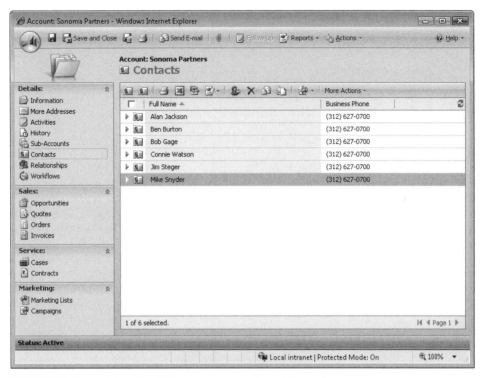

FIGURE 5-25 Contact Associated View as seen on an Account record

Therefore, if you want to add a Contact's title to the view in Figure 5-25, you would edit the Contact Associated View even though you're actually viewing an Account record. Because only one Associated View exists per entity, you cannot display different views based on the related entity. For example, both Lead and Opportunity reference the Activity Associated View. If you change the Activity Associated View, this change appears on both Leads *and* Opportunities.

Advanced Find View   With the Advanced Find View for an entity, you can define the default columns that appear when users use the Advanced Find feature. Figure 5-26 shows the Advanced Find View for Contacts.

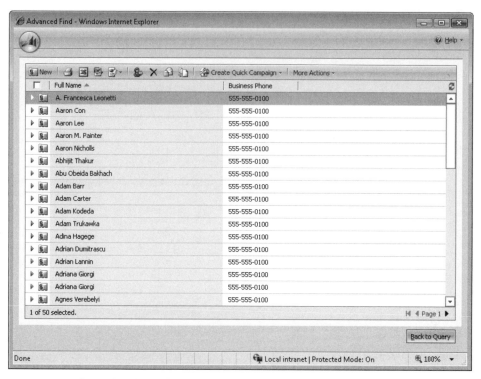

FIGURE 5-26 Advanced Find View for Contacts

Note that users can easily edit the columns that appear in the Advanced Find results, as shown in Figure 5-27, but their updates will not change the Advanced Find View for the entity.

So, every time a user creates a new Advanced Find, the columns from that entity's Advanced Find View are the default results.

Lookup View When users click the Lookup button (the magnifying glass), a Look Up Records dialog box appears in which users can search for a particular record. Figure 5-28 shows the Contact Lookup View that users see when they select a Primary Contact for an Account.

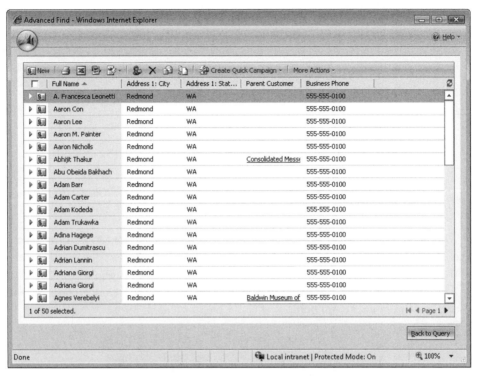

FIGURE 5-27 Advanced Find columns that have been edited by a user

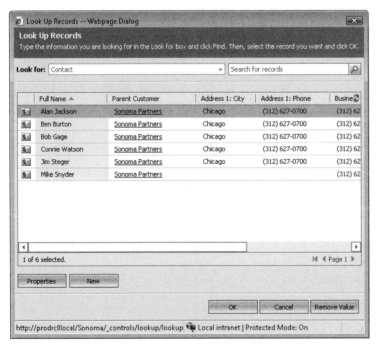

FIGURE 5-28 Contact Lookup View

You can define the columns that appear in the Look Up Records dialog box by editing the Lookup View for an entity. In addition to modifying the columns in the view, you can also add Find Columns to the view. By adding Find Columns, Microsoft Dynamics CRM will search for data in all of the Find Columns when users enter text to search for. For example, the default Find Columns for Contact are the following:

- E-mail
- First Name
- Middle Name
- Last Name
- Full Name

When a user searches for a record by entering text into the Look Up Records dialog box, Microsoft Dynamics CRM queries data in the Find Columns to retrieve matching records. Therefore, if you search for a Contact by entering the Contact's phone number in the Look Up Records dialog box, Microsoft Dynamics CRM will not return any records because the phone number field is not one of the Find Columns (Figure 5-29).

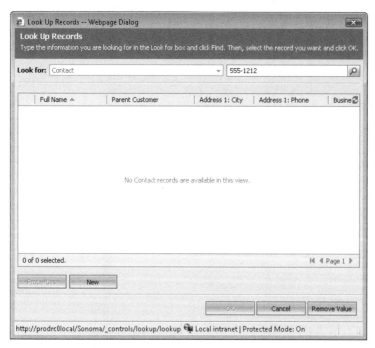

FIGURE 5-29 Results of a phone number search using the default Find Columns

However, if you edit the Lookup View by adding Business Phone as a Find Column, your users can search for customers by entering the customers' phone numbers.

Adding the Business Phone number as a Find Column in the Contact Lookup View

1. In the Customization section of Microsoft Dynamics CRM, click Customize Entities.

2. Double-click the Contact entity, and click Forms and Views in the navigation pane.

3. Double-click the Contacts Lookup View, and then click Add Find Columns in the Common Tasks pane. The Add Find Columns dialog box opens.

4. In the list of attributes for the Contact, select the Business Phone check box, and then click OK.

5. Click the Save and Close button on the View Editor toolbar.

6. In the entity editor, publish the Contact entity by clicking Publish under the Actions menu bar button.

The next time a user enters a phone number in the Look Up Records dialog box, Microsoft Dynamics CRM will also search the Business Phone column for matching records. Figure 5-30 shows the search results.

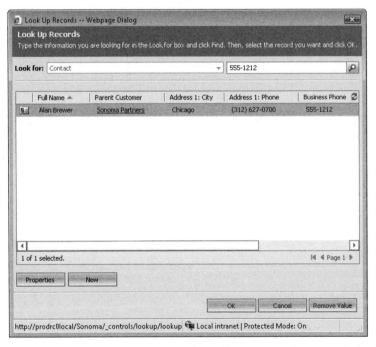

FIGURE 5-30 Contact record returned after adding Business Phone as a Find Column

 Caution Use care when adding Find Columns. If your database contains many records, adding additional Find Columns can have a performance impact because those columns may not necessarily be indexed in the database. Only include the columns you require, or work with the Microsoft Dynamics CRM support team to add the proper indexes.

In addition to phone numbers, you may also want to add the Contact's Social Security number or a unique customer number (ID) as a Find Column to help users find records more quickly.

> **Important** When users enter search values, please note that Microsoft Dynamics CRM will search for the value as is; it will not search for substrings by default. For example, if you search for "555-1212" and the Contact's Business Phone is "(312) 555-1212," Microsoft Dynamics CRM will not find a match. The software tries to find all records that start with "555-1212," but this record doesn't start with that value. To return this Contact record in a search result, you would need to search for "(312) 555-1212" or "(312)." Obviously, there may be times when you don't know the exact value you're searching for. Therefore, in Microsoft Dynamics CRM you can enter an asterisk (*) as a wildcard character in your searches (both Quick Find and Lookup). So, if you do not know the phone number area code, you could search for "*555-1212" and Microsoft Dynamics CRM would find the matching record.

Quick Find View On the main entity pages, users can search for records by using the Quick Find feature. To do this, simply type a search value in the Look For box and click Find. Microsoft Dynamics CRM then searches for matching records and returns the results using the Quick Find View of the entity. Note that the Quick Find View in the View Filter appears as "Search Results." Figure 5-31 shows the Account's Quick Find View.

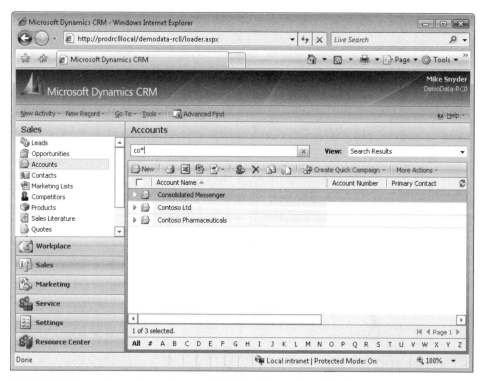

FIGURE 5-31 Accounts search results using Quick Find View and a wildcard character

As with the Lookup View, you can customize the Find Columns of the Quick Find View, allowing users to search for records across the entity attributes that you specify.

Preview   When you are looking at records in a grid, the Preview shows additional information about a record without requiring you to open the record in a new window. Users can display the Preview for a record, as shown in Figure 5-32, by clicking the arrow in the far left column.

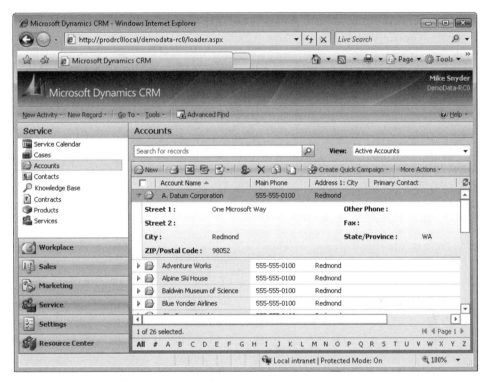

FIGURE 5-32 Preview of an Account record

If you double-click the Preview record in the Forms and Views grid of the entity editor, you'll see the Preview form editor, which looks and behaves like the form editor. Editing the Preview will update the information that users see when they click the Preview arrow. For the Preview form, you can only add fields, remove fields, and change field properties. Not every entity in Microsoft Dynamics CRM includes a Preview.

Saved Views

As a reminder, you do not manage Saved Views in the Customization section of Microsoft Dynamics CRM. When users create new views using the Advanced Find feature, they can save their work as a Saved View. Saved Views have many of the same attributes as the Public and System-Defined Views, but they also have a couple of unique distinctions.

Saved Views can be activated or deactivated, unlike Public and System-Defined Views. Only active views appear in the view name filter. This feature is very beneficial when you are creating a new view and you don't want to see it in your view name filter until it's complete.

Saved Views also have user ownership. This means that they can be assigned to a specific user, and they will follow the Microsoft Dynamics CRM security rules. The Saved View permission is part of the Security Role configuration, so you can specify which security roles can, for example, read, write, or delete Saved Views. The Saved View ownership and Microsoft Dynamics CRM security configuration determine the Saved View records that users can access. However, the Public and System-Defined Views exist across the entire system so that all users can access them. If you create a Saved View that you want to share with everyone, one way to accomplish this is to share the Saved View with a team that every user belongs to or create it as a Public View.

Customizing Views

Now that you understand the different view types, we will discuss in detail how to customize these views to show the data that you want to see. To edit a view, simply double-click the view name in the Forms and Views grid of the entity editor. All of the views use the same editor tool, shown in Figure 5-33.

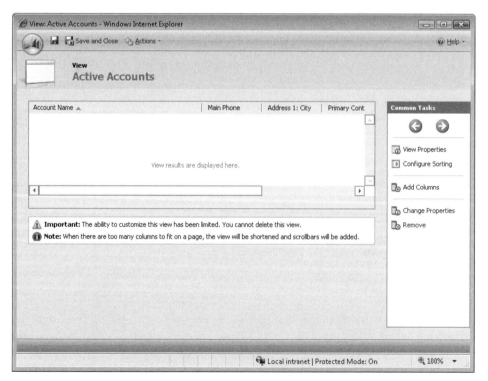

FIGURE 5-33 Active Accounts view editor

Similar to the form editor, the Common Tasks pane offers several tools to customize a view:

- **Directional arrows**   Select a column header, and then use these arrows to move it to the left or right in your view.

- **View Properties**   Use this tool to change the name of the view. The view's name appears in the View Filter.

- **Edit Filter Criteria**   The Edit Filter Criteria tool gives you the opportunity to create complex criteria that refine the data that each view returns. You can specify view filter criteria only if you create a new view; you cannot use this feature on the System-Defined views installed with Microsoft Dynamics CRM (like the view shown in Figure 5-33). The Edit Filter Criteria tool uses the same user interface as the Advanced Find feature to create your data query.

- **Configure Sorting**   Use this tool to specify the default order in which the view should sort the records. You can choose to sort by any one column in ascending or descending order. If you closely examine the view editor, you may notice that the default sort order column header has a small arrow that points up (for ascending) or down (for descending). Unfortunately, there is no way to automatically add a second or third sort order.

- **Add View Columns**   Use this feature to add additional columns to the view. In addition to adding attributes of the entity to the view, Microsoft Dynamics CRM allows you to add attributes from related entities. For example, you could choose to display the account relationship type attribute in a contact view. To access the attributes of related entities, select the entity name in the picklist and Microsoft Dynamics CRM will update the list of attributes you can choose from.

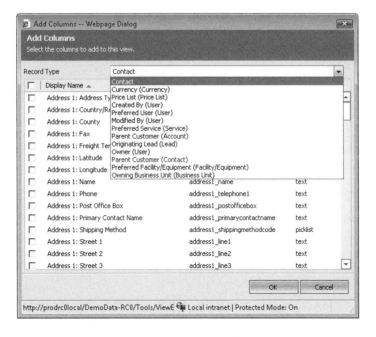

By default, new columns are added to the far right. For views in which you cannot add Find Columns, Microsoft Dynamics CRM labels this tool as Add Columns. If you select a column header and then add a View Column, Microsoft Dynamics CRM places the new column to the right of the selected column. This tip can save you some clicks if you have a view with many columns.

- **Add Find Columns**   As discussed previously, with this feature you can specify which columns Microsoft Dynamics CRM should search for matching records. The Add Find Columns feature does not apply to all views.

- **Change Properties**   If you want to change the width of a column in the view, select the column header, and then click Change Properties. You can specify the column's width in pixels (abbreviated as "px" in the user interface). For certain types of columns, you can select the Enable presence for this column check box if you want to display the Microsoft Office SharePoint Server 2007 presence indicator in the view.

- **Remove**   Use this option to remove a column from the view.

Tip Even though you can add columns from related entities to a view, you can only configure the default view sorting using attributes from the primary entity.

When you install Microsoft Dynamics CRM, the software creates System-Defined Views for each entity. To make sure that the software always functions correctly, Microsoft Dynamics CRM restricts your ability to customize these views. When you edit one of these restricted views, Microsoft Dynamics CRM displays a warning as shown earlier in Figure 5-33.

Caution When you add a column to a view, Microsoft Dynamics CRM displays the attribute name as that column's header. If you add a column from a related entity, Microsoft Dynamics CRM automatically appends the related entity's name in parentheses after the attribute name in the column header. Unfortunately, you cannot customize the column header names in the view.

Now we walk through creating two sample views to show you how to create custom views:

- My Direct Reports' Overdue Activities
- Opportunity Relationships

Sample View: My Direct Reports' Overdue Activities

Managers commonly want to view which of their direct reports are falling behind schedule and which are completing their activities on time. We show you how to create an Activity view to quickly mine the Microsoft Dynamics CRM database for this information.

Creating an Overdue Activities custom view

1. In the Customization section of Microsoft Dynamics CRM, click Customize Entities.

2. Double-click the Activity entity, and click Views in the navigation pane of the entity editor.

3. Click New on the grid toolbar to create a new view.

4. In the Properties dialog box, type the view name **My Direct Reports' Overdue Activities**, and then click OK.

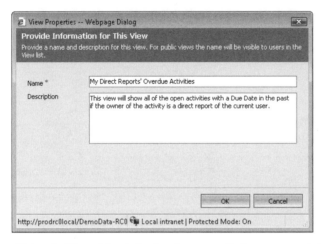

5. Click Edit Filter Criteria in the Common Tasks pane, and the Edit Filter Criteria dialog box opens.

6. Rest the cursor on (or click) Select. Under the Fields group of the picklist, select Activity Status. Next, click Enter Value and click the ellipsis button (…) that appears.

7. The Select Values dialog box opens. Under the Available Values section, select Open, and then click the **>>** button. Click OK to close the Select Values dialog box. With the Activity Status filter set to Open, the view will select only records that have not been completed or canceled.

8. To filter the open Activities to show only those with a Due Date in the past, rest the cursor on (or click) Select, and then select Due Date, which is listed under the Fields group.

9. Click to the right of the Due Date picklist. Microsoft Dynamics CRM will display a picklist of different date operators from which you can select. However, notice that there is no "in the past" or "overdue" option. If you try to choose On or Before, Microsoft Dynamics CRM prompts you to enter a specific date. Therefore, if you use On or Before

and enter a date value, you would have to update the view every day to show overdue activities. You obviously don't want to do this, so use this simple workaround: Set the Due Date evaluation picklist to Last X Years and type **99** in the Enter Value field. Now Microsoft Dynamics CRM will display all open Activities with a Due Date in the last 99 years.

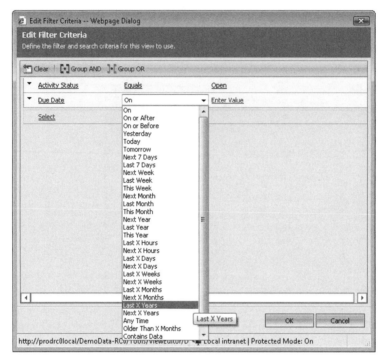

10. So far, the view will return open Activities with a Due Date in the last 99 years, but you want to only see the activities assigned to the manager's direct reports. To add this filter, rest the cursor on (or click) Select again. In the picklist, scroll down to the Related grouping and choose Owner.

11. Rest the cursor on (or click) the Select link that appears under Owner. Under the Fields group, select Manager, leave the default operator value of Equals Current User selected, and click OK to close the Edit Filter Criteria dialog box.

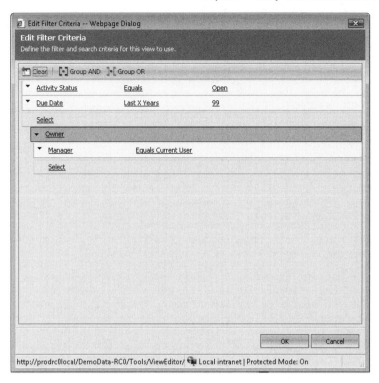

12. Add the columns you want to display in your view. By default, Microsoft Dynamics CRM includes the Subject in new Activity views, so just add the following columns by clicking Add Columns in the Common Tasks pane: Activity Type, Date Created, Due Date, Last Updated, Owner, and Priority.

13. Reorder the columns in the view. Use the left and right arrows to put the columns in the following order from left to right: Activity Type, Subject, Priority, Date Created, Last Updated, Due Date, Owner.

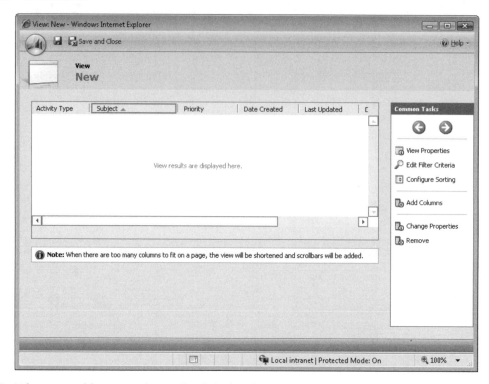

14. When you add a new column, the default column width is 100 pixels (100px). Click Change Properties to change the width of the columns so that the width of the Priority column is 75 pixels (75px) and the width of the Due Date column is 125 pixels (125px).

15. Specify the default sort order to show the most overdue activities first. To do so, click Configure Sorting and select Due Date in ascending order. Click OK.

16. Click Save and Close on the view editor toolbar to complete the view customization.

17. To publish the view, click Activity in the Customize Entities list, and then click Publish on the grid toolbar.

18. A "Publishing customizations" message appears. When the message disappears, you can use your new view.

19. Browse to the Activities section in the Workplace area and select My Direct Reports' Overdue Activities in the View Filter.

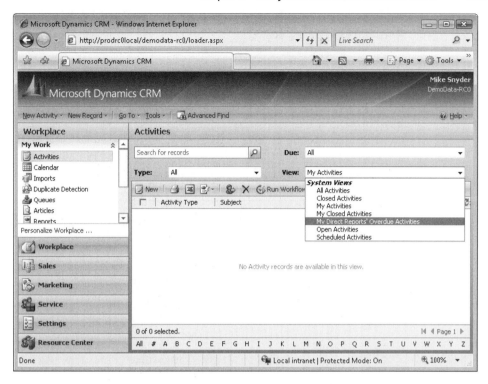

If you don't see the records you expect, confirm that each user's manager record is set correctly. You can view a user's manager in his or her user record. To view a user's record, go to the Settings section of Microsoft Dynamics CRM and click Users. Then, double-click the user's name to open the record and set the user's Manager by using the Change Manager feature located on the Actions menu.

Sample View: Opportunity Relationships

Microsoft Dynamics CRM allows users to enter Opportunity relationships to track Accounts and Contacts related to each Opportunity. For example, if you want to track the many different influencers (contacts) on a potential sale, you would set up and configure an Opportunity Relationship for the influencers. If you later want to run a marketing campaign to thank these influencers for helping you win new business this year, a view would be a good way to find these key people quickly.

Creating a Referred Deal custom view

1. In the Customization section of Microsoft Dynamics CRM, click Customize Entities.

2. Double-click the Contact entity, and then click Forms and Views in the navigation pane.

3. Click New on the grid toolbar to create a new view, and enter the view name **Influenced Deals We Won**.

4. Click Edit Filter Criteria in the Common Tasks pane, and the Edit Filter Criteria dialog box opens.

5. Scroll down the picklist to the Related grouping, and select Opportunity Relationships (Customer). Rest the cursor on (or click) the Select link that appears under Opportunity Relationships (Customer), and choose the Customer Role value that appears under the Fields grouping. Leave the default criterion condition of Equals, and then click the Lookup button. Use the Lookup dialog box to select Influencer.

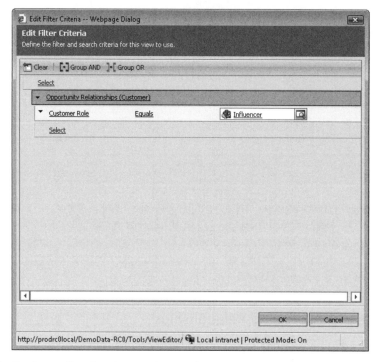

6. Further refine the view to show only those Contacts that referred an Opportunity that turned into revenue. Rest the cursor on (or click) the Select link that appears under the Clear button. Scroll down to the Related grouping values, and select Opportunities (Potential Customer). Note that there is also an Opportunity under Fields, but you want the value listed under Related.

7. Rest the cursor on (or click) the Select link that appears under the Opportunities (Potential Customer), and select the picklist value of Status. Next, set the criterion to Won.

8. Repeat this process and select Actual Close Date with a criterion of This Year.

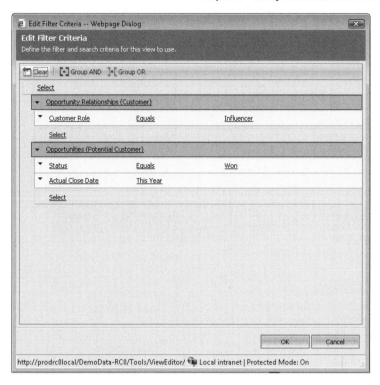

9. When your criteria are identical to those shown in the preceding screen shot, click OK to return to the view editor.

10. Now add any additional columns you'd like to include by clicking Add Columns in the Common Tasks pane.

11. Click Save on the view editor toolbar, and then publish the Contact entity.

12. When you browse to the Account records, you will see the Influenced Deals We Won view in the View Name List. From this view, you could easily click Create Quick Campaign to automatically assign Phone Call activities to ensure that you personally thank each contact for his or her influence on a deal.

Customizing Activities

Activities are the heart and soul of any customer relationship management (CRM) system, including Microsoft Dynamics CRM. The main purpose of any CRM system is to effectively track and manage all of the sales, service, and marketing data related to your customers, and Microsoft Dynamics CRM stores the vast majority of this data (also known as *touch points*) as Activities. As with the Lead, Account, Contact, and Opportunity entities, you can perform many of the customizations we've discussed so far on Activities, such as adding attributes, customizing views, and renaming entities.

> **Important** Microsoft Dynamics CRM uses an entity named Activity (schema name of *activity-pointer*) to act as the parent of multiple other entities such as Task, Fax, Phone Call, E-mail, and so on. Microsoft Dynamics CRM also refers to these subentities as Activities because they're child entities of the parent Activity entity.

However, because Activities are so important to Microsoft Dynamics CRM, we want to explicitly cover some Activity-specific customizations. The default Microsoft Dynamics CRM installation contains approximately 16 different types of Activities (child entities of the Activity entity):

- Task
- Fax
- Phone Call
- E-mail
- Letter
- Appointment
- Service Activity
- Campaign Response
- Campaign Activity
- Order Close
- Quote Close
- Opportunity Close
- Quick Campaign
- Case Resolution
- System Job
- Bulk Operation Log

Microsoft Dynamics CRM predefines all of the system relationships between the Activity and its related children entities. Because the Activity entities manage many of the software's inner workings, Microsoft Dynamics CRM restricts your ability to customize some of these entities. Consequently, you cannot add any custom attributes to the Activity entity or modify any of the relationships between the Activity entity and its related entities. As a matter of fact, the Activity entity doesn't even have a form for you to customize.

> **Tip** Microsoft Dynamics CRM automatically creates some Activities such as Order Close and Opportunity Close when users close those records. You can reference these autocreated Activities for reporting purposes and viewing a record's history.

Figure 5-34 summarizes the differences between the Activity entity and its child entities.

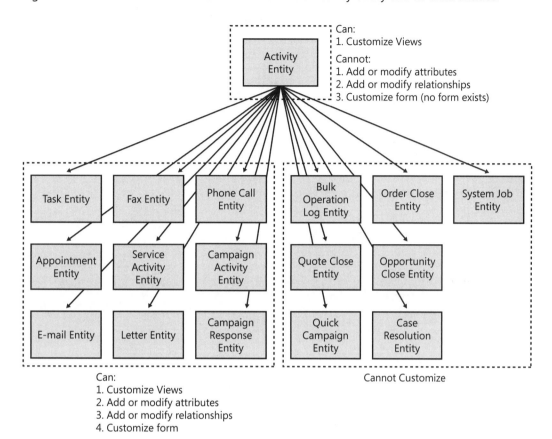

FIGURE 5-34 Differences between the Activity entity and some of its related entities

However, just because Microsoft Dynamics CRM restricts customization of the parent Activity entity, don't make the mistake of thinking that Activities cannot be customized. So, even though you cannot add attributes to the Activity entity, you can add attributes to the child Activity entities such as Task, Phone Call, and Letter.

> **Important**   You add custom Activity attributes on the different activity entities, such as Task, Phone Call, Appointment, and so on, but you cannot add attributes to the Activity entity. Although you cannot add attributes to the Activity entity, you can customize the Activity entity views.

Activity Views

You use the same process to customize the views of Activities that you use for the other customizable entities, but we want to highlight a few view customization nuances.

Workplace Activities

When users first log on to Microsoft Dynamics CRM, the default start page is the Activities page in the Workplace.

 Tip Each user can specify a different start page by clicking the Tools menu, and then clicking Options.

From the Activities page, users can quickly and easily filter through all of their Activity records. In addition to the View Filter and the Quick Find feature that appear on the other pages, the Activities page also allows users to filter the records by using the Type and Date criteria, as shown in Figure 5-35.

FIGURE 5-35 The Activities page, showing Type and Date filters

The Type and Date activity filters are hard-coded into Microsoft Dynamics CRM, so you cannot add your own custom values into these filter picklists. However, you can modify the data columns that Microsoft Dynamics CRM searches when users use the Quick Find feature. In addition, you can create new views that appear in the View Filter. However, the View Filter behaves differently on the Activities page from how it behaves on other pages in the system: Changing the Activity Type filter changes the list of view names that users can select in the View Filter. Everywhere else in Microsoft Dynamics CRM, the View Filter list always contains the same list of views, and it does not update dynamically. From the Activities page, users can immediately access more than 30 different activity views.

When you want to customize the default Activity views or start creating new views, you need to know that the Activity entity controls the views for the All filter, but all of the other Activity views are contained in their individual entity record. This is important to consider because the Activity entity contains only attributes that are common to all of the entities. So, you could not add a child entity–specific attribute such as Phone Call Phone Number to any of the views that appear in the All filter. The same constraint applies to the Quick Find feature on the Activities page. You can include Find Columns only from an Activity entity that includes common Activity attributes but does not include any of the attributes unique to the individual Activity types.

Entity Activity Views

In addition to the Workplace Activity views, two additional Activity views that contain special features are the Activities and History views that appear for the following entities: Lead, Contact, Account, Opportunity, Quote, Order, Invoice, Case, and Contract. Figure 5-36 shows the Activities views on the Account entity.

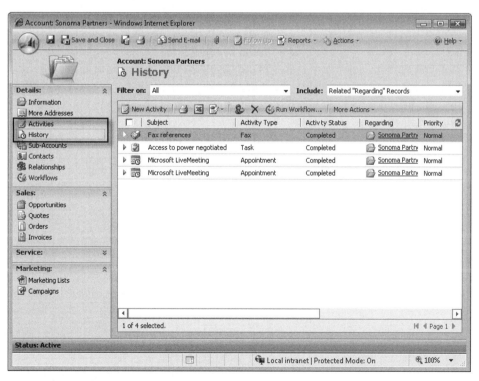

FIGURE 5-36 Activities views on an Account record

Even though both of these views display Activities related to the entity, clicking History in the navigation pane shows only completed Activities. Clicking Activities in the navigation pane displays only open activities. To customize the columns that appear when users click Activities in the navigation pane, you must edit the Open Activity Associated View of the Activity entity. To customize the view that appears when users click History in the navigation pane, you must edit the Closed Activity Associated View of the Activity entity. Again, because these views display different types of Activities entities (Phone Call, Task, Fax, and so on), you can display only the columns from the parent Activity entity.

Activity Attributes and Forms

As we just explained, some of the Activity views behave a little differently from the non-Activity views in Microsoft Dynamics CRM. Likewise, customizing the Activity attributes and forms involves a few additional wrinkles that you should be aware of. You can, of course, customize the form for most of the child Activity entities. However, Microsoft Dynamics CRM uses several special system fields that appear on most of the Activity forms (such as Duration and Due Date Time) that behave differently from regular attributes and forms. The following subsections discuss some of the Activity attribute and form restrictions.

Adding Picklist Values to the Duration Field

Some of the Activity entities use a special Duration field that appears on their form. This Duration field displays more than 20 picklist values such as 1 minute, 5 minutes, and 1 hour. If you want to add a new value of 2 minutes, you might expect that you could simply add a new picklist value for the Duration attribute. However, if you browse to the attributes of the Phone Call entity, you will notice that both the *Scheduled Duration* and *Actual Duration* attributes are read-only integers, not a *picklist* data type, so you cannot add a new value. If this was a standard picklist attribute, you could simply edit the picklist values from this screen, which you obviously can't do here.

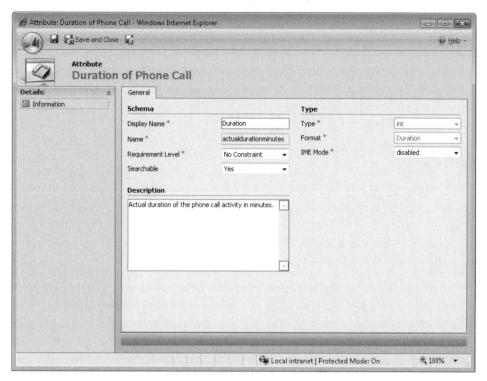

Even though you can't add new picklist values to the Duration attribute, users can simply type a new value in the field when they are entering Activity data. To do so, they simply select a value in the picklist, and then click in the Duration field to enter a new value, such as 2 minutes. This data is saved correctly in the database as 2 minutes. The database stores the duration in whole minutes, so you can enter 2.25 hours (135 minutes), but you cannot enter 15.25 minutes; Microsoft Dynamics CRM automatically converts 15.25 minutes to 15 minutes.

Adding Picklist Values to Due Date Time

The default picklist values are every 30 minutes for the Due Date Time field, and you cannot add new interval values. However, as with the Duration field, users can simply type their own values (such as 12:15 P.M.) in the Due Date Time field.

Organizing Category and Sub-Category data

The default data type for the Category and Sub-Category data fields is *nvarchar*, so users can enter any text value in these fields. This free-form text option can make it difficult for companies to track and filter Activities by category because users might type different values to mean the same thing. For example, one person may type "Sales," and another user may type "Sales Calls." You could enforce a more standardized approach by creating new attributes or even creating a relationship to a new custom entity. In addition, the Category and Sub-Category fields in Microsoft Dynamics CRM do not correlate or link with the Category field for tasks that the Microsoft Dynamics CRM client for Microsoft Office Outlook synchronizes to your Outlook tasks.

Summary

In this chapter, you learned more about entity customization, with a focus on forms and views. Each customizable entity has a form that you can customize by adding fields, tabs, and sections. You also learned how to use the form and field events, *onLoad*, *onSave*, and *onChange*, to add more advanced customizations with scripts. You learned the details and benefits of adding an IFrame to the form of an entity.

Each of the view types that Microsoft Dynamics CRM uses to display data throughout the system were reviewed. You saw what each of the system-defined views does, and how you can customize the views to show only the data that you want to see. Finally, you learned about some of the nuances related to activity customization, such as the activity views and attributes.

Chapter 6
Entity Customization: Relationships, Custom Entities, and Site Map

> **In this chapter:**
>

In Chapter 4, "Entity Customization: Concepts and Attributes," and Chapter 5, "Entity Customization: Forms and Views," you learned how to customize entities by modifying their attributes, forms, and views. Those chapters primarily focus on customizing the entities that Microsoft Dynamics CRM installs by default. However, in Microsoft Dynamics CRM, you also can create entirely new entities to track and manage additional categories of data in your system. The new entities that you create are called *custom entities*. Before you create custom entities, you should understand how Microsoft Dynamics CRM uses and manages entity relationships.

In this chapter, we cover all of the details related to entity relationships, including data relationships, relationship behavior, and entity mapping. When you understand how to create custom entity relationships, you're ready to create custom entities. We walk you through the steps and configuration settings necessary to create custom entities, show you how to integrate custom entities with the default Microsoft Dynamics CRM entities, and highlight some of the tricks we've learned.

After you start creating custom entities, you will want to tweak and modify where they appear in the Microsoft Dynamics CRM application navigation. The last topic in this chapter explains how to use the Microsoft Dynamics CRM site map to customize and revise the user interface to blend in your custom entities and custom Web pages.

Understanding Entity Relationships

An *entity relationship* in Microsoft Dynamics CRM defines how two entities interact with each other. A Microsoft Dynamics CRM entity relationship definition includes multiple parameters:

- **Relationship definition** Specifies the nature of the data relationship between two entities (one-to-many, and many-to-many)

- **Relationship attribute**   Specifies the schema name and requirement level

- **Relationship navigation**   Determines how the entity relationships should appear in the Microsoft Dynamics CRM user interface

- **Relationship behavior**   Specifies how Microsoft Dynamics CRM manages data when users take actions against one of the entities in the relationship

- **Entity mapping**   Specifies how Microsoft Dynamics CRM maps common attributes that two entities share

Microsoft Dynamics CRM includes hundreds of default entity relationships, and you can modify these default relationships or create entirely new entity relationships. You will almost always create at least one relationship between a custom entity and the Microsoft Dynamics CRM default system entities. In reality, you will probably create between 5 and 50 custom entity relationships for each custom entity that you create, depending on the complexity of your data model. Consequently, it's critical that you understand entity relationships before you create any custom entities.

> **Important** You won't need to write a single line of programming code to create custom entities, but you do need a thorough understanding of the different entity relationship types and the custom relationships that Microsoft Dynamics CRM supports.

You can view all of an entity's relationships by using the entity editor in Microsoft Dynamics CRM. Figure 6-1 shows the some of the default entity relationships for the Lead entity.

This grid lists all the Lead entity relationships that Microsoft Dynamics CRM creates by default. To view the details of any one relationship, double-click a record in the grid. For example, double-click the record with the primary entity of Lead and the related entity of Contact, and you'll see the entity relationship editor shown in Figure 6-2.

You can use the relationship editor to view and configure all of the entity relationship parameters. In the next subsections, we review each component of an entity relationship definition, starting with the data relationship.

Relationship Definition

One purpose of entity relationships is to define the *data relationship* between two entities in the system. Unlike a traditional database, in which you might configure primary and foreign keys to manage data relationships, you use entity relationships in Microsoft Dynamics CRM to manage how data interacts in the system metadata. This metadata design gives you the opportunity to customize and manage the data relationships easily without having to touch the underlying system data (and database keys) in Microsoft SQL Server.

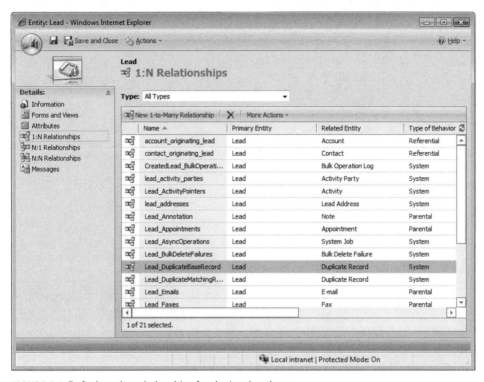

FIGURE 6-1 Default entity relationships for the Lead entity

Microsoft Dynamics CRM uses three types of data relationships:

- One-to-many
- Many-to-one
- Many-to-many

We review these concepts in more detail.

One-to-Many

One-to-many (abbreviated as 1:N) describes a relationship between two entities in which a single entity can possess multiple (many) related entities. For example, consider the default relationship between the Account and Contact entities in Microsoft Dynamics CRM. Each Account can have many Contacts, but you can assign only one Account to each Contact.

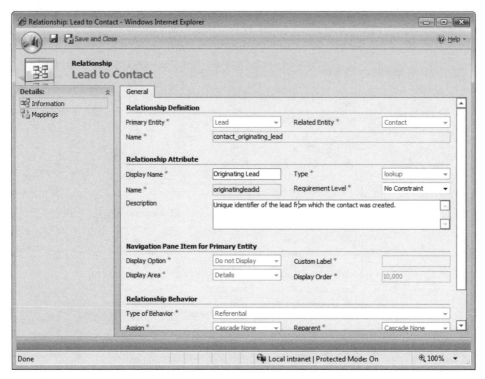

FIGURE 6-2 Relationship editor

As you browse through the Microsoft Dynamics CRM customization section, you might notice that the user interface uses different terminology interchangeably to describe the one-to-many data relationship (as shown in Table 6-1).

TABLE 6-1 Relationship Terminology

Perspective	Example 1	Example 2	Example 3
Account	One-to-many relationship to Contact	Parent relationship to Contact	Primary entity
Contact	Many-to-one relationship to Account	Child relationship to Account	Related entity

Although Microsoft Dynamics CRM uses different terminology to describe the one-to-many relationship, the user interface on an entity's form always displays one-to-many entities in a consistent manner. Figure 6-3 shows an example of the relationship between the Account and Contact entities on the Contact form. On the related entity's form (Contact), a *lookup field* labeled Parent Customer appears so that users can select the primary entity (Account).

Conversely, the related entity (Contact) does not appear on the form of the primary entity (Account). Rather, Microsoft Dynamics CRM adds a link in the navigation pane of the primary entity to a page that displays all of the related entities in a grid view, as shown in Figure 6-4.

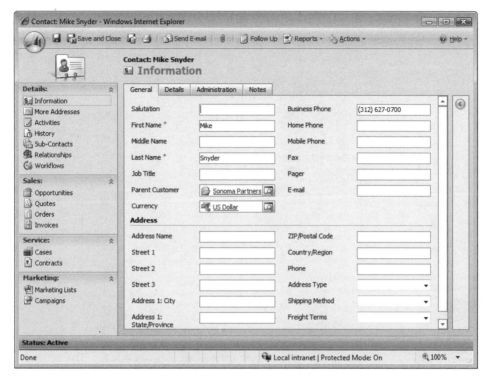

FIGURE 6-3 The primary entity displayed as a lookup on the related entity's form

Remembering how Microsoft Dynamics CRM displays primary and related entities in the user interface can help eliminate some confusion when you try to decide how to set up your custom entity relationships.

Many-to-One

As you would expect, many-to-one relationships (abbreviated as N:1) behave in the exact opposite manner as one-to-many relationships do. You refer to the relationship type (many-to-one or one-to-many) depending on which entity you're talking about.

Many-to-Many

Many-to-many is the third type of data relationship between entities in Microsoft Dynamics CRM. Consider the relationship between the Marketing List entity and the Marketing List members. You can create many marketing lists in Microsoft Dynamics CRM, and then you can assign multiple members to each list. In addition, you can add members to multiple marketing lists. You can describe this relationship as *many-to-many*. The Microsoft Dynamics CRM user interface always uses grids to display many-to-many relationships between two entities. Therefore, any time you see a lookup field on a form, you know that a one-to-many relationship exists between the two entities.

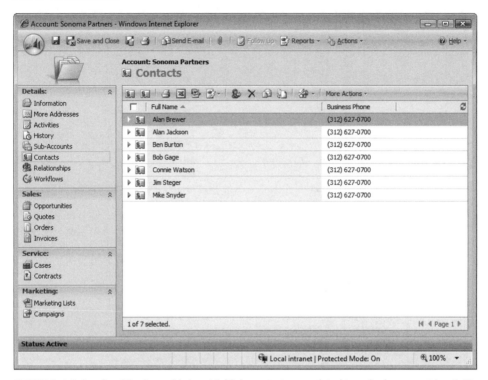

FIGURE 6-4 Related entities in a grid view. Multiple contacts are related to a single account in a 1 :N relationship between Account and Contact.

Relationship Attribute

The relationship attribute applies to one-to-many and many-to-one entity relationships. When you configure the relationship attribute, you specify the following parameters: Display name, Name (schema name), Requirement level, and Description. You might notice that these are the same parameters you specify when you add a custom attribute to an entity. Because these parameters behave the same way for the relationship attribute as they do for custom attributes, we don't recap how to use them, but you can refer to Chapter 4 for additional information.

> **Tip** Sometimes you might be confused about which name to enter in the Display Name field. Enter a name that describes the primary entity's relationship to the related entity, and remember you can easily modify the Display Name later, if necessary.

Relationship Navigation

As you saw in Figure 6-4, Microsoft Dynamics CRM links related entities in the navigation pane of the entity record. In that figure, the Contacts link displays all of the Contacts related to the Account. Microsoft Dynamics CRM offers you the flexibility of configuring how related entity information appears in the navigation pane. For all types of relationships, you can configure the following:

- Display option
- Display area
- Display order

We look at each of these options in more detail.

Display Option

You can choose from one of three options here:

- **Do not Display**   As you might guess, this option hides the related entity link in the navigation pane of the primary entity.

- **Use Custom Label**   When you select this option, the Custom Label field becomes active and you can enter the name that you want to appear in the navigation pane. Even though you can enter up to 50 characters in this field, only the first 17 characters fit in the navigation pane link. However, users can view the entire custom label name by resting their mouse on the navigation pane link to see the alt tag text.

- **Use Plural Name**   If you select this option, the plural name of the related entity will appear in the navigation pane. This can cause confusion for your users if multiple relationships exist between two entities; therefore, we recommend that you only use this option if one relationship exists between two entities.

Display Area

With this option, you can specify in which navigation pane group the related entity link will appear. The default navigation pane groups for all entities are as follows: Details, Sales, Service, and Marketing.

> **Tip** You cannot add new groups in the entity navigation pane, but you can rename these groups using the site map (as explained later in this chapter).

Display Order

If you add multiple links to the navigation pane, you may also want to specify in which order the links appear. For example, you might want the most frequently used links at the top and the less frequently used links at the bottom. Microsoft Dynamics CRM orders the additional links in the navigation pane from the lowest to the highest value of the display order. Therefore, to reorder the links simply enter new values in this field.

Relationship Behavior

In addition to understanding how Microsoft Dynamics CRM structures the data relationship between entities, you must understand the *relationship behavior* of entity relationships before you can map out your own custom entities and custom relationships. Entity relationships always exhibit one of two behaviors:

- Parental
- Referential

In the case of parental relationship behavior, actions that you take against the primary entity also apply to its related entities. With referential relationship behavior, any actions against the primary entity apply only to that entity, and none of its related entities. In Microsoft Dynamics CRM, only five actions are affected by relationship behaviors:

- Delete
- Assign
- Reparent
- Share
- Unshare

Consequently, if you take any other action against an entity in Microsoft Dynamics CRM (such as running a workflow rule), that action is not affected by the entity's parental or referential relationship behavior.

> **Tip** You might be wondering what the difference is between the assign action and the reparent action. When you assign an entity, you change the owner of the record from one user to a different user. When you reparent an entity, you change a record's parent entity by using the lookup tool. Changing the parent account of an Account is an example of reparenting an entity.

It's important to understand the differences between parental and referential behavior because you need to specify relationship behavior any time you create a relationship between two entities. Usually, you create at least one entity relationship for every custom entity. However, in Microsoft Dynamics CRM you also can modify the default relationship behavior between the default system entities. In the following subsections, we review parental and referential behavior in more detail. We also review a special kind of referential behavior known as Referential, Restrict Delete.

Parental Behavior

If the relationship between entities exhibits parental behavior, actions applied to the parent entity propagate down to all of its child entities. If you delete an Account record (the primary entity) such as the sample record for Coho Vineyard shown in Figure 6-5, Microsoft Dynamics CRM deletes all of that record's related data, including its Activity, Note, custom entity, and Opportunity records, because of the parental relationships those entity records have with the Account entity. Likewise, when Microsoft Dynamics CRM deletes the custom entity record and the Opportunity record, it determines whether it should also delete their related entities based on the various relationship behaviors specified.

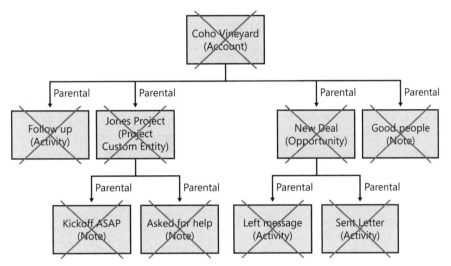

FIGURE 6-5 Parental relationships between entities

In the Coho Vineyard example, Microsoft Dynamics CRM deletes the Notes and Activities related to the custom entity record and the Opportunity because a parental relationship behavior exists between those entities. The software refers to this concept of working down the primary and related entity tree as *cascading*.

> **More Info** All of the default system entities, such as Leads, Accounts, and Contacts, possess a parental relationship with Activities and Notes by default. Therefore, any action you take against the parent entity cascades down to all of its Activities and Notes. For example, if five active and two completed Tasks exist for an Account and you reassign that Account to a new user, all of the Tasks (active and completed) will also be assigned to the new user. Many customers want to reconfigure this default relationship behavior between system entities because they do not want to change the owner of completed Activity records. We explain how to make this change in the section titled "Behavior Configuration Options" later in this chapter.

Referential Behavior

In the case of referential relationships, actions taken against the primary entity do not cascade down to its related entities. To demonstrate referential relationship behavior, we modified the previous example by adding a custom entity B with a referential child relationship to the Project custom entity (see Figure 6-6).

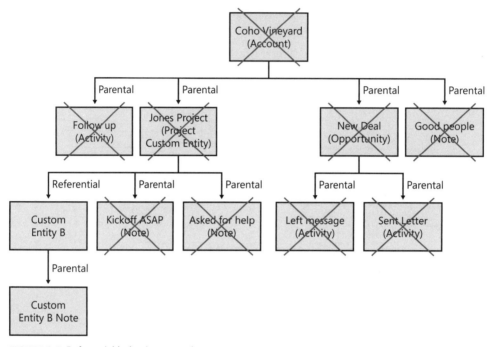

FIGURE 6-6 Referential behavior example

If you delete the Coho Vineyard Account shown in Figure 6-6, Microsoft Dynamics CRM deletes all of the records except custom entity B and its Note. Microsoft Dynamics CRM does not delete custom entity B because that entity has only a referential relationship to the Project custom entity. Microsoft Dynamics CRM deletes the Project custom entity because of the parental relationship behavior to its primary entity Account.

> **Important** Parental relationship behavior applies only to one-to-many and many-to-one entity relationships. All many-to-many relationships exhibit referential behavior.

Behavior Configuration Options

Now that you understand the difference between parental and referential relationship behavior, we examine how you use the relationship editor to configure these relationships in Microsoft Dynamics CRM. Figure 6-7 shows the relationship editor that appears when you create a new one-to-many relationship.

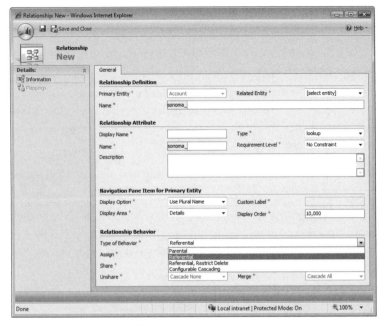

FIGURE 6-7 Entity relationship editor

In the Relationship Behavior section, you can choose from one of four values in the Type of Behavior list:

- Parental

- Referential

- Referential, Restrict Delete

- Configurable Cascading

Again, entity relationships can exhibit only parental or referential behavior, but Microsoft Dynamics CRM includes four options in this list because they represent different configuration options for how the parental and referential behavior should apply to the various actions.

Selecting Parental or Referential applies that behavior type to the entity relationship for all actions.

However the Referential, Restrict Delete option describes a special kind of referential behavior. If you choose Referential, Restrict Delete behavior, Microsoft Dynamics CRM does not allow the user to delete the parent entity if that entity has any related entities. Rather, Microsoft Dynamics CRM displays this error message to the user stating that "The record cannot be deleted because it is associated with another record." Consequently, Microsoft Dynamics CRM applies referential behavior to all of the other actions *except* the delete action.

If you choose Configurable Cascading, you can specify different cascading behaviors depending on the action that users take against the parent entity. For example, you can set up parental cascading behavior for delete actions against the parent, and then assign referential behavior for the assign action. For the assign, share, unshare, and reparent actions, you can configure one of four cascading rules:

- **Cascade All**   Perform the action on the parent entity and all of its child entities; equivalent to parental behavior.

- **Cascade Active**   Perform the action on the parent entity and all of its child entities where the status is active or open. You might select this option if you want to maintain a history of which users owned the previously completed Activities (Tasks, Phone Calls, and so on).

- **Cascade User Owned**   Perform the action on the parent entity and only those child entities for which the entity owner matches the parent entity owner.

- **Cascade None**   Perform the action on the parent entity only; equivalent to referential behavior.

A simple example can illustrate how these cascading rules work in the real world. Figure 6-8 shows an Account with four Tasks (two active, two completed) attached to it.

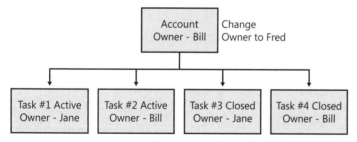

FIGURE 6-8 Account with four Tasks

If you take an action against the Account (the parent entity), such as changing the Account owner from Bill to Fred, the cascading behavior of the relationship between the Account and Task entities determines how Microsoft Dynamics CRM applies the same action (assign) to the children entities. Table 6-2 shows how Microsoft Dynamics CRM would assign the owners of the four tasks for each of the cascading behavior settings.

TABLE 6-2 Ownership Determined by Cascading Behavior

Type	Entity	Status	Original owner	Final owner			
				Cascade All (parental)	Cascade Active	Cascade User Owned	Cascade None (referential)
Parent	Account	Active	Bill	Fred	Fred	Fred	Fred
Child	Task 1	Active	Jane	Fred	Fred	Jane	Jane
Child	Task 2	Active	Bill	Fred	Fred	Fred	Bill
Child	Task 3	Closed	Jane	Fred	Jane	Jane	Jane
Child	Task 4	Closed	Bill	Fred	Bill	Fred	Bill

For the delete action, you can configure one of three behaviors:

- **Cascade All**   Delete the parent entity and all of its child entities; equivalent to parental behavior.

- **Remove Link**   Delete the link between the parent entity and the child entities, but do not delete the child entities; equivalent to referential behavior.

- **Restrict**   Prevent the user from deleting an entity that possesses child entities; equivalent to referential, restrict delete behavior.

Although a Merge picklist appears in the Relationship Behavior section, you cannot configure different relationship behaviors for that action. Merge always uses the cascade all (parental) behavior.

Note The merge functionality applies only to the Lead, Contact, and Account entities.

Entity Mapping

Entity mapping is another component of the relationship definition between two entities. Not every relationship between two entities includes an entity mapping, although every relationship must include a data relationship and relationship behavior. By using mapping, you can specify common attributes that two entities share. Entity mapping provides the benefits of saving your users time and reducing data entry errors by automatically *mapping* data from the primary entity to its related entity at the time the related record is created in Microsoft Dynamics CRM.

For example, if you add a related Contact to an Account, the default entity mapping between these entities automatically populates the address of the Contact with the same address as the Account. Without mappings, the user would have to retype the address information into the Contact even though it's identical to the address of the Account.

Important Microsoft Dynamics CRM maps entity attributes only at the time that it creates a related entity. Mapping does not continually keep data synchronized. Therefore, if the address of the Account (primary) record changes, Microsoft Dynamics CRM will not automatically map these changes to the Contact (related) records. This type of synchronization requires additional system customization with custom programming. We demonstrate an example of this custom programming in Chapter 9, "Microsoft Dynamics CRM 4.0 SDK." Or you can also use the bulk edit feature in Microsoft Dynamics CRM to update the address of multiple Contact records at one time.

Some of the scenarios in which Microsoft Dynamics CRM uses entity mappings include the following:

- Adding a related entity to a primary entity (clicking New on the grid toolbar of an associated view)

- Adding an Activity to an entity by using actions (clicking Add Activity from Actions on the entity menu bar)

- Converting a Lead to an Account, Contact, or Opportunity

To view the entity relationships that include a mapping, open the entity editor and click the Type list in the appropriate relationship list, and then select Mappable. When you open the relationship editor for any mappable relationship, you see a Mappings link in the left navigation pane. Click the Mappings link to display the mapped attributes for the relationship. Figure 6-9 shows the attribute mappings between the Account and Contact entities.

Each mapping consists of a source attribute and a target attribute, and you can see that Microsoft Dynamics CRM already mapped attributes such as the address information between Account and Contact. Therefore, when you create a related Contact for an Account, Microsoft Dynamics CRM automatically prepopulates the target attributes of the Contact with the values from the source entity (Account). Figure 6-10 shows a graphical representation of the Account and Contact mapping.

We did not include all of the Account and Contact attributes in this figure because of space considerations, but you can see that the Account entity includes attributes (such as *account-number* and *credit limit*) that do not map to the Contact entity. Likewise, the Contact entity includes attributes such as *birthdate* and *childrensnames* that don't apply to the Account entity. The point is, you don't have to map *all* of the attributes from one entity to another, just the ones that make sense.

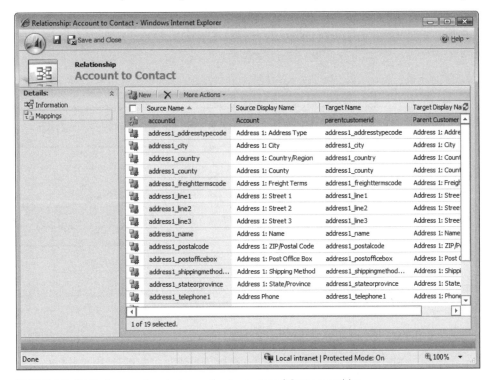

FIGURE 6-9 Attribute mappings between the Account and Contact entities

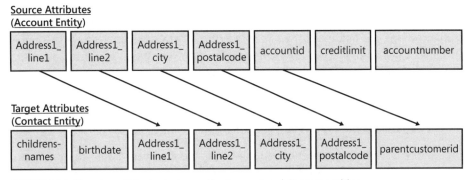

FIGURE 6-10 Mapping attributes between the Account and Contact entities

Creating Custom Mappings

Microsoft Dynamics CRM includes thousands of attribute mappings by default, but at some point you will probably need to create new attribute mappings or modify the default mappings. Consider an example in which you add a custom picklist attribute with a schema name of *new_customerrating* to both the Account and Contact entities (see Figure 6-11). Although both entities use the same schema name of *new_customerrating*, you must still create a mapping between these two attributes if you want Microsoft Dynamics CRM to automatically populate the *new_customerrating* field when you create a related Contact from an Account.

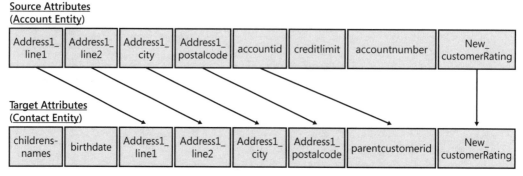

FIGURE 6-11 Mapping custom attributes between the Account and Contact entities

To create a custom mapping between two attributes, you must meet the following conditions:

- Both attributes must use the same data type.

- The length of the target attribute must be equal to or greater than the source attribute.

- You can specify an attribute as the target value only one time. However, you can map an attribute from the source entity to multiple target schema names.

Microsoft Dynamics CRM provides two methods for creating mappings. You can manually map attributes one at a time, or you can use the Generate Mappings feature to let Microsoft Dynamics CRM automatically generate mappings for you. When you use the Generate Mappings feature, Microsoft Dynamics CRM creates an attribute map if two attributes share a schema name and data type.

Manually creating a mapping

1. In the Customization section, double-click an entity record and click the type of relationship you want in the navigation pane.

2. Double-click the entity relationship for which you want to modify the relationship mapping, including adding a new mapping.

3. In the relationship editor window, click Mappings in the navigation pane.

4. To add a new mapping, click New on the grid toolbar. To modify an existing mapping, double-click the mapping you want to modify.

5. A dialog box appears with the source entity attributes on the left and the target entity attributes on the right.

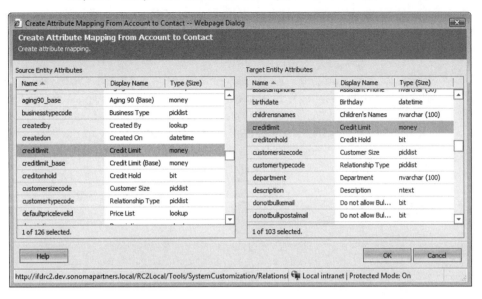

6. Select the source and target attributes that you want to map, and then click OK.

7. An "Attribute Mapping" message appears.

8. Save the relationship, and then publish the entities that you customized.

> **Tip** You can map two attributes even if they use different schema names.

To use the Generate Mappings feature instead of manual mapping, simply click More Actions on the grid toolbar, and then click Generate Mappings. Please note that when you generate mappings Microsoft Dynamics CRM removes all of the existing mappings between the entities.

Mapping Picklist Attributes

Creating mappings for attributes of the *picklist* data type requires additional steps to ensure that the values map correctly. When you map two picklist attributes together, you must also make sure that the picklist values match up accurately. When a user looks at a drop-down list on a form, Microsoft Dynamics CRM displays the *picklist label* to the user. However, when Microsoft Dynamics CRM maps two picklist fields together, it uses the *picklist value*, not the picklist label.

To demonstrate this nuance, we will add a new value to the Industry picklist on the Lead entity. Microsoft Dynamics CRM includes a default mapping between the Industry attribute of Lead to the Industry attribute of Account. When you convert a Lead and create an Account, Microsoft Dynamics CRM uses this mapping to automatically populate the Account industry with the same value as the Lead industry. If you want to add a new industry to the picklist called Software, you must add this value to both the Lead and Account attributes to keep the values in sync.

When you click Add (see Figure 6-12), you enter the picklist text **Software** in the Label box. The text in the Label box is what the user sees in the drop-down list on the form. However, note that Microsoft Dynamics CRM also uses an integer picklist value along with the picklist label. When Microsoft Dynamics CRM maps the Lead industry to the Account industry, it uses the picklist integer value to set the value on the Account. Table 6-3 shows how Microsoft Dynamics CRM maps different picklist values.

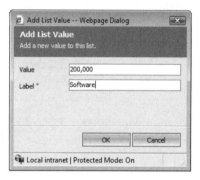

FIGURE 6-12 Adding a new picklist value

TABLE 6-3 Picklist Mapping Examples

Source picklist value (Lead)	Source picklist label (Lead)	Target picklist attribute value (Account)	Target picklist attribute label (Account)	Match?	Resulting picklist value (Account Record)	Resulting picklist label (Account Record)
1	Consulting	1	Consulting	Yes	1	Consulting
1	Consulting	1	Professional Services	Yes	1	Professional Services
1	Consulting	2	Consulting	No	Blank	Blank
1	Consulting	None	None	No	Blank	Blank

> **Important** Microsoft Dynamics CRM always uses the picklist value to determine matches for picklist fields. Consequently, *it is critical that you make sure that the integer values of the picklist always match correctly.*

Microsoft Dynamics CRM automatically provides a default picklist integer value when you add a new option, but you can edit the suggested integer value as necessary. It's important to note that Microsoft Dynamics CRM treats system-created picklists differently from custom picklists that you create:

- **System-created picklists** When you add a new option to a system-created picklist, you can use picklist values only between 200,000 and 2,147,483,646.

- **Custom picklists** When you add a new custom picklist attribute, you can assign picklist values between 1 and 2,147,483,646.

To see where you need to be mindful of this distinction, consider an example in which you want to create a custom Category picklist attribute on the Opportunity entity, and map the opportunity Category values to the Account attribute Category. Also, assume that you want to add a new category option named VIP. If you accept the default picklist values that Microsoft Dynamics CRM suggests, you would have the scenario shown in Figure 6-13.

Category Attribute Account Entity	Category Attribute Opportunity Entity
Preferred Customer (value = 1) Standard (value = 2) VIP Customer (value = 200,000)	Preferred Customer (value = 1) Standard (value = 2) VIP Customer (value = 3)

FIGURE 6-13 Mapping custom picklists to system-created picklists

With this configuration, the Category picklist fields would map from the Account to the Opportunity only for Preferred Customers and Standard customers. However, the Category field would not map to the Opportunity record for VIP accounts because the picklist values don't match. To correct this, you need to modify the VIP picklist value on the Opportunity category attribute to equal 200,000. Remember, you cannot modify the value of the VIP picklist option to 3 because Microsoft Dynamics CRM allows you to use only values starting at 200,000 on system-created picklists.

More Info On system-generated fields, customers who upgraded from Microsoft Dynamics CRM 3.0 to Microsoft Dynamics CRM 4.0 can have custom picklist values less than 200,000 because they carried over from the previous version.

This same concept of matching picklist values also applies to entities with status reasons and state attributes such as Account, Lead, and Opportunity. Please remember to make sure that you match up the values for all of the status reasons for each of the different states between two entities.

Tip Don't worry if you skip integer values in the picklist because you deleted an option—just make sure that the values you want to match always use the same integer value.

Creating Custom Relationships

Now that you understand some of the details behind entity relationships, we explore how to create custom relationships in more detail and examine some real-world scenarios. Microsoft Dynamics CRM supports a wide range of custom entity relationships, such as the following:

- **One-to-many and many-to-one** Create primary and related entity relationships between system to system, custom to custom, and system to custom entities.

- **Many-to-many** Create two related entity relationships between entities.

- **Self-referencing** Create a relationship between an entity and itself so that you can have parent:child record support.

- **Multiple references** Create multiple references between the same two entities. For example, you can create multiple references between the Contact and Account entities.

- **System to system** Create new relationships between existing Microsoft Dynamics CRM system entities.

Although Microsoft Dynamics CRM supports all of these custom relationships in some shape or form, not all of the entities behave the same way. Consider the following examples of unique entity relationship constraints:

- On the Appointment and Campaign Response entities, you can create custom N:1 relationships, but you cannot create custom 1:N or N:N relationships.

- On the Business Unit and Subject entities, you can create custom 1:N relationships, but you cannot create custom N:1 or N:N relationships.

- You cannot create custom self-referencing relationships on the Business Unit and Subject entities because they already include those types of relationships.

Microsoft Dynamics CRM includes too many unique entity circumstances to list in entirety. Conseqently, you should *not* assume that you can apply all types of custom entity relationships to all types of entities. Please double-check the entity Customization section to verify what Microsoft Dynamics CRM allows before finalizing an entity relationship design.

To illustrate the benefits of custom relationships, we explore two commonly requested real-world scenarios:

- Adding multiple user references per account
- Creating parent and child cases

Adding Multiple User References per Account

Many customers who deploy Microsoft Dynamics CRM do so because they want to track the various interactions they have with their customers. As more and more people from your company interact with a single customer, managing that interaction becomes more and more complicated. Consequently, many customers want the ability to assign multiple employees to a single account and to designate their individual roles in relation to the account.

By default, each Microsoft Dynamics CRM Account record includes a single owner record. Fortunately, you can use custom relationships to add the additional references you need to the Account entity. Assume that in addition to the account owner, you want to add a sales-person reference and a customer service reference to each Account.

Add additional user references

1. In the Customization section of Microsoft Dynamics CRM, click Customize Entities.

2. Double-click the Account entity to open the entity editor.

3. Because a single user can have the same role with multiple accounts, you will create a many-to-one (N:1) relationship between the Account and User entities. Click the N:1 Relationships link in the navigation pane.

4. Click the New Many-to-1 Relationship button on the grid toolbar.

5. Select User for the Primary entity and type **sales_user_account** in the Name field.

6. For the Display Name, type in **Sales Person**. This is the name that will appear on the form, in the views, and so forth.

7. For Display Option, select the Do not Display option because you don't want to see the related accounts on the user's record.

8. On the Type of Behavior drop-down menu, select Referential so that Microsoft Dynamics CRM does not apply the cascading actions such as assign, share, and delete to the user's related accounts when action is taken against the User record.

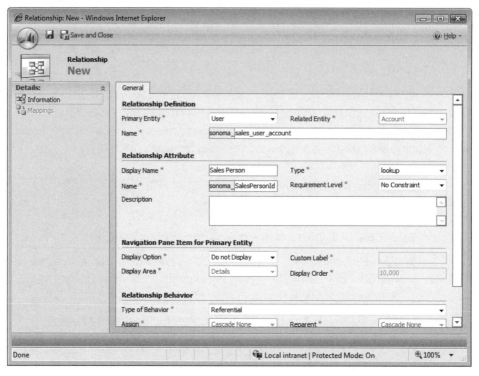

9. Click the Save and Close button. You just created a new custom relationship between the User and Account entities to track which user is the account's salesperson.

10. Repeat the process to create the relationship to the account's service manager.

11. In the navigation pane, click the N:1 Relationships link.

12. On the grid toolbar, click the New Many-to-1 Relationship button.

13. Select User for the Primary entity, and type **service_user_account** in the Name field.

14. For the Display Name, type in **Service Manager**.

15. For the Display Option, select Do not Display.

16. For the Type of Behavior, select Referential.

17. Click the Save and Close button.

18. Next, you need to add the new fields to the Account form so that users can select records for each account.

19. In the navigation pane, click Forms and Views, and then double-click Form. The form editor opens.

20. In the Common Tasks pane, click Add Fields. Scroll down and select the Sales Person and Service Manager fields that you just added.

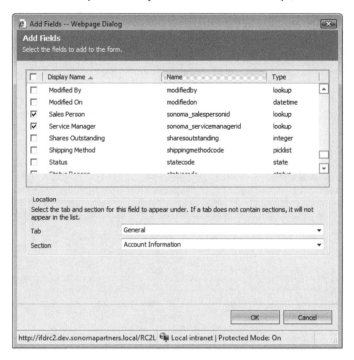

21. Click Save and Close, and then publish the Account entity (on the Actions menu).

Now when you browse to an Account record, you can specify the salesperson and the service manager (using Microsoft Dynamics CRM User records) for each account, as shown in Figure 6-14.

As you learned in Chapter 3, "Managing Security and Information Access," the Microsoft Dynamics CRM security settings are partly determined by each record's owner. So, even though you added additional users to the Account in this example, Microsoft Dynamics CRM still references the original Owner field to determine the security settings.

Creating Parent and Child Cases

As the previous example shows, adding custom relationships to entities gives you the flexibility to track additional relationship data about how records interact with other entities. You can also use custom relationships to track and manage how records of one entity type interact with records of the same entity type. Microsoft Dynamics CRM 4.0 supports these types of self-referencing custom relationships, and we walk through a real-world example of these relationships using the Case entity.

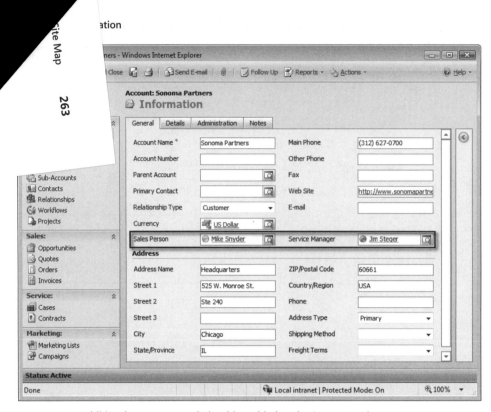

FIGURE 6-14 Additional custom user relationships added to the Account entity

As you know, the Microsoft Dynamics CRM customer service module allows a company to capture data about requests and issues that they want to resolve using a case record. As a company starts to build a database with a large number of cases, they quickly see that many of the cases relate to one another. Consequently, the company might want to create a link between these related cases so that once they resolve a single case, they can quickly apply that same resolution to the related cases. In the following exercise, you use custom relationships to create a parent and child relationship between cases records.

Create a self-referencing relationship for the Case entity

1. In the Customization section of Microsoft Dynamics CRM, click Customize Entities.

2. Double-click the Case entity to open the entity editor.

3. In the navigation pane, click the 1:N Relationships link, and then on the grid toolbar click the New 1-to-Many Relationship button.

4. Select Case for the related entity, and type **sonoma_incident_incident** in the Name field. This name is the schema name.

5. For the Display Name, type **Parent Case**. This is the name that will appear on the form, in the views, and so forth.

6. For the Display Option, select the Use Custom Label option, and type **Child Cases** into the Custom Label text box.

7. For the Type of Behavior, select Referential so that Microsoft Dynamics CRM does not apply the cascading actions such as assign, share, and delete to the child cases when an action is taken against the parent case record.

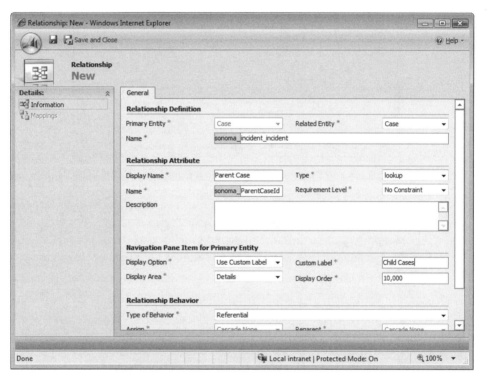

8. Click the Save and Close button.

9. Next, add the new Parent Case field to the case form so that users can select the Parent Case for a record. In the navigation pane, click Forms and Views, and then double-click Form. The form editor opens.

10. In the Common Tasks pane, click Add Fields. Scroll down the list and select the Parent Case field that you just added. Click OK.

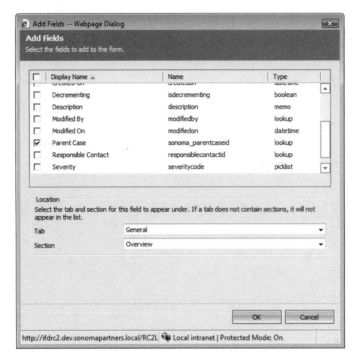

11. Click Save and Close, and then publish the case entity (on the Actions menu).

When users work with a case record now, they can track how a single case relates to other cases so that they can manage the list of issues more efficiently. For example, customer service representatives can select a Parent Case for each record using the lookup on the form, and in addition they can click Child Cases in the navigation pane to see a list of child records related to the case (Figure 6-15).

> **Tip** In this example, you set up a referential relationship between the parent and child cases. However, you might want to configure the cascading behavior so that when you reassign the parent case, Microsoft Dynamics CRM automatically assigns all of the child cases to the same case owner.

These two custom relationship examples show you how quickly and easily you can configure entity relationships in Microsoft Dynamics CRM to manage your customer data. As you can imagine, you can get very creative with these custom relationships to develop a system that perfectly suits your unique business needs.

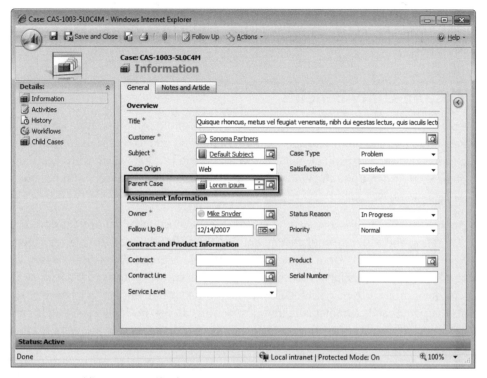

FIGURE 6-15 Adding custom self-referencing relationships to the Case entity to track parent and child case information

Creating Custom Entities

Now that you understand entity relationships and how to create your own custom relationships, we can explore custom entities. Microsoft Dynamics CRM creates more than 150 entities when you install the software, and you can add an almost unlimited number of custom attributes to the customizable entities. However, you will almost certainly want to track business data that does not fit neatly into one of these existing entities. With most other customer relationship management (CRM) applications, tracking new categories of data usually requires a custom application development project in which consultants create new custom databases and user interface forms that they try to blend into the host CRM application.

In addition to the obvious downsides of using development time and costing money, these customized CRM application projects usually result in less-than-ideal functionality for system administrators and end users. Plus, when the host CRM application releases an updated version, the consultants must reprogram the business logic code, update the customized databases, and revise the user interface forms. Add all these factors up and you can understand why CRM customization projects in the past required lots of time, money, and effort.

Custom Entity Benefits

Fortunately, Microsoft Dynamics CRM solves many of the common CRM customization issues related to tracking new categories of data by allowing you to create custom entities. Even more beneficial, Microsoft Dynamics CRM allows you to create custom entities and manage their relationships using the Web-based administration interface (so that no custom programming is required).

So, how might you use custom entities? You have almost unlimited options on how you can set up and structure your custom entities. For example, an apartment management company might use custom entities to track its various property locations, leases, and rental applications. A professional services firm can create custom entities to track its various customer projects. A magazine publisher might use custom entities to capture data about its magazines and customer subscriptions. As you can see, how you can use custom entities depends on the nature of your business and the types of data that you want to capture in Microsoft Dynamics CRM.

When you create a custom entity to store a new category of data, Microsoft Dynamics CRM automatically adds the entity to the metadata and its underlying system data. This means that custom entities behave as "first-class" system entities, sharing almost all of the functionality of the default system entities created on installation. Some common benefits of custom entities and the default entities include the following:

- You can customize the custom entity attributes, forms, and views with the same Web-based administration tools that you use to customize the default entities.

- Users can use the Advanced Find feature to create and save custom queries on custom entities.

- You can add client-side events such as *onChange*, *onLoad*, and *onSave* to the custom entity's form.

- You can import and export custom entities and their customizations with the same import/export tool and the metadata application programming interface (API) that you use for the default entities.

- Users can access custom entities in the Microsoft Dynamics CRM client for Microsoft Office Outlook, and they can work with custom entities offline using the Microsoft Dynamics CRM client for Microsoft Office Outlook.

- You can add custom relationships and mappings to custom entities, just as you can with the default entities.

- Custom entities fully participate in the Microsoft Dynamics CRM security framework, so you can set privileges such as Create, Read, and Write on an entity-by-entity basis.

- Developers can programmatically access custom entities through the Microsoft Dynamics CRM software development kit (SDK), including Create, Retrieve, and Update operations.

- Microsoft Dynamics CRM supports plug-ins on custom entities.

- Users can use the batch edit feature on custom entity records.

- You can configure duplicate detection to check against custom entity records.

- Microsoft Dynamics CRM creates filtered views for custom entities in the SQL Server database that you can use for creating reports.

- Users can export custom entities to Microsoft Office Excel as a dynamic PivotTable or dynamic worksheet.

- You can modify the Microsoft Dynamics CRM application navigation and menu structure to blend custom entities into the user interface seamlessly.

This list illustrates that custom entities behave almost identically to the default entities in the Microsoft Dynamics CRM system.

Custom Entity Limitations

Despite all of the similarities between custom entities and default entities, a few notable limitations exist for custom entities:

- You cannot merge two custom entity records together.

- The Microsoft Dynamics CRM system entities include a relationship to Customer in which users can select an Account or a Contact. For custom entities, you can specify a relationship with the Account entity and the Contact entity, but you cannot create a relationship to the composite Customer entity (in which users can select an Account or a Contact on a single lookup).

- Custom entities don't appear in an entity rollup (showing activities from child entities on the parent entity's record).

- Custom entities cannot have parental relationship behavior with system entities.

As you can see, only a few limitations exist regarding custom entities, so you will probably make heavy use of them in your Microsoft Dynamics CRM deployment. We explain setting up and configuring custom entity relationships (and their corresponding) limitations next.

Custom Entity Example

To better understand the benefits of custom entities, let's map out a real-world example of creating custom entities and relationships for a fictional property management firm called Litware, Inc.

Litware manages 15 apartment buildings on the East Coast. The apartment complexes range in size from 25 to 75 apartments per building, including one-bedroom, two-bedroom, and three-bedroom apartments. As part of the rental process, each prospective tenant must complete a rental application and submit to a credit check. After receiving credit approval, all of the tenants sharing an apartment (roommates) sign a lease. Litware uses Microsoft Dynamics CRM to manage its current tenants and track potential tenants.

Based on this description, we created an initial design proposal in which Litware would use the following entities in Microsoft Dynamics CRM:

- **Building**   Custom entity with attributes such as name and address.

- **Apartment**   Custom entity with attributes such as number of bedrooms, number of bathrooms, square footage, monthly rent, and floor number.

- **Lease**   Custom entity with attributes such as monthly rent, start date, end date, and security deposit. Up to two people can share a single lease.

- **Lease Application**   Custom entity with attributes such as employment information and previous addresses. Each tenant provides his or her own application.

- **Contact**   System entity used to track tenants and applicants.

- **Opportunity**   System entity used to track a potential rental opportunities.

When you map out an entity design like this one, you should consider different scenarios because no hard rules exist to let you know whether you should create a custom entity or add attributes to an existing entity. We recommend that you try to map out all of the proposed entities and relationships that you think you'll need in your solution before you start entering changes in Microsoft Dynamics CRM. Making changes to your entity relationships in a modeling tool such as Microsoft Office Visio is much easier and more efficient than making changes in Microsoft Dynamics CRM. Figure 6-16 shows the proposed entity map for Litware.

Based on this initial design, we created visual mockups of the Building, Apartment, Lease, and Lease Application forms as shown in Figures 6-17 through 6-20.

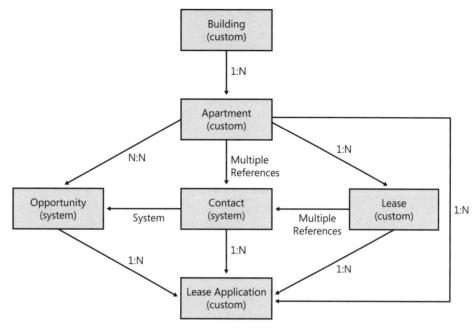

FIGURE 6-16 Proposed entity relationship map for Litware

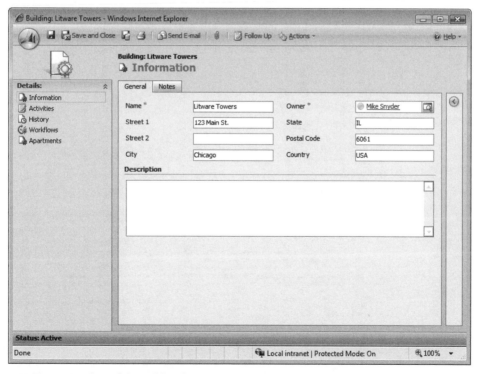

FIGURE 6-17 Mockup of the Building form

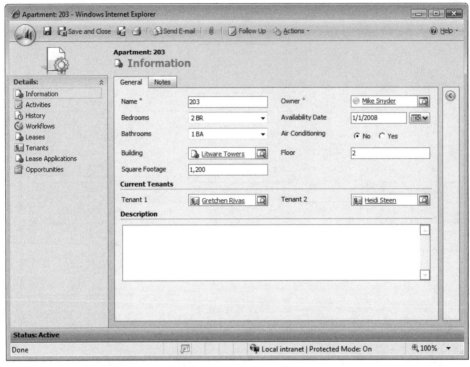

FIGURE 6-18 Mockup of the Apartment form

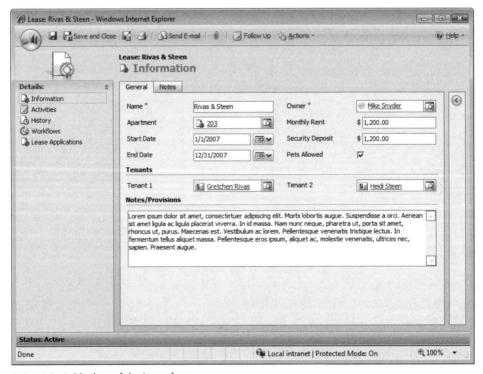

FIGURE 6-19 Mockup of the Lease form

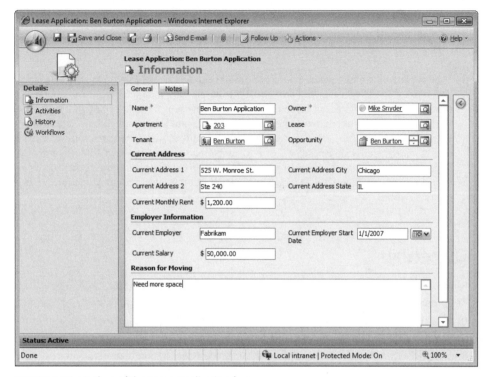

FIGURE 6-20 Mockup of the Lease Application form

You can immediately see how some of the proposed entity relationships manifest in the user interface. For example, the proposed design includes the following benefits and caveats:

- You can track multiple tenant records per lease because of the multiple relationships created between Lease and Contact (Tenant 1 and Tenant 2). This also allows you to track a contact who rented from the company multiple times and consequently has multiple leases on file.

- For any single apartment, you can view all of the related Opportunities because of the many-to-many relationship between Apartment and Opportunity. This relationship can show you which apartments a group of tenants might rent in addition to telling you which potential tenants are considering a single apartment.

- The proposed design allows each tenant to complete his or her own lease application independently, yet you can still link tenants together using the Opportunity and Apartment records.

When Litware reviews the proposed relationship design, the reviewers might decide to make changes to the entity relationships based on their specific business needs. Fortunately, Microsoft Dynamics CRM makes it easy to create custom entities and modify their relationships.

We created all of the custom entities, attributes, relationships, and forms for this example in less than 20 minutes!

> **Tip** When you create a many-to-many relationship directly between two entities, you can't customize that relationship with additional attributes. Also, a direct many-to-many relationship does not appear in Microsoft Dynamics CRM workflow, which might not fit your business requirements. As an alternative, you can effectively create a many-to-many relationship between two entities (A and B) by creating an intermediate entity (C), and then creating two custom one-to-many relationships: Create a one-to-many relationship between A and C, and also create a many-to-one relationship between C and B. You can consider using this technique when you want to capture additional data (add attributes) about the many-to-many relationship between the two entities.

Ownership

Microsoft Dynamics CRM assigns an owner to almost all of the records in its database. Records such as Leads, Accounts, Activities, and Contacts have a Microsoft Dynamics CRM user as their owner. However, Microsoft Dynamics CRM assigns ownership of records such as products, sales literature, and sites to the organization. These types of records store information that theoretically applies to all of the users in the organization, regardless of the business unit.

For each custom entity you create, you must specify one of two ownership types:

- User-owned
- Organization-owned

Make the entity ownership decision carefully because you cannot change the entity ownership type after you create the entity.

Some of the differences between user ownership and organization ownership include the following:

- User-owned entities can be assigned to other users; organization-owned entities cannot.
- User-owned entities can be shared with one or more teams; organization-owned entities cannot.
- Because user-owned entities belong to a user and each user belongs to a business unit, you have more flexibility when configuring security on user-owned entities than you do when configuring security on organization-owned entities. When you configure a security role for organization-owned entities, you can specify only None and Organization

access levels. For user-owned entities, you can specify one of five d
levels: None, User, Business Unit, Parent:Child Business Units, or Organ

- Organization-owned entities can require less work to administer because t
to the company. However, you must always assign a user-owned entity to a sp
user record.

As this list illustrates, making custom entities user-owned provides you with more options and greater configurability. However, user ownership does require that you carefully assign each entity to the correct owner and configure the security roles appropriately. If users frequently change business units or job functions, you must update entity ownership accordingly. In such scenarios, the work of maintaining the correct user ownership information might offset the additional configurability benefits.

Entity Icons

Microsoft Dynamics CRM uses different icons in the user interface to represent each of the default system entities. These icons appear in the navigation pane, in various views, and on a related entity's form. In addition to improving the visual aesthetics, these entity icons help users navigate the system by providing graphical indicators about each type of record they are working with. By default, Microsoft Dynamics CRM assigns the same icon to all new custom entities.

When you have more than a few custom entities in your system, using the same default icon for all of the custom entities diminishes the aesthetic benefit of icons and might cause confusion with your users. Fortunately, in Microsoft Dynamics CRM you can upload your own custom icons for each custom entity. We highly recommend that you use custom icons for each custom entity in your system. You can upload three types of entity icons for each custom entity:

- **Web application**   Image that appears in the grids and navigation pane
- **Microsoft Dynamics CRM client for Microsoft Office Outlook**   Image that appears in the Outlook client
- **Icon in entity forms**   Image that appears at the top of each entity form

If possible, use files with transparent backgrounds for entity icon files. When the icons appear on dark backgrounds or when Microsoft Dynamics CRM highlights the record, failure to use transparency in your images creates an unpleasant effect.

Most graphics editing programs provide the tools to create these icons to Microsoft Dynamics CRM's specifications. When you have your icon files ready, uploading them to the custom entity is easy.

…ies, and Site Map

…fferent access

…ization.

…ey belong

…ecific

275

…ity icons

…r, click Actions, and then click Update Icons. The Select New Icons
…s:

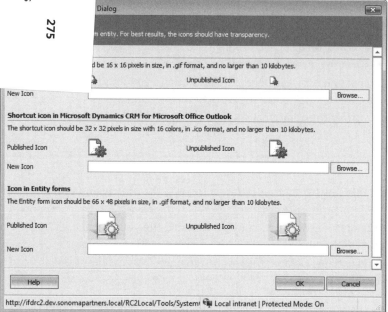

2. For each file type, browse and upload the appropriate icon files that you want to use, and then click OK. A preview of the icon that you uploaded appears, in addition to the current published icon.

3. Publish the entity so that users can see the new icons.

In Microsoft Dynamics CRM, you can upload icons for custom entities, but you can also change the entity icons by using the site map. Even though you can technically update an entity icon with the site map, using the Select New Icons tool is the preferred method to change the icons. We recommend using the icon feature in the site map just for custom links that you add to the navigation. We explain the site map in more detail in the section titled "Site Map" later in this chapter.

> **Tip** Even though we strongly recommend it, you might not want to take the time to create and upload custom icons. If you're in a rush, one quick and dirty way to get custom icons is to upload image files you find in the Microsoft Dynamics CRM Web folder. By default, you can find this folder at C:\Inetpub\wwwroot_imgs on the Microsoft Dynamics CRM Web server. There are lots of images in there to choose from! The Microsoft Dynamics CRM SDK also includes image files that you can use in the client\images folder. Of course, it is better to create your own custom icons, but reusing the Microsoft Dynamics CRM icons can provide a better user experience than leaving the default custom entity icon can.

Creating a Custom Entity

By now you should understand the concepts, benefits, and limitations related to custom entities. Now we go through the steps that you will follow to create a custom entity in Microsoft Dynamics CRM. For every custom entity you create, you must configure the following parameters:

- Entity definition
- Offline availability
- Duplicate detection
- Relationships
- Display areas
- Primary attribute

Figure 6-21 shows the user interface for creating a new entity; we provide more information about each parameter in the following subsections.

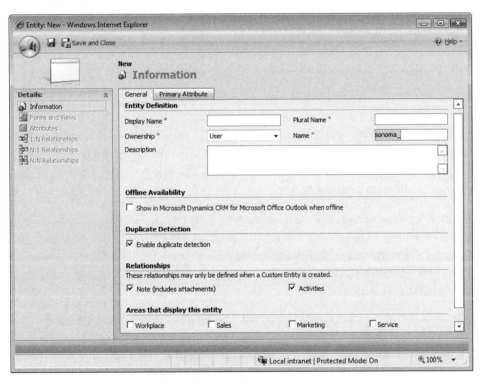

FIGURE 6-21 Creating a new custom entity

Entity Definition

In the Entity Definition section, you enter basic parameters about the custom entity, including the following:

- Name
- Plural name
- Ownership (user or organization)
- Schema name
- Description (optional)

In Chapter 4, we discussed how the name, plural name, schema name, and description parameters work in regard to renaming entities, so you should be familiar with these concepts. Remember that you cannot change the schema name after you create the entity, but you can modify the name, plural name, and description at any time.

> **Tip** You can change the default schema name prefix from *new_* to a different value by configuring the schema-name prefix. To alter this value, browse to Settings, click Administration, System Settings, and then click Customization.

For the ownership parameter, you must specify whether the entity will be user-owned or organization-owned, as discussed earlier in this chapter.

Offline Availability

As you know, Microsoft Dynamics CRM includes two different Outlook clients: Microsoft Dynamics CRM for Microsoft Office Outlook and Microsoft Dynamics CRM for Microsoft Office Outlook with Offline Access.

With the offline version, users can access Microsoft Dynamics CRM data even when they disconnect from the network. Microsoft Dynamics CRM refers to this concept of working disconnected from the network as *working offline*. The nonoffline client works only when users are connected to the server. You have the option to use one, none, or both of the Outlook clients in your deployment.

When you create a custom entity, you can choose whether you want your users to be able to work offline with that custom entity. Obviously, this parameter affects you only if your organization deploys the offline client because only that client can go offline. The offline availability option has no impact on the nonoffline client.

> **Tip** Even if you decide to include a custom entity for offline availability, the default synchronization settings for Microsoft Dynamics CRM for Microsoft Office Outlook with Offline Access will not include any custom entities. Therefore, users must also manually configure their offline filters to include the custom entity to access that data offline. You can also modify the Microsoft Dynamics CRM security roles to allow only certain users to take data offline.

You have the option to toggle the offline availability of a specific custom entity off and on at any time.

Duplicate Detection

As you can probably guess, by selecting this option you can allow users to configure and use the Microsoft Dynamics CRM duplicate detection functionality on the custom entity records. Again, you can enable and disable this option for a particular entity at any time.

Relationships

When you create a custom entity, you can choose whether you want to enable Notes and Activities for the entity. Notes and Activities for custom entities behave just like Notes and Activities for the default system entities. Therefore, if you enable Activities, users can add any type of Activity record (such as Task, Phone Call, or Letter) that their security credentials allow.

You must configure Notes and Activities at the time that you create a custom entity. You cannot change the associated entity settings later.

> **More Info** Because you can't change these settings later, you might be tempted always to include Notes and Activities on your custom entities. One thing to remember is that when you include Activities on a custom entity, that entity appears as an option in the Regarding list for Tasks, Phone Calls, and so on. If you don't want people to select the custom entity as a regarding value, make sure that you do not include Activities. If you really need to toggle the availability for Notes and Activities on an entity at a later time, you can export the entity's customization.xml file and manually edit that file to change the Notes and Activities settings. Microsoft might not consider this technically supported, but we know several people who have successfully used this technique.

Display Areas

With Microsoft Dynamics CRM, you can specify where to display the custom entity to users in the application navigation. The default display area options include Workplace, Sales, Marketing, Service, Settings, and Resource Center. You can choose to display the custom entity in all, some, or none of the areas. When you choose to include a custom entity, Microsoft Dynamics CRM adds a link in the navigation pane and a link in the application menu bar. You can toggle the display settings whenever you want, not just during entity creation.

r customize the user interface and application navigation by using the site
er later in this chapter. By modifying the site map, you can include additional
ea options.

oute

uding the default system entities, needs a primary attribute that Microsoft
uses to display on the lookup field in related entities. If you reference back to
Figure 6-20, the schema field *name* is the primary attribute of the Apartment entity, so the
name of the apartment record appears in the lookup field of its related records.

Most custom and default entities use a name field as the primary attribute, but you are not
required to do so. However, you will notice that Microsoft Dynamics CRM does require
you to create a primary attribute with a data type of *nvarchar* and a format of text. You
can set up a maximum length and business requirement level for the primary attribute that
makes sense for your business.

> **Tip** After you create a custom entity, the data fields in the Primary Attribute tab become read-
> only, so it appears that you cannot edit the primary attribute. However, if you navigate to the list
> of attributes for the custom entity and double-click the primary attribute, you can modify the
> primary attribute's name, business requirement level, and maximum length in the attribute
> editor. Although you can edit some of the primary attribute's values, you cannot change the
> primary attribute of a custom entity.

Other than the data type and data format requirement, the rules and restrictions for creating
a primary attribute are the same as they are for creating any attribute for an entity.

Deleting a Custom Entity

If you decide that you no longer need to use a custom entity, you can easily delete it from
Microsoft Dynamics CRM. Just like deleting attributes, you must remove all existing references to the custom entity in forms and views before Microsoft Dynamics CRM allows you to
delete it. To remove references to an entity, do the following:

- Remove references to the entity from the form of any related entities, and then delete
  any relationships linking to the custom entity.

- Remove the entity from any reports.

- Remove the entity from any script or code references.

Warning Deleting a custom entity also deletes all of the data stored in that entity, and you can never retrieve that data without a database backup in place. Microsoft Dynamics CRM also permanently deletes all of the Notes and Activities related to that entity. Make sure that you take the appropriate steps to back up all of your data before deleting an entity or attribute.

Just like when you delete attributes, Microsoft Dynamics CRM checks for existing references to custom entities in forms and relationships before it allows you to delete an entity, but you must remove references to deleted entities in reports.

Application Navigation

Because of the flexibility and power of custom entities, you will find yourself creating multiple custom entities in your Microsoft Dynamics CRM system. Simple deployments might use just a few custom entities, but a complex deployment might contain 25, 50, or 100 custom entities! By default, Microsoft Dynamics CRM adds custom entities to the user interface and site navigation in the order in which you create them, listing the first custom entity at the top of the list. In addition, Microsoft Dynamics CRM lists the custom entities together under an Extensions group in the navigation pane. If you use more than a handful of custom entities, you can alter where and how they appear in the user interface. Microsoft Dynamics CRM uses multiple tools to configure how users access entities and navigate in the application. These application navigation customization tools include the following:

- Site map
- Entity display areas
- ISV.config

Microsoft Dynamics CRM combines data from these three tools to create the user interface on a system-wide level. After it determines the system navigation, Microsoft Dynamics CRM also provides a Personalize Workplace feature in which each individual user can customize the groups that appear in their workplaces. Before we discuss what each application navigation tool configures, we quickly review the Microsoft Dynamics CRM terminology for the screen region names in the Web application and the Microsoft Dynamics CRM client for Microsoft Office Outlook application. Figure 6-22 shows the user interface screen regions and Figure 6-23 shows the entity record screen regions.

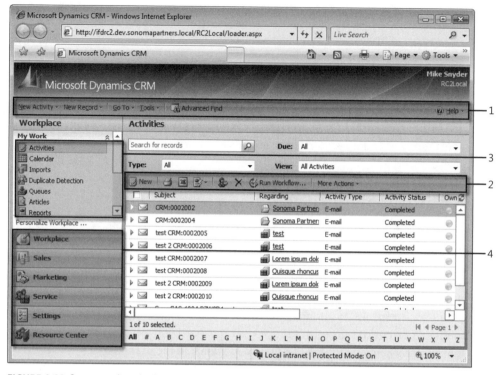

FIGURE 6-22 Screen regions in the Microsoft Dynamics CRM user interface

1. Application menu toolbar

2. Grid toolbar

3. Application navigation pane

4. Wunderbar (also referred to as Application Areas)

5. Entity menu toolbar

6. Entity navigation pane

Table 6-4 summarizes which customization tool you can use to modify the Microsoft Dynamics CRM application navigation depending on the type of customization that you require and where in the application navigation that customization resides.

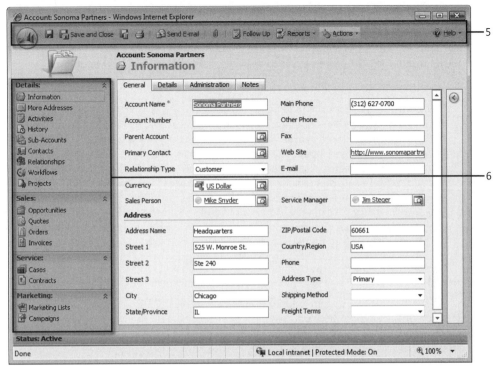

FIGURE 6-23 Screen regions on a Microsoft Dynamics CRM entity record

TABLE 6-4 Application Navigation Customization Tool Summary

Screen region name	Site map	ISV.config	Entity display areas (custom entities only)	Personalize Workplace
Application menu toolbar	Add, modify, and reorder items on Go To menu	Add new menu items and custom buttons	Choose the areas in which to display an entity	No
Application navigation pane	Add, modify, and reorder items	No	Choose the areas in which to display an entity	Users can specify the groups in which to display their workplace
Grid toolbar	No	Add new menu items and custom buttons	No	No
Wunderbar	Add, modify, and reorder items	No	No	No
Entity menu toolbar	No	Add new menu items and custom buttons	No	No
Entity naviga-tion pane	No	Add custom links only	No	No

By using these four tools, you can customize almost every part of the user interface. In general, with the site map you can add, reorder, and remove items in the application navigation pane and the wunderbar. Use ISV.config to add new links and buttons to the application menu toolbar in addition to adding new links and buttons to individual entities.

> **More Info** You might be wondering what ISV.config means. Unlike the site map, the name of the ISV.config feature does not indicate its purpose. Microsoft Dynamics CRM 4.0 uses the ISV. config terminology as a carryover from earlier versions of Microsoft Dynamics CRM. The ISV.config file originally allowed independent software vendors (ISVs) to configure their enhancements in the Microsoft Dynamics CRM interface. The term *ISV* refers to third-party companies that develop software enhancements and add-ons for the Microsoft Dynamics CRM platform. Although ISVs do make heavy use of the ISV.config file, customers can also use ISV.config for their own internally developed customizations and enhancements. Because the ISV.config file deals mostly with extending Microsoft Dynamics CRM, we discuss how to work with it along with the other extension features in Chapter 10, "Client-Side SDK."

Now that you understand which tools to use to customize the navigation components of Microsoft Dynamics CRM, we can discuss the details of how to edit the site map and Personalize Workplace features.

Site Map

By modifying the site map, you can customize the user interface of the application navigation pane, the wunderbar, and parts of the application menu toolbar. As discussed earlier, if you add more than a few custom entities, you will probably want to modify the site map so that your custom entities appear in the user interface exactly where you want them. Conceptually, the site map is just an .xml file that you edit (with the XML editing tool of your choice) to configure different parts of the Microsoft Dynamics CRM navigation. Before we explain how to edit the site map, it will help to further define the screen components in the application navigation pane and the wunderbar (as shown in Figure 6-24) because the site map uses new terms to describe these areas of the user interface.

By default Microsoft Dynamics CRM displays six buttons in the wunderbar: Workplace, Sales, Marketing, Service, Settings, and Resource Center.

When you are working with the site map, Microsoft Dynamics CRM refers to these six buttons as *areas*. When users click an area, Microsoft Dynamics CRM updates the application navigation pane to show the appropriate links for that area. As the example in Figure 6-24 shows, the Workplace area contains three main elements: My Work, Customers, and Marketing.

FIGURE 6-24 Screen components of the application navigation pane and the wunderbar

The site map refers to these elements as *groups*. Microsoft Dynamics CRM formats groups in the Web client's application navigation pane with the expand/collapse control. In each group are additional links that the site map refers to as *subareas*. For example, the My Work group in Figure 6-24 includes eight subareas:

- Activities
- Calendar
- Imports
- Duplicate Detection
- Queues
- Articles
- Reports
- Announcements

In addition to updating the application navigation pane and the wunderbar, editing the site map also concurrently updates the Go To menu on the application menu toolbar. Figure 6-25 shows the Go To menu for this example.

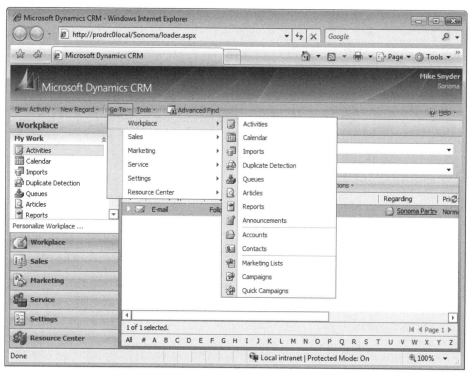

FIGURE 6-25 The Go To menu for the Workplace area

As you can see, the application menu toolbar lists the same areas that appear in the wunderbar (and in the same order). In addition, the application menu bar also displays all of an area's subareas that are nested. However, notice that the application menu bar does not display the group name. Instead of the group name, Microsoft Dynamics CRM displays a horizontal line to divide the groups graphically.

Important Editing the site map updates the Web client's application navigation pane, the wunderbar, and the Go To menu on the application menu toolbar all at the same time.

Although the Outlook client uses some of the same screen region names as the Web client, it also includes a few unique region names. Figure 6-26 shows the Microsoft Dynamics CRM desktop client for Outlook, and the region names are identified in the subsequent list.

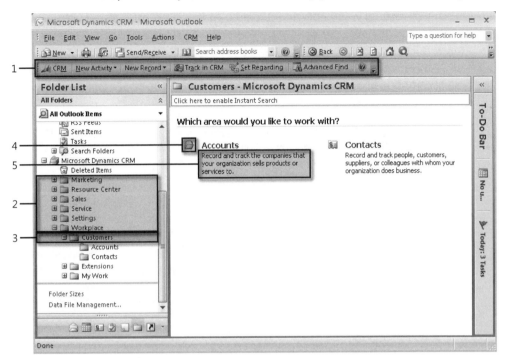

FIGURE 6-26 Screen regions in Microsoft Dynamics CRM for Microsoft Office Outlook

1. Application toolbar

2. Areas

3. Subareas

4. Icon

5. Description

You can see that the Outlook client displays areas and subareas in the Outlook navigation pane as folders instead of the buttons and links that the Web client uses. Also notice that the Outlook client does not display groups at all.

 Important Remember that the Web client and the Outlook client share the same site map to configure the application navigation. Therefore, you should always consider how changes you make in the site map will appear to Web and Outlook users.

Sitemap.xml

Now that you understand the terminology that Microsoft Dynamics CRM uses for the site map, we show you how to modify the site map to meet your needs. As explained earlier, the site map is simply an .xml configuration file that you can edit manually. To get a copy of the current site map of your deployment to edit, you must export it from Microsoft Dynamics CRM. As with any customization, you export the site map by browsing to Settings, clicking Customization, and then clicking Export Customizations. Select the Site Map record, and then click Export Selected Customizations. Microsoft Dynamics CRM prompts you to open or save the file. Because you want to edit the site map file, save a copy to your local drive.

> **Best Practices** Microsoft Dynamics CRM uses customizations.xml as the default file name for all exported customizations. When you export the site map customizations and unzip the file, a best practice is to rename the customizations.xml file to sitemap.xml. Although it is not required, using this naming convention makes the contents of the file obvious to you and others.

You can edit .xml files by using any text editor, such as Notepad or WordPad, but using an XML-specific editor such as Microsoft Visual Studio makes the editing process much easier because you can expand and collapse the different XML elements (see Figure 6-27). You can use Microsoft Internet Explorer to view an .xml file, but you won't be able to edit it there.

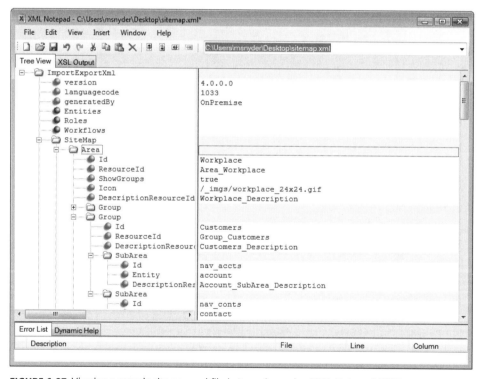

FIGURE 6-27 Viewing a sample sitemap.xml file in tree view using XML Notepad 2007

> **Tip** If you don't have access to Microsoft Visual Studio, we highly recommend that you find some other XML editing application. Fortunately, Microsoft offers a free XML editor named XML Notepad 2007. Microsoft designed XML Notepad 2007 as a very lightweight application (less than 2-MB download) for basic editing and manipulation of XML files. With this tool, you can view and edit files such as the Microsoft Dynamics CRM site map. You can download XML Notepad 2007 at *http://www.microsoft.com/downloads*.

By default, Microsoft Dynamics CRM creates a sitemap.xml file with the XML structure shown in Figure 6-28.

Only the *SiteMap* and *Languages* elements in the sitemap.xml file contain any data. The *Entities*, *Roles*, *Workflows*, *EntityMaps*, and *EntityRelationships* elements should be empty. We discuss each of the *SiteMap* elements and their attributes in detail in the following subsections.

> **Important** The default site map that you export does not include any of the following elements: *Title*, *Titles*, *Description*, *Descriptions*. However, you need to use these elements if you add any new areas to the application navigation. Microsoft Dynamics CRM doesn't require these elements for the six default areas, but you can add them if you want. Consequently, even though the *Title* and *Description* attributes are deprecated, you can still edit these values on the *Area*, *Group*, and *SubArea* elements for the six default areas if you want a quick update. Microsoft Dynamics CRM ignores the *Title* and *Description* attribute values if the *Titles* and *Descriptions* elements exist. The *Title*, *Titles*, *Description*, and *Descriptions* elements apply to the *Area*, *Group*, and *SubArea* elements.

FIGURE 6-28 XML element structure of default sitemap.xml export

Figure 6-29 shows an updated XML element structure of the sitemap.xml file that includes the *Title*, *Titles*, *Description*, and *Descriptions* elements. Microsoft Dynamics CRM includes these four areas in the sitemap to support the ability to use multiple languages within a single Microsoft Dynamics CRM organization.

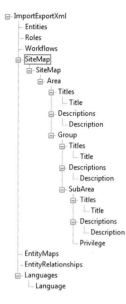

FIGURE 6-29 XML element structure of sitemap.xml

SiteMap

It might seem a little confusing initially, but Microsoft Dynamics CRM uses the name SiteMap as the root node of the *SiteMap* element (illustrated in Figure 6-29). Your sitemap.xml file can include only one occurrence of the *SiteMap* node under the *SiteMap* elements. Table 6-5 lists the only attribute for the *SiteMap* node.

TABLE 6-5 *SiteMap* **Attribute**

Name	Description	Data type	Required?	Applies to Web client?	Applies to Outlook clients?
Url	Specifies a URL that Microsoft Dynamics CRM will display in the Outlook clients when users click the Microsoft Dynamics CRM folder **Valid values:** Any valid URL	*string*	No	No	Yes

By using the SiteMap *Url* attribute, you can display the Web page of your choice when users click the Microsoft Dynamics CRM folder in the Outlook client. Figure 6-30 shows an example in which we specified the URL *http://sharepoint* to display a Microsoft Office SharePoint Services intranet Web site.

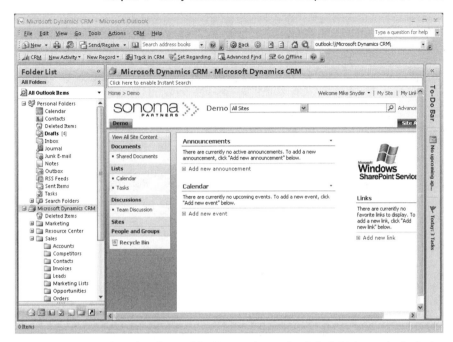

FIGURE 6-30 Using the *Url* attribute of SiteMap to change the default Web page in Outlook

To implement the example in Figure 6-30 you can change the *SiteMap* node from the default value.

```
<SiteMap>
```

Simply add the *Url* attribute to the node so that it looks like the following example.

```
<SiteMap Url="http://sharepoint">
```

In the real world, you might want to display a custom Web page such as a dashboard or some other intranet site. Note that changing this attribute affects the Outlook client, but it does not affect users who access Microsoft Dynamics CRM through the Web client.

Area

The default sitemap.xml file includes six area elements (*Workplace*, *Sales*, *Marketing*, *Service*, *Settings,* and *Resource Center*), and you can modify, reorder, or remove any of these areas. You can also add entirely new areas to the Microsoft Dynamics CRM navigation by adding new area elements to sitemap.xml. Remember, Microsoft Dynamics CRM displays areas in the wunderbar, on the application menu toolbar, and in the Outlook client folders.

> **Caution** Although technically you can remove the Settings area from the application navigation by removing it from the site map, you might accidentally lock yourself out of the Customizations section by doing so. Therefore, we strongly recommend that you *never* remove the Settings area from the site map. If you do not want users to see this area in the application navigation, you should change their security role settings instead of modifying the site map.

Table 6-6 lists the attributes for the *Area* node.

TABLE 6-6 *Area* Attributes

Name	Description	Data type	Required?	Applies to Web client?	Applies to Outlook clients?
Description	Deprecated. Text that Microsoft Dynamics CRM displays in the Outlook client when users click the parent folder. Use the *Descriptions* element instead.	*string*	No	No	Yes
DescriptionResourceID	For internal use only	*string*	No	Yes	Yes
Icon	Specifies a URL to an image; allows you to display a different icon for the area	*string*	No	Yes	Yes
ID	Specifies a unique identifier in ASCII; spaces are not allowed. Valid values: a–z, A–Z, 0–9, and underscore (_)	*string*	Yes	Yes	Yes
License	Deprecated	*string*	No	Yes	Yes
ResourceId	For internal use only	*string*	No	Yes	Yes
ShowGroups	Specifies whether Microsoft Dynamics CRM will display an area's groups in the navigation pane. Valid values: *true* *false*	*boolean*	No	Yes	Yes

TABLE 6-6 *Area* **Attributes**

Name	Description	Data type	Required?	Applies to Web client?	Applies to Outlook clients?
Title	Deprecated. Allows you to enter a different text label for the area. Use the *Titles* element instead.	*string*	No	Yes	Yes
Url	Specifies a URL that Microsoft Dynamics CRM will display in the Outlook clients when users click the folder that represents the area.	*string*	No	No	Yes

Group

In each area of the site map, you can specify multiple groups (or no groups at all). By using groups, you can categorize the subareas in a manner that makes the most sense for your end users. The *Group* element in sitemap.xml uses the attributes listed in Table 6-7.

TABLE 6-7 *Group* **Attributes**

Name	Description	Data type	Required?	Applies to Web client?	Applies to Outlook clients?
Description	Deprecated. Text that Microsoft Dynamics CRM displays in the Outlook client when users click the parent folder. Use the *Descriptions* element instead.	*string*	No	No	Yes
DescriptionResourceID	For internal use only	*string*	No	Yes	Yes
Icon	Specifies a URL to an image; allows you to display a different icon for the area	*string*	No	No	Yes

TABLE 6-7 *Group* **Attributes**

Name	Description	Data type	Required?	Applies to Web client?	Applies to Outlook clients?
ID	Specifies a unique identifier in ASCII; spaces are not allowed. Valid values: a–z, A–Z, 0–9, and underscore (_)	*string*	Yes	Yes	Yes
IsProfile	Controls whether this group represents a user-selectable profile for the workplace. Valid values: *true* *false*	*boolean*	No	Yes	No
License	Deprecated.	*string*	No	Yes	Yes
ResourceId	For internal use only.	*string*	No	Yes	Yes
Title	Deprecated. Allows you to enter a different text label for the group. Use the *Titles* element instead.	*string*	No	Yes	Yes
URL	Specifies a URL that Microsoft Dynamics CRM will display in the Outlook clients when users click the folder that represents the group.	*string*	No	No	Yes

Most of these attributes behave in exactly the same way as the *Area* element's attributes do. We want to highlight one attribute unique to the *Group* element: *IsProfile*.

When users navigate to the Workplace area, they can click a Personalize Workplace link in the navigation pane. Microsoft Dynamics CRM displays the Set Personal Options dialog box, as shown in Figure 6-31.

In this dialog box, users can select the groups that they want to see in their personal workplaces. Changing the groups displayed affects what they will see, but it does not affect what other users see.

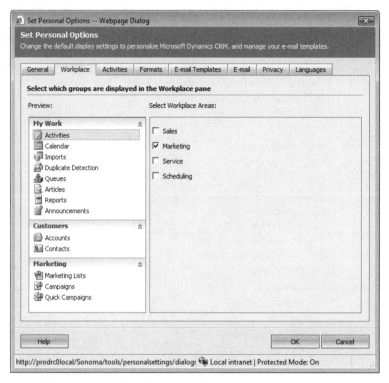

FIGURE 6-31 Set Personal Options dialog box

Tip The Microsoft Dynamics CRM user interface uses the phrase "Select Workplace Areas," but users actually select which workplace *groups* they want to display.

Microsoft Dynamics CRM does not display all of the groups in the Personalize Workplace area; it shows only groups with an *IsProfile* attribute value of *true*. So, if you want a particular group in the Workplace area to always appear for all users, set the *IsProfile* attribute of the group to *false* so that Microsoft Dynamics CRM won't allow users to clear the selection of the group in the Personalize Workplace area.

Tip Although users can personalize their workplace only by using the Web client, their changes will also appear in the Outlook client.

SubArea

Each group element in the sitemap.xml file can contain multiple *SubArea* elements (or no *SubAreas* elements at all). *SubArea* elements possess the attributes shown in Table 6-8.

TABLE 6-8 *SubArea* Attributes

Name	Description	Data type	Required?	Applies to Web client?	Applies to Outlook clients?
AvailableOffline	Specifies whether to display a subarea when the user is offline in Outlook client. Valid values: *true* *false*	*boolean*	No	No	Yes (offline client only)
Client	Specifies whether to display the subarea depending on the type of client with which the user is accessing Microsoft Dynamics CRM. Valid values: *All* (the default value) *Outlook* *OutlookLaptopClient* *OutlookWorkstationClient* *Web* Multiple values can be used separated by a comma and without any spaces.	*string*	No	Yes	Yes
Description	Deprecated. Text that Microsoft Dynamics CRM displays in the Outlook client when users click the parent folder (group). Use the *Descriptions* element instead.	*string*	No	No	Yes
DescriptionResourceID	For internal use only.	*string*	No	Yes	Yes
Entity	Allows you to enter the schema name of the entity that you want to display when users click the sub-area link.	*string*	No	Yes	Yes
Icon	Specifies a URL to an image; allows you to display a different icon for the subarea.	*string*	No	Yes	Yes

TABLE 6-8 *SubArea* **Attributes**

Name	Description	Data type	Required?	Applies to Web client?	Applies to Outlook clients?
ID	Specifies a unique identifier in ASCII, with no spaces. Valid values: a–z, A–Z, 0–9, and underscore (_)	*string*	Yes	Yes	Yes
License	Deprecated.	*string*	No	Yes	Yes
PassParams	Specifies whether information about the organization and language context are passed to the URL. Valid values: 0 = don't pass parameters [default] 1 = pass parameters				
OutlookShortcutIcon	Specifies the icon to display in the Outlook client.	*string*	No	No	Yes
ResourceId	Used internally to address a localized label to display. Valid values: a–z, A–Z, 0–9, and underscore (_)	*string*	No	Yes	Yes
Title	Deprecated. Allows you to enter a different text label for the subarea. Use the *Titles* element instead.	*string*	No	Yes	Yes
URL	Specifies a URL that Microsoft Dynamics CRM will display in the Outlook client when users click the folder that represents the subarea; overrides the schema name if you specify both a schema name and a *Url* attribute.	*string*	No	Yes	Yes

In regard to the *Client* attribute, the name values refer to older names of the Microsoft Dynamics CRM client for Outlook, but you can probably figure out what they refer to:

- **Outlook**   Refers to both the online and offline Outlook clients

- **OutlookLaptopClient**   Refers to just Microsoft Dynamics CRM for Outlook with Offline Access

- **OutlookWorkstationClient**   Refers to Microsoft Dynamics CRM for Outlook (no offline access)

Privilege

The last element of the sitemap.xml document is the *Privilege* element. Using the *Privilege* element in a *SubArea* element is optional, and you can include multiple *Privilege* elements if you desire. By using the *Privilege* element, you can specify security criteria that Microsoft Dynamics CRM evaluates to determine whether it will display a subarea to a user.

It's important to note that the *Privilege* element does not override the Microsoft Dynamics CRM security settings for custom and system entities. Therefore, even if you try to assign Display (Read) rights to a user by adding a site map permission, the Microsoft Dynamics CRM security settings would not display the subarea to a user who does not have Read rights to that entity.

So, if the Microsoft Dynamics CRM security settings always make the final determination on whether to display a subarea to a user, you might wonder why anyone would ever need to use a *Privilege* element. We think the most obvious benefit of the *Privilege* element is that you can use it to configure security display rights for custom Web pages that you integrate with Microsoft Dynamics CRM (which you cannot do by using the native Microsoft Dynamics CRM security settings).

The *Privilege* element has the attributes listed in Table 6-9.

TABLE 6-9 *Privilege* **Attributes**

Name	Description	Data type	Required?	Applies to Web client?	Applies to Outlook clients?
Entity	Allows you to enter the schema name of the entity that you want to reference for the permissions check.	string	Yes	Yes	Yes
Privilege	Specifies the permissions needed to display this subarea. Valid values: A comma-separated list with no spaces, made up of these possible values:	string	No	Yes	Yes

TABLE 6-9 *Privilege* **Attributes**

Name	Description	Data type	Required?	Applies to Web client?	Applies to Outlook clients?
	All				
	AllowQuickCampaign				
	Append				
	AppendTo				
	Assign				
	Create				
	Delete				
	Read				
	Share				
	Write				

Here is an example that uses the *Privilege* element.

```
<SubArea Id="test_subarea" Url="custompage.aspx">
   <Privilege Entity="account" Privilege="Delete, Write"/>
</SubArea>
```

In this example, if the user has Delete and Write permissions for the Account entity, Microsoft Dynamics CRM will display the subarea in the application navigation pane. Conversely, if you add the custom Web page Custompage.aspx to your system and you don't want a particular user to see this page, you can simply use the *Privilege* element in your site map to specify a security permissions that you know the user does not have.

Site Map Editing Tips and Tricks

Here are a few tips and tricks that might save you some time when editing the sitemap.xml file:

- **Editing the order of elements in the site map works only in the Web client**   The Microsoft Dynamics CRM Web client displays navigation elements (such as subareas) in the order that you specify in the site map. However, the Microsoft Dynamics CRM Outlook clients use folders to display the navigation. Outlook always displays folders in alphabetical order, not in the order that you specify in the site map.

- **Don't confuse the *Titles* and *Descriptions***   It's easy to confuse what the *Titles* and *Descriptions* elements do. The *Descriptions* elements appear only in the Microsoft Dynamics CRM Outlook client; the *Titles* elements appear in both the Web and Outlook clients.

- **The site map is case-sensitive**   Because the site map uses XML, which is case-sensitive, you must ensure that you have used correct casing for all of your attributes.

- **Watch out for default attributes**   When we first opened the sitemap.xml file to edit the name of a group or area (such as Sales), we looked for the text "Sales" so that we could change it. However, that text does not appear in the default sitemap.xml file. Instead, the *Area* element for sales looks like this:

```
<Area Id="SFA" ResourceId="Area_Sales" Icon="/_imgs/sales_24x24.gif"
DescriptionResourceId="Sales_Description">
```

It isn't obvious what text you need to change because the word to be updated ("Sales") does not appear anywhere in this element. Because Sales is one of the six default areas, you can change this text by adding a *Title* attribute to the *Area* element.

```
<Area Id="SFA" ResourceId="Area_Sales" Icon="/_imgs/sales_24x24.gif"
DescriptionResourceId="Sales_Description" Title="New Sales Title">
```

For custom entities, you need to add the *Titles* and *Title* elements to configure the text that appears. Because neither the *Titles* nor *Title* elements or the *Title* attribute appear in any of the default elements, Microsoft Dynamics CRM uses a behind-the-scenes translation to display the titles of the default entities. In this example, you can describe the *Title* as defaulted from Microsoft Dynamics CRM because it doesn't exist in the site map. So, if you're looking in the site map and you can't find the correct attribute to update in the sitemap.xml file, it's probably a default attribute that you need to add explicitly.

- **Id attributes must be unique**   Each element requires an *Id* attribute. Remember that it must be unique from all of the other *Id* attributes in the site map.

- **Beware of conditionally required attributes**   Earlier in this chapter, we outlined the attributes of each element and identified whether Microsoft Dynamics CRM requires them. In some cases, an attribute might become required depending on the settings of other elements. Microsoft Dynamics CRM usually prompts you with a good description of the error, but you should know that these conditional requirement possibilities exist.

- **How to recover from a site map error**   Although Microsoft Dynamics CRM validates the sitemap.xml file before the import, you might accidentally import a sitemap.xml file that modifies the navigation so that you cannot access the import customizations tool. If you cannot access the import tool, you obviously can't import a corrected site map file! In Microsoft Dynamics CRM, you can access the import customizations tool directly at the following URL: *http://<crmserver>/<organizationname>/tools/systemcustomization/ ImportCustomizations/importCustomizations.aspx*

- **Refreshing site map changes**   When you import a new site map, sometimes clicking the Refresh button in Internet Explorer does not update Microsoft Dynamics CRM with your changes. This depends on the type of change you have made. If you don't see the changes you expect, we recommend closing the Web browser window and opening a new one.

- **Do not change the home page of Microsoft Dynamics CRM Outlook folders**   You might think that you can also customize the Microsoft Dynamics CRM clients for

Outlook by changing the home page of a folder in Outlook (accessed by right-clicking a folder and selecting Properties).

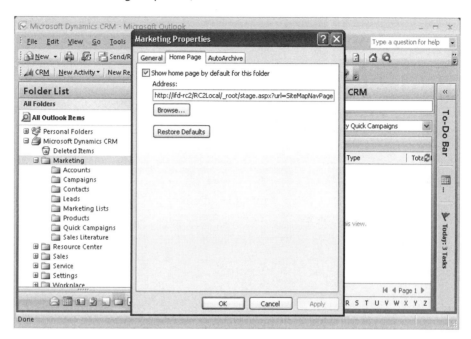

Although making this change is technically possible, it might adversely affect how the Microsoft Dynamics CRM client for Outlook interacts with the site map, so we strongly discourage you from trying this.

- **Consistent attribute ordering saves editing time**   You can put the attributes in any order you want, but putting them in a consistent order will save you time later when you want to edit them.

- Always export the latest site map and create a backup copy before making any edits.

Entity Display Areas

As you learned earlier in this chapter, you can select the areas where you want Microsoft Dynamics CRM to display your custom entities. You select or clear the appropriate areas by using the entity editor in the Web client. When you select new areas or remove existing areas by using the entity editor, Microsoft Dynamics CRM automatically edits the site map for you. Because of this nuance, you should *always* export the site map before you edit it to make sure that you are working with the latest version.

Conversely, editing the different areas of the site map to include different entities and then importing the new file automatically updates the custom entity in Microsoft Dynamics CRM.

Therefore, the display area check boxes update accordingly the next time you access this Web page.

Summary

Microsoft Dynamics CRM includes many powerful features, but the ability to create custom entities and custom data relationships through a Web-based administration tool ranks as one of the more important ones. By using custom entities, you can easily track additional types of information related to your customers. Custom entities behave almost exactly like the default system entities. Understanding how Microsoft Dynamics CRM structures entity relationships can help you plan and map your system to ensure that there is a smooth implementation. By using the site map in Microsoft Dynamics CRM, you can reconfigure almost every area of the application navigation (Web client and Outlook client) to hide or show the entities and links that make the most sense for your users.

Chapter 7
Reporting and Analysis

Customer relationship management (CRM) systems capture data about your customers' interactions, and your database will quickly grow to thousands (or millions) of data records about your customers. Although it's beneficial to capture these customer interactions in a database, this customer data provides real value only if you can easily extract it and present it to your users in a simple and easy-to-read format. Microsoft Dynamics CRM offers multiple reporting and analysis options, and you can decide which tool to use based on factors such as the desired output format and the type of user who will create the analysis.

Everyone defines the expression *report* differently. When people in information technology departments hear the term, most immediately think of powerful report-writing tools such as Microsoft SQL Server Reporting Services. However, most nontechnology users such as managers and executives think of reports as simply *getting their data*; they typically don't care how they get it, as long as they get it on time and accurately. The Microsoft Dynamics CRM user interface uses the term *report* to refer to any type of data analysis file, regardless of its origin and type. Therefore, a report may be a Microsoft Office Excel file, a SQL Server Reporting Services report, a third-party reporting file, or a link to an external Web page report.

 Note Although Microsoft Dynamics CRM does not explicitly refer to entity views and the Advanced Find feature as reports, we consider them important data reporting and analysis tools because of their flexibility and ease of use. Therefore, we discuss their use as reporting tools in this chapter.

Reporting and Analysis Tools

Microsoft Dynamics CRM offers several reporting and analysis tools:

- Entity views and the Advanced Find feature
- Dynamic Excel files
- SQL Server Reporting Services reports
- Filtered views
- Third-party reporting tools

Each of these tools provides a unique set of benefits and drawbacks, so you should determine the most appropriate tool for each type of analysis. As you can see from the list of reporting tools, Microsoft Dynamics CRM even lets you integrate third-party reporting tools in the user interface. Table 7-1 summarizes the reporting tools and their features.

TABLE 7-1 **Reporting and Analysis Tools in Microsoft Dynamics CRM**

	Entity views and Advanced Find	Dynamic Excel files	Microsoft Dynamics CRM Report Wizard	SQL Server Reporting Services reports	Filtered views	Third-party reporting tools
Report output	Microsoft Dynamics CRM grids	Excel PivotTables and PivotCharts	Web-based Reporting Services reports created from the Microsoft Dynamics CRM user interface.	Web-based reports that can be exported to additional formats, such as Excel, PDF, and CSV	SQL Server database view	Varies
Skill level required to create or modify reports	Beginner	Beginner	Beginner	Advanced	Advanced	Varies
Ability to schedule reports for e-mail delivery	No	No	Yes (with Reporting Services Report Manager)	Yes	No	Varies
Supports charts and graphs	No	Yes (with Excel charts or PivotCharts)	Yes	Yes	No	Varies

TABLE 7-1 **Reporting and Analysis Tools in Microsoft Dynamics CRM**

	Entity views and Advanced Find	Dynamic Excel files	Microsoft Dynamics CRM Report Wizard	SQL Server Reporting Services reports	Filtered views	Third-party reporting tools
Report results can be cached for better performance	No	No	Yes	Yes	No	Varies
Supports subreports and drill-through reports	No	No	Yes	Yes	No	Varies
Can include data from multiple entities in results	Yes	Yes	Yes	Yes	Yes	Yes
Can include data from multiple entities in the report query	Yes	Yes	Yes	Yes	Yes	Yes
Supports report snapshots	No	No	Yes	Yes	No	No
Can prompt users to enter parameters before running reports	No	No	Yes	Yes	No	Varies
Allows for user access restrictions	Yes	Yes	Yes	Yes	Does not apply	Varies
Respects Microsoft Dynamics CRM security settings by default	Yes	Yes	Yes	Yes	Yes	No
Ability to run reports contextually from an entity list or form	No	No	Yes	Yes	No	No
Users can access from Reports list	No	Yes	Yes	Yes	Yes	Yes

SQL Server Reporting Services reports clearly offer the most benefits and functionality, but they also typically require an advanced user to author new reports. In addition, Reporting Services reports can take additional time to configure and manage compared to the simpler reporting tools. The entity views and dynamic Excel tools offer less functionality than Reporting Services does, but any beginner user can quickly and easily author new reports. We review each of these reporting tools in more detail in the following sections.

Note   Your reporting options and access vary depending on the deployment model being used. Customers using the Microsoft Dynamics CRM on-premise deployment model will have the most access to all of the features available. Microsoft Dynamics CRM Live and Internet-facing deployment customers face more constraints. We focus the discussion in this chapter on the Microsoft Dynamics CRM on-premise deployment model unless otherwise noted.

Entity Views and Advanced Find

We explained how to set up and configure entity views in Chapter 5, "Entity Customization: Forms and Views," but we want to emphasize that you can use entity views in conjunction with the Advanced Find feature as an entry-level reporting and analysis tool. Entity views and the Advanced Find feature offer the following reporting benefits:

- Users of all skill levels can set up and configure views by using the Advanced Find feature, but Advanced Find also offers powerful query features such as Group AND and Group OR that more sophisticated report writers will want.

- Users can save any views that they create using the Advanced Find feature so that they can quickly run that same report later.

- By default, only the user who creates an Advanced Find view can access it. However, in Microsoft Dynamics CRM you can share Advanced Find views with other users or with a team. Therefore, you can explicitly control access to a view so that only a select group of users has access.

- Entity system views (but not saved Advanced Find views) can be imported or exported along with the other system customizations.

- Users can sort the records in their views in ascending or descending order by clicking the column headers.

- Users can export the records in their views to Excel, and they can create dynamic worksheets that link to the Microsoft Dynamics CRM database.

- You can query on attributes of related entities, and also display columns of related entities in your view. For example, you can display columns from the Contact entity in an Opportunity view, and you can use columns from Contact as part of the view filter criteria.

However, using entity views for reporting and analysis involves the following restrictions:

- You have very little control over output formatting because Microsoft Dynamics CRM displays the data in the grid. You can't include charts, graphs, or subtotals when using views.

- Although you can include columns from related entities in your display, you cannot sort on them.

- You can't schedule reports or deliver them by e-mail when using views.

Note Of course, you can export your data to Excel, and use that application to sort data and create charts, graphs, subtotals, PivotTables, and so on.

Remember, although Microsoft Dynamics CRM doesn't refer to entity views and the Advanced Find feature as *reports*, they're still powerful reporting and analysis tools.

Dynamic Excel Files

Many people consider Excel to be the world's most popular reporting and analysis tool, and we wholeheartedly agree with that statement. With its broad range of features and ease of use, we expect that your users use Excel for a lot (or most) of their data analysis needs. Fortunately, Microsoft Dynamics CRM provides excellent integration with Excel so that your users can create reports and perform analysis of CRM data with a tool that they're already comfortable using.

To export data from Microsoft Dynamics CRM to Excel, users can simply click the Export to Excel button on the grid toolbar and Microsoft Dynamics CRM will export the data from the current view. When users export data to Excel, Microsoft Dynamics CRM provides three types of export options:

- Export to static worksheet

- Export to dynamic PivotTable

- Export to dynamic worksheet

We review the difference between static and dynamic exports in the following subsection.

Note All examples and references to Excel in this chapter assume you use Microsoft Office Excel 2007. Microsoft Dynamics CRM also supports Microsoft Office Excel 2003 SP3.

Static vs. Dynamic Exports

If you choose one of the dynamic export options, Microsoft Dynamics CRM creates a live link between the data in your Excel file and the view data in Microsoft Dynamics CRM. When the data in Microsoft Dynamics CRM changes, you can automatically update the data in your dynamic Excel file by simply refreshing the external data. Exporting data to a static worksheet takes a snapshot of data at the time that you export it, but you can't automatically update the data in Excel like you can with a dynamic export.

> **Important** Dynamic Excel files update Microsoft Dynamics CRM data only when Excel refreshes external data. When you export a dynamic Excel file from Microsoft Dynamics CRM, Excel prompts you on whether you want to enable automatic data refresh for this file.

In addition to creating a live link between the Excel file and the Microsoft Dynamics CRM database, the dynamic Excel files also respect the Microsoft Dynamics CRM security settings. Each user sees only his or her permissible data allowed in the dynamic Excel file. For example, assume that you have two customer support representatives named Scott Bishop and Eli Bowen. If Scott exports a dynamic worksheet of the view My Active Cases, the Excel file shows the cases that Scott owns. Now imagine that Scott creates several additional customizations and additions to the Excel file and then e-mails the modified Excel file to Eli. When Eli opens the worksheet, Excel refreshes the Microsoft Dynamics CRM view data to show only the cases that Eli owns. Although both Scott and Eli use the same Excel file, Microsoft Dynamics CRM automatically displays the correct data to them based on their security settings. Because static Excel files don't maintain a link to the Microsoft Dynamics CRM database, they don't update the data based on the user's security settings.

> **Tip** If you choose to disable automatic refresh, and multiple users share the same file (through e-mail or a network share, for example), it's possible for users to view records to which they should not have access. In this example, if Scott disables the automatic refresh option and then e-mails the file to Eli, Eli would see all of Scott's active cases upon opening the file because the data would not refresh with Eli's credentials. Excel would show the appropriate data the next time that Eli refreshes external data, but this clearly isn't an ideal scenario. Because of this potential issue, we recommend that you enable the automatic refresh option if multiple users may access the same Excel file.

At first, you may wonder why anyone would want to export a static worksheet. We can think of several instances in which you may prefer a static export over a dynamic export:

- If you want to capture data at a specific time, you should use a static worksheet. For example, you may want to run a weekly report every Monday and compare the results to the previous week. With a dynamic Excel file, the numbers in the report may change because it's always pulling live data.

- If you want to share an Excel file exported from Microsoft Dynamics CRM with a non–Microsoft Dynamics CRM user, you must use a static worksheet. When a user opens a dynamic Excel file, Excel retrieves the latest data from Microsoft Dynamics CRM based on the user's security settings. If the person opening the file (such as an external vendor or partner) doesn't have an active account, he or she encounters a login error.

- Similarly, if the person viewing the report isn't logged on to the computer with the same credentials used for his or her Microsoft Dynamics CRM user account, that user also receives a login error message. For on-premise deployments, Microsoft Dynamics CRM uses Integrated Windows authentication, passing the domain and user name with which the user logs on to the computer to retrieve the appropriate dynamic data. Even if the person has a Microsoft Dynamics CRM license, he or she might be logged on under a different name or domain. This could happen if a user tries to open a dynamic Excel file from a personal home computer not registered to the user's work domain.

- Microsoft Dynamics CRM Live customers must install Microsoft Dynamics CRM for Microsoft Office Outlook to take advantage of the dynamic export options.

Now that you understand the differences between static and dynamic exports, we explain how to use the Export to Excel feature in the user interface.

> **Caution** Remember that when users export dynamic Excel files, they run their reports on your *live* production database. Therefore, it's possible for a user unknowingly to create a complex query that seriously degrades the performance of your server. Because all Microsoft Dynamics CRM users share the server, a renegade query or report could destroy the performance of Microsoft Dynamics CRM for all of your users. If you're concerned about this scenario, you can disable the Export to Excel security privilege for certain roles in Security Settings as explained in Chapter 3, "Managing Security and Information Access."

Refreshing external data in Excel

When you export data to a dynamic Excel file, Microsoft Dynamics CRM automatically creates a link in the Excel file to the Microsoft Dynamics CRM SQL Server database. The process of refreshing external data in Excel isn't unique to Microsoft Dynamics CRM, but we briefly want to explain some tips on how to do it. We will review a couple of methods for refreshing external data in Excel:

- Right-click the dynamic data range, and then click Refresh.

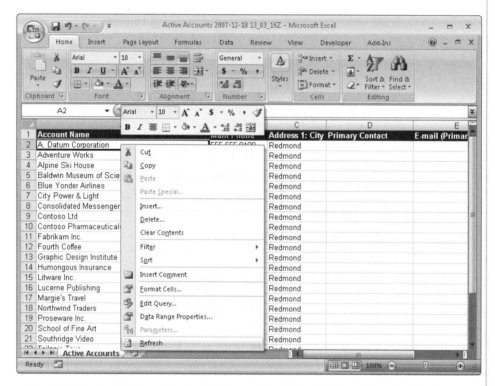

- Click the Data tab on the Excel ribbon. Click Refresh All, and Excel refreshes the external data for all of the dynamic ranges in your workbook.

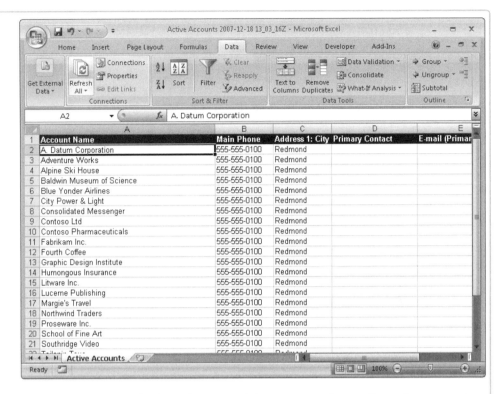

In addition to manually refreshing the external data, you can also configure the automatic refresh control by editing the data range properties. You access the data range properties by right-clicking a cell in the dynamic data range, and then selecting Data Range Properties. You can also access the properties by clicking Properties in the Data tab.

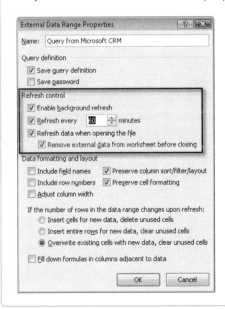

In the External Data Range Properties dialog box, you can enable an auto-refresh at a specified time interval or force a data refresh every time someone opens the Excel worksheet.

Exporting

To export data from Microsoft Dynamics CRM to Excel, you simply click the Excel button on the grid toolbar, as shown in Figure 7-1.

FIGURE 7-1 Excel button on the grid toolbar

Note   To access the Excel button on the grid toolbar, users must have the Export to Excel security privilege enabled for at least one of their assigned security roles.

After you click the Excel button, Microsoft Dynamics CRM prompts you to select the type of Excel file that you want to export. As we reviewed, you can choose to export data to Excel in one of the following formats:

- Static worksheet (one page or all pages)
- Dynamic PivotTable
- Dynamic worksheet

Static Worksheet

This option exports a snapshot of the CRM data at the time the user created the export. If data changes in Microsoft Dynamics CRM after the export, the new data will not be reflected in the user's Excel file.

If you view a grid with multiple pages, Microsoft Dynamics CRM prompts you with the additional option of exporting to a static worksheet with records from all pages in the current view (see Figure 7-2). You can then determine whether you want all the records in the view or just the records displayed on the current page.

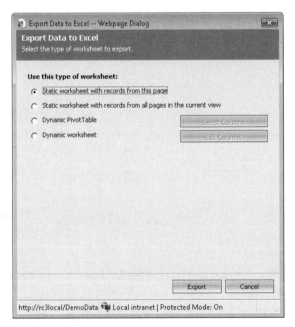

FIGURE 7-2 Exporting records from one page or all pages

When you export a static worksheet, Microsoft Dynamics CRM automatically creates a column in Excel for each column in your view.

Dynamic PivotTable

If you choose to export data as a dynamic PivotTable, Microsoft Dynamics CRM automatically creates a blank PivotTable using the view's data as its source data. By default, Microsoft Dynamics CRM includes all of the view's columns in the PivotTable source data, but you can add or remove columns by clicking the Select Columns button before you click the Export button. Figure 7-3 shows a sample PivotTable created by exporting the All Opportunities view.

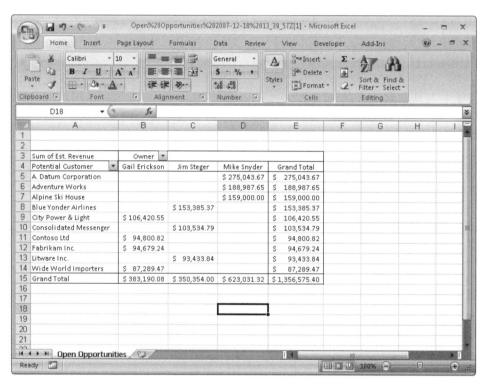

FIGURE 7-3 Sample dynamic PivotTable using the All Opportunities view

As you can see, with PivotTables you can sort, summarize, and group data into meaningful reports. From any PivotTable in Excel, you can easily create a chart by right-clicking the PivotTable, and then clicking PivotChart on the shortcut menu. Figure 7-4 shows the sample chart created with one click from the dynamic PivotTable in Figure 7-3.

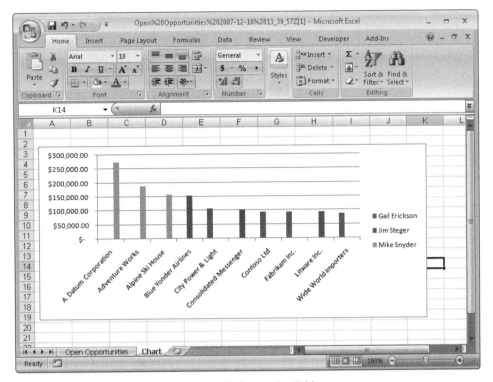

FIGURE 7-4 Sample chart created with one click from a PivotTable

> **Tip** PivotTables may appear intimidating to new users, but they're actually quite easy to use, and they provide excellent data analysis and charting options. The Microsoft Office Web site (*http://office.microsoft.com*) offers several excellent free tutorials that introduce PivotTables. We highly recommend these online tutorials if you're not comfortable using PivotTables as a data analysis tool.

Dynamic Worksheet

Exporting a view to Excel as a dynamic worksheet creates a worksheet of rows and columns in Excel similar to a static worksheet export. However, by using the dynamic worksheet option you can select additional data columns to include in your Excel worksheet before you click the Export button. And, of course, it automatically creates the live link to the Microsoft Dynamics CRM database. By exporting a dynamic worksheet, you can use the data in that dynamic worksheet to create your own PivotTables, charts, and additional calculations as necessary.

You will receive a warning when opening the Microsoft Dynamics CRM exported file in Excel 2007. Microsoft Dynamics CRM saves the exported Excel file with an older .xls extension, prompting the warning shown in Figure 7-5. Simply click Yes and continue loading the file.

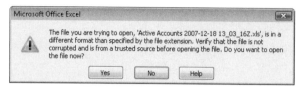

FIGURE 7-5 Excel 2007 opening file warning

Once done, the default security setup for Excel 2007 will prompt a security warning as shown in Figure 7-6.

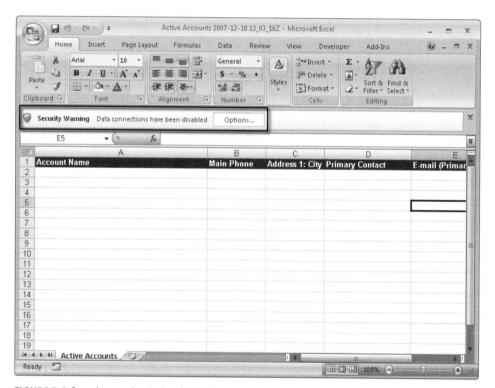

FIGURE 7-6 Security warning in Excel 2007

Click the Options button, and enable the content from the data connection (Figure 7-7). Once done, the worksheet loads with the Microsoft Dynamics CRM data.

FIGURE 7-7 Enabling dynamic content in Excel 2007

A closer look at exported Excel files

When you export an Excel file from an on-premise Microsoft Dynamics CRM deployment, the file is saved with an .xls extension. However, Microsoft Dynamics CRM does not export a typical Excel file. Microsoft Dynamics CRM actually exports an *XML file* that it saves with an .xls extension to maintain correct file associations. Just like any .xml file, you can open and edit the exported Excel file with any text editor or XML editor. If you tried to open a regular (non-XML) Excel file in a text editor, you would see a bunch of strange characters.

For example, if you export the default My Active Accounts view as a dynamic worksheet and open the exported file in an XML editor, you would see something like this.

Note Editing the SQL connection does not apply to exported files from Microsoft Dynamics CRM Live or for files exported from Internet-facing deployment servers. Those deployment models do not have direct access to the SQL Server and therefore will use a Web service connection to retrieve data.

```
<?xml version="1.0"?>
<?mso-application progid="Excel.Sheet"?>
<Workbook xmlns="urn:schemas-microsoft-com:office:spreadsheet"
 xmlns:o="urn:schemas-microsoft-com:office:office"
 xmlns:x="urn:schemas-microsoft-com:office:excel"
 xmlns:dt="uuid:C2F41010-65B3-11d1-A29F-00AA00C14882"
 xmlns:ss="urn:schemas-microsoft-com:office:spreadsheet"
 xmlns:html="http://www.w3.org/TR/REC-html40">
 <DocumentProperties xmlns="urn:schemas-microsoft-com:office:office">
  <Author>Jim Steger</Author>
  <Created>2007-12-17T19:12:02Z</Created>
  <Version>12.00</Version>
 </DocumentProperties>
 <ExcelWorkbook xmlns="urn:schemas-microsoft-com:office:excel">
  <WindowHeight>9090</WindowHeight>
  <WindowWidth>13260</WindowWidth>
  <WindowTopX>480</WindowTopX>
  <WindowTopY>45</WindowTopY>
  <ProtectStructure>False</ProtectStructure>
  <ProtectWindows>False</ProtectWindows>
 </ExcelWorkbook>
 <Styles>
  <Style ss:ID="Default" ss:Name="Normal">
   <Alignment ss:Vertical="Bottom"/>
   <Borders/>
   <Font ss:FontName="Arial"/>
   <Interior/>
   <NumberFormat/>
   <Protection/>
  </Style>
  <Style ss:ID="s62">
   <Font ss:FontName="Arial" x:Family="Swiss"/>
  </Style>
  <Style ss:ID="s63">
   <Font ss:FontName="Arial" x:Family="Swiss" ss:Color="#FFFFFF" ss:Bold="1"/>
   <Interior ss:Color="#333399" ss:Pattern="Solid"/>
  </Style>
 </Styles>
 <Worksheet ss:Name="My Active Accounts">
  <Names>
   <NamedRange ss:Name="Query_from_Microsoft_CRM"
    ss:RefersTo="='My Active Accounts'!R2C1:R3C6"/>
  </Names>
  <Table ss:ExpandedColumnCount="6" ss:ExpandedRowCount="3" x:FullColumns="1"
   x:FullRows="1" ss:StyleID="s62">
   <Column ss:StyleID="s62" ss:Width="225"/>
   <Column ss:StyleID="s62" ss:Width="75" ss:Span="1"/>
   <Column ss:Index="4" ss:StyleID="s62" ss:Width="111.75" ss:Span="1"/>
   <Column ss:Index="6" ss:StyleID="s62" ss:Hidden="1"/>
   <Row ss:StyleID="s63">
    <Cell><Data ss:Type="String">Account Name</Data></Cell>
    <Cell><Data ss:Type="String">Main Phone</Data></Cell>
    <Cell><Data ss:Type="String">Address 1: City</Data></Cell>
    <Cell><Data ss:Type="String">Primary Contact</Data></Cell>
```

From here you could manually edit various properties of the Excel XML file as you see fit. You probably won't ever have to edit an exported Excel file, but it's nice to know that the option exists.

> **Caution** Only advanced users should attempt to edit an Excel XML file manually. If you do edit the file, you could very easily make a change that prevents Excel from opening the file correctly, so be very careful. Make sure that you have a backup in case something goes wrong.

One instance in which you may want to edit the Excel XML file occurs when you need to change the connection string information of a file in Excel 2003. Exporting a dynamic worksheet or PivotTable creates a live link to the originating Microsoft Dynamics CRM database, but no user interface exists in Excel 2003 to change the SQL Server database that the file references. However, you can change the connection string by editing the Excel XML file. If you examine the XML nodes, you'll see a node called *<Worksheet>* with a child element called *<QueryTable>*. Under the *<QueryTable>* node, you will see a node called *<QuerySource>*. *<QuerySource>* contains an element called *<Connection>* that will look similar to this.

```
<Connection>DRIVER=SQL Server;APP=Microsoft Office 2003;Network=DBMSSOCN;Trusted_
Connection=Yes;SERVER=sqlserver;DATABASE=organizationname_MSCRM</Connection>
```

Simply enter your updated *SERVER* and *DATABASE* values, save the file, and then open it in Excel. Voila! You just changed the connection string.

Microsoft Dynamics CRM also exports static worksheets as XML, but manually editing those files obviously won't provide as much benefit as editing the dynamic files because the data in a static worksheets won't change.

Note Excel 2007 provides a mechanism for changing the connection properties in the user interface.

The ability to export Microsoft Dynamics CRM data directly to Excel provides a powerful reporting and analysis option that users can employ to quickly create ad-hoc analyses. We want to share three advanced techniques for working with dynamic Excel files:

- Updating the server connection and SQL statement in dynamic Excel files
- Using Microsoft Query to edit columns in exported dynamic Excel files
- Running Excel as a different user

After you export your dynamic worksheet or PivotTable to Excel, you may want to change the connection properties or alter the query of your file. If you're comfortable manually editing SQL syntax, you can follow these steps to change the SQL Server and default database. In addition, you can add (or remove) the columns that Excel queries from Microsoft Dynamics CRM in your dynamic files.

Updating the server connection and SQL statement in exported dynamic Excel files

1. In your dynamic Excel file, click the Data tab, and then click Connections.

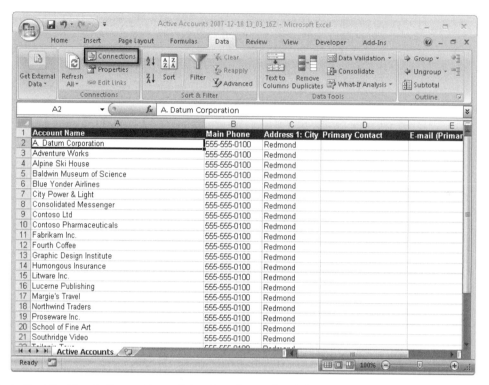

2. In the Workbook Connections dialog box, leave the default Connection value selected, and click Properties.

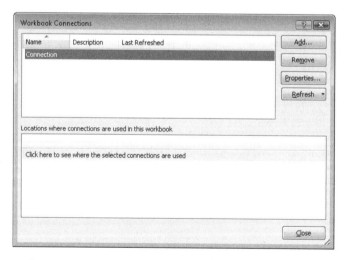

3. In the Connection Properties dialog box, click the Definition tab.

4. You can now alter the connection string and change values, such as the server and database.

5. In the Command text box, you will see the data query and all of the columns that Excel pulls from Microsoft Dynamics CRM. You can alter the query here, adding or removing the columns that want you to appear in your Excel file.

The Command text box of the Definition tab does not provide a useful environment in which to edit your SQL query. Fortunately, Excel 2003 and Excel 2007 provide the Microsoft Query Excel component to assist you with changing SQL queries. You must have Microsoft Query Excel installed on your computer to perform these steps. Excel 2003 and Excel 2007 can automatically install this component for you.

Using Microsoft Query to edit columns in exported dynamic Excel files

1. In your dynamic Excel file, right-click the data range, and then click Edit Query.

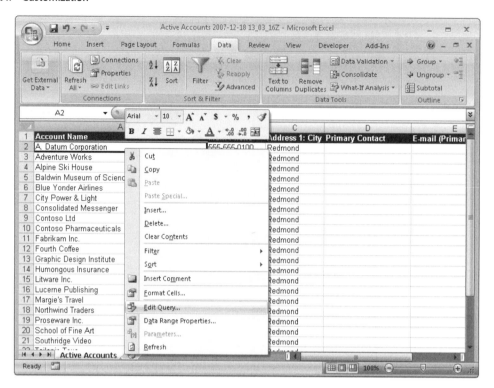

Note You can also click the Edit Query button in the Connection properties Definition tab.

2. A message appears that says, "This query cannot be edited by the Query Wizard." Click OK.

3. In the Microsoft Query editor, click the SQL button on the toolbar.

4. In the SQL editor, you will see the data query and all of the columns that Excel pulls from Microsoft Dynamics CRM. From here, you can manually add or remove the columns that you want to appear in your Excel file.

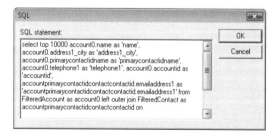

5. After editing the columns in SQL, click OK. You may see another message that says, "SQL Query can't be represented graphically. Continue anyway?" Click OK.

6. On the File menu, click Return Data to Microsoft Office Excel. Excel returns the modified columns in your data set.

> **Tip** Consider using Microsoft SQL Server Management Studio to edit and test yo
> updating it in Excel.

The dynamic Excel files exported from an on-premise Microsoft Dynamics CRM deploym
connect to the database using Integrated Windows authentication. This means that Excel
uses your current user credentials to query the Microsoft Dynamics CRM database when you
open dynamic Excel files. This works great for your end users, but as an administrator you
may want to run dynamic Excel files as if you're a different user to confirm the data that your
users will see. If you use the default Microsoft Windows authentication, you would have to
log off of your computer, and then log on as the user that you want to impersonate. If you
have to do this frequently, the process can take too much time. Fortunately, you can follow
these steps to impersonate a different user when running Excel 2007. The following steps
should work on Microsoft Windows XP and the Windows Vista operating system.

Running Excel as a different user

1. Open a new text file in Notepad by clicking Start, and then clicking Run. Type **notepad**, and press Enter.

2. In the Notepad file, enter the following command. Replace *domain\username* with the credentials of the user you wish to impersonate.

```
runas /profile /user:domain\username "C:\Program Files\Microsoft Office\Office12\
EXCEL.EXE"
```

> **Note** If you use Excel 2003, simply replace the *Office12* in the preceding script with *Office11*.

3. Save the file with a .bat extension, such as runas_excel.bat.

4. Double-click the newly created .bat file, and you will be prompted for the account's password.

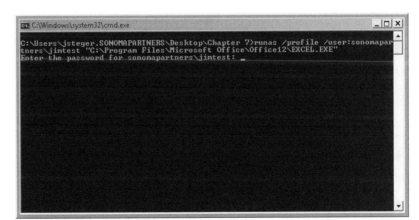

password, Excel will start. Open your exported dynamic file as before, xternal data, Excel retrieves data from Microsoft Dynamics CRM using at you just supplied.

rst time you run an Office application (such as Excel or Microsoft Office Word) computer, Office will prompt you to set up your profile. If you cannot do this mpersonated user, you may need to log on to the computer one time as the ser, and then start Excel to set up your profile. Then, you can log back on as se the technique previously described.

Accessing Reports with Microsoft Dynamics CRM

As you learned earlier, the term *reports* in Microsoft Dynamics CRM can refer to different types of files, including the following:

- Any type of report files (such as Excel, Word, or Microsoft Office Access) that you upload to the server

- Reporting Services reports

- Links to Web pages (categorized as reports)

- Third-party report files

Regardless of the report type, Microsoft Dynamics CRM stores all the reports in the Microsoft Dynamics CRM SQL Server database. You can access the Microsoft Dynamics CRM Reports list by navigating to the Reports subarea of the Workplace area. Almost all of your common tasks will be handled through the Microsoft Dynamics CRM user interface.

We now discuss the following:

- Report security

- Reports in the user interface

- Running Reporting Services reports

Report Security

Reports exist in Microsoft Dynamics CRM as an entity just like the other system entities such as Leads, Accounts, Contacts, and so on. As such, the Report entity also adheres to the standard security characteristics that apply to all entities as described in Chapter 3 with a few notable caveats.

Each report in Microsoft Dynamics CRM contains a *Viewable By* attribute, with values of *Organization* or *Individual*. If the report's *Viewable By* value equals *Organization*, all users will be able to run the report, provided they have minimal Report Read privileges. If the *Viewable By* value equals *Individual*, the Report Read privilege will determine each user's access to the report. To create, view, and update a report, users must have the appropriate Report privileges assigned to at least one of their assigned user roles.

> **Note** You can find the Report entity privileges in the Security Role form's Core tab.

Two additional privilege settings exist for reports, Publish Reports and Add Reporting Services Reports.

- **Publish Reports**   Allows a user to make a report available (or viewable) to the entire organization. For Reporting Services reports, this privilege also allows the user to publish the report to the Reporting Services Web server for external use.

- **Add Reporting Services Reports**   Permits the user to upload an existing Reporting Services report file to Microsoft Dynamics CRM. Reporting Services files use the Report Definition Language (RDL) format. This privilege differs from the Create privilege of the Report entity, which refers to creating a new report by using the Report Wizard or by adding another file type (such as an Excel file or PDF report).

An additional level of security exists for Reporting Services reports to protect the data the reports display. Provided a report uses the Microsoft Dynamics CRM filtered views, the report will only display the data that each user should see. This means that even if a user has access to run a report, that user will see only the data he or she has rights to view as defined by the user's Microsoft Dynamics CRM security role. We discuss filtered views in more detail later in the chapter.

> **More Info** Microsoft Dynamics CRM uses the term *Reporting Services reports* to mean reports in the format of the Report Definition Language (RDL), as opposed to an Excel file or link to another report. Reporting Services reports have additional built-in functionality with Microsoft Dynamics CRM. As you will soon learn, you can create Reporting Services reports through the new Microsoft Dynamics CRM Report Wizard or with a tool such as Microsoft Visual Studio 2005.

Reports in the User Interface

You can run reports in the Microsoft Dynamics CRM user interface from one of three areas:

- Reports list
- Entity list
- Entity form

Reports List

The default Microsoft Dynamics CRM installation creates a subarea called Reports in the My Work group of the Workplace area (see Figure 7-8). In addition to listing all of the available reports, you can use this Reports list to administer reports, assuming that you have the appropriate security permissions.

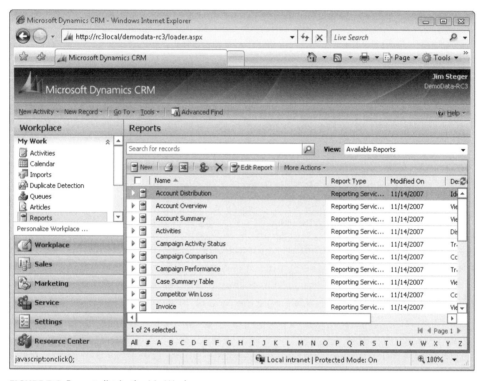

FIGURE 7-8 Reports list in the My Work group

Tip Remember that you can modify the site map to make the Reports list appear wherever you want in the application navigation; for example, you can create a new area called Reports in the Application Areas section. You enter **Url="/CRMReports/home_reports.aspx"** to display the Reports list.

Entity List

In addition to the Reports list, you can also allow users to run Reporting Services reports from the toolbar of an entity's grid by clicking the Report button, as shown in Figure 7-9 for the Account entity.

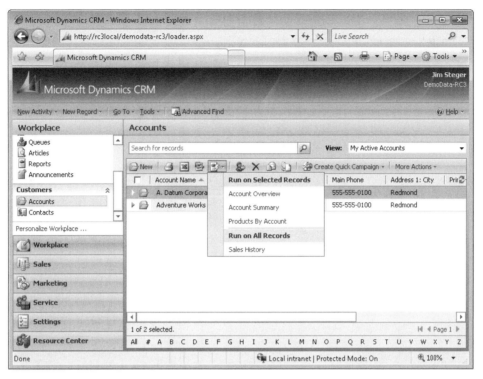

FIGURE 7-9 Accessing reports from an entity's grid toolbar

This figure shows reports listed among one of two groups: Run on Selected Records or Run on All Records. If the user chooses to run one of the reports listed under Run on Selected Records, Microsoft Dynamics CRM prompts users to select which records they want to apply to the report. Microsoft Dynamics CRM displays three options:

- All applicable records
- The selected records
- All records on all pages in the current view

By selecting one of these three options, users can prefilter the records that they want Microsoft Dynamics CRM to include in the report results.

If the user selects a report listed under the Run on All Records group, Microsoft Dynamics CRM will run the report independently of the selected records or the records that appear in the view.

Important We refer to reports that run for Run on Selected Records as *contextual reports* because they run in the context of particular records. You must create the report query using the correct technique to create your own custom contextual reports. We explain this technique later in this chapter.

Entity Form

Similar to running reports from the entity list, you can also run reports directly from the entity form by clicking the Reports button on the menu bar (Figure 7-10).

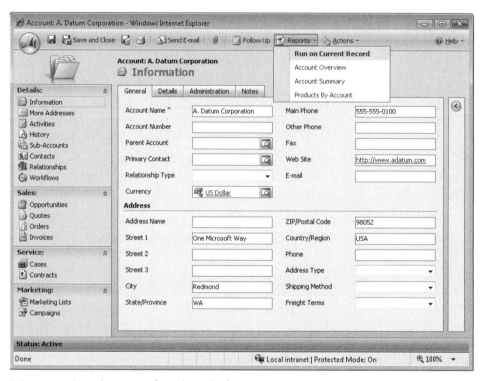

FIGURE 7-10 Accessing reports from the entity form

Unlike running reports from the entity list, you can choose to run only a contextual report. On the entity form, Microsoft Dynamics CRM lists all possible contextual reports under the Run on Current Record grouping. If you choose to run a report from the entity form, Microsoft Dynamics CRM will not prompt you (like the entity list report) to further refine the record set because only one record exists to run the report. Figure 7-11 shows the output if you run the Account Overview report directly from the A. Datum Corporation Account record.

Without the contextual report feature, if you wanted to run the Account Overview report for a single Account, you would need to navigate to the Reports list, pick the report you want to run, and then manually specify an Account. Instead, Microsoft Dynamics CRM allows users to run a contextual report directly from the entity menu bar of an Account record, saving numerous clicks every time they run a report.

 Tip Create contextual reports for your custom reports whenever possible to save your users extra clicks in the application navigation.

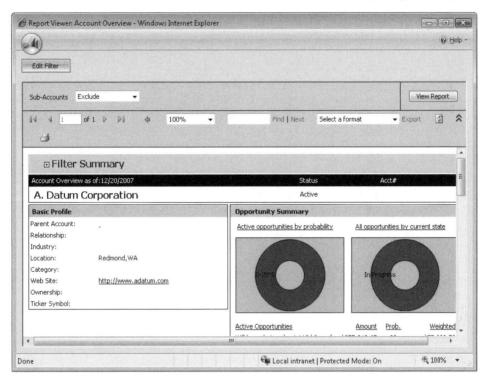

FIGURE 7-11 Sample Account Overview report

We explain later in this chapter how to configure contextual reports and specify where you want them to appear in the application navigation.

Running a Reporting Services Report

From the Reports list, simply double-click the name of the report that you want to run. You can run contextual reports by clicking the report name on the form or grid toolbar.

Now we examine what your users see when they run Reporting Services reports:

- Report prefiltering
- Results navigation
- Export options

Report Prefiltering

In Microsoft Dynamics CRM, you can create Reporting Services reports with a prefiltering option. *Prefiltering* gives users the opportunity to set up and modify filter criteria before running the report. By prefiltering a report, users can drastically reduce the number of records that Reporting Services must manipulate, which provides a noticeable increase in the report's and overall system's performance. When users run a report with prefiltering enabled, they see the report filtering criteria on the Report Viewer page. Figure 7-12 shows the default prefilter page for the Account Distribution report.

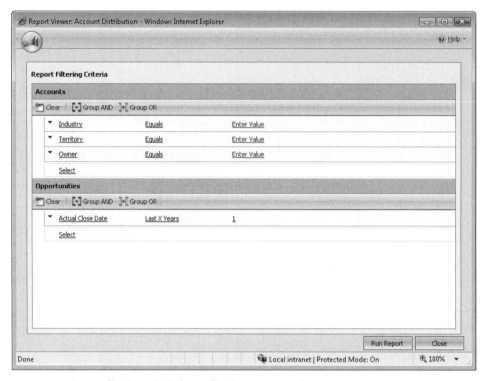

FIGURE 7-12 Report filtering criteria for prefiltering report results

As you can see, this report prefilter allows the user to enter values for multiple default filters against multiple entities before running the report. If the user does not enter values when prompted by the Enter Value text (Industry, Territory, and Owner), the report will run as if that filter does not exist.

Important The report prefiltering functionality exists only through the Microsoft Dynamics CRM user interface. If you navigate directly to the Reporting Services Web server and run a report from there, the prefiltering option is not displayed. Likewise, you must create or upload reports through Microsoft Dynamics CRM to include the prefiltering feature. You should not upload the reports directly to Reporting Services.

In addition to the default prefilter parameters that appear on the Report Viewer page, users can further modify the prefilter criteria. The report prefilter uses the same user interface as the Advanced Find feature (as shown in Figure 7-10), so users should be able to manipulate the prefilter settings easily. Just as with the Advanced Find feature, you can create highly complex report filters to search for the exact type of results that interest you.

Results Navigation

After you set the prefilter criteria for your reports, click the Run Report button to execute the report. Microsoft Dynamics CRM displays a status message to the user while it creates the report. After executing the report, Microsoft Dynamics CRM updates the Report Viewer page with the completed report. Figure 7-13 shows the output for the Account Distribution report.

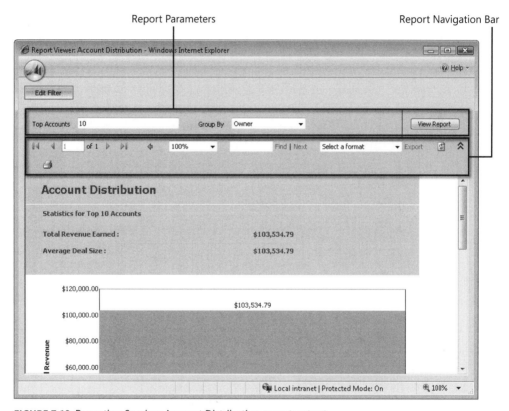

FIGURE 7-13 Reporting Services Account Distribution report output

In Figure 7-13, we highlight two areas of the report output. By using the report navigation bar, you can navigate records, change the zoom level, find text in the report output, export the results, and refresh and print the data. The navigation bar exists with all Reporting Services reports.

The report parameters unique to the report appear above the report navigation bar. By using report parameters, you can further refine the results in your report. Reporting Services supports many types of parameters, including text fields and drop-down lists, as shown in the Account Distribution example.

Important Report parameters behave differently from prefilter criteria. In Microsoft Dynamics CRM, you use prefilter criteria to reduce the number of records returned in your report. After Reporting Services generates the report, you use report parameters to filter the report records already contained in the result set. You define report parameters in the report's .rdl file; you define prefilter criteria in Microsoft Dynamics CRM.

If you double-click any of the columns in the Account Distribution chart, a new report appears on the Report Viewer page. Reporting Services refers to this nested report as a *subreport*. By using subreports, you can link reports together so that users can examine a specific area of a report to get more detailed information. You can configure a subreport to accept parameters dynamically from its parent report.

Tip Creating subreports and drill-throughs on your custom reports takes more work to develop and test, but users absolutely love this feature. Consider adding this drill-through feature on some of the most popular or important custom reports in your deployment.

Export Options

After you manipulate the report results to display the records that you want, you can easily export the report data to multiple formats. To export a report, simply choose a format from the Select a format list on the report navigation bar, and then click Export, as shown in Figure 7-14.

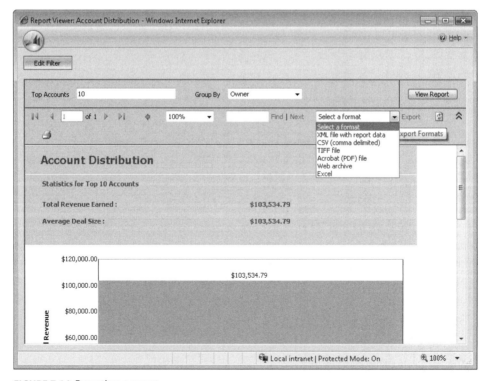

FIGURE 7-14 Exporting a report

You can export the report in any of the following formats from a standard Reporting Services installation.

- XML file with report data
- CSV (comma delimited)
- TIFF file
- Acrobat (PDF) file
- Web archive
- Excel

Creating Reports in Microsoft Dynamics CRM

Numerous tools exist for creating Reporting Services reports, including an add-in for Visual Studio 2005, Reporting Services Report Builder, and multiple third-party tools. In addition to these options, Microsoft Dynamics CRM also provides you a simple, yet powerful wizard to create custom reports. In this section, we focus on the Microsoft Dynamics CRM Report Wizard. Later in the chapter, we cover creating and modifying Reporting Services reports with Visual Studio 2005.

All users have access to the Report Wizard to create a report for their personal use, assuming they have any level of access to the Report Create privilege. The installation enables the Report Create privilege on all security roles by default. By default, the Report Wizard creates the report as a personal (individual viewable) report.

You access the Report Wizard by creating a new report from the Reports grid. In addition to creating a report, you can use the Report Wizard to edit an existing Report Wizard report. We cover all the report properties and actions in the next section.

 Note Microsoft Dynamics CRM Live customers can also take advantage of the Microsoft Dynamics CRM Report Wizard to create new ad-hoc reports.

Starting the Report Wizard

1. Navigate to the Reports subarea in the Workplace area to view the Reports list.

2. Click New, and in the resulting New Report dialog box, click the Report Wizard button to start the Report Wizard.

The Report Wizard contains the following steps:

- Get Started
- Report Properties

- Select Records to Include in the Report
- Lay Out Fields
- Format Report
- Select Chart Type (optional)
- Customize Chart Format (optional)
- Report Summary
- Confirmation

Get Started

You can start with a new report or select an existing report created by the Report Wizard, as shown in Figure 7-15. If you choose an existing Report Wizard report, you can select to overwrite it so that you can edit a previously created report. The existing report lookup displays only reports created by the Reporting Wizard that you have access to edit.

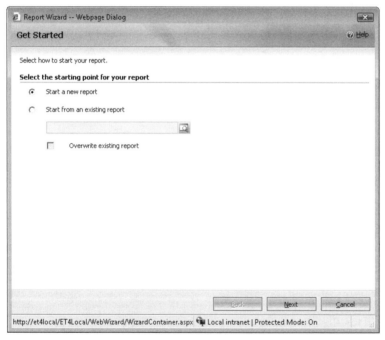

FIGURE 7-15 Get Started step

Report Properties

Figure 7-16 shows the properties you will set on this step. Specify the name of your report and enter a description. We highly recommend taking the time to enter a meaningful description for your report. Finally, you need to choose the primary entity for your report's data. You may optionally select a related entity should you need to display or filter on data from a related entity.

FIGURE 7-16 Report Properties step

Select Records to Include in the Report

Microsoft Dynamics CRM next asks to create a default filter for the report. The standard Advanced Find screen (Figure 7-17) appears next. You can choose from an existing saved view or create a new filter.

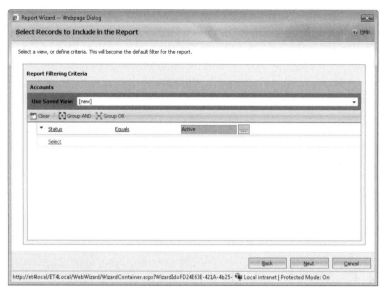

FIGURE 7-17 Defining default filter step

Lay Out Fields

In the Lay Out Fields step, you can add report display columns, groupings, and totals in the report. You can also configure the default sorting of the data and limit the number of records returned. As Figure 7-18 shows, the form contains the familiar Common Tasks pane.

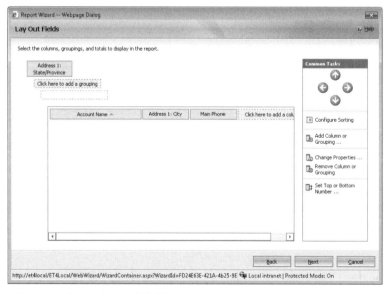

FIGURE 7-18 Report layout definition

From this area, you can do the following:

- Move existing fields and columns (Green Arrows)
- Configure sorting
- Add columns or groupings
- Change properties
- Remove columns or groupings
- Set top or bottom numbers

Green Arrows

The up and down arrows move existing fields placed from the grouping section to the display columns and vice versa. The left and right arrows move display columns accordingly.

Configure Sorting

The Configure Sorting button allows you to choose one attribute to use as the default sort.

Add Column or Grouping

The Add Column or Grouping button adds a new grouping attribute or display column depending on where your focus resides. If you click in the grouping area and then click this button, you will get the Add Grouping dialog box.

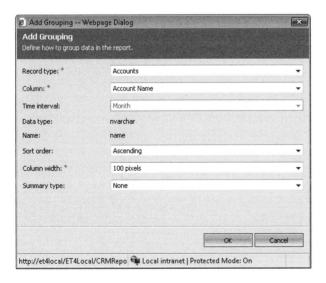

Likewise, if you were to click in the display column area and then click the Add Column or Grouping button, you would see the Add Column dialog box.

> **Note** You can also click the *Click here* rectangles to open the corresponding dialog boxes.

When you add a column or grouping, you can specify the following:

- **Record type**   Choose the primary entity, secondary entity, or any related entities to the primary or secondary entity.

- **Attribute**   Choose the attribute to group or display. The attribute's data type will determine some of your remaining options.

- **Time interval**   The time interval groups *datetime* attributes by day, week, month, or year. This option exists only for grouping attributes with a *datetime* data type.

- **Column width**   Select from a preset list of widths specified in pixels.

- **Sort Order**   Determines which attribute to default the sort order. This option displays only available for grouping attributes. The Configure Sorting action handles column display sorting.

- **Summary Type**   Optionally determines how to aggregate the data. The choices vary by the chosen attribute's data type and the column type (grouping or display). You can choose from the following options: Count, Average, Maximum, Minimum, and Percent of Total.

Change Properties

You can use this action to alter the details of an existing display column or grouping.

Remove Column or Grouping

Select an existing column or grouping to remove it from the layout.

Set Top or Bottom Number

The Set Top or Bottom Number option filters the number of summary groups to display in the final report. You can select to keep the top or bottom group and also specify how many groups to show. You set this option if you have a numeric attribute with a summary type set.

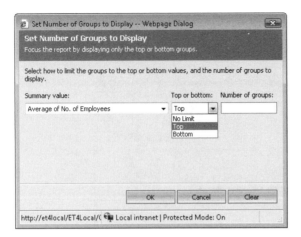

For instance, assume a report groups accounts by the average number of employees by state and the final output would have four total groupings. If you were to configure to display only the top two groups, your report will only display the two states with the highest average number of employees.

Format Report

As you can see in Figure 7-19, if you do not include a numeric column with a summary type, you will not be able to add a chart to your report. If your report does not need a chart, you can just click Next and continue to the next step.

FIGURE 7-19 Report format step with chart warning

In this simple Account report example, we went back to the previous step and added a new attribute, *No. of Employees*. This column is an *integer* data type, and we set the *Summary* value to *Average*. Figure 7-20 shows the new layout.

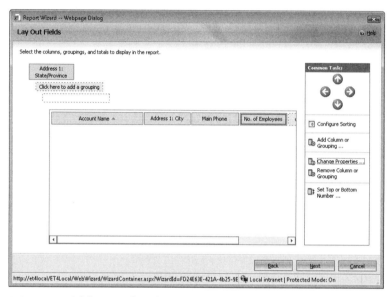

FIGURE 7-20 Adding *No. of Employees* attribute in the Lay Out Fields dialog box

Figure 7-21 shows the updated report format screen. You now can choose a chart option.

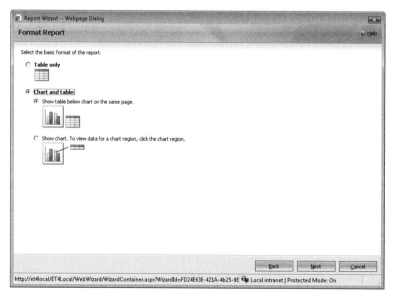

FIGURE 7-21 Format report chart selection after summary of an *integer* attribute added

Select Chart Type

The Select Chart Type page is displayed only if you have chosen to include a chart in your report. As Figure 7-22 shows, you choose from the following chart types:

- Vertical bar chart
- Horizontal bar chart
- Line chart
- Pie chart

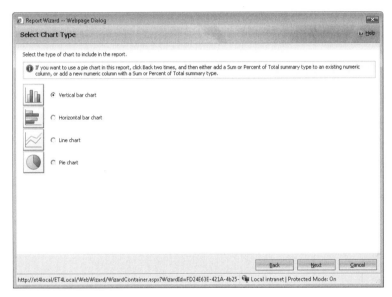

FIGURE 7-22 Chart type selection

The Pie chart requires a summary of type Sum or Percent to be used. Microsoft Dynamics CRM automatically disables the option if you don't have the proper fields in your layout.

Customize Chart Format

The Customize Chart Format page (as shown in Figure 7-23) is displayed when you include a chart in the report. This step presents you with standard charting options. The drop-down menus dynamically update based on your form layout selections. This prevents you from choosing an incorrect value for your axes.

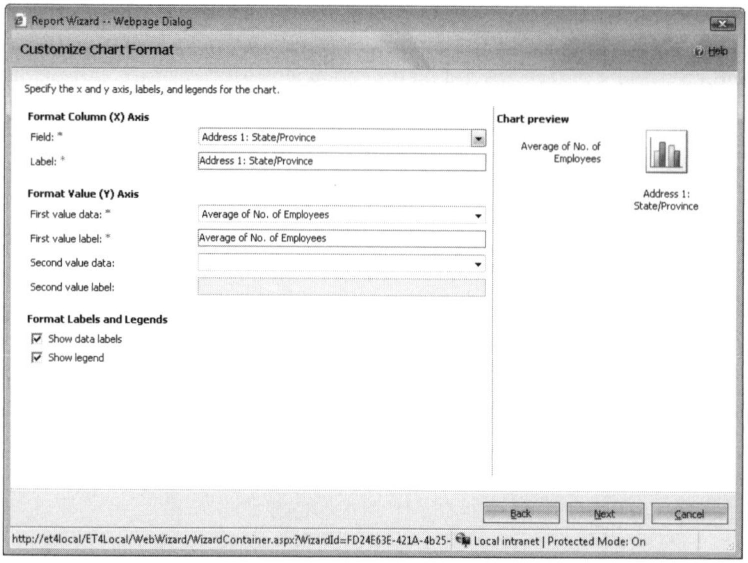

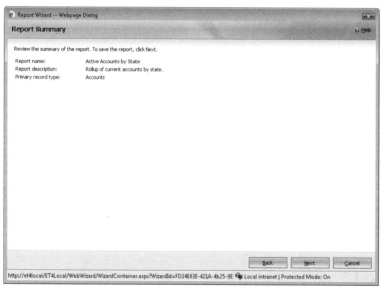

FIGURE 7-23 Customize chart format

Report Summary

The Report Summary step describes your basic report options, as shown in Figure 7-24. Click Next to create the report.

FIGURE 7-24 Summary step

Confirmation

If the report is created successfully, you see the Confirmation page, as shown in Figure 7-25. If any errors were encountered, the error and explanation are displayed and you can go back and correct the problem.

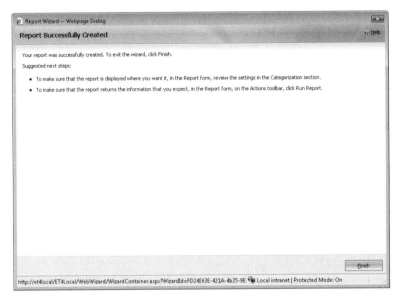

FIGURE 7-25 Confirmation step

After the report generates, you click Finish. You return to the standard report form, as shown in Figure 7-26.

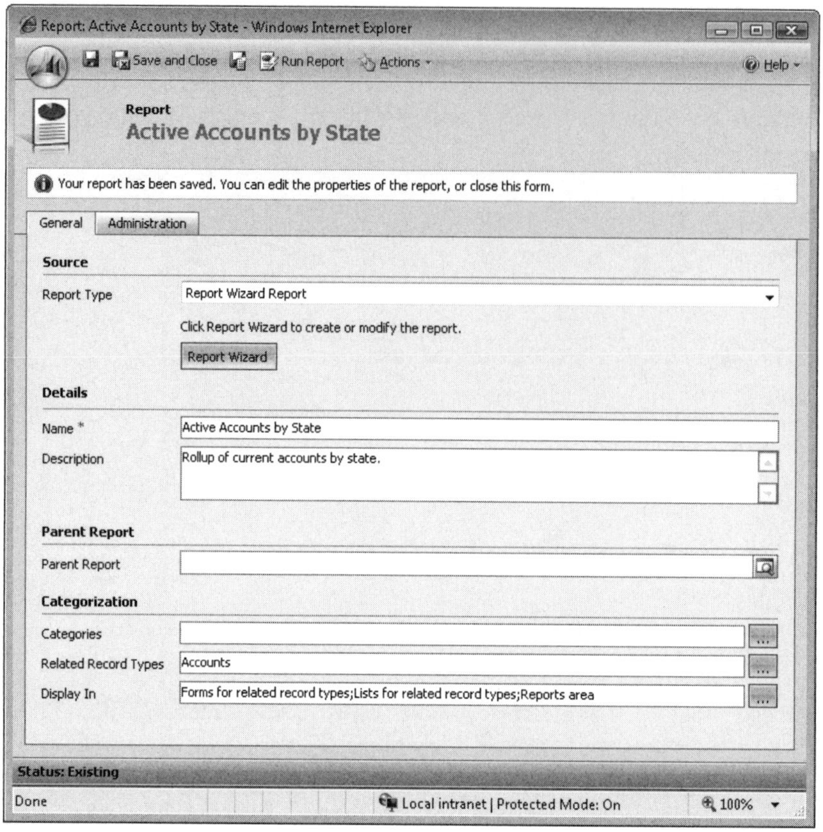

FIGURE 7-26 Report form

Figure 7-27 shows this report's two-page output. The first page displays the chart listing the average employees by state. The second page shows the account list by state. Notice that accounts that don't have a state specified conveniently are grouped in a Not Specified category automatically.

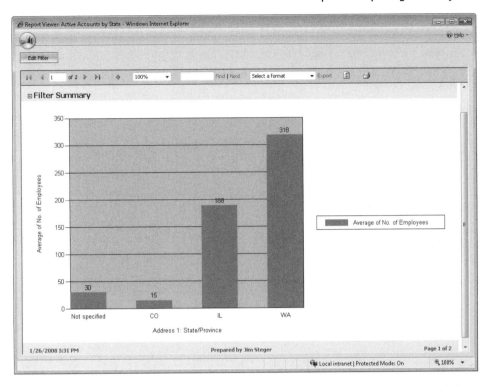

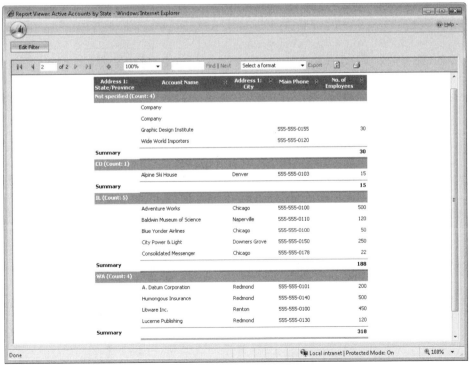

FIGURE 7-27 Active Accounts by State report

Managing Reports with Microsoft Dynamics CRM

You now know how to run reports, specifically Reporting Services reports, in Microsoft Dynamics CRM. You also learned how to use the new Reporting Wizard to create powerful, custom reports quickly. We now discuss the options you have to manage reports in Microsoft Dynamics CRM. We cover the following report options:

- Reports List Management
- Edit Report Properties
- Edit Report Actions
- Report Categories

Reports List Management

You can perform the following management tasks from the Reports list More Actions menu:

- Run report
- Edit the default filter
- Schedule the report
- Share the report

Remember that you can access the Reports list by browsing to the Workplace area and clicking Reports. You should already know how to run and share a report. Therefore, we focus on the remaining two actions, editing the default filter and scheduling a report.

Editing the Default Filter

Microsoft Dynamics CRM allows users to prefilter their results when they run Reporting Services reports. If you upload a new Reporting Services report with a query built with a special *CRMAF_* alias, Microsoft Dynamics CRM creates a default prefilter of "Modified in the last 30 days" for that report.

> **Note** We discuss this concept further later in the chapter.

You can edit the default prefilter to include additional default parameters that will automatically be displayed to your users. Of course, users can still edit the prefilter on the fly when they run the report, but you can save them clicks by editing a report's default filter to include the parameters that users will likely want.

Editing the default filter

1. Navigate to the Reports subarea in the Workplace area to view the Reports list.

2. Select the report that you would like to edit.

3. On the More Actions menu, click Edit Default Filter.

4. The Report Viewer page appears with the current prefilter settings in Detail mode. Simply edit the filter values to fit your needs.

5. Click Save Default Filter.

The next time a user runs this report, he or she will see the report prefilter that you just configured.

> **Note** Report prefilters apply only to Reporting Services reports, so you can edit the default filter only for reports of this type.

Scheduling a Report

Running complex reports can drastically reduce the performance of your reporting server. If you install Microsoft Dynamics CRM and Reporting Services on the same server, these complex reports can negatively affect performance for *all* of your Microsoft Dynamics CRM users, including those users not running reports. Therefore, it's ideal for you to install Reporting Services on a dedicated computer separate from Microsoft Dynamics CRM so that you can isolate the reporting demands from standard Microsoft Dynamics CRM usage. Regardless of the Reporting Services configuration, you can use the Microsoft Dynamics CRM Report Scheduling Wizard to reduce the impact of report execution on your Microsoft Dynamics CRM server performance. By using this technique, you can execute a report and cache the results, providing a performance boost at run time when viewing the report, according to a predefined schedule. In addition to caching report results, with this execution setting you also can take a report *snapshot* that freezes the report results as of a specific time (useful for quarterly progress reports, monthly quotas, and so on).

> **Note** Microsoft Dynamics CRM Live does not allow scheduled reports.

To use the Report Scheduling Wizard, you need to select the report you want to modify in the Microsoft Dynamics CRM Reports grid, click More Actions, and then click Schedule Report to start the wizard. We show you an example of how this works.

> **More Info** Microsoft Dynamics CRM actually configures a snapshot of the report in Reporting Services. The options you define in the Report Scheduling Wizard correspond to the options you have in Reporting Services.

Scheduling the Neglected Accounts report to execute monthly

1. Click the Neglected Accounts report in the Reports list.

2. Click More Actions, and then choose Schedule Report to open the Report Scheduling Wizard.

3. Choose whether you will schedule the report snapshot manually or per a defined schedule. Each option takes you through different, but self-explanatory pages. For this example, select On a schedule, and click Next.

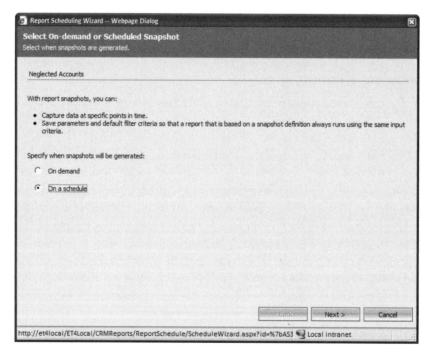

4. Next, select the frequency the report should execute. Each option (once, hourly, daily, weekly, monthly) provides additional unique parameters for you to configure. Select Monthly, and leave the default options. Click Next.

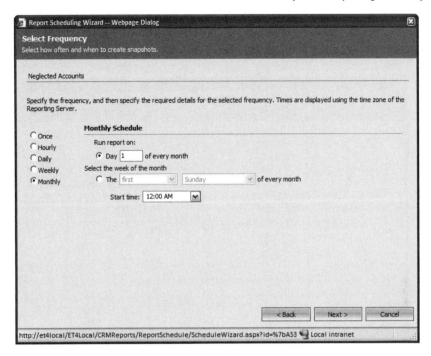

5. Next, you define the report parameters you want to use in your snapshot. This page displays the parameters specific to the report you scheduled. The step also provides an Edit Filter button. Click this button to further refine the filter used for the report snapshot. Keep the defaults, and click Next.

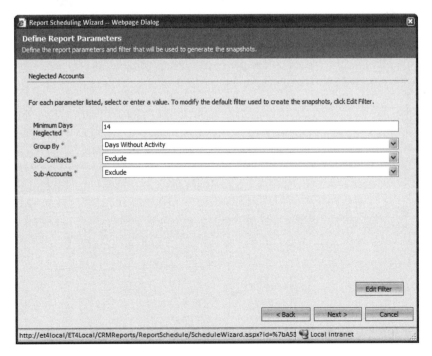

6. On the next page, you can review all of your selections. Pay special attention to the note listed. Only the most recent eight snapshots of your report will be stored. Click Create to complete the report snapshot.

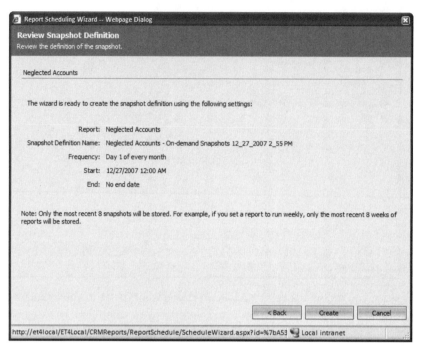

7. After processing the report, the final page appears, letting you know whether your report was properly scheduled or detailing any error the wizard encountered. Click Finish to complete the process.

If you try to view the report before the snapshot has completed, you will receive the error shown in Figure 7-28.

FIGURE 7-28 Reporting error

After the report snapshot completes, you cannot edit the schedule from the Microsoft Dynamics CRM user interface. However, you can update the schedule through the Reporting Services Report Manager interface. We demonstrate how to do this later in the chapter.

The user who created the snapshot becomes the report's owner. The report *Viewable By* attribute defaults to *Individual*. When you configure report caching or snapshots, the report runs under the context of the report owner.

If you want the report to be viewable by the organization, you must consider the owner of the report and the data that the owner can view. If the report runs in the context of a user with higher privileges (such as a system administrator), every person who views that report will see the same data that the system administrator would see regardless of the user's individual business unit and security roles. Consequently, a lower-level user may see data in the report that he or she would not be able to see through the Microsoft Dynamics CRM user interface.

Conversely, if you choose to cache a report or take a snapshot with a user who has lower-level privileges, a higher-level user may miss data that he or she should be able to view. Therefore, you must carefully consider the owner of the scheduled report and the report's intended audience when you configure report caching and snapshots.

Edit Report Properties

For every report in Microsoft Dynamics CRM, you can configure the report properties to set up where you want the report to appear in the user interface. To access a report's properties, select a report name in the Reports list, and then click the Edit Report button located on the Report grid toolbar. Figure 7-29 shows the properties editor.

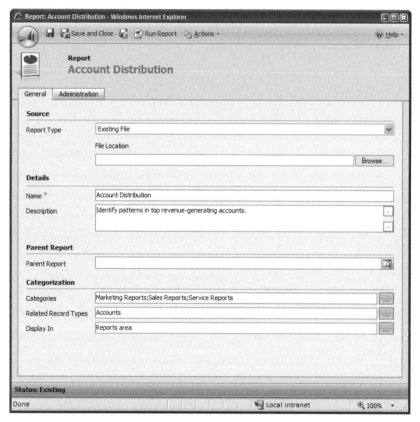

FIGURE 7-29 Report properties editor

 More Info The Reports list grid behaves differently from the other grids in Microsoft Dynamics CRM. Usually, if you double-click a record, you open the form to edit. With reports, double-clicking a record opens the Report Viewer and allows you to run the report. You must click the Edit Report button on the report grid's toolbar to edit the properties of any report.

You can alter the following properties when adding or editing a report:

- **Report Type** Microsoft Dynamics CRM includes the following report types: Report Wizard Report, Existing File, and Link to Web page. The Existing File option uploads a report file to Microsoft Dynamics CRM. The Link to Web page option stores a link pointing to a Web address. The Web page address can be either an internal or external URL.

- **File Location**   This displays as an upload dialog box or a simple text box, depending on the report type that you specify.

- **Name**   The name of the report. The report name appears in the navigation and the Reports lists, so try to be as descriptive as possible. If you enter the name of an existing report, Microsoft Dynamics CRM will ask if you want to overwrite the existing report file.

- **Description**   This optional field allows you to enter more information about what the report does. The description information appears in the Reports list.

- **Parent Report**   If the report is a subreport, you must specify its parent report for the report's drill-through functionality to work. The parent report must already exist in Microsoft Dynamics CRM.

- **Categories**   Select one or more report categories to which the report will belong.

- **Related Record Types**   This attribute allows you to associate the report with system and custom entities. For example, the Account Overview displays information about an Account record, so you would select Account in the Related Record Types field. You must configure this property in conjunction with the Display In property.

- **Display In**   After you specify the related record types for a report, you can choose how you want the report to be displayed for those entities. You can select any combination of Reports area, Lists for related record types, and Forms for related record types. Reports Area displays the report in the General reporting tab list for access. Lists for Related Record Types allows the report to be run against the entity list (grid). Forms for Related Record Types displays the report as an option from an individual entity's form page.

> **Note**   The Display In settings apply to all of a report's related record types. For example, you can't specify to display a report on entity A's form and list but only display the report on entity B's list. The Display In setting applies to all of the related record types.

- **Owner**   As with most records, the owner of the report helps determine the access permissions.

- **Viewable By**   Defines whether the organization or just an individual owner can run the report as defined by the user's report security settings.

- **Languages**   If you enable multiple languages, you need to specify a language. The report will be displayed for all users who have selected that language in their personal options. Select All Languages to make this report available to all users.

> **Note**   The Languages option does not change the language displayed inside the report output.

In addition to the editable report properties, Microsoft Dynamics CRM displays information about who created the report and the last time a user modified the report. You cannot edit these fields because Microsoft Dynamics CRM automatically populates them for you.

Edit Report Actions

The report edit form provides some additional actions, if you have the proper security enabled. These actions include standard record options such as Delete Report, Assign, Sharing, Copy Shortcut, and Send Shortcut. We discuss these report-specific actions:

- Download Report
- Revert to Personal Report/Make Report Available to Organization
- Publish Report for External Use

Downloading a Report

You can download individual report files from the Report list in the Microsoft Dynamics CRM user interface. This action saves the actual report's RDL file to your computer so that you can make copies, redistribute, or edit as you see fit.

Revert to Personal Report/Make Report Available to Organization

The Revert to Personal Report and Make Report Available to Organization actions require the user to have the Report Create and Read privileges and the Publish Reports to Organization privilege enabled. Microsoft Dynamics CRM displays the action based on the value of the *Viewable By* attribute. Table 7-2 shows the options available.

TABLE 7-2 *Viewable By* **Actions**

Viewable By attribute value	Action displayed in Microsoft Dynamics CRM
Individual	Make Report Available to Organization
Organization	Revert to Personal Report

Remember that the data displayed will still be filtered based on the user's record security settings.

Publish Report for External Use

The *Publish Report for External Use* action creates a copy of the report at the root of the organization's folder in Reporting Services. This will then more conveniently expose the report to additional features of Reporting Services, such as creating a subscription to e-mail the report on a scheduled basis. We walk through this particular example later in the chapter.

For on-premise deployments using the data connector, reports cannot be run directly from the Reporting Services server. The Microsoft Dynamics CRM data connector sets the security context on the report viewer when accessing the report. To allow other applications, such as Reporting Services, Microsoft SharePoint Server, or custom Microsoft .NET Framework pages to use a report, you must publish the report to the parent directory of Reporting Services, which uses traditional Windows authentication to connect. This approach requires that you properly configure trust for delegation.

You should be aware that when you publish the report for external use, you make a copy of the report in Reporting Services. Any changes to the original report will need to be republished. Also, any subreport will also be published, but the name will be displayed as the Microsoft Dynamics CRM report's globally unique identifier (GUID), as shown in Figure 7-30.

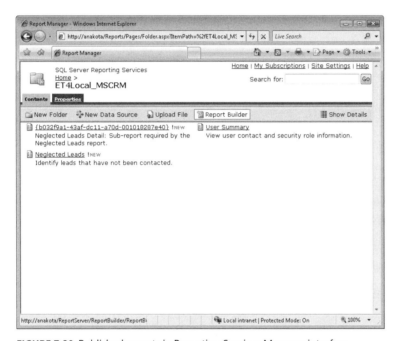

FIGURE 7-30 Published reports in Reporting Services Manager interface

We recommend that you go into the Reporting Services manager and hide any published subreports to avoid confusion with your users.

Report Categories

By using report categories, you can group similar reports together so that users can filter the Reports list based on these categories, as shown in Figure 7-31.

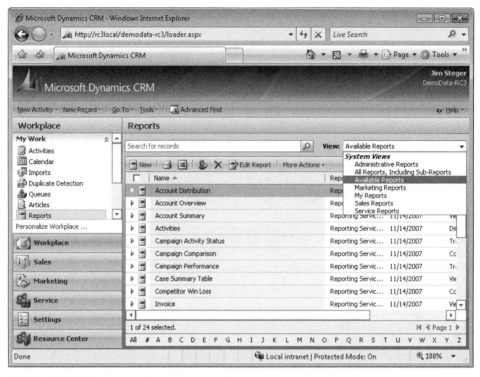

FIGURE 7-31 Filtering reports by report categories

You can assign a report to a single category, or you can assign a report to multiple categories if necessary. Microsoft Dynamics CRM includes four report categories in the default installation:

- Sales Reports
- Service Reports
- Marketing Reports
- Administrative Reports

Of course, you can add, modify, or delete these report categories to fit your business needs. Here we review how to manage report categories.

Managing report categories

1. Browse to the Settings area of Microsoft Dynamics CRM, and click Administration.

2. Click System Settings, and Microsoft Dynamics CRM will open the System Settings dialog box.

3. In the Reporting tab, you will see the familiar list for editing the categories. From here, you can add, modify, delete, and sort the various report categories. You can also assign a default category for any new reports.

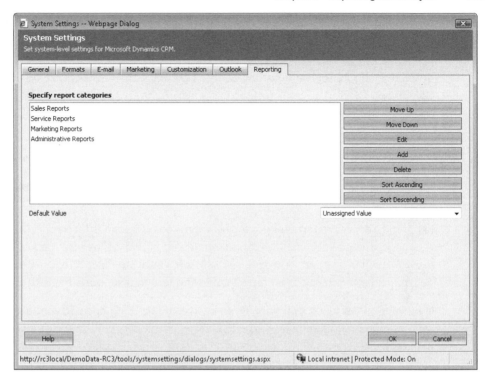

Remember the following when you edit report categories:

- Your changes will appear immediately in the user interface; you don't need to publish your changes.

- If a report belongs to just one category and you delete that category, you can still access the report by using the Available Reports filter.

- Microsoft Dynamics CRM currently ignores the order you set.

SQL Server Reporting Services

SQL Server Reporting Services (SSRS) provides a complete server-based platform for the delivery, creation, and administration of reports. Microsoft Dynamics CRM uses SQL Server Reporting Services as its reporting engine and takes advantage of many Reporting Services built-in features such as report scheduling, exporting reports to multiple formats, and report snapshots.

 Important This information applies to on-premise deployments only. Microsoft Dynamics CRM Live customers do not have access to Reporting Services.

SQL Server Reporting Services manages all parts of reporting, including report authoring, data source management, report security, output formats, and multiple delivery mechanisms.

In addition to SQL Server, Reporting Services supports other data source types, such as OLE DB and ODBC. This book focuses exclusively on the SQL Server data source because Microsoft Dynamics CRM uses SQL Server to store its data.

> **Important** Because Reporting Services supports multiple data sources, you can create a single report that combines Microsoft Dynamics CRM data with other non–Microsoft Dynamics CRM data (assuming Reporting Services supports the data type that you want to combine in the report).

Reporting Services report files use an .rdl extension. RDL stands for Report Definition Language, an open-schema XML language definition that defines the data retrieval and display layout of a report. You can use Microsoft Visual Studio 2005 to create report .rdl files, but you can also use any other report authoring tool that supports the RDL schema.

In addition to the report authoring flexibility created by using open-schema .rdl files, Reporting Services offers a programming model that allows developers to further customize and enhance the Reporting Services functionality, and Microsoft Dynamics CRM uses this with its integration.

This section covers just some aspects of Reporting Services and how it pertains to Microsoft Dynamics CRM. The breadth of Reporting Services functionality prevents us from covering it adequately in this text, and we encourage you to review the Reporting Services Online Help installed with the product and the following links for additional information:

- Product overview: *http://www.microsoft.com/sql/technologies/reporting/overview.mspx*
- Report Definition Language: *http://msdn2.microsoft.com/en-us/library/aa237626.aspx*

Reporting Services Versions

Microsoft Dynamics CRM 4.0 supports the following Reporting Services editions:

- SQL Server 2005, Standard Edition with Service Pack 2 (SP2)
- SQL Server 2005, Enterprise Edition SP2
- SQL Server 2005, Workgroup Edition SP2
- SQL Server 2005, Standard Edition, x64 SP2
- SQL Server 2005, Enterprise Edition, x64 SP2

> **Important** Microsoft Dynamics CRM 4.0 does not support SQL Server 2000 Reporting Services editions.

You will need Reporting Services installed prior to the installation of Microsoft Dynamics CRM 4.0. Please reference the Implementation Guide for further details.

Reporting Services comes with SQL Server, so no additional charge exists for the Reporting Services software if you have a valid SQL Server license and you install the Reporting Services web on the same server as SQL Server. However, for the most current licensing information, please visit *http://go.microsoft.com/fwlink/?LinkID=92675*.

Microsoft Dynamics CRM 4.0 Connector for Microsoft SQL Server Reporting Services

Remember that the on-premise deployment of Microsoft Dynamics CRM uses Integrated Windows authentication and filtered views to determine which data to display in the Reporting Services report. To help mitigate authentication issues in a multiple-server environment, Microsoft Dynamics CRM created the Microsoft Dynamics CRM 4.0 Connector for Microsoft SQL Server Reporting Services. This service installs as a separate component after Microsoft Dynamics CRM, and Microsoft Dynamics CRM uses this component to communicate with Reporting Services.

For the purposes of this book, just be aware that a separate reporting connector exists that allows you to connect properly to the Reporting Services server from on-premise and Internet-facing deployment configurations. Also, this component must be properly installed for you to run Reporting Services reports from the Microsoft Dynamics CRM user interface. Please review the Microsoft Dynamics CRM Implementation Guide for further details.

Interaction with SQL Server Reporting Services

Even though Microsoft Dynamics CRM 4.0 uses Reporting Services as its engine, you might not ever need to log on to the Reporting Services Report Manager tool. If you did access the Reporting Services Report Manager by navigating to *http://<reportserver>/reports* and clicking the *<organizationname>_*MSCRM folder for a new installation of Microsoft Dynamics CRM, you will see what appears to be an empty folder, as shown in Figure 7-32.

> **Note** If you upgrade your system from Microsoft Dynamics CRM 3.0, you will see all of the existing reports in this folder.

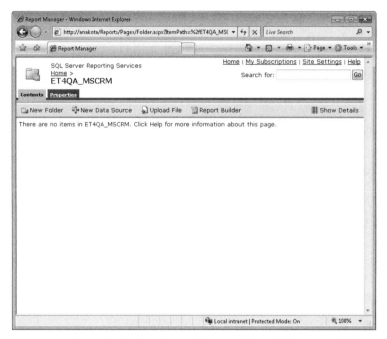

FIGURE 7-32 Reporting Services Report Manager Microsoft Dynamics CRM empty folder

However, when you click the Show Details button, you will see a 4.0 folder and the CRM data source. All Reporting Services reports created through the Microsoft Dynamics CRM Report Wizard or uploaded from an external RDL file will be stored in the hidden 4.0 folder with the name of the report being the report GUID as stored in the Microsoft Dynamics CRM database (Figure 7-33). We explore some of the actions best done with the Reporting Services manager later in the chapter.

> **Tip** If you need to determine the GUID for a report, simply open the Edit Report form in Microsoft Dynamics CRM and press F11 twice. This technique will provide you the URL in the browser's address bar where you can view the identifier. You will learn more about this technique in Chapter 9, "Microsoft Dynamics CRM 4.0 SDK."

Microsoft Dynamics CRM needs to keep the reports in its database in sync with the report files in Reporting Services. The two systems can become unsynchronized from time to time (for instance, if the Reporting Services isn't available for a period of time or from an import of a new organization). If this were to occur, you will need to synchronize the systems manually using the publishreports.exe tool provided with Microsoft Dynamics CRM. The publishreports.exe tool exists in the *<install drive>*:\Program Files\Microsoft Dynamics CRM\Tools.

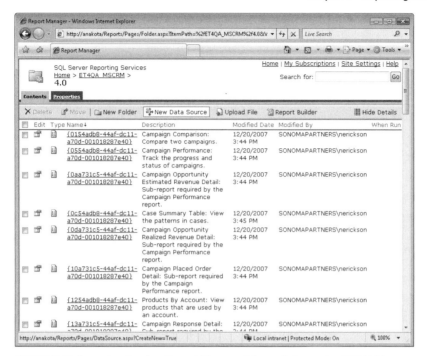

FIGURE 7-33 Reporting Services Report Manager Microsoft Dynamics CRM hidden contents

Note The path will be *<install drive>*:\Program Files\Microsoft CRM\Tools for upgraded systems.

Open a command prompt in the Tools directory, and type **Publishreports *Organization_ Name***, where *Organization_Name* is the unique name of the organization. See the Microsoft Dynamics CRM Implementation Guide for additional details.

Note The publishreports.exe in Microsoft Dynamics CRM 4.0 does not behave the same as with Microsoft Dynamics CRM 3.0. Microsoft Dynamics CRM 4.0 does not provide a downloadreports. exe. You need to write your own tool using the Microsoft Dynamics CRM SDK if you wish to transfer reports from one system to another.

Filtered Views

At this point in the book, we have warned you many times not to interact with the SQL Server database directly. Now we tell you about the one (just one) time it's permitted to retrieve data directly from the SQL Server database.

> **Note** Filtered views does not apply to reports accessed from Microsoft Dynamics CRM Live or Microsoft Dynamics CRM Internet facing deployment scenarios.

If you were to browse the Microsoft Dynamics CRM SQL Server database (with a tool such as SQL Server Management Studio), you may notice multiple data objects related to Accounts, including the following:

- AccountBase table
- AccountExtensionBase table
- AccountLeads table
- Account view
- FilteredAccount view

When you want to write your own custom report about Accounts, you may wonder which of these database objects includes the information you're looking for. In addition to the Account entity, you'll find that the Microsoft Dynamics CRM database has a similar setup for all of its entity data. It stores all of the data in a highly normalized and efficient layout, but that doesn't necessarily simplify your reporting and analysis needs.

Fortunately, instead of forcing you to spend hours investigating what types of entity data Microsoft Dynamics CRM stores in these various database objects, Microsoft Dynamics CRM greatly simplifies reporting and analysis by offering you filtered views. *Filtered views* perform the cumbersome task of denormalizing multiple tables and relationships into a streamlined view of entity and system data. In addition, filtered views respect the Microsoft Dynamics CRM security settings so that users who query filtered views (or run reports that query filtered views) will see only the data that they're allowed to see. Also, filtered views translate lookup fields and picklist values, and they calculate all *datetime* values in both Coordinated Universal Time (UTC) and the user's localized value. For example, the *createdon* field will display the user's local time and the *createdonutc* field will display the field with the Coordinated Universal Time.

When you create reports that use Integrated Windows authentication (such as SQL Server Reporting Services), the filtered views automatically filter the data that the report displays to each user based on the user's logged-on credentials, business unit, and security roles. Two different users viewing the same report may see entirely different results depending on the Microsoft Dynamics CRM security settings. This feature can save you hours of headaches if you try to determine the security and data settings of each custom report manually.

> **Important** Filtered views simplify the complex Microsoft Dynamics CRM data model for use with reporting and analysis while maintaining user security and access to data. All of your custom reports should read data from the database filtered views exclusively. You should avoid writing reports that query any other database table or view.

You can easily recognize filtered views in the database because their name always starts with the text "Filtered." For the most part, you can also determine to which entity each filtered view relates by simply looking at its name. Every entity has a filtered view, but Microsoft Dynamics CRM also includes some filtered views that do not map directly to an entity.

As you customize your system by adding custom attributes to the system entities, Microsoft Dynamics CRM automatically updates the filtered views for you. It also creates entirely new filtered views for each custom entity that you add to your installation.

Microsoft Dynamics CRM automatically configures all of the filtered view permissions to allow only SELECT (read-only) operations against them. Even though a database administrator could technically change the default permissions, you should *never* change the filtered view permissions to allow INSERT, DELETE, or UPDATE operations. Attempting to perform any non-SELECT operation against a filtered view can cause irrecoverable damage to your Microsoft Dynamics CRM database.

SQL Server Reporting Services Reports

In this section, we explain more about Reporting Services and how you can use it with Microsoft Dynamics CRM. Unlike the Report Wizard, you have much more flexibility and customization capabilities when authoring your own Reporting Services report. We explore modifying existing Microsoft Dynamics CRM reports, as well as creating your own Reporting Services report from scratch using Visual Studio 2005. We also briefly examine the Reporting Services Manager and some common scenarios where you will want to use its interface.

Microsoft Dynamics CRM includes approximately 24 Reporting Services reports in the default installation, and those reports include an additional 28 subreports. However, you will definitely want to create new reports (or modify the default reports) as you customize your Microsoft Dynamics CRM database with new entity attributes and custom entities.

As we explained earlier in this chapter, Reporting Services includes powerful reporting features and functionality in Microsoft Dynamics CRM, and creating or modifying Reporting Services reports typically requires a more experienced report writer. Therefore, we don't expect to tell you everything you need to know about Reporting Services in this chapter, but we do want to demonstrate a few simple examples and highlight some unique areas of Microsoft Dynamics CRM that relate to Reporting Services.

Note Microsoft Dynamics CRM Live customers cannot upload new Reporting Services reports, so this section applies only to on-premise deployments. Microsoft Dynamics CRM Live customers can use the Microsoft Dynamics CRM Report Wizard and Link to Web Page options for creating new reports.

Report Authoring Tools

Although you can use any RDL-compliant report authoring tool, most Microsoft Dynamics CRM customers will use Visual Studio 2005 with the Business Intelligence Development Studio add-in to author Reporting Services reports. We use Visual Studio 2005 for the reporting examples.

> **More Info** Use the tools provided for the version of Reporting Services you have installed. If your environment uses SQL Server 2008, use the Reporting Services tools associated with that edition. At the time this book went to press, Microsoft Dynamics CRM supports SQL Server 2005.

You can install the Business Intelligence Development Studio components from SQL Server 2005 Developer Edition. Please review MSDN for additional information and licensing requirements.

Installing the Business Intelligence Development Studio add-in for Visual Studio 2005

1. Navigate to the Tools folder of the SQL Server 2005 Developer Edition installation disc.

2. Double-click Setup.exe and follow the installation wizard.

3. Begin the wizard, accepting all of the default settings until you arrive at the Feature Selection page. Ensure that you install the Business Intelligence Development Studio component.

4. After installation completes, confirm that the component installed correctly. Open Visual Studio 2005.

5. On the File menu, point to New, and then click Project.

6. Under Project Types, look for a project type called Business Intelligence Projects. If you see this project type, the Business Intelligence Development Studio component installed successfully.

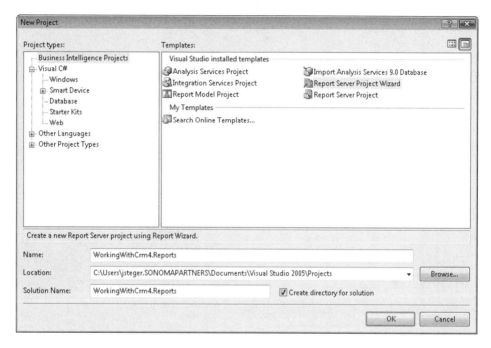

 Important You should avoid installing the Business Intelligence Development Studio on the Microsoft Dynamics CRM server or Reporting Services server. Rather, you should always edit the report .rdl files on a client computer, and then upload the files to the server when you're finished.

Editing a Reporting Services Report

We now show you how to use Visual Studio 2005 and the Report Designer to edit one of the Microsoft Dynamics CRM default reports and then upload the modified report back to Microsoft Dynamics CRM. You may need to edit the default Microsoft Dynamics CRM reports if you add custom attributes and you want to modify the report layout to include these new fields.

 Tip The default Reporting Services reports in Microsoft Dynamics CRM use complex data sets and advanced reporting features. You should edit these reports only if you're extremely comfortable authoring Reporting Services reports. Beginner or intermediate report writers may feel more comfortable creating new reports from scratch instead of trying to edit the default Microsoft Dynamics CRM reports.

In the following example, we show you how to modify the Account Overview report. Assume you would like to add the number of employees as a field in the Basic Profile section of the report. Figure 7-34 shows the final report with the field added.

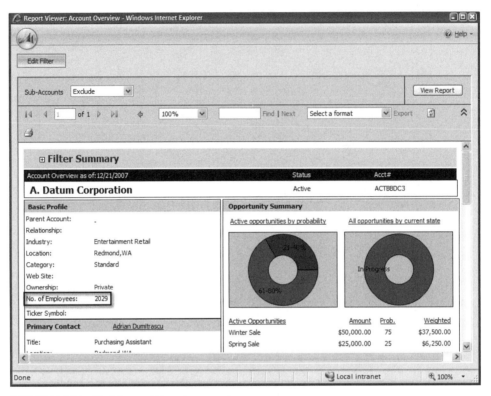

FIGURE 7-34 Modified Account Overview report

Most of the default Microsoft Dynamics CRM reports use a subreport to display the report details, and the Account Overview report is no different. Therefore, you need to modify the Account Overview Sub-Report to add the number of employees field to the report layout.

Warning Whenever you update a report, make sure that you save a backup of the original so that you can roll back to the original version should you have any problems.

Modifying the Account Overview report

1. Click the Reports subarea in the Workplace area.

2. Change the View to All Reports, Including Sub-Reports, select the Account Overview Sub-Report, and then click Edit Report.

3. After the Account Overview Sub-Report dialog box appears, click Actions, and then click Download Report. Save the report to your desktop, making sure that the file you download has an .rdl extension.

4. In Visual Studio 2005, click the File menu, point to New, and then click Project.

5. In the Project Types section, select Business Intelligence Projects, and in the Templates section, select Report Server Project.

6. Give your Visual Studio project the name **WorkingWithDynamicsCrm4.Reports**, and then click OK. Visual Studio creates a Reporting Services project with two empty folders: Shared Data Sources and Reports.

7. Right-click the Reports folder, point to Add, and then click Add Existing Item.

8. In the Look in list, click Desktop. Select the Account Overview Sub-Report.rdl file, and then click Add.

9. Visual Studio adds the report to your project. Double-click the report to open it in Layout mode.

10. Click the Data tab to verify your data connection. If your data connection does not work, you will receive an error.

11. If your preview does not generate an error, you do not need to edit your data connection and you can skip to step 14. To edit your data connection, click the Data tab, and then click the ellipsis (...) button on the toolbar.

12. In the Dataset dialog box, click the ellipsis (...) button next to Data Source: CRM to open the Data Source dialog box.

13. Make sure you enter the correct data source and initial catalog values in the Connection String text box for your environment. When you download reports, sometimes Microsoft Dynamics CRM sets the data source to localhost and the initial catalog to Adventure_Works_Cycle_MSCRM. You will need to change these default values to the correct values for your deployment. The data source should be the name of your Microsoft Dynamics CRM SQL Server. The initial catalog should be the name of the Microsoft Dynamics CRM database. The initial catalog name should appear as *organizationname*_MSCRM, where *organizationname* is the organization name used when Microsoft Dynamics CRM was installed. After you edit these values, click OK to close the Data Source dialog box, and then click OK in the Dataset dialog box. If you click the Preview tab, it should display a blank Account Overview report. If you still receive an error, review your data source settings.

14. Before you can add the number of employees field to the report, you must modify the report's dataset so that the report query includes the number of employees field in the result set. As we mentioned earlier, most of the default Microsoft Dynamics CRM reports include multiple data sets, so you need to know which data set to edit. You already determined that you want to add the number of employees field to the ds_BasicProfile data set. To edit the query, click the Data tab and select ds_BasicProfile from the Dataset list. The SQL query text will be displayed in the Generic Query window.

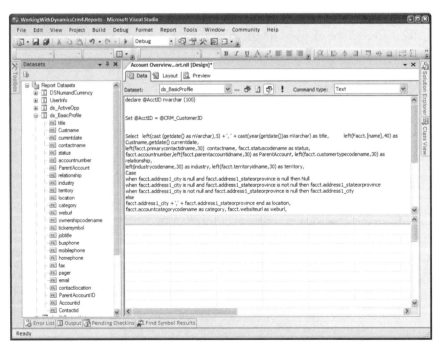

15. To add the number of employees field to the query, you need to know the schema name of the attribute. Remember that one method to look up attribute schema names is to browse to: *http://<crmserver>/sdk/list.aspx*, replacing *<crmserver>* with the name of your Microsoft Dynamics CRM server. We need the schema name *numberofemployees* for our example. To add this field to the query, add the following text after the SELECT keyword in the query:

```
facct.numberofemployees,
```

This is a complex query that we won't explain in detail; however, *facct* is an alias that the query uses to reference the FilteredAccount database view. A snippet of the final code with the new field added looks like the following.

```
DECLARE @AcctID nvarchar(100)
SET @AcctID = @CRM_CustomerID
SELECT
  facct.numberofemployees,
LEFT(cast(getdate() AS nVarchar), 5) + ', ' + cast(year(getdate()) AS nVarchar)
AS title, LEFT(Facct.[name], 40) AS Custname,getdate() currentdate,
…
```

16. After you add the field to the query, click the Save button on the Visual Studio 2005 toolbar. Make sure that you save before you click the Layout or Preview tab again; otherwise, you may receive a warning message.

17. Now that the report query results include the number of employees data field, you can add that field to the report output in the Layout section. Click the Layout tab, and then click the text box that contains *Ownership*.

18. In the table outline, right-click the icon with the three horizontal lines next to Ownership, and then click Insert Row Below to insert a new row between Ownership and Ticker Symbol.

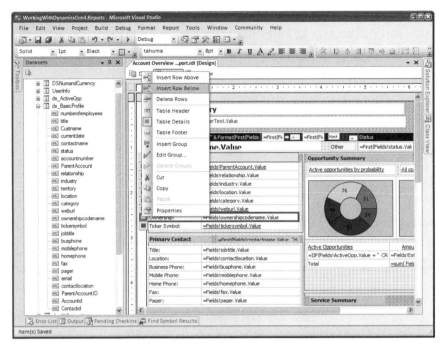

19. Click the text box under Ownership, and type **No. of Employees:**.

20. Right-click the box to the right of the No. of Employees field, and then click Properties.

21. In the Textbox Properties dialog box, do the following:

    a. In the Name box, type **numberofemployees**.

    b. In the Value list, select =Fields!numberofemployees.Value. This should be at the top of the list because you added it as the first field in the query. If this field doesn't appear automatically, you can manually type it into the Value box.

    c. Click OK.

22. Click the =Fields!numberofemployees.Value field, and then select the text alignment for this field to the left to remain consistent with the other fields in this column. You can set the text alignment from the toolbar or by modifying the TextAlign property in the Properties window.

23. Save your report by clicking Save All on the File menu. If you try to preview the report, you won't see any data because the report needs an Account ID value to run correctly. You must upload the report to Microsoft Dynamics CRM to see it work.

24. In the Web client, navigate to the Microsoft Dynamics CRM Reports list.

25. Select the Account Overview Sub-Report (in the All Reports, Including Sub-Reports category), and click Edit Report.

26. In the Source section, under File Location, click Browse, select the Account Overview Sub-Report that you just edited, and then click Save and Close. You see a warning message reminding you that you will overwrite an existing report.

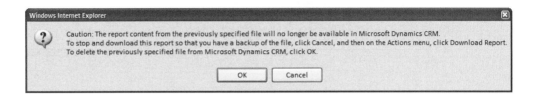

Note Do not select the file you downloaded to your desktop. You must select the up-dated .rdl file from the directory in which Visual Studio stores your project files.

27. In the Reports grid, double-click Account Overview report, and you'll now see No. of Employees in the Basic Profile section of the report.

As you can see, an inexperienced report author can make simple modifications to add custom attributes, make minor formatting changes, and so on despite the default Microsoft Dynamics CRM complexity. You can imagine how to carry this same concept through to adding additional fields to a report or modifying where fields appear in the report layout.

Creating a New Reporting Services Report

As you saw with the Account Overview report example, the default Microsoft Dynamics CRM Reporting Services reports use complex queries, multiple data sets, and subreports, so you may not feel comfortable making significant changes to those reports. Therefore, we recommend that beginner report writers create entirely new reports, and we walk you through this process.

The sample report you will create lists all the Activity records for an Account. This report can help users because it will display both open and closed Activities for an Account on a single page. We also show you how to use some of the special reporting fields such as the prefilter field that Microsoft Dynamics CRM provides to include additional functionality in your report.

Tip When creating a new Reporting Services report, consider starting with a similar report using the Microsoft Dynamics CRM Report Wizard so that you can create a report with the formatting already in place.

Creating a new report

1. Open the same reporting project you created in the Account Overview example, right-click the Reports folder, and then click Add New Report.

2. If this is your first time creating a new report, you should see the Report Wizard. Click Next.

3. You create a new data source first:

   a. In the Name box, type **CRM**.

   b. In the Type list, select Microsoft SQL Server.

   c. To enter the Connection String, click the Edit button, which opens the Data Link Properties dialog box.

   d. In the Connection tab, enter or select the name of the computer running SQL Server on which you installed Microsoft Dynamics CRM.

   e. Select the Use Windows NT Integrated security option.

   f. Select your database (<*organizationname*>_MSCRM).

   g. Click OK.

   h. If you select the Make this a shared data source check box, you can reuse this data source for additional reports in the Visual Studio Report Designer. However, you cannot deploy a report to Reporting Services through Microsoft Dynamics CRM with a shared data source, so you must manually reset the data source for each report before you deploy it.

   i. Click Next.

4. On the Design the Query page, enter the following SQL statement, and then click Next.

```
SELECT    FilteredActivityPointer.activitytypecodename,
FilteredActivityPointer.subject, FilteredActivityPointer.modifiedonutc,
FilteredActivityPointer.modifiedbyname,
FilteredActivityPointer.statecodename,
FilteredActivityPointer.statuscodename,
FilteredActivityPointer.owneridname, FilteredAccount.name
FROM FilteredAccount
INNER JOIN FilteredActivityPointer ON FilteredAccount.accountid =
FilteredActivityPointer.regardingobjectid
ORDER BY FilteredActivityPointer.modifiedonutc DESC
```

5. You can continue through the Report Wizard to adjust the report formatting, or just click Finish to accept the default formatting.

6. For the report name, type **Account Activities**, and then click Finish. You will see the report in Layout mode. You can adjust the report column widths by dragging the columns to the left or right. You can also click the Preview tab to see what your report will look like.

7. On the File menu, click Save to save your new report. Now add it to Microsoft Dynamics CRM.

8. In the Microsoft Dynamics CRM Web client, navigate to the Reports list, and click New on the grid toolbar.

9. Select Existing File for the Report Type, and in the File Location field, select your new Account Activities.rdl and give the report a name. Remember that the report name must be unique.

10. Enter a description and optionally chose any categorization.

11. Click Save, and then click Run your new report. The report output shows as the following, if you accept the default layout formatting for the Adventure Works sample database.

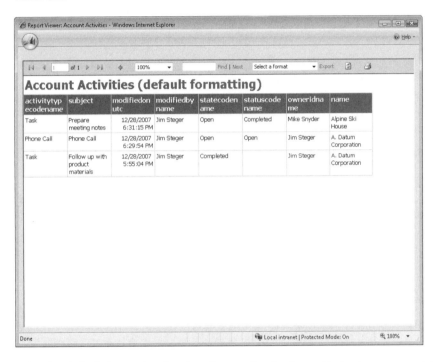

Obviously, the default Reporting Services formatting looks pretty bad, so we would never deploy a report that looked like this. However, we wanted this example to demonstrate how quickly and easily you can create a custom report for Microsoft Dynamics CRM. The example uses the default Reporting Services formatting, but you would obviously want to edit the report formatting (fonts, colors, and so on) to match all of the other reports used in Microsoft Dynamics CRM.

Reporting Parameters

In the example report you just finished, you created a simple stand-alone report that didn't use any report parameters. Reporting Services uses *parameters* to allow you to dynamically alter the report query and output based on incoming variables. In addition to the standard parameter functionality that Reporting Services supports, Microsoft Dynamics CRM offers a few additional special report parameters, as listed in Table 7-3.

TABLE 7-3 Microsoft Dynamics CRM Reporting Parameters

Parameter	Description	Usage
CRM_<filteredentityview>	■ Adds prefiltering to the report	Add to query expression (Data tab)
CRM_FilterText	■ Passes any filtered values to a text box in your report	Add to report layout
CRM_URL	■ Tells Microsoft Dynamics CRM the path to the Web server ■ Important to set when using drill-through capabilities	Add to report layout
CRM_Locale	■ Sets the language of the report	Add to report layout
CRM_SortField	■ Defines the attribute to use for custom sorting in the report	Add to report layout
CRM_SortDirection	■ Defines the direction of the sort	Add to report layout
CRM_FormatDate	■ Formats date	Add to report layout
CRM_FormatTime	■ Formats time	Add to report layout

As you can see from this table, you use the CRM_ parameter in the query of your report. You use the other parameters in the report layout mostly to help format data. Explaining how to use the report layout Microsoft Dynamics CRM report parameters would require detailed explanations of using the Reporting Services Report Designer and is therefore beyond the scope of this book. You can also use the CRMAF_ alias to add a prefilter to your report.

Prefilters and Contextual Reports

To use the CRMAF_ alias, you simply need to modify the report query by prepending CRMAF_ to the name of the filtered view the report references. So, instead of using the following query syntax:

```
Select industry, numberofemployees from FilteredAccount
```

you would use this syntax in the query:

```
Select CRMAF_FilteredAccount.industry,
CRMAF_FilteredAccount.numberofemployees from FilteredAccount as
CRMAF_FilteredAccount
```

When you include the CRMAF_<filteredentityview> in your SQL query, you're telling Microsoft Dynamics CRM that you want to display the prefilter option to users before it runs the report. As you learned earlier, the prefilter option allows your users to modify the filter criteria before they run the report. If you don't include this parameter in your query, Microsoft Dynamics CRM will skip the prefilter option and immediately run the report for all of the records in the query.

In addition to displaying the prefilter option, you also use the *CRMAF_* alias in your queries to create contextual reports that users can run from the entity form or the entity list.

> **Note** When users run a report contextually, Microsoft Dynamics CRM will not display the prefilter criteria to the users. It will automatically include the prefilter criteria as part of the report results. Users can modify the prefilter criteria by clicking the Edit Filter button after they run a report. Or they can modify the default prefilter criteria for the report as explained later in this chapter.

The criteria to create a contextual report include the following:

1. Create a report that queries data from a filtered view using the alias *CRMAF_ <filteredentityview>*, and then join your related filtered views (entities) in the report query.

2. Make sure you include the *CRMAF_* alias name on all of the fields in your query.

3. When you upload the report to Microsoft Dynamics CRM, include the filtered entity and the other filtered entities from your query in the Related Record Types.

4. Display the report using the Lists for related record types and the Forms for related record types.

The following procedure shows the steps for creating a custom report that uses the *CRMAF_* alias to create contextual reports and reports that use the prefilter.

Adding prefiltering to your custom Activity report

1. Open the Account Activities report that you created in the previous example.

2. In the Data tab, change your query to add the *CRMAF_ <filteredentityview>* as shown.

```
SELECT
CRMAF_FilteredActivityPointer.activitytypecodename,
CRMAF_FilteredActivityPointer.subject,
CRMAF_FilteredActivityPointer.modifiedonutc,
CRMAF_FilteredActivityPointer.modifiedbyname,
CRMAF_FilteredActivityPointer.statecodename,
CRMAF_FilteredActivityPointer.statuscodename,
CRMAF_FilteredActivityPointer.owneridname,
CRMAF_FilteredAccount.name
FROM FilteredAccount AS CRMAF_FilteredAccount
INNER JOIN FilteredActivityPointer AS CRMAF_FilteredActivityPointer ON
accountid = CRMAF_FilteredActivityPointer.regardingobjectid
ORDER BY CRMAF_FilteredActivityPointer.modifiedonutc DESC
```

3. Save the report file, and then upload it to Microsoft Dynamics CRM using the Reports form we showed earlier. Make sure that you select the Activities and Accounts entities for the Related Record Types and select all options for the Display In areas so that users can also run this report contextually.

4. Now when you run your report from the Reports list, you will see the prefilter option. If you run the report directly from the report edit form, you will bypass the prefilter, although you can go back and edit it. The prefilter screen displays only when you run the report directly from the Reports list.

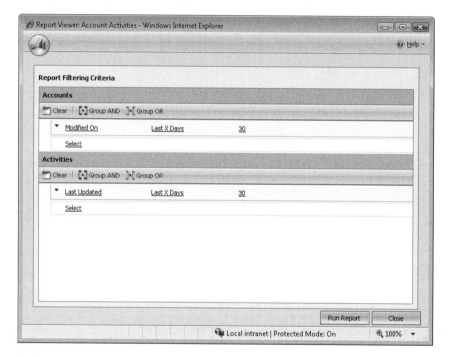

5. When you open an Account record, users will see this report listed under the Use Current Record grouping on the Reports button on the toolbar. Therefore, when they run this report from the Account form, Microsoft Dynamics CRM will run the report contextually for just the Account record viewed.

Troubleshooting If your custom report appears under the Run Report grouping, you did not configure the report or the query to run correctly contextually. Go back and double-check your query and report configuration.

By default, Microsoft Dynamics CRM creates a prefilter of Modified On in the Last 30 days for each entity in your report with the *CRMAF_* prefix. As you learned earlier in this chapter, you can modify the default prefilter options to include additional variables and change the default values.

Best Practices   Using contextual reports will save your users time and provide powerful reports and analysis options as they work with various records in Microsoft Dynamics CRM. By using the *CRMAF_* alias, you can easily create custom reports to take advantage of this feature. Therefore, as a best practice you should try to make your custom reports available to run contextually from their related entities.

Using Reporting Services Manager

Until now, we've only discussed administering reports using the Microsoft Dynamics CRM Reports list. Although we recommend that you continue to use the Microsoft Dynamics CRM interface for your report management, some of the report administration functions and tasks require you to access the Reporting Services Report Manager Web site at *http://* <reportserver>/*reports*. You can use the Reporting Services Report Manager for numerous tasks, including the following:

- Scheduling reports for e-mail delivery

- Managing report snapshot schedules

- Adding additional or alternate data sources

- Managing additional Reporting Services report security

We elaborate further on the two most common tasks you will use the Reporting Services Manager for, scheduling e-mail delivery of a report and updating an existing report snapshot schedule.

Scheduling Reports for E-Mail Delivery

With Reporting Services, you can schedule reports (hourly, daily, weekly, and so on) and deliver the report results by e-mail by using a notification list. You can send the reports to any valid e-mail address in any of the output formats that Reporting Services supports. As with report caching and snapshots, when you deliver reports through e-mail, you must run them from the context of a single user.

Caution   All e-mail recipients will see identical report results, so make sure that you don't accidentally send confidential information to an inappropriate user.

We walk through a simple example of scheduling a report that Reporting Services will deliver by e-mail. To deliver reports by e-mail, first you must configure an e-mail server for your Reporting Services server. Then, you publish the report you wish to e-mail to the Reporting Services server. Finally, you create a subscription in the Reporting Services administration interface to schedule the report for e-mail delivery.

Important To schedule reports, you must have the SQL Agent service running on the Reporting Services computer.

Configuring a SQL Reporting Services 2005 e-mail server

1. Log on to the Reporting Services server.

2. Click Start, click All Programs, Microsoft SQL Server 2005, Configuration Tools, and finally Reporting Services Configuration.

3. Click the E-mail Settings tab.

4. Update the Sender Address and SMTP Server with valid information, and click Apply.

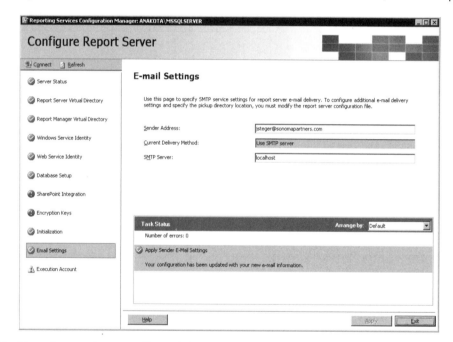

5. Now that you have configured the e-mail server for the Reporting Services server, you can schedule a report for e-mail delivery.

 More Info Refer to the Reporting Services Help or the following article for more information about configuration of e-mail services: *http://msdn2.microsoft.com/en-us/library/ms159155.aspx.*

Publishing the report for external use

1. Click the Reports link in the Workplace area.

2. Select the Neglected Leads report, and click Edit Report.

3. Click Actions, and then select Publish Report for External Use.

Scheduling an e-mail report

1. Open Reporting Services Manager (*http://*<reportserver>*/reports*).

2. Click the *<organizationname>*_MSCRM folder.

3. Click the Neglected Leads report.

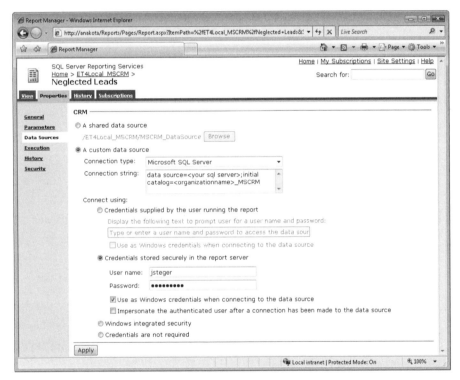

4. In the Properties tab, click Data Sources. To schedule the report, you must specify a user under which Reporting Services will execute the report. To do this, you will create a new data source and store the credentials securely with the report.

5. Click A custom data source.

   a. In the Connection Type box, select Microsoft SQL Server.

   b. In the Connection String box, type **data source=*<your sql server>*;initial catalog=*<organizationname>*_MSCRM**.

    c. In the Connect Using section, select Credentials stored securely in the report server, enter a valid user name (domain\username) and password, and ensure that you select the Use as Windows credentials when connecting to the data source check box.

6. Click Apply.

7. To test the credentials you just entered, click the View tab and confirm that the report renders correctly. If it does not, you must modify the data connection settings until the report renders correctly.

8. In the Subscriptions tab, click the New Subscription button to begin creating the subscription for this report.

> **Note** You can create subscriptions only for reports where the data source uses stored credentials or no credentials.

9. Change the Delivered By option to E-Mail. If this option does not appear, you must properly configure Reporting Services with an e-mail server. (See the preceding procedure.)

10. Enter valid e-mail addresses in the To, Cc, and Bcc boxes. Separate multiple e-mail addresses with a semicolon.

11. Enter a subject for the e-mail.

> **Tip** Reporting Services will replace the special tokens *@ReportName* and *@ExecutionTime* with the report name and the time the report was generated before sending the e-mail message. We recommend that you leave these tokens in the Subject field.

12. For this example, select Web archive for the render format (although you can pick different formats), and leave the Include Report and Include Link options selected. The Include Report option tells Reporting Services to include the report as an attachment. The Include Link option allows for a link back to the report on the Reporting Services server in the body of the e-mail. The render formats include the same options as exporting a report from the report viewer.

13. To select a schedule, click the Select Schedule button.

14. On the schedule page, enter the day, time, and recurrence that you would like for delivery of this report, and then click OK.

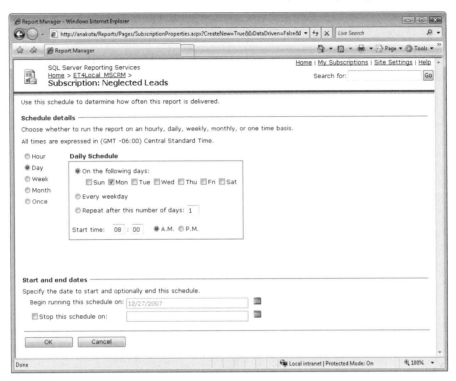

15. You now have the option to alter the query and report parameters for this scheduled report. For this example, leave everything as is. Click OK.

16. Click the Subscriptions tab to see your new e-mail report.

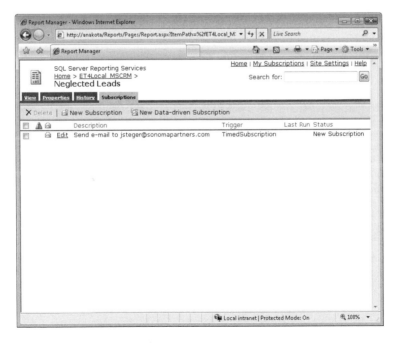

17. After Reporting Services sends the report, you will receive an e-mail message resembling the one shown in Figure 7-35.

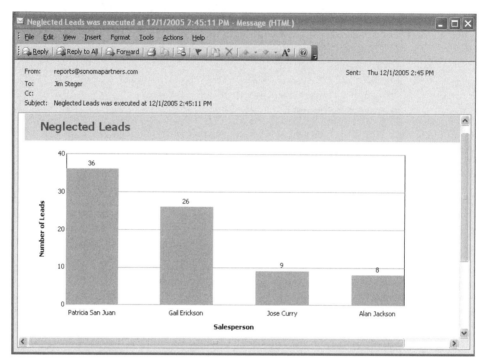

FIGURE 7-35 E-mailed report

Note The Web archive option for rendering will display the report in the body of the e-mail message for HTML-capable browsers. Other rendering options, such as Acrobat (PDF) and Excel, will arrive as e-mail attachments.

Updating the Schedule of an Existing Snapshot Report

We mentioned earlier that you cannot change the snapshot schedule of a report from the Microsoft Dynamics CRM user interface. However, because Microsoft Dynamics CRM integrates into Reporting Services, you can update the snapshot schedule through Reporting Services Report Manager by following these steps.

1. Open Reporting Services Report Manager (*http://*<reportserver>*/reports*).

2. Click the *<organizationname>_*MSCRM folder.

3. Click the Show Details button to display the hidden 4.0 folder.

4. Click the 4.0 folder link.

5. You will need to know the GUID of the report you wish to alter. You can retrieve this by going to the Edit Report form in Microsoft Dynamics CRM and pressing F11 twice to display the page's address bar. Once you have the GUID, find it in the Reports list and click the Properties icon.

6. You will now be able to alter the properties of the report. Click the Execution link to change the schedule of the report. Note that any change will not appear back in the Microsoft Dynamics CRM user interface.

Tips

Your users will love their Microsoft Dynamics CRM system if they have quick access to all of the reports they need. Unfortunately, most people wait until just before going live with Microsoft Dynamics CRM to start thinking about and creating reports. Consequently, reports frequently get rushed and short-changed on development and testing. So, don't wait to address reporting until the end of your implementation process. Reports always take longer to develop and test than you expect!

Keep in mind the following tips when you work with Microsoft Dynamics CRM reports.

General

- Always keep backups of your report files, and never edit the live reports. If possible, save your reports in a version-control mechanism such as Microsoft Visual SourceSafe or Subversion, so that you can roll back to previous versions if necessary.

- Adding images or logos to your report will help improve their appearance, but adding too many can slow down the report's performance. Therefore, be mindful of the number of images used and their file sizes. Embedding images in the report or database (instead of referencing an external URL) provides for better portability.

- When using the Reporting Services Designer, be sure you select the layout or data view if you click the Save button on the toolbar. If you click Save in the Preview tab, Visual Studio tries to save the output of the report instead of the report itself.

- If you create custom stored procedures or views for your reports, you should not add them in the Microsoft Dynamics CRM databases. Remember, Microsoft does not support modifying or altering the SQL Server databases directly; you should create a separate database for this type of situation.

- Microsoft Dynamics CRM conveniently creates two columns for each lookup and pick-list field in the filtered view. You can reference the lookup or picklist value, or just reference the name directly. Make sure that your report writers know this so that they don't waste time trying to join filtered views to display the names.

- Two additional views (FilteredStringMap and FilteredStatusMap) provide the picklist and status reasons, respectively. You may need to reference these views for custom parameter lists.

Performance

- If possible, you should try to use an entirely separate server for your reporting needs instead of the live production database. Keeping reporting on a separate database server is absolutely critical for larger organizations, databases with large amounts of data, and companies with complex, time-consuming report queries. Moving reporting to a separate database server provides the following benefits:

  - ❑ You will see performance gains in the transactional queries on the Microsoft Dynamics CRM database because SQL Server tunes itself to those types of requests. Further, you will have less concurrency or locking issues.

  - ❑ You can add indexes specific to the needs of the report queries without adverse effects on the transactional database.

  - ❑ If any particular report or load creates a performance bottleneck, you won't affect other Microsoft Dynamics CRM users when the report runs. Data caching and snapshots can also help alleviate this problem.

  - ❑ You can create custom stored procedures and views as necessary.

  - ❑ You can configure refined security for report authors. For instance, you can limit which stored procedures and views a particular report author can access.

- When creating queries in your reports, do not use select * (to return all of the columns in your query). You will get better performance by selecting only the columns you need returned.

- Make sure that you modify the default prefilters for each custom Reporting Services report you create to further limit the amount of data returned (thus improving performance).

- Perform filtering, calculations, and grouping in SQL Server rather than in Reporting Services when possible. SQL Server performs grouping operations more efficiently and quickly than Reporting Services does.

- Because filtered views return a UTC and a local date for each date field, make sure that you also reference the UTC date when comparing dates in a report.

Summary

Microsoft Dynamics CRM offers many different reporting and analysis tools. The tools range from simple options such as views and Excel exports to a sophisticated enterprise-class reporting tool such as SQL Server Reporting Services. And, of course, you can extend the reporting options even further to include your own third-party reporting tool if necessary. Add all of these options together and you have almost unlimited flexibility to get your customer data out of Microsoft Dynamics CRM.

Microsoft Dynamics CRM includes more than 20 different Reporting Services reports as part of the default installation, and you can modify all of these reports as necessary. You can also create entirely new reports by using the Microsoft Dynamics CRM Report Wizard or the Report Designer add-in for Visual Studio 2005. You manage all of your reports easily from the Microsoft Dynamics CRM user interface. Reporting Services also allows you to deliver reports by e-mail and manage existing reporting subscriptions and snapshot schedules.

Chapter 8
Workflow

Microsoft Dynamics CRM includes a workflow module that you can use to automate your business processes based on the rules, logic, and actions that you design. Microsoft revamped the workflow functionality in Microsoft Dynamics CRM 4.0 so that it uses the Microsoft Windows Workflow Foundation whereas previous versions of Microsoft Dynamics CRM use their own proprietary workflow engine. The results of the revised workflow functionality will impress you: Users, administrators, and developers can design and create powerful business processes using the workflow tools with new features and a new user interface for creating and monitoring the workflow processes.

Workflow Basics

Many companies try to adopt and implement standardized business processes to help their operations run more consistently and smoothly. For example, the CEO might say, "All customer service cases must be resolved within 24 hours," or, "We're implementing a new sales process for all deals over $100,000." However, the communication of these business processes often gets delivered to employees in an ad hoc and unregulated manner. A process document may exist on a network file share, but people don't know that it's there. And some employees might rely on word-of-mouth information from co-workers to learn the processes for their jobs. Consequently, standardizing business processes can prove challenging for some companies, particularly larger organizations. So, what benefit does workflow offer for these scenarios? Microsoft Dynamics CRM workflow provides a tool to help you set up and define business process activities (including the proper sequencing) that employees should use when working with Microsoft Dynamics CRM data.

> **Important** Conceptually, you can think of Microsoft Dynamics CRM workflow as an application or service that runs in the background, 24 hours a day, 7 days a week, constantly evaluating your Microsoft Dynamics CRM data and the multiple workflow rules in your deployment. When the workflow service encounters a trigger event, it fires the appropriate workflow rules to run the workflow actions. Typical workflow actions include sending an e-mail message, creating a task, and updating a data field on a record.

By implementing workflow processes in your Microsoft Dynamics CRM deployment, you can enjoy the following benefits:

- Ensure that you track and manage your customer data and processes in a consistent fashion. Instead of relying on your users to remember the appropriate steps for processing data, you can create workflow rules that will automatically determine the next required steps and assign activities as necessary.

- Process your customer data more quickly so that new sales leads or customer service requests are assigned and routed immediately upon record creation.

- Allow your users to focus on more valuable activities instead of having to perform a large number of manual repetitive steps.

Organizations of all sizes can benefit greatly from workflow processes, so we cover the details of using workflow in Microsoft Dynamics CRM. In the following subsections, we discuss the following basic workflow concepts as they pertain to Microsoft Dynamics CRM:

- High-level architecture
- Running workflow rules
- Workflow security
- Understanding the workflow interface

High-Level Architecture

Windows Workflow Foundation provides a comprehensive programming model, run-time engine, and tools to manage workflow logic and applications. Microsoft Dynamics CRM workflow uses the Windows Workflow Foundation framework for its core infrastructure. Fortunately, the Microsoft Dynamics CRM workflow user interface abstracts users and administrators from needing to interact with Windows Workflow Foundation directly; therefore, you do not have to understand Windows Workflow Foundation to create workflow logic in

Microsoft Dynamics CRM. However, we want to highlight the Microsoft Dynamics CRM benefits of using this standardized workflow engine.

Another important component of Microsoft Dynamics CRM workflow is the Microsoft Dynamics CRM Asynchronous Processing Service that is automatically installed with Microsoft Dynamics CRM. The Asynchronous Processing Service executes long-running operations in Microsoft Dynamics CRM, including processing the workflow rules. If you're not familiar with the term *asynchronous*, it means that operations take place in a nonblocking manner so that the system can continue processing additional events without waiting for one action to complete. Conversely, *synchronous* actions need to complete entirely before the system proceeds to the next step.

Microsoft Dynamics CRM workflows execute asynchronously; consequently, the Asynchronous Processing Service must be running for any Microsoft Dynamics CRM workflows to execute. Chapter 9, "Microsoft Dynamics CRM 4.0 SDK," discusses these concepts further, as well as provides examples of custom workflow activities based on the Windows Workflow Foundation, which allows you the flexibility to provide more complex logic.

> **Caution** Because of the asynchronous nature of Microsoft Dynamics CRM workflow, you may notice a slight delay between the time that you apply a rule and the time that the rule is implemented. Depending on the workflow action, you may also have to refresh the record you're viewing to see new or updated values. As you will see, Microsoft Dynamics CRM provides multiple ways for you to monitor the execution of the workflow rule as it is running.

Running Workflow Rules

Microsoft Dynamics CRM initiates workflow rules in one of three ways:

- Manually by the user
- Automatically from a trigger event
- From another workflow process

First, we discuss how users can manually execute workflows. Assume that you've already designed multiple workflow rules for the Opportunity entity. When users look at an opportunity view, they can select one or more records, and then click the Run Workflow button located on the grid toolbar, as shown in Figure 8-1.

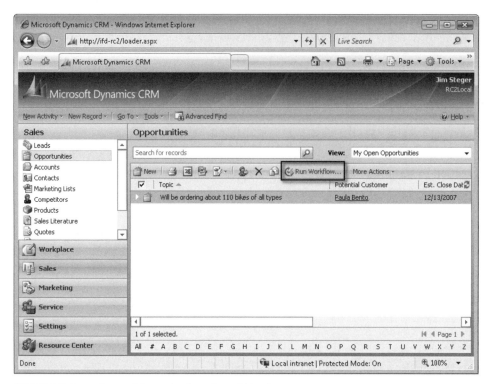

FIGURE 8-1 Accessing workflow rules from the grid toolbar

Note Microsoft Dynamics CRM displays the Run Workflow button only if the entity has at least one published workflow rule with the *On demand* option selected and the user has the Execute Workflow Job and minimal Workflow read permissions.

When the user clicks the Run Workflow button, a dialog box appears like the one shown in Figure 8-2.

In this dialog box, the user can select one of the published workflow rules to run against the records selected in the Opportunity view. After users select the rule that they want to apply and click OK, Microsoft Dynamics CRM runs that rule for each of the selected records and takes the actions that the rule specifies. Users can select and run only one workflow rule at a time in this dialog box.

In addition to manually applying workflow rules, Microsoft Dynamics CRM can also automatically run rules based on a trigger event you specify, or it can run them as a subprocess in another workflow rule. As you may expect, designing workflow rules that run automatically provides you with more benefits.

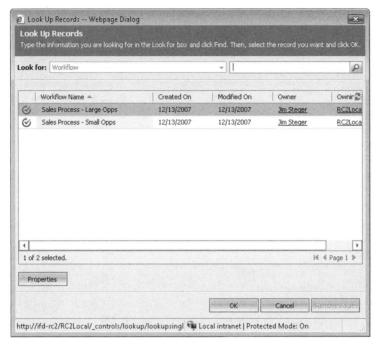

FIGURE 8-2 Run Workflow dialog box

Workflow Security

Just like the other features in Microsoft Dynamics CRM, you can set up and configure detailed security settings for workflow rules. You can secure workflow rules from two different perspectives:

- Creating and editing workflow rules
- Running workflow rules

Creating and Editing Workflow Rules

Configuring Microsoft Dynamics CRM workflow security to specify which users can create and edit workflow rules is the same as configuring Microsoft Dynamics CRM security for the other entities such as leads, accounts, and contacts. Each workflow rule has an owner, and the owner of the workflow rule combined with a user's security role determines which actions the user can take on that rule.

Most default security roles created by Microsoft Dynamics CRM upon software installation include basic workflow editing rights. Just as with any Microsoft Dynamics CRM security privilege you can alter the access levels or create new roles to match your specific business needs.

Running Workflow Rules

When Microsoft Dynamics CRM runs a workflow rule, it runs that rule under one of two security settings depending on how the rule started.

- **Manually started rules**   These rules run under the context of the user who applied the rule.

- **Automatically started rules**   These rules run under the context of the workflow rule owner.

Consider an example in which a user with the System Administrator security role owns a workflow rule, but a nonadministrative user manually applies that workflow rule through the user interface. Because the rule is started manually, Microsoft Dynamics CRM executes the rule under the security settings of the nonadministrative user, not the user with the System Administrator role. If the workflow rule actions require it to delete a record and the non-administrative user does not have permission to delete a record, the deletion step of the workflow rule will fail. Therefore, you should confirm that a user has permission to execute all of the steps in a workflow rule, including any child workflow steps, if you let users run that rule manually.

On the other hand, when workflow automatically starts a workflow rule from one of the event triggers, Microsoft Dynamics CRM uses the security credentials of the rule owner.

> **Important** The workflow rule owner plays a key role because automatically started workflow rules run in the security context of the user who owns the rule. However, if a user manually applies a workflow rule by using the user interface, the rule runs under the context of that user's security credentials (not under the security context of the rule owner). If you're not sure how the rule started (and consequently which security credentials it is using), you can view the workflow job owner with the monitor tools we explain later in this chapter.

So, when a workflow rule runs correctly when started automatically but does not work properly when run manually, 9 times out of 10 you can solve this problem by making sure that the user who instantiated the rule has the security credentials necessary to execute all of the actions contained in the rule.

Understanding the Workflow Interface

You can use the Microsoft Dynamics CRM Web client as the primary user interface for creating and managing workflow rules. However, you may encounter a business need for which you want workflow to do something that can't be accommodated through the Web interface tools. In such scenarios, you can use Microsoft Visual Studio 2008 to create workflow assemblies that perform custom business logic per your requirements. After they are properly registered, you can access the workflow assemblies through the workflow Web interface to perform almost any type of action or calculation required. Chapter 9 includes an example of using Visual Studio 2008 to create a custom workflow activity assembly and shows how to use that assembly in the workflow Web interface.

> **More Info** You cannot use workflow assemblies with Microsoft Dynamics CRM Live. This option applies only to on-premise or partner-hosted deployments of Microsoft Dynamics CRM.

You access workflow rules by navigating to Settings, and then Workflow. A familiar Microsoft Dynamics CRM grid will appear showing you the workflow rules, as shown in Figure 8-3.

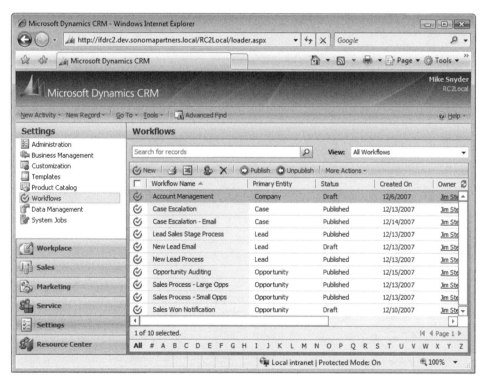

FIGURE 8-3 Workflow grid

To create a new workflow rule, click the New button, enter a workflow name, and then choose an entity to which the rule should apply. You also can choose to create an original rule or select an existing workflow rule template. If you create a new blank rule and click OK, Microsoft Dynamics CRM displays the workflow editor tool (Figure 8-4).

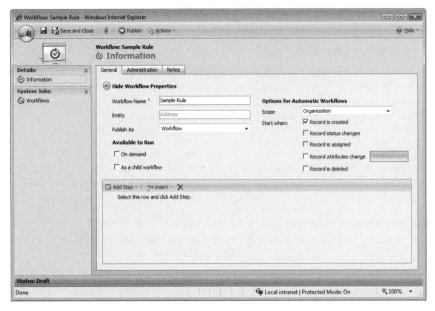

FIGURE 8-4 Workflow editor form

In addition to creating new workflow rules, you can use the workflow grid to perform other administrative tasks such as follows:

- Publish
- Unpublish
- Delete
- Share
- Assign

This section of the user interface displays only the workflow rules and the workflow templates. After Microsoft Dynamics CRM runs a workflow rule against a particular record, you can access information about that process in the System Jobs section or by clicking the Workflow link in the navigation pane of a specific rule (Figure 8-4). We explain monitoring running workflow processes later in this chapter.

Workflow Templates

Workflow templates provide a convenient mechanism for reusing common rules. Templates can save you time by simplifying the creation of new workflow rules, and creating a workflow template is easy. Simply select the Workflow template from the Publish As option when creating the workflow.

After you have workflow templates in place and published, you can select a workflow template when you create a new workflow rule. Do this by selecting Workflow Template as the Type, and then select from any published workflow template for the entity selected. When the workflow rule record opens, it will contain all of the steps and settings from the saved template.

As you would expect, workflow templates can save you a lot of time if your system uses a large number of workflow rules that contain similar steps and actions.

Workflow Properties

When you create a workflow rule, you must specify several parameters about the rule:

- Basic workflow properties
- Workflow execution options
- Scope
- Trigger events

Basic Workflow Properties

For the basic properties, you can alter the workflow's name and publishing type (either a workflow rule or a workflow template). In addition, by using other tabs, you can change the owner of the rule (important for security), add a workflow description, and add notes.

 Tip The workflow editor does allow you to enter duplicate workflow names for a given entity. However, this can be confusing when you troubleshoot or update rules, so try to provide unique descriptive names for your rules.

Workflow Execution Options

When you create a workflow rule, you need to specify how Microsoft Dynamics CRM can execute that rule. As Figure 8-4 shows, you can configure multiple options to trigger the workflow rule automatically. We cover the options for automatic execution in the section titled "Trigger Events" later in this chapter.

In addition to specifying automatic triggers, you can also configure a workflow rule with two additional execution options:

- **On demand**   Allows a user to execute a workflow rule manually on a group of records or a single record

- **As a child workflow** Allows workflow rule designers to reference the workflow rule as a child in a different workflow rule

You can mix and match these execution options appropriately, so you can create a large number of combinations regarding how you want Microsoft Dynamics CRM to execute your workflow rules.

Scope

By using workflow scope, you can further refine which records the workflow rule affects. The scope options are the familiar Microsoft Dynamics CRM security access levels:

- User
- Business Unit
- Parent: Child Business Units
- Organization

These scope options appear for workflow rules on user-owned entities such as Leads, Accounts, and Contacts. For organization-owned entities such as Address or Product, Microsoft Dynamics CRM provides an Organization scope option.

When running an automatic workflow rule, Microsoft Dynamics CRM uses the combination of the workflow rule owner's privileges and the scope of the workflow rule to determine the records affected by the workflow.

Important The scope option applies only to workflow rules instantiated automatically by an event in Microsoft Dynamics CRM. Scoping a workflow rule cannot elevate a user's rights. It can only further restrict the number of records typically affected.

Consider an example of how modifying the workflow scope affects the records the rule runs on. Say you have a workflow rule that updates a lead, and a user named Alan owns the workflow rule. If Alan has Organization update rights to leads, but the rule's scope is set to User, only the lead records that Alan owns will be updated by this rule as limited by the scope of the workflow rule. Likewise, if Alan's update access level is set to User but the workflow rule's scope is set to Organization, the workflow rule updates only leads owned by Alan as limited by the scope of Alan's security rights. Workflow cannot elevate (or allow access to) the privileges of Alan as defined by his security roles.

Tip When creating workflows intended to execute on any record in the organization, set the scope to Organization. If you are creating a personal workflow rule to execute against records you own, set the scope to User.

Trigger Events

When you create a workflow rule, you must define the event that will trigger it. In other words, you must specify which actions in the Microsoft Dynamics CRM system will start the workflow rule. For each rule, you can specify one or more of the following triggers:

- *Record is created*   Creating a new record of an entity

- *Record status changes*   Changing the status (state) of a record

- *Record is assigned*   Changing the owner of a record in Microsoft Dynamics CRM

- *Record attributes change*   Changing one or more values on a record

- *Record is deleted*   Deleting a record

Most of these triggers are self-explanatory, but we want to clarify the *Record status changes* event. We've been working with Microsoft Dynamics CRM for years, but sometimes we still get confused between the *state* of a record and the *status reason* of a record. So, don't worry if you need to look this up, too! The *Record status changes* event refers to the status (schema name of statecode) of an entity, but not the status reason (schema name of statuscode). Table 8-1 displays some sample status and status reason values to illustrate the differences.

TABLE 8-1 Status and Status Reason Values for Select Entities

Entity	Status values	Status reason values
Account	Active Inactive	Active Inactive
Case	Active Resolved Canceled	In Progress On Hold Waiting for Details Researching Problem Solved Canceled
Lead	Open Qualified Disqualified	New Contacted Qualified Lost Cannot Contact No Longer Interested Canceled
Phone Call	Open Completed Canceled	Open Sent Received Canceled

Many people assume that the *Record status changes* event will execute when changing the status reason of a record. However, changing only the status value will trigger the workflow.

> **Tip** If you want to trigger a workflow rule from a change of the status reason attribute, use the *Record attributes change* event and select Status Reason (statuscode).

With the *Record attributes change* event, you can select one or more attributes of the entity for workflow to monitor. After you select the *Attribute change* option, simply click the Select button, and then select the attributes you wish to have monitored (see Figure 8-5).

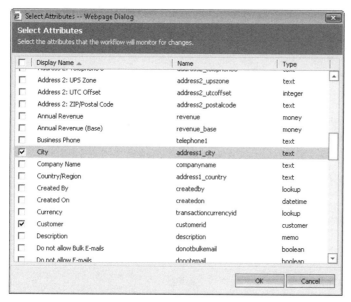

FIGURE 8-5 Choosing attributes to monitor

> **Caution** Updates to records happen regularly in the system. Consider this when choosing workflow rules using the *Record attributes change* event to avoid unnecessary stress on the system. Further, avoid using *Wait* conditions in workflow rules triggered from this event.

Workflow Step Editor

This section covers how you create workflow logic and actions in the workflow form using the step editor. On the step editor toolbar, you can add various step types, choose whether the newly entered step comes before (above) or after (below) the selected step (the default is after the selected step), and delete steps. Everything in this editor frame is contextual, meaning that Microsoft Dynamics CRM determines which actions you can take based on the step selected (which is highlighted in the user interface).

When you add any step (conditions or actions), the text box shown in Figure 8-6 appears so that you can enter a step description.

FIGURE 8-6 Step description

We strongly recommend that you take the time to enter a description. The step description is used with monitoring workflow, custom workflow actions, and reporting. Adding a short and meaningful description greatly improves the overall process visibility to the organization. We cover the following Add Step choices available to you with the workflow editor:

- Check conditions

- Wait conditions

- Workflow actions

- Stages

> **Tip** Be sure you select the correct row before removing a step. Click the desired row, and it will turn a darker shade of blue when selected.

Check Conditions

By using conditions, you can add business logic to manage the actions of your workflow rule. You have the ability to create simple or complex logical statements that control when actions should be taken. Typical scenarios include sending an e-mail message when a record status changes, creating different sets of activities based on potential revenue of an opportunity, or updating a sales stage when all activities are completed.

After you open a workflow record, click Add Step, and select Check Condition, as shown in Figure 8-7.

You can create three different check condition branches:

- *Check Condition*   The first *if-then* statement

- *Conditional Branch*   An *else-if-then* statement displayed as *Otherwise-if-then* in the user interface

- *Default Action*   An *else* statement displayed as *Otherwise* in the user interface

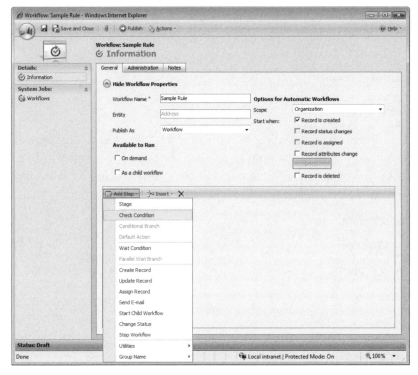

FIGURE 8-7 Adding a workflow check condition

Figure 8-8 shows how each of these steps looks in the editor.

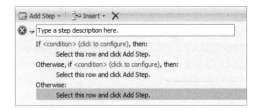

FIGURE 8-8 Check condition steps

Microsoft Dynamics CRM automatically determines which condition option you can insert into a workflow rule, depending on which step you select in the statement box. For instance, you can use the Conditional Branch option only when adding a step with an existing Check Condition step.

 Caution You need to be sure to select the condition's row to enable the Conditional Branch or Default Action options.

After you add a Check Condition step, you need to specify the business logic by clicking the *<condition>* (click to configure) link to open the Specify Workflow Condition Web dialog box (Figure 8-9).

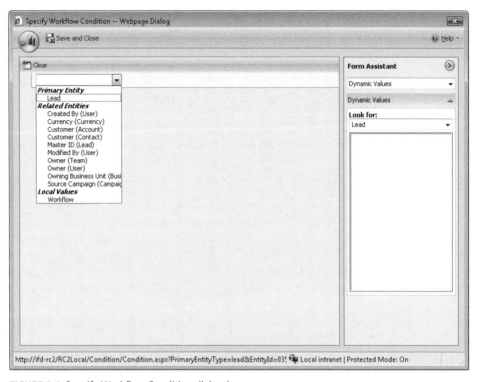

FIGURE 8-9 Specify Workflow Condition dialog box

In the Specify Workflow Condition dialog box, you can add many different conditions using the familiar Advanced Find interface, such as the following:

- Values from primary records on which workflow has been triggered.

- Values from uniquely related records (including custom entities).

- Values from externally created workflow activities.

- Values from records created inside workflows (such as follow-up tasks). Microsoft Dynamics CRM displays these under the Local Values grouping.

- Special workflow conditions such as activity count and execution time.

You may notice that the interface used to insert dynamic values in a check condition behaves a little differently from the interface for inserting dynamic values in entity records. In particular, you can insert dynamic values in a check condition by placing your cursor in the appropriate field and simply selecting the dynamic value in the Form Assistant. The user interface does not require you to click the OK button like it does when you insert dynamic values in an entity record.

Wait Conditions

By using wait conditions, you can configure your workflow logic to respond to time-based conditions. Common situations in which you can use wait conditions include sending an e-mail message a certain amount of time before a service contract expires, creating tasks after a field is updated with a value, or just waiting a given amount of time before following up on a lead.

You configure wait conditions the same way as you configure check conditions. However, you have one extra option named Timeout available to you when you configure the wait duration. By using the Timeout option, you can have the workflow step wait a specified period of time before continuing. Figure 8-10 shows a condition for a step that waits one month before it proceeds to the next step.

FIGURE 8-10 Wait condition using a timeout

> **Note** The Timeout option replaces the Microsoft Dynamics CRM 3.0 Wait for Timer condition.

A parallel wait branch works similarly to the condition branch described earlier.

Workflow Actions

Now that you understand conditions, we'll explain the workflow actions that you can execute. After all, using conditions without any actions does not really provide any benefits! After you select a row, click Add Step to see the list of workflow actions available, as shown in Figure 8-11.

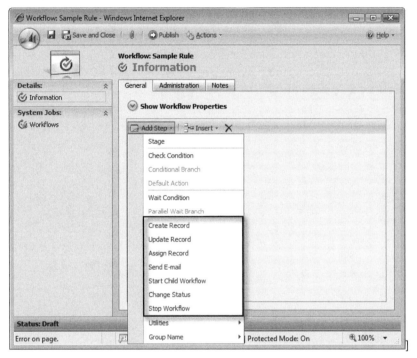

FIGURE 8-11 Workflow actions

You can use the following workflow actions when you create workflow rules:

- Create Record
- Update Record
- Assign Record
- Send E-mail
- Start Child Workflow
- Change Status
- Stop Workflow
- Custom workflow activity actions

We include a few custom workflow activity actions (accessed from Utilities and Group Name) in Figure 8-11 to illustrate how they will appear in the Microsoft Dynamics CRM user interface. However, you will not see these or other custom options in your system until you register custom workflow activities.

Create Record

You use the Create Record action to create a Microsoft Dynamics CRM record, including activities and custom entity records. After you select this action, choose the entity type for the record you want to create, and click Set Properties to open a form in which you can specify default attribute values for the newly created record. Figure 8-12 shows an example Task form to create a new Task record in the workflow.

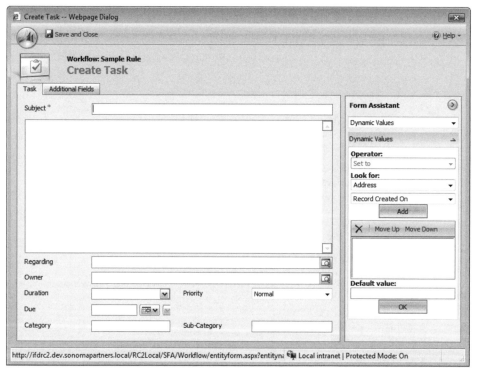

FIGURE 8-12 Workflow Create Task dialog box

You can enter data in the various entity fields so that Microsoft Dynamics CRM workflow automatically creates the new record with the values that you specify. In some situations, you may want the same data to appear for all of the created records so that you can simply enter the desired data. In other cases, you will probably want Microsoft Dynamics CRM to populate the fields with dynamic data depending on your business rules. Because of the power and sophistication of dynamic values, we explain their usage in detail later in this chapter.

Update Record

By using the Update Record action, you can update data in the workflow entity record. For example, you can create an Opportunity workflow rule that automatically changes the Opportunity priority attribute to *High* if the estimated value of a deal is greater than $100,000.

In addition, you can use the Update Record action to update data values in entity records related to the primary workflow entity. For example, you can create a workflow rule that updates the relationship type field of an account record to a value of *Prospect* if someone creates an Opportunity record for that account. Microsoft Dynamics CRM automatically determines which related entities you can update using this technique. For the most part, you can update values in related entities only if the entity has a primary relationship to the workflow entity. Because Account is the primary entity in relation to the Opportunity entity, Microsoft Dynamics CRM lets you update data on the Account record in Opportunity work-flow rules. However, the inverse is not true. You cannot update the value of an Opportunity record for workflows attached to the Account entity.

After you select an entity, you select the fields that you want to update, and then set the new values.

Important Updating an entity will trigger any plug-ins or workflow rules registered to the entity.

Assign Record

Use the Assign Record action to change the assignment or owner of the workflow entity. You can assign records to a specific user or queue, or you can use dynamic values to perform more advanced record assignment. Figure 8-13 shows an example of using dynamic values to assign a workflow entity to the manager of a lead record's owner.

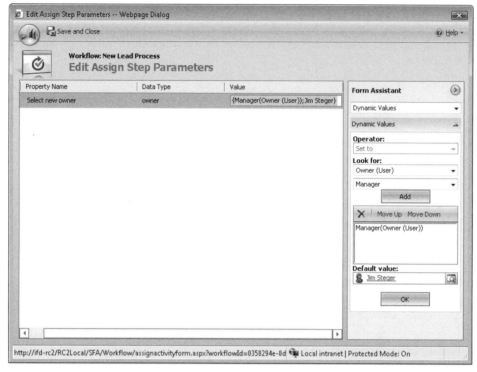

FIGURE 8-13 Workflow Edit Assign Step Parameters dialog box

To assign an entity to the manager, you must first specify someone as the manager in the user record. If a manager isn't specified, workflow will generate an error when it tries to complete the assignment.

If you assign the entity to the manager or to a user, Microsoft Dynamics CRM actually changes the owner of the entity. However, if you assign the entity to a queue, Microsoft Dynamics CRM does not change the owner—it just adds the record to the queue.

> **Caution** You can assign only certain types of entities to a queue, such as cases and activities, so Microsoft Dynamics CRM automatically disables this option for non-queue-supported entities.

Send E-mail

Use the Send E-mail action when you want to send an e-mail message automatically as part of your workflow rule. When you select the Send E-mail action, you first need to specify whether you wish to create a new message or use an existing template. When you click Set Properties, the dialog box shown in Figure 8-14 appears.

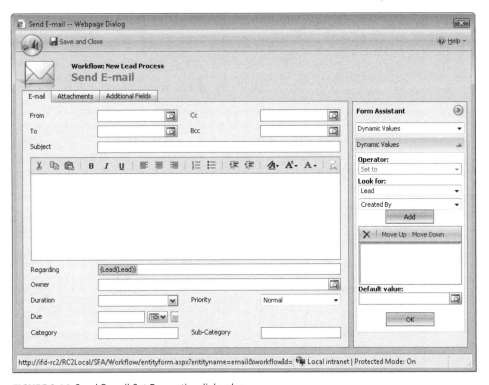

FIGURE 8-14 Send E-mail Set Properties dialog box

From here, you can configure the key attributes of the message, such as the recipients, the subject, and the body. The following are some of the key details and constraints related to sending e-mail messages with workflow:

- You can select an e-mail template if the entity of the workflow rule offers a template. You will need to specify the e-mail message To and From values. Failure to provide To and From values will generate an error when the workflow executes.

- Although Microsoft Dynamics CRM sends the message as HTML (instead of plain text), the workflow e-mail editor toolbar does not include buttons to insert images or hyperlinks. However, you can select images and hyperlinks in a Web browser and then copy and paste them into the Description box (body) of the e-mail message.

- For e-mail tracking, Microsoft Dynamics CRM can append the tracking code to the Subject line of your workflow messages depending on how you configured e-mail tracking in your system.

- On the Attachments tab, you can specify as many file attachments per e-mail message as you wish.

- You may encounter formatting differences between the e-mail text shown during creation of the message and the actual message sent. To ensure that e-mail text is generated correctly, be sure to send yourself a test e-mail.

Tip You can use the e-mail recipient fields (To, CC, BCC) to add multiple individuals, including dynamic values. However, once you add a dynamic value to one of these fields, you'll notice that Microsoft Dynamics CRM hides the lookup button in that field, preventing you from selecting a specific record such as a Contact or User. If you do want to send an e-mail message to a dynamic value and a static record, don't worry, we have a solution for you.

Assume you want to create a workflow e-mail message that includes a dynamic value to carbon copy the account owner, but you also want to carbon copy a user named Alan Brewer. To accomplish this, first add a dynamic value to the CC field that includes the account owner. After you do this, the lookup button in the CC field disappears. Next, add a second dynamic value to the CC field but do not actually select a dynamic field in the Dynamic Values box. Instead, simply select the user Alan Brewer using the Default value lookup button (Figure 8-15) and click OK.

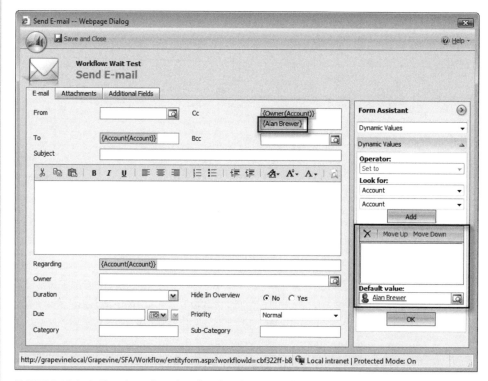

FIGURE 8-15 Including dynamic and static values in an e-mail recipient field

When Microsoft Dynamics CRM runs this workflow rule, it will always include Alan Brewer as a CC recipient because it won't find a dynamic value for that field and Alan Brewer is the default value.

Start Child Workflow

By using the Child Workflow action, you can execute an entirely separate workflow rule as an action in the original workflow rule. You can reference a workflow rule as a child only if it has the As a child workflow option selected in the Available to run section.

> **Note** The child workflow rule is analogous to the subprocess option in Microsoft Dynamics CRM 3.0.

When you start to develop a large number of workflow rules, you may find that multiple rules perform the same subset of actions. To help make workflow rules easier to manage, you can create a workflow rule that performs this subset of actions, and then have all other rules run this subset workflow rule as a child workflow. Then, if you need to change the subset of actions, you have to edit only the subset workflow rule for the new logic to be applied immediately to all of the workflow rules that reference this rule.

When you're using child workflow rules, be sure to remember that child workflow runs *asynchronously*. Therefore, the parent workflow rule will execute the child workflow rule and then continue to the next step without waiting for the child workflow to finish its logic. The simplest way to ensure that execution in a workflow rule is synchronous is to rewrite the rule to avoid using a child workflow. If you require a child workflow to execute synchronously, use a custom workflow activity in the child workflow. When a workflow rule executes a custom workflow activity, it does not proceed to the next step in the workflow rule until Microsoft Dynamics CRM completes the entire process related to the activity.

Finally, the child workflow rule will execute under the security context of the executing instance of the parent rule. In the case of manual execution, the child workflow rule will run under the security context of the user who triggered the parent rule.

Loop Detection

When you use child workflow rules, you may accidentally create a situation in which a workflow rule can't ever complete because it's stuck in a loop. Or you may accidentally create a loop by designing a workflow rule that updates a field on your record triggered by changes to that field. If a workflow rule gets stuck in an infinite loop, obviously it negatively affects the performance of your Microsoft Dynamics CRM server, so you clearly want to avoid these situations.

Fortunately, Microsoft Dynamics CRM includes loop detection logic to help minimize the possibility of infinite loops occurring in the system. Microsoft Dynamics CRM uses two mechanisms to manage loop detection behavior:

- Depth
- Time expiration boundary

Microsoft Dynamics CRM automatically tracks a variable known as *depth counter* and it increments the depth counter each time it executes a rule. By default, Microsoft Dynamics CRM allows the workflow rule to continue up to eight times before automatically halting the rule. However, you may, for example, have a workflow that each year updates a contract's renewal date. In this situation, you would not want the workflow to stop operating on that record after eight successive actions. Microsoft Dynamics CRM handles this situation by using a concept known as the *time expiration boundary*. If the workflow is still active and hasn't been executed for a specified period of time, Microsoft Dynamics CRM resets the depth counter to zero.

Even though Microsoft Dynamics CRM provides this behavior, you should always carefully examine your business logic and test your complex workflow rules in a development environment to avoid accidental infinite loops.

Note The depth and time expiration boundary values are stored in the DeploymentProperties table of the mscrm_config database. Changing these values manually is considered an unsupported change.

Change Status

You can use the Change Status action to change the status and status reason of an entity record. You can change the status of the entity record that triggered the workflow rule instance, a related record, or a record created from within the workflow process.

Stop Workflow

A workflow rule processes all of the conditions and actions that you configure, and then it considers the rule finished. However, you may face a situation in which you want to stop a workflow rule somewhere in the middle of its process (typically based on a condition evaluation). You can use the stop action in such situations. When you insert a stop action, you can select from one of the following two options:

- **Succeeded**   Immediately stops the workflow rule with a status of *Succeeded*
- **Canceled**   Immediately stops the workflow rule with a status of *Canceled*

Best Practices By including a stop workflow action in all of your rules, you can make sure that Microsoft Dynamics CRM closes all of your rules completely. We recommend including either the Succeeded or Canceled stop workflow action in all of your workflow rules.

Custom Workflow Plug-in Actions

If none of the preceding workflow actions meet your business requirements, Microsoft Dynamics CRM offers you the option of creating custom workflow logic actions and using those actions in steps and conditions. Custom workflow actions appear in the step editor only after you properly register them against the entity used in your workflow rule. Figure 8-16 shows an example of two custom workflow action groups named Utilities and Group Name, in addition to a custom workflow action named Url Builder. You can configure how these custom workflow actions and groups appear in the step editor. We discuss how you create custom workflow plug-in assemblies in Chapter 9.

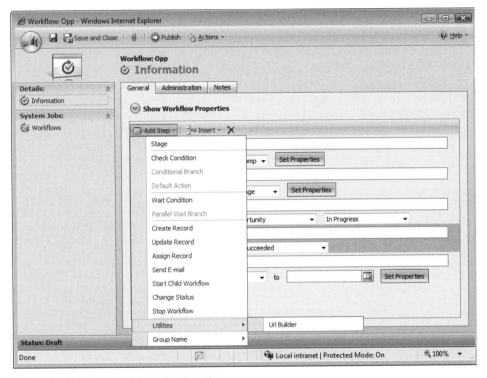

FIGURE 8-16 Custom workflow plug-in action

More Info Currently, you cannot use custom workflow actions with Microsoft Dynamics CRM Live. This option applies only to on-premise or partner-hosted deployments of Microsoft Dynamics CRM.

Stages

Stages act as groups for workflow steps, and you can add a stage to encapsulate common business steps. To add a stage to a workflow rule, click Add Step, and then click Stage. In the blue background box, you can then add a stage description. Just as with steps, we recommend you take the time to describe each of the stages that you add.

> **Note** If you add a stage to a workflow rule, all steps in that rule must be part of a stage. Microsoft Dynamics CRM informs you of this requirement when you add your first stage to a new workflow rule.

In Microsoft Dynamics CRM, you can add stages to any entity in workflow. If you want, you can add wait conditions to each stage so that Microsoft Dynamics CRM won't proceed to the next stage until the workflow rule satisfies the wait conditions. Figure 8-17 shows a sample workflow rule with stages.

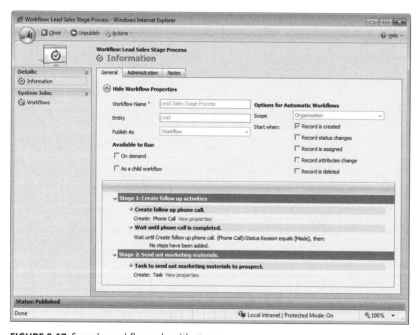

FIGURE 8-17 Sample workflow rule with stages

In this example, the workflow rule creates a new Phone Call activity after a new Lead is created. The last step of the first stage is to wait until that Phone Call activity is closed and completed before moving to stage 2 (see Figure 8-18). You can design your workflow wait conditions based on many different attributes in workflow, not just whether or not a task was completed.

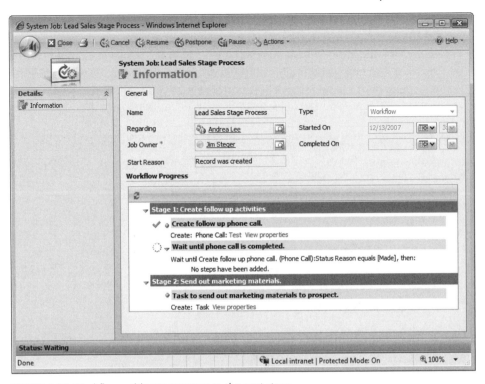

FIGURE 8-18 Workflow waiting to progress to the next stage

Note The concept of workflow stages in Microsoft Dynamics CRM 4.0 replaces the Opportunity Sales Process concepts in previous versions of Microsoft Dynamics CRM.

Dynamic Values in Workflow

Now that you understand the concepts involved in using, creating, and managing workflow, we will describe some of the details related to creating rules and actions. One of the most important workflow features that you will use (probably in every single rule that you create) is *dynamic values*. You can use dynamic values in your workflow rules to populate your conditions, actions, and so on with data specific to the workflow entity or its related entities.

To help illustrate the benefits of dynamic values, consider a common business scenario. You want to implement a new process in which Microsoft Dynamics CRM automatically sends a case acknowledgment e-mail message to a customer every time the customer logs a service request. In the case acknowledgment e-mail message, you want to include information specific to the customer's case such as the case number and the phone number of the case owner. Because the information you want to include in the message changes for each case, you must use dynamic values in the Send E-mail workflow action. We will explain the details behind setting dynamic values shortly, but Figure 8-19 shows the final Send E-mail workflow configuration. The highlighted fields include the dynamic data.

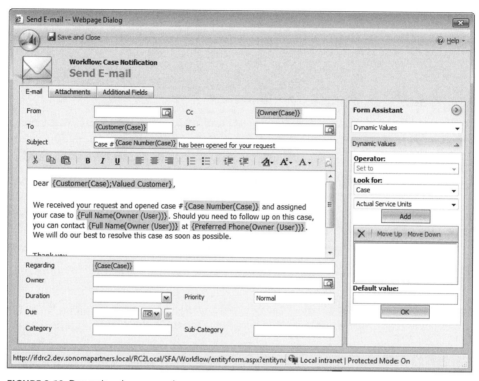

FIGURE 8-19 Dynamic values example

You access dynamic values in workflow from the Form Assistant. Microsoft Dynamics CRM automatically changes the dynamic values choices based on multiple criteria. To insert a dynamic value in workflow, select a field on the form where you want the dynamic value to appear, use the Form Assistant to select the value, and then click OK.

Tip Because the dynamic values Form Assistant automatically updates the options depending on your context, we must admit it can cause a little confusion when you initially start working with workflow rules. However, you can rest assured that you will quickly become comfortable using dynamic values in workflow rules.

In addition to including dynamic values in the form, you can also use dynamic values to update data fields even if the attribute does not appear on the entity form. You can access nonform attributes in the Additional Fields tab.

In the Form Assistant pane, you can see the following aspects of dynamic values:

- Operator
- Look for options
- Dynamic Values box
- Default value

Operator

Microsoft Dynamics CRM automatically updates the operator values based on the form field with the current focus. So, if you select a numeric field on the form, Microsoft Dynamics CRM shows you operator options specific to numeric fields; when you select a date field, Microsoft Dynamics CRM shows you options specific to date fields. Table 8-2 shows the operator options and when you can apply them.

TABLE 8-2 Operator Options

Operator	Description
Set to	The default operator. Simply assigns the dynamic value to the field. For *DateTime* fields, additional time options are displayed.
Increment by	Available in certain field situations. Can be used to increase the current value by the selected dynamic value. Available only for numeric fields for the Update Record action.
Decrement by	Can be used to reduce the current value by the selected dynamic value. Available only for numeric fields for the Update Record action.
Multiply by	Used to multiply the current value by the selected dynamic value. Available only for numeric fields for the Update Record action.
Clear	Removes the current value from the field. Available only with the Update Record action.

Important The *Set to* operator is the only option displayed unless you are using the Update Record step.

As mentioned, when you select a date field, Microsoft Dynamics CRM displays different operator options, as shown in Figure 8-20. By using the date-specific options, you can define the dynamic value for dates to be a certain amount of time before or after a custom date field.

FIGURE 8-20 Additional date-based dynamic values options

Look for Options

Microsoft Dynamics CRM splits the Look for options into entity and attribute lists. The entity list displays the current primary entity, all related entities, a workflow option, and any custom assembly steps configured in the workflow rule (Figure 8-21). The attribute list is contextually driven by the choice of the entity list and displays only attributes of the data type available for the field currently in focus. Almost all attributes are available, including custom attributes.

If you select the Workflow option in the Look for picklist as shown in Figure 8-21, the user interface displays these special attribute choices (depending on the field with focus):

- *Activity Count*   The current number of activities associated with the primary entity excluding any created by the workflow rule.

- *Activity Count Including Workflow*   The current number of activities associated with the primary entity plus any activities specifically created by the workflow rule.

- *Execution Time*   The amount of time elapsed on the current workflow step. The execution time value resets each time a step is taken.

If you configure a wait condition and select the Workflow option, Microsoft Dynamics CRM will give you a fourth option, Timeout. If you select Timeout, you can also access a special Duration dynamic value in addition to the typical Before and After values (Figure 8-22). By using the Duration option, you can specify an amount of time that the workflow rule should wait before it proceeds to the next step.

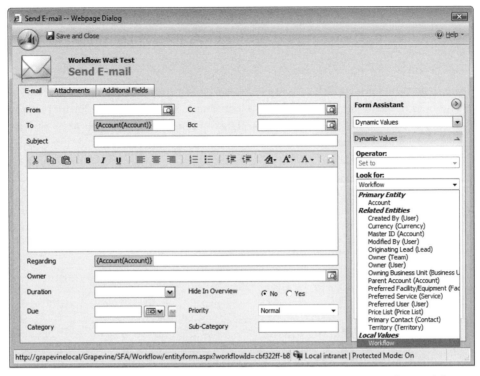

FIGURE 8-21 Accessing primary entity, related entity, and local values in dynamic values Look for

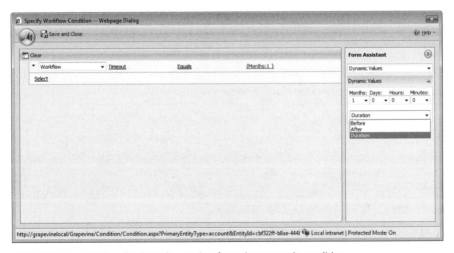

FIGURE 8-22 Accessing the Duration option for a timeout wait condition

Tip For wait conditions, you will almost always want to use the Timeout option to ensure that the workflow rule waits the correct amount of time before proceeding to the next step.

Dynamic Values Box

The Dynamic Values box stores the values you add. Most of the time, you will have only one value; however, the design allows for multiple values should one of them be null. A common use for this technique is choosing a customer value for an Opportunity or Case. Because the customer of an Opportunity can either be an Account or a Contact, you may want to configure dynamic values to accommodate either scenario (Figure 8-23). In this example, Microsoft Dynamics CRM will try to populate the top value in the box (Account Name) as the dynamic value. If no account name value exists because the customer of the Opportunity is a Contact, Microsoft Dynamics CRM will try to populate the dynamic value with the next value in the box. If that value doesn't exist either, workflow will populate the dynamic value using the default value that you specify.

FIGURE 8-23 Multiple values selected in the Dynamic Values box

Default Value

If your dynamic value doesn't return any data from the database, you can use the default value to ensure that the value contains some data. You should strongly consider specifying a default value unless you are certain the data field chosen will always have a value. Default values do not apply to workflow wait conditions.

Monitoring Workflow

As we explained previously, the Microsoft Dynamics CRM Asynchronous Processing Service runs constantly behind the scenes, evaluating your workflow rules, Microsoft Dynamics CRM data, and events. You can use the Microsoft Dynamics CRM Web interface to monitor workflow jobs (including those in progress) from the workflow record, the affected Microsoft Dynamics

CRM record, or System Jobs. This flexibility provides you the information you need to quickly determine which jobs have been executed and also to help you troubleshoot any failures.

In this section, we review the following:

- Monitoring workflow jobs from the workflow record

- Accessing workflow jobs from a Microsoft Dynamics CRM record

- Accessing workflow jobs from System Jobs

- Reviewing the log details on an existing workflow process instance

- Actions available for workflow processes

Monitoring Workflow Jobs from the Workflow Record

The workflow record contains a convenient Workflows link that lists all executed instances of the rule in the system, including their status, as shown in Figure 8-24.

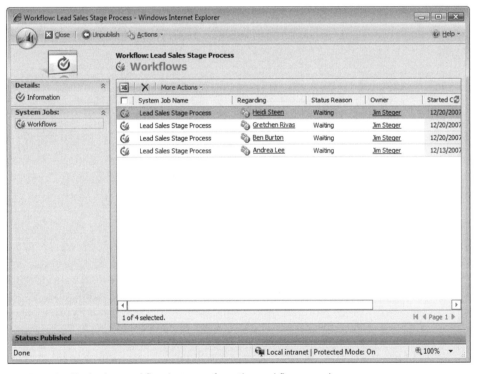

FIGURE 8-24 Reviewing workflow instances from the workflow record

Because workflow security behaves similarly to the other entity, you have access to see instantiated workflow rules from the workflow record only if you have Read privileges on the workflow entity.

Accessing Workflow Jobs from a Microsoft Dynamics CRM Record

Microsoft Dynamics CRM conveniently lets you view and access any workflow processes running against a record directly from the record. You can click the Workflows link (Figure 8-25) in a record to show all workflow processes that have been executed (or that are executing) against that record.

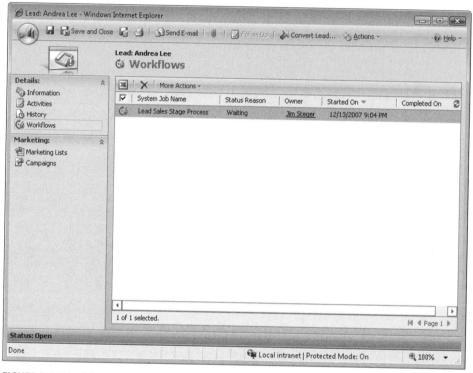

FIGURE 8-25 Workflows associated view from a record

Caution If a user opens an entity record in Microsoft Dynamics CRM, he or she can view a list of all the workflow jobs related to that individual record in the Workflows associated view if the user's security role includes *any level* of Read access to the System Jobs entity. So, even if a user has only User level access to read System Jobs records, he or she can view all of the workflow rules running on the record from that record. This security behavior is unique because you would expect this user would be able to see only the system jobs that he or she owns. This exception exists to allow users to see all jobs that pertain to records they have access and to provide backward compatibility with the Microsoft Dynamics CRM 3.0 Sales Processes. Fortunately, if a user tries to open the workflow job and see the details, Microsoft Dynamics CRM will let the user view that record if his or her security role allows it.

Accessing Workflow Jobs from System Jobs

You can also view all instantiated workflow processes from the System Jobs link in the Settings area. Any user with the proper access level for the Read permission on System Jobs is able to access this area. In this view, an administrator can monitor all asynchronous jobs executed against Microsoft Dynamics CRM. One of these job types is Workflow, as shown in Figure 8-26. When filtered, Microsoft Dynamics CRM will only display workflow process instances.

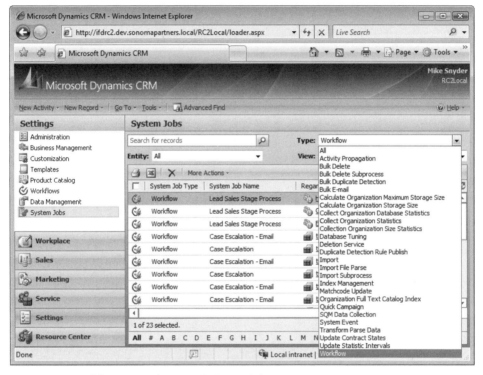

FIGURE 8-26 Workflow process instances in System Jobs

System Jobs (such as workflow) can have one of the following status reasons:

- Canceled

- Canceling

- Failed

- In Progress

- Pausing

- Succeeded

- Waiting

- Waiting for Resources

Reviewing Log Details

Regardless of where you access the executed workflow processes, you can review the details of any step by resting the mouse on the icon to the left of each step (see Figure 8-27).

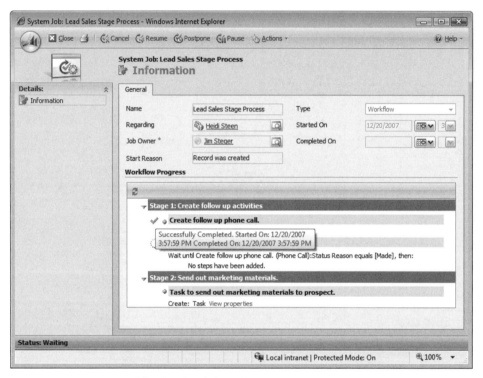

FIGURE 8-27 Accessing workflow log details from the step's tooltip

If your workflow job includes a large number of steps, resting your mouse on each step can become tedious. Fortunately, if you access the print view of a workflow job (from the Dynamics jewel/circle in the upper left corner), you can view all of the workflow details in a single layout. Figure 8-28 shows a sample print view, and you can see that it includes the details of each step.

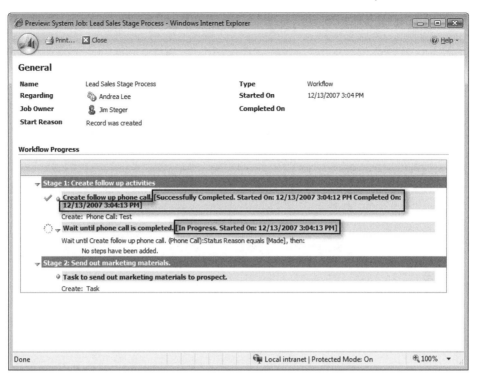

FIGURE 8-28 Workflow print details

Actions Available for Workflow Jobs

When you view a workflow process, provided that you have the correct permissions, you can take the following actions:

- **Cancel**   You can terminate an instance. No further steps will be executed.

- **Resume**   Resumes a paused instance. If the Workflow service paused the instance because of an error, you must correct the error before resuming.

- **Postpone**   You can delay the execution of the instance until a future date and time.

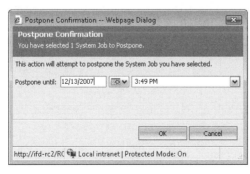

- **Pause**   You can manually pause an instance at any time.

Importing and Exporting Workflow

Just as with most of the Microsoft Dynamics CRM customizations and settings, you can import and export workflow rules from one Microsoft Dynamics CRM system to another. Therefore, you can create and test all of your workflow rules on a development system and deploy them to your production environment.

Each workflow rule (even draft rules) appear in the Export Customizations grid, as shown in Figure 8-29.

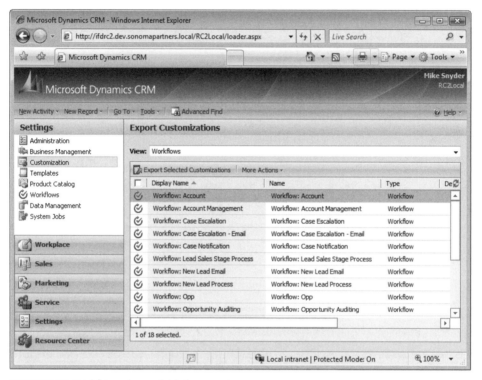

FIGURE 8-29 Workflow rules available for export

When you import workflow rules into a system, you need to be mindful that some references may be specific to the original system. Some potential workflow import issues include the following:

■ **Missing entities or attributes**   If you import a workflow rule that includes references to custom entities or custom attributes that don't exist in the target system, Microsoft Dynamics CRM experiences an error and prevents you from importing the workflow rule.

■ **Missing custom workflow activities**   If you import a workflow rule that references a custom workflow activity, make sure the target system has the custom workflow activity assembly registered. If the custom workflow activity is missing, the rule will import, but it will contain a warning message that you must correct the missing activity before you can publish the workflow rule.

- **User references**   If workflow rules include references to specific users, Microsoft Dynamics CRM will maintain the user reference if you import the rule to a target system on the same Microsoft Active Directory domain. If you import workflow rules between two different domains, you need to update all of the user references manually before you can publish the imported rule.

Don't forget that you will need to publish the imported workflow rules before they will start to work in your system.

Workflow Examples

Now that you understand the concepts and details related to Microsoft Dynamics CRM workflow, a few examples can show you how to pull everything together in real-world workflow scenarios. This section demonstrates the following common scenarios:

- Creating a business process for a new lead

- Escalating overdue service cases

- Adding simple data auditing for the Account entity

Creating a Business Process for a New Lead

Assume that your company would like to use a standardized process to handle each Lead created in the system. However, the business process varies depending on the Lead source and the location of the prospective client. Assume that the sales manager gives you the following requirements:

- If the Lead comes from the Web, send the Lead an e-mail acknowledgment.

- For all Leads (regardless of origin), create a Phone Call follow-up activity due one day after lead creation.

- Wait 14 days and determine if the Lead is still open. If yes, create a follow-up task due one day later to reconnect.

- Wait 30 days and evaluate the Lead status again. If it's still open, disqualify the Lead by marking it as lost.

This example will demonstrate the following features in workflow:

- Using conditions to create different sets of activities

- Using the Send E-mail action to send an e-mail template

- Using the Create Activity action to generate activity records for the Lead owner

- Using the Wait condition to perform subsequent checks on the record

Creating the rule

1. Log on to the Microsoft Dynamics CRM Web application, click Settings, and then click Workflows.

2. Click New on the Workflow grid toolbar. This opens a new workflow dialog box.

3. In the Create Workflow dialog box, type **New Lead Process** in the Name box, and select Lead in the Entity list. Ensure that New blank workflow is selected, and click OK.

> **Note** The following steps assume that After Step is selected for the Insert type. With this option selected, Microsoft Dynamics CRM creates each new step after the currently highlighted step.

Sending the response for Web site leads

1. Click Add Step, and click Check Condition.

2. For the step description, type **Check for Web lead**, and then click the *<condition>* (click to configure) link.

3. In the Specify Workflow Condition dialog box, create a condition as shown in the following image, and then click Save and Close.

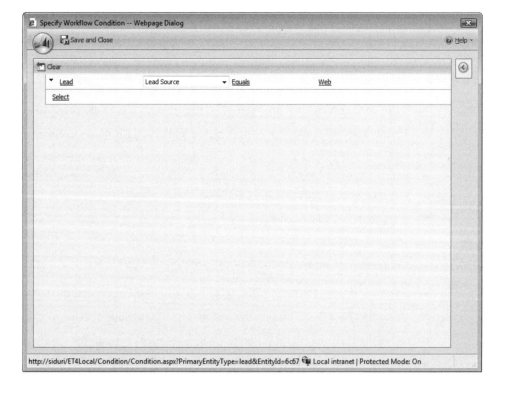

4. Click Select this row, click Add Step, and then click Send E-mail.

5. For the step description, type **Send Web Template E-mail**. To use one of the default templates provided by Microsoft Dynamics CRM, select Template, Lead, and then click Set Properties.

6. In the Send E-mail dialog box, click the To field to set the focus, and then in the Form Assistant panel, select Lead and Owner in the Look for list. Click Add, and then click OK. This will use dynamic values to send the e-mail message to the Lead owner. Repeat this process for the From field.

7. Select Lead Template from the Template Type list. Microsoft Dynamics CRM will display all of the e-mail templates that apply to the Lead entity. Select the Lead Reply-Web Site Visit from the Template list. Your page should resemble the one in the following image. Click Save and Close when done.

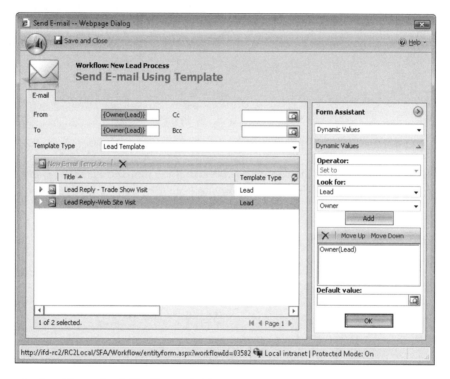

Your rule should now look like Figure 8-30.

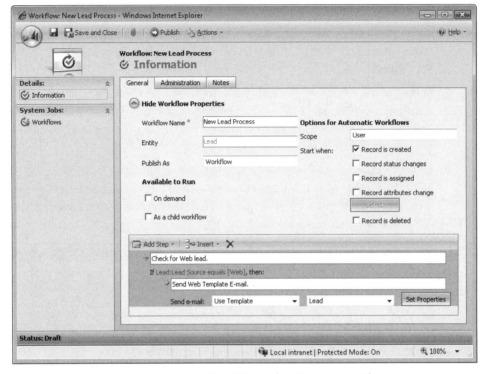

FIGURE 8-30 Workflow rule after Web lead condition and actions are entered

The next step is to add the common actions that the new Lead process expects. You want to create a Phone Call activity so that someone from your company will contact and attempt to qualify the lead.

Creating phone call actions

1. To add a Phone Call activity, click the area just to the left of the first step name to select that step, click Add Step, and then click Create Record.

2. For the step description, type **Create phone call activity**.

3. Select Phone Call from the Entity list, and click the Set Properties button.

4. In the Subject box, type **Follow up on new Web lead -** . Leave the cursor at the end of the space in the Subject box.

5. Next, you will add a new dynamic value for the lead topic. In the Form Assistant, for the dynamic value, select Lead, and then click Topic in the attribute list. Click Add. Microsoft Dynamics CRM will add the dynamic value (highlighted in yellow) in your phone call subject.

6. Type **No topic** in the Default Value box, and then click OK.

7. Click in the Due field. You want this phone call to be made quickly, so give it a due date one day after the Lead creation date. In the Form Assistant, click 1 day, and select After in the picklist. Next, select the Lead entity and the Created On attribute, and click Add. Leave the default value blank, and then click OK.

8. Next, follow a similar process to add dynamic values for the phone number and sender fields as shown in the following image. Click Save and Close to complete.

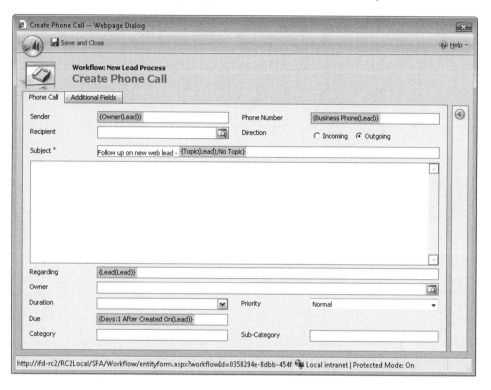

In the last sequence of steps, you will add some additional follow-up activities and cleanup steps. You will add a wait condition step to make the rule wait for 14 days. Then, you will check to see whether the Lead is still open. If it is, you will create a Task to reconnect with the Lead and assign it to the Lead owner. Then, you will add a final wait condition step with the duration of one month. If the Lead is still open after one month, you will send an e-mail message to the manager and close the Lead.

Adding the follow-up steps

1. Click the area just outside of the phone call step to highlight it, click Add Step, and then click Wait Condition.

2. For the step description, type **Lead cleanup**, and then click the *<condition>* (click to configure) link.

3. In the Specify Workflow Condition dialog box, create a condition as shown in the following image, and then click Save and Close.

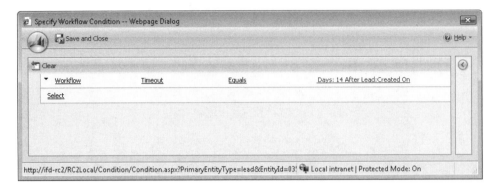

4. Next, click the Select this row and Add Step text under the timeout check you added. Click the new *<condition>* (click to configure) link. Configure the check condition as shown in the following image.

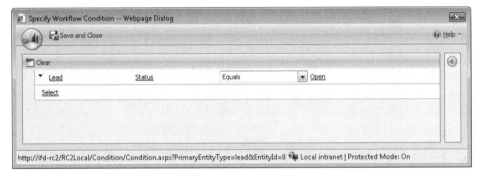

5. Click the Select this row and Add Step text under the check condition you added. Click Add Step, select Create New Record, and select Task in the picklist. Give the step a description of **Create follow up task to reconnect with Lead**.

6. Click Set Properties and configure the task as follows.

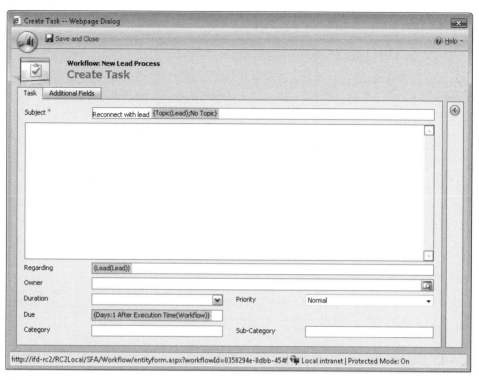

7. Select the task step and add another wait condition with the duration of 1 month. Give it a description of **Wait 1 more month**. When you configure the wait condition, make sure you select Workflow timeout equals duration of 1 month. Click Save and Close.

8. Click Select this row and Add Step, and then add another check condition. Click the *<condition>* (click to configure) link and configure the picklists to check if the Lead status equals Open. Click Save and Close.

9. Click Select this row and Add Step, click Add Step, and add a Change Status action. Give it a description of **Disqualify lead**. Change the state to Lost and save the workflow rule. Now publish the new rule. The final workflow rule should appear as shown.

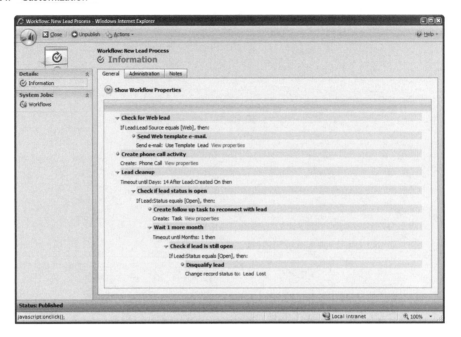

Escalating Overdue Service Cases

Every company would like to provide quick turnaround time when responding to and resolving their customers' support cases. For the purposes of this example, assume that the organization would like to ensure that it reacts to all cases within one day. After one day, they will check to see whether the case is still open. If it is, they will e-mail the owner's manager. They will then wait another day to see whether or not the status changes. If it does not, they will send another e-mail message to the manager of the case owner and assign the case to Level 2 support. This loop will continue until the case is resolved. Figure 8-31 shows the process graphically.

In addition to creating conditionals and actions that you are already familiar with, this example will highlight additional features in workflow:

- Using the Stop Workflow action
- Using the Start Child Workflow action
- Creating a looping process

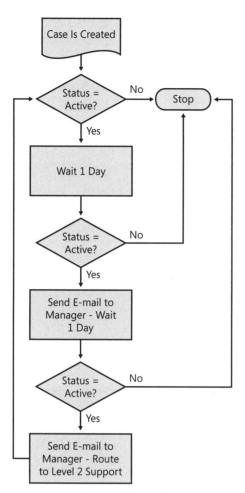

FIGURE 8-31   Case escalation logic

By now you should be familiar with the basics of creating a workflow, so we focus on only the new actions used for this example. You will create two workflow rules for the case entity in the following order:

- **E-mail rule**   A manual rule that simply sends an e-mail message to the owner's manager.

- **Escalating logic rule**   A child workflow rule that contains the logic for the case escalation. This rule calls itself, creating a looping situation.

You will manually create the e-mail message as a separate workflow rule because you want to use this message twice in the escalation logic rule. By using a separate rule, you also can make changes to the message in one centralized place.

Creating the e-mail rule

1. Log on to the Microsoft Dynamics CRM Web application, click Settings, and then click Workflows.

2. Click New on the workflow grid toolbar. This opens a new workflow dialog box.

3. In the Create Workflow dialog box, type **Case Escalation - Email** in the Name box, and select Case in the Entity list. Ensure that New blank workflow is selected, and then click OK.

4. Create a rule that matches the following figure.

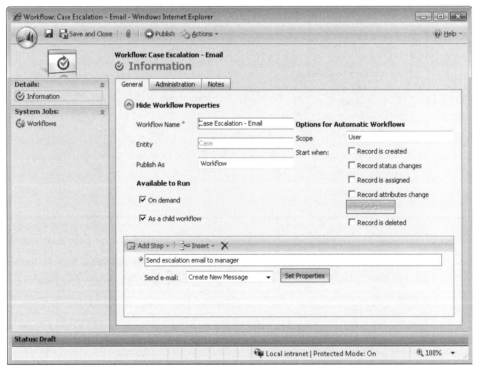

5. Click Set Properties and create an e-mail message with the following parameters:

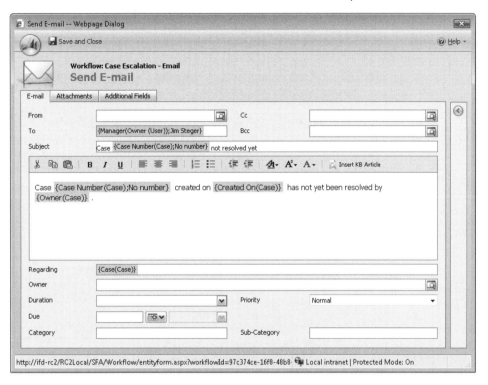

6. Save and publish the rule.

The next step is to create the main escalating logic. You will use the flow chart from Figure 8-31 as the blueprint. This workflow appears very simple, but notice that at the end, the workflow rule calls itself, creating a looping situation.

Use extreme care when creating a loop in workflow, especially one that calls additional child processes. You can accidentally create a situation in which the workflow rule enters an infinite loop. An infinite loop will create performance bottlenecks until it is terminated manually or by the Microsoft Dynamics CRM loop detection. Test the rule in a development environment. If you find yourself in an infinite loop, immediately terminate the step, deactivate the rule, and correct the problem.

Creating the escalating logic rule

1. Create a new workflow rule for the case entity called **Case Escalation - Logic**.

2. Change the scope to be Organization; leave the Record is created trigger, and set the Available to Run option to be As a child workflow.

3. Add your initial condition, checking the status of the case. If the case is not active (meaning that it has been resolved or canceled), you want to exit immediately with a stop command, marking the process as Succeeded.

4. Add a Wait for timer condition and set it for one day from when the case was created, and then add a check condition immediately after that checks whether the case status is still Active.

5. For the actions of this condition, add the child e-mail process. Click Add Step, and then click Start Child Workflow. Select Case Escalation – Email from the list.

6. Add a default condition to stop the process if the case is not active.

7. Continue to add the logic shown in Figure 8-31.

8. At the end, you want to create a recursive loop, so add one more child action. This time, though, call the Case Escalation - Logic rule.

9. Save and publish your rule.

The final rule should look like that shown in Figure 8-32.

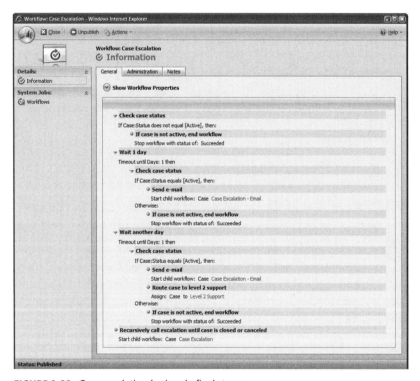

FIGURE 8-32   Case escalation logic rule final steps

Adding a Simple Data Audit for the Account Entity

Microsoft Dynamics CRM automatically records the date, the time, and the user who last modified a record. However, it does not record the specific values that the user changed in the record. This lack of detailed data auditing may cause some concern for your management and executives in today's intense Sarbanes-Oxley world. Fortunately, you can save the day for management by adding a data auditing feature to your Microsoft Dynamics CRM implementation with the combination of a new custom entity and a simple workflow rule. When you're done with this example, you'll be able to view a list of changes made to a single Account record, as shown in Figure 8-33.

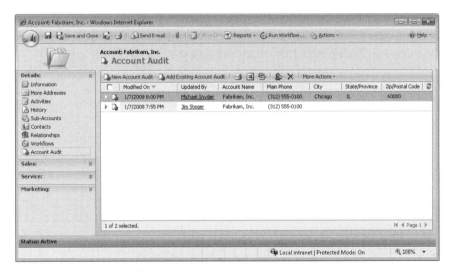

FIGURE 8-33   Account Audit example

To summarize the customizations necessary for this example, you will do the following:

- Create a new entity called Account Audit and customize it to your needs, including creating a many-to-one relationship with the Account entity.

- Update the Account Audit entity's associated view to display inactive records.

- Create a workflow rule to create a new account audit record, capturing the values of the account form.

Creating and customizing an Account Audit entity

The first step is to create a custom entity called Account Audit that will store the account-based auditing information. You will use this custom entity to record the field-level changes for attributes you specify. For this example, you will audit changes to the Account entity, so you will add a one-to-many relationship from the Account entity to the Account Audit entity.

Finally, as with all new custom entities, you must update your security roles to allow the appropriate access to the Account Audit entity. Since this workflow rule will trigger automatically, it will execute under the security context of the workflow rule owner. Therefore, for the Account Audit entity security privileges, make sure the workflow rule owner's security role includes Create, Read, Append, and Assign privileges to the Account Audit entity. For the remaining users, you should make sure their security role includes Read privileges to the Account Audit entity. To maintain the integrity of the account audit records, you should not grant Delete or Update permissions on the Account Audit entity to any role except the System Administrator role, which has access by default.

1. Create a new entity called Account Audit, as shown in the following graphic. Be sure to change the primary attribute's maximum length to 160 characters (to match the Account name attribute length), change the requirement level to No Constraint, and clear the Enable Duplicate Detection, Notes, and Activities check boxes.

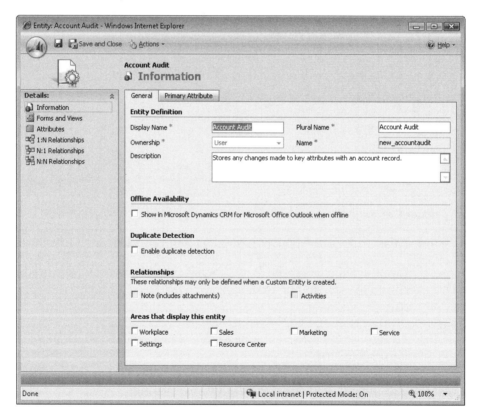

Note We recommend that you make this entity user-owned to determine who made the changes and to provide the business greater security flexibility with the audit records it wants to display to the user.

2. Click *Attributes*, and then add the custom attributes shown in Table 8-3. To show the time that the record was changed in the native grid, change the *modifiedon* attribute display to Date & Time. Finally, change the Owner attribute's Display Name to Updated By.

> **Note** Because the workflow will execute automatically as the workflow owner, the *createdby, modifiedby*, and *owner* attributes of the Account Audit record will default to the workflow owner. However, you want to know which user updated the account record. To capture the user who made the changes, you will assign the Account Audit record to the last user who modified the Account.

TABLE 8-3 Account Audit Entity Attributes

Display name	Schema name	Type
Main Phone	*new_telephone1*	*nvarchar(50)*
City	*new_address1_city*	*nvarchar(50)*
State/Province	*new_address1_stateorprovince*	*nvarchar(50)*
Zip/Postal Code	*new_postalcode*	*nvarchar(20)*

> **Note** Be sure to match the data types for any attribute you wish to audit.

3. Click N:1 Relationships, and add a many-to-one, referential relationship to the Account entity.

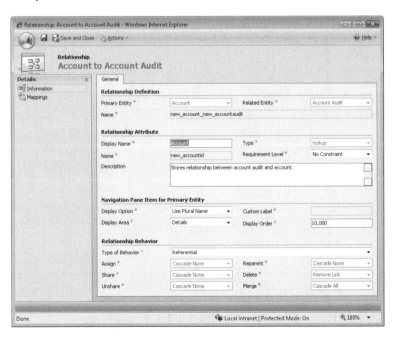

4. Click Forms and Views, double-click Form, and add the fields as shown in the following graphic. Rename the section by typing in the following text: **The system generates this information.** Click Save and Close on the toolbar.

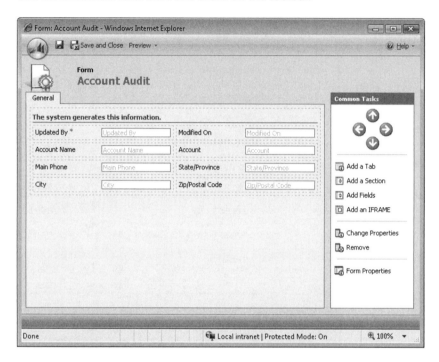

Note Later, you will modify these attributes to make them read-only on the form so that users can't modify the audit records. However, you need to leave them enabled now to create the workflow rule properly. You will go back and disable them once you complete the workflow rule.

5. Open the Associated View editor and add the columns and default sort as shown in the following graphic.

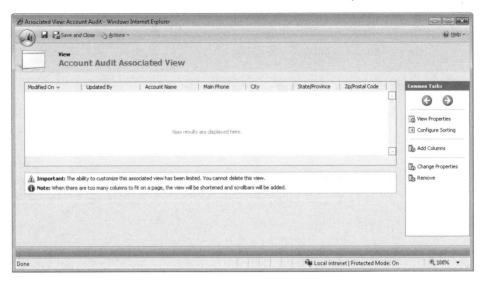

6. Publish the entity.

Important Don't forget to add the appropriate security settings for this new entity in your system. By default, only the System Administrator role can access the newly created custom entities.

Modifying the Account Audit associated view to display inactive records

By default, Microsoft Dynamics CRM only displays active records in an associated view. However, we would recommend that you create the account audit records in the inactive state so that users cannot modify them and it's clear that these records should not be modified. Unfortunately Microsoft Dynamics CRM doesn't include an option in the user interface to associated views to display inactive records. Therefore, you will need to export the account audit entity and manually modify the customization XML file.

1. Click Settings, and select Customization. Select the Account Audit record, then click Export Selected Customizations.

2. Open the customization file in your favorite XML editor and search for the name Account Audit Associated View. After you find this saved query, navigate to the *<columnset>* node and remove the *<filter>...</filter>* nodes.

Note Be sure to update the correct *<columnset>*. The *<localizednames>* node is actually at the end of the *<savedquery>* node set, so its corresponding *<columnset>* is actually above it in the file.

3. Save the file and import it into Microsoft Dynamics CRM.

4. Publish the Account Audit entity.

Creating the Account Audit workflow rule

With the account audit entity ready, now you need to create the workflow rule that will automatically create audit records when users create or change an Account record. The final workflow rule will resemble the one shown in Figure 8-34.

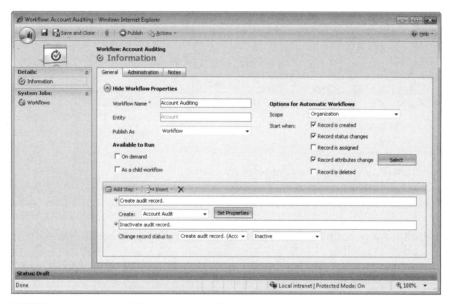

FIGURE 8-34 Account workflow rule for auditing

1. Log on to the Microsoft Dynamics CRM Web application, click Settings, and then select Workflows.

2. Click New on the workflow grid toolbar. This opens a new workflow dialog box.

3. In the Create Workflow dialog box, type **Account Auditing** in the Name box, and select Account in the Entity list. Ensure that New blank workflow is selected, and click OK.

4. Select Organization as the Scope. We want the workflow rule to execute for everyone in the organization.

5. Select Record is created, Record status changes and Record attributes change. For Record attributes change, select Account Name, Address1: City, Address1: State/Province, Address 1: Zip/Postal Code, Main Phone as the attributes to monitor.

6. Click Add Step, and select Create Record. Type **Create audit record** in the step description box.

7. Select Account Audit for the entity, and click Set Properties.

8. Add dynamic values to the Account Audit as shown in the following graphic.

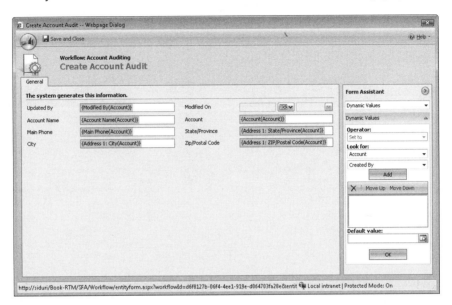

9. Click Add Step, and select Change Status. Type **Inactivate audit record** in the step description box.

10. Select your previous step (should be the last choice), and set the status to Inactive.

11. Save and publish your workflow rule.

Now that you completed configuring the workflow rule, you need to go back to the account audit entity to disable the attributes on the form because you do not want users to be able to create or alter these records manually. By disabling the attributes on the field (instead of using security roles to control access to the entity), no users can modify these fields. This even applies to users with a system administrator role who can edit every record in Microsoft Dynamics CRM.

Disable the Account Audit form attributes

1. Update the properties of each attribute displayed on the Account Audit to be disabled on the form.

2. Publish the Account Audit entity.

Finally, you must update your security roles to allow the appropriate access to the Account Audit entity. At a minimum, you will have to allow for Create, Read, Append, and Assign privileges for the workflow owner. For all remaining users, allow for Read privileges to the Account Audit entity.

Create a new Account and you will see that the values you enter for Name, Main Phone, City, State/Province, and Zip/Postal Code are captured in the new Account Audit entity. After you save the changes, click the Workflows link to see the status of your workflow rule (see Figure 8-35).

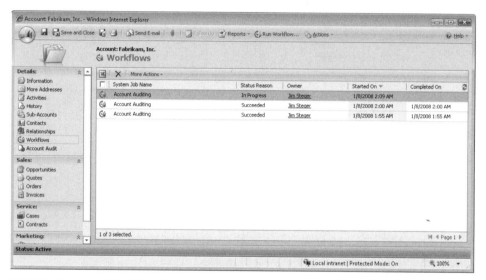

FIGURE 8-35 Account Audit workflow process status

Note Remember that the workflow rules run asynchronously and you may need to wait a few seconds to see the new Account Audit record. Click the refresh icon for the grid to see the new record, or check the workflows grid of the record for the status of the workflow process.

Navigate to the Account Audit grid to see your changes after the workflow rule shows the status as *Succeeded* (Figure 8-36).

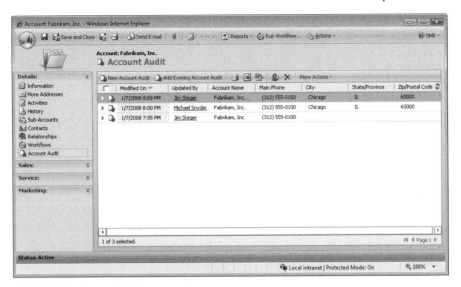

FIGURE 8-36 Account Audit record changes

Summary

Microsoft Dynamics CRM includes powerful workflow functionality that you can set up and configure to implement standardized business processes in an automated fashion. You configure and manage workflow in the Microsoft Dynamics CRM user interface, so users and administrators can quickly create complex business rules without being required to have any programming knowledge. You can create workflow rules for most of the entities in Microsoft Dynamics CRM, including custom entities. By using workflow rules, you can specify criteria and business logic for how Microsoft Dynamics CRM should execute the rule. In addition to configuring the workflow trigger event, you can insert conditions and actions in each rule. Workflow rules follow the Microsoft Dynamics CRM security model, so you can configure the rules and security roles for your organization to restrict user access.

Part III
Extending Microsoft Dynamics CRM

When we work with prospects considering a Microsoft Dynamics CRM purchase, we hear lots of stories about complex business rules and sophisticated programming requirements. Usually at least one time in the sales process the prospect will ask a question along the lines of "Is this even possible to program in Microsoft Dynamics CRM?" That's when a big smile crosses our face as we say "Of course!" This isn't just tough talk to win a deal, we mean it when we say that you can program almost anything with Microsoft Dynamics CRM.

This part of the book goes into the details of how you can use the Microsoft Dynamics CRM software development kit (SDK) to create your own custom code. By working within the SDK framework, your custom solutions will be supported by the Microsoft Dynamics CRM support team, and stand a very good chance of upgrading smoothly when Microsoft releases new versions and updates of Microsoft Dynamics CRM. The Microsoft CRM SDK opens all sorts of programming interfaces into the software, so any experienced Web developer can be up and running with custom solutions in very little time.

We wrote all of the examples in this part of the book so that you can download the sample code and deploy the software to your organization if you wish. The book's introduction explains how you can download the sample code off of the book's Web site.

Chapter 9
Microsoft Dynamics CRM 4.0 SDK

In addition to all of the Web-based configuration and customizations tools discussed so far, Microsoft Dynamics CRM provides a programming interface that you can use to create *even more* complex and sophisticated customizations. Information about accessing the Microsoft Dynamics CRM programming interface is published in a document called the Microsoft Dynamics CRM software development kit (SDK). To create customizations and integrations by using the information in the SDK, you must be comfortable developing Web-based applications using tools such as Microsoft Visual Studio. We assume you have working knowledge of Visual Studio and Web application configuration with Microsoft Internet Information Services (IIS). If you're not a developer, we still recommend that you read the chapters in this part of this book to gain an understanding of the types of customizations that the Microsoft Dynamics CRM programming model makes possible.

 Note Our examples and references use Visual Studio 2008. You can also use Visual Studio 2003 or Visual Studio 2005 for your development.

The SDK defines all of the supported interaction points, also known as application programming interfaces (APIs), that you can access when writing code that integrates with Microsoft Dynamics CRM. Using the APIs for your customizations provides several significant benefits:

- **Ease of use** The APIs include hundreds of pages of documentation complete with real-world examples, code samples, and helper classes to help you write code that works with Microsoft Dynamics CRM.

- **Supportability** If you encounter technical problems or issues using the APIs, you can contact Microsoft technical support or use the Microsoft Dynamics CRM public newsgroup for assistance.

- **Upgrade support** Microsoft makes every effort to ensure that code that you create for Microsoft Dynamics CRM using the APIs will upgrade smoothly with future versions of the product, even if the underlying Microsoft SQL Server database changes radically. This is also true for any hotfixes that Microsoft might release for Microsoft Dynamics CRM.

- **Certification** By following the documented APIs, you can submit your customizations to a third-party testing vendor to certify that your application works within the confines of the SDK. This certification provides comfort and reassurance for people evaluating your customizations.

> **Caution** As discussed in Chapter 4, "Entity Customization: Concepts and Attributes," it is techni-
> cally possible for you to create programming customizations that bypass the Microsoft Dynamics
> CRM APIs and interact directly with the SQL Server database. However, we strongly discourage
> anyone from attempting to do this for all of the reasons just listed.

In addition to the SDK Help file, you will also find an SDKReadme.htm file. This document contains many known issues regarding the SDK, and we recommend that you review it before working with the SDK.

Chapter 10, "Form Scripting and Extensions," covers the form and scripting customizations in detail. Don't forget that you can download all of the sample code included in this book (the book's Introduction specifies the download URL).

Overview

As you learned in Chapter 1, "Microsoft Dynamics CRM 4.0 Overview," Microsoft Dynamics CRM uses a metadata and server platform layer to abstract the application and extensibility points from the SQL Server database tier. The platform layer also controls security, event management, and extensibility points (such as plug-ins and workflow) while enforcing the proper constraints for interacting with the underlying schema of the database. By providing a supported API, Microsoft Dynamics CRM allows developers to customize the application and continue to use those customizations after future upgrades.

Figure 9-1 shows a graphical representation of the Microsoft Dynamics CRM architecture.

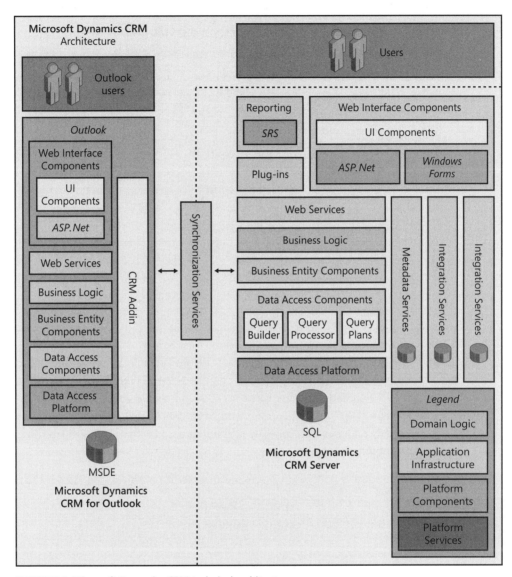

FIGURE 9-1 Microsoft Dynamics CRM technical architecture

New Features of the Microsoft Dynamics CRM 4.0 SDK

Microsoft Dynamics CRM has always been committed to making it possible for system developers to interact programmatically with the software. The Microsoft Dynamics CRM 4.0 SDK provides great new functionality with an easy to use programming model.

Table 9-1 outlines a few of the new additional key features the 4.0 SDK has to offer.

TABLE 9-1 Notable Microsoft Dynamics CRM 4.0 SDK Improvements

Feature	Description
Multitenancy support	Multiple organizations can now be hosted on a common set of hardware, and the Web Services Description Language (WSDL) APIs are now unique per organization. Microsoft Dynamics CRM introduces a new DiscoveryService API to return the organizations' APIs.
Multilanguage support	Additional languages are now installed in convenient language packs. The metadata API service has been extended to retrieve language information.
Unified event model	Plug-ins and workflow now use the same event framework, allowing for even more extensibility.
Offline API	The SDK has been expanded to include offline access.
Enhanced metadata	Now you can programmatically create, read, update, and delete the Microsoft Dynamics CRM metadata such as entities, attributes, and relationships with ease.

Microsoft Dynamics CRM uses a service-oriented approach for its APIs, making use of three WSDL-compliant Web services (DiscoveryService, CrmService, and MetadataService). As you can see in Figure 9-1, Microsoft Dynamics CRM controls data access for the application interface, reports, and extensibility through the use of these Web services. As you learned in Chapter 7, "Reporting and Analysis," Microsoft Dynamics CRM also allows for direct and secure retrieval of data from SQL Server through the use of filtered views. Filtered views provide read-only access of data directly to the database layer, but they still honor the security rights of the calling user.

The shaded, rounded rectangles in Figure 9-2 denote the business logic extension areas available to you.

Three API Web services exist for you to extend Microsoft Dynamics CRM:

- CrmService Web service
- MetadataService Web service
- DiscoveryService Web service

This chapter focuses on these core API services available for custom integration and application development in Microsoft Dynamics CRM, as well as platform-based events and customization points.

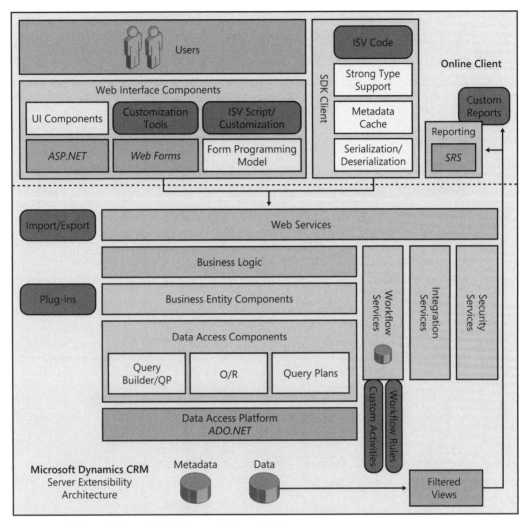

FIGURE 9-2 Microsoft Dynamics CRM extensibility architecture

Accessing the APIs in Visual Studio 2008

Before you can programmatically use the methods and logic available in Microsoft Dynamics CRM, you must first add the Web service API references to your project.

With the Web service APIs, you have a choice of either referencing the service endpoint directly or you can connect to an exported WSDL file. We discuss both approaches shortly. Table 9-2 lists the three Web service–based APIs available and the recommended namespaces when referencing by the Web, and where you can download the WSDL file.

TABLE 9-2 Available Microsoft Dynamics CRM Web Service APIs

API name	Namespace name	WSDL location
CrmService	CrmSdk	Download from Microsoft Dynamics CRM user interface for each organization
MetadataService	MetadataSdk	Download from Microsoft Dynamics CRM user interface for each organization
DiscoveryService	CrmSdk.Discovery	Included in the WSDL folder of the Microsoft Dynamics CRM SDK

Table 9-3 lists the Microsoft Dynamics CRM Web service API URL locations for on-premise deployments.

TABLE 9-3 Available Microsoft Dynamics CRM Web Service API End Points

API name	On-premise deployment endpoint
CrmService	http://<crmserver>/mscrmservices/2007/crmservice.asmx
MetadataService	http://<crmserver>/mscrmservices/2007/metadataservice.asmx
DiscoveryService	http://<crmserver>/mscrmservices/2007/ad/crmdiscoveryservice.asmx

Note Microsoft Dynamics CRM Live uses a unique address for the DiscoveryService Web service: *https://dev.crm.dynamics.com/mscrmservices/2007/passport/crmdiscoveryservice.asmx*.

If you don't plan to use the Web service APIs, Microsoft also offers three assemblies that you can use to programmatically interact with Microsoft Dynamics CRM instead (with some benefits and constraints):

- Microsoft.Crm.Sdk.dll
- Microsoft.Crm.SdkTypeProxy.dll
- Microsoft.Crm.Outlook.Sdk.dll

The Web service APIs can provide a dynamic, strongly typed development reference. This provides a more robust development experience. However, you must keep the Web references up-to-date and you need to access the latest WSDL at compile time.

On the other hand, the assembly references wrap the Web service functionality and provide you most of the core functionality (and default entity access), but you will not know about any schema customizations made to the system. Further, these assemblies provide additional helper functionality. When using the assembly references, you take advantage of the Microsoft Dynamics CRM's *DynamicEntity* concept (we discuss this further later in the chapter). By using this approach, you will have an easier time deploying common solutions across multiple and changing environments.

When developing assembly-based solutions, such as plug-ins and workflow assemblies, we recommend the assembly reference approach as the preferred method. For Web development applications, you can use either the WSDL or assembly reference approach. We discuss ASP.NET Web development further in Chapter 10.

> **Note** You can access the DiscoveryService functionality only as a Web-based WSDL reference.

As mentioned, you must add references in your Visual Studio 2008 project to programmatically access the APIs functionality. You can add any of the APIs by using one of the following methods:

- Access the Web reference URL directly in Visual Studio 2008

- Download the WSDL definition to the file system and add the Web reference locally

- Reference the Microsoft.Crm.Sdk and Microsoft.Crm.SdkTypeProxy assemblies

When you add a Web reference, we recommend using the same naming convention described earlier in Table 9-2, but you can choose whatever naming convention you wish. Next, we show you an example of adding references for the CrmService and Microsoft.Crm. Sdk using each of the various techniques. You would use a similar technique for the other API references.

Adding the CrmService Web reference URL directly in your project

1. Open a project in Visual Studio 2008 and target the .NET Framework 3.0.
2. Right-click the project, and then click Add Service Reference.
3. Click the Advanced button in the Add Service Reference box.
4. In the Service Reference Settings box, click Add Web Reference.
5. In the Add Web Reference dialog box, add the CrmService reference:
   a. In the URL box, type **http://<*crmserver*>/mscrmservices/2007/crmservice. asmx**.
   b. In the Web reference name box, type **CrmSdk** (note that if you are using C#, this is case-sensitive).
   c. Click Add Reference.

Adding an on-premise CrmService service WSDL reference to your project

1. Open Microsoft Dynamics CRM in a Web browser, click Settings, click Customization, and then select Download Web Service Description Files.

2. Click the icon of the CrmService.asmx file to download. The file will open in a Web browser window.

3. In the Web browser, save the page to your file system as an XML file (in Internet Explorer 7, click Page, and then click Save As). Be sure to change the file name to end with the .xml or .wsdl extension, for example, CrmServiceWsdl.xml.

4. Open a project in Visual Studio 2008 and target the .NET Framework 3.0.

5. Right-click the project, and then click Add Service Reference.

6. Click the Advanced button in the Add Service Reference box.

7. In the Service Reference Settings box, click Add Web Reference.

8. In the Add Web Reference dialog box, add the CrmService reference:

   a. In the URL box, type the location of your downloaded WSDL file (for example, **c:\CrmServiceWsdl.xml**).

   b. In the Web reference name box, type **CrmSdk** (note that if you are using C#, this is case-sensitive).

   c. Click Add Reference.

Note   The Visual Studio 2005 Add Web Reference command will automatically appear in Visual Studio 2008 when you target the .NET Framework 2.0.

Adding the SDK assembly references to your project

1. Open a project in Visual Studio 2008.

2. Right-click the project, and then click Add Reference.

3. In the Add Reference dialog box, click the Browse tab.

4. Navigate the file system and find the Microsoft.Crm.Sdk.dll assembly. The SDK assemblies reside in the SDK's bin folder or the GAC folder of the Microsoft Dynamics CRM server installation CD. Click OK to add.

After the references are added to your project, you are ready to begin development.

Caution   Do not add *both* the WSDL-based reference and the Microsoft.Crm.* assemblies to your project and reference them in your classes. The references share the same namespace and many of the same properties and methods, which will force to you fully qualify all of your commands. We recommend you use one approach per class file.

Before we begin to code, we first review the key functionality of each Web service API.

CrmService Web Service

The CrmService Web service is the core API mechanism for programmatically interacting with all entities in Microsoft Dynamics CRM. This service contains six common methods that work on all entities, and an *Execute* method that is available for all other needs. The service is strongly typed and WSDL compliant, and can be updated with any changes to the schema directly through Visual Studio 2008.

> **Important** Microsoft Dynamics CRM automatically updates its API interfaces as you add custom entities and custom attributes using the Web-based administration tools. Therefore, if you add multiple custom attributes to the Account entity, you can reference these new attributes programmatically through the API and can even use IntelliSense updates to reflect these new attributes in Visual Studio 2008 when using the WSDL-based API.

The CrmService Web service is located at *http://<crmserver>/mscrmservices/2007/crmservice .asmx*, where *<crmserver>* is the Microsoft Dynamics CRM Web server.

In addition, we recommend you initialize the service *Url* property in your code, as shown in the following code example.

```
public CrmService GetCrmService(string orgName, string server)
{
  // Standard CRM Service Setup
  CrmAuthenticationToken token = new CrmAuthenticationToken();
  token.AuthenticationType = 0; //AD (On-premise)
  token.OrganizationName = orgName;

  CrmService service = new CrmService();
  service.Credentials = System.Net.CredentialCache.DefaultCredentials;

  // If you know you are using the default credentials,
  // you can replace the service.Crendentials line with the following line
  // service.UseDefaultCredentials = true;

  service.CrmAuthenticationTokenValue = token;
  service.Url = string.Format("http://{0}/mscrmservices/2007/crmservice.asmx",server);

  return service;
}
```

> **Note** Because of page length considerations, we reuse the *GetCrmService()* method in some of the examples.

With the service's *Url* property, you can access the Web service URL that may be different from the URL specified in your project's Web reference. Set the *Url* property of service by using a configuration approach so that you can deploy to different environments without having to recompile your code. You can accomplish this using the registry or using DiscoveryService Web service. We demonstrate setting the service *Url* property using the DiscoveryService later in the chapter.

> **Tip** Specifying a valid organization name in the token for your service's URL is critical. If you receive a 401: Unauthorized error, first check to see that you have the correct organization name for your service's endpoint and the user accessing the service has a valid account with that organization.

Now that you have a little background on the CrmService Web service, we can review these additional topics related to the CrmService:

- Authentication

- Impersonation

- Common methods

- *Execute* methods

- *Request* and *Response* classes

- *DynamicEntity* class

- Attributes

Authentication

Microsoft Dynamics CRM provides a pluggable authentication model so that you can use the proper authentication mechanism for accessing the API services, depending on the Microsoft Dynamics CRM deployment. The three deployment types currently available for Microsoft Dynamics CRM are on-premise, Microsoft Dynamics CRM Live, or Internet-facing deployment (IFD). The examples in this book focus on the on-premise deployment model.

> **Note** Microsoft Dynamics CRM Live uses Windows Live Authentication (Passport). Please refer to the SDK for additional information.

We discuss the on-premise authentication in three areas:

- Authenticating to the API services

- Configuring the security token

- Understanding the security context of the method call

Authenticating to the API Services

With an on-premise deployment, you are required to pass valid Active Directory credentials to communicate properly with the Microsoft Dynamics CRM Web service APIs. You will commonly see this handled with the following *Credentials* lines of code:

```
CrmService service = new CrmService();
service.Credentials = System.Net.CredentialCache.DefaultCredentials;
```

This code uses the logged-in user's credentials for validation. The Microsoft Dynamics CRM APIs by default will then translate the domain credentials to the proper customer relationship management (CRM) system user and use the CRM user id (usually referred to as the *systemuserid*) throughout the life of that service's instantiation.

You could also choose to specify a user by passing in a valid set of credentials as shown in the following line of code:

```
service.Credentials = new NetworkCredential("UserName","UserPassword","UserDomain");
```

Obviously, try to avoid hard-coding any credential set, and if you do have to use this approach, be sure to encrypt the information. We provide this information so that you can understand that authenticating to the Web service is network dependent, not Microsoft Dynamics CRM dependent. As long as a user has a valid Active Directory credential set, the user can authenticate to the service APIs, even if that user is not a valid Microsoft Dynamics CRM user. However, to actually retrieve any data you must provide a valid Microsoft Dynamics CRM *systemuserid*. This concept is discussed further shortly.

Configuring the Security Token

Given the multiple security models and tenants available for Microsoft Dynamics CRM, the Web services require an authentication token to be constructed and passed as part of the SOAP header. The code for the token typically is the following:

```
CrmAuthenticationToken token = new CrmAuthenticationToken();
token.AuthenticationType = 0; //AD (On-premise)
token.OrganizationName = "<ValidOrganizationName>";
```

You need to set the authentication type and specify the name of the organization you wish to access. Table 9-4 lists the possible values for the *AuthenticationType* property. Choose the type appropriate for your deployment.

TABLE 9-4 *AuthenticationType* **Values**

Description	Value
Active Directory	0
Microsoft Dynamics CRM Live	1
Internet-facing deployment (IFD)	2

Finally, you can set the service's *CrmAuthenticationTokenValue* property to your newly created token, as shown in the following code:

```
service.CrmAuthenticationTokenValue = token;
```

Understanding the Security Context of a Method Call

Now that you have properly connected to the service, you need to understand the Microsoft Dynamics CRM security context under which the call is being made. This is often overlooked because Microsoft Dynamics CRM implicitly defaults to the user defined with the *Credentials* property if you don't explicitly pass a value for the token's *CallerId* property.

The security context being used by Microsoft Dynamics CRM determines which actions can be performed with the API. For instance, if you have logic that should create a new lead, the calling user must have rights to create a lead.

> **Important** Context also varies depending on how you are accessing the API. For instance, plug-ins execute under the same identity of the Microsoft Dynamics CRM Web application pool. Workflow context execution varies depending on how the rule is initiated.

Microsoft Dynamics CRM recognizes that at times you might need to perform actions on behalf of a user with rights in the Microsoft Dynamics CRM application different from the user who triggered the logic. This can be performed by employing a concept known as impersonation, which we discuss next.

Impersonation

As you just learned with an on-premise deployment, you need to authenticate to the Microsoft Dynamics CRM Web service APIs. When used in the context of Web pages, code executes under the security credentials of the user browsing the Web page. At times, you might want to execute code using different security credentials from those of the user browsing the Web page. In Microsoft Dynamics CRM, you can execute business logic on behalf of another user through a technique called impersonation.

To do this, you need to do the following:

- Explicitly set the authentication token's *CallerId* property using a valid Microsoft Dynamics CRM system user

- Ensure the network credentials of the user used to authenticate to the Web service is a member of the *PrivUserGroup* in the Active Directory directory service

You can set the *CallerId* very easily by adding the following line of code after your standard service setup.

```
token.CallerId = new Guid("00000000-0000-0000-0000-000000000000");
```

Replace the string of zeros (also referred to as an empty GUID) with the actual *systemuserid* globally unique identifier (GUID) of the Microsoft Dynamics CRM user whom you wish to impersonate. Microsoft Dynamics CRM ignores an empty GUID and uses the security credentials of the user browsing the Web page. If you specify a GUID that does not exist, Microsoft Dynamics CRM will throw an exception.

Also, the authenticating user of the API Web service must be a member of the *PrivUserGroup* in Active Directory. These are the network credentials specified in the *service.Credentials* property. The *PrivUserGroup* is an Active Directory group added during the installation of Microsoft Dynamics CRM.

Important The user that corresponds to the *systemuserid* specified in the *CallerId* property is *not* the user who needs to be a member of the *PrivUserGroup*. The Active Directory user specified in the *service.Credentials* property is the user who must be added.

Although this is a powerful technique, any time you impersonate you open a potential security risk and add configuration challenges to your implementation. We recommend that you try to avoid using impersonation whenever possible. In most cases, you can find an alternative way to execute the logic required by altering the user's Microsoft Dynamics CRM security permissions or by changing the logic's design.

Warning Impersonation is not supported with workflow assemblies, when the code is executed in offline mode, or with Microsoft Dynamics CRM Live.

Common Methods

The following six methods provide the basic create, read, update, delete (CRUD) operations for entities, including custom entities:

- **Create**   Creates a new record for a given entity.

- **Retrieve**   Returns a single record based on the entity ID passed in.

- **RetrieveMultiple**   Returns multiple records based on a query expression.

- **Update**   Edits an existing record.

- **Delete**   Removes a record.

- **Fetch**   Returns multiple records based on a FetchXML query. The FetchXML query syntax mirrors that of previous Microsoft Dynamics CRM versions.

Consider a simple example of how you would use one of the common methods. This example retrieves the topic, first name, last name, and industry for a single Lead record, and then displays the information. You will work with the Lead record shown in Figure 9-3. For simplicity, this example will just run in a console application.

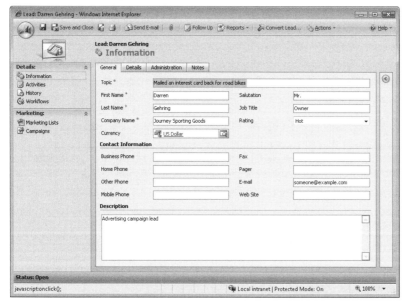

FIGURE 9-3 Lead form

Because this is the first SDK example, we walk you through the process of creating a basic console application in Visual Studio 2008.

Creating a new console project

1. Open Visual Studio 2008.

2. On the File menu, click New, and then click Project.

3. Under Project Types, select Visual C# Projects, and then click Console Application under Templates.

4. In the Name box, type **WorkingWithDynamicsCrm4.SdkExamples**.

5. Using either WSDL-based approach to add the service reference explained earlier in this chapter, add a Web reference to the CrmService Web service, calling it **CrmSdk**.

> **Note** You reuse this console application concept for other examples later in the book.

Now that you have the basic console application in place, add the logic to return values from a Lead using the Microsoft Dynamics CRM *retrieve* method.

Retrieving a Lead record from Microsoft Dynamics CRM

1. In the default Program.cs file, add the code shown in Listing 9-1.

2. Open an existing Lead record in your Microsoft Dynamics CRM system. After you have the record open, press the F11 key *twice* to open Microsoft Internet Explorer. In the address bar, you can retrieve the Lead unique identifier.

3. Replace the leadId value with your own.

4. Update the organization name with the correct organization name of your Microsoft Dynamics CRM system.

5. Save the class file.

6. On the Build menu, click Build Solution.

Listing 9-1 shows the code for retrieving the Lead record. If you were to run this example, you might have to update the namespace of your CrmSdk depending on the name of your project.

Listing 9-1 Retrieving a Lead record

```
using System;
using System.Text;
using System.Net;
using WorkingWithDynamicsCrm4.SdkExamples.CrmSdk;

namespace WorkingWithDynamicsCrm4.SdkExamples
{
  class Program
  {
```

```
static void Main(string[] args)
{
  // Replace the default guid with a specific lead from your system.
  Guid leadId = new Guid("2B1689A5-8194-DC11-A8E4-0003FF9456FD");
  RetriveLead(leadId);
}

public static void RetriveLead(Guid leadId)
{
  // Use generic GetCrmService method from earlier
  // Replace <organization> and <server> with your values
  CrmService service = GetCrmService("<organization>","<server>");

  // Set the columns to return.
  ColumnSet cols = new ColumnSet();
  cols.Attributes = new string [] {"subject", "firstname", "lastname",
"industrycode"};

  try
  {
    // Retrieve the record, casting it as the correct entity.
    lead oLead = (lead)service.Retrieve(EntityName.lead.ToString(), leadId, cols);

    // Display the results.
    // Because you have a strongly typed response, you can access the properties of
the object.
    Console.WriteLine("Topic: {0}", oLead.subject);
    Console.WriteLine("First Name: {0}", oLead.firstname);
    Console.WriteLine("Last Name: {0}", oLead.lastname);
    Console.WriteLine("Industry: {0}", oLead.industrycode.Value);
    Console.ReadLine();
  }
  catch (System.Web.Services.Protocols.SoapException ex)
  {
    Console.WriteLine(ex.Detail.InnerText);
  }
}
}
}
```

After you add this code, compile it, and run the project, you might receive the following error message:

```
Object reference not set to an instance of an object.
Console.WriteLine(oLead.industrycode.Value);
```

This error occurs because Microsoft Dynamics CRM does not return an object reference for any attribute that has a value of null. You received this error because the sample Lead does not have an *Industry* value selected in the picklist, hence its value is null in the database. So, when your code tries to access the *industrycode* value property, you get an exception.

Important Microsoft Dynamics CRM will not return a requested field if the field has a null value in the database.

To account for the possibility that Microsoft Dynamics CRM might not return a field that your code is expecting, you should ensure that the attribute you want to access is not null. This code example shows one way to check for null values.

```
Console.Write("Industry: ");
if (oLead.industrycode != null)
        Console.WriteLine(oLead.industrycode.Value);
```

After the code in Listing 9-1 is updated to check for a null value and refreshed, you'll receive output similar to that shown in Figure 9-4.

FIGURE 9-4 Lead retrieval example.

The SDK contains many more examples that demonstrate how to use each of the six common methods.

Execute Method

The *Execute* method allows you to run any special commands or business logic not addressed by the common methods. Unlike the common methods, the *Execute* method works on *Request* and *Response* classes. You pass a *Request* class as a parameter to the *Execute* method, which then processes the request and returns a response message. Though the *Execute* method can perform most of the actions of the common methods, its real purpose is to provide you the functionality that the common methods lack. Typical actions for which you might use the *Execute* method are to retrieve the current user, assign and route records, and send e-mail messages through Microsoft Dynamics CRM. For instance, the following code example shows how to retrieve the current user using the *Execute* method.

```
// Use generic GetCrmService method from earlier
// Replace <organization> and <server> with your values
CrmService service = GetCrmService("<organization>","<server>");

// Get current user object.
WhoAmIRequest userRequest = new WhoAmIRequest();
WhoAmIResponse user = (WhoAmIResponse) service.Execute(userRequest);
```

Note You must always cast the returning message to the appropriate instance of the *Response* class.

Request and *Response* Classes

Microsoft Dynamics CRM uses a *Request* and *Response* message class model for the *Execute* method. You must create a *Request* class message, set the properties that you require, and pass the request a target message. You then send the *Request* object to the platform by using the *Execute* method. The platform runs the request and sends back an instance of a *Response* class message.

Microsoft Dynamics CRM *Request* and *Response* classes support generic, targeted, specialized, and dynamic entity requests. These *Request* classes always end in the word *Request*, such as *WhoAmIRequest*, *CreateRequest*, and *SendEmailRequest*. Generic requests are not dependent on a specific entity and do not contain an entity name in their class name. Generic requests can work across multiple entities (such as the *AssignRequest*) in addition to sometimes working with no entities (such as the *WhoAmIRequest*).

Generic requests that apply to entities require a target message class to specify which entity should receive the action. A target class name begins with the word *Target* and, once instantiated and configured, is then applied to the *target* property of a generic class. This code example shows how a *TargetQueuedIncident* could apply to the *RouteRequest* to send a case to a support queue.

```
// Use generic GetCrmService method from earlier
// Replace <organization> and <server> with your values
CrmService service = GetCrmService("<organization>","<server>");

// Create the Target object (case or incident for this example)
TargetQueuedIncident target = new TargetQueuedIncident();

// EntityId is the GUID of the case record being routed.
// We are using a known case GUID. In practice, this will be passed in to your
routines.
target.EntityId = new Guid("D5F7CAE8-D51E-40EF-9EFC-592B484BCCFF");
```

```
// Request object
RouteRequest route = new RouteRequest();
route.Target = target;
route.RouteType = RouteType.Queue;

// EndPointId is the GUID of a non-work-in-progress queue or user to whom the case is
being routed.
// You are using a known case GUID. In practice, this is passed in to your routines.
route.EndpointId = new Guid("922F63E8-6585-DA11-8D43-0003FF12CD51");

// SourceQueueId is the GUID of the queue the case is coming from.
// We are using a known case GUID. In practice, this will be passed in to your
routines.
route.SourceQueueId = new Guid("E8B77049-13C1-41FE-93B0-B3B8031F089C");

try
{
  // Execute the Request.
  RouteResponse routed = (RouteResponse)service.Execute(route);
}
catch(System.Web.Services.Protocols.SoapException ex)
{
  // Handle error.
}
```

Specialized requests are similar to targeted requests except that they work only on a specific entity to perform a distinct action. Their naming convention is *<Action><Entit yName>Request*. Good examples of these requests are the *SendEmailRequest* and the *LoseOpportunityRequest*.

With the dynamic entity request, you can use requests at run time for any entity. By setting the parameter *ReturnDynamicEntities* to *True*, your results will be returned as a *DynamicEntity* class instead of the *BusinessEntity* class. Not all requests permit the *DynamicEntity* option, and you should refer to the SDK for the complete list that does. We go into more detail about the *DynamicEntity* class next.

DynamicEntity Class

The *DynamicEntity* class, derived from the *BusinessEntity* class, provides run-time access to entities and attributes even if those entities and attributes did not exist when you compiled your assembly. The *DynamicEntity* class contains the logical name of the entity and a property-bag array of the system attributes. In programming terms, this can be thought of as a loosely typed object. With the *DynamicEntity* class, you can access entities and attributes created in Microsoft Dynamics CRM even though you might not have the actual entity definition from the WSDL.

The *DynamicEntity* class must be used with the *Execute* method, and it contains the following properties:

- **Name**   Sets the entity schema name

- **Properties**   Array of type *Property* (which is a name/value pair)

Review the syntax of the *DynamicEntity* class to create a Lead. You create a *string* property to store the subject text, which you pass into the *DynamicEntity dynLead*. After you create the *DynamicEntity* object and set its name to *lead*, you create a *TargetCreateDynamic* class to serve as the target message for the *CreateRequest* call.

```
// Use generic GetCrmService method from earlier
// Replace <organization> and <server> with your values
CrmService service = GetCrmService("<organization>","<server>");

// Set up dynamic entity.
DynamicEntity dynLead = new DynamicEntity();

dynLead.Name = "lead";
dynLead.Properties = new Property[] {
   CreateStringProperty("subject","New Lead Using Dynamic Entities"),
   CreateStringProperty("lastname","Steen"),
   CreateStringProperty("firstname","Heidi")
};

// Standard target request, passing in the dynamic entity.
TargetCreateDynamic target = new TargetCreateDynamic();
target.Entity = dynLead;
CreateRequest create = new CreateRequest();
create.Target = target;
CreateResponse response = (CreateResponse)service.Execute(create);

// Helper method that creates a string property based on passed-in values
private Property CreateStringProperty(string Name, string Value)
{
   StringProperty prop = new StringProperty();
   prop.Name = Name;
   prop.Value = Value;
   return prop;
}
```

Obviously, you would not use the dynamic entity approach over the common *Create* method to create a Lead record if you have access to the CrmService Web service because the dynamic entity approach is not as efficient and requires more code. However, Microsoft Dynamics CRM provides this class for run-time situations in which you might not know the entity, or when new attributes might be added to an existing entity.

You will make heavy use of the *DynamicEntity* class with Microsoft Dynamics CRM because it will be your primary entity class when writing plug-ins and workflow assemblies, as you will see later in this chapter.

We also want to highlight the helper method used in this example for creating the properties that you wanted to set. In this particular example, you knew you were working with a *string* property, but in some scenarios, you might not know the property type. To address this, you would have to query the metabase and determine the data types of your desired attributes at run time. With Microsoft Dynamics CRM, you can do this with the MetadataService Web service, as you will see shortly.

> **More Info** The SDK provides helper classes that contain many useful methods. Be sure to review them and add them to your projects to ease development.

Attributes

Remember that when using an individual WSDL, the Microsoft Dynamics CRM attributes will be strongly typed. Therefore, you must create a typed attribute when setting values for an entity, unless you are using the *DynamicEntity* class. The SDK documentation lists examples of each type and how to use them, so we won't list them here. However, you will see examples of this throughout the sample code.

MetadataService Web Service

In addition to the CrmService Web service, the Microsoft Dynamics CRM SDK includes a MetadataService Web service that you can use to programmatically access the metadata. You can perform the following types of actions with the MetadataService Web service:

- Retrieve the metadata for a specific entity, either system or custom.
- Retrieve the attributes for an entity.
- Retrieve the metadata for a specific attribute such as the possible state names or picklist values for an attribute.
- Create a custom entity.
- Add or update an attribute for an entity, either system or custom.
- Create or delete a relationship between two entities.
- Retrieve all the metadata to create a metadata cache in a client application.
- Determine whether the metadata has changed since a previous retrieve.
- Retrieve all the entities and determine which ones are custom entities.
- Add or remove an option from a picklist attribute.
- Write an install and uninstall program for your custom solution.

The MetadataService Web service is located at *http://<crmserver>/mscrmservices/2007/ metadataservice.asmx*, where *crmserver* is the Microsoft Dynamics CRM Web server. As with the CrmService Web service, you need to add a Web reference in your project to access the methods and properties available.

However, unlike the previous Microsoft Dynamics CRM versions, the MetadataService Web service allows for write requests as well. Therefore, you can now use this service to manipulate the underlying metadata programmatically. As you will see, you can add, modify, or delete Microsoft Dynamics CRM underlying metadata such as managing entities, attributes, and even relationships.

The MetadataService Web service has numerous messages available for use. We review a few of them here to demonstrate some typical uses. Please refer to Microsoft Dynamics CRM SDK documentation for all possible messages.

Listing 9-2 shows how you would use the MetadataService Web service to access information about a picklist attribute. This example also shows some of the information that you can retrieve about this attribute and that you can use in your own application.

Listing 9-2 Retrieving picklist metadata information

```
public static void RetrievePicklistMetadata()
{
  MetadataSdk.CrmAuthenticationToken token = new MetadataSdk.CrmAuthenticationToken();
  token.AuthenticationType = 0;
  token.OrganizationName = "<organization>"; // Replace with your organization name
  MetadataService metadataService = new MetadataService();
  metadataService.Credentials = CredentialCache.DefaultCredentials;
  metadataService.CrmAuthenticationTokenValue = token;

  try
  {
    RetrieveAttributeRequest attributeRequest = new RetrieveAttributeRequest();
    attributeRequest.EntityLogicalName = EntityName.account.ToString();
    attributeRequest.LogicalName = "accountcategorycode";
    attributeRequest.RetrieveAsIfPublished = true;

    RetrieveAttributeResponse attributeResponse = (RetrieveAttributeResponse)metadataService
.Execute(attributeRequest);

    // Access the retrieved attribute
    PicklistAttributeMetadata attMetaData = (PicklistAttributeMetadata)attributeResponse.
AttributeMetadata;
    Console.WriteLine("DisplayName: \t\t{0}", attMetaData.DisplayName.UserLocLabel.Label);
    Console.WriteLine("DefaultValue: \t{0}", attMetaData.DefaultValue);
    Console.WriteLine("DisplayMask: \t{0}", attMetaData.DisplayMask.Value);
    Console.WriteLine("IsCustomField: \t\t{0}", attMetaData.IsCustomField.Value);
    Console.WriteLine("Name: \t\t\t{0}", attMetaData.EntityLogicalName);
    Console.WriteLine("RequiredLevel: \t\t{0}", attMetaData.RequiredLevel.Value);
    Console.WriteLine("Type: \t\t\t{0}", attMetaData.AttributeType.Value);
    Console.WriteLine("ValidForCreate: \t{0}", attMetaData.ValidForCreate.Value);
```

```
      Console.WriteLine("ValidForRead: \t\t{0}", attMetaData.ValidForRead.Value);
      Console.WriteLine("ValidForUpdate: \t{0}", attMetaData.ValidForUpdate.Value);
      Console.WriteLine("Options:");

      foreach (Option o in attMetaData.Options)
      {
        Console.WriteLine("{0}={1}", o.Value.Value,o.Label.UserLocLabel.Label);
      }
      Console.ReadLine();
  }
  catch (System.Web.Services.Protocols.SoapException ex)
  {
      // Handle error.
  }
}
```

Figure 9-5 shows the output when you run this console application in Visual Studio 2008.

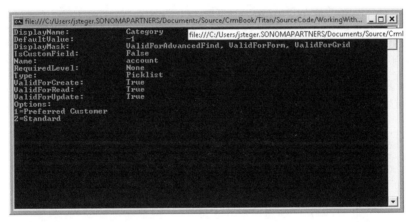

FIGURE 9-5 Picklist metadata

Microsoft Dynamics CRM now provides even more information when retrieving entity information by using the *MetadataItems* property. Table 9-5 shows the values that can be retrieved and their descriptions.

TABLE 9-5 *MetadataItems* **Information**

Name	Value	Description
All	0x10	Retrieves all information about an entity
EntitiesOnly	1	Retrieves base information about an entity
IncludeAttributes	2	Returns base entity information and attribute details
IncludePrivileges	4	Returns base entity information and security credential details
IncludeRelationships	8	Returns base entity information and relationship details

> **Caution** When retrieving metadata entities, choose the metadata items flag based on the needs of your application while keeping in mind that Microsoft Dynamics CRM provides these different options for performance reasons. The more data items you request from the metabase, the longer it will take to process and return the results.

Again, we won't list all of the properties and methods of the MetadataService Web service because of space considerations, but you can use the SDK or the Visual Studio IntelliSense feature to discover all of its available properties and methods.

Discovery Web Service

The CrmDiscoveryService Web service can provide a list of organizations and their corresponding Web service endpoint URLs. You will use this information to configure the CrmService and MetadataService Web service proxies and call Web service methods that access an organization's data. The discovery service URL is fixed per installation so that you can programmatically configure solutions for multiple organizations in a single environment.

The Discovery Web service is most applicable for multitenant installations of Microsoft Dynamics CRM, installations that have the Web service APIs installed on a server different from the Microsoft Dynamics CRM Web server, or for independent software vendors (ISVs) solutions.

> **More Info** A multitenant installation is one in which multiple CRM organizations are configured against a common set of hardware. Remember that each organization contains a unique database that contains the custom configuration and all of the business data.

The CrmDiscoveryService Web service for an Active Directory installation is located at *http://<crmserver>/mscrmservices/2007/AD/CrmDiscoveryService.asmx*.

> **Note** Microsoft Dynamics CRM Live uses a different URL for the discovery service. If you are working with a Microsoft Dynamics CRM Live implementation, use the following URL instead: *https://dev.crm.dynamics.com/MSCRMServices/2007/Passport/CrmDiscoveryService.asmx*.

Listing 9-3 shows some basic code using the CrmDiscoveryService to retrieve organizations and their API Web service URLs.

Listing 9-3 Example using the CrmDiscoveryService

```
// Create and configure the CrmDiscoveryService Web service proxy.
CrmDiscoveryService discoveryService = new CrmDiscoveryService();
```

```
discoveryService.UseDefaultCredentials = true;
discoveryService.Url = "http://localhost/MSCRMServices/2007/AD/CrmDiscoveryService.asmx";

// Retrieve the list of organizations to which the logged-on user belongs.
RetrieveOrganizationsRequest orgRequest = new RetrieveOrganizationsRequest();
RetrieveOrganizationsResponse orgResponse =
    (RetrieveOrganizationsResponse)discoveryService.Execute(orgRequest);

// Loop through list to locate the target organization.
OrganizationDetail orgInfo = null;
foreach (OrganizationDetail orgDetail in orgResponse.OrganizationDetails)
{
    if (orgDetail.OrganizationName.Equals("AdventureWorksCycle"))
    {
        orgInfo = orgDetail;
        break;
    }
}

// Check whether a matching organization was not found.
if (orgInfo == null)
    throw new Exception("The specified organization was not found.");
```

After you obtain the organization details, you can then access the CrmService and
MetadataService Web services to perform your business logic using the following code.

```
CrmAuthenticationToken token = new CrmAuthenticationToken();
token.AuthenticationType = 0;  //AD authentication type
token.OrganizationName = orgInfo.OrganizationName;

CrmService crmService = new CrmService();
crmService.Url = orgInfo.CrmServiceUrl;
crmService.CrmAuthenticationTokenValue = token;
crmService.Credentials = System.Net.CredentialCache.DefaultCredentials;
```

Queries

With any custom code that you create, of course you'll need to programmatically query
data from Microsoft Dynamics CRM. Microsoft Dynamics CRM offers three data retrieval
mechanisms: *QueryExpression*, FetchXML, and filtered views.

QueryExpression Class

Microsoft Dynamics CRM provides a powerful, typed *QueryExpression* class. You initialize
QueryExpression like all other classes.

```
QueryExpression query = new QueryExpression();
```

You then set the entity that you want to query and any other query parameters required for your search. Table 9-6 lists the main fields (each with their own properties) that are available with this class. For more details on the *QueryExpression* fields, consult the SDK.

TABLE 9-6 *QueryExpression* **Fields**

Field	Description
ColumnSet	Property that contains an array of columns to return. Set to an instance of *AllColumns* to return all possible fields for an entity. If left null, only the primary key is returned.
Criteria	Contains the filters of your query.
Distinct	Determines whether duplicate records should be returned.
EntityName	Sets the name of the entity to search.
LinkEntities	Used to join across other entities.
Orders	Specifies the order of the results.
PageInfo	Sets the number of pages and number of records per page for the result set.

You will now create a sample query that you can execute against the sample database. This query starts by retrieving all Leads created this week. The results should be identical to the Leads Opened This Week view on the Leads grid. You can sort this grid by the Name (*fullname*) column, as shown in Figure 9-6.

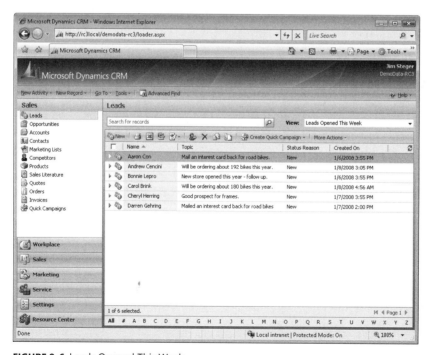

FIGURE 9-6 Leads Opened This Week

```
// Use generic GetCrmService method from earlier
// Replace <organization> and <server> with your values
CrmService service = GetCrmService("<organization>","<server>");

  try
  {
    QueryExpression query = new QueryExpression();
    query.EntityName = EntityName.lead.ToString();
    ColumnSet cols = new ColumnSet();
    cols.Attributes = new string[] { "subject", "fullname", "createdon" };

    ConditionExpression condition = new ConditionExpression();
    condition.AttributeName = "createdon";
    condition.Operator = ConditionOperator.ThisWeek;

    FilterExpression filter = new FilterExpression();
    filter.FilterOperator = LogicalOperator.And;
    filter.Conditions = new ConditionExpression[] { condition };

    OrderExpression order = new OrderExpression();
    order.OrderType = OrderType.Ascending;
    order.AttributeName = "fullname";

    query.ColumnSet = cols;
    query.Criteria = filter;
    query.Orders = new OrderExpression[] { order };

    BusinessEntityCollection retrieved = service.RetrieveMultiple(query);

    foreach (lead leadResult in retrieved.BusinessEntities)
    {
      Console.Write(leadResult.fullname.ToString() + "\t");
      Console.Write(leadResult.createdon.date.ToString() + "\t");
      Console.WriteLine(leadResult.subject.ToString());
    }
    Console.ReadLine();
  }
  catch (System.Web.Services.Protocols.SoapException ex)
  {
    // Handle error.
  }
```

If you parsed the results in a Web page (as shown in Figure 9-7), you see the same data returned by the grid view.

FIGURE 9-7 Leads returned from *QueryExpression*

> **Tip** You could also perform simple queries by using the *QueryByAttribute* class. See the SDK for sample code.

FetchXML

FetchXML defines a custom query language from the original version of Microsoft Dynamics CRM. Using the FetchXML syntax, you create a string containing your query statement. You then pass that string using the common method *Fetch*.

We generally recommend that you use *QueryExpression* over FetchXML for better performance in addition to the fact that the *QueryExpression* results are strongly typed. However, the FetchXML option still exists to ease the upgrade path for users of earlier versions of Microsoft Dynamics CRM and also provides more advanced query options not yet available in *QueryExpression* (such as returning attributes from a link entity).

The following code example shows an example FetchXML call using the *Fetch* method.

```
// Use generic GetCrmService method from earlier
// Replace <organization> and <server> with your values
CrmService service = GetCrmService("<organization>","<server>");

// Retrieve the full name of any contact whose first name equals "Alan".
string fetch = @"
 <fetch mapping=""logical"">
  <entity name=""contact"">
   <attribute name=""fullname""/>
    <filter>
     <condition attribute=""firstname"" operator=""eq"" value=""Alan""/>
    </filter>
```

```
  </entity>
 </fetch>";

try
{
 // Retrieve the results.
 string result = service.Fetch(fetch);
}
catch (System.Web.Services.Protocols.SoapException ex)
{
 // Handle error.
}
```

The resulting string of this query when run against the Microsoft Dynamics CRM sample database is similar to the following:

```
<resultset morerecords="0" paging-cookie="&lt;cookie
page=&quot;1&quot;&gt;&lt;contactid last=&quot;{5C9507B8-3496-DC11-A8E4-
0003FF9456FD}&quot; first=&quot;{127290B1-3496-DC11-A8E4-0003FF9456FD}&quot;
/&gt;&lt;/cookie&gt;"><result><fullname>Alan
Waxman</fullname><contactid>{127290B1-3496-DC11-A8E4-
0003FF9456FD}</contactid></result><result><fullname>Alan
Brewer</fullname><contactid>{5C9507B8-3496-DC11-A8E4-
0003FF9456FD}</contactid></result></resultset>
```

Filtered Views

In addition to *QueryExpression* and FetchXML, you can also use SQL filtered views to retrieve data from Microsoft Dynamics CRM. We introduced filtered views in Chapter 7, so we won't review them in detail again. In the context of creating custom code that reads data from Microsoft Dynamics CRM, you can connect to the filtered view tables in SQL Server directly instead of using the API.

> **Important** Accessing data in filtered views is the only case in which your code should ever connect directly to SQL Server. For all other calls, you should use the methods provided in the Microsoft Dynamics CRM SDK.

Filtered views were originally developed for reporting purposes, but you can take advantage of them in your code as well. However, remember that you must connect to SQL Server by using Microsoft Windows authentication, not SQL Server authentication, because the views join against the systemuser base table based on the domain name of the calling user to determine to which data rows the user has access.

When working with plug-in assemblies, you need to take this into account because, as you will see in the next section, plug-ins typically run as the network service account. As such, the calling context is the server's system account and it won't return any data when accessing the filtered views. You should use *QueryExpression* or FetchXML to retrieve the data that you require whenever possible.

> **More Info** You can also use context switching by placing the *context_info()* function in your SQL statement to return data directly from the filtered views in a plug-in assembly. We expand on this topic later in the chapter.

Plug-ins

Plug-ins provide a server-based mechanism to run custom logic or spawn custom processes both before and after Microsoft Dynamics CRM executes a request against the platform layer in either a synchronous or asynchronous fashion. Figure 9-8 shows the event execution pipeline approach.

Microsoft Dynamics CRM 4.0 supports both pre-event plug-ins (events that fire before an action is taken against the platform) and post-event plug-ins. Further, the Microsoft Dynamics CRM 4.0 plug-in architecture is fully Microsoft .NET Framework compliant, which means it's more stable and easier to use for developing and deploying solutions.

> **Tip** When developing integration to and from other applications, you will typically make heavy use of the Microsoft Dynamics CRM plug-in model.

Development

In this section, we review the process of developing plug-ins. Plug-ins are simple .NET class assemblies, and most people develop plug-ins using Visual Studio. We assume you are using Visual Studio 2008 and C# as the programming language for the discussion and examples.

Creating the Plug-in Project

First, create a new C# class library project targeting Microsoft .NET Framework 3.0 version, and then immediately add references to the Microsoft.Crm.Sdk and Microsoft.Crm.SdkTypeProxy assemblies. These files are located in the /bin folder of Microsoft Dynamics CRM 4.0 SDK files. After you add these references to your project, you are now ready to build a custom plug-in class.

We recommend that you try to avoid creating explicit Web references to the Microsoft Dynamics CRM API services to avoid having to re-create the authentication. As you will soon see, you will create the CrmService and MetadataService from the plug-in's context, and by using *DynamicEntities* you can compile your project entirely from the SDK assemblies.

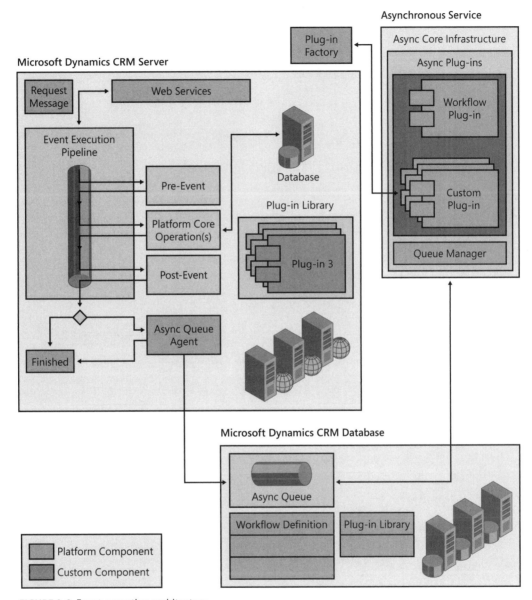

FIGURE 9-8 Event execution architecture

 Important In your projects, you should not reference any Microsoft Dynamics CRM assembly files other than ones approved by Microsoft. The only assemblies currently supported are Microsoft.Crm.Sdk.dll, Microsoft.Crm.SdkTypeProxy.dll, and the Microsoft.Crm.Outlook.Sdk. dll. Please refer to the Microsoft Dynamics CRM 4.0 SDK for the most current information.

Digitally Signing Your Assembly

Your must digitally sign your custom plug-in (and workflow) assemblies to register them with Microsoft Dynamics CRM. Digital signing creates a strong name for your assembly and further strengthens its identity to the server.

The simplest way to sign your assembly is to use Visual Studio 2008.

Signing an assembly using Visual Studio 2008

1. Right-click the project, and click Properties.

2. Click Signing.

3. Select the Sign the Assembly check box, and select <New> from the Choose a strong key name file list.

4. Enter any name in the key file name box, and clear the Protect my key file with a password option.

Your result should resemble the one shown in Figure 9-9.

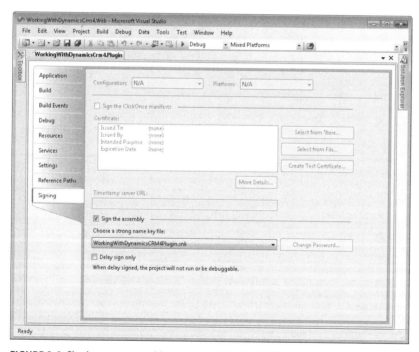

FIGURE 9-9 Signing your assembly with Visual Studio 2008

You can also use the strong name tool that comes with Visual Studio 2008. On the Start menu, click Program Files, Microsoft Visual Studio 2008, Visual Studio Tools, and then open a Visual Studio 2008 command prompt. At the prompt type the following:

```
sn -k <file name>
```

Then, attach the newly created file to your project by using the Signing tab described in the previous procedure. For more information about the Strong Name tool, read the article titled "Strong Name Tool (Sn.exe)" on Microsoft MSDN at *http://msdn2.microsoft.com/en-us/library/k5b5tt23(VS.90).aspx.*

For more information about digitally signing assemblies, review the Building Secure Assemblies section on MSDN at *http://msdn2.microsoft.com/en-us/library/aa302423.aspx.*

Adding the Class File

Next, create a simple class file. Be sure to add the appropriate *using* statements to the CRM assemblies, and remember that your class file must inherit from the *IPlugin* interface. To run your custom logic, you must override the *Execute* method, as the following example shows.

```
using System;
using Microsoft.Crm.Sdk;
using Microsoft.Crm.SdkTypeProxy;

namespace SonomaPartners.Plugins
{
    public class SamplePluginClass : IPlugin
    {
        public void Execute(IPluginExecutionContext context)
        {
            // Execute your custom logic here.
        }
    }
}
```

Now that your class file is in place, we review programming with the plug-in's context.

Plug-in Context

The plug-in context contains all sorts of useful information. The SDK lists all of the methods and properties available for use, but we want to discuss the way you would create services from the context.

We previously mentioned that you will want to use the passed-in context when instantiating your service. To do this, use the following lines:

```
ICrmService service = context.CreateCrmService(false);
IMetadataService mdService = context.CreateMetadataService(false);
```

Both methods return an interface, which means you don't need to cast the return type. Even better, the context returns the service instance already authenticated for you. The parameter the method takes determines whether you should impersonate the calling user or just allow the service to execute as the system account. We discuss this further in the next section.

Because you are creating the service from the context, and because you won't have an updated Web service WSDL to use to compile your code when interacting with the API, you need to use the *DynamicEntity* class.

Please reference the SDK, the samples provided, and our examples for additional information.

Plug-in Impersonation

Plug-ins execute under the security context of the Web application's application pool identity, which is typically the network service account.

> **More Info** The network service account typically translates to the generic *SYSTEM* Microsoft Dynamics CRM user.

Therefore, your plug-in logic will typically execute as the CRM *SYSTEM* user. For many plug-in scenarios, this works fine. However, you might find that you need to use the credentials of the user making the request in your plug-ins.

To use impersonation in your plug-in code, you simply need to create the service from the plug-in's context as usual, but then set the parameter to *true*.

```
ICrmService service = (ICrmService)context.CreateCrmService(true);
```

Your service calls will now use impersonation. The security context of the user used will depend on the value specified in the *impersonatinguserid* attribute during the plug-in registration. If you leave the *impersonatinguserid* field null (blank) during registration, the impersonated user will be the calling user; otherwise, the security context will be the user specified in this field.

> **Important** Plug-in impersonation does not work offline. The actions offline will always be taken by the logged-on user.

Deployment

Now that Microsoft Dynamics CRM 4.0 supports multitenancy and offline execution of assemblies, the process of deploying plug-ins and workflow assembly files involves a bit more work.

Deployment Security

The user account registering the plug-in must exist in Microsoft Dynamics CRM and in the Deployment Administrators group. You manage the Deployment Administrators group with the Deployment Manager tool.

Adding a new user to the Deployment Administrators group

1. Log on to the Microsoft Dynamics CRM Web server directly or by a Remote Desktop Connection using the installation user account or any user account already added to the Deployment Administrators group.

2. Open the Deployment Manager tool, and click Deployment Administrators on the left.

3. In the right pane, click New Deployment Admin.

4. Enter the user in the Select User dialog box.

The registration user must also have the following Microsoft Dynamics CRM organization security privileges:

- prvCreatePluginAssembly
- prvCreatePluginType
- prvCreateSdkMessageProcessingStep
- prvCreateSdkMessageProcessingStepImage
- prvCreateSdkMessageProcessingStepSecureConfig

These privileges are not exposed in the Microsoft Dynamics CRM user interface. However, any user in the Microsoft Dynamics CRM System Administrator or System Customizer role will automatically have these privileges set.

Registration Methods and Tools

Microsoft Dynamics CRM provides API methods for you to properly register your assemblies with the application. Rather than having to investigate and write your own code for this purpose, Microsoft offers a command-line tool (PluginDeveloper) that ships with the SDK sample code; we use that project for examples later in the chapter.

> **Important** Please refer to the SDK documentation for the most current information and tools available to deploy plug-in and workflow assemblies.

The documentation that comes with the command-line registration tool details what you will need to build the project. Please refer to it so that you can properly build the project. The tool then uses a simple XML file (called register.xml) that contains all the information required to register your assembly information with Microsoft Dynamics CRM. The XML file is well documented and should be relatively simple for you to configure. Any references to custom assemblies need to be placed in the Microsoft Dynamics CRM assembly folder for on-disk deployments prior to registration. For database deployments, you will either need to register any referenced assemblies in the global assembly cache (GAC) or use the ILMerge tool to create a single assembly.

> **Tip** The ILMerge tool is a great way to create a single assembly to use in database deployment of plug-ins and workflow assemblies. See the section titled "Coding and Testing Tips" later in this chapter for more information about the ILMerge tool.

During development, we recommend that you open the PluginDeveloper project in Visual Studio and run it in debug mode. This way you can quickly trap any errors with registration and correct them, as shown in Figure 9-10.

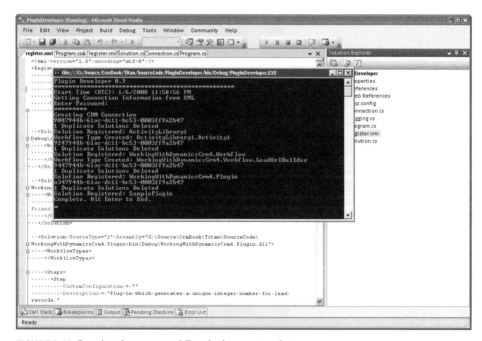

FIGURE 9-10 Running the command-line deployment project

When developing, plan on deploying the assembly, including a matching project database (PDB) file, using the on-disk option so that you can debug your files using Visual Studio. To do this, copy your assembly files to the Microsoft Dynamics CRM Web server to the following directory: *<crm install drive>*\Program Files\Microsoft Dynamics CRM\server\bin\assembly.

> **Important** You should copy the files to the server prior to registering them for the first time.

As you make updates, you might find that you are unable to copy the files because of an error resulting from a file already in use. This can happen because IIS still has the assembly in memory, and you should either recycle the application pool or perform an *iisreset* to free the file. Also, if you deploy in asynchronous mode, the Microsoft Dynamics CRM asynchronous processing service might have the file locked. By restarting this service, you can properly update your assembly files.

> **Note** You do not have to deploy Microsoft.Crm.Sdk.dll and Microsoft.Crm.SdkTypeProxy.dll. Microsoft Dynamics CRM automatically installs these assemblies to the GAC of the Web server during the installation process, which makes them available to your assemblies.

We demonstrate coding examples of the plug-in at the end of the chapter and provide you the appropriate code for your registration configuration file to install the samples properly.

Plug-in Registration Properties

As users work in the application, their actions cause Microsoft Dynamics CRM to trigger events that developers can use to execute custom logic through the use of plug-ins. With Microsoft Dynamics CRM, you can add your own custom code that will execute if a user action triggers one of the events.

Microsoft Dynamics CRM 4.0 enhances the plug-in model over Microsoft Dynamics CRM 3.0 by providing more configuration options for the developer. Plug-ins now support additional events (or messages), can run synchronously or asynchronously, offer deployment options to the file system of the server or the database, and can run offline in Microsoft Dynamics CRM for Microsoft Office Outlook with Offline Access.

We review the following options available for plug-in registration:

- **Mode**   A plug-in can execute either synchronously or asynchronously.
- **Stage**   This option specifies whether the plug-in will respond to pre or post events.
- **Deployment**   A plug-in can execute only on the server, with the Outlook client, or both.

- **Messages**   This option determines the Microsoft Dynamics CRM events that should trigger your logic, such as Create, Update, and even Retrieve.

- **Entity**   A plug-in can execute against most of the entities, including custom entities.

- **Rank**   This option is an integer that specifies the order in which all plug-in steps should be executed.

- **Assembly Location**   This option tells Microsoft Dynamics CRM whether the assemblies are stored in the database or on the Web server's file system.

- **Images**   You may pass attribute values from the record as either pre or post certain messages for certain message types.

You configure these plug-in properties when you register the plug-in with Microsoft Dynamics CRM.

Mode

Microsoft Dynamics CRM 4.0 introduces the concept of asynchronous execution of plug-in assemblies. In previous versions, plug-ins (previously known as callouts) only executed synchronously. So, for longer-running processes or business logic, developers in Microsoft Dynamics CRM 3.0 were forced to create their own asynchronous queuing mechanisms or attempt to use custom workflow assemblies. Now in Microsoft Dynamics CRM 4.0, you simply need to configure the plug-in upon installation as asynchronous and Microsoft Dynamics CRM will automatically execute it as part of its asynchronous service.

We recommend that you configure your plug-in to run asynchronously when you have a longer-running process that does not need to be completed immediately. This will allow the user to continue using the application and provide a faster user experience.

> **Warning** Microsoft Dynamics CRM does not support pre-event plug-ins configured for asynchronous operation.

Stage

You can register your plug-ins to run before or after submitting data to the database. Pre-event plug-ins are useful when you wish to validate or alter data prior to submission. With post-event plug-ins, you can execute additional logic or integration after the data has been safely stored in the database.

Deployment

One of the great new features of Microsoft Dynamics CRM 4.0 is the ability to have your plug-in logic execute offline with the Outlook client, further extending your existing solution. You can choose to have the plug-in execute only against the server, run offline with the Outlook client, or both.

Remember that when a client goes offline and then returns online, any plug-in calls are executed after the data synchronizes with the server. If you choose to have your logic execute both with the server and offline, be prepared for Microsoft Dynamics CRM to execute your plug-in code twice!

> **Caution** Microsoft Dynamics CRM does not support an asynchronous implementation of the plug-in with offline deployment. If you wish to have your plug-in work offline, you need to register it in synchronous mode.

Messages

In the documentation, Microsoft Dynamics CRM 4.0 refers to server-based trigger events as *messages*. The Microsoft Dynamics CRM 4.0 SDK also supports all of the events from Microsoft Dynamics CRM 3.0 such as *Create*, *Update*, *Delete*, and *Merge*. In addition, Microsoft Dynamics CRM 4.0 includes some new messages such as *Route*, *Retrieve*, and *RetrieveMultiple*.

Please reference the SDK for all available messages. You can also use the API to write code to see if Microsoft Dynamics CRM supports a particular message.

Entities

As with messages, Microsoft Dynamics CRM 4.0 greatly increases the number of entities that support plug-ins. Most system and all custom entities are available for plug-in execution. Please reference the SDK for all available entities.

Rank

Rank merely denotes the order in which a plug-in should fire. Rank is simply an integer, and Microsoft Dynamics CRM starts with the lowest one first and then cycles through all available plug-ins. You should definitely consider the order of the plug-ins, depending on the logic they are performing.

> **Note** The registration tool supplied with the SDK code samples does not include rank in the registration file. You can easily update the sample code to accommodate it though.

Images

Images provide you with the record attribute values. Images exist as pre (before the core platform operation) and post values. Not all messages allow images. Table 9-7 lists the available messages that allow images and the associated *MessagePropertyName* value.

TABLE 9-7 Plug-in Image Message List

Message	*MessagePropertyName* value
Assign	*Target*
Create	*Id*
Delete	*Target*
DeliverIncoming	*EmailId*
DeliverPromote	*EmailId*
Merge	*Target*
Merge	*SubordinateId*
Route	*Target*
Send	*EmailId*
SetState	*EntityMoniker*
SetStateDynamic	*EntityMoniker*
Update	*Target*

Assembly Location

You have two options for where you can store your plug-in assembly files: (1) the database, or (2) the file system. For production-level deployments, we recommend that you use the database. This deployment option will allow for offline access, easier distribution across Web farm deployments, and better isolation in multitenant configurations.

The file system deployment option exists to allow backward compatibility with previous Microsoft Dynamics CRM solutions and, more important, so that developers can have the ability to debug their solutions in Visual Studio 2008. You can even debug plug-ins from multiple organizations on the same server.

Just as with Microsoft Dynamics CRM 3.0, you copy your assembly files, including the program database (.pdb) file if debugging, to the Microsoft Dynamics CRM assembly folder on the Web server.

> **Tip** This folder typically is c:\Program Files\Microsoft CRM\Server\bin\assembly on upgraded Microsoft Dynamics CRM 3.0 deployments or c:\Program Files\Microsoft Dynamics CRM\Server\ bin\assembly on new Microsoft Dynamics CRM 4.0 installations.

We recommend that you use the file system deployment model while developing your plug-ins, and then switch to database deployment after testing.

Debugging Your Custom Assemblies

When you use Visual Studio 2008 to debug your code you can drastically improve your development efficiency. However, if you do not want to install Visual Studio 2008 on your Web server, we show you how you can set up remote debugging of plug-in assemblies.

First, you need to deploy your plug-in using the on-disk option. Then, ensure that an up-to-date project database (PDB) file is available for your plug-in assembly and that you have added breakpoints appropriately in the plug-in.

The next step is to start remote debugging on the server. Run msvsmon.exe on the server. You can instantiate this from any location that has Visual Studio installed (for example, your local development computer). Msvsmon.exe is installed with Visual Studio 2008 in the following directory: *Install path*\Microsoft Visual Studio 9.0\Common7\IDE\Remote Debugger\x86. Figure 9-11 shows the monitor after it starts.

> **Tip** You can also install the remote debugger directly on the Microsoft Dynamics CRM Web server without installing the full Visual Studio 2008 product. Look for the remote debugger tool on the Visual Studio 2008 disc and follow the installation steps.

FIGURE 9-11 Starting remote debugging on the Web server

Once the monitor is running on the server, you use Visual Studio 2008 to attach to the remote process.

Using Visual Studio 2008 for interactive debugging

1. In Visual Studio 2008, on the Debug menu, click Attach to Process.

2. In the Attach to Process dialog box, set the following options:

   a. Transport: Select Default.

   b. Qualifier: Enter the name of the CRM Web server (when you do, you will see the domain\name@server as shown in the following image).

   c. Attach To: Select Managed Code. This eliminates some annoying pop-up errors from Visual Studio 2008.

   d. Available Processes: Once this is attached, select the W3WP.exe process from the list of options.

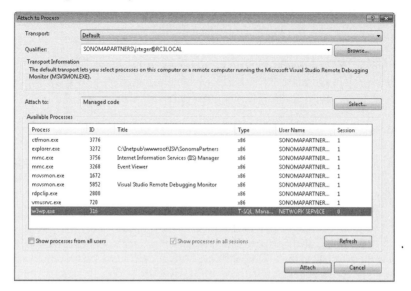

Note If W3WP.exe doesn't appear in the list, it hasn't started yet (probably because of iisreset), so you can just refresh any Microsoft Dynamics CRM page to get it started.

After you attach the debugger, the breakpoints should hit when the plug-in fires, which occurs when you access the Microsoft Dynamics CRM Web pages that trigger the event for the plug-in.

If you would like additional information about remote debugging, review the SDK and the following link: *http://msdn2.microsoft.com/en-us/library/bt727f1t.aspx*.

Additional Plug-in Tips and Information

We list a few other plug-in tips and information here. Please refer to the SDK documentation for more details about plug-in development.

- The SetState message refers only to native entities. SetStateDynamic can apply to both native and custom entities. Unfortunately, you might not know definitively which message Microsoft Dynamics CRM triggers. In general, the SetStateDynamic message is executed for any state-based events. To be sure you cover all possibilities, you can add both SetState and SetStateDynamic for all state-based events.

- You can share variable information between multiple plug-ins using the *SharedVariables* property bag.

- Be cautious when registering plug-ins for both offline and online access. You will want to guard against the logic executing twice. Remember that offline plug-ins have to be synchronous. Microsoft Dynamics CRM does not support offline, asynchronous plug-in execution.

- To display a custom error message, your plug-in should throw an *InvalidPluginExecution Exception* with the custom message as the *Message* property value.

Workflow Assemblies

As you learned in Chapter 8, "Workflow," with the Microsoft Dynamics CRM workflow module, you can create powerful business rules that help automate your sales, marketing, and customer service processes. In addition to the default workflow actions, you can also create custom assemblies and reference them directly in a workflow rule user interface. This feature opens a wide array of extensibility possibilities.

Workflow assemblies can accept values from a workflow rule and then return values to the workflow logic to be used in other actions, or they can execute actions on their own. You deploy workflow assemblies to Microsoft Dynamics CRM just as you do plug-ins. Then, you can reference the assemblies directly from the workflow record's step editor.

Custom Workflow Assembly Development

Unlike plug-in assembly development, Microsoft Dynamics CRM workflow uses the Windows Workflow Foundation (WF) framework. As such, you create a Workflow Activity project instead of a standard class library that you would create with plug-ins. We provide additional links to WF resources at the end of this section, but you won't need to be an expert in WF to develop Microsoft Dynamics CRM workflow assemblies. Similar to plug-in assemblies, make sure you include references to the Microsoft.Crm.Sdk and Microsoft.Crm.SdkTypeProxy assemblies and digitally sign your assembly.

First, you start with the creation and setup of the project file.

Creating a workflow assembly project

1. Create a new Workflow Activity Library in Visual Studio 2008 targeting .NET Framework 3.0, as shown in the following image.

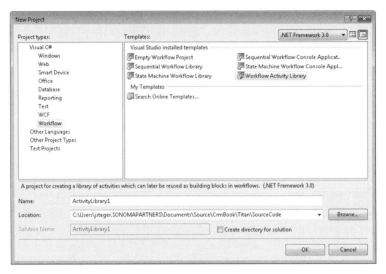

2. Add standard references to the Microsoft.Crm.Sdk and Microsoft.Crm.SdkTypeProxy assemblies.

3. Create a strong key, and sign your assembly.

4. Delete the default activity created.

5. Right-click the project, click Add, then select Class. Name the new class file **Activity1**.

6. Update the class file with the code in Listing 9-4.

> **Note** If you use Visual Studio 2005, you need to add the Windows Workflow Foundation framework first.

Now that your project is created and ready, we review a basic activity class. Listing 9-4 shows the basic structure of a workflow class, including optional input and output parameters.

Listing 9-4 Workflow Sample Class File

```
using System;
using System.Workflow.ComponentModel;
using System.Workflow.Activities;
using Microsoft.Crm.Workflow;

namespace ActivityLibrary1
{
  [CrmWorkflowActivity("Workflow Step", "Group Name")]
  public partial class Activity1 : SequenceActivity
  {

    protected override ActivityExecutionStatus Execute(ActivityExecutionContext
executionContext)
    {
      //Get context
```

```
      IContextService contextService =
(IContextService)executionContext.GetService(typeof(IContextService));
      IWorkflowContext ctx = contextService.Context;

      // Execute custom logic here

      // Access your input and output properties as shown
      this.InputExample = "foo";
      this.OutputExample = this.InputExample + " bar";

      return base.Execute(executionContext);
    }

    // Set input property
    public static DependencyProperty InputExampleProperty = DependencyProperty
.Register("InputExample", typeof(string), typeof(Activity1));
    [CrmInput("InputExample")]
    public string InputExample
    {
      get
      {
        return (string)base.GetValue(InputExampleProperty);
      }
      set
      {
        base.SetValue(InputExampleProperty, value);
      }
    }

    // Set output property
    public static DependencyProperty OutputExampleProperty = DependencyProperty.Register
("OutputExample", typeof(string), typeof(Activity1));
    [CrmOutput("OutputExample")]
    public string OutputExample
    {
      get
      {
        return (string)base.GetValue(OutputExampleProperty);
      }
      set
      {
        base.SetValue(OutputExampleProperty, value);
      }
    }
  }
}
```

Your class should inherit from *SequenceActivity*, and the *CrmWorkflowActivity* decorator of the class will determine how your assembly appears to a user in the Microsoft Dynamics CRM application interface, as shown in the following code.

```
[CrmWorkflowActivity("Workflow Step", "Group Name")]
public partial class Activity1 : SequenceActivity
```

You perform all custom business logic in the *Execute* method. Simply override this method as shown here:

```
protected override ActivityExecutionStatus Execute(ActivityExecutionContext
executionContext)
```

Create a reference to the *IContextService* interface and use its *GetService()* method. Then, grab the context as shown here:

```
IContextService contextService =
(IContextService)executionContext.GetService(typeof(IContextService));
IWorkflowContext ctx = contextService.Context;
```

You define input and output parameters as standard decorated properties, as shown in Listing 9-4. However, you also need to register these properties as a Workflow *DependencyProperty* property.

You access the new input and output properties in other classes by using code similar to the following:

```
this.InputExample = "foo";
this.OutputExample = this.InputExample + "bar";
```

Deploying a Workflow Assembly

You deploy workflow assemblies by using a registration technique similar to plug-in registration. However, you will configure the *<Workflow>* nodes in the registration configuration file. As with plug-ins, you can also deploy workflow assemblies using the on-disk option to allow for integrated debugging. Remember to restart the CRMAsyncService service when deploying updated files.

> **Tip** When using the integrated debugging in Visual Studio 2008, attach to the CRMAsyncService.exe process. This process should appear in the list when you select the Show processes from all users option.

See the SDK documentation for more details.

Using a Workflow Assembly with the Workflow User Interface

Now that you have an example workflow assembly developed and deployed to Microsoft Dynamics CRM, we show you how you can interact with it in the workflow user interface.

After you create a new workflow rule, you will see a new step option, as shown in Figure 9-12. As you can see, the class decorator defines the actual step as *Workflow Step* and it is grouped under *Group Name*.

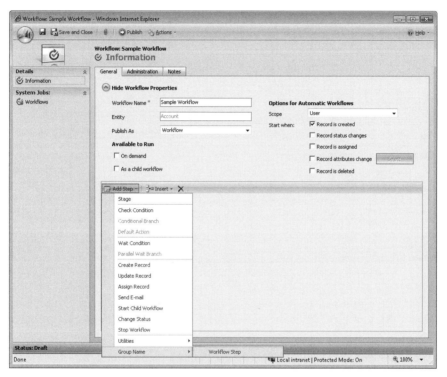

FIGURE 9-12 Custom assembly in the Workflow application interface

Figure 9-13 shows the step after the sample step was selected. As with any step, you still have the opportunity to enter a description and set the properties.

When you click Set Properties, Microsoft Dynamics CRM displays a custom step window in which you enter values for any of the defined *CrmInput* properties defined in your workflow assembly (see Figure 9-14).

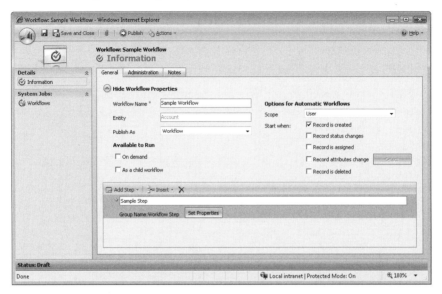

FIGURE 9-13 Workflow assembly step

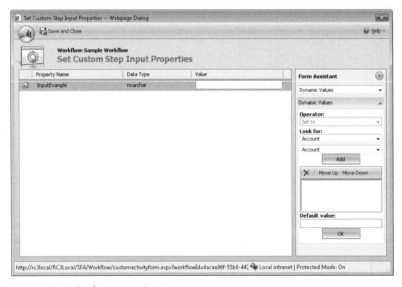

FIGURE 9-14 Configure your inputs

Now that your step is configured, it shows up as an option in the workflow Dynamic Values picklist, as shown in Figure 9-15, assuming there is an output property specified.

Tip Microsoft Dynamics CRM displays the workflow assembly description name in the Dynamic Values picklist. Be sure to create a description for each custom assembly step, and try to keep the description short.

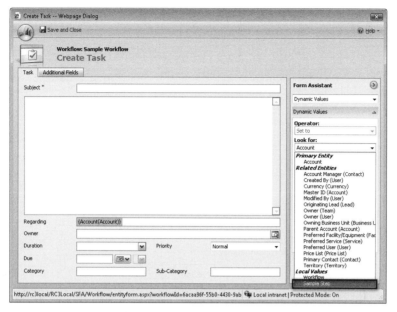

FIGURE 9-15 Accessing the output value in another workflow step

Workflow Assembly Example

In this example, we show you how to create a basic workflow assembly with which you can construct a URL of a record to include in workflow-generated e-mail messages.

Creating a custom URL builder workflow solution

1. Create a new Workflow Activity Library project targeting version .NET Framework 3.0. Call it **WorkingWithDynamicsCrm4.Workflow**, sign it, and add the references to the Microsoft Dynamics CRM SDK assembly files.

2. Create a new class, and name it **UrlBuilder**.

3. Replace the default code in the UrlBuilder class with the code in Listing 9-5.

4. Build the solution.

5. Register the solution with Microsoft Dynamics CRM using the registration configuration XML provided in Listing 9-6.

Listing 9-5 URL builder workflow activity

```
using System;
using System.Workflow.ComponentModel;
using System.Workflow.Activities;
using Microsoft.Crm.Workflow;

namespace WorkingWithDynamicsCrm4.Workflow
```

```
{
  [CrmWorkflowActivity("Url Builder", "Utilities")]
  public partial class UrlBuilder: SequenceActivity
  {
    // Override this method with custom logic
    protected override ActivityExecutionStatus Execute(ActivityExecutionContext
executionContext)
    {
      //Get context
      IContextService contextService =
(IContextService)executionContext.GetService(typeof(IContextService));
      IWorkflowContext ctx = contextService.Context;

      // Get the record id
      Guid id = ctx.PrimaryEntityId;

      // Configure the Url and pass back to the output parameter
      string fullUrl = this.RecordUrl = this.Url + id;
      this.RecordUrl = string.Format(@"<a href=""{0}"">{0}</a>",fullUrl);

      return base.Execute(executionContext);
    }

    // Allow the user to set the Url with this input parameter
    public static DependencyProperty UrlProperty = DependencyProperty.Register("Url",
typeof(string), typeof(UrlBuilder));
    [CrmInput("Url")]
    public string Url
    {
      get
      {
        return (string)base.GetValue(UrlProperty);
      }
      set
      {
        base.SetValue(UrlProperty, value);
      }
    }

    // Returns the final record Url to the workflow rule for use
    public static DependencyProperty RecordUrlProperty = DependencyProperty.
Register("RecordUrl", typeof(string), typeof(UrlBuilder));
    [CrmOutput("RecordUrl")]
    public string RecordUrl
    {
      get
      {
        return (string)base.GetValue(RecordUrlProperty);
      }
      set
      {
        base.SetValue(RecordUrlProperty, value);
      }
    }
  }
}
```

Listing 9-6 URL builder workflow activity registration XML

```
<Solution SourceType="1" Assembly="G:\Source\CrmBook\Titan\SourceCode\
WorkingWithDynamicsCrm4.Workflow\bin\Debug\WorkingWithDynamicsCrm4.Workflow.dll">
    <WorkflowTypes>
      <WorkflowType TypeName="WorkingWithDynamicsCrm4.Workflow.UrlBuilder"
FriendlyName="Lead Url Builder"/>
    </WorkflowTypes>
  </Solution>
```

Now that the custom solution is complete and registered with Microsoft Dynamics CRM, the next step is to use it in a workflow rule.

Using the URL builder in workflow

1. Create a new workflow rule for the Lead entity called **New Lead Notification**.

2. Add a step, selecting the new Url Builder assembly step located in the Utilities group.

3. Enter **Url Builder** as the step's description.

4. Click Set Properties, and enter the correct URL to the Lead's edit page as the Value of the *Url* property. For example:

   http://<crmserver>/<organization name>/sfa/leads/edit.aspx?id=

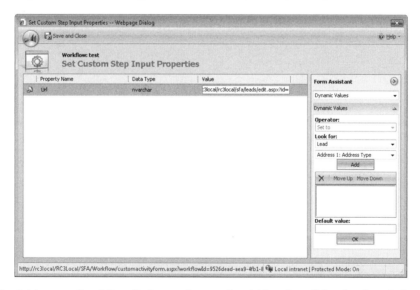

5. Add a new Send E-mail step and enter *Send Alert E-mail* for the description.

6. Leave the Create New Message option selected, and click Set Properties.

7. In the Send E-mail dialog box, configure the e-mail message, and in the body, add the new Url Builder dynamic value.

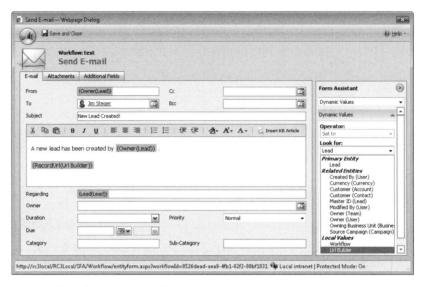

8. Save and publish your workflow rule.

Now create a new Lead and you will see that an e-mail message containing a hyperlink to the record is sent, as shown in Figure 9-16.

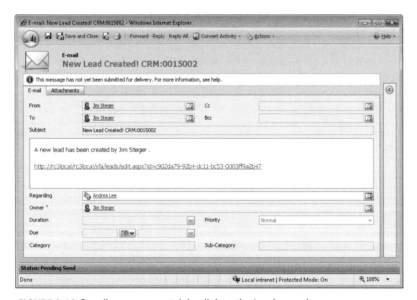

FIGURE 9-16 E-mail message containing link to the Lead record

Plug-in vs. Workflow

You might find yourself wondering when you should use a plug-in versus when you should use a workflow rule. As you would expect, the answer depends on your situation. For instance, if you need to take an action before the data reaches the platform, you have to use a plug-in (pre-event plug-in, in this case). If you would like the user to instantiate the action manually, use a manual workflow rule.

Remember that with the new unified model, you can use either workflow or a plug-in on just about any action or event available, although the plug-in offers some extra messages. Regardless of the model you choose, you should strive to keep your synchronous plug-in routines as simple and fast as possible. If processes become long, you can transfer them to an asynchronous process or a workflow rule for background processing.

We recommend the following guidelines to help you decide when to use a plug-in and when to use a workflow assembly:

- Use plug-ins

    - To alter data prior to submission to the platform

    - When you need to validate data prior to submission to the platform and possibly cancel the submission

    - When you need a synchronous transaction and an immediate response

    - To take action before or after the merging of two records

- Use workflow

    - For simple common tasks. The Workflow Manager has a list of actions already built and available for use, requiring no custom application development. Some of the actions available include creating new records (such as Activities, Notes, or Accounts), sending e-mail messages, and updating values on related entities.

    - To allow more configuration options for the end user creating the workflow logic. Because the user builds the workflow rule with the rule editor, he or she can also alter it without necessarily requiring programmatic interaction.

    - When you need a user to manually execute the necessary logic.

Development Environment Considerations

Now that we've reviewed the key server-side integration points in the SDK, we hope that you're excited to actually create your own code that will work with Microsoft Dynamics CRM. Even if you're an expert developer, setting up and configuring a development environment for Microsoft Dynamics CRM requires you to know a trick or two unique to the software.

When you're creating custom code with the SDK, you obviously don't want your development coding to interfere with your Microsoft Dynamics CRM users when they're using the system. Therefore, you should plan on creating at least two Microsoft Dynamics

CRM installations to minimize the impact of any production downtime on your users. We refer to the system that your clients use as the *production* environment, and you'll write your code in the *development* environment. If possible, we recommend creating a third Microsoft Dynamics CRM environment, commonly known as *staging* or *testing*, for testing your changes before you push them live to production.

Your ideal development environment depends on multiple factors. Some of them include the following:

- Microsoft Dynamics CRM product you own (Workgroup Edition, Professional Edition, Enterprise Edition)

- Configuration options (on-premise, Internet-facing deployment, Microsoft Dynamics CRM Live, offline Outlook client, and so forth)

- The number of projects you development and support

- The number of developers and quality assurance personnel working with the product

As you would expect, you could set up your development and testing environments in numerous ways. Although we cannot explore every possible permutation in this book, we list some considerations as you plan and maintain a development environment.

- Please thoroughly review the Implementation Guide for installation and configuration details about Microsoft Dynamics CRM deployment and environment options.

- Understand the business requirements for your Microsoft Dynamics CRM project and how they will affect development and testing. You should have an environment for each configuration you plan to support.

- Create both a development and a staging environment.

- Use a source control system (for example, Visual Source Safe, Subversion) for your custom files and consider an automated build tool (such as CruiseControl .NET) as well.

- Back up your databases and any custom source files. You can use the Microsoft Dynamics CRM API to easily export your customizations and include that in your backup procedures.

- We recommend that you keep the development domain separate from the production domain. However, you can reuse the development domain for the staging environment.

- Multitenant installation requires Microsoft Dynamics CRM 4.0 Enterprise Edition.

- You can add and delete organizations only through the Deployment Manager installed on the Microsoft Dynamics CRM Web server.

- Microsoft Dynamics CRM creates a SQL Server database for each organization but only one configuration database (mscrm_config) that manages the different organizations and their settings installed on that SQL Server instance.

- Microsoft Dynamics CRM 4.0 allows only one installation per SQL Server instance. You need to install another brand-new Microsoft Dynamics CRM environment to another SQL Server instance or a completely separate SQL Server.

- You can share SQL Server, Reporting Services, and Exchange Server hardware between your staging and development environments, provided you use multitenancy.

- You can use virtual servers to create complete instances of Microsoft Dynamics CRM or any of the components. Try to avoid putting a large SQL Server on a virtual server because you might experience mediocre performance.

- Remember that each organization is an isolated environment of customizations and data. You cannot natively share data/records between organizations, although you can write tools (or find third-party tools) to synchronize the data.

- Create organizational units (OUs) in your development Active Directory domain for each separate installation so that it is easier to keep track of your installation groups in Active Directory.

- As you develop your solutions, always consider IFD, multiple organization, and users working offline.

- Use the new import organization feature of the Deployment tool to synchronize your data between Microsoft Dynamics CRM deployments in different domains. You will not be able to restore the databases because the system GUIDs will not match between domains.

 Note If you set up your production, staging, and development environments in the same domain, you can expedite migrations by simply restoring the SQL Server databases from one environment to another. Despite this potential benefit, we generally recommend against the single-domain setup. By using two different domains, you minimize the chances of accidentally damaging the production environment during testing and development. Further, you can update data between domains much more easily now with the new Import Organization tools for Microsoft Dynamics CRM. However, if you're a risk-taker, maybe the single-domain installation fits you better!

Coding and Testing Tips

This section contains development and testing tips that we use when working on Microsoft Dynamics CRM projects. We hope you find them as useful as we do. We review the following topics:

- Microsoft .NET Framework versions

- Application mode and Loader.aspx

- Enabling the default Internet Explorer shortcut menu
- Viewing query string parameters
- Referencing the Microsoft Dynamics CRM assemblies or files
- Web files deployment and configuration considerations
- Authentication and coding with filtered views
- WSDL reference
- IFD development considerations
- Offline plug-in assembly configuration
- Finding available plug-in messages by entity
- Using ILMerge with plug-in or workflow assembly references
- Testing different users and roles
- Enabling platform-level tracing
- Enabling development errors

Microsoft .NET Framework Versions

Microsoft built Microsoft Dynamics CRM 4.0 against .NET Framework 3.0. Microsoft recommends you build your solutions with Visual Studio 2008 targeted at .NET Framework 3.0. Note that the ASP.NET version configured in IIS will probably be 2.0.50727, but this is the run-time version of .NET. The run-time versions of the .NET Framework version 3.0 (and 3.5) are identical to those of version 2.0, so any code developed in .NET Framework 3.0 will run properly on the 2.0.50727 run-time engine.

Please review the latest SDK for the most up-to-date information on support for .NET Framework versions.

Application Mode and Loader.aspx

Previous versions of Microsoft Dynamics CRM opened the application in a special Internet Explorer window that did not contain the menu bar, address bar, toolbar, and so on. Microsoft Dynamics CRM refers to this as *application mode*, and it ran in this mode by default. Often, however, developers need the additional Internet Explorer features that application mode hides. You can open Microsoft Dynamics CRM in a standard Internet Explorer window by browsing to *http://<crmserver>/loader.aspx*.

> **Note** A new installation of Microsoft Dynamics CRM 4.0 has application mode disabled. However, an upgraded installation assumes the setting from the Microsoft Dynamics CRM 3.0 environment, which in most cases has application mode enabled.

Using the Loader.aspx page disables application mode for that single Web session. You can also enable or disable application mode for *all* users and *all* sessions by updating the settings for your organization.

Disabling application mode

1. In the Microsoft Dynamics CRM application, navigate to Settings, click Administration, and then click System Settings.

2. Click the Customizations tab, and clear the Open Microsoft Dynamics CRM in Application Mode option.

Enabling the Default Internet Explorer Shortcut Menu

In addition to running in application mode, Microsoft Dynamics CRM modifies standard Internet Explorer behavior by displaying its own shortcut menu when you right-click in the application. Right-clicking a grid gives you options unique to Microsoft Dynamics CRM, such as Open, Print, and Refresh List. However, right-clicking a form won't display a shortcut menu like you would see on a normal Web page. When you're troubleshooting and debugging, you might find that you want to access the standard Internet Explorer shortcut menu so that you can use features such as View Source, Properties, or Open in New Window. You can activate the Internet Explorer shortcut menu by editing the Global.js file.

Activating the Internet Explorer standard shortcut menu

1. On the Microsoft Dynamics CRM Web server, navigate to *<Web installation path>*_common\scripts (typically C:\Inetpub\wwwroot_static_common\scripts), where *Web installation path* is the location of the Microsoft Dynamics CRM Web files.

2. Open the Global.js file in Notepad (or any text editor). Note: Do not double-click this file because it will attempt to execute the JavaScript file.

3. Use the Find feature of the text editor to locate the document.oncontextmenu() function.

4. Add **event.returnValue = true;** and comment out the code in this function by adding **/*** and ***/** as shown in the following code. You can undo this change later if required.

```
function document.oncontextmenu()
{
event.returnValue = true;
/*
var s = event.srcElement.tagName;
// Only allow shortcut menus if:
// the element is not disabled AND
// the element is either a TextArea OR a TextBox OR a user selection in some
TextBox/TextArea
event.returnValue =
(!event.srcElement.disabled &&
(document.selection.createRange().text.length > 0 ||
s == "TEXTAREA" ||
s == "INPUT" && event.srcElement.type == "text"));
*/
}
```

5. Save the file.

6. Open a page in Microsoft Dynamics CRM and right-click it. You will see the familiar
   Internet Explorer shortcut menu.

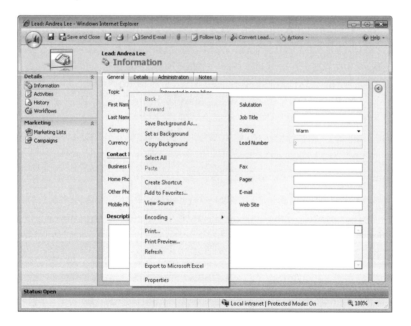

Caution Use this technique on development servers only. This change affects all organizations
for that Web server. Do not modify the Global.js file in a production or staging environment; this
unsupported change might cause unpredictable behavior. Microsoft Dynamics CRM prevents use
of the shortcut menu for the user's benefit and to maintain a predictable navigation structure in
the application interface.

Viewing Query String Parameters

When testing or debugging code, you will frequently need the GUID of an entity record or want to see the query string parameters that Microsoft Dynamics CRM passed to the window. You can accomplish this from the browser a few ways:

- You can access the URL of any page and view its GUID by pressing the F11 key twice. The first press makes the window full screen. The second press reduces the window back to usual size but includes the address bar.

- Another way to access the URL and GUID of a page is by pressing Ctrl+N. Internet Explorer opens a new window, and the address bar displays the window's query string parameters. You can also press the F11 key twice when viewing a record to toggle the display so that the URL address bar appears.

- If you activated the Internet Explorer shortcut menu, you can also view the URL and GUID information by right-clicking the page and selecting Properties. You can then copy the URL from the Properties dialog box.

- Internet Explorer 7.0 displays the address bar by default if your Microsoft Dynamics CRM Web site is not listed as a trusted site or an Intranet site with Internet Explorer.

Referencing the Microsoft Dynamics CRM Assemblies or Files

When developing plug-in custom workflow assemblies, you should plan on referencing the Microsoft.Crm.Sdk.dll and Microsoft.Crm.SdkTypeProxy.dll assemblies and avoid adding specific Web service API references. Microsoft Dynamics CRM will provide you the context as part of the plug-in, which is already instantiated and authenticated. As such, you then need to use *DynamicEntities* for any service calls that interact with the Microsoft Dynamics CRM API.

> **Note** Any compile-time code needed should be contained in the SDK assemblies so that you can properly build your solution.

When developing Web or other external applications, you can use either WSDL references or the Microsoft Dynamics CRM SDK assemblies.

You should never explicitly reference any Microsoft Dynamics CRM assemblies other than Microsoft.Crm.Sdk.dll, Microsoft.Crm.SdkTypeProxy.dll, and Microsoft.Crm.Outlook.Sdk.dll. You also should not import any of the JavaScript, style sheets, or behavior files into your project. Microsoft does not support this type of code reuse, and you will probably experience significant code problems when Microsoft Dynamics CRM releases hotfixes, updates, and patches.

> **Caution** Because you're not supposed to even *reference* any of the Microsoft Dynamics CRM assemblies other than the ones just mentioned, it should be pretty obvious that you shouldn't attempt to *modify* any of the Microsoft Dynamics CRM assembly files either.

If you want to mimic any look or functionality of Microsoft Dynamics CRM, you must re-create it yourself. The SDK provides a UI style guide and also has a sample style sheet, but if you want to review and understand the native script files, you can find most of them in *<Web installation path>*_static_common. If you want to review styles or code, copy these files to your own directory.

Web File Deployment and Configuration Considerations

If you create custom pages that work with Microsoft Dynamics CRM 4.0 (see Chapter 10 for additional information), Microsoft now recommends that you deploy your Web files to your own custom folder inside a new *ISV* directory in the Microsoft Dynamics CRM Web folder structure (for example: c:\Inetpub\wwwroot\ISV\SonomaPartners\). Following this recommendation allows for the proper path translation in multitenant deployments and also gives you the opportunity to ease the security and authentication complexity between on-premise and IFD and offline implementations.

Once the files are placed in this directory, any custom assemblies they reference should be installed in Microsoft Dynamics CRM's /bin folder on the Web server.

Please review Chapter 10 for more in-depth information regarding ASP.NET application development and deployment.

Authentication and Coding with Filtered Views

SQL Server filtered views provide an excellent method for you to retrieve Microsoft Dynamics CRM data quickly and easily by using standard SQL Server connections. However, the filtered views respect the Microsoft Dynamics CRM security settings and as such require a valid system user.

If you were to go under the hood of a filtered view in SQL Server and look at its script, you would see that it uses a custom function to determine the Microsoft Dynamics CRM system user with which to enforce the proper security settings.

```
create function [dbo].[fn_FindUserGuid] ()
returns uniqueidentifier
as
begin
    declare @userGuid uniqueidentifier
```

```
    --- test whether the query is running by privileged user with user role of
CRMReaderRole
    --- if it is dbo, we trust it as well.
    --- There is an issue in SQL. If the user is a dbo, if it not member of any role
    if (is_member('CRMReaderRole') | is_member('db_owner')) = 1
    begin
            select @userGuid = cast(context_info() as uniqueidentifier)
    end

    if @userGuid is null
    begin
            select @userGuid = s.SystemUserId
                    from SystemUserBase s
                    where s.DomainName = SUSER_SNAME()
    end
    return @userGuid
end
```

The functions, *context_info()* and *SUSER_SNAME()* are special functions in SQL that are used to provide mechanisms for Microsoft Dynamics CRM to find the *systemuserid* identifier to apply to the filtered views. If your code doesn't authenticate to SQL Server by using Windows authentication or it passes a valid user context, your queries will not return any data because all of the filtered views perform an inner join using *systemuserid* returned from this function.

In most cases, you can simply connect to the database by using Windows authentication instead of SQL Server authentication. Your connection string would include the following parameter: *Integrated Security=SSPI*. The full string looks something like this.

```
server=databaseserver;database=yourcustomdatabase;Integrated Security=SSPI
```

More Info Remember that Microsoft doesn't support changes to the Microsoft Dynamics CRM databases, including adding your own routines or stored procedures. The preferred recommendation is to create your own database to store your custom routines.

This SSPI authentication approach presents numerous challenges in environments with multiple servers because it relies on Kerberos and delegation. What we have seen in practice is that these networking issues can be very problematic to maintain and troubleshoot.

As we explained earlier, another consequence of the integrated security features in filtered views is that it becomes more difficult to use filtered views in plug-ins and workflow assemblies.

However, as you have probably deduced from the *fn_FindUserGuid()* function, SQL Server has a concept of the *context_info()* function. With this function, you can programmatically switch the user context in your query.

Given that the SDK provides you a mechanism for finding the current *systemuserid*, you can use *content_info()* to impersonate a user. First, create SQL Server authentication with an account that has access to the custom and Microsoft Dynamics CRM databases. Then, use this account when connecting to the database with a connection string such as the following:

```
server=databaseserver;database=yourcustomdatabase;uid=sqluser;pwd=sqlpwd
```

With SQL Server 2005, you can add synonyms to the Microsoft Dynamics CRM filtered views to query from your custom database. Synonyms provide a pointer (or alias) to its target, in this case the filtered views, so that you don't have to refresh the synonym when Microsoft Dynamics CRM updates the filtered views. Then, you can use the command in a routine such as the following:

```
create procedure MyStoredProcedure
(
  @userid uniqueidentifier
)
as

declare @original uniqueidentifier
set @original = context_info() -- store original value

set context_info @userid

/* Do stuff with this new context value */
-- Example: This will pull only the accounts that the @userid has read access
-- select name from filteredaccount

-- Set context back to original value
if @original is null
      set context_info 0x
else
      set context_info @original
end
```

Because *context_info()* persists for the entire session, you simply capture what it was before you changed it, and then set it back after the query logic is complete.

 Tip You won't be able to set the *context_info()* directly to null. If you wish to null out the context, use the following command: *set context_info 0x*.

WSDL Reference

Earlier we showed you how to add the CrmService reference to Visual Studio 2008 one project at a time. However, instead of adding the Web references individually to each project, you can also create a common assembly that contains the CrmService, MetadataService, and DiscoveryService Web references. Then, you can reference the common assembly in your other projects, and you can update these service APIs in a single place should you ever need to update this information.

> **Tip** Are your custom entities or new attributes not appearing in IntelliSense in Visual Studio? Make sure that you have published your changes *and* updated your Web reference in Visual Studio 2008. Updating the reference will depend on the technique you used to reference the WSDL. If you used the URL, you can update the reference right from Visual Studio 2008. If you referenced the file, you will need to first export a new WSDL and replace the existing one before you will see the change.

As you saw in the section titled "Discovery Web Service" earlier in this chapter, you can use the DiscoveryService Web service to query for the CrmService and MetadataService API endpoints and set them as variables for your service URLs. You should consider using the DiscoveryService for the following situations:

- You are an independent software vendor (ISV) writing a generic module

- You use a multitenant environment

- You installed the API endpoints on a separate server (referred to as an application server)

If you use a single-tenant installation, you might find it easier and faster to build the service URLs directly from the registry. The SDK contains examples of this. The following code example shows one such class.

```
public class CrmEnvironment
{
  bool isoffline;
  string orgname;
  string crmserviceurl;
  string metadataserviceurl;

  public CrmEnvironment(System.Web.HttpRequest Request)
  {
    //Determine Online/Offline State using Host Name
    if (Request.Url.Host.ToString() == "127.0.0.1")
    {
      isoffline = true;
    }
    else
    {
      isoffline = false;
    }
    if (isoffline == true)
    {
```

```
        //Retrieve the Port and OrgName from the Registry
        RegistryKey regkey =
Registry.CurrentUser.OpenSubKey("Software\\Microsoft\\MSCRMClient");
        orgname = regkey.GetValue("ClientAuthOrganizationName").ToString();
        string portnumber = regkey.GetValue("CassiniPort").ToString();

        //Construct the URLs
        StringBuilder url = new StringBuilder();
        url.Append("http://localhost:");
        url.Append(portnumber);
        url.Append("/mscrmservices/2007/");
        crmserviceurl = url.ToString() + "crmservice.asmx";
        metadataserviceurl = url.ToString() + "metadataservice.asmx";
    }
    else
    {
        //Retrieve the URLs from the Registry
        RegistryKey regkey =
Registry.LocalMachine.OpenSubKey("SOFTWARE\\Microsoft\\MSCRM");
        string ServerUrl = regkey.GetValue("ServerUrl").ToString();
        crmserviceurl = ServerUrl + "/2007/crmservice.asmx";
        metadataserviceurl = ServerUrl + "/2007/metadataservice.asmx";

        //Retrieve the Query String from the current URL
        if (Request.QueryString["orgname"] == null)
        {
          orgname = string.Empty;
        }
        else
        {
          //Query String
          string orgquerystring = Request.QueryString["orgname"].ToString();
          if (string.IsNullOrEmpty(orgquerystring))
          {
            orgname = string.Empty;
          }
          else
          {
            orgname = orgquerystring;
          }
        }
        if (string.IsNullOrEmpty(orgname))
        {
          //Windows Auth URL
          if (Request.Url.Segments[2].TrimEnd('/').ToLower() == "isv")
          {
            orgname = Request.Url.Segments[1].TrimEnd('/').ToLower();
          }
          //IFD URL
          if (string.IsNullOrEmpty(orgname))
          {
            string url = Request.Url.ToString().ToLower();
            int start = url.IndexOf("://") + 3;
            orgname = url.Substring(start, url.IndexOf(".") - start);
```

```
            }
          }
        }
      }

    public bool IsOffline
    {
      get { return isoffline; }
    }

    public string OrgName
    {
      get { return orgname; }
    }

    public string CrmServiceUrl
    {
      get { return crmserviceurl; }
    }

    public string MetadataServiceUrl
    {
      get { return metadataserviceurl; }
    }
  }
}
```

IFD Development Considerations

If you develop for IFD, you should use the *CrmImpersonator* class when instantiating your
service objects. See the SDK documentation for more information about this technique.

```
using (new CrmImpersonator())
{
    CrmAuthenticationToken token;
    if (offline == true)
    {
        token = new CrmAuthenticationToken();
        token.OrganizationName = orgname;
        token.AuthenticationType = 0;
    }
    else
    {
        token = CrmAuthenticationToken.ExtractCrmAuthenticationToken(Context,
orgname);
    }

    //Create the Service
    CrmService service = new CrmService();
    service.Credentials = System.Net.CredentialCache.DefaultCredentials;
```

```
    service.CrmAuthenticationTokenValue = token;
    service.Url = <CrmServiceUrl>; //Pass in a valid CrmService URL

    account account = new account();
    account.name = "Offline Impersonator: " + DateTime.Now.TimeOfDay.ToString();

    if (offline == false)
        account.ownerid = new Owner("systemuser", token.CallerId);

    service.Create(account);
}
```

Offline Plug-in Assembly Configuration

If you develop a plug-in to execute offline, in addition to properly setting the deployment value when you register the plug-in, you will also need to configure each client's registry. On each client, you need to add your assembly's public key as a new empty registry key located at HKEY_CURRENT_USER\Software\Microsoft\MSCRMClient\AllowList. The name of the key should be your assembly's public key, as shown in Figure 9-17.

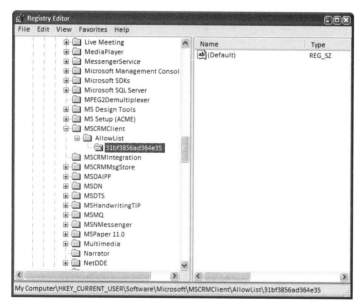

FIGURE 9-17 The AllowList client key

One way to determine the public key is to add the assembly to the GAC and view it there, as shown in Figure 9-18. The public key token is unique to the assembly and does not change as you deploy to other environments.

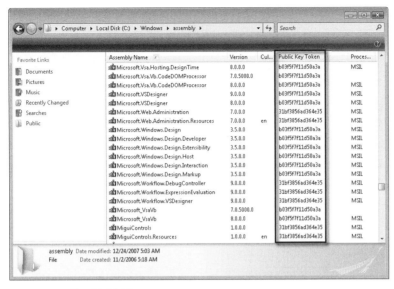

FIGURE 9-18 The GAC folder

Finding Available Plug-in Messages by Entity

Microsoft Dynamics CRM provides numerous messages and entities available for plug-in development and registration. The SDK documents many of these, but there are more than 650 possible combinations. If you are unsure whether you can trigger custom code against a particular message for an entity, the following script can be a handy reference. Run the following query against the *<organization>*_mscrm database to return all possible plug-in message and entity combinations.

```
select m.name as MessageName,  e.name as EntityName, f.PrimaryObjectTypeCode
FROM  SdkMessage  m
inner join SdkMessageFilter f on m.SdkMessageId = f.SdkMessageId
inner join Entity e on e.ObjectTypeCode = f.PrimaryObjectTypeCode
where f.IsCustomProcessingStepAllowed = 1
order by m.name asc,  f.PrimaryObjectTypeCode asc
```

Using ILMerge with Plug-in or Workflow Assembly References

Microsoft prefers that you deploy your production plug-in and workflow assemblies to the database. Database deployment allows for the following advantages:

- Offline execution
- Ease of deployment

- Ease of backup

- Ease of use in Web farm scenarios

However, if your plug-in or workflow assembly code references an external assembly (for instance, a custom business logic assembly or a third-party tool), you will be forced to deploy the referenced assemblies to each Microsoft Dynamics CRM Web server's and client computer's global assembly cache (GAC). This hurdle negates the last three advantages that you get with database deployment of plug-ins and workflow assemblies.

Instead of deploying these files to GAC, you could merge them with your plug-in/workflow assembly into a single assembly that can then be deployed to the database.

ILMerge is a downloadable tool that can be used with a post-build event to merge all required assemblies into a single file suitable for database deployment. For more information about ILMerge, see the following links:

http://www.microsoft.com/downloads/details.aspx?FamilyID=22914587-B4AD-4EAE-87CF-B14AE6A939B0&displaylang=en
http://research.microsoft.com/~mbarnett/ILMerge.aspx

Authenticating as Different Users and Roles

When testing, you will often need to review users with different roles to validate security and custom functionality. Because Microsoft Dynamics CRM uses your domain information for its authentication credentials, by default you access the application under the Windows account that you use to access your computer. If you want to check the functionality of a different role, you have to change the role of your account or log on using a different account.

Chapter 3, "Managing Security and Information Access," showed you in detail how to force the browser to prompt for credentials. By using this technique, you can authenticate as different users without having to log off of your computer. Remember that this affects all intranet Web applications that you currently access.

Another approach available to you is to use the *runas* command of the Windows operating system. With this handy command, you can start an application, such as Internet Explorer, under the context of another user. You can then create batch files to start browsers under various test accounts. To perform this, execute the following statement in a command prompt, filling in your user name and Microsoft CRM Web server information:

```
runas /user:<domain\user> "C:\Program Files\Internet Explorer\iexplore
http://<crmserver:[port]>/<orgname>/loader.aspx"
```

Tip Add the preceding command to a .bat file for easy access.

Enabling Platform-Level Tracing

You might need to track down issues at the platform level to debug plug-ins, workflow, or even the Outlook client. Enabling this type of tracing requires a registry change. The locations of the registry settings are listed in Table 9-8.

TABLE 9-8 **Registry Settings Locations**

Web server	HKEY_LOCAL_MACHINE\Software\Microsoft\MSCRM
Outlook client	HKEY_CURRENT_USER\Software\Microsoft\MSCRMClient

To enable tracing, you must create the registry values listed in Table 9-8 in the appropriate key, as specified in Table 9-9.

TABLE 9-9 **Registry Values**

Name	Type	Data
TraceEnabled	Dword	1
TraceRefresh	Dword	1

Tracing will be enabled immediately when the *TraceEnabled* value is set to 1. The *TraceRefresh* value is in minutes. The trace logs will be stored on the Microsoft Dynamics CRM Web server at *<installation drive>*:\Program Files\Microsoft Dynamics CRM\Trace. If you have upgraded from Microsoft Dynamics CRM 3.0, the path is *<installation drive>*:\Program Files\Microsoft CRM\Trace.

Remember that tracing negatively affects performance, so be sure to turn it off when it is no longer required. To do this, change *TraceEnabled* to 0 and perform an *iisreset* and restart the CRMAsyncService for it to take effect. Please review the Implementation Guide for further details about platform tracing.

> **Caution** We would be remiss if we didn't provide the obligatory warning from Microsoft regarding editing the registry:
>
> "Using Registry Editor incorrectly can cause serious, system-wide problems that may require you to re-install Windows to correct them. Microsoft cannot guarantee that any problems resulting from the use of Registry Editor can be solved. Use this tool at your own risk."

Enabling Viewing of Development Errors

By default, Microsoft Dynamics CRM displays a nice, user-friendly error message if it encounters a problem while trying to execute a request. However, as you develop and troubleshoot your code, you'll want to see more descriptive information about errors. You can enable viewing of detailed development errors (Figure 9-19) with a setting in the Microsoft Dynamics CRM web.config file.

Enabling viewing of development errors in the web.config file

1. On the Microsoft Dynamics CRM Web server, navigate to *<web installation path>*\ (typically C:\Inetpub\wwwroot\).

2. Open the web.config file in Notepad (or any text editor).

3. Look for the DevErrors key, and change its value to On.

4. Save the web.config file.

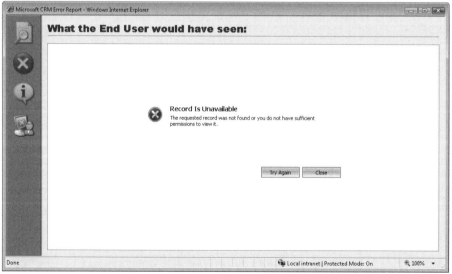

FIGURE 9-19 Development errors enabled

Sample Code

The Microsoft Dynamics CRM SDK includes great code samples and examples that you can reference when you develop your own solution. In this book, we include additional code examples that address some common requests. In this section, we demonstrate how to do the following tasks:

- Create an auto number field
- Validate a field when converting an Opportunity
- Synchronize a contact's address with its parent account
- Copy a system view

Creating an Auto Number Field

Microsoft Dynamics CRM uses a GUID to uniquely identify each record in the database, and it also gives you the ability to add custom attributes. However, Microsoft Dynamics CRM does not provide a way to create an automatically incrementing field (typically referred to as an *Identity* field in SQL Server). Although some objects (such as Cases, Invoices, and Quotes) include a numbering scheme that neatly identifies a unique record to the user, entities such as Lead, Account, and Contact do not include a numbering method. If your users want to reference records by a simple integer number instead of the unfriendly looking GUID, you can create custom code that manages a numbering scheme for the entities that you want to uniquely identify with a number.

This example code simulates the SQL Server identity concept to give end users a Lead entity numbering scheme using the pre-event plug-in. You will first create a new integer attribute on the Lead form. Then, you will develop a query to get the maximum Lead number and use that method in a pre-event plug-in routine to set the value of the Lead number before saving a new Lead record to the database.

Configure the Lead form

1. Add a new integer attribute to the Lead form called **new_leadnumber**.

2. Add this field to the form, and make sure that it is disabled to the user because you will be populating the value automatically.

Building a plug-in assembly project

1. Create a new C# Class Library project in Visual Studio 2008 targeted at the .NET Framework 3.0 and call it **WorkingWithCrm4.Plugin**.

2. Be sure to check for the System.Web.Services reference. If it doesn't exist, add a reference to the System.Web.Services namespace.

3. Add references to the Microsoft.Crm.Sdk and Microsoft.Crm.SdkTypeProxy assemblies.

4. Add a new Class file called **LeadAutoNumber**.

6. Enter the code shown in Listing 9-7.

Listing 9-7 details the plug-in code you will use for this example, but we review a few key points with this sample before reviewing the code.

- You need to ensure that you retrieve the highest existing Lead number. Therefore, we do not want to impersonate as the user creating the lead because that user might not have rights to retrieve all leads.

- While in offline mode, you will not be able to guarantee uniqueness because the user might not have all the latest data. Therefore, you will not allow the Lead number to be created while offline.

- Use the query expression paging option to limit the number of records returned for performance reasons.

- This technique will not *guarantee* uniqueness. It will work in most cases you encounter, but if you need a more robust scheme, you will have to consider alternate approaches.

Listing 9-7 Creating a Lead auto number field

```
using System;
using System.Collections.Generic;
using System.Text;
using Microsoft.Crm.Sdk;
using Microsoft.Crm.SdkTypeProxy;
using Microsoft.Crm.Sdk.Query;

namespace WorkingWithDynamicsCrm4.Plugin
{
  public class LeadAutoNumber : IPlugin
  {
    /// <summary>
    /// This sample automatically creates a unique integer based number for the lead entity.
    /// </summary>

    public void Execute(IPluginExecutionContext context)
    {
      // Verify we have an entity in the target
      if (context.InputParameters.Properties.Contains("Target") &&
context.InputParameters.Properties["Target"] is DynamicEntity)
      {
        // Obtain the target business entity from the input parmameters.
        DynamicEntity entity =
(DynamicEntity)context.InputParameters.Properties["Target"];

        // Verify that the entity represents an lead.
        if (entity.Name == EntityName.lead.ToString())
```

```
      {
        ICrmService service = context.CreateCrmService(false);

        // If lead number was not set, generate a new one
        // Use "contains" because the indexer will throw an error if the column is not
found
        if (entity.Properties.Contains("new_leadnumber") == false)
        {
          CrmNumber crmLeadNumber = new CrmNumber();
          crmLeadNumber.Value = NextLeadNumber(service);
          CrmNumberProperty leadNumber = new CrmNumberProperty("new_leadnumber",
crmLeadNumber);
          entity.Properties.Add(leadNumber);
        }
        else
        {
          // Throw an error, because lead number must be system generated
          throw new InvalidPluginExecutionException("The lead number can only be set by
the system.");
        }
      }
    }
  }

  private int NextLeadNumber(ICrmService service)
  {
    // Create a set of columns to return
    ColumnSet cols = new ColumnSet();
    cols.AddColumns(new string[] { "leadid", "new_leadnumber" });

    // To improve performance, we will only pass back the top record
    // This will return only 1 page with 1 record per page
    PagingInfo pages = new PagingInfo();
    pages.PageNumber = 1;
    pages.Count = 1;

    // Create a query expression and set the query parameters
    QueryExpression query = new QueryExpression();
    query.EntityName = EntityName.lead.ToString();
    query.ColumnSet = cols;
    query.AddOrder("new_leadnumber", OrderType.Descending);
    query.PageInfo = pages;

    // Retrieve the values from CRM as a dynamic entity
    RetrieveMultipleRequest request = new RetrieveMultipleRequest();
    request.ReturnDynamicEntities = true;
    request.Query = query;

    RetrieveMultipleResponse retrieved = (RetrieveMultipleResponse)
service.Execute(request);

    int nextNumber = 1; // Default 1 for first record.

    // Check to see if we have any records
    if (retrieved.BusinessEntityCollection.BusinessEntities.Count > 0)
    {
```

```
        // Cast results dynamic entity and only retrieve first entity
        DynamicEntity results = (DynamicEntity)retrieved.BusinessEntityCollection.
BusinessEntities[0];

        // Return the next value lead number.
        // If there are records, but none have a number, the attribute won't exist in the
dictionary, so just pass back 1 (the default)
        if (results.Properties.Contains("new_leadnumber") == true)
          nextNumber = ((CrmNumber)results.Properties["new_leadnumber"]).Value + 1;
      }
      return nextNumber;
    }
  }
}
```

After you build your assembly, you must deploy your plug-in using the technique you learned earlier. Listing 9-8 displays only the solution node necessary for the plug-in registration tool's register.xml file.

Listing 9-8 Lead auto number plug-in registration details

```xml
<Solution SourceType="1" Assembly="WorkingWithDynamicsCrm4.Plugin.dll">
  <WorkflowTypes></WorkflowTypes>
  <Steps>
    <Step
      CustomConfiguration = ""
      Description = "Plug-in which generates a unique integer number for lead records."
      FilteringAttributes = "sonoma_leadnumber,leadid"
      ImpersonatingUserId = ""
      InvocationSource = "0"
      MessageName = "Create"
      Mode = "0"
      PluginTypeFriendlyName = "Lead Auto Number"
      PluginTypeName = "WorkingWithDynamicsCrm4.Plugin.LeadAutoNumber"
      PrimaryEntityName = "lead"
      SecondaryEntityName = ""
      Stage = "10"
      SupportedDeployment = "0" >

      <Images>
        <Image
          EntityAlias = "PreImage"
          ImageType="1"
          MessagePropertyName="id"
          Attributes ="sonoma_leadnumber,leadid">
        </Image>
      </Images>
    </Step>
  </Steps>
</Solution>
```

Validating a Field When Converting an Opportunity Record

Imagine that as part of your sales process, you want every salesperson to enter the start date of a project (a custom Opportunity attribute) before the salesperson can close an

Opportunity as won. However, you don't want to make the project start date field required on the Opportunity form because that would force the salesperson to enter a value before he or she could save a record. In this example, the user won't know the project start date until the customer agrees to purchase, so it doesn't make sense to configure this as a required field. However, your business requirement dictates that the salespersons must enter the project start date field before they can close the Opportunity as won. This example walks through all the steps necessary to develop a customization that will perform this type of check.

For simple form validation, we typically recommend using client-side scripting methods, as demonstrated in Chapter 10, instead of the pre-event plug-in because they are better for performance and easier to develop and deploy between environments. Using pre-event plug-ins does have some advantages though, such as consolidating the validation logic to work in cases where sources other than the Microsoft Dynamics CRM Web page (such as imports) alters the data.

This particular example is a unique case in which you must use the pre-event plug-in for validation. In this example, you want to perform a validation when the user interacts with a Web dialog box. As you will learn in Chapter 10, Microsoft Dynamics CRM does not include client-side events in Web dialog boxes such as converting Leads or closing Opportunities. Fortunately, the pre-event plug-in provides the appropriate hook for you to perform this type of Web dialog box validation. If the user tries to close an Opportunity without entering a project start date, a simple error message (shown in Figure 9-20) will be returned instructing him or her to correct the oversight.

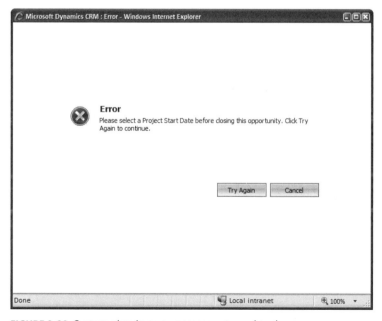

FIGURE 9-20 Custom plug-in error message returned to the user

Configure the Opportunity form

1. Add a new datetime attribute to the Opportunity form called **new_projectstartdate**. This field will be used for reporting and reference, but it doesn't need to be complete until the Opportunity is closed.

2. Add this field to the form, and select the Lock field on the form check box to prevent anyone from accidentally removing it from the form.

3. Publish the Opportunity entity.

> **Caution** When you deploy the pre-event plug-in assembly in this example, the user must enter a value in this field prior to closing an Opportunity record. If someone accidentally removes this field from the form, no one will be able to close an Opportunity. We recommend that you lock any fields that you reference in a custom event, plug-in, or workflow assembly so that other users who might edit the form know to leave that field on the form.

Next, you must create the plug-in code. The business requirements dictate that the mode be synchronous and the stage be a pre-event. You also need the value of the *new_projectstartdate* field and the *statecode* field because you don't want to validate unless the user is closing the Opportunity record (changing the state).

Next, you need to decide the message and entity to use for the custom validation logic. The plug-in model offers many possible messages, so we examine the possible choices. Because you are looking to validate when the state of the record changes, you should start with the SetStateDynamic message. For most entities, this would work flawlessly; however, the Opportunity entity behaves differently. When an Opportunity record is closed (marked as either Won or Lost), Microsoft Dynamics CRM uses two special messages called Win and Lose. Additionally, a special OpportunityClose activity record is created and logged with the Opportunity record. When you register the plug-in for the Win message, you discover that you cannot register any image attributes, meaning you will have to retrieve the *new _projectstartdate* with an extra SDK call.

Now examine another approach. Because you know that an opportunity close record is being created, you can configure the plug-in method against the Create message of the OpportunityClose entity.

The OpportunityClose activity triggers during the Opportunity Win (and Lose) transaction, meaning that it executes in the child pipeline. Yet, you require the *new_projectstartdate* field from the Opportunity record. Although you can access the Opportunity through the *ParentContext* collection, it doesn't contain the *new_projectstartdate* value, meaning you still would have to retrieve it manually using the SDK.

Important If you attempt to instantiate the CrmService object in a child transaction, Microsoft Dynamics CRM will throw an error. Microsoft Dynamics CRM restricts custom code from creating another service call in the child pipeline to prevent possible deadlocks in the system.

Because the OpportunityClose activity entity event will not work in this example, you have to accomplish the task using the Opportunity WinOpportunity message and manually retrieving the *new_projectstartdate* value using the opportunity id you retrieve from the *InputParameters*.

Microsoft Dynamics CRM no longer passes the record id (also known as the instance id) directly in the parent pipeline by default. For some messages, you pass the record id by the *Image* collection. In this example, you have to use the OpportunityClose entity passed in through the *InputParameters* collection. Microsoft Dynamics CRM uses the same entity Request message model for plug-ins. The plug-in serializes the Request object for the entity registered and places the results in the *InputParameters* property bag. For instance, the WinOpportunityRequest provides an instance property of the OpportunityClose and the Status of the opportunity.

 Tip Use Visual Studio 2008 remote debugging and a basic plug-in to examine the Microsoft Dynamics CRM properties exposes.

Plug-in development and deployment

1. Add a new Class file to the WorkingWithCrm.Workflow plug-in project, and call it **ValidateOpportunity**. Remember that this project already has references to the Microsoft.Crm.Sdk and Microsoft.Crm.SdkTypeProxy assemblies.

2. Replace the default code in ValidateOpportunity.cs with the code shown in Listing 9-9.

3. Build and deploy the solution assemblies to the Microsoft Dynamics CRM Web server's assembly folder for remote debugging during testing. The assembly folder is typically located at c:\Program Files\Microsoft Dynamics CRM\server\bin\assembly.

4. Register the solution with Microsoft Dynamics CRM by adding the solution XML in Listing 9-10 to your register.xml file.

Listing 9-9 Using a pre-event plug-in to validate a form field

```
using System;
using System.Collections.Generic;
using System.Text;
using Microsoft.Crm.Sdk;
using Microsoft.Crm.SdkTypeProxy;
using Microsoft.Crm.Sdk.Query;

namespace WorkingWithDynamicsCrm4.Plugin
{
```

```csharp
public class ValidateOpportunity : IPlugin
{
    /// <summary>
    /// This sample validates a field on the opportunity has a value prior to the
opportunity being closed.
    /// </summary>

    public void Execute(IPluginExecutionContext context)
    {
        // Verify we have a dynamic entity
        if (context.InputParameters.Properties.Contains("OpportunityClose") &&
context.InputParameters.Properties["OpportunityClose"] is DynamicEntity)
        {
            // Since the opportunityid is not passed with the "Win" messsage, we will retrieve
the opportunityid from the child opportunityclose entity
            DynamicEntity oppClose =
((DynamicEntity)context.InputParameters.Properties["opportunityclose"]);

            // Verify that we are working with an opportunityclose record
            if (oppClose.Name == EntityName.opportunityclose.ToString())
            {
                Guid opportunityId = ((Lookup)oppClose.Properties["opportunityid"]).Value;

                ICrmService service = context.CreateCrmService(false);

                // Retrieve the project start date from the opportunity checking if it has a value
                bool validStartDate = ValidateProjectStartDate(service, opportunityId);
                if (! validStartDate)
                {
                    // Throw an error, because the project start date didn't have a value prior to
closing the opportunity
                    throw new InvalidPluginExecutionException("Please select a Project Start Date
before closing this opportunity. Click Try Again to continue.");
                }
            }
        }
    }

    private bool ValidateProjectStartDate(ICrmService service, Guid opportunityId)
    {
        ColumnSet cols = new ColumnSet();
        cols.AddColumns(new string[] { "new_projectstartdate" });

        TargetRetrieveDynamic targetRetrieve = new TargetRetrieveDynamic();
        targetRetrieve.EntityName = "opportunity";
        targetRetrieve.EntityId = opportunityId;

        RetrieveRequest retrieve = new RetrieveRequest();
        retrieve.Target = targetRetrieve;
        retrieve.ColumnSet = cols;
        retrieve.ReturnDynamicEntities = true;

        RetrieveResponse retrieved = (RetrieveResponse)service.Execute(retrieve);
        DynamicEntity entity = (DynamicEntity)retrieved.BusinessEntity;
```

```
      // if new_projectstartdate is null then it won't exist in the properties collection
      return entity.Properties.Contains("new_projectstartdate");
    }
  }
}
```

You can deploy to the solution using the on-disk option (*SourceType="1"*). Use the solution node listed in Listing 9-10 with your plug-in deployment application's register.xml file to have your Opportunity validation routine ready for testing.

Listing 9-10 Validate Opportunity plug-in registration details

```
<Solution SourceType="1" Assembly="WorkingWithDynamicsCrm4.Plugin.dll">
  <WorkflowTypes></WorkflowTypes>
  <Steps>
    <Step
      CustomConfiguration = ""
      Description = "Plug-in which validates the opportunity fields prior to closing."
      FilteringAttributes = ""
      ImpersonatingUserId = ""
      InvocationSource = "0"
      MessageName = "Win"
      Mode = "0"
      PluginTypeFriendlyName = "Validate Opportunity"
      PluginTypeName = "WorkingWithDynamicsCrm4.Plugin.ValidateOpportunity"
      PrimaryEntityName = "opportunity"
      SecondaryEntityName = ""
      Stage = "10"
      SupportedDeployment = "0" >
    </Step>
  </Steps>
</Solution>
```

Synchronize a Contact's Address with Its Parent Account

As you know, you can assign each Contact record in Microsoft Dynamics CRM to an Account record. If you create the contact from an existing Account record, Microsoft Dynamics CRM will default certain fields on the Account based on the mappings between those entities (such as address fields). However, if you edit the Account address later, Microsoft Dynamics CRM will *not* automatically update the address information of the Account's related contacts. Consequently, many companies using Microsoft Dynamics CRM request a method to synchronize the Contact address information with the parent Account record. We now show you a simple way to accomplish this request using plug-ins.

You will create an asynchronous plug-in to find all Contacts associated with an Account, and then update each Contact's address with changes from the parent.

First, add an attribute to the Contact to let you know whether you should synchronize the address from the Account. This allows you to configure which Contacts attached to each Account should stay synchronized with the parent Account record.

Configure the Contact form

1. Add a new bit attribute to the Contact form called **new_syncaddresswithparent**.

2. Set the default value to **Yes**.

3. Add this field to the form, and select the Lock field on the form check box.

4. Publish the Contact entity.

Now that you updated the contact entity, you can start working on the plug-in code. Listing 9-11 details the plug-in code you will use for this example. In this listing, you will create generic properties for all of the changed address fields. If you have at least one changed address field, you can then find all Contacts that need to be updated and modify them using the *DynamicEntity* class.

Listing 9-11 Synchronizing a Contact address with its parent

```
using System;
using System.Collections.Generic;
using System.Text;
using System.Web.Services.Protocols;
using Microsoft.Crm.Sdk;
using Microsoft.Crm.SdkTypeProxy;
using Microsoft.Crm.Sdk.Query;

namespace WorkingWithDynamicsCrm4.Plugin
{
  public class AddressSync : IPlugin
  {
    /// <summary>
    /// This sample synchronizes a contacts address with its parent account
asynchronously.
    /// </summary>
    public void Execute(IPluginExecutionContext context)
    {

      // Verify you have an entity to work with
      if (context.InputParameters.Properties.Contains("Target") &&
context.InputParameters.Properties["Target"] is DynamicEntity)
      {
        ICrmService service = context.CreateCrmService(false);

        // Obtain the target business entity from the input parameters.
        DynamicEntity entity =
(DynamicEntity)context.InputParameters.Properties["Target"];

        // Verify that the entity represents an account.
        if (entity.Name == EntityName.account.ToString())
        {
          Dictionary<string, Property> changedValues = new Dictionary<string,
Property>();         changedValues = SetChangedAddressValues(entity);

          // If you have a changed address value, continue with the update
          if (changedValues.Count > 0)
```

```
        {
            Guid accountId = ((Key)entity.Properties["accountid"]).Value;

            // Retrieve applicable contact ids
            BusinessEntityCollection contactsToUpdate =
RetrieveContactsForAddressSync(service, accountId);

            // Update all contacts found
            UpdateContactAddress(service, contactsToUpdate, changedValues);
        }
      }
    }
  }

  private Dictionary<string, Property> SetChangedAddressValues(DynamicEntity entity)
  {
    Dictionary<string, Property> changedValues = new Dictionary<string, Property>();

    AddStringPropertyToDictionary(entity, "address1_name", changedValues);
    AddStringPropertyToDictionary(entity, "address1_line1", changedValues);
    AddStringPropertyToDictionary(entity, "address1_line2", changedValues);
    AddStringPropertyToDictionary(entity, "address1_line3", changedValues);
    AddStringPropertyToDictionary(entity, "address1_city", changedValues);
    AddStringPropertyToDictionary(entity, "address1_address1_stateorprovincename",
changedValues);
    AddStringPropertyToDictionary(entity, "address1_postalcode", changedValues);
    AddStringPropertyToDictionary(entity, "address1_country", changedValues);
    AddStringPropertyToDictionary(entity, "address1_telephone1", changedValues);
    AddPicklistPropertyToDictionary(entity, "address1_addresstypecode",
changedValues);
    AddPicklistPropertyToDictionary(entity, "address1_shippingmethodcode",
changedValues);
    AddPicklistPropertyToDictionary(entity, "address1_freighttermscode",
changedValues);
    return changedValues;
  }

  private void UpdateContactAddress(ICrmService service, BusinessEntityCollection
contactsToUpdate, Dictionary<string,Property> newAddressValues)
  {
    foreach (DynamicEntity retrievedContacts in contactsToUpdate.BusinessEntities)
    {
      try
      {
        DynamicEntity oContact = new DynamicEntity();
        oContact.Name = EntityName.contact.ToString();

        KeyProperty contactId = new KeyProperty();
        contactId.Name = "contactid";
        contactId.Value = ((Key)retrievedContacts.Properties["contactid"]);
        oContact.Properties.Add(contactId);

        foreach (KeyValuePair<string, Property> prop in newAddressValues)
        {
```

```
          oContact.Properties.Add(prop.Value);
        }

        TargetUpdateDynamic target = new TargetUpdateDynamic();
        target.Entity = oContact;

        UpdateRequest update = new UpdateRequest();
        update.Target = target;
        UpdateResponse response = (UpdateResponse)service.Execute(update);
      }
      catch (SoapException ex)
      {
        throw new Exception(ex.Detail.InnerXml.ToString());
      }
    }
      }

  private BusinessEntityCollection RetrieveContactsForAddressSync(ICrmService service,
Guid accountId)
    {
      ColumnSet cols = new ColumnSet();
      cols.AddColumns(new string[] { "contactid" });

      QueryByAttribute query = new QueryByAttribute();
      query.EntityName = "contact";
      query.Attributes = new String[] { "parentcustomerid",
"sonoma_syncaddresswithparent" };
      query.Values = new Object[] { accountId, true };
      query.ColumnSet = cols;

      try
      {
        // Retrieve the values from CRM as a dynamic entity
        RetrieveMultipleRequest request = new RetrieveMultipleRequest();
        request.ReturnDynamicEntities = true;
        request.Query = query;

        RetrieveMultipleResponse matchingContacts =
(RetrieveMultipleResponse)service.Execute(request);
        return matchingContacts.BusinessEntityCollection;
      }
      catch (SoapException ex)
      {
        throw new Exception(ex.Detail.InnerText);
      }
    }
    private void AddStringPropertyToDictionary(DynamicEntity entity, string attribute,
Dictionary<string, Property> newValue)
    {
      if (entity.Properties.Contains(attribute))
      {
        StringProperty prop = new StringProperty();
        prop.Name = attribute;
        prop.Value = entity.Properties[attribute].ToString();
        newValue[attribute] = prop;
```

```
      }
    }
    private void AddPicklistPropertyToDictionary(DynamicEntity entity, string attribute,
Dictionary<string, Property> newValue)
    {
      if (entity.Properties.Contains(attribute))
      {
        Picklist picklist = new Picklist();
        picklist.name = attribute;
        picklist.Value = ((Picklist)entity.Properties[attribute]).Value;

        PicklistProperty prop = new PicklistProperty();
        prop.Name = attribute;
        prop.Value = picklist;
        newValue[attribute] = prop;
      }
    }
  }
}
```

After you build the assembly, you must deploy the plug-in using the technique you learned previously. Listing 9-12 displays just the solution node required for the register.xml file.

Listing 9-12 Synchronize address plug-in registration details

```xml
<Solution SourceType="1" Assembly="WorkingWithDynamicsCrm4.Plugin.dll">
  <WorkflowTypes></WorkflowTypes>
  <Steps>
    <Step
      CustomConfiguration = ""
      Description = "Plug-in which synchronizes contact addresses with its parent
account address."
      FilteringAttributes = ""
      ImpersonatingUserId = ""
      InvocationSource = "0"
      MessageName = "Update"
      Mode = "1"
      PluginTypeFriendlyName = "Synchronize Contact Address"
      PluginTypeName = "WorkingWithDynamicsCrm4.Plugin.AddressSync"
      PrimaryEntityName = "account"
      SecondaryEntityName = ""
      Stage = "50"
      SupportedDeployment = "0" >
      <Images>
        <Image
          EntityAlias = "PreImage"
          ImageType="1"
          MessagePropertyName="Target"
          Attributes
="accountid,address1_name,address1_line1,address1_line2,address1_line3,address1_
city,address1_stateorprovince,address1_postalcode,address1_country,address1_
telephone1,address1_addresstypecode,address1_shippingmethodcode,address1_freighttermscode">
        </Image>
        <Image
```

```
            EntityAlias = "PostImage"
            ImageType="1"
            MessagePropertyName="Target"
            Attributes
="accountid,address1_name,address1_line1,address1_line2,address1_line3,address1_
city,address1_stateorprovince,address1_postalcode,address1_country,address1_
telephone1,address1_addresstypecode,address1_shippingmethodcode,address1_freighttermscode">
         </Image>
      </Images>
   </Step>
  </Steps>
</Solution>
```

Copy a System View

With Microsoft Dynamics CRM system views, you can display a group of views to all of the users in your organization. However, unlike with Advanced Find views, Microsoft Dynamics CRM does not allow you to copy an existing system view to create a new view. Consequently, creating a new system view in Microsoft Dynamics CRM always involves creating the view from scratch! Fortunately, the Microsoft Dynamics CRM API provides tools you can use to write a simple program to clone an existing system view. You can then use the Microsoft Dynamics CRM user interface to alter the copied view to your specific needs.

As you might remember, system views are created through the Customizations area of Microsoft Dynamics CRM, as shown in Figure 9-21.

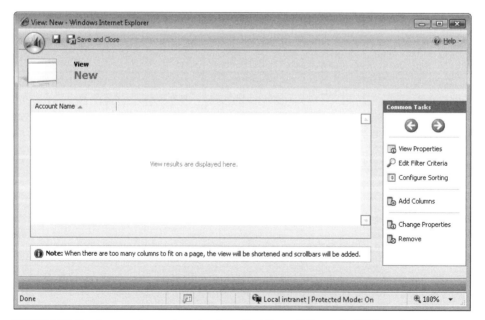

FIGURE 9-21 Creating a custom system view from the Microsoft Dynamics CRM user interface

This implementation uses a command-line application, but this concept could easily be migrated into a more formal application or Web page to allow for easier access or wider distribution. Simply create a console application project and replace the code in the default Program.cs with the code shown in Listing 9-13.

Listing 9-13 Clone a system view

```
using System;
using System.Web.Services.Protocols;
using System.Xml;
using System.Globalization;

using WorkingWithDynamicsCrm4.CloneView.CrmSdk;

namespace WorkingWithDynamicsCrm4.CloneView
{
  class Program
  {
    static readonly int MainApplicationView = 0;

    static void Main(string[] args)
    {
      if (args.Length != 4)
      {
        DisplayUsage();
        return;
      }

      Uri crmServerUri = new Uri(args[0], UriKind.Absolute);
      string entityName = args[1];
      string viewName = args[2];
      string newViewName = args[3];

      Console.WriteLine("Initiating connection to server...");
      CrmService crmService = CreateCrmService(crmServerUri);

      savedquery view = GetViewByName(crmService, entityName, viewName);
      if (view != null)
      {
        CreateCopyOfView(crmService, view, newViewName);
        Console.WriteLine("Created view '{0}'", view.name);
      }
    }

    static void DisplayUsage()
    {
      Console.WriteLine("CloneView.exe <crmServerUrl> <entityName> <viewName>
<newViewName>");
      Console.WriteLine("ex: CloneView.exe http://crmserver/orgname account \"Active
Accounts\" \"New Active Accounts\"");
    }

    static CrmService CreateCrmService(Uri crmServerUri)
    {
```

```
            UriBuilder uriBuilder = new UriBuilder(crmServerUri);

            CrmAuthenticationToken token = new CrmAuthenticationToken();
            token.OrganizationName = uriBuilder.Path.Trim('/');

            uriBuilder.Path = "/MSCrmServices/2007/CrmService.asmx";

            CrmService crmService = new CrmService();
            crmService.CrmAuthenticationTokenValue = token;
            crmService.Url = uriBuilder.ToString();

            // use credentials of user running application
            crmService.UseDefaultCredentials = true;

            return crmService;
        }

        static savedquery GetViewByName(CrmService crmService, string entityName, string
    viewName)
        {
            QueryByAttribute query = new QueryByAttribute();
            query.EntityName = EntityName.savedquery.ToString();
            query.Attributes = new string[] { "name", "returnedtypecode", "querytype" };
            query.Values = new object[] { viewName, entityName, MainApplicationView };

            ColumnSet cols = new ColumnSet();
            cols.Attributes = new string[]
            {
              "columnsetxml", "description", "fetchxml", "layoutxml", "name", "querytype",
              "returnedtypecode"
            };
            query.ColumnSet = cols;

            savedquery view = null;
            BusinessEntityCollection entities = crmService.RetrieveMultiple(query);

            switch (entities.BusinessEntities.Length)
            {
              case 0:
                Console.WriteLine("No view with name '{0}' for entity '{1}' exists.", viewName,
    entityName);
                break;
              case 1:
                Console.WriteLine("Found view with name '{0}' for entity '{1}'.", viewName,
    entityName);
                view = (savedquery)entities.BusinessEntities[0];
                break;
              default:
                Console.WriteLine("More than one view with name '{0}' for entity '{1}' exists.",
    viewName, entityName);
                break;
            }
            return view;
        }
```

```
static void CreateCopyOfView(CrmService crmService, savedquery view, string newViewName)
{
  string originalName = view.name;
  view.name = newViewName;
  view.savedqueryid = null;

  try
  {
    crmService.Create(view);
  }
  catch (SoapException ex)
  {
    throw new Exception(ex.Detail.InnerXml.ToString());
  }
}
}
}
```

Summary

This chapter provided you a firm understanding of the programming touchpoints available to you when working with the Microsoft Dynamics CRM SDK. You can create and include custom processes and logic at various points in the application, notably through the use of plug-ins and custom workflow assemblies.

The Microsoft Dynamics CRM APIs provide clear, scalable methods for accessing entities and manipulating data in the system without requiring you to understand the underlying mechanisms of the platform. By using these techniques, you have almost unlimited possibilities for customizing Microsoft Dynamics CRM to your specific business needs.

Chapter 10

Form Scripting and Extensions

In Chapter 5, "Entity Customization: Forms and Views," we explained how to perform basic form customizations on each entity. You can easily add fields, tabs, and sections to a form by using the Web-based administration tool without having to do any programming. However, if you want to set up more complex form customizations than the Web-based administration tool allows, Microsoft Dynamics CRM offers a rich form scripting and extension programming model.

In the context of Web-based applications, the term *client-side* typically refers to code that executes on the user's Web browser. Microsoft Dynamics CRM allows for business logic code to work offline and on the client, expanding the notion of client-side code. In addition to the offline business logic code, you can use scripting functionality on an entity's form. Microsoft Dynamics CRM includes a software development kit (SDK) that explains the supported methods you can use to create custom scripts that tap into form and field events, such as *onLoad*, *onSave*, and *onChange*. This chapter examines these advanced form programming techniques. We also review the use of IFrames in the Microsoft Dynamics CRM forms and the ISV.config file and how you can use these two features to extend the Microsoft Dynamics CRM interface with your own custom Web pages. In addition, we supply numerous examples of how you might implement some customizations that these powerful form scripting and extensions allow.

Because of the nature of the form scripting programming model, this chapter contains a significant amount of dynamic HTML (DHTML) and scripting code. However, even if you're not an expert with these technologies, this chapter can help you understand the types of customizations possible in Microsoft Dynamics CRM.

We created the samples in this chapter so that you could deploy them to your own Microsoft Dynamics CRM system. You can download all of the sample code directly from the download site mentioned in the book's Introduction. We also provide references to additional information regarding scripting syntax and methods later in this chapter.

Form Scripting Overview

After reading Chapter 9, "Microsoft Dynamics CRM 4.0 SDK," you should be familiar with the application programming interfaces (APIs) and general architecture. We now focus on the many events and programmatic possibilities available to you by using the form scripting techniques. We cover the following topics in this section:

- Definitions

- Understanding scripting with Microsoft Dynamics CRM

- Referencing Microsoft Dynamics CRM elements

- Available events

Definitions

Before we get too deep in the form scripting SDK and examples, we review a few key expressions and their definitions.

- **Client-side scripting**   Code that executes on a user's Web browser instead of a centralized Web server.

- **Hypertext Markup Language (HTML)**   A tag-based language used to render content in an Internet browser.

- **Cascading style sheet**   A definition document that describes how a Web document should display formats and styles to the user.

- **Document Object Model (DOM)**   An application programming interface designed to access HTML documents, representing elements in the document in an object-oriented model.

- **Dynamic HTML (DHTML)**   A technology that extends regular HTML with client-side scripting and cascading style sheets, exposing the elements on an HTML document so that you can manipulate them programmatically by using the DOM.

- **Globally unique identifier (GUID)**   A string that represents a unique value. Microsoft Dynamics CRM uses a GUID as the unique identifier for each record.

Understanding Client-Side Scripting with Microsoft Dynamics CRM

Client-side scripting helps distribute the application processing load between the client computer and the Web server. Because Microsoft Dynamics CRM uses a Web-based architecture, it displays all of its data on Web pages. However, the Microsoft Dynamics CRM pages don't appear as typical Web pages that users see when browsing the Internet. Rather, Microsoft Dynamics CRM relies heavily on DHTML to achieve a more advanced and functional user interface. Because the DOM treats each HTML element as an object, a developer may use traditional DHTML programming techniques to access the Microsoft Dynamics CRM forms to create even more customized and sophisticated Web pages in Microsoft Dynamics CRM.

Microsoft Dynamics CRM supports a specialized subset of DOM methods and events as defined in the client-side SDK. We examine many of the available properties and methods here, but you can refer to the Microsoft Dynamics CRM SDK for a complete list of supported methods.

Referencing Microsoft Dynamics CRM Elements

The "Client Programming Guide" section of the Microsoft Dynamics CRM SDK provides information regarding the client methods, properties, and events available to a programmer. In Table 10-1 through Table 10-9, we highlight a few of the key actions that you will probably use frequently in your own scripts.

TABLE 10-1 **Global Variables**

Name	Description
SERVER_URL	Returns the URL of the CRM Web server
USER_LANGUAGE_CODE	Provides the language code set by the user in Microsoft Dynamics CRM
ORG_LANGUAGE_CODE	Returns the base language for the organization
ORG_UNIQUE_NAME	Returns the organization name

TABLE 10-2 **Global Methods**

Method	Description
IsOnline	Gets a Boolean value indicating whether the form is currently online
IsOutlookClient	Gets a Boolean value indicating whether the form is currently being displayed in one of the Microsoft Office Outlook clients
IsOutlookLaptopClient	Gets a Boolean value indicating whether the form is currently being displayed in Microsoft Dynamics CRM for Outlook with Offline Access
IsOutlookWorkstationClient	Gets a Boolean value indicating whether the form is currently being displayed in Microsoft Dynamics CRM for Outlook

TABLE 10-3 *crmForm* **Properties**

Property	Description
all	A collection of CRM fields on the form.
IsDirty	Gets or sets a value indicating whether any of the fields on the form have been modified.
FormType	Gets an integer value designating the mode of the form. Possible values are: 0 = Undefined Form Type 1 = Create Form 2 = Update Form 3 = Read-Only Form 4 = Disabled Form 5 = Quick Create Form 6 = Bulk Edit Form
ObjectId	Gets the entity GUID that the form is displaying. This property returns null if the form is in Create mode.
ObjectTypeName	Gets the entity name of the displayed form.

TABLE 10-4 *crmForm* **Methods**

Method	Description
Save()	Executes the save function (simulates a user clicking *Save*).
SaveAndClose()	Executes the save and close function (simulates a user clicking *Save and Close*).
SetFieldReqLevel(sField, bRequired)	Sets a field as required. Note that this is unsupported and may change or not be available in future releases.

TABLE 10-5 *crmForm.all* **Field Collection Properties**

Property	Description
Precision	Gets the number of digits to display for *currency* and *float* data types.
DataValue	Gets or sets the value of the field.
Disabled	Gets or sets a value indicating whether the field is available for user entry.
ForceSubmit	Gets or sets a value indicating whether the field should be submitted to the database on a save. By default, any enabled, modified field will be submitted. This property is useful when you need to submit a disabled field.
IsDirty	Gets a value indicating whether the field has been modified.
Min	Gets the minimum allowable value for *currency*, *float*, and *integer* data types.
Max	Gets the maximum allowable value for *currency*, *float*, and *integer* data types.
MaxLength	Gets the maximum length of a string or memo field.
RequiredLevel	Gets the required status of the field. Possible values are 0 = No Constraint 1 = Business Recommended 2 = Business Required

TABLE 10-6 *crmForm.all* **Field Collection Methods**

Method	Description
SetFocus()	Moves the mouse cursor to the field, making it active on the form
FireOnChange()	Executes the Microsoft Dynamics CRM OnChange event for the attribute specified

The lookup and picklist field types differ from the other fields because they act as arrays (a collection of name/value pairs). The value that Microsoft Dynamics CRM stores in the database (a GUID for lookup fields and an integer for picklist fields) is not the value that the user will see on the form. Because you probably don't want to reference the GUID or integer value, Microsoft Dynamics CRM includes the following additional attributes of the *DataValue* property for displaying the translated value as shown in the next three tables.

TABLE 10-7 *crmForm.all.<lookupfield>.DataValue* **Attributes**

Attribute	Description
id	Gets or sets the GUID identifier. Required for set.
type	Gets or sets the object type code. Required for set.
name	Gets or sets the name of the record to be displayed in the lookup field on the form. Required for set.

TABLE 10-8 *crmForm.all.<picklistfield>* **Properties and Methods**

Syntax	Description
DataValue	Gets or sets the currently selected option, returning an integer.
SelectedText	Gets the text displayed with the currently selected option.
GetSelectedOption	Gets a picklist.
Options	Returns an array of picklist objects and sets new options for a drop-down list by specifying an array of picklist objects.
AddOption(option)	Adds a new option at the end of the picklist collection. *DataValue* and *Name* must have valid values.
DeleteOption(value)	Removes a picklist option based on the integer value passed in.

TABLE 10-9 *crmForm.all.<picklistfield>.DataValue* **Attributes**

Attribute	Description
Name	Gets or sets the text displayed in the picklist
Data	Gets or sets the data

Available Events

Microsoft Dynamics CRM supports three client-side events that you can reference in your custom scripts:

- **Form *onLoad* event**   Executes immediately before the form loads in the browser. By using this event, you can manipulate the form before Microsoft Dynamics CRM displays it to the user.

- **Form *onSave* event**   Triggers when the user clicks the Save, Save and Close, or Save and New button. This event happens before the form is submitted to the server and can be used to cancel the save. Also, this event always fires, even if the user did not change any of the fields on the form.

- **Field *onChange* events**   Fires when the user navigates away from a form field (clicks elsewhere or presses the Tab key) in which he or she has changed the value.

> **Tip** If you want to cancel the save, use the following syntax: *event.returnValue = false;*.

We introduced adding client-side scripts to an entity form in Chapter 5, but here we go through a quick refresher.

Adding event code

As a System Administrator or System Customizer role, you will navigate to the Settings section, click Customizations, and then click Customize Entities.

1. In the Customize Entities section, double-click the entity that you want to customize.

2. In the navigation pane, click Forms and Views.

3. Double-click Form from the resulting list.

The form editor page is displayed and shows all of the tabs and fields that the form will display to the user.

Customizing form events

To customize the form events (*onLoad* and *onSave*), follow these steps:

1. Click Form Properties in the Common Tasks area. A dialog box appears that lists the *onLoad* and *onSave* events.

2. Select the event to which you want to add code, and then click Edit.

3. Enter your custom script in the Event Detail Properties dialog box (shown in Figure 10-1), select the Event is enabled check box, and then click OK.

Adding scripts to the field event

Adding scripts to the field event (*onChange*) works the same way as it does for form events:

1. In the form editor, double-click the field where you will add your code. Or you can select a field, and then click Change Properties.

2. The Field Properties dialog box opens. Click the Events tab.

3. Click Edit. You will see the Event Detail Properties dialog box, as shown in Figure 10-1.

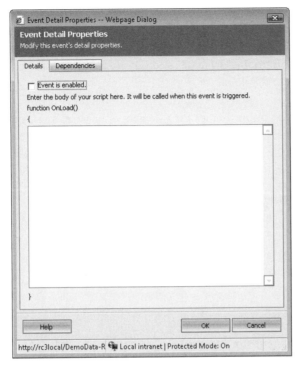

FIGURE 10-1 The Event Detail Properties dialog box

Remember these key points related to configuring your client-side scripts on the entity forms:

- You must enable your script by selecting the Event is enabled check box in the Event Detail Properties dialog box. This check box tells Microsoft Dynamics CRM to run the script the next time the event is triggered.

- Although not required, it's a good practice to specify the fields your script uses in the Dependencies tab. Specifying dependent fields will block users from accidentally removing fields from the form that your script requires.

- You can test and debug your scripts by using one of the form preview options: Create, Update, and Read-Only.

- Microsoft Dynamics CRM provides a Simulate Form Save button on the preview that will trigger the *onSave* event. You can use this button to test your onSave custom scripts.

- Of course you need to remember to publish your customizations when you're done.

We show lots of examples of client-side customizations later in this chapter; we just wanted to give you a quick background on the customization process and terminology.

IFrames and Scripting

With Microsoft Dynamics CRM, you can add an IFrame (also known as an *inline frame*) to the form of an entity. Chapter 5 introduced IFrames and described how to set up a simple IFrame in a form, but now we go into the details of how to really take advantage of this powerful feature with client-side customization techniques. The IFrame feature creates tremendous integration and customization opportunities for a developer in Microsoft Dynamics CRM. Because you can programmatically access an IFrame document from the Microsoft Dynamics CRM form through the DOM, your enhancements can appear seamless to the user. Figure 10-2 shows a sample IFrame that references a Microsoft Windows SharePoint Services Web site.

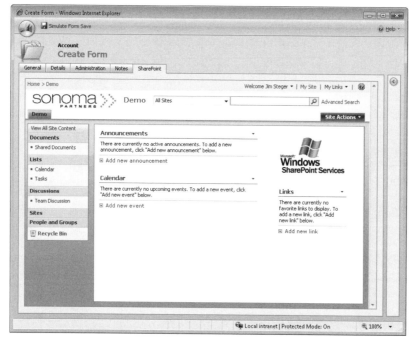

FIGURE 10-2 IFrame example

IFrames can reference any URL or Web page, regardless of whether they are hosted on your Web server or any other any Web server. Common uses might include displaying SharePoint sites, adding mapping functionality through external Web sites, and custom application integration.

Caution Remember that Microsoft Dynamics CRM for Microsoft Office Outlook with Offline Access users can work offline, so they might experience an issue with a form if the IFrame references a Web page that they can't access offline. Therefore, don't include any key functionality in an IFrame that offline users will require unless you plan on deploying that functionality locally to the client.

Security

We couldn't possibly provide a comprehensive analysis on Web application security in the scope of this book, but we want to touch upon the notion of Microsoft Dynamics CRM cross-site scripting and its IFrame-related security issues. Cross-site scripting provides a powerful (and potentially dangerous) feature in Web applications, including Microsoft Dynamics CRM. In most cases, DHTML and the user's browser settings permit scripting access to and from IFrame documents that reside on the same domain and reference matching protocols (such as FTP, HTTP, or HTTPS).

For example, consider an HTML document called Main.htm located on the www.adatum.com domain (*http://www.adatum.com/main.htm*). A second Web page called Frame.htm located on the same domain includes an IFrame that references Main.htm. The protocol in this example is HTTP for both pages, and because they both reside on the same domain, the browser will permit the scripts from the Frame.htm page to access and manipulate content on the Main.htm document. Microsoft Internet Explorer will disable scripting access to IFrame URLs that refer to a page on another domain or reference the page through a different protocol. So, if the IFrame source is *https://www.adatum.com/frame.htm* (accessed by using the Secure Sockets Layer (SSL) protocol) or *http://www.contoso.com/frame.htm* (located on another domain), Internet Explorer will prevent script access between the pages. Figure 10-3 shows a graphical representation of this.

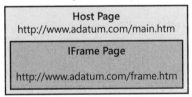

Cross-Site Scripting Allowed

Same domain (www.adatum.com)
and protocol (http)

Host Page
http://www.adatum.com/main.htm

IFrame Page

http://www.adatum.com/frame.htm

Cross-Site Scripting Denied

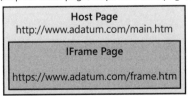

Same domain (www.adatum.com),
but different protocols
(http for main page, https for frame page)

Host Page
http://www.adatum.com/main.htm

IFrame Page

https://www.adatum.com/frame.htm

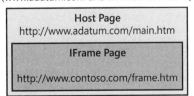

Same protocol (http),
but different domains
(www.adatum.com and www.contoso.com)

Host Page
http://www.adatum.com/main.htm

IFrame Page

http://www.contoso.com/frame.htm

FIGURE 10-3 Default Internet Explorer IFrame security

> **Important** If you are a Microsoft Dynamics CRM Live customer, you should carefully consider how these cross-site scripting security constraints will affect your IFrames. We cover developing for Microsoft Dynamics CRM Live in more detail later in this chapter.

In addition to the default Internet Explorer security behavior, with Microsoft Dynamics CRM, you can add another layer of security by using the Restrict cross-frame scripting setting. Behind the scenes, this option sets the value of the *security* attribute of the IFrame tag to *restricted*. Under default conditions, this setting has the following effects:

- Restricts JavaScript and Microsoft Visual Basic Scripting Edition (VBScript) from executing on the IFrame page.

- All hyperlinks will open in a new browser window.

So, even if Internet Explorer would have allowed cross-frame scripting, you can disable this for a specific IFrame in Microsoft Dynamics CRM. By default, Microsoft Dynamics CRM restricts cross-frame scripting on new IFrame pages. If you want your scripts to run across the Microsoft Dynamics CRM form and your custom page, you must clear the cross-frame scripting setting. Obviously, for security purposes we recommend that you leave selected the default setting of not allowing cross-frame scripting unless you have a specific need for this feature.

> **More Info** For additional information about the IFrame *security* attribute, visit *http://msdn2.microsoft.com/en-us/library/ms534622.aspx*.

CRM IFrame Scripting Example

We now demonstrate how the Web page domain and the Microsoft Dynamics CRM IFrame property settings affect the form's display and scripting capabilities between the IFrame document and the Microsoft Dynamics CRM Contact form. For this example, we integrate a custom Web page that calculates monthly mortgage payments assuming you deployed Microsoft Dynamics CRM on-premise. The custom Web page in the IFrame accepts values entered by a user, calculates the correct mortgage payment, and then populates that payment value back into a native Microsoft Dynamics CRM field.

The resulting form should look like the one shown in Figure 10-4.

Adding attributes

In this example, you will add a new attribute (Mortgage Payment) to the Contact entity.

1. Browse to the Customization area of Microsoft Dynamics CRM, and double-click the Contact entity. Click Attributes in the navigation pane.

2. Add a money attribute called mortgagepayment (the schema name will be *new_mortgagepayment*, provided that you haven't changed your default schema name prefix).

3. Type **Mortgage Payment** in the Display Name box.

4. Change the Type field to money. Leave the money value defaults, and then click Save and Close.

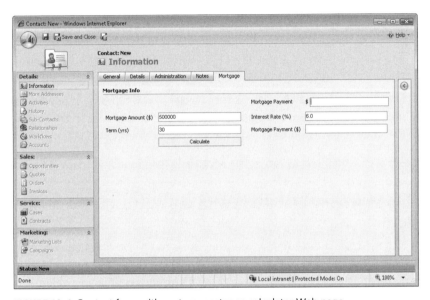

FIGURE 10-4 Contact form with custom mortgage calculator Web page

Modifying the form

1. In the navigation pane, click Forms and Views, and then click Form to open the Form Editor window.

2. Add a new tab called **Mortgage** on the Contact form. This tab will contain an automatically expanding IFrame that points to a custom HTML page and two currency fields.

3. Add a section called **Mortgage Info**. Select both the label and the divider line options.

4. Add the new Mortgage Payment field that you just created.

5. Add a section called **iframe**. This section will contain an automatically expanding IFrame.

6. Select the newly created section, and then click the Add an IFrame link. You will change the properties of the IFrame to see the impact that they have on the form. Initially, set the following properties:

   a. Name: mortgage

   b. URL: /ISV/SonomaPartners/WorkingWithCRM4/mortgage.htm. (We explain how to deploy the mortgage.htm file later.)

    c. Label: Leave blank.

    d. Security: Clear the Restrict cross-frame scripting check box. You will start by allowing the two pages scripting access so that the IFrame page can update a field on the Microsoft Dynamics CRM form.

7. Switch to the Formatting tab, and set the following properties:

    a. Number of Rows: Select Automatically expand to use available space.

    b. Scrolling: Select Never. You have created a form to mirror the existing Microsoft Dynamics CRM form. If you allow scrollbars, Internet Explorer will allocate space for this, shifting the IFrame form, as shown in Figure 10-5.

    c. Border: Clear Display Border. As with scrolling, you don't want to alert users to the fact that they are looking at a different page. You want to create the illusion that they are working on the native Microsoft Dynamics CRM form.

8. Switch to the Dependencies tab, select Mortgage Payment, and make it dependent.

Blending an IFrame Web Page with the Microsoft Dynamics CRM Form

In the mortgage calculator example, you want users to believe that they are using one form. You don't want (or need) them to know that some of the fields in the Mortgage tab are actually hosted in an IFrame. Therefore, it's important that you modify the IFrame settings to make the page blend in as much as possible.

Figure 10-5 shows how the IFrame page would look with the border enabled and scrolling set to As Necessary. If you look to the right, Microsoft Dynamics CRM automatically allotted space for a scrollbar should it need it. Therefore, the Interest Rate and Mortgage Payment fields in the IFrame shift to the left and they don't line up with the native Mortgage Payment form field. In addition, with the border enabled, a blue outline frames the IFrame page.

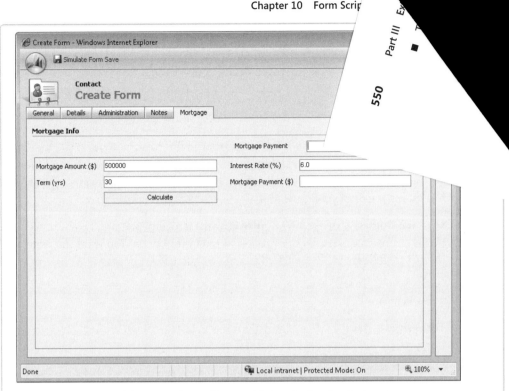

FIGURE 10-5 IFrame with automatic scrolling enabled and a border displayed

Because we like our Web pages and forms neat and tidy with all of the fields lined up correctly, you're going to tweak the IFrame configuration options. By setting the scroll-bars to Never and disabling the border, you can then format the custom IFrame Web page to blend in with the Microsoft Dynamics CRM form, creating the illusion of one page and a consistent interface to the user, as shown earlier in Figure 10-4.

Custom HTML Page

Now you need to create the custom Mortgage.htm Web page that contains the mortgage calculator in the IFrame. The Web page takes three financial inputs, and then it calculates a monthly mortgage payment by using a custom JavaScript method. It then attempts to write the value back to the Microsoft Dynamics CRM form, allowing the value to be saved with the Contact record.

You should take note of the following in regard to the Mortgage.htm file:

- The styles of the custom Web page mirror those of the native Microsoft Dynamics CRM form so that you can seamlessly integrate the IFrame page into the form.

- This example includes a simple JavaScript page, but you can create much more sophis-ticated Web pages and display in an IFrame.

- The custom page also contains a Mortgage Payment field to demonstrate the interac-tion between the Microsoft Dynamics CRM form and the custom Web page.

The script attempts to send the monthly payment result back to the Microsoft Dynamics CRM form. The Microsoft Dynamics CRM form is unnamed, but it will always be the first item in the forms collection. So, you can reference it by using the following syntax:

```
parent.document.forms[0]
```

- In this example, you use a submit button on the custom page. In the section titled "Client-Side Scripting Code Examples" later in this chapter, the Custom Interface For Multi-Select Lists sample shows how you can also use cross-frame scripting to force a submit event of your custom page.

The code for the Mortgage.htm page is shown in Listing 10-1.

Listing 10-1 mortgage.htm HTML Code

```html
<html>
<head>
 <title>Mortgage Calculator</title>
 <script type="text/javascript">
  function calculate()
  {
    // Gather inputs from form
    var mortgageamount = document.getElementById("mortgageamount").value;
    var interestrate = document.getElementById("interestrate").value;
    var term = document.getElementById("term").value;

    // Calculate payment and assign to field on form
    var mortgagepayment = calculatePayment( interestrate, term * 12, mortgageamount)
    document.getElementById("mortgagepayment").value = mortgagepayment;

    // Also assign back to the Microsoft Dynamics CRM form
    parent.document.forms[0].all.new_mortgagepayment.DataValue = mortgagepayment;
  }

  function calculatePayment(rate, nummonths, presentvalue)
  {
    var intRate = rate /100 / 12;
    var pmt = Math.floor((presentvalue*intRate)/(1-Math.pow(1+intRate,
(-1*nummonths)))*100)/100;
    return pmt;
  }
</script>

<style type="text/css">
 ...styles for page...
</style></head>
<body><form>
<div style="padding:0px;">
<table class="layout" cellspacing="0" cellpadding="3" border="0">
  <col width="115"/><col/><col width="135" style="padding-left:20px;"/><col/>
  <tr>
    <td>Mortgage Amount ($)</td>
    <td><input type="text" id="mortgageamount" name="mortgageamount" value="500000" /></td>
```

```
  <td>Interest Rate (%)</td>
  <td><input type="text" id="interestrate" name="interestrate" value="6.0" /></td>
</tr>
<tr>
  <td>Term (yrs)</td>
  <td><input type="text" id="term" name="term" value="30" /></td>
  <td>Mortgage Payment ($)</td>
  <td><input type="text" id="mortgagepayment" name="mortgagepayment" value="" /></td>
</tr>

<tr>
  <td> </td>
  <td><input type="button" id="btnSubmit" name="btnSubmit" value="Calculate"
onclick="calculate();" /></td>
</tr>
</table>
</div></form></body></html>
```

After you complete the page, you must deploy it to the location specified by the IFrame URL property (the ISV/SonomaPartners/WorkingWithCrm4/). Navigate to the root Microsoft Dynamics CRM Web location (typically C:\Inetpub\wwwroot\) on your Microsoft Dynamics CRM Web server and create a SonomaPartners and then a WorkingWithCrm4 directory. Then, copy the Mortgage.htm file to this location using whatever method is easiest (such as Xcopy or FTP).

After you save the form, you can preview it to see the results. Using the Create Form preview functionality, you can also test how the Restrict cross-frame scripting setting works. Because of the multicurrency functionality in Microsoft Dynamics CRM, you will need to first select a currency in the General tab. Switch back to the Mortgage tab, enter some values in the mortgage calculator, and click Calculate. You will see that both Mortgage Payment ($) fields on the custom page and the native Microsoft Dynamics CRM form update, as shown in Figure 10-6.

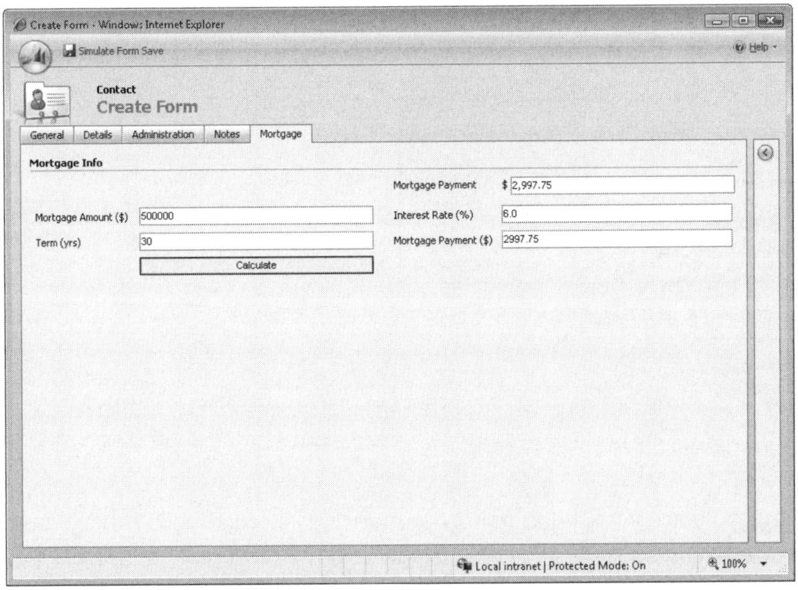

FIGURE 10-6 Mortgage tab preview

Also, notice that with the border turned off and the scrolling set to Never, the form looks as if it is part of the native page. Because you allowed cross-frame scripting in the IFrame properties, you can execute the custom page's JavaScript routines. Also, because you deployed and referenced the page using the same domain and protocol as the Microsoft Dynamics CRM server, you will be able to access elements on the Microsoft Dynamics CRM form and populate the monthly payment results back to Microsoft Dynamics CRM.

What would happen if you restrict cross-frame scripting? When a user clicks the Calculate button, the IFrame's monthly payment field will not be populated. The Microsoft Dynamics CRM form also remains blank, and no error message is displayed. All scripting on the custom IFrame page was disabled and prevented from executing.

> **Important** Remember that when you disable cross-site scripting in Microsoft Dynamics CRM, your referenced IFrame page will also be restricted from running any scripts (even if those scripts don't try to go cross-frame into Microsoft Dynamics CRM).

Enable cross-frame scripting again, but move the IFrame form to another server and access it in a different URL domain. Update the *URL* property of the IFrame to *http://crmserver2/ workingwithcrm/iframe-example.htm*. Then, preview the form and try the mortgage calculation again. The Mortgage Payment field correctly populates, but a script error appears in the browser (similar to the one shown in Figure 10-7). Internet Explorer displays the access denied message because it doesn't allow scripting across two Web pages hosted on different domains: crmserver and crmserver2.

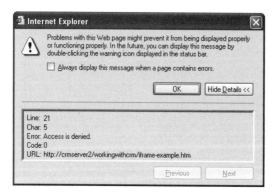

FIGURE 10-7 Scripting access denied error

> **Caution** Because any IFrame page will be hosted on another server under a different URL, you will not be able to take advantage of cross-site scripting techniques for Microsoft Dynamics CRM Live.

Of course, you could accomplish this particular mortgage calculation in this example by using alternate methods. For example, you could simply add the mortgage fields from the IFrame to the native Contact form and use the *onChange* event to do the same calculations. Another option is to add the fields to the native form and call a Web service or Web page from the *onChange* event. With simple business logic, you really don't need the overhead of a custom IFrame, but you can see that in more complex situations, the IFrame element with cross-frame scripting can be a valuable tool.

> **More Info** For more information about security of DHTML, visit *http://msdn2.microsoft.com/en-us/library/ms533047.aspx*.

Dynamic IFrame URLs

Even though you enter a URL address for an IFrame when you add it to a form, you can still programmatically change this URL on the fly. For example, you might need to change the IFrame URL based on user form selections, or even update the protocol of the URL based on the protocol of Microsoft Dynamics CRM. To do this, you can update the *src* property of the IFrame from either the *onLoad*, *onSave*, or *onChange* events. The code would look like this:

```
crmForm.all.<iframe_name>.src = <URL reference>
```

ASP.NET Application Development

The previous example discusses how to deploy a simple HTML page in an IFrame; however, we expect that most of your Web application development will involve ASP.NET Web pages. When you're ready to deploy your ASP.NET Web pages to Microsoft Dynamics CRM, you should deploy your Web files to the following folders:

- **Server**   *<installation root>*\ISV*<company name>**<application name>* where the *<installation root>* is the default directory of the Microsoft Dynamics CRM Web files (typically c:\Inetpub\wwwroot), *<company name>* is the name of your company, and *<application name>* is the name of your application.

- **Client**   *<Installation Program Files Folder>*\Microsoft Dynamics CRM\Client\res\web\ISV*<company name>**<application name>* where the *<Installation Program Files Folder>* is the default directory of the Microsoft Dynamics CRM client files (typically c:\Program Files), *<company name>* is the name of your company, and *<application name>* is the name of your application.

> **Important** Do not place your files directly beneath the ISV folder. Always create a subfolder first. Creating a subfolder helps reduce the risk of your custom application conflicting with other custom applications deployed to your Microsoft Dynamics CRM (such as third-party add-ons and so on).

Keep in mind the following points when developing ASP.NET applications that you will deploy to the ISV folder:

- If you reference the Microsoft Dynamics CRM Web Service WSDL in your application, you must compile your Web application to an assembly and place the assembly in the Microsoft Dynamics CRM bin folder for the reference to load properly.

- You could add the SDK assembly references and use the Dynamic Entity approach. Using this approach, you could just deploy your .aspx and .cs files. We demonstrate an example of this later in the chapter.

- Use strong naming and digitally sign all of your assemblies.

- If you develop your application to work offline, you will need to determine when the application is running in an offline state because offline uses different references. The SDK provides examples of how to implement this.

- Microsoft Dynamics CRM offers a new *CrmImpersonator* class. With this class, you can take advantage of the current security context that Microsoft Dynamics CRM uses. This class is ideal for Internet-facing deployments (IFDs).

- When you link your custom pages from the ISV.config or site map using a relative path, Microsoft Dynamics CRM will engage a virtual path provider to insert the organization name to the URL. Once this occurs, you will be unable to use a custom web.config file.

Tip If your application requires the use of a web.config file, you can use */../* in your relative URL path to bypass the virtual path provider (for example: *Url="/../ISV/SonomaPartners/Elements/ sample.aspx"*. The */../* tells the Web browser to back up a folder, effectively removing the organization name from the URL and bypassing the virtual path provider. Conveniently, the Web browser also gracefully handles the case where no subfolder exists in the path. However, this method limits you to the default organization when using the *CrmImpersonator* class.

By deploying your custom Web pages to the ISV folder, your application should work in various types of environments such as in a local intranet, over an Internet-facing deployment, and offline in Microsoft Dynamics CRM for Outlook with Offline Access.

However, if your users will only access your custom Web application over a local intranet, you can use a Microsoft Internet Information Services (IIS) virtual directory, instead of the ISV folder, to deploy your ASP.NET files.

With the virtual directory approach, you create your own Web application and deploy it to the Microsoft Dynamics CRM Web server as a virtual directory in IIS. The virtual directory approach provides some advantages. You can set your own application pool identity and Microsoft .NET Framework run-time version, providing isolation of your code from Microsoft Dynamics CRM. In addition, you can take advantage of all the functionality of your own web. config file, use your own bin directory for assembly reference, and have a way to configure the application deployment to your needs in a supported manner with Microsoft Dynamics CRM.

However, you should only use this virtual directory deployment model in certain circum-stances because it includes several significant drawbacks. First, your custom Web applica-tion will not work in offline mode. Microsoft Dynamics CRM for Outlook uses the Cassini Web server for its offline client implementation, and Cassini doesn't allow virtual directories. Second, it will require your custom Web pages to reauthenticate in the Internet-facing deployment model. IFD uses forms-based authentication and IIS does not seamlessly pass that authentication properly to the virtual directory pages. Finally, you will need to either specify the full URL to your pages or use the /../ technique mentioned earlier to access your pages.

Therefore, we recommend you use this virtual directory deployment approach only when you can be sure you will never need to access your custom pages offline or from an IFD server.

Regardless of which method (ISV folder or virtual directory) that you choose to deploy your ASP.NET files, please keep the additional following best practices in mind when developing your custom Web pages:

- Target the .NET Framework version 3.0 for your application for consistency with the Microsoft Dynamics CRM application. You can target different versions of the .NET Framework if necessary.

- Do not modify the Microsoft Dynamics CRM root web.config file. This is an unsupported change and any changes you make could place the entire Microsoft Dynamics CRM application in an unstable state.

Microsoft Dynamics CRM Virtual Path Provider

For those of you familiar with creating custom Web pages for the previous version of Microsoft Dynamics CRM, you know that Microsoft did not allow developers to deploy *any* files to the Microsoft Dynamics CRM Web folders. Instead, deploying custom pages to a virtual directory was the preferred and recommended deployment method. However, to support multiple organizations in a single deployment, Microsoft Dynamics CRM 4.0 uses a virtual path provider to dynamically insert the organization name in the URL. So, instead of a URL like *http://<crmserver>/loader.aspx*, you would see *http://<crmserver>/<organization>/loader.aspx* in your Web browser address bar. Microsoft Dynamics CRM automatically adds the *<organization>* name to the URL when users access Web pages from the site map or ISV.config.

> **Note** Microsoft Dynamics CRM does not insert the organization name with custom IFrame references.

Developers need to consider how the virtual path provider affects their custom ASP.NET applications. First, consider the case where you try to use a custom virtual directory called CustomWeb under the Microsoft Dynamics CRM Web site and you reference your ASP.NET web page with a relative path as */CustomWeb/custompage.aspx*. When you click this link in Microsoft Dynamics CRM, you will receive an error that IIS cannot find the Web page. The reason is that Microsoft Dynamics CRM will translate the URL to *http://<crmserver>/<organization>/CustomWeb/custompage.aspx* and because your page actually resides at *http://<crmserver>/CustomWeb/custompage.aspx*, IIS will not find the file. So, clearly this won't meet your needs.

Second, even if you try to avoid the virtual directory approach and just add your custom files to a folder in Microsoft Dynamics CRM, when Microsoft Dynamics CRM enages the virtual path provider, IIS will not execute any web.config file in a subfolder. This means you cannot rely on custom web.config settings in your application, load assemblies, modules, and so on. Again, this is clearly not an ideal situation.

> **Caution** Common HTML files (with extensions of .htm, .html, .css, .js, etc.) will not load when accessed through the virtual path provider.

Consequently, the virtual path provider changes to Microsoft Dynamics CRM 4.0 caused Microsoft to modify the supported methods to deploy custom ASP.NET Web pages to Microsoft Dynamics CRM, allowing developers to deploy their web files to the /ISV folder and their compiled assemblies to the Microsoft Dynamics CRM /bin folder.

Your best options are either to reference your URLs with /../ and bypass the virtual path provider (when deploying to single tenant environments) or to compile your Web logic to a signed assembly and deploy the assembly to the Microsoft Dynamics CRM /bin folder.

ISV.config

With the ISV.config file, you can integrate custom Web pages into the Microsoft Dynamics CRM application. By editing the ISV.config file in conjunction with the site map functionality you learned about in Chapter 6, "Entity Customization: Relationships, Custom Entities, and Site Map," you can create a highly customized application navigation for your Microsoft Dynamics CRM users. Some of the functionality available in the Microsoft Dynamics CRM ISV.config file includes the ability to add buttons and action menu links to the grid toolbar, JavaScript code support for menus and buttons, and access to the parent window. Microsoft Dynamics CRM includes a default ISV.config, but the ISV features are disabled by default.

> **More Info** You can get more information about the ISV.config XML reference in the SDK.

Integration Areas

Figure 10-8 shows the areas in the main application window that you can customize with the ISV.config file. As you can see in this figure, we added some sample buttons and menu items to illustrate how the ISV.config customizations will appear in the user interface. You can add custom buttons or menu items to the following areas of the application navigation:

1. Application menu toolbar

2. Application toolbar

3. Grid toolbar

4. Grid actions menu

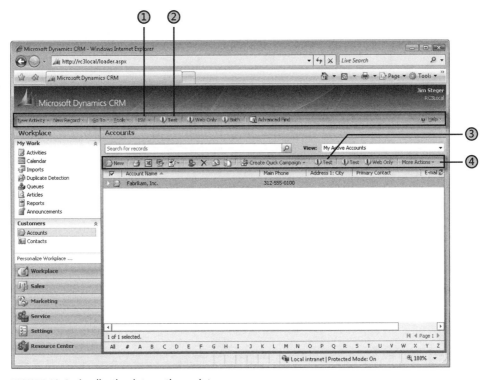

FIGURE 10-8 Application integration points

In addition to the application navigation, you can also customize the entity form. Figure 10-9 displays the integration areas that the ISV.config offers in an entity form window. You can add customizations to the following:

1. Form toolbar buttons

2. Form toolbar menu

3. Navigation pane

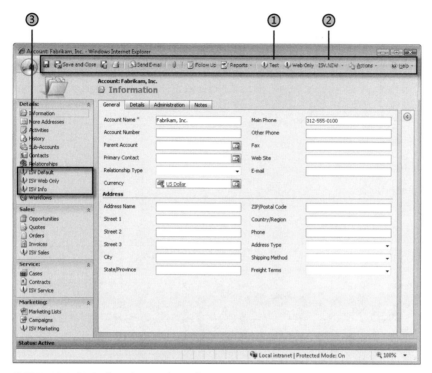

FIGURE 10-9 Entity form integration points

Note You can't customize the *application* navigation pane by using the ISV.config file, but you can customize the *entity* navigation pane. Chapter 6 explains how to customize the application navigation pane by using the site map.

The following code shows a partial sample from the ISV.config file that ships with Microsoft Dynamics CRM. We discuss the meaning of the elements available in this file next.

```
<IsvConfig>
 <configuration version="3.0.0000.0">
  <Root>
   <MenuBar>
    <CustomMenus>
     <Menu>
      <Titles>
       <Title LCID="1033" Text="ISV" />
      </Titles>
      <MenuItem Url="http://www.microsoft.com">
       <Titles>
        <Title LCID="1033" Text="New Window" />
```

```
                </Titles>
              </MenuItem>
              <MenuSpacer />
            </Menu>
          </CustomMenus>
        </MenuBar>
      </Root>
      <Entities>
        <Entity name="account">
          <NavBar>
            <NavBarItem Icon="/_imgs/ico_18_debug.gif"
    Url="http://www.microsoft.com" Id="navItem">
              <Titles>
                <Title LCID="1033" Text="ISV Default" />
              </Titles>
            </NavBarItem>
          </NavBar>
        </Entity>
      </Entities>
    </configuration>
  </IsvConfig>
```

Tip Don't be confused by the ISV.config version number of 3.0.0000.0. That is the correct version even though it refers to Microsoft Dynamics CRM 4.0.

Nav Bar Areas

Four named areas (Details, Sales, Service, and Marketing) exist with Microsoft Dynamics CRM form navigation. You cannot add additional form navigation areas. However, by using the <NavBarAreas> element, you can change the labels for these areas to something more meaningful for your business. Unfortunately, this change is global across all entity forms. Therefore, the display label used should be sufficiently general to apply to the other forms in the applications.

```
<NavBarAreas>
  <NavBarArea Id="Sales">
    <Titles>
      <Title LCID="1033" Text="New Sales Label" />
      <Title LCID="1031" Text="Deush Sales Label" />
    </Titles>
  </NavBarArea>
  <NavBarArea Id="Service">
    <Titles>
      <Title LCID="1033" Text="New Service Label" />
    </Titles>
  </NavBarArea>
</NavBarAreas>
```

Figure 10-10 shows the preceding customizations on an English language form of Microsoft Dynamics CRM. Notice that the Sales and Service areas are now labeled as New Sales Label and New Service Label, respectively.

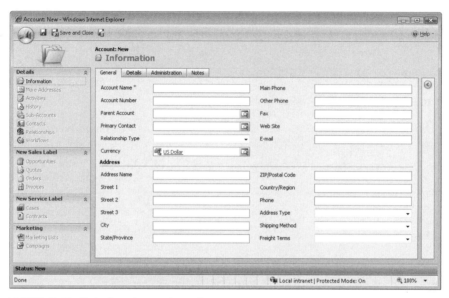

FIGURE 10-10   Entity form integration points

The *Id* attribute of the *<NavBarArea>* elements defines which area to customize. Valid values for the *Id* attribute are *Details*, *Sales, Service*, and *Marketing*.

As you know, Microsoft Dynamics CRM supports multiple languages in a single organization. Therefore, defining a new label for the *NavBarArea* requires the use of the *<Titles>* element. The *<Title>* element contains the language code (*LCID* attribute) and display text (*Text* attribute) for each language you have installed. The *<Titles>* element will contain one or more child *<Title>* elements. The *<Titles>* element is a child of any ISV.config element in the application that displays text to the user.

Some final notes about the *<NavBarArea>* and *<Title>* elements:

- Changes will apply globally to all entity forms. Be sure to consider this before making a change.

- You can add language translations to the ISV.config file even if the language pack is not yet installed on the Microsoft Dynamics CRM server. After the language pack is installed and the user configures the preferred language, the translated label will then be displayed properly.

- Changes appear to the users immediately after importing; you don't have to publish the ISV.config file. However, you will probably need to refresh your Web browser to see the changes.

Menu Bar

By editing the ISV.config file you can add menu links to the main application, the entity form, and a grid's Actions menu. If you add a *<MenuBar>* node beneath the *<Root>* node, you can add custom menus to the application. To create a custom menu on the entity's form, you need to place a *<MenuBar>* directly beneath the *<Entity>* node.

The *<MenuBar>* node requires a *<CustomMenu>* node. The *<CustomMenu>* node can contain one or more *<MenuItem>* nodes that have the attributes listed in Table 10-10 to further define your custom menu links.

TABLE 10-10 *<MenuItem>* **Attributes**

Attribute	Description
AccessKey	Specifies a keyboard shortcut. When a single character is specified, the user would be able to access the menu item by using ALT+*<key>*.
AvailableOffline	Defines whether the link should appear in the Outlook client if the client is offline. Valid options are *True* and *False*.
Client	Defines which client applications the link should appear in. Valid options are *Web* and *Outlook*. If you leave this blank or ignore the node, the menu item will display in both client applications.
JavaScript	If populated, Microsoft Dynamics CRM will execute the JavaScript. If populated, the *Url* attribute will be ignored.
PassParams	If set to 1, Microsoft Dynamics CRM will pass information about the record, organization name, and language context to the new window. Valid options are 0 (don't pass parameters) and 1 (pass parameters).
Url	Microsoft Dynamics CRM will open a window to the path specified in this attribute. If the *JavaScript* attribute is populated, the *Url* attribute will be ignored.
ValidForCreate	Displays menu item when the entity form is in create mode. Valid options are 0 (don't display) and 1 (display).
ValidForUpdate	Displays menu item when the entity form is in update mode. Valid options are 0 (don't display) and 1 (display).
WinMode	Determines the type of window to open. Valid options are ■ 0 (normal window) ■ 1 (modal dialog box) ■ 2 (modeless dialog box)
WinParams	Defines additional JavaScript *window.open* options (see Table 10-12 and Table 10-13). The parameters are dependent on the *WinMode* value.

The following code example shows how to add a custom menu that is displayed in the main application window.

```
<IsvConfig>
  <configuration version="3.0.0000.0">
    <Root>
      <MenuBar>
        <CustomMenus>
          <Menu>
            <Titles>
              <Title LCID="1033" Text="Sonoma Partners" />
            </Titles>
            <MenuItem Url="http://www.microsoft.com">
              <Titles>
                <Title LCID="1033" Text="Custom Menu Item" />
              </Titles>
            </MenuItem>
            <MenuSpacer />
          </Menu>
        </CustomMenus>
      </MenuBar>
    </Root>
  </configuration>
</IsvConfig>
```

Figure 10-11 displays the result of this configuration.

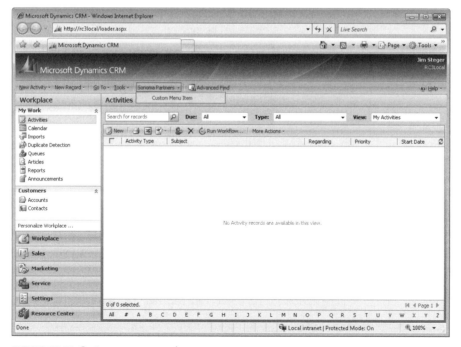

FIGURE 10-11 Custom menu example

Likewise, you could add a custom menu to an entity menu bar (instead of the application menu bar) by adding code such as the following under the *<Entity>* node.

```xml
<Entities>
 <Entity name="account">
  <MenuBar>
     <CustomMenus>
        <Menu>
          <Titles>
            <Title LCID="1033" Text="ISV.NEW" />
          </Titles>
          <MenuItem Url="http://www.microsoft.com" PassParams="0" WinMode="1">
            <Titles>
               <Title LCID="1033" Text="Coming Soon..." />
            </Titles>
          </MenuItem>
        </Menu>
     </CustomMenus>
  </MenuBar>
 </Entity>
</Entities>
```

Navigation Pane

You can also use the ISV.config file to add links in the entity navigation pane. The *<NavBar>* node of the ISV.config file controls the entity navigation pane, which resides under the *<Entities>* and *<Entity>* nodes. Table 10-11 describes the *<NavBarItem>* attributes available to you.

Note Remember that to add links to the application's navigation pane, you have to use the site map.

TABLE 10-11 *<NavBarItem>* **Attributes**

Attribute	Description
Area	Defines the navigation area where the link will appear. Valid options are Sales, Marketing, Service, and Info. Note that Info corresponds to the Details area.
AvailableOffline	Defines whether the link should appear in the Outlook client if the client is offline. Valid options are *True* and *False*.
Client	Defines which client applications the link should appear in. Valid options are *Web* and *Outlook*. If you leave this blank or ignore the node, the menu item will be displayed in both client applications.
Id	Defines the HTML ID of the link. This string value must be unique and is required.

TABLE 10-11 *<NavBarItem>* **Attributes**

Attribute	Description
Icon	Defines a path to an image file. Image size should be 16 x 16. This value is required.
PassParams	If set to 1, Microsoft Dynamics CRM will pass the organization name, organization language code, and the user's language code. Valid options are 0 (don't pass parameters) and 1 (pass parameters). Note that the entity id, and entity name will be included by default.
Url	Microsoft Dynamics CRM will open a window to the path specified in this attribute. This parameter is required.

Toolbar

The *<ToolBar>* node contains the *<Button>* and *<ToolBarSpacer />* nodes. These buttons are available from the main application toolbar as well as from an entity form's toolbar. Here's an example of a *<ToolBar>* node.

```
<ToolBar ValidForCreate="0" ValidForUpdate="1">
  <Button Icon="/_imgs/ico_18_debug.gif" Url="http://www.microsoft.com"
PassParams="1" WinParams="" WinMode="1">
    <Titles>
      <Title LCID="1033" Text="Test" />
    </Titles>
    <ToolTips>
      <ToolTip LCID="1033" Text="Info on Test" />
    </ToolTips>
  </Button>
</ToolBar>
```

The *<ToolBar>* node also contains the *ValidForCreate* and *ValidForUpdate* attributes. Just as with menu items, you can apply these attributes selectively at the button level. The *<Button>* element contains the same attributes as *<MenuItem>*, plus the *Icon* and *WinParams* attributes. The *Icon* attribute defines an image that will appear with the button. This image size should be 16 by 16 pixels. By using the *WinParams* attribute, you can define additional JavaScript *window.open* options (see Table 10-12 and Table 10-13); it's dependent on the *WinMode* selected. You add options and their values in a comma-separated string, such as the following.

```
WinParams="height=350,width=600,toolbars=0,menubar=0,location=0"
```

As with the menu items, a separate *<Titles>* element exists for the display text and language information. However, unlike the menu, a *<ToolTips>* element also exists to provide language-specific tooltip information. A tooltip defines what is displayed to the user when the user rests the mouse on the button.

> **Note** You have to specify parameters only if you want to specify values different from the Microsoft Dynamics CRM default settings.

TABLE 10-12 *WinMode = 0* Parameters

Parameter	Valid options	Description
Height	Number in pixels	Determines the height of the window
Left	Number in pixels	Determines the horizontal placement of the window relative to the upper-left corner of the screen
Location	Yes or no 1 or 0 Default: yes	Displays the Internet Explorer address bar in the browser window
Menubar	Yes or no 1 or 0 Default: yes	Displays the Internet Explorer topmost menu bar in the browser window
Resizable	Yes or no 1 or 0 Default: yes	Allows the window to be resized and will display the corner handles at the bottom of the window
Scrollbars	Yes or no 1 or 0 Default: yes	Allows for the vertical and horizontal scroll-bars to appear
Status	Yes or no 1 or 0	Displays the status bar at the bottom of the browser window
Toolbar	Yes or no 1 or 0	Displays the Internet Explorer toolbar in the browser window
Top	Number in pixels	Determines the vertical placement of the window relative to the upper-left corner of the screen
Width	Number in pixels	Determines the width of the window

TABLE 10-13 *WinMode = 1 or 2* Parameters

Parameter	Valid options	Description
dialogHeight	Number in pixels	Determines the height of the window
dialogLeft	Number in pixels	Determines the horizontal placement of the window relative to the upper-left corner of the screen
Center	Yes or no 1 or 0 Default: yes	Determines whether the window should open in the center of the screen

TABLE 10-13 *WinMode = 1 or 2* **Parameters**

Parameter	Valid options	Description
Edge	Sunken or raised Default: raised	Determines the type of window edge style to use
Help	Yes or no 1 or 0 Default: yes	Determines whether the *Help* icon should appear
Resizable	Yes or no 1 or 0 Default: yes	Allows the window to be resized and will display the corner handles at the bottom of the window
Scroll	Yes or no 1 or 0 Default: yes	Allows for the vertical and horizontal scroll-bars to appear
Status	Yes or no 1 or 0	Displays the status bar at the bottom of the browser window
Toolbar	Yes or no 1 or 0	Displays the Internet Explorer toolbar in the browser window
dialogTop	Number in pixels	Determines the vertical placement of the window relative to the upper-left corner of the screen
dialogWidth	Number in pixels	Determines the width of the window

Grid Toolbar

You can also use the ISV.config to add links to the Actions menu and add buttons to the grid toolbar. The grid configuration merges both the *<MenuBar>* and *<Button>* elements, so we won't repeat all the available attributes. You customize the grid toolbar by adding a *<Grid>* to an *<Entity>* node, as shown here.

```
<Grid>
  <MenuBar>
    <ActionsMenu>
      <MenuItem Url="http://www.microsoft.com" WinMode="1">
        <Titles>
          <Title LCID="1033" Text="Coming Soon..." />
        </Titles>
      </MenuItem>
    </ActionsMenu>
    <Buttons>
      <Button Icon="/_imgs/ico_18_debug.gif" Url="http://www.microsoft.com"
WinParams="" WinMode="2">
        <Titles>
          <Title LCID="1033" Text="Test" />
        </Titles>
        <ToolTips>
          <ToolTip LCID="1033" Text="Info on Test" />
```

```
        </ToolTips>
      </Button>
    </Buttons>
  </MenuBar>
</Grid>
```

For custom Web pages accessed from a grid toolbar button or menu, you can programmatically access the selected records in the grid by using the *windows.dialogArguments* method. For example, the following Web page will display to the user the GUIDs of the selected records in a grid when accessed from the *<Grid>* node of an entity.

```
<!DOCTYPE HTML PUBLIC "-//W3C//DTD HTML 4.0 Transitional//EN">
<html>
<head>
<title>Custom Grid Page</title>
<script language="javascript">
function window.onload()
{
  if(window.dialogArguments != null)
  {
    var arr = new Array(window.dialogArguments.length -1);
    arr = window.dialogArguments;

    for(i=0; i< arr.length; i++)
    {
      alert(arr[i]);
    }
  }
  else
  {
    alert("No records were selected");
  }
}
</script>
</head>
<body>
</body>
</html>
```

Deploying

To deploy your ISV.config customizations, you need to import the ISV.config file by using the Web client interface in the Customization area under Import Customizations. Again, always make a backup copy of the file prior to altering it, in case you need to roll back your changes. You can also import and publish the ISV.config file programmatically using the Microsoft Dynamics CRM API.

> **Tip** Back up the default ISV.config file before you make your first set of changes. The default ISV.config file included with the Microsoft Dynamics CRM installation contains examples of how to use the various nodes. Of course, you can retrieve all the information that you need from the SDK, but sometimes it is useful to review a sample when adding new and unfamiliar nodes.

Enabling the ISV.config

After you update and import the ISV.config file to Microsoft Dynamics CRM, you still need to enable it in the Microsoft Dynamics CRM settings. To enable your ISV.config customizations, navigate to Settings, then Administration, and finally System Settings. Click the Customization tab (see Figure 10-12), and then click the ellipsis (...) button in the Custom menus and toolbars section.

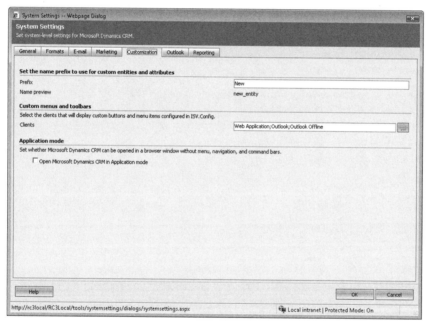

FIGURE 10-12 Displaying the ISV Extensions in the user interface

In the Custom menus and toolbars section, you can choose from one or more of the following possible values:

- **Outlook** Enable customizations for both versions of the Microsoft Dynamics CRM for Outlook client, but not the Web client.

- **Outlook Offline** Enable customizations for Microsoft Dynamics CRM for Outlook with Offlince Access when in offline mode.

- **Web Application** Enable customizations for the Web client only.

After you configure the ISV menus and toolbars for the application, you must also make sure that you enable the ISV Extensions privilege for the user's security role so that the user can see the extensions, as shown in Figure 10-13. The ISV Extensions privilege is listed in the Customizations tab as a miscellaneous privilege.

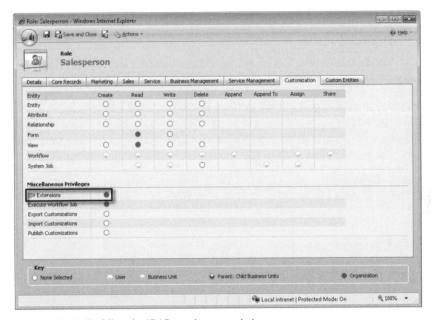

FIGURE 10-13   Enabling the ISV Extensions permission

> **Caution**   If you configure your extensions for Microsoft Dynamics CRM for Outlook with Offline Access, make sure that your users can access those links when they're offline.

Microsoft Dynamics CRM Client-Side Scripting Tips

In this section, we review some useful tips we've discovered when working with client-side scripts. These topics include the following:

- Development environment
- Scripting languages
- Testing and debugging
- Additional resources

Development Environment

We recommend that you create your scripts in an external editor instead of attempting to write code directly in the Microsoft Dynamics CRM Event Detail Properties dialog box. Common script editor choices are Microsoft Visual Studio 2008, Microsoft Office FrontPage, and Notepad. We recommend that you write your scripts in an external editor for the following reasons:

- The Tab key do not function as expected in the Microsoft Dynamics CRM text area. This makes it extremely difficult to write well-formatted and easy-to-read code.

- External editors provide a myriad of tools to assist in development (such as Microsoft IntelliSense, syntax highlighting, and integrated debugging). The Microsoft Dynamics CRM form is simply an HTML form text area that doesn't provide any of these development features.

- With an external editor, you can use a version control program (such as Microsoft Visual SourceSafe) to archive and back up your scripts.

Scripting Languages

Microsoft Dynamics CRM renders event scripts on the client side of the browser, so you must use a scripting language compatible with Internet Explorer (such as Microsoft JScript or JavaScript). Therefore, you can use the scripting language that you're most comfortable with or that your business logic requires.

Testing and Debugging

Any developer who has received an emergency call on the weekend about a coding or system problem knows the importance of thoroughly testing code! Because Microsoft Dynamics CRM does not validate any script code, you are responsible for ensuring that your scripts will work with Microsoft Dynamics CRM.

Debugging JavaScript

Even though Microsoft Dynamics CRM supports different scripting languages, we use JavaScript for most of our client extensions. The most efficient way to debug your JavaScript code in Microsoft Dynamics CRM is to use the JavaScript *debugger;* statement. Here is how you can use this useful statement in conjunction with Internet Explorer to achieve an integrated script debugging experience.

First, you need to configure Internet Explorer to allow for script debugging.

Configuring Internet Explorer

1. Open Internet Explorer, click Tools, and then Internet Options.

2. In the Advanced tab, clear the Disable script debugging (Internet Explorer) option.

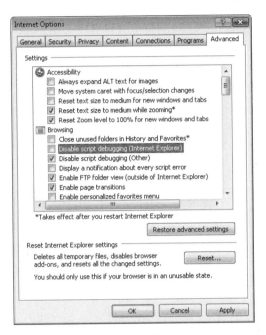

Now you just need to add the *debugger;* command in the JavaScript code and refresh the page in the browser to start the debugging process.

Here is a quick example of how this works. Add the simple JavaScript e-mail validation code shown in Listing 10-2 to the *onChange* event of an account's e-mail address. Notice that we added a *debugger;* statement in the first line.

Listing 10-2 JavaScript Debugging Example

```
debugger;
var oEmailAddress1 = document.crmForm.all.emailaddress1;
var sCleanedEmailAddress = oEmailAddress1.DataValue.replace(/[^0-9,A-Z,a-z,\@,\.]/g, "");
var regexEmail = /^.+@.+\..{2,3}$/;

// Test the cleaned e-mail string against the e-mail regular expression
if ( (regexEmail.test(sCleanedEmailAddress)) )
{
 oEmailAddress1.DataValue = sCleanedEmailAddress;
}
else
{
 alert("The E-mail Address appears to be invalid. Please correct.");
}
```

Preview the account form and enter an e-mail address in the E-mail field, as shown in Figure 10-14.

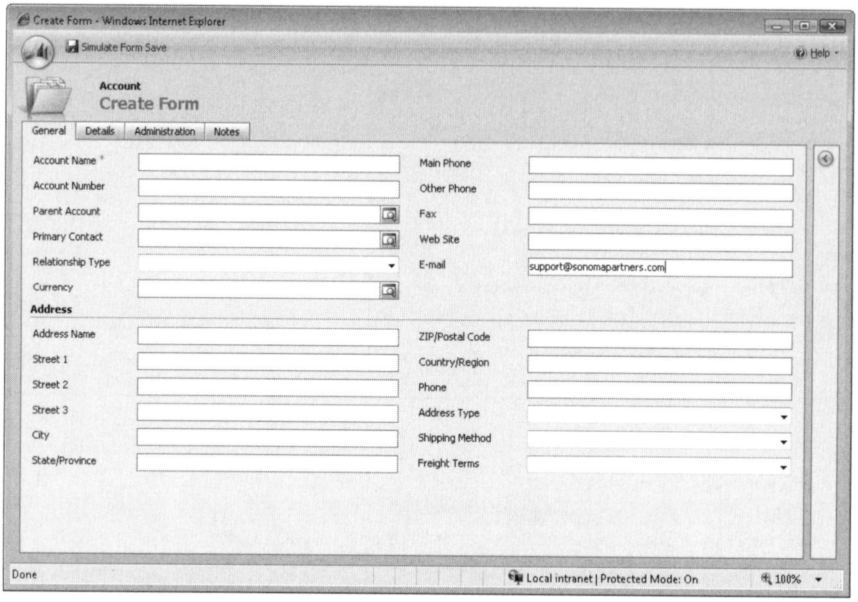

FIGURE 10-14 Entering an e-mail address to test JavaScript debugging

After you leave the field, the *onChange* code will execute and your debugger statement will display the Visual Studio dialog box shown in Figure 10-15.

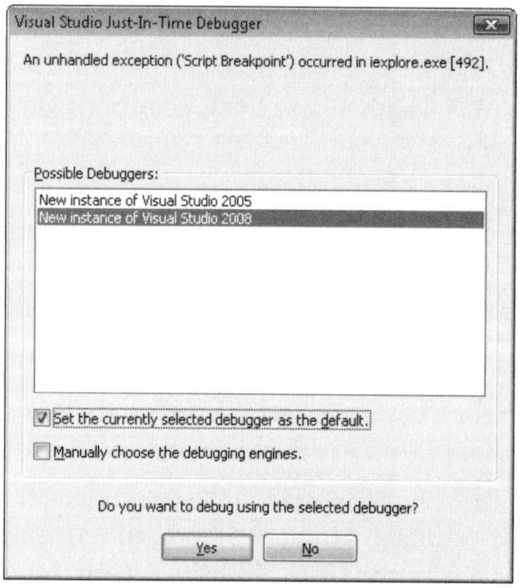

FIGURE 10-15 JavaScript debugging dialog box

You can start a new instance of Visual Studio 2008, and then you can perform real-time debugging of the JavaScript code, as shown in Figure 10-16.

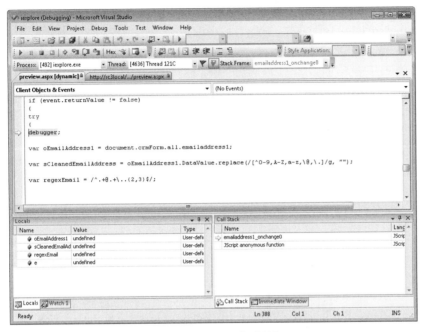

FIGURE 10-16 Debugging JavaScript in Visual Studio 2008

Additional Testing and Debugging Tips

We recommend the following additional testing and debugging techniques when developing your custom scripts:

- Always test your scripts in a development Microsoft Dynamics CRM environment and not on production servers.

- When possible, set up a simple Web page with a test form, and test your JavaScript outside of Microsoft Dynamics CRM. This will provide for faster development and debugging. Then, copy and paste the final code into the appropriate Microsoft Dynamics CRM event.

- Use the *Preview* command to test your client-side scripts before publishing.

- If it appears that your code doesn't work as expected, first ensure that you enabled your event. You should then use the JavaScript integrated debugging technique mentioned earlier. If you have trouble getting the integrated debugging working, you can use the *alert()* method to output various logic points, and try to eliminate the interaction with Microsoft Dynamics CRM first. In many cases, the flaw may be contained in the code logic itself, independent of the integrated properties of Microsoft Dynamics CRM.

- Add an external script reference. You can inject a reference to an external script file from the form's *onLoad()* event (refer to the examples later in this chapter for syntax). By doing this, you can update the JavaScript directly and test against the actual Microsoft Dynamics CRM form on a development server, instead of constantly opening the preview form. We recommend referencing an external script only during the development phase of your project; don't do this in production environments because Microsoft does not support this technique.

- When making updates to your script and reviewing them in a preview form, you must close and open a new preview form with each script change. Microsoft Dynamics CRM caches the form, so simply refreshing your existing preview form will not show your changes.

- Always export a backup copy of the entity that you are updating so that you can roll back if your updates cause an irreversible error.

- Be sure to keep backups of your scripts and store them with in a source control system.

- Disable the Microsoft Dynamics CRM Error Notification feature. You can update this by clicking the Tools menu, clicking Options, and in the Privacy tab, selecting Never send an error report to Microsoft about Microsoft Dynamics CRM.

> **Tip** If you are new to scripting languages, you should be aware that both JavaScript and JScript are case-sensitive. So, *<field>.SetFocus()* will properly move the mouse cursor to the field, whereas *<field>.setfocus()* will do nothing!

Additional Resources

The following list provides some additional information regarding the topics discussed in this section:

- **Microsoft Dynamics CRM SDK** Available with Microsoft Dynamics CRM and includes detailed information regarding the client-side integration options, as well as additional coding examples *http://www.microsoft.com/downloads/details. aspx?FamilyID=82e632a7-faf9-41e0-8ec1-a2662aae9dfb&DisplayLang=en*

- **DHTML overview** *http://msdn2.microsoft.com/en-us/library/ms533045.aspx*

- **DHTML object reference** *http://msdn2.microsoft.com/en-us/library/ms533054.aspx*

- **JScript User's Guide** *http://msdn2.microsoft.com/en-us/library/4yyeyb0a.aspx*

- **Regular expressions** *http://msdn2.microsoft.com/en-us/library/28hw3sce.aspx*

- **Debugger** *http://msdn2.microsoft.com/en-us/library/0bwt76sk(vs.85).aspx*

Developing for Microsoft Dynamics CRN

Given that Microsoft Dynamics CRM Live currently does not a
assemblies, you will probably rely heavily on the client-side se
customized business logic. Here, we review the following top
for Microsoft Dynamics CRM Live:

- Client-side script
- Custom Web pages
- Accessing the Microsoft Dynamics CRM Web service with client-side script
- Using Fiddler to capture Microsoft Dynamics CRM SOAP XML
- Sending a request and handling the result

 Important The functionality of Microsoft Dynamics CRM Live may and probably will change in the future. If something is not available now, it doesn't mean it won't be available in the future. Be sure to check the Microsoft Dynamics CRM Live Web site for the most up-to-date information regarding Microsoft Dynamics CRM Live restrictions and programming options.

Client-Side Script

JavaScript code will execute in a Microsoft Dynamics CRM Live environment. Performing simple validation, updating fields, and so forth are commonly used and supported tasks. Client-side scripting is your primary tool for programmatically extending and enhancing Microsoft Dynamics CRM Live.

Avoid or use care when attempting to use your own external JavaScript references. For one, you will have to be sure to host them somewhere because you currently won't be able to host them on Microsoft Dynamics CRM Live. Also, the browser will load these separate JavaScript files asynchronously, so you need to ensure that no logic is dependent on the file until you are confident the file is completely loaded.

Custom Web Pages

Microsoft Dynamics CRM Live does not currently host custom Web pages. As such, if you wish to include a custom IFrame or Web page, you must find an alternate method for hosting. Consider the following when using this externally hosted page approach:

- Cross-site scripting will not be available to you. Therefore, any data manipulation or business functionality must use the Microsoft Dynamics CRM Live Web service application programming interface (API).

will be responsible for authentication of the custom pages and any communication back to the Microsoft Dynamics CRM Live Web service API.

- If the information provided by your custom pages is business critical, be sure to host the pages at a reliable hosting company.

Accessing the Microsoft Dynamics CRM Web Service with Client-Side Script

Fortunately in Microsoft Dynamics CRM Live, you can use JavaScript to execute Web service methods. By using this handy technique, you can perform rather complex logic in JavaScript. For example, Listing 10-3 shows the SOAP XML used for a simple retrieve of an existing contact record.

Listing 10-3 SOAP XML Request for Microsoft Dynamics CRM Contact Retrieve

```
<?xml version="1.0" encoding="utf-8"?>
<soap:Envelope xmlns:soap="http://schemas.xmlsoap.org/soap/envelope/"
xmlns:xsi="http://www.w3.org/2001/XMLSchema-instance"
xmlns:xsd="http://www.w3.org/2001/XMLSchema">
  <soap:Header>
    <CrmAuthenticationToken xmlns="http://schemas.microsoft.com/crm/2007/WebServices">
      <AuthenticationType
xmlns="http://schemas.microsoft.com/crm/2007/CoreTypes">0</AuthenticationType>
      <OrganizationName
xmlns="http://schemas.microsoft.com/crm/2007/CoreTypes">Prod72840rg01</OrganizationName>
      <CallerId xmlns="http://schemas.microsoft.com/crm/2007/CoreTypes">00000000-0000-0000-
0000-000000000000</CallerId>
    </CrmAuthenticationToken>
  </soap:Header>
  <soap:Body>
    <Retrieve xmlns="http://schemas.microsoft.com/crm/2007/WebServices">
      <entityName>contact</entityName>
      <id>b07be4aa-f87b-dc11-8276-0003ff8a2b47</id>
      <columnSet xmlns:q1="http://schemas.microsoft.com/crm/2006/Query"
xsi:type="q1:ColumnSet">
        <q1:Attributes>
          <q1:Attribute>fullname</q1:Attribute>
        </q1:Attributes>
      </columnSet>
    </Retrieve>
  </soap:Body>
</soap:Envelope>
```

Using Fiddler to Capture Microsoft Dynamics CRM SOAP XML

Using SOAP directly with JavaScript can be pretty handy, especially in the Microsoft Dynamics CRM Live environment. You might be asking yourself how you find the SOAP XML for the various Web service calls you wish to make.

To accomplish this, we recommend using a program called Fiddler to capture the requests Microsoft Dynamics CRM makes, and then use the information you captured to construct your own SOAP XML. Fiddler is a free tool that will log all HTTP traffic between your computer and the rest of the network (including the Internet).

We walk you through a brief example on how to use Fiddler in conjunction with a custom console application to find the SOAP XML used by Microsoft Dynamics CRM quickly. You will do the following:

- Download and install Fiddler.
- Create a simple console application.
- Review the HTTP traffic captures from Fiddler.

The first step is to download and install Fiddler. The program is very small and should take you only a few minutes to download and install.

Download and install Fiddler

1. Download the latest version of the Fiddler tool at *http://www.fiddlertool.com*.

2. Install Fiddler on your workstation computer.

Next, you will create an application to test various Microsoft Dynamics CRM API method calls to capture the resulting request/response SOAP envelopes passed from the browser to the Microsoft Dynamics CRM Web server.

Create a simple console application

1. Start Visual Studio 2008.

2. Create a new console application in Microsoft Visual C# and name it **CrmHttpTester** and target .NET Framework 3.0.

3. Add a new Web reference to the Microsoft Dynamics CRM CrmService API and call it **CrmSdk**.

4. Replace the contents of the default Program.cs file with the code listed in Listing 10-4.

5. Build the console application and ensure that there are no errors.

The following code simply retrieves the full name of an existing contact record. Be sure to put a valid contact ID and organization name.

Listing 10-4 Retrieve Contact Example

```
using System;
using System.Collections.Generic;
using System.Text;
using System.Net;
using CrmHttpTester.CrmSdk;

namespace CrmHttpTester
{
  class Program
  {
    static void Main(string[] args)
    {
      Guid contactId = new Guid("B07BE4AA-F87B-DC11-8276-0003FF8A2B47");
      RetriveContact(contactId);
    }
    public static void RetriveContact(Guid contactId)
    {
      CrmAuthenticationToken token = new CrmAuthenticationToken();
      token.AuthenticationType = 0;
      token.OrganizationName = "<organization name>";
      CrmService service = new CrmService();
      service.Credentials = CredentialCache.DefaultCredentials;
      service.CrmAuthenticationTokenValue = token;

      ColumnSet cols = new ColumnSet();
      cols.Attributes = new string[] { "fullname" };
      contact oContact = new contact();
      oContact = (contact) service.Retrieve("contact", contactId, cols);

      Console.WriteLine(oContact.fullname.ToString());
      Console.ReadLine();
    }
  }
}
```

Review the HTTP traffic captures from Fiddler

1. Open the Fiddler application.

2. Go back to Visual Studio 2008 and run your console application.

3. After the application finishes running, return to Fiddler.

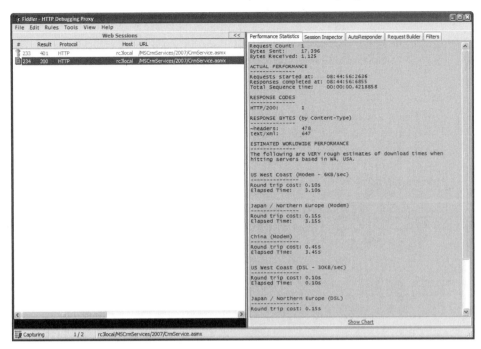

4. Click the second HTTP capture to your CRM server that has a result of 200. The two panes on the right will have all the information you need to construct a valid SOAP request and response for Microsoft Dynamics CRM. The top pane shows information regarding the request, and the bottom pane displays information about the response.

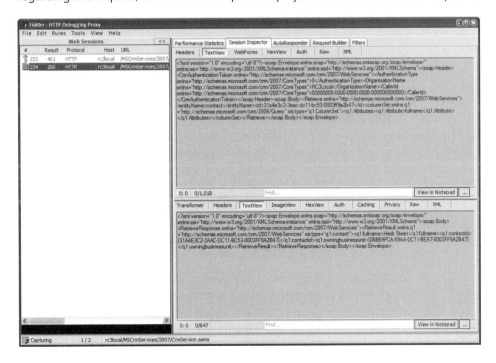

Note You can ignore the first request with a 401 result caused by Internet Explorer first making the request to the server without any credentials, which fails. The request is then automatically tried again with credentials. The second request properly authenticates and returns an approved result of 200, and it is this approved request that you should examine.

In the request results pane, start by clicking the Session Inspector tab and reviewing the Headers section. Figure 10-17 shows the SOAP action you will need when constructing your request in JavaScript.

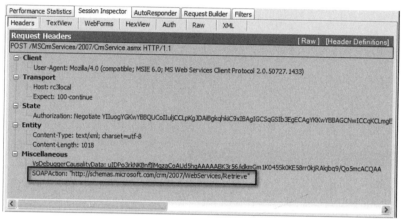

FIGURE 10-17 Finding the SOAP action from Fiddler

Next, click the TextView section in both the request and response panes. This will show you the SOAP XML the browser passed to the Web server. In this example, the request is the same as previously shown in Listing 10-3.

Listing 10-5 displays the response returned. You can see that the *<q1:fullname>* node contains the full name of the contact.

Note Although you asked only for the full name in the query, the ID and business unit ID were also returned. These two values will always be returned, even if you don't explicitly request them.

Listing 10-5 SOAP XML Response for Microsoft Dynamics CRM Contact Retrieve Example

```
<?xml version="1.0" encoding="utf-8"?>
<soap:Envelope xmlns:soap="http://schemas.xmlsoap.org/soap/envelope/"
xmlns:xsi="http://www.w3.org/2001/XMLSchema-instance"
xmlns:xsd="http://www.w3.org/2001/XMLSchema">
  <soap:Body>
    <RetrieveResponse xmlns="http://schemas.microsoft.com/crm/2007/WebServices">
      <RetrieveResult xmlns:q1="http://schemas.microsoft.com/crm/2007/WebServices"
xsi:type="q1:contact">
        <q1:fullname>Test Test</q1:fullname>
        <q1:contactid>{B07BE4AA-F87B-DC11-8276-0003FF8A2B47}</q1:contactid>
```

```
        <q1:owningbusinessunit>{86288A0C-367B-DC11-9029-
0003FF8A2B47}</q1:owningbusinessunit>
      </RetrieveResult>
    </RetrieveResponse>
  </soap:Body>
</soap:Envelope>
```

Sending a Request and Handling the Result

After a little practice, you should feel comfortable using Fiddler to assist you in constructing the various SOAP requests to send to Microsoft Dynamics CRM. In addition, you can also use Fiddler to understand the response Microsoft Dynamics CRM sends back.

Listing 10-6 shows an example of how to use the SOAP XML in JavaScript.

Listing 10-6 Using SOAP XML in JavaScript

```
var serverUrl = "/mscrmservices/2007/crmservice.asmx";
var xmlhttp = new ActiveXObject("Microsoft.XMLHTTP");
xmlhttp.open("POST", serverUrl, false);
xmlhttp.setRequestHeader("Content-Type", "text/xml; charset=utf-8")
xmlhttp.setRequestHeader("SOAPAction",
"http://schemas.microsoft.com/crm/2007/WebServices/Retrieve")

var message =
[
  "<?xml version='1.0' encoding='utf-8'?>",
  "<soap:Envelope xmlns:soap='http://schemas.xmlsoap.org/soap/envelope/'
xmlns:xsi='http://www.w3.org/2001/XMLSchema-instance'
xmlns:xsd='http://www.w3.org/2001/XMLSchema'>",
  "  <soap:Header>",
  "    <CrmAuthenticationToken
xmlns='http://schemas.microsoft.com/crm/2007/WebServices'>",
  "      <AuthenticationType
xmlns='http://schemas.microsoft.com/crm/2007/CoreTypes'>0</AuthenticationType>",
  "      <OrganizationName
xmlns='http://schemas.microsoft.com/crm/2007/CoreTypes'>Prod7284Org01</OrganizationName>
",
  "      <CallerId xmlns='http://schemas.microsoft.com/crm/2007/CoreTypes'>00000000-0000-
0000-0000-000000000000</CallerId>",
  "    </CrmAuthenticationToken>",
  "  </soap:Header>",
  "  <soap:Body>",
  "    <Retrieve xmlns='http://schemas.microsoft.com/crm/2007/WebServices'>",
  "      <entityName>contact</entityName>",
  "      <id>b07be4aa-f87b-dc11-8276-0003ff8a2b47</id>",
  "      <columnSet xmlns:q1='http://schemas.microsoft.com/crm/2006/Query'
xsi:type='q1:ColumnSet'>",
  "        <q1:Attributes>",
  "          <q1:Attribute>fullname</q1:Attribute>",
  "        </q1:Attributes>",
  "      </columnSet>",
  "    </Retrieve>",
  "  </soap:Body>",
```

```
    "</soap:Envelope>"
].join("");

xmlhttp.send(message);
var result = xmlhttp.responseXML.xml;

var doc = new ActiveXObject("MSXML2.DOMDocument");
doc.async = false;
doc.loadXML(result);
var returnNode = doc.selectSingleNode(«//fullname»);
if( returnNode != null )
{
  alert( returnNode.text );
}
else
{
  return null;
}
```

Consider the following in the preceding code example:

- You are setting the request header's SOAPAction parameter with the SOAP action you saw in the Fiddler header section.

- You will need to authenticate to the Microsoft Dynamics CRM Web server. The actual SOAP XML for this is shown in this listing. You need to input the correct organization name for the *OrganizationValue* node. You should use the *GenerateAuthenticationHeader()* global method from Microsoft Dynamics CRM to simplify this (see Listing 10-7 for an example).

- You should replace the GUID listed in the *<id>* node with your GUID (or pass it in with a variable).

- For a slight performance improvement, you can join an array of strings to store the SOAP XML, as opposed to concatenating the strings.

- You are using XPATH in JavaScript to extract the result from the response XML returned. You could use alternative methods, but we find this a very simple way to retrieve your value.

Listing 10-7 shows how you can use the Microsoft Dynamics CRM global method *GenerateAuthenticationHeader()* to provide the proper authentication header for your SOAP calls. Using this method is a convenient way to provide authentication information, but it has to be executed in a Microsoft Dynamics CRM form.

Listing 10-7 Authenticating with *GenerateAuthenticationHeader()*

```
var message =
[
  "<?xml version='1.0' encoding='utf-8'?>",
  "<soap:Envelope xmlns:soap='http://schemas.xmlsoap.org/soap/envelope/'
xmlns:xsi='http://www.w3.org/2001/XMLSchema-instance'
```

```
    xmlns:xsd='http://www.w3.org/2001/XMLSchema'>",
     GenerateAuthenticationHeader(),
     "<soap:Body>",
     "<Retrieve xmlns='http://schemas.microsoft.com/crm/2007/WebServices'>",
     "<entityName>contact</entityName>",
     "<id>b07be4aa-f87b-dc11-8276-0003ff8a2b47</id>",
     "<columnSet xmlns:q1='http:/schemas.microsoft.com/crm/2006/Query'
    xsi:type='q1:ColumnSet'>",
     "<q1:Attributes>",
     "<q1:Attribute>fullname</q1:Attribute>",
     "</q1:Attributes>",
     "</columnSet>",
     "</Retrieve>",
     "</soap:Body>",
     "</soap:Envelope>"
    ].join("");
```

Client-Side Scripting Code Examples

Now that you understand the framework and the details of the Microsoft Dynamics CRM client-side SDK, we want to get into the fun of coding examples and real-world usage of these features. We have included a variety of script samples for reference and to provide a starting point for your own customization needs. The following examples are just a sampling of the many ways in which you can integrate custom logic by using the information in the client-side SDK:

- Formatting and translating U.S. phone numbers

- Custom interface for multiselect lists

- Accessing API commands through JavaScript

- Hiding tabs and fields

- Referencing external script files

- Dynamically changing picklist values

 Note Because of page length restrictions, we are displaying the code with limited comments and in some cases as partial listings. You can review the full code samples at the book's companion download site specified in the Introduction.

Formatting and Translating U.S. Phone Numbers

You can add the following script to the *onChange* event of any field used for a phone number. The script will automatically format any 7- or 10-digit number as 555-1212 or (312) 555-1212. In addition, it will translate a phone number entered as letters to its numeric equivalent; for example, if the user enters 866-555CODE, the script converts the letters in the phone number to (866) 555-2633.

Figure 10-18 shows an example phone number entered by a user.

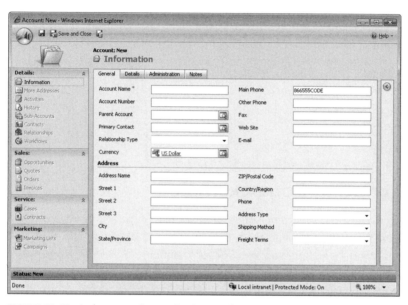

FIGURE 10-18   A phone number on the Contact form as entered by a user

Figure 10-19 shows how the script will translate the Business Phone entry as soon as the user changes focus from the phone number field.

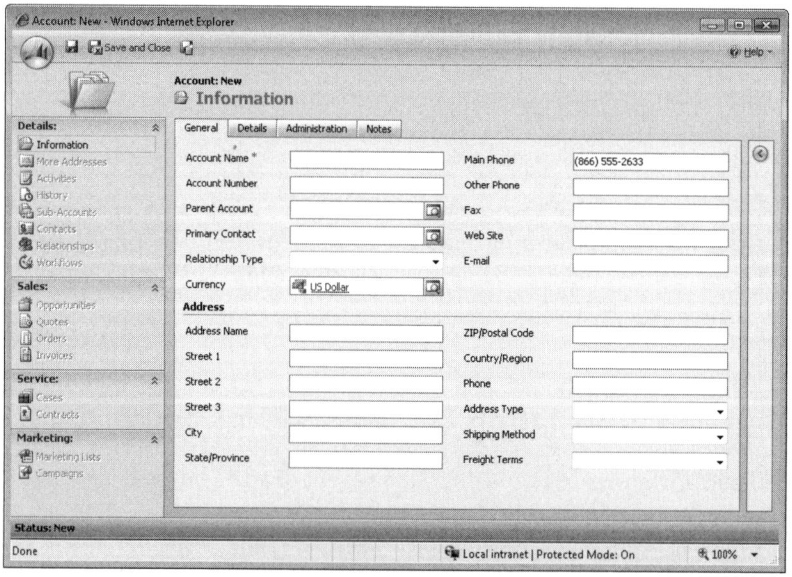

FIGURE 10-19   The translated and formatted phone number

The script fires as soon as the user enters a phone number and the cursor exits the field, which is referred to as *losing focus* or *changing focus*, either because the user clicks elsewhere on the form or presses the Tab key. When fired, the script first removes any special characters from the entered text. It then passes the first 10 characters of the modified text through a translation function that exchanges any letters for their equivalent phone digits. Finally, it takes that result, formats it, and assigns it back to the field. To account for the possibility of people entering extensions, the script outputs any characters after the 10th digit as they were entered. Listing 10-8 shows the phone number formatting script.

Listing 10-8 Formatting and Translating U.S. Phone Numbers

```
// Installation: Add this script to onChange event of any phone number field.
var oField = event.srcElement;

// Verify that the field is valid
if (typeof(oField) != "undefined" && oField != null)
{
  if (oField.DataValue != null)
  {
    // Remove any special characters
    var sTmp = oField.DataValue.replace(/[^0-9,A-Z,a-z]/g, "");

    // Translate any letters to the equivalent phone number, if method is included
    try
    {
      if (sTmp. Length <= 10)
      {
      sTmp = TranslateMask(sTmp);
      }
      else
      {
        sTmp = TranslateMask(sTmp.substr(0,10)) + sTmp.substr(10,sTmp.length);
      }
    }
    catch(e)
    {
    }

    // If the number is a length you expect and support,
    // format the translated number
    switch (sTmp.length)
    {
    case 1:
    case 2:
    case 3:
    case 4:
    case 5:
    case 6:
    case 8:
    case 9:
      break;
    case 7:
      oField.DataValue = sTmp.substr(0, 3) + "-" + sTmp.substr(3, 4);
      break;
    case 10:
```

```
        oField.DataValue = "(" + sTmp.substr(0, 3) + ") " + sTmp.substr(3, 3) + "-" +
sTmp.substr(6, 4);
        break;
    default:
        oField.DataValue = "(" + sTmp.substr(0, 3) + ") " + sTmp.substr(3, 3) + "-" +
sTmp.substr(6, 4) + " " + sTmp.substr(10,sTmp.length);
        break;
    }
  }
}

function TranslateMask( s )
{
  var ret = "";

  //Loop through each char, and pass it to the translation method
  for (var i=0; i<s.length; i++)
  {
    ret += TranslatePhoneLetter(s.charAt(i))
  }

  return ret;
}

function TranslatePhoneLetter( s )
{
  ...Letter to phone number translation code...
}
```

Custom Interface for Multiselect Lists

The next example walks you through one option for creating a more convenient user interface for a multiselect list. Natively, you are not able to add a multiple-selection list to a Microsoft Dynamics CRM form, but you can create a many-to-many relationship. In this example, you will create a new entity called Lead Source to track all of the company's possible lead sources. You will then add a many-to-many relationship to the Lead entity. After the customizations are published, you are able to add multiple lead sources to a Lead record through the Microsoft Dynamics CRM native user interface. Great, right? Well, although this certainly captures the proper data relationships, it is not very convenient for your users. Instead of offering this approach, you will use an IFrame to display a check box list of your lead sources from which users can select right on the form.

For this example, you will do the following:

- Create a new Lead Source entity and relationship to Lead.
- Create a custom .aspx page to display lead source options as a check box list.
- Add an IFrame to the Lead form.
- Add an onSave event to save the IFrame.
- Deploy to the server.
- Wrap up.

Figure 10-20 shows the final output of the check box display.

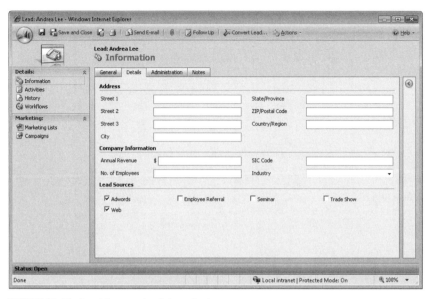

FIGURE 10-20   Lead Source check box display

Create a new Lead Source entity and relationship to Lead

1.   Create a new entity called Lead Source as shown in the following graphic:

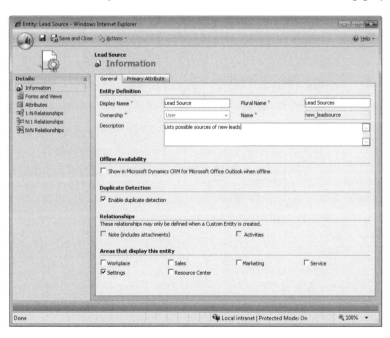

2.   Add an *N:N* relationship to the Lead entity.

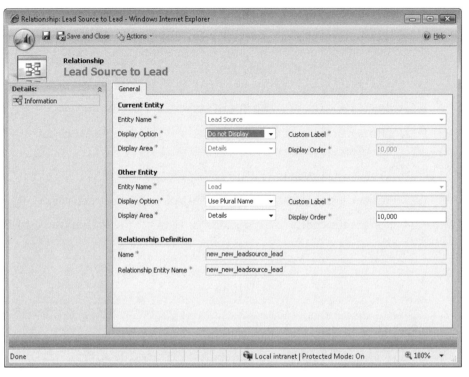

3. Publish the entity.

4. In the Settings pane, click Lead Sources, and add some new lead sources.

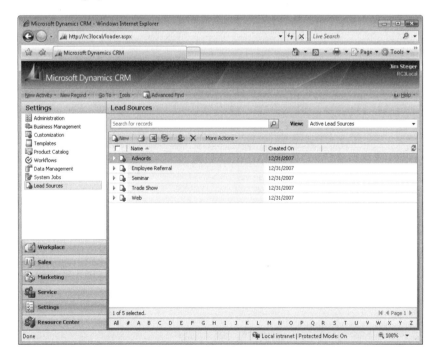

The entity is now properly configured and you have added some data. It is time to work on the custom IFrame page to properly display the lead source data. You will use the SDK assemblies and Dynamic Entities instead of referencing the Microsoft Dynamics CRM API WSDL. This approach will simplify your deployment.

Create a custom .aspx page to display Lead Source options as a check box list

1. Create a new Web application and add references to the Microsoft.Crm.Sdk and Microsoft.Crm.SdkTypeProxy assemblies.

2. Create a new Web form page called LeadSourceList.aspx.

3. Replace the code in LeadSourceList.aspx with the code in Listing 10-9.

4. Replace the code in LeadSourceList.aspx.cs with the code in Listing 10-10.

Listing 10-9 LeadSourceList.aspx

```
<%@ Page Language="C#" AutoEventWireup="true" CodeFile="LeadSourceList.aspx.cs"
Inherits="LeadSourceList" EnableViewState="true" %>

<!DOCTYPE html PUBLIC "-//W3C//DTD XHTML 1.0 Transitional//EN"
"http://www.w3.org/TR/xhtml1/DTD/xhtml1-transitional.dtd">

<html xmlns="http://www.w3.org/1999/xhtml" >
<head runat="server">
  <title>Lead Source List</title>
  <style type="text/css">
    body { font-size:11px; font-family:"Tahoma,Verdana"; margin:0px; border:0px;
background-color:#eaf3ff; cursor:default; }
    td { font-size:11px; font-family:"Tahoma,Verdana"; width:25%; }
    table { table-layout:fixed; width:100%; }
    input { font-size:8pt; width:auto; height:19px; border:0px solid #7b9ebd; }
  </style>
</head>
<body>
  <form id="crmForm" runat="server">
  <asp:Label ID="notificationText" runat="server" Font-Names="Tahoma" Font-Size="8pt"
Visible="false" Text="Please first save your record." />
  <asp:CheckBoxList runat="server" ID="checkboxlist" RepeatColumns="4" RepeatLayout="Table"
RepeatDirection="horizontal" EnableViewState="true" Font-Names="Tahoma" Font-Size="X-Small"
/>
  </form>
</body>
</html>
```

Listing 10-10 LeadSourceList.aspx.cs

```
using System;
using System.Collections.Generic;
using System.Data;
using System.Configuration;
using System.Collections;
using System.Web;
using System.Web.Security;
```

```
using System.Web.UI;
using System.Web.UI.WebControls;
using System.Web.UI.WebControls.WebParts;
using System.Web.UI.HtmlControls;
using System.Net;
using Microsoft.Crm.SdkTypeProxy;
using Microsoft.Crm.Sdk;
using Microsoft.Crm.Sdk.Query;

public partial class LeadSourceList : System.Web.UI.Page
{
  protected void Page_Load(object sender, EventArgs e)
  {
    // get querystring values
    string orgName = (Request.QueryString["orgname"] == null) ? "RC3Local" : Request.
QueryString["orgname"];
    Guid leadId = (Request.QueryString["id"] == null) ? Guid.Empty : new Guid(Request.
QueryString["id"]);

    // create service object
    CrmAuthenticationToken token = new CrmAuthenticationToken();
    token.AuthenticationType = 0; //AD (on-premise) authentication
    token.OrganizationName = orgName;
    CrmService service = new CrmService();
    service.Credentials = CredentialCache.DefaultCredentials;
    service.CrmAuthenticationTokenValue = token;

    // retrieve from registry, discoveryservice, or some other configurable mechanism in
production
    service.Url = "http://rc3local/MSCrmServices/2007/CrmService.asmx";


    if (Page.IsPostBack)
    {
      Guid leadSourceId;
      foreach (ListItem listItem in checkboxlist.Items)
      {
        leadSourceId = new Guid(listItem.Value.ToString());

        if (listItem.Selected)
        {
          // add checked values
          AddLeadSourceList(service, leadId, leadSourceId);
        }
        else
        {
          // remove value if it exists
          RemoveLeadSourceList(service, leadId, leadSourceId);
        }
      }

      // to eliminate leaving the form in a posted-back state, redirect back to itself
      Response.Redirect(Request.Url.ToString(), true);
    }
    else
    {
```

```csharp
    if (leadId == Guid.Empty)
    {
      notificationText.Visible = true;
    }
    else
    {
      try
      {
        Dictionary<Guid, DynamicEntity> leadSourceMap;
        leadSourceMap = GetLeadSourceForLead(service, leadId);

        BusinessEntityCollection leadSources = GetLeadSources(service);
        if (leadSources.BusinessEntities.Count > 0)
        {
          for (int i = 0; i < leadSources.BusinessEntities.Count; i++)
          {
            DynamicEntity leadSourceResult = (DynamicEntity)leadSources.
BusinessEntities[i];
            Key leadSourceId = (Key)leadSourceResult.Properties["new_leadsourceid"];
            string leadSourceName = (string)leadSourceResult.Properties["new_name"];

            ListItem oListItem = new ListItem(leadSourceName.ToString(),
leadSourceId.Value.ToString());
            oListItem.Selected = leadSourceMap.ContainsKey(leadSourceId.Value);
            checkboxlist.Items.Add(oListItem);
          }
        }
      }
      catch (System.Web.Services.Protocols.SoapException ex)
      {
        Response.Write(ex.Detail.InnerText);
      }
    }
  }
}

public BusinessEntityCollection GetLeadSources(CrmService service)
{
  ColumnSet cols = new ColumnSet();
  cols.AddColumns(new string[] { "new_leadsourceid", "new_name" });

  QueryExpression query = new QueryExpression();
  query.EntityName = "new_leadsource";
  query.ColumnSet = cols;
  query.AddOrder("new_name", OrderType.Ascending);

  RetrieveMultipleRequest request = new RetrieveMultipleRequest();
  request.ReturnDynamicEntities = true;
  request.Query = query;

  RetrieveMultipleResponse retrieved = (RetrieveMultipleResponse)service.Execute(request);

  return retrieved.BusinessEntityCollection;
}

public Dictionary<Guid, DynamicEntity> GetLeadSourceForLead(CrmService service, Guid leadId)
```

```csharp
{
  ColumnSet cols = new ColumnSet();
  cols.AddColumns(new string[] { "new_leadsourceid" });

  ConditionExpression condition = new ConditionExpression();
  condition.Operator = ConditionOperator.Equal;
  condition.AttributeName = "leadid";
  condition.Values = new object[] { leadId };

  FilterExpression filter = new FilterExpression();
  filter.FilterOperator = LogicalOperator.And;
  filter.AddCondition(condition);

  LinkEntity link = new LinkEntity();
  link.LinkToAttributeName = "new_leadsourceid";
  link.LinkToEntityName = "new_new_leadsource_lead";
  link.LinkFromAttributeName = "new_leadsourceid";
  link.LinkFromEntityName = "new_leadsource";
  link.LinkCriteria = filter;

  QueryExpression query = new QueryExpression();
  query.EntityName = "new_leadsource";
  query.LinkEntities.Add(link);

  query.ColumnSet = cols;

  try
  {
    // Retrieve the values from Microsoft Dynamics CRM as a dynamic entity
    RetrieveMultipleRequest request = new RetrieveMultipleRequest();
    request.ReturnDynamicEntities = true;
    request.Query = query;

    RetrieveMultipleResponse existingLeadSources = (RetrieveMultipleResponse)service.
Execute(request);

    Dictionary<Guid, DynamicEntity> leadSourceMap = new Dictionary<Guid, DynamicEntity>();
    for (int i = 0; i < existingLeadSources.BusinessEntityCollection.BusinessEntities.Count;
i++)
    {
      DynamicEntity leadSource = (DynamicEntity)existingLeadSources.
BusinessEntityCollection.BusinessEntities[i];
      leadSourceMap[((Key)leadSource.Properties["new_leadsourceid"]).Value] = leadSource;
    }

    return leadSourceMap;
  }
  catch (System.Web.Services.Protocols.SoapException ex)
  {
    throw new Exception(ex.Detail.InnerText);
  }
}

public void AddLeadSourceList(CrmService service, Guid leadId, Guid leadSource)
{
```

```
    try
    {
      AssociateEntitiesRequest associate = new AssociateEntitiesRequest();
      associate.RelationshipName = "new_new_leadsource_lead";
      associate.Moniker1 = new Moniker();
      associate.Moniker1.Name = "lead";
      associate.Moniker1.Id = leadId;
      associate.Moniker2 = new Moniker();
      associate.Moniker2.Name = "new_leadsource";
      associate.Moniker2.Id = leadSource;
      service.Execute(associate);
    }
    catch (Exception ex)
    {
      //Do nothing
    }
}

public void RemoveLeadSourceList(CrmService service, Guid leadId, Guid leadSource)
{

    try
    {
      DisassociateEntitiesRequest disassociate = new DisassociateEntitiesRequest();
      disassociate.RelationshipName = "new_new_leadsource_lead";
      disassociate.Moniker1 = new Moniker();
      disassociate.Moniker1.Name = "lead";
      disassociate.Moniker1.Id = leadId;
      disassociate.Moniker2 = new Moniker();
      disassociate.Moniker2.Name = "new_leadsource";
      disassociate.Moniker2.Id = leadSource;
      service.Execute(disassociate);
    }
    catch (Exception ex)
    {
      //Do nothing
    }
  }
}
```

You then need to deploy the files to the server so that you can access the page from an IFrame in Microsoft Dynamics CRM.

Deploying custom files to the server

1. On the Microsoft Dynamics CRM Web server, navigate to the Microsoft Dynamics CRM Web files (typically c:\inetpub\wwwroot).

2. Navigate to the ISV folder.

3. Create a new folder called SonomaPartners for your custom files.

4. Copy the LeadSourceList.aspx and LeadSourceList.aspx.cs files to this new folder.

Add an IFrame to the Lead entity's form

1. Open the form editor for the Lead entity.

2. Click the Details tab and remove the existing Lead Source field (if it exists).

3. Change the name of the section to be **Lead Sources**.

4. Add a new IFrame with the properties shown in the following graphic. Also, clear the Display border option in the Formatting tab.

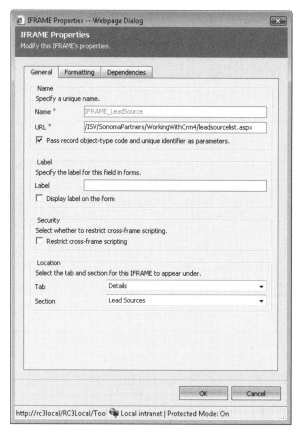

5. Save the form.

Add an *onSave* event to save the IFrame

1. Add the following line to the Lead form's *onSave* event:

```
document.frames("IFRAME_LeadSource").document.crmForm.submit();
```

2. Publish the Lead entity.

After the files are on the server and your form is published, you can add multiple lead sources conveniently from the Lead record itself. Keep in the mind the following points though:

- Because the onSave client event occurs prior to the record being saved, users will not be able to select from the check box list until after the record is first saved.

- If you have only a handful of options, you might consider adding bit fields for each option. Although this approach is simpler from a data model perspective, it is less flexible and normalized.

Accessing API Commands Through JavaScript

You might find times when it is more convenient to access a Microsoft Dynamics CRM Web service API command (or any Web service for that matter) directly from JavaScript. This technique becomes extremely handy with Microsoft Dynamics CRM Live because Microsoft Dynamics CRM Live currently limits you to only JavaScript calls from the form events for custom logic. You previously learned how to use Fiddler to capture and reconstruct SOAP XML requests and responses. Now we walk through an example of updating the phone number field for a blank phone call record when you add a recipient.

More Info Accessing the Web service API through JavaScript provides convenience for deployment and portability purposes but comes at the price of code fragility, maintenance, and development experience. You should determine when it is best to use this approach.

Listing 10-11 shows the JavaScript code to default the phone number from the first recipient on the Phone Call form. On the Phone Call form, add the code in Listing 10-11 to the *onChange* event of the *to* attribute.

Listing 10-11 Default Phone Number on Phone Call Record

```
// Default phone number based on first recipient SetDefaultPhoneNumber();


function SetDefaultPhoneNumber()
{
  var phoneNumberField = document.crmForm.all.phonenumber;
  if (phoneNumberField.DataValue == null)
  {
    var customer = new Array;
    customer = document.crmForm.all.to.DataValue;

    if (customer != null)
    {
      // You will evaluate the first customer in the list
      var customerId = customer[0].id;
      var typeName = customer[0].typename;

      var phoneNumber = GetPhoneNumber(customerId, typeName);
```

```
      if (phoneNumber  != null)
      {
        phoneNumberField.DataValue = phoneNumber;

      }
    }
  }
}

function GetPhoneNumber(customerId, typeName)
{
  var serverUrl = "/MSCrmServices/2007/CrmService.asmx";
  var xmlhttp = new ActiveXObject("Microsoft.XMLHTTP");
  xmlhttp.open("POST", serverUrl, false);
  xmlhttp.setRequestHeader("Content-Type", "text/xml; charset=utf-8");
  xmlhttp.setRequestHeader("SOAPAction", "http://schemas.microsoft.com/crm/2007/WebServices/
Retrieve");

  var message =
  [
    "<?xml version='1.0' encoding='utf-8'?>",
    "<soap:Envelope xmlns:soap=\"http://schemas.xmlsoap.org/soap/envelope/\" xmlns:
xsi=\"http://www.w3.org/2001/XMLSchema-instance\" xmlns:xsd=\"http://www.w3.org/2001/
XMLSchema\">",
    GenerateAuthenticationHeader(),
    "<soap:Body>",
    "<Retrieve xmlns='http://schemas.microsoft.com/crm/2007/WebServices'>",
    "<entityName>",
    typeName,
    "</entityName>",
    "<id>",
    customerId,
    "</id>",
    "<columnSet xmlns:q1='http://schemas.microsoft.com/crm/2006/Query' xsi:type='q1:
ColumnSet'>",
    "<q1:Attributes><q1:Attribute>telephone1</q1:Attribute></q1:Attributes>",
    "</columnSet></Retrieve>",
    "</soap:Body></soap:Envelope>"
  ].join("");

  xmlhttp.send(message);
  var result = xmlhttp.responseXML.xml;
  var doc = new ActiveXObject("MSXML2.DOMDocument");
  doc.async = false;
  doc.loadXML(result);
  var telephone1Node = doc.selectSingleNode("//q1:telephone1");
  if( telephone1Node != null )
  {
    return telephone1Node.text;
  }
  else
  {
    return null;
  }
}
```

Hiding Tabs and Fields

Unfortunately, Microsoft Dynamics CRM does not allow you to create forms based on a user's security role or some other custom logic natively; everyone will see the same form. Some customers would like to display different information on the entity form depending on the security role of the user viewing the form. One technique, albeit unsupported, to accomplish this is to implement your own business logic and use DHTML to hide form tabs and/or fields based the user's security role.

> **Warning** This technique is considered unsupported by Microsoft. You are not supposed to reference the form elements directly using the DOM because these elements could change in a future release. Use it at your own risk.

Hiding a Tab

Before we show the finished product, we show you how to start by hiding an entire tab of data. To hide a tab, we recommend you use the *display* property of the element's *style* attribute. The following JavaScript example can be used to hide a tab:

```
tabnTab.style.display = 'none';
```

tabnTab refers to the ID of the tab. The *n* is the number of the tab starting with 0 from the left. In Figure 10-21, the Administration tab is *tab2Tab*.

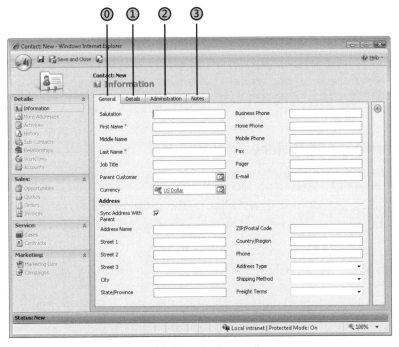

FIGURE 10-21 Determining a tab's ID on the Contact form

To show a hidden tab, you can use the following script:

```
tabnTab.style.display = 'inline';
```

Caution This approach assumes that the tab order won't change in the future. For instance, if someone were to add another tab in between the first one and the tab you are using, you will end up hiding the wrong tab!

Hiding and Showing a Field and Label

The same approach used to hide a tab can be used for hiding and showing a field and its label. However, unlike the tab example, you typically do not want to collapse the area and have the elements shift. So, you will instead use the style's *visibility* property. Just as with the tab, you need to find the ID of the element you wish to toggle and set its *visibility* property to *hidden* or *visible* as appropriate.

Use the following script to hide a field and label, replacing *attributename* with the name of the attribute you wish to hide.

```
crmForm.all.attributename_c.style.visibility = 'hidden'; //label
crmForm.all.attributename_d.style.visibility = 'hidden'; //data
```

You can use the following script to show a field and label by replacing *attributename* with the name of the attribute you wish to show.

```
crmForm.all.attributename_c.style.visibility = 'visible'; //label
crmForm.all.attributename_d.style.visibility = 'visible'; //data
```

Understanding CSS Display vs. Visibility

It is easy to confuse the *display* and *visibility* properties. When the *display* property is set to *none*, the browser will remove the entire element from the page upon rendering and shift all remaining elements as appropriate. The *visibility* property can also hide an element, but the element will still occupy its proper space on the page.

When hiding tabs, we recommend that you use the *display* property so that the other tabs after the target tab will shift over and look normal to the user. If you were to use the *visibility* approach, you could end up with a gap if the tab you are hiding is a middle tab. Figure 10-22 shows the result of the following: *tab2Tab.style.visibility = 'hidden';*.

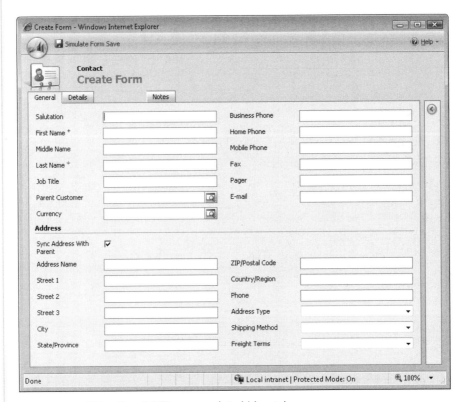

FIGURE 10-22 Using the *visibility* approach to hide a tab

With fields and labels, the choice of which CSS approach to take is up to you. Generally speaking, if you wish to preserve layout of the field or label, use the *visibility* property.

> **Tip** Remember that when an item is hidden it will not receive any events.

Hiding a Tab Based on User Security

Now that you know the techniques to hide a tab, field, and label, let's review how to show or hide one of those elements based on the security role of the user viewing the record. For this example, you will hide the administrative tab (third tab) on the contact form for all users unless the user has either the System Administrator or the Sales Manager security role.

Simply add the code in Listing 10-12 to the *onLoad* event of the Contact form. Save the form and publish the Contact entity once complete.

Listing 10-12 Hiding a Tab

```
HideTab();

function HideTab()
{
  var allowedRoles = [ "System Administrator", "Sales Manager" ];
  var roleAllowed = IsRoleAllowed(allowedRoles);

  if (! roleAllowed)
  {
    // hide Administrative tab
    tab2Tab.style.display = 'none';
  }
}

function IsRoleAllowed(allowedRoles)
{
  var result = RetrieveUserRoles();
  var foundResult = false;

  for (i=0;i<=allowedRoles.length;i++)
  {
    if (result.indexOf(allowedRoles[i]) > -1 )
    {
      foundResult = true;
      break;
    }
  }
  return foundResult;
}

function RetrieveUserRoles()
{
  var serverUrl = "/mscrmservices/2007/crmservice.asmx";
  var xmlhttp = new ActiveXObject("Microsoft.XMLHTTP");
  xmlhttp.open("POST", serverUrl, false);
  xmlhttp.setRequestHeader("Content-Type", "text/xml; charset=utf-8");
  xmlhttp.setRequestHeader("SOAPAction", "http://schemas.microsoft.com/crm/2007/WebServices/
RetrieveMultiple");

  var message =
  [
  "<?xml version='1.0' encoding='utf-8'?>",
  "<soap:Envelope xmlns:soap=\"http://schemas.xmlsoap.org/soap/envelope/\" xmlns:
xsi=\"http://www.w3.org/2001/XMLSchema-instance\" xmlns:xsd=\"http://www.w3.org/2001/
XMLSchema\">",
  GenerateAuthenticationHeader(),
    "<soap:Body>",
    "<RetrieveMultiple xmlns='http://schemas.microsoft.com/crm/2007/WebServices'>",
    "<query xmlns:q1='http://schemas.microsoft.com/crm/2006/Query' xsi:type='q1:
QueryExpression'>",
    "<q1:EntityName>role</q1:EntityName>",
    "<q1:ColumnSet xsi:type='q1:ColumnSet'><q1:Attributes><q1:Attribute>name</q1:
Attribute></q1:Attributes></q1:ColumnSet>",
    "<q1:Distinct>false</q1:Distinct>",
```

```
      "<q1:LinkEntities><q1:LinkEntity>",
      "<q1:LinkFromAttributeName>roleid</q1:LinkFromAttributeName>",
      "<q1:LinkFromEntityName>role</q1:LinkFromEntityName>",
      "<q1:LinkToEntityName>systemuserroles</q1:LinkToEntityName>",
      "<q1:LinkToAttributeName>roleid</q1:LinkToAttributeName>",
      "<q1:JoinOperator>Inner</q1:JoinOperator>",
      "<q1:LinkEntities><q1:LinkEntity>",
      "<q1:LinkFromAttributeName>systemuserid</q1:LinkFromAttributeName>",
      "<q1:LinkFromEntityName>systemuserroles</q1:LinkFromEntityName>",
      "<q1:LinkToEntityName>systemuser</q1:LinkToEntityName>",
      "<q1:LinkToAttributeName>systemuserid</q1:LinkToAttributeName>",
      "<q1:JoinOperator>Inner</q1:JoinOperator>",
      "<q1:LinkCriteria><q1:FilterOperator>And</q1:FilterOperator>",
      "<q1:Conditions><q1:Condition>",
      "<q1:AttributeName>systemuserid</q1:AttributeName>",
      "<q1:Operator>Equal</q1:Operator>",
      "<q1:Values>",
      "<q1:Value xmlns:q2='http://microsoft.com/wsdl/types/' xsi:type='q2:guid'>",
      GetUserId(),
      "</q1:Value></q1:Values></q1:Condition></q1:Conditions>",
      "</q1:LinkCriteria></q1:LinkEntity></q1:LinkEntities>",
      "</q1:LinkEntity></q1:LinkEntities></query></RetrieveMultiple>",
      "</soap:Body></soap:Envelope>"
  ].join("");

  xmlhttp.send(message);
  return xmlhttp.responseXML.text;
}

function GetUserId()
{
  var serverUrl = "/mscrmservices/2007/crmservice.asmx";
  var xmlhttp = new ActiveXObject("Microsoft.XMLHTTP");
  xmlhttp.open("POST", serverUrl, false);
  xmlhttp.setRequestHeader("Content-Type", "text/xml; charset=utf-8");
  xmlhttp.setRequestHeader("SOAPAction", "http://schemas.microsoft.com/crm/2007/WebServices/
Execute");

  var message =
  [
    "<?xml version='1.0' encoding='utf-8'?>",
    "<soap:Envelope xmlns:soap=\"http://schemas.xmlsoap.org/soap/envelope/\" xmlns:
xsi=\"http://www.w3.org/2001/XMLSchema-instance\" xmlns:xsd=\"http://www.w3.org/2001/
XMLSchema\">",
    GenerateAuthenticationHeader(),
    "<soap:Body>",
    "<Execute xmlns='http://schemas.microsoft.com/crm/2007/WebServices'>",
    "<Request xsi:type='WhoAmIRequest' />",
    "</Execute>",
    "</soap:Body>",
    "</soap:Envelope>"
  ].join("");

  xmlhttp.send(message);
  var result = xmlhttp.responseXML.xml;
  var doc = new ActiveXObject("MSXML2.DOMDocument");
```

```
doc.async = false;
doc.loadXML(result);
var returnNode = doc.selectSingleNode("//UserId");

if( returnNode != null )
{
  return returnNode.text;
}
else
{
  return null;
}
}
```

Referencing an External Script File

As we discussed earlier, you can add code against the form's *onLoad* event that references an external script file. The main reason to do this is for ease of script administration and code reuse. For example, if you add the phone number formatting script from an earlier example to 20 or 30 different phone number fields in the Lead, Account, and Contact entities, and then you need to modify the script, you would have to update the script in all 20 or 30 locations manually. Referencing an external script saves you this headache because you only need to make one update. However, Microsoft doesn't support referencing an external script for the following reasons:

- **Deployment overhead**   Script code added directly to the events can be deployed with the built-in import/export mechanisms. By referencing an external file, you will be responsible for deployment and updating the references in the Microsoft Dynamics CRM form events, including the offline clients.

- **Access issues**   When referencing a file on an external Web site, if that site is not available or if there is a delay in loading the file, the required methods might not be available to your code and might cause errors.

- **Web browser caching**   The Web browser can cache external files. After you deploy a modification to an external file, users may need to delete their browser's cache to load the changes.

> **Note** Microsoft considers this approach unsupported, so use at your own risk.

With the code in Listing 10-13, you can use DHTML to add an external script reference. You will need to update the *url* variable with the proper path to your script file, and then add the script to the form's *onLoad* event.

Listing 10-13 Referencing a Basic External Script File

```
// Define your script URL
```

```
var url = "/ISV/SonomaPartners/custom/scripts/script.js";

// Create the script element
var scriptElement = document.createElement("<script src='" + url + "' language='javascript'
>");
document.getElementsByTagName("head")[0].insertAdjacentElement("beforeEnd", scriptElement);
```

> **Note** Adding the following code directly to the *onLoad* event will not work:
>
> ```
> <script language="JavaScript"
> src="http://<crmserver>/ISV/SonomaPartners/custom/scripts/script.js"></script>
> ```
>
> The manner by which Microsoft Dynamics CRM injects the *onLoad* script code into the form's
> output prevents this line from executing.

As mentioned previously, one of the drawbacks to this file reference is that the browser will
load the JavaScript files asynchronously. As such, if you need to execute logic in the form's
onLoad event that relies on a method residing in your external script, you could end up with
an error if that script hasn't loaded in time.

You can help mitigate the asynchronous loading concern in a couple of ways. One approach
is to take advantage that the Web browser reads the files sequentially (that is, from top to
bottom). Place any logic that requires a method from the external JavaScript file at the bottom of that file. This will ensure that the dependent logic loads correctly.

Another option would be to use the *onreadystatechange* event when you load your script.
The *onreadystatechange* event will fire after the script has fully loaded, allowing you to
execute additional code safely. The code sample below shows how you can use a custom
Script_OnLoad function in conjunction with the *onreadystatechange* event.

```
// Create the script element
var scriptElement = document.createElement("<script type='text/javascript'>");
scriptElement.src = "/ISV/SonomaPartners/custom/scripts/script.js";
scriptElement.attachEvent("onreadystatechange", Script_OnLoad);
document.getElementsByTagName("head")[0].insertAdjacentElement("beforeEnd",
scriptElement);

function Script_OnLoad()
{
   if (event.srcElement.readyState == "loaded" || event.srcElement.readyState ==
"complete")
   {
     // Safely call functions defined in your external script file.
   }
}
```

Dynamically Changing Picklist Values

The default behavior of picklist attributes in Microsoft Dynamics CRM is that each field operates totally independently of other values on the form. In reality, you might want to dynamically alter the picklist values of a record based on other values selected in the record. For example, if the user selects that a contact's shipping method is Will Call, it doesn't make sense to let the user select FOB (Freight on Board) as the Freight Terms for that contact.

This example shows how you can dynamically change values of the Freight Terms picklist field based on the selection of the Shipping Method picklist. If the user selects Will Call as the shipping method, you will use the client-side SDK to programmatically remove the FOB (Freight on Board) option from the Freight Terms list and automatically set the option to Free of Charge. If the user then changes the Shipping Method to a new value, you must programmatically add the FOB (Freight on Board) option back to the Freight Terms list.

> **Tip** You can use the code and concepts from this example to extend your company's Microsoft Dynamics CRM deployment to dynamically update different sets of picklist values depending on the needs of your organization.

As you saw earlier, Microsoft Dynamics CRM provides two routines for managing picklist options: *AddOption()* and *DeleteOption()*. You will use *DeleteOption()* to remove the FOB option when Will Call is selected. When any other value is selected, you will add FOB (if it has been removed). This example demonstrates how you would access and work with picklist fields. Figure 10-23 shows the results on the form.

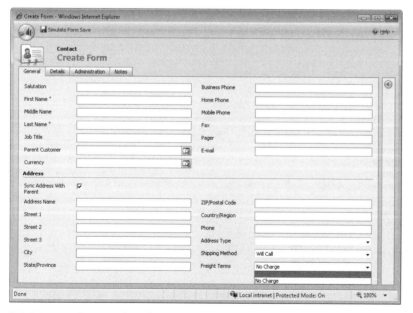

FIGURE 10-23 Form preview of Shipping Method picklist script

Important You should not progr...
Microsoft Dynamics CRM. Technic...
method, but if the value has not ...
Dynamics CRM will not be able t...

For this example, you will nee...
Change event. You must also ...
form's update mode to addr...
script for this example can ...

Listing 10-14 Dynamically ...

```
// Installation: Add this
onChange() event.
// Ensure that these mat
var SHIPPINGMETHODCODE_'
var FREIGHTTERMSCODE_F(
var FREIGHTTERMSCODE_N
var oShipMethod = even...
var oFreightTerms = crmForm.al...
var freightTerms = oFreightTerms.Options
var fobExists = false;

// Loop through existing options and determine whether the FOB optiv.
for (var i=0; i<freightTerms.length; i++)
{
 if (freightTerms[i].DataValue == FREIGHTTERMSCODE_FOB)
 fobExists = true;
}

if (oShipMethod.DataValue == SHIPPINGMETHODCODE_WILLCALL)
{
 // Default to No Charge
 oFreightTerms.DataValue = FREIGHTTERMSCODE_NOCHARGE;

 // Remove FOB as an option
 oFreightTerms.DeleteOption(FREIGHTTERMSCODE_FOB);
}
else
{
 // Default to blank
 oFreightTerms.DataValue = null;

 // If the FOB option is missing, add it back
 if (! fobExists)
 oFreightTerms.AddOption("FOB",FREIGHTTERMSCODE_FOB);
}

//Installation: Add this script to the Contact form's onLoad() event.

// Set up the constants
var CRM_FORM_TYPE_CREATE = "1";
var CRM_FORM_TYPE_UPDATE = "2";
// Ensure that these match the codes in Microsoft Dynamics CRM
```

```
var SHIPPINGMETHODCODE_WILLCALL = 7...
var FREIGHTTERMSCODE_FOB = 1;
var FREIGHTTERMSCODE_NOCHARGE =

// Only check if form is in
if (crmForm.FormType == CRM
{
 if (document.crmForm.a
 WILLCALL)
 {
 // Remove FOB as
 document.crmFo
 }
}
```

Tip
D...

```
                      2;

            pdate mode
        _FORM_TYPE_UPDATE)

    1.address1_shippingmethodcode.DataValue == SHIPPINGMETHODCODE_


    an option
m.all.address1_freighttermscode.DeleteOption(FREIGHTTERMSCODE_FOB);
```

When you need to find the value of a picklist item, navigate to the entity's Attributes page.
Double-click the picklist attribute. On the right, you will see the list of options. Double-click an
option name, and a dialog box displays the corresponding value, as shown in Figure 10-24.

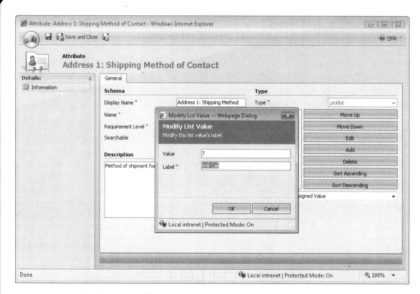

FIGURE 10-24 Retrieving picklist values

Summary

This chapter discusses the methods and options available to a script developer attempting
to enhance and extend the application forms. In addition to the events available in Microsoft
Dynamics CRM, the use of the IFrame element further enhances your ability to add custom
functionality without requiring the user to leave the form. By using scripts and the touch
points opened by Microsoft Dynamics CRM, you can easily create user-friendly and complex
application integration.

Index

Symbols

About the Authors

Mike Snyder

Mike Snyder is co-founder and principal of Sonoma Partners, a Chicago-based consulting firm that specializes in Microsoft Dynamics CRM implementations. Sonoma Partners won the Global Microsoft CRM Partner of the Year award in both 2005 and 2003. Recognized as one of the industry's leading Microsoft Dynamics CRM experts, Mike is a member of the Microsoft Dynamics Partner Advisory Council, and he writes a popular blog about Microsoft Dynamics CRM.

Before starting Sonoma Partners, Mike led multiple product development teams at Motorola and Fortune Brands. Mike graduated with honors from Northwestern's Kellogg Graduate School of Management with a Master of Business Administration degree, majoring in marketing and entrepreneurship. He has a bachelor's degree in engineering from the University of Notre Dame. Mike lives in Naperville, Illinois, with his wife and three children. He enjoys ice hockey and playing with his kids in his free time.

Jim Steger

Jim Steger is also a co-founder and principal of Sonoma Partners. He is a Microsoft Certified Professional and has architected multiple award-winning Microsoft Dynamics CRM deployments, including complex enterprise integration projects. He has developed solutions and code for Microsoft Dynamics CRM since the version 1.0 beta.

Before starting Sonoma Partners, Jim designed and led various global software development projects at Motorola and Acco Office Products. Jim earned his bachelor's degree in engineering from Northwestern University. He currently lives in Naperville, Illinois, with his wife and two children. In his free time, Jim enjoys volleyball, ice hockey, and spending time with his family.

About Sonoma Partners

This book's authors, Mike Snyder and Jim Steger, are co-owners of the Chicago-based consulting firm Sonoma Partners. Sonoma Partners is a Microsoft Gold Certified Partner that sells, customizes, and implements Microsoft Dynamics CRM for enterprise and midsize companies throughout the United States. Sonoma Partners has worked exclusively with Microsoft Dynamics CRM since the version 1.0 prerelease beta software. Founded in 2001, Sonoma Partners possesses extensive experience in several industries, including financial services, professional services, health care, and real estate.

Sonoma Partners is unique because of the following reasons:

- We are 100 percent focused on the Microsoft Dynamics CRM software product. We do not spread our resources over any other products or services.

- We have successfully implemented more than 100 Microsoft Dynamics CRM deployments, and we received the Global Microsoft CRM Partner of the Year award in 2005 and 2003 for our past work.

- More than half of our staff includes application and database developers so that we can perform very complex Microsoft Dynamics CRM customizations and integrations.

- We were named one of 101 Best and Brightest Companies to Work for in Chicago in 2007.

- We are a member of Microsoft Dynamics Partner Advisory Council.

In addition to the books we've written for Microsoft Press, we share our Microsoft Dynamics CRM product knowledge through our e-mail newsletter and online blog. If you're interested in receiving this information, you can find out more on our Web site at *http://www.sonomapartners.com*.

Even though our headquarters is in Chicago, Illinois, we work with customers throughout the United States. If you're interested in discussing your Microsoft Dynamics CRM system with us, please don't hesitate to contact us! In addition to working with customers who want to deploy Microsoft Dynamics CRM for themselves, we also act as a technology provider for Independent Software Vendors (ISVs) looking to develop their solution for the Microsoft Dynamics CRM platform.

Sometimes people ask us where we got our name. The name *Sonoma Partners* was inspired by Sonoma County in the wine-producing region of northern California. The wineries in Sonoma County are smaller than their more well-known competitors in Napa Valley, but they have a reputation for producing some of the highest quality wines in the world. We think that their smaller size allows the Sonoma winemakers to be more intimately involved with creating the wine. By using this hands-on approach, the Sonoma County wineries can deliver a superior product to their customers . . . and that's what we strive to do as well.

What do you think of this book?

We want to hear from you!

Do you have a few minutes to participate in a brief online survey?

Microsoft is interested in hearing your feedback so we can continually improve our books and learning resources for you.

To participate in our survey, please visit:

www.microsoft.com/learning/booksurvey/

...and enter this book's ISBN-10 or ISBN-13 number (located above barcode on back cover*). As a thank-you to survey participants in the United States and Canada, each month we'll randomly select five respondents to win one of five $100 gift certificates from a leading online merchant. At the conclusion of the survey, you can enter the drawing by providing your e-mail address, which will be used for prize notification only.

Thanks in advance for your input. Your opinion counts!

* Where to find the ISBN on back cover

ISBN-13: 000-0-0000-0000-0
ISBN-10: 0-0000-0000-0

0 00000 000000

Example only. Each book has unique ISBN.

www.microsoft.com/learning/booksurvey/

Microsoft®
Press